NIKOLAUS
PEVSNER

A HISTORY OF
BUILDING
TYPES

NIKOLAUS PEVSNER

A HISTORY OF BUILDING TYPES

THAMES AND HUDSON

LONDON

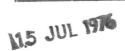
Copyright © 1976 by the Trustees of the National Gallery
of Art, Washington, D.C.
The A. W. Mellon Lectures in the Fine Arts, 1970, delivered
at the National Gallery of Art, Washington, D.C.

First published in Great Britain in 1976 by Thames and Hudson Ltd, London
Published in the United States of America in Bollingen Series by
Princeton University Press, Princeton, N.J.

Filmset by Keyspools Ltd, Golborne, Lancashire
Printed by the Alden Press, Oxford
Bound by Webb Son & Co. Ltd, Glamorgan

CONTENTS

FOREWORD

THIS BOOK is an extended version of the Mellon Lectures which I gave in the National Gallery of Art in Washington early in 1970. Their endeavour was to compile an outline history of building types with due stress on the nineteenth century which was the crucial century in that respect. The lectures were eight and they included sixteen types. This book adds four more, but even that does not cover all types by any means. My attempt to justify this at the beginning of the Introduction is, as I am aware, only convincing up to a point. My main reason has simply been a fervent wish to see publication.

There is, to the best of my knowledge, no history of building types in existence. What come nearest are the historical sections, short or long as the case may be, in the surveys of types which traditionally formed part of the architectural courses of the nineteenth and the early twentieth centuries. J.-N.-L. Durand's *Précis des leçons d'architecture données à l'Ecole Polytechnique* published in 1802–09 is the earliest in the nineteenth century. It stands in the tradition of Jacques-François Blondel's *Cours d'architecture civile*, whose second volume of 1771 has treatment by types. Durand's *Précis* had been preceded by another help for students, a historical case-book by types, his *Recueil et parallèle des édifices de tous genres, anciens et modernes*, issued in 1801. This was followed by Charles Gourlier and others' *Choix d'édifices publiques projetés et construits en France depuis le commencement du XIXᵉ siècle* of 1825–50, by Léonce Reynaud's *Traité d'architecture* of 1850–58 and P. Planat's *Encyclopédie de l'architecture et de la construction* in six volumes, published in 1888–95. The climax was reached by Julien Guadet's *Eléments et théorie de l'architecture* of 1902–04. A German parallel is Ludwig Klasen's *Grundriss-Vorbilder in Gebäuden aller Art* of

1884–96. There is no English parallel. The *Dictionary of Architecture* published by the Architectural Publication Society in 1853–92 (editor Wyatt Papworth) is a dictionary, not a treatise. So is *Wasmuths Lexikon der Baukunst* of 1929–32. And as for the gigantic *Handbuch der Architektur*, edited by R. Durm, part IV deals with types in many *Halbbänden*, often of several *Hefte*, but only some of the authors take in the history of the types properly. Finally, when the late Talbot Hamlin's *Forms and Functions of Twentieth-century Architecture* was brought out in 1952, though it was intended to replace Guadet, the demand for such encyclopedic treatment had all but disappeared, and historically in this one case Hamlin proved weak.

So there seemed to me scope for a book such as this. The history of building types had fascinated me for many years, because this treatment of buildings allows for a demonstration of development both by style and by function, style being a matter of architectural history, function of social history. I lectured on the subject at Göttingen in 1930, and held seminars on it at Cordova in the Argentine in 1960 and at the Courtauld Institute of Art of the University of London several times in the sixties.

At that time mine was still a lonely pursuit; but that – to the great advantage of this book – has changed now, and histories of single types have begun to appear, books such as Elias Cornell's *De stora Utställningarnas Arkitekturhistoria* of 1952 (on exhibitions), the late Carroll Meeks's *The Railroad Station* of 1956, J. F. Geist's *Passagen* of 1969, Simon Tidworth's *Theatres* and M. C. Donnelly's *A Short History of Observatories*, both of 1973, and K. H. Schreyl's *Zur Geschichte der Baugattung Börse* (on exchanges) of 1963. Dr Schreyl's book is a doctoral thesis, and more theses on building types have been undertaken or are being undertaken. They will be quoted in their appropriate places. Here it is enough to add *The Architectural Review* as the journal in which consistently, even if sporadically, papers on building types have been published. They are on prisons T. Markus, 'The Pattern of the Law', CXVI, 1954, 251 ff.; on libraries my 'Nutrimentum Spiritus', CXXX, 1961, 240 ff.; on hospitals H. Rosenau, 'The Functional and the Ideal in late eighteenth-century French Architecture', CXL, 1966, 253 ff.; and on museums H. Seling, 'The Genesis of the Museum', CXLI, 1967, 103 ff. (see below, chapter 8, note 1).

For the other building types I was on my own. Most of my research was done in the British Museum Library, the Library of Congress, where I was greatly helped by Edgar Breitenbach and Alan Fern, the New York Public Library, where my chief support was Etta Arntzen and Joseph T. Rankin, and the Avery Library of Columbia University in New York, where Adolf Placzek, the director, and Neville Thompson made things wonderfully easy for me. Many of the slides for the Mellon Lectures were made for me by the Courtauld Institute of Art, and more during the weeks of the lectures thanks to the kindness of Professor Phoebe Stanton and Anne von Rebhan. Also during the weeks of the lectures Margaret Bouton was my greatest help inside the National Gallery. In London Richard Haslam did much reading, extracting and sifting for me in the course of the winter preceding the lectures, and in 1971–72 he helped on the illustrations. He did it extremely well, and as for the typing of my illegible and labyrinthine manuscript, Marjorie Sutherland did that miraculously well.

My thanks are also due to my secretary, Fiona Dobson, for a variety of helpful work, to Professor Henry-Russell Hitchcock, Professor Elias Cornell, Bo Berntsson and many others for the loan or gift of photographs, to Brian Blackwood who photographed much for me, to Professor Robert Judson Clark for a number of corrections, to Dr H. Seling for permission to re-use much of his thesis on museum buildings, to M. Maurice Culot for valuable material on Belgian factories, to Professor Günter, Michael Weisser and H. H. Schmitz for information on, and photographs of, German factories, to F. D. Lethbridge for verifying dates and architects' names for public buildings in Washington, D. C., and to many others gratefully referred to in footnotes.

In addition a special paragraph must be made to record my gratitude to Emily Lane, who saw the book through the proof stage and undertook plenty of research to find solutions to hundreds of niggly queries. Her patience knew no bounds.

Yet, however much I was helped, the book appears with many faults. Had I another few years for preparation, most of them could be corrected. The search for suitable material which might be hidden in novels, in letters, in memoirs could have gone on, and friends could have gone on drawing my attention to such sources. However, at my age one is anxious to see a book come out, better faulty than not at all.

Even as it is, I am intensely grateful to Providence for having made it possible for me to work in the best libraries. While the book grew I had for all the day-to-day work the British Museum less than five minutes from my office, the Warburg Institute, the University Library and the library of my own college, Birkbeck College, within a ten-minute range and even the Royal Institute of British Architects at walking distance. Such a book as this just could not be written at Dundee or Dunedin, at Keele or Kiel, at St Davids or St Louis.

NP

1 Oslo, Royal Palace, 1824–48, by H. P. F. Linstow

2 Athens, Royal Palace, 1834–38, by F. Gärtner

3, 4 Munich, Residenz, Königsbau, 1826–35, and Festsaalbau, 1832–42, both by Leo von Klenze

5 Osborne, Isle of Wight, 1845–49, by Prince Albert and
Thomas Cubitt

6 Balmoral, 1853–55, by William Smith

7 Schwerin, begun 1843
by G. A. Demmler and
continued by F. A. Stüler

Introduction

IF ONE looks at any book on the history of Western architecture from the beginnings to the middle of the eighteenth century, one will find that it is almost entirely made up of churches and castles and palaces. In addition there are a few medieval town halls, especially in Italy, there is the sixteenth-century town hall of Antwerp, and the seventeenth-century one of Amsterdam. More frequently theatres of the sixteenth to the eighteenth centuries have survived, rarely a hospital like that of Beaune, and more rarely still a library like the Laurenziana in Florence. All this changed in the course of the nineteenth century so that today what the architect is concerned with is a multitude of building types. This is how Henry van Brunt, that eminently intelligent American late nineteenth-century architect, put it in 1886:[1]

The architect, in the course of his career, is called upon to erect buildings for every conceivable purpose, most of them adapted to requirements which have never before arisen in history . . . Railway buildings of all sorts; churches with parlors, kitchens and society rooms; hotels on a scale never before dreamt of; public libraries the service of which is fundamentally different from any of their predecessors; office and mercantile structures, such as no pre-existing conditions of professional and commercial life has ever required; school houses and college buildings, whose necessary equipment removes them far from the venerable examples of Oxford and Cambridge; skating-rinks, theatres, exhibition buildings of vast extent, casinos, jails, prisons, municipal buildings, music halls, apartment houses, and all the other structures which must be accommodated to the complicated conditions of modern society . . . Out of [the] . . . eminently practical considerations of planning must grow elevations, of which the essential character, if they are honestly composed, can have no precedent in architectural history.

My selection from all these possible types has been to some extent arbitrary. Churches have been exhaustively covered in general histories of architecture. Schools and university buildings, observatories, concert halls and barracks, for instance, would have been rewarding but would have swelled the book to unmanageable proportions. Dwellings, including apartment houses and suburban villas, would have needed another volume altogether.

Almost alone among building types, the palaces of rulers of countries have declined and are now down to nothing; but for the nineteenth century they make an interesting sequence and introduce the styles which we shall find imitated for other types. The series starts with the Classicism of Oslo by H. P. F. Linstow, 1824–48, and Athens by Gärtner of Munich, of 1834–38. Norway had become independent in 1814, Greece in 1832. So palaces were needed. The King of Greece was the son of Ludwig I of Bavaria, who paid much of the cost of his son's palace. At home King Ludwig – Bavaria had become a kingdom as recently as 1806 – extended the existing palace by two large ranges, and they are no longer Neo-Greek or Neo-Roman but Neo-Italian Renaissance: The Königsbau of 1826–35 and the Festsaalbau of 1832–42, both by Klenze, but the first shaped on the pattern of the Palazzo Pitti in Florence, i.e. the Quattrocento, the second of a grander and freer High Renaissance, indeed heralding Baroque features remarkably early.

The Italianate style appeared in two guises – the palazzo and the villa, though the so-called Italianate villas have little to do with Italian villas such as those by Palladio. They are characterized instead by asymmetrical plans and a tower somewhere as a main accent. The fashion started in England with Charles Barry's Trentham Park of 1833–42 and was taken up by Prince Albert at Osborne on the Isle of Wight in 1845–49. A little later Balmoral was built, in 1853–55, in the Scottish Baronial style.

So here are Grecian, Italian palazzo, Italian villa and Scottish Baronial. But more styles served as inspiration, e.g. the French Renaissance. Almost a freak is the French Renaissance Schloss at Schwerin, begun in 1843 by G. A. Demmler and continued by Stüler of Berlin;[2] for in 1843 the Neo-French Renaissance was still an exception even in France. It became popular only more than a decade later, when Napoleon III completed the Louvre – and not as a palace but for government offices. Meanwhile – and this is what one finds in every country – the older styles carried on. In our case the Greek Revival was carried on by Schinkel till he died in 1841, and handled as superbly as ever but with a new sense for bold planning in landscape. The two dream-palaces which Schinkel designed, one in 1834 for the King of Greece, the other in 1838 for the Empress of Russia at Orianda on the Crimea, are examples of how the interpenetration of interior and exterior space can act as a solvent to the compact solidity of the Greek Revival. Other ways of achieving the same loosening will be found in later chapters of this book.

The Gothic Revival was considered less suitable for palaces. The paramount example is indeed not a new building but the restoration of a genuine castle, though a very drastic restoration: Viollet-le-Duc's Pierrefonds of 1858–79, done for Napoleon III. To build castles totally afresh at so late a date is another freak. I am referring to Neuschwanstein, built in 1868–86 for Ludwig II of Bavaria.[3] He was a fervent admirer of Richard Wagner but also of Louis XIV, and as moreover he suffered from a *bâtissomanie* as rampant as that of any German eighteenth-century ruler, he built Linderhof as well and Herrenchiemsee, the one in 1870–

74, the other in 1878–86. Linderhof is a French *maison de plaisance*, Herrenchiemsee a new Versailles. Linderhof was ready when the King committed suicide, Neuschwanstein was completed (though never finished inside) after his death, Herrenchiemsee, grand as it is, is only a fragment. Neuschwanstein was behind its time, but Linderhof and Herrenchiemsee represent the Neo-Baroque which was internationally typical of their date.

So here in terms of royalty is a synopsis of styles imitated during the nineteenth century. We shall find the same sequence in building types other than palaces, and one of the intentions of my chapters is to watch for each type the order in which styles follow one another. But that is only one of two intentions of equal importance. The other, as has already been pointed out, is to follow changes in function and changes in planning.

The arrangement of types is to be from the most monumental to the least monumental, from the most ideal to the most utilitarian, from national monuments to factories.

8 K. F. Schinkel, design for a palace for the Empress of Russia at Orianda in the Crimea, 1838

9 Neuschwanstein, 1868–86, by E. Riedel and C. Jank

10 Herrenchiemsee, Gallery of Mirrors, 1878–86, by G. Dollmann

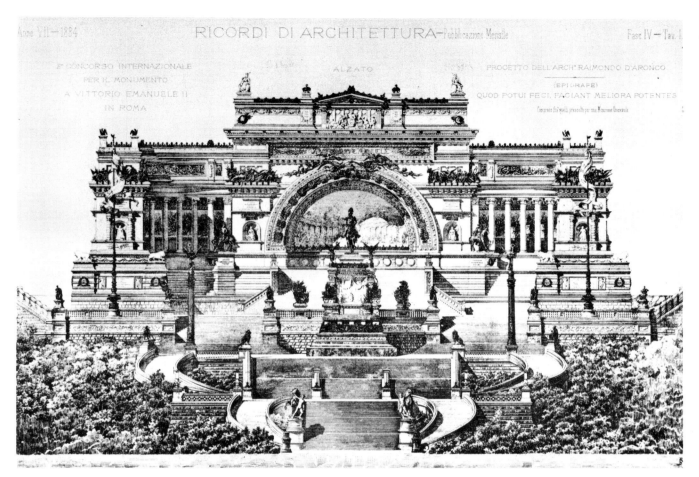

1.1 Raimondo d'Aronco, design for a monument to Victor Emanuel II, 1884

I
National monuments and monuments to genius

IT HAS always been customary in monarchies to erect monuments to kings or princes after their death. Such monuments do not qualify for inclusion in this chapter unless the king or prince created the nation or made it understand itself as a nation. In these cases it is the nation celebrating itself in the person of its creator. Such monuments therefore are on a par with monuments which a nation – or indeed a private individual – may erect to great men. The nineteenth century being the era of *l'Europe des nations* was the era *par excellence* for national monuments, though the story begins in the eighteenth.

The eighteenth and nineteenth centuries had inherited three types of commemorative structures from the Romans: the column of the type of Trajan's column, the triumphal arch, and the equestrian statue. They were never forgotten, not even in the Middle Ages. From Trajan's column the way leads to Bishop Bernward's bronze column at Hildesheim, from the arches of

Titus and Constantine to the curious contraption of Einhard, Charlemagne's biographer,[1] from the equestrian statue of Marcus Aurelius on the Capitol to the mid-thirteenth-century statue in the market place at Magdeburg, symbol no doubt of imperial privileges. The Renaissance did not take up the narrative column or the triumphal arch (except for temporary pageants), though the entry frontispiece of Alfonso I of Aragon, built *c.* 1445–55 and leading into the Castel Nuovo in Naples, comes near the type. However, the equestrian statue remained an accepted memorial type, from Donatello's Gattamelata (Padua) and Verrocchio's Colleoni (Venice) to Giovanni da Bologna's Cosimo I in the Piazza della Signoria and Giovanni da Bologna and Pietro Tacca's Ferdinando I in the Piazza dell' Annunziata (both in Florence), Henri IV on the Pont Neuf (Paris) by the same two, Philip III and Philip IV in Madrid, Charles I by Le Sueur in Whitehall (London), and finally Falconet's swagger Peter the Great in St

1.2

1.2 St Petersburg (Leningrad),
Peter the Great, 1766–76,
by E. M. Falconet

1.2 Petersburg of 1766–76 with rocky base and prancing horse.[2] Peter the Great may well be called the creator of a Russian nation, a new Westernized Russia, and so he would stand at the beginning of national monuments in the sense of this chapter.

But his is not quite the earliest date. The first monuments to national genius had preceded Falconet's Peter by a generation, and they are English of the decades of Whig ascendancy. Poets' Corner in Westminster Abbey was created in the 1730s. Addison in *The Spectator* calls it the Poets' Quarter. Gibbs's and Rysbrack's Matthew Prior is of *c.* 1723, Scheemakers' Dryden of 1731, Rysbrack's John Gay of *c.* 1733, his Milton of 1737, his Ben Jonson probably of the same year and Scheemakers' Shakespeare of 1740.

1.3 However, the first monument to national genius built specially as such is William Kent's Temple of British Worthies in the grounds of Viscount Cobham's Stowe. The monument was put up in 1733. It is built on a curve with in the middle a pyramid and a niche originally containing a statue of Hermes Psychopompos. On either side are busts, and they represent not only Elizabeth I, William III, King Alfred and the Black Prince, but also Gresham, Drake, Raleigh, Hampden,

Sir John Barnard (Lord Mayor of London from 1727 and MP for the City from 1722 to 1761), Inigo Jones, Shakespeare, Bacon, Milton, Locke, Newton, who had died only a few years before, and Pope, who was still alive.[3] Eight of the busts were transferred from a former 'Saxon Temple' of 1732. So here princes and statesmen stand side by side with scientists, the philosopher, the architect and the poets, and on the same level.[4]

In exactly the same years Queen Caroline built her Hermitage at Richmond and furnished it with busts of great men. The busts, possibly designed by Guelfi, were mostly carved by Rysbrack. Vertue's notebooks under 1731 call them 'to be made'. In 1733 they were installed. They represented Bacon, Boyle, Dr Samuel Clarke, Locke, Newton and William Wollaston.[5] Locke and Newton are also commemorated in the famous set of painted and engraved allegorical cenotaphs commissioned by Owen McSwiny mainly from Venetian and Bolognese artists. What was carried out belongs to the 1720s and 1730s.[6]

Among these worthies there is one whose genius was admired as much abroad as in Britain. The Newton cult created monuments of the first order in France, even if they remained on paper and were bound to remain on

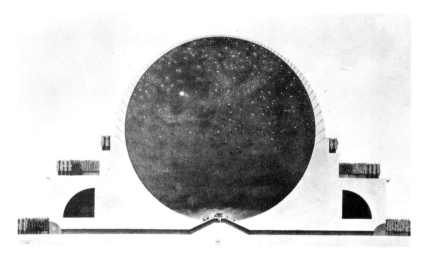

1.4, 5 E.-L. Boullée; design for a monument to Newton, *c.* 1785: elevation (top) and section *(Paris, Bibliothèque Nationale)*

1.3 Stowe, Bucks., Temple of British Worthies, 1733, by William Kent

1.4,5 paper because of their huge size. The first and by far the most important is by Etienne-Louis Boullée, who lived from 1728 to 1799.[7] His monument forms part of a treatise which was never published. It can be assigned to 1784 or 1785. It is in the form of a globe intended to be about 400 feet in height, if one can go by the tiny figures in the foreground. These megalomaniac dimensions are characteristic of French architects of Boullée's age and 8.14–18 even permeate the Grand Prix designs of the academy. They derive ultimately from Piranesi and from Mylne.[8] Boullée's sphere is girt by three rings of cypress trees. The entrances are small, the upper one indeed tiny. One version has an armillary sphere suspended inside, the 1.5 other has the starry sky, much like the planetaria of today.[9] Now why should Boullée have wanted to celebrate Newton and why in this form? The answer to the first question can be given in two quotations. Alexander Pope's epitaph in 1732 is the first:

> Nature and Nature's laws lay hid in night
> God said: Let Newton be! and all was light.

The second quotation is from the dedicatory poem to Voltaire's *Elemens de la Philosophie de Neuton* of 1738:

> Le compas de Neuton mesurant l'univers
> Lève enfin ce grand voile, et les Cieux sont ouverts.

The universe is immense and was uncharted. Newton proved that it is governed by laws which can be understood. The immensity thus has horrors no longer. In this lay the fascination of Newton, a fascination attested for instance by Count Algarotti's elegant *Neutonianismo per le Dame* which came out in 1737 (for Algarotti see pp. 79, 114) and by Quentin de la Tour's portrait of Mademoiselle Ferrand of 1753 meditating on Newton.[10] In 1759 Madame du Châtelet brought out her translation of the *Principia*.[11]

In the text to his Newton plates Boullée is explicit and enthusiastic:

Esprit sublime! Génie vaste, et profond! Etre Divin! Newton! Daigne agréer l'hommage de mes foibles talens! Ah! Si j'ose le rendre publique, c'est à cause de la persuasion que j'ai de m'être surpassé dans l'ouvrage dont je vais parler. O Newton! Si par l'étendue de tes lumières et la sublimité de ton Génie, tu as déterminé la figure de la terre: moi j'ai conçu le projet de t'envelopper de ta découverte. C'est en quelque façon t'avoir enveloppé de toi même.

(Sublime spirit! Vast and profound genius! Divine being! Newton! Accept the homage of my poor talents! Ah! If I dare to make it

1.6 Ermenonville, Rousseau Island, *c.* 1780

1.7 Heinrich Gentz, design for a monument to Luther, 1804

1.8 Hans Christian Genelli, design for a monument to Frederick the Great, 1787

public, it is only because I am convinced that in this work of which I shall speak I surpassed myself. O Newton! You, by the extent of your vision and the sublimity of your genius, have determined the shape of the world: I have conceived the idea of enveloping you within your discovery. I shall envelope you within yourself!)

The sphere, ever since Parmenides, has been regarded as the most perfect form. Hence for instance the curious idea of some Early Christian Palestinian monks that at the resurrection of the dead the body will be spherical.[12] Boullée took over from Plato the faith in the perfection of the sphere. So, when it came to honouring Newton, only the sphere would do.

That is one aspect, but there is also another, concerning the position of the Newton Monument in the history of style. For the perfection of the sphere is the most complete contrast to the arbitrariness and the flippancy of the Rococo, just as the enormous scale is the answer to the *petitesse* of the Rococo. These are the answers of a Classicist, but the starry sky, the awesomeness of the night are the answer of a Romantic, and the Boullée-Ledoux generation was in fact both, radically Classical and radically Romantic.

1.6 Romantic genius was celebrated at the same time in the Rousseau Island at Ermenonville, where Rousseau had lived and where he died in 1778. The grounds of Ermenonville were landscaped in the English way, and a hermitage, a grotto, a *temple rustique* were provided. On the island is the grave, a sarcophagus designed by Hubert Robert, set amid Lombardy poplars and with the inscription: 'Ici repose l'homme de la Nature et de la Vérité.'[13] A few years later Duke Leopold Franz Friedrich of Anhalt-Dessau at Wörlitz imitated the island and the poplars and placed a cenotaph on it commemorating Rousseau, 'who conducted back with manly eloquence the *Witzlinge* to sound reason, the lechers to true joys, errant art to the simplicity of nature, and those who doubted to the revelation'.[14]

Classicist and Romantic elements worked on in unison right down to the 1830s. A paramount example is the design by Heinrich Gentz (1766–1811) of Berlin 1.7 for a monument to Luther, one of the great men of Germany. It combines the Classical obelisk with a rocky sub-structure.[15] Gentz also contributed to the designs for a national monument to Frederick the Great, who 1.10 made provincial Prussia into a great nation.[16] Frederick had died in 1786. The Berlin Akademie der Wissenschaften early in 1787 proposed an architectural monument. So the astronomer Professor Bode, who produced the splendid idea of naming a constellation of stars 'Frederick's Honour', did not qualify.[17] Nor did – though on a narrower interpretation of 'architectural' – Karl Ludwig Fernow's proposal of 'a pyramid without any decoration, and, graven in, just the word *Frederico*'. The choice of a pyramid shows that Fernow must have known what was happening in France, as Gentz and Gilly did ten years later and George Dance less than 1.21 five years after that. But their proposals cannot occupy

1.9 Friedrich Gilly, design for a monument to Frederick the Great, 1797

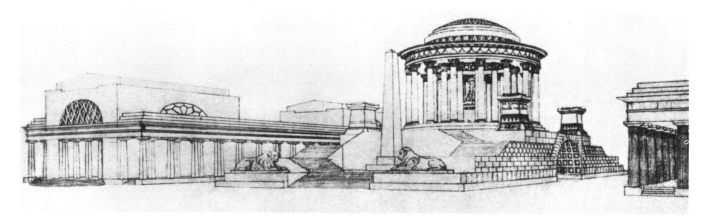

1.10 Heinrich Gentz, design for a monument to Frederick the Great, 1797

us yet. What is of interest here is that the pyramid was considered in the Boullée circle in Paris to have qualities of elementary geometry almost as perfect as the sphere. Boullée used it for cenotaphs, for a 'Chapel of the Dead' and, truncated, for the monument to Turenne; Ledoux, truncated, for Maupertuis (1780), for his cannon forge (in the four corners) and his *four à bois*; and Fontaine for the cenotaph for which he received a second prize of the French Academy in 1785.[18] The pyramid story then goes on, for instance, to the mausoleum at Blickling in Norfolk by Bonomi, 1793; a design by Hans Christian Genelli of 1808 to commemorate Kant;[19] a design of 1813 for a memorial to Napoleon on Mont Cenis by Selva, the leading Venetian architect;[20] a design by Thomas Harrison to commemorate the golden jubilee of George III (with an Egyptian portico this time);[21] and the monument of the founder of Karlsruhe in the Market Place of that city. This dates from 1823–25. Weinbrenner, its designer, belonged to the Gentz-Gilly circle, to which Genelli also belonged.

To return now to Frederick the Great and the initiative of 1787: Genelli and the sculptor Schadow sent a design from Rome. The proposal, however, was shelved, and a new batch of designs came in only in 1797. Gentz's was one of these, Friedrich Gilly's another. Genelli's design had been a temple of moderate size with a hexastyle portico of Greek Doric columns – the earliest example of such columns in Germany.[22] Inside the temple a sarcophagus was to be placed with

the reclining effigy of the King and allegories below. There were to be niches in the walls of the temple with statues.[23] Gentz's rotunda is a little less radical, but he went far beyond Genelli in suggesting a whole precinct, and the elements of this are as uncompromising and novel as those of Gilly, to whom we shall turn presently. The Greek Doric columns occur in Gentz as well, and the semicircular entrance into the basement of the rotunda is totally unrelieved. One of the subsidiary buildings has an entrance in the form of a coffered apse behind a screen of columns, the area above the architrave remaining open. That is a Robert Adam motif (see e.g. the Kenwood library of 1767–69) taken over by Ledoux in one of his toll-houses of the eighties for Paris, the Barrière des Bonshommes. Gentz had travelled in Italy and Sicily from 1790 and ended in Paris and London in 1795. His style, like that of Gilly, as we shall see, presupposes knowledge of Parisian designers, perhaps of Ledoux, certainly of Peyre whose *Oeuvres d'architecture* had been published in 1765.

Friedrich Gilly, Gentz's brother-in-law, left Berlin for Paris only in April 1797, and by then his design for the national monument to Frederick the Great had been delivered to the Academy. It is one of the most beautiful and most original designs of its age. In his descriptive notes Gilly calls it a sanctuary.[24] It consists chiefly of a Greek Doric temple, containing the image of Frederick enthroned, and raised on a high, severely cubic platform, and a triumphal arch. The choice of the Greek

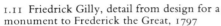

1.11 Friedrick Gilly, detail from design for a
monument to Frederick the Great, 1797

1.12 Paris, the Madeleine, decreed 1806, begun 1809 by Pierre Vignon, completed 1845

Doric order for a monument to the Prussian national hero may at first seem incongruous, but in terms of the evocative qualities of styles it makes sense. The style of the Parthenon was regarded as the noblest of all styles, the style of the age of highest human achievement. No other could be elevated enough for Frederick the Great.

The architecture of the nineteenth century cannot be fully appreciated without taking evocative or associational elements into consideration. This is how Francesco Milizia, the famous Italian theoretician of architecture, expressed it in 1787: 'Le fabbriche come le figure nella pittura e nella scultura hanno d'avere ciascuna la sua fisionomia. . . . Se gli artisti interrogheranno le nature di ciascun monumento, sapranno dargli il suo proprio carattere e in modo che il popolo le riconosca.'[25] (Buildings, like the figures in painting and sculpture, must have their own physiognomy. . . . If only artists would inquire into the nature of each monument, they would know how to give it its own character, in such a way that people would recognize it.) So, in the nineteenth century, if a school was given Grecian features, that linked it with *Academe*, whereas Gothic features would conjure up the learning of the cloister. Architects of the nineteenth century were aware of the suggestiveness of the various styles. Gottfried Semper, the greatest Neo-Renaissance architect of Central Europe, wrote in 1846: 'The impression made on the masses by a building is partly founded on reminiscences',[26] and Andrew Jackson Downing, the American architect and writer, said in 1852 that styles, such as Roman, Italian, Venetian, Swiss or Rural Gothic please less 'from the beauty of form or expression' than 'from personal or historical associations connected with them'.[27]

But Gilly's triumphal arch could not benefit from evocation; for its general shape has no ties with any style of the past, even if the Greek Doric columns, the Roman coffered tunnel vault and the Palladian semicircular

windows have. To propose so unrelieved a block was as daring as any of Soane's inventions and surpassed them in monumentality. As Gilly said in his submitted explanation, the monument was to be 'without any playful decoration'. The temple incidentally was to have light coming in from above – a totally un-Grecian feature. The design, needless to say, remained on paper. In the end all that was done was an equestrian monument, iconographically traditional, though excellent in the execution. Rauch was commissioned; the dates of beginning and end are 1839 and 1851. In 1829 Schinkel had tried his hand at something at least approaching the scale of Gilly's design. Schinkel proposed different sites and different possibilities of commemoration. Of his six designs, four have Greek Doric columns, two Corinthian. One has a giant column in the middle, one a square pillar with reliefs, one an equestrian statue, one a quadriga, and one has a broad tower of three tiers of colonnading.[28]

But it is time to return to France. Napoleon in 1806 decreed that the unfinished church of the Madeleine should be built as a peripteral temple to serve as a memorial to the French army. Article I of the decree states: 'Il sera établi, sur l'emplacement de la Madeleine de notre bonne ville de Paris . . . un monument à la Grande Armée, portant sur le frontispice: L'Empereur Napoléon aux Soldats de la Grande Armée.' (On the site of the Madeleine in our good city of Paris shall be built . . . a monument to the Grande Armée bearing on its façade the words: the Emperor Napoleon to the Soldiers of the Grande Armée.) But the columns were no longer Greek Doric; the moment of uncompromising rigour had passed. The Corinthian order chosen by Vignon is more ornate, and of course also more slender.[29] The interior here is as unconnected with the exterior as in Gilly's temple. The Madeleine (for that is what the monument is now) is covered by three

1.12

1.13 Paris, Arc de Triomphe de l'Etoile, 1806–36, by J.-F.-T. Chalgrin

1.14 Paris, Panthéon, begun 1757 by
J.-G. Soufflot, transformed 1791

saucer domes. Incidentally, Napoleon wanted the roof to be of iron, and we shall follow the march of iron in other chapters. In a characteristically vague way the decree goes on to stipulate that inside the monument on the anniversaries of the battles of Jena and Austerlitz a concert should be given and a discourse held on the 'vertus nécessaires aux soldats' with an *éloge* of the fallen.

Napoleon erected two more major national monuments in Paris, the Colonne Vendôme on the pattern of Trajan's column, built in 1806–10, and the Arc de Triomphe de l'Etoile, also begun in 1806 but completed only in 1836. The Colonne Vendôme was 'monumentum belli germanici' and had a statue of Napoleon on the top. (Napoleon was always tempted into self-glorification. Canova made him a nude hero.[30]) The Arc de Triomphe was dedicated 'à la gloire des armées impériales'. Chalgrin, its designer, had been among the leaders of the Neo-Classical taste ever since his church of St Philippe du Roule of 1774–84. It is not a straightforward imitation of Roman arches. In its own rhetorical way it is as original as Gilly's design. What characterizes Chalgrin's Arc de Triomphe is its blockiness, i.e. the absence of columns, the scarcity of relief and the heavy attic. Precedents are not lacking but are few: in the first place Bullet's Porte St Martin in Paris of 1674–75, d'Orbay's Porte Peyrou at Montpellier of 1691–93, some provincial later eighteenth-century arches (e.g. Châlons-sur-Marne), Ledoux's gate arch of the Hôtel Thélusson of 1778–81 and Boullée's design of *c.* 1780 for a fortified-looking gatehouse. But Chalgrin's closest predecessor is Cellerier's triple entry arch of 1790 to the Champ de Mars. Finally, a more immediate antecedent is Durand's triumphal arch in his *Précis des leçons d'architecture* of 1802–09. In his text Durand pronounces against 'de froides colonnes' and calls for something 'à échauffer l'âme du spectateur'.[31]

But Paris had already before Napoleon created a national monument to her great men. The church of Ste Geneviève, begun in 1757 to Soufflot's design, was the first building in France to abandon Baroque plans and features in favour of the new Classicism.[32] The plan is central with very little extra stress on the east-west axis, and that stress an afterthought. Moreover, the main vessels are separated from aisles and ambulatories by columns carrying a straight entablature instead of arches. In 1791 the Assemblée Constituante changed the purpose from a church to a commemorative building. Above the entrance it now said: 'Aux grands hommes la patrie reconnaissante.' The name was changed from Ste Geneviève to Panthéon.[33]

At this point we leave France and turn back to the North, where the Pantheon idea had caught on too. About 1813 or 1814 Thomas Harrison, one of the best English Grecians and one who must have been aware of the style of the French *pensionnaires* of the Académie de France in Rome and of Boullée and Ledoux, made designs for a monument to commemorate the defeat of Napoleon, and they have the excessively long rows of Greek Doric columns and the Pantheon dome.[34]

The long colonnade and the Pantheon dome are also the principal elements of Schinkel's masterly museum in Berlin (on which see p. 127). Now it was Schinkel's intention to put into the colonnade along the front of his museum 'monuments . . . to those who are of special public interest',[35] and in a design of 1835 for a palace he wanted to provide 'premises for the commemoration of famous men of our country by monuments for enjoyment and for instruction in all the sciences and arts, with a view to the participation of the people in such an institution',[36] an eminently characteristic programme in so far as it marks the transition from palace to public institution. We shall find other such transitions in the development of the theatre, the library and the museum.

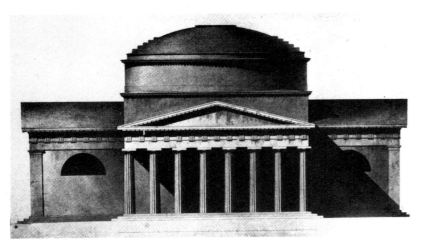

1.17 Karl Freiherr Haller von Hallerstein, design for the Walhalla, near Regensburg, 1814–15

1.15, 16 Karl von Fischer, two designs for the Walhalla, near Regensburg, 1809 (top) and 1810

But while these plans of Schinkel remained a dead letter, two national monuments were actually built.

The scene is Bavaria, the patron Ludwig I, whom we have already met in connection with his enlargements to the palace and whom we shall meet again in a later chapter (pp. 9, 123–24). He had succeeded Maximilian I as king in 1825. As crown prince he had visited Rome and lived there with the young German artists on terms of easy friendship. He was interested in Classical archaeology too and managed to acquire for Munich the sculpture of Aegina. In 1806, when he was twenty, he visited Paris and saw the Panthéon. In the next year, so he wrote himself much later, i.e. 'in days of deepest disgrace', he conceived the idea of 'marble portraits of the fifty most gloriously excellent Germans'. He intended to call the collection Pantheon, but the historian Johannes von Müller suggested Walhalla, and this Germanic term convinced the Prince. The effect of the building, as Ludwig wrote, should be 'that the German should leave it more German'. In spite of these intentions and in spite of the name the building was to be Grecian. The first designs were made in 1809–10 by Karl von Fischer, Ludwig's architect during those years.[37] The earliest had an eight-column Greek Doric portico but a domed centre on the pattern of the Pantheon in Rome. The second design was a peripteral Doric temple, eight by eighteen columns in size.

After the liberation of Germany from Napoleon – on whose side, incidentally, Bavaria had been – the idea was taken up again by the Crown Prince, and now a competition was held. Ludwig stipulated 'the purest antique taste after the most beautiful patterns of ancient temples'. Not everyone believed that this choice of style was right. Johann Martin von Wagner, sculptor and connoisseur of art,[38] wrote from Rome: 'Why has one not given this building, dedicated to German glory, a German form or style? The Gothic style, it may well be said, even if its origin is not German, is yet most akin to the German people. I for one am convinced that one can make anything out of the Gothic style and that it is capable of any form.' Schinkel indeed submitted a kind of Gothic *Campo Santo*. But Ludwig would not budge, and his choice of style was reinforced by sketches which he received from Athens and which were made by Karl Freiherr Haller von Hallerstein,[39] who had been trained as an architect in Berlin by Friedrich Gilly and his father David Gilly in 1798–1805. He had gone to Rome in 1808 and to Athens in 1810. He was a friend of C. R. Cockerell and belonged to the group which discovered the sculpture of Aegina, which, only owing to

1.16

1.15

1.17

1.18 Walhalla near Regensburg, 1821–42, by Leo von Klenze

1.9

a blunder of the British agent, escaped the British Museum and, as we have seen, went to Munich. The story really belongs to another chapter of this book, a chapter in which we shall also meet Johann Martin von Wagner again (p. 124). Haller von Hallerstein's sketches were patently inspired by Gilly's Frederick the Great monument, but he transferred the buildings into the open country. For several years no beginning was made. Karl von Fischer died in 1820. He had been replaced in Ludwig's favour by Leo von Klenze, who was now for some time going to be the Prince's chief executant.

Klenze was born in 1784, had studied in Berlin under David Gilly just after Friedrich Gilly's death, and worked in 1802–03 in Paris under Percier and Fontaine and also Durand. Percier and Fontaine became Napoleon's own architects; Durand, who taught at the Ecole Polytechnique, belonged to the Boullée-Ledoux group. In 1804 Klenze, only twenty years old, became architect to Napoleon's brother Jérome at Kassel. After Napoleon's defeat in 1814, he was by chance introduced to Ludwig and thereupon settled down in Munich for the rest of his life. In 1816 he was commissioned to design the Walhalla. He tried for some years to persuade Ludwig that a Doric temple was 'not wholly suited to represent at first glance a Walhalla, a German Ely-

sium'.[40] But again the Prince insisted. So Klenze gave in, and the final plan was agreed in 1821. In 1825 Ludwig succeeded to the throne, in 1830 the foundation stone was laid on a beautifully wooded site above the Danube near Regensburg, and in 1842 the Walhalla was complete. Turner painted the opening celebrations.

The Walhalla is marble-faced and has eight by seventeen columns carrying a roof of cast iron, as Napoleon had wanted for the Madeleine. The pediments, carved by Schwanthaler, show Arminius, or Hermann, defeating the Romans and Germania welcoming back the provinces lost to Napoleon. Inside, broad projections with paired pilasters articulate the long walls. In the recessed parts are the busts of the great Germans – for instance Leibniz, Schiller, Goethe (who had died in 1832), Mengs, Gluck, Mozart. Along a frieze Wagner carved scenes from early German history ending at the conversion to Christianity. Yet higher up are name plates for those whose likeness was unknown and above the pilasters free-standing Valkyries, again carved by Schwanthaler. The interior is polychrome; in 1820 Hittorff had discovered the polychromy of Greek architecture. Even the Valkyries have lilac garments, gilded bear-skins and fair hair.

The choice of a Doric temple for the Walhalla did not,

1.18

1.19, 20 Kelheim, Befreiungshalle, 1842–63, by Leo von Klenze

as we have seen, go unnoticed and unargued. Franz Kugler, the art historian, wrote in 1843 in its defence: 'We must not object to the choice of style. As our age has not yet produced an architectural style of its own which would be the expression of our thoughts and feelings today, the choice is justifiable . . . Only a fool could deny the higher purity, beauty and dignity of the works of the Greeks.'[41] But according to others that was not the point. The point was, as Cornelius, the leading monumental painter of Germany, had already expressed it in 1820: Why 'ignore the superb fully original German style?' And if Gothic were excluded, why not 'the free development' of the Classical styles in Brunelleschi and Bramante?[42]

So here – may it be noted at once in this very first chapter – were the three stylistic possibilities of the first half of the nineteenth century: Grecian, Gothic, Italianate.

But there was yet another possibility – a Classical yet not imitative style. And this is precisely what Klenze chose for his second national monument, the Befreiungshalle or Hall of Liberation above Kelheim, also on the Danube. Liberation of course meant liberation from Napoleon. As the earliest designs are of 1833 and the decision to build was taken only in 1836, the building

seems somewhat belated. The commission went to Friedrich von Gärtner.[43] He designed a rotunda, and the King laid the foundation stone in 1842, on the day of the opening of the Walhalla. The first designs were inspired by the Pantheon, but later the *Rundbogenstil* was preferred, with arcades instead of straight entablatures. Gärtner died in 1847, and Klenze took over. He built on Gärtner's foundations, but changed the elevation radically. King Ludwig abdicated in 1848 but carried on with the Hall of Liberation at his own private expense. The building was complete in 1863; Klenze died in 1864, Ludwig in 1868.

The Hall of Liberation is one of the most telling examples of Neo-Classicism leaving the stage of imitation, as represented by the Walhalla, and exploring original possibilities. This stage, reached usually in the 1840s, will be noted in other chapters as well. The building is round and in its lower two-thirds articulated by buttresses carrying allegorical statues. There are no windows. Higher up runs a colonnade and the top, slightly recessed, has short buttresses with trophies. Inside at ground level are deep niches, their arches segmental, not round – which once more is characteristic of the last stage of Neo-Classicism. Winged white marble Victories stand in front of the arcade, holding hands and

1.21 George Dance, design for a monument to Washington, 1800
1.22 Baltimore, Washington Monument, 1815–29, by Robert Mills
1.23 Washington, D.C., Washington Monument, 1877–84 by Robert Mills

forming a ring. They have golden shields with the names of battles. Above are plaques with the names of generals and in the architrave names of fortresses. A colonnade with straight entablature leads on to the coffered dome, glazed in the centre. It is once more the Pantheon motif. The glazed oculus is indeed the only source of light. The coffering in comparison with that of the Pantheon is restless and in this again reaches beyond strict historicism.

At this point it is advisable to go for a while outside Europe to have a good look at the Washington Monument in Washington, a legitimate national monument as it celebrates the founder of a nation. It had been preceded by a design of George Dance, commissioned in 1800, one year after Washington's death. It was commissioned by Benjamin West, American but at the time President of the Royal Academy in London. Dance's 1.21 design is far too little known.[44] With its two symmetrical giant pyramids and further back a low pavilion of vaguely Indian character, it belongs to the Boullée-Ledoux-Lequeu group.[45]

In America efforts to commemorate Washington started a full fifteen years later. They take us to Balti-1.22 more.[46] The monument erected there in 1815–29 is a column 130 feet high, in the tradition of the Colonne

Vendôme of 1806–10 and that other Napoleonic column in Paris, the Colonne de Victoire in the Place du Châtelet of 1808, and the Nelson Columns, the earliest of which were those in Edinburgh, begun in 1805, and in Dublin, erected in 1808. The Baltimore column was designed by Robert Mills, and he also designed the Washington obelisk.[47] For obelisks there was of course 1.23 the tradition of Rome – most familiar the obelisk in front of St Peter's – but America also had a famous precedent: the Bunker Hill Monument by Samuel Willard or Horatio Greenough, 221 feet high and put up in 1825–42.

The story of the Washington Monument in Washington is familiar. It was begun in 1848. Mills's design had a Greek Doric rotunda wrapped round the foot of the obelisk. The rotunda was soon given up, and all work stopped in 1855. It was only resumed in 1877; 1884 is the year of final completion. It cost $1,300,000 and is 1.23 555 feet high, the highest monument ever.[48] The material is marble. The walls are 15 feet thick at the base, tapering to 18 inches at the top. Horatio Greenough was critical of it. He wrote:[49]

A national monument to Washington has been designed, and is in process of construction. A lithographic print of this design is before

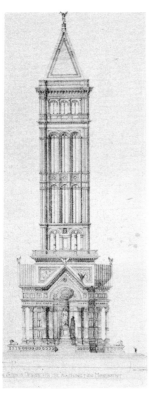

1.24, 25, 26 Designs for a monument to Washington by William Story (left), H. R. Searle (centre), and M. P. Hapgood, *c.* 1879

the public. It represents an obelisk rising out of a low circular build-ing whose exterior presents a Greek colonnade of the Doric order. A facsimile of the endorsement of some of our most distinguished citizens recommends this design to their fellow countrymen. I propose to examine the invention.

The prominent peculiarity of the design before us is the inter-marriage of an Egyptian monument – whether astronomical, as I believe, or phallic, as contended by a Boston critic, matters not very much – with a Greek structure, or one of Greek elements. I do not think it is in the power of art to effect such an amalgamation with-out corrupting and destroying the special beauties and characters of the two elements. The one, simple even to monotony, may be defined a gigantic expression of unity; the other, a combination of organized parts assembled for a common object. The very perfec-tion of their forms as exponents of so distinct characters makes them protest against juxtaposition.

The obelisk has to my eye a singular aptitude, in its form and character, to call attention to a spot memorable in history. It says but one word, but it speaks loud. If I understand its voice, it says, Here! It says no more. For this reason it was that I designed an obelisk for Bunker Hill, and urged arguments that appeared to me unanswerable against a column standing alone. If this be the expres-sion of the obelisk, I object to the site of the proposed monument.

I protest also against the enormous dimensions of this structure. It is another example of the arithmetical sublime – an attempt to realize in art the physical truth that many little things united form one great one; which *in art is not true.*

A structure which rises five hundred feet from the ground and bears the name of Washington must form a unique feature in this metropolis. It must command the attention of everyone, be he American or foreigner, who sees its lofty shaft towering into the blue and holding the sunshine after twilight is gray below. What will be its effect artistically speaking? Kneading into incongruous contact elements hitherto only jumbled by conquest and ruin – truncated – bare – without gradation and without finale – standing upon crumbling detail – heavy above and light below – it will be a symbol of huge aspiration and chaotic impotence.

One reads with respect anything Greenough wrote, but one remains baffled. There is the obelisk in the middle of the capital whose name is Washington. Surely this calls for the one word 'Here' spoken loud.

Another comment on the obelisk worth reporting comes from an essay of the American architect Henry van Brunt, written in 1889:[50]

By an act of hardy rebellion against the authority of a mighty nation unjustly exercised, a certain people, after a long and bloody war, were once set aside from the rest of the world to form a true re-public; and, because of the wisdom and prudence of its founders, this republic eventually became one of the greatest nations of the earth. There was one, the leader in this rebellion, and chief among these founders by the greatness of his services, the dignity of his character, and the pre-eminence of his virtues, upon whom has been conferred by the common voice of mankind a singular title – 'The Father of his country.'

The sentiment of nations with respect to their greatest bene-factors, whether it has contented itself with natural emotions of gratitude and admiration or found more satisfactory expression in acts of adoration, has always been among the most fruitful inspira-tions of art; indeed, its only adequate utterance has been in visible monuments.

1.27 Anonymous design for a monument to Washington, *c.* 1879

1.28 Edinburgh, monument to the Napoleonic Wars on Calton Hill, begun 1822, by W. H. Playfair

And as for a monument to Washington,

no theme other than a religious one has ever been presented more worthy of treatment by a form of art.

But what was the outcome? Height alone, although

the degree and quality of the height resides in its essential composition from the beginning, and is foreshadowed even in the lowest stages of the monument, as in the Giralda at Seville – which, though begun by the Moors in the Saracenic style and completed by the Christians some two centuries later in the style of the Renaissance – is still remarkable for unity of effect, in the brick tower of Saragossa, the Campanile of Santa Maria del Fiore at Florence and that of St Mark at Venice, and in all the later medieval spires without exception. In these each part is essential to the whole.

Not so in the case of an obelisk which can 'express bigness but not . . . grandeur'. The Egyptian prototype

has fixed proportions and . . . was intended to convey a concrete idea by the hieroglyphics which filled its four polished sides . . . It was conspicuously an historic record. The American invention fulfilled none of these conditions, and its pyramidion was so ignorantly debased in the geometrical elevation as to be entirely invisible from any near point . . . In fact it was not an obelisk; it was a chimney without an outlet.

And if Winthrop in laying the foundation stone said: 'Build it to the skies, you cannot outreach the loftiness of his principles', he forgot the fact that an obelisk cannot be 'in any respect significant of Washington'.

So in the end 'a misquotation barbarously misapplied' was van Brunt's verdict, and he proceeded in a second essay to comment on some 'of the suggestions which were volunteered from time to time with a view to develop, for architectural expression, the possible capacities of the shaft'. As examples of the stylistic variety of Late Victorian design four may here be illustrated, all by minor designers. H. R. Searle made 1.25 the shaft into an Italianate chimney, similar to the chimneys of English mid-nineteenth-century waterworks. William Story, the sculptor, living in Italy, 1.24 suggested a derivation from Giotto's campanile of Florence Cathedral and detailed it knowledgeably. M. P. Hapgood, a student, proposed a more ornate 1.26 Gothic, and an anonymous contributor did a wild 1.27 design not remotely dependent on any one style of the past. Van Brunt calls it 'modern French Renaissance' and 'enthusiastically overloaded'.

For the rest of this chapter we can be briefer. Edinburgh after its Nelson Column began work in 1822 on a national monument to the Napoleonic Wars. W. H. 1.28 Playfair designed it, and, like the Walhalla, it was to be a Doric temple. It was left unfinished and has thereby acquired a power to move which in its complete state it could not have had. It was followed by G. Meikle Kemp's Walter Scott Monument, a statue under a 1.29 Gothic canopy, inspired by Melrose Abbey and garnished with statuettes of principal characters. The dates are 1840–44.

The Albert Memorial in London developed the same 1.30 *parti*. It was designed by Sir George Gilbert Scott and

1.29 Edinburgh, Walter Scott Memorial, 1840–44, by G. Meikle Kemp

1.30 London, Albert Memorial, 1863–72, by Sir George Gilbert Scott

1.30   built in 1863–72.[51] At first sight it may not qualify as a national monument and be regarded as yet another monument to a ruler. What justifies its inclusion here is that the inscription cites Prince Albert's 'life devoted to the public good' and that all the sculptural and pictorial representations are devoted to the arts of peace. The four large groups above the relief-clad base are Agriculture, Manufactures, Commerce and Engineering, the figures against the pillars of the canopy Astronomy, Chemistry, Geology and Geometry, the figures in the niches above the pillars Rhetoric, Medicine, Philosophy and Physiology, the mosaic of the gables Poetry and Music, Painting, Architecture and Sculpture. The reliefs on the base are assemblies of the great men of Music, Poetry, Painting, Architecture and Sculpture.[52] It is entertaining and instructive to see what unobvious men were included: in music e.g. Auber and Méhul, Mendelssohn and Weber, Josquin des Prés and Guido d'Arezzo, Arne, Boyce and Sir Henry Bishop; in poetry Corneille and Molière (not Racine), Goethe and Schiller;[53] in painting Wilkie and Turner (not Constable), Lochner, Orcagna, Masaccio (not Giorgione), Géricault, Delacroix, Delaroche, Decamps; in architecture William of Sens, William of Wykeham, Suger, Robert de Courcy, Jean de Chelles, Erwin von Steinbach, Arnolfo di Cambio,

Delorme, Mansart, John Thorpe, Wren and Vanbrugh, and Chambers (not Adam), Barry, Cockerell, Pugin (though Catholic) and Scott himself; in sculpture Torel, William of Ireland (of the Eleanor Crosses), Cibber, Bird, Bushnell, Roubiliac, Flaxman, Bandinelli and Giovanni da Bologna, Bernini, Canova and Thorwaldsen, Peter Vischer (the only German), Palissy, Bontemps, Puget and David d'Angers. A comparison of the Scott and Albert Memorials brings out the contrast of Early and High Victorian, the latter being more intricate, more colourful and more determined in its accents.

Next in order of time comes the Statue of Liberty, given to the United States by the French Republic in honour of the centenary of independence. The actual dates are 1871–86, the structural skeleton is by Eiffel, the bronze statue by F. A. Bartholdi, the base by R. M. Hunt. The statue is 157 feet high and has inside an iron framework. In 1885 work on the monument to Victor Emanuel II – he too founder of a nation – began in Rome. The executed design was by Count Giuseppe Sacconi, though the first prize had gone to P. H. Nénot, architect of the vast new Sorbonne in Paris. Among the competitors was Raimondo d'Aronco, soon to be one of the leaders in the Stile Liberty, the Art Nouveau of

1.31

1.36

1.1

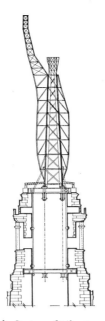

1.31 New York, Statue of Liberty, 1871–86, the skeleton by Gustave Eiffel

1.34 Moscow, Lenin Memorial, 1929–30, by A. Shchusev

1.32 Leipzig, Völkerschlachtsdenkmal, 1896–1913, by Bruno Schmitz

1.35 Ankara, Atatürk Memorial, 1944–53, by Emin Onat

1.33 Voortrekker Monument, near Pretoria, completed in 1949, by Gerhard Moerdyk

Italy. His is an exuberant, undisciplined Neo-Baroque design.

The largest national monument of the early twentieth century is Bruno Schmitz's Völkerschlachtsdenkmal in Leipzig commemorating Napoleon's defeat in 1813. The choice of Schmitz was the right one. Born in 1858, he had already in 1881 won a silver medal for the Victor Emanuel Monument; in 1888 he won the competition for the Soldiers' and Sailors' Monument at Indianapolis,[54] and in the nineties did the monumental architectural memorials to the Emperor Wilhelm I on the Kyffhäuser, at the Porta Westfalica and at the confluence of Rhine and Moselle at Koblenz. He also had a share in the Bismarck Towers, the German equivalent to American Washington monuments.[55] The Völkerschlachtsdenkmal was begun in 1898 and inaugurated in the centenary year 1913.[56] Its height is 300 feet and it has a hall inside 223 feet high. The vault of this hall and that of the crypt below are of reinforced concrete. (More on concrete will be found in the chapters to follow.) The style is no longer in imitation of the past – a cyclopean granite structure of impressive outline, self-confident and threatening in mood. Bruno Schmitz interpreted it himself: 'The subject of the monument is the whole German people which rose and never rested in its struggle until the Corsican and his army were chased from German soil. Hence the monument also had to rise on a broad base in clear contours and to a great height, in vigorous forms, like a great nation rising.'[57]

Evidently derived from the Völkerschlachtsdenkmal is the Voortrekker Monument outside Pretoria, by Gerhard Moerdyk, completed only in 1949.

This leaves two more national monuments of the twentieth century, both to creators of national self-consciousness and pride: the Lenin Monument in Moscow, 1929–30 by Shchusev, a black unrelieved cube, and the Atatürk Monument outside Ankara, 1944–53 by Emin Onat, a hall with subsidiary buildings in a style similar to Mussolini's and Hitler's (no offence meant): travertine outside, marble inside, a gilded ceiling and the tomb block weighing forty tons.

1.36 Rome, monument to Victor Emanuel II, 1885–1911, by Count Giuseppe Sacconi

2.1 Florence, Uffizi, 1560–71, by Giorgio Vasari

2
Government buildings from the late twelfth to the late seventeenth century

DIFFERENTIATION is a theme which will run through many of the chapters of this book. Nowhere is the development from multiple functions to single, rigidly special functions more patent than in medieval government buildings. Before the late twelfth century administration in general and the administration of law took place in the palace of emperor, king, prince, bishop, and if for some purpose extra space was needed, the churches and of course any public square were available.

Something to correspond to the Greek *bouleuterion*[1] came into existence only when the towns of North and a little later Central Italy had achieved independence, even if nominally they remained under the Emperor. Dr Jürgen Paul, in an excellent thesis,[2] has traced the development. Names of councils, and officials, varied widely among different towns and among different phases at the same time. Buildings are mentioned from the late twelfth century onwards and preserved from the early thirteenth.

The oldest dated government building is the Palazzo del Broletto at Como, inscribed 1215. 'Broletto' comes from *brolium* or *brolum*, a fenced-in area. The plan became standard: an open ground floor with arcades and one large room above. The type was derived from such palaces as Goslar of the mid-eleventh century and Brunswick of the late twelfth. An eleventh-century Italian example is at Pomposa. At Como the ground floor served as an extension of the market held in front of the building; the upper floor was town hall as well as law court.[3] Novara and Bergamo are of the same type and about the same time. In Milan the provision was more elaborate.[4] To the west of the cathedral a spacious area, now called the Piazza de' Mercanti, was isolated by a high wall. In its middle was and still is the Palazzo della Ragione, dated 1233, of the same type as the Broletto of Como. *Render ragione* is to administer justice; so the law court aspect rather than the town hall aspect was stressed. Facing the long sides of the building were two open markets. On the east side of the area was the Palazzo del Podestà, built in 1251 and also housing the prison (like the markets it no longer survives). On the south side is the Loggia degli Osii, mentioned in 1257 but rebuilt in 1316. It served for announcements. There is also the fourteenth-century Palazzo dei Notai and, in its present form dated 1564, the Palazzo dei Giureconsulti. Differentiation of functions had obviously set in.

Early medieval town halls, under divers names, abound in Italy and also exist in other countries. Ex-

2.3 Siena, Palazzo Pubblico, 1298–1348

2.4 Florence, Palazzo Vecchio, 1299–1314

2.2 Como, Palazzo del Broletto, 1215

amples in France are Trie-Château of *c.* 1160 and La Réole in the Gironde of *c.* 1200; in Germany Gelnhausen, also of *c.* 1200, and Minden in Westphalia of the late thirteenth century.[5] The ground floor at Minden has the same arcading as the Italian town halls, the upper floor was altered after the Reformation. Italy, however, remained the leading country for town halls into the fourteenth century. The great hall could be much larger than at Como – 260 feet long at Padua, 200 feet at Bologna – and wings could be added at the back with more halls, until they formed the inner courtyard of a building of four ranges (Brescia, Verona, Cremona, Piacenza – the latter begun only in *c.* 1281 and never completed).

Between 1250 and 1300 a new type was developed in Tuscany. It is first heralded by the Bargello in Florence, the core of which dates from 1250–60.[6] It consists of two halls, one on top of the other, but the lower hall is no longer open, which means that the market function was now splitting off. Its further development concerns a much later chapter (p. 235ff). The Bargello was built for the newly created post of the Capitano del Popolo.[7] One generation later Florence built the Palazzo Vecchio[8] and Siena the Palazzo Pubblico.[9] The date of beginning was 1298 in Siena, 1299 in Florence, the date of completion 1314 in Florence, 1348 in Siena. Both are no longer of the predominantly horizontal type of a ground-floor and a first-floor hall, but let height dominate. In Siena at first only the centre was built, rightly called Torrione. The wings followed in 1307–10, one storey less than they are now, the tower in 1325–48. The centre contained two large halls and subsidiary rooms, the right wing the offices and dwellings of the Signori Nove, the left wing, round a small inner courtyard, the palace of the Podestà. Market space was no longer provided. The markets began to demand a building to themselves (pp. 236–37). Here and even more in Florence it is obvious that more office space and more specialized office accommodation had become necessary. The largest hall in Siena is the Sala di Mappamondo, with Simone Martini's *Maestà* and his *Guidoriccio da Fogliano* – the oldest of all secular portraits. The assembly hall of the Nove which adjoins the Mappamondo has Ambrogio Lorenzetti's *Good and Bad Regimen*.

In Florence the Palazzo Vecchio – or rather Palazzo dei Signori, whose authority consisted of the Gonfaloniere and six Priori – is more compact than the Siena Town Hall, and with its mightily machicolated top and its tower growing right out of the block has a decidedly

2.3

2.4

2.3, 4

2.5 Minden, Town Hall, ground floor late 13th century

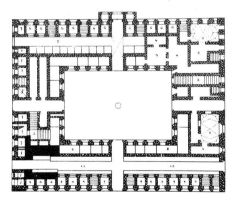

2.6, 7 Thorn (Torun), Town Hall, tower begun *c.* 1250, top
1385; surrounding building begun 1393, upper storey 1602–03:
plan (left) and exterior

fortress-like character. There is no ground floor arcading at all. The plan is complex. The north third had
three assembly rooms one on top of the other, the south
two-thirds a spacious courtyard with a cloister at
ground level and rooms above. Few original details
survive. Apart from the Priori and the Gonfaloniere,
the Consiglio Generale and the Consiglio Speciale met
in the palace. The staff of the Priori is recorded as forty-
three. As in Siena, no markets were held in the new
building.[10] When the republic came to an end and
Alessandro Medici became the first Duke, the palace
became the Palazzo Ducale; when the first Grand-Duke
moved into the Palazzo Pitti, the name Palazzo Vecchio
became a sensible denomination.

North of the Alps there is only one fourteenth-
century town hall to stand comparison with those of
Florence and Siena, and that is politically as well as
architecturally an exception. It is the town hall of Thorn
(now Torun in Poland).[11] Generally speaking German
town halls are much more varied than Italian. Brunswick, e.g., is L-shaped and has upper as well as lower
arcading all along the front and a gable for every bay
above the elaborate tracery of the upper arcade. It dates
from 1393–96 and 1447–68. Lübeck, the mightiest of the
Hanseatic towns, is even more complex, with parts of

every century from the thirteenth to the sixteenth.[12]
But Thorn is just one brick block with an inner courtyard and a grand tower. There is hardly any decoration,
only consistent blank arcading to frame each window
bay. The tower was begun *c.* 1250, the rest is of 1393
et seq., except for the top floor which is an addition of
1602–03. The explanation of this exceptional plan and
elevation lies in the fact that Thorn was in the territory
of the Prussian Order and in fact the most prosperous
town in their territory. Already in 1280 it had its share in
the Hanseatic League. The plan and elevation are not in
the line of development of town halls, but of the castles
of the Order, for instance Marienwerder as rebuilt
c. 1320–40. We know the functions of the building from
the licence for the rebuilding of 1393. The licence was
issued by the High Master of the Order on condition
that all the following rooms should be inside the one
building: town hall, market hall, law courts, general
retailers' shops, bakers' shops, weigh-house and other
rooms.[13] The shops were all on the ground floor. They
were for the cloth trade, which was the staple trade of
Thorn, for haberdashers, potters, soap makers, linen
sellers, bakers and cake bakers. So here, as against Siena
and Florence, the market function had not yet split off.
On the first floor were the great hall, the council room

2.6, 7

2.6, 7

2.8 Middelburg, Town Hall, largely 1506 et seq., by Antony I and Rombout Keldermans

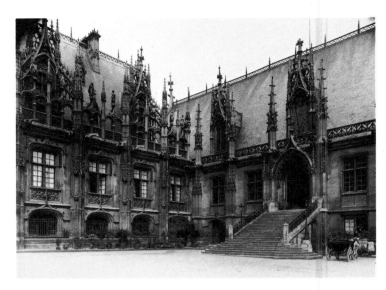

2.9 Rouen, Palais de Justice, 1499–1543

and chancellery rooms. One room for law cases was on the upper, another (with a figured vault) on the ground floor.

It is not necessary to follow the town halls through the later Middle Ages in all countries. A fine crop survives in the Netherlands and the north of France, where as a rule the cloth hall and other halls built by guilds are separate buildings. Ypres, as we shall see in a much later chapter (p. 236), had the grandest of all cloth halls, and at Bruges also the Halles are larger than the town hall, and there were extra buildings for the chancellery (Greffe) and the town hall of the liberties, i.e. suburbs (Le Franc). Brussels, Louvain and Ghent all have fifteenth-century town halls with ornate Late Gothic façades. So have Douai of the late fifteenth and Arras of the early sixteenth century in the part of France bordering on the Netherlands,[14] and so has Middelburg in Holland, which was built mostly in 1506 and after to designs of two members of the Flemish Keldermans family, Antony I and Rombout.[15]

At least as ornate as the Late Gothic town halls of the Netherlands is the building at Rouen known as the Palais de Justice. It has an interesting story.[16] It was begun as the Parloir aux Bourgeois, and it was to be the equivalent of a town hall, with shops and market below and the great hall above. But when building had only just started Louis XII decided to make it the seat of the Echiquier des Causes of Normandy, later called the Parlement, i.e. the Law Courts of Normandy. So a wing was added at right angles. The centre dates from 1508–09. Building went on till 1543, and many altera-

tions followed from the seventeenth to the nineteenth century.[17] The great hall is 158 feet long and has a grand timber roof in the shape of a tunnel-vault. In details of the building Early Renaissance forms appear.

The town hall of Paris has a complicated architectural history.[18] The medieval Parloir aux Bourgeois was on the left bank. In 1357 Etienne Marcel, Prévost des Marchands, bought a house of the thirteenth century in the Place de Grève to serve as a larger town hall. It was known as the Maison aux Piliers because of its open ground floor – the familiar medieval pattern. It was replaced by a more stately building only in 1535 and – gradually – into the seventeenth century. The style was that of the French Early Renaissance. The designer was Domenico da Cortona, called Boccador, the executant master mason Pierre Chambiges.[19] There was a court-yard behind the façade with ranges to west (the façade range), south and east. To the north were the premises of the Hôpital du St Esprit; to the east was the church of St Jean. This being so the town hall could not expand, and even the building on this site was completed only in 1628. The architect of that time was Marin de La Vallée, father and grandfather of the two famous Swedish La Vallées. Marin to a remarkable degree kept to the Early Renaissance style.

English town halls do not deserve more than a sentence or two. For political reasons towns never built on the scale of Italy and the Netherlands. The one exception is the London Guildhall of *c.* 1410–40, with a great hall about 165 feet long and a vaulted undercroft.

The Renaissance brought no immediate changes. The

2.8

2.9

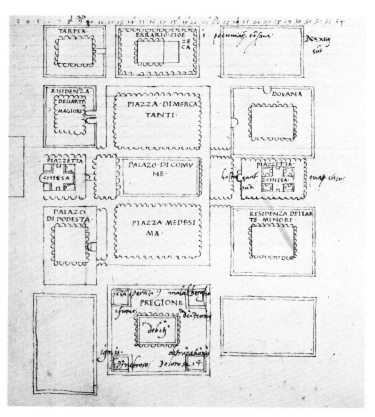

2.10 Filarete, design for a town centre, from his *Treatise*, early 1460s (*Florence, Biblioteca Nazionale Centrale*)

2.11 Francesco di Giorgio, designs for civic offices, from his *Treatise*, c. 1480 (*Florence, Biblioteca Nazionale Centrale*)

town halls of Pienza (by Bernardo Rossellino), Verona (by Fra Giocondo), Bologna, Brescia, Padua follow the medieval tradition of the open arcaded ground floor and the council chamber above. Only on paper did Italian fifteenth-century architects have a chance to demonstrate axial compositions of separate buildings to satisfy the various developing needs. Antonio Filarete was the first – his *Treatise on Architecture* having been written in the early 1460s in Milan.[20] He visualizes a large 'Piazza di Mercatanti' (*dei mercanti*), in its middle the town hall ('Palazzo di Comune'), along its top the treasury ('Tarpea' and 'Errario cioè zeca'), along its bottom the prison, along its left side the major guilds, a small church or chapel and the Palazzo del Podestà, and along its right side the customs house, another chapel (symmetry before reason!) and the minor guilds. The market buildings are separate and will occupy our attention much later (p. 237).

About thirty years later, we learn from a famous letter of Summonte to Marcantonio Michiel[21] that Alfonso II of Naples intended to build near the Castel Nuovo 'a great palace where the various law courts would have been located' and 'men of affairs could transact their business'. So that would have been a combined exchange and law courts. Charles VIII's invasion of Italy foiled the plan.

At the same time Francesco di Giorgio, who was a painter and sculptor besides being architect and author, wrote a treatise while he lived at Urbino. Most probably he knew Filarete's treatise.[22] He wants the Signoria to be near the main square and higher than the other buildings. Opposite the Signoria should be the loggia for the merchants. Nearby also should be the 'case degli officiali', the prison, the customs house, the salt magazine and other shops and warehouses ('banchi e fondachi').[23] Francesco drew two versions of 'case et Palazi di republica', with a large council chamber, a courtyard with columns, a chapel with vestry, a small council chamber ('consistorio') in one, a chancellery in the other, a room marked 'riformagioni' and some others. In his text Francesco goes more into details. The 'casa della repubblicha' should lie at the back of the main square and be fully detached. It should have only one entry, and this should lead into an atrium and from there to the courtyard from where 'tutti li offici' should be accessible. Francesco also mentions the armoury. A staircase leads to the council chamber and 'all the other rooms'. They include the 'consistorio overo audienza' with the chancellery next door, a chapel with vestry and lavatories ('necessari').[24] Francesco also provides a kitchen and dining room (called 'ticrino', i.e. *triclinio*), a barber's room, and on the third floor rooms for the council members (Priori) and more rooms for 'notaries, scribes and other officials'. Francesco's 'sala o andata circum circa per sollazzo et esercizio de' signori' must be a kind of long gallery.

In the description of the city centre Francesco mentioned a 'casa degli officiali'. One is tempted to interpret this as a term for an office building. And this may well be the correct interpretation considering that one of the most famous Italian buildings of the sixteenth century was just that. Everybody knows it, although few people

2.12 Antwerp, Town Hall, 1561–65, by Cornelis Floris

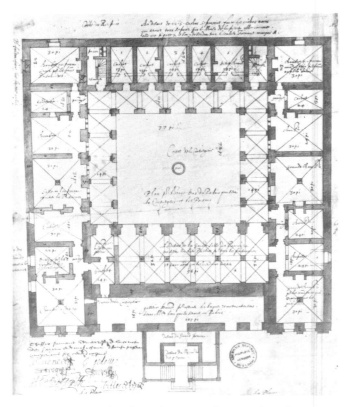

2.13, 14 Rennes, Palais de Justice, 1618–after 1626, by Salomon de Brosse: view and plan (Rennes, Archives)

2.1 realize that the Uffizi in Florence were built to be 'uffizi'. The architect is Vasari, the date 1560–71. The occupants of the offices were many, the most important being the nine Conservatori, with their Scriptori, their Audienza and their Chancellery. Others were the major and some minor guilds, i.e. Mercatanti, Cambio, Seta, Speziale and Fabbricanti, the Commercial Tribunal, the Commissioners of the Militia, and of Public Demeanour (including the control of prostitution), the Conservatori delle Leggi, dei Pupilli, della Grascia, delle Decime e Vendite – thirteen bodies in all.[25]

In exactly the same years or, to be more precise, in 1561–65, the proudest town hall of the sixteenth century 2.12 was being built: Cornelis Floris' Antwerp Town Hall, 256 feet long and 184 feet high.[26] We know something of the main rooms inside and their function from an inventory of 1570. A little to the right of the centre a tunnel-vaulted passage led into the courtyard. Off the passage a wide staircase designed by Nicolo Scarini went up to the great hall. Near this was the conciergerie and the kitchen. The top landing of the staircase was the place from which decisions of the council were announced. Carrying on to the south one came to the large and the small rooms where the aldermen conferred on matters civil and juridical. The remaining two rooms

along the façade were the quarters of the Ambtman, i.e. the Public Prosecutor, and the court of justice. If one went back from this side of the building to the courtyard, one could now go up the staircase of honour to reach the conciergerie and the small and the large council chambers. The latter was the sanctuary of the City Council. Next to it was the chapel and behind this the Treasurer's office. The description is not very clear, but what results from it undoubtedly is that the functions of town hall and of law courts were still mixed up.

The case of the next government building of comparable monumentality is different. Salomon de Brosse's Palais de Justice at Rennes was built as the Palais du 2.13, 1 Parlement, and that in the seventeenth century meant law courts. It will be remembered that that was so already at the time of the Rouen Palais de Justice. Salomon de Brosse[27] in 1618 took over the building which had been originally designed by Germain Gauthier, François Mansart's brother-in-law, in 1609. It was still far from complete when de Brosse died in 1626. The building is square, 200 by 200 feet, but the façade has angle bays moderately projecting. They frame the principal room, the Salle des Procureurs. Beyond is a spacious courtyard with a cloister below, galleries above. The Salle is elevated and was originally

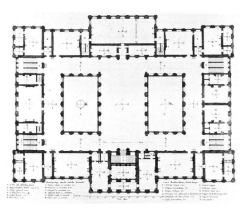

2.15,16 Amsterdam,
Town Hall (now Royal Palace),
1648–55, by Jacob van Campen:
plan and Burgerzaal

reached by a large outer staircase. On the ground floor were prisons, with a common room, also used for visitors. That sounds humane, but at the north end is the ominous annotation: 'au dessous . . . se pourront faire les cachots noirs', i.e. windowless cells (pp. 160, 161). On the main floor to the west of the Salle were the Greffe (chancellery), chapel, Salle de la Tournelle (i.e. inter-rogation chamber) and the council room for the Tournelle; east of the Salle de la Tournelle were the Chambre des Requêtes, the Greffe Civile and the audience chamber. Finally, the north range repeats Chambre des Requêtes and adds a Greffe des Requêtes. A 'buvette' is also provided. But the importance of the building is less in its internal accommodation than in its style. De Brosse's name is most familiar as that of the architect of the Luxembourg. There, in 1615, he was still working in the style of Henri IV with restless surfaces and a broken skyline. The Palais de Justice, only three years later, has an even skyline and a much reduced variety of façade motifs. It is closer to Mansart's Orléans range at Blois, i.e. French seventeenth-century classicity, than to the Luxembourg.

The Rennes stage in France is that of Jacob van Campen in Holland, as is patent in his Amsterdam Town Hall, the grandest of all seventeenth-century town halls. Its grandeur was justified; for Amsterdam had taken over the leading role in North European commerce which in Floris's time had been Antwerp's. Jacob van Campen's building, now the Royal Palace, went up in 1648–55.[28] It is 263 feet long and 167 feet high. The façade is less convincing than that of Ant-werp. The order of windows in five tiers, square, oblong, square, oblong, square, and the two orders of pilasters are a weak way of articulating. The plan, however, is of great monumentality. The block is a parallelepiped with two courtyards separated by a wide range which lies in axis with the centre of the façade and contains the Burgerzaal or *salle des pas perdus*, a splendid apartment such as no previous town hall had possessed, high, wide, ashlar-faced and tunnel-vaulted, with sumptuous sculptural decoration. The principal sculptor of the town hall was Artus Quellien or Quellin. One entered left and right of the actual centre and passed through the vestibules between which is the Vierschar, i.e. the hall for public announcements and especially those of death sentences. Behind this is the staircase up to the *piano nobile* and foremost the Burgerzaal. This served as waiting room, distribution centre and general promenade. From it issue wide tunnel-vaulted corridors which run round the courtyards and have the entries to

2.13

2.15–17

2.17

2.15

2.16

all the main rooms. They also are amply decorated as are the other principal rooms. To the façade are on the left from left to right the Treasury and the Burgomasters' Suite, on the right from right to left the Trustees of Orphans, the Council Room and the Court Room. In the left range the centre is the Secretariat, in the right range the Insurance Office, the Bankruptcy Office (where Rembrandt attended in 1656) and the Accounts. They are at the corner, and the back range then continued to the left with the Magistrates' Chamber, the large, centrally placed Magistrates' Court, the Chamber of the Commissioner for Petty Affairs and in the corner the Treasury Extraordinary. On the ground floor beneath the Burgerzaal is the Arsenal. To the right of the entrance are guard rooms, to the left are other guard rooms and then the City Bank (see p. 199). Round the corner in the left range the City Bank continues and a smaller room is for the Assayer. The left half of the back range is the caretaker's flat. The right half of the back range and the right range are for legal business. In the corner is the gaoler's flat, and in the back range the Torture Chamber, in the right range the Whipping Chamber and the prison cells. One would not at once connect either the age of Rembrandt or this cool and civilized building with flogging and torture.

To the end of the seventeenth century government buildings were, as we have seen, nearly all town halls. Council meetings, administrative offices and courts of justice were located in the same building. A separate building for offices such as the Uffizi was an exception. In the course of the eighteenth century that was to change. Differentiation of functions continued, and by 1800 houses of parliament, buildings for ministries, town halls and law courts all went their own way. In the next three chapters I shall follow them in their development.

2.17 Amsterdam, Town Hall (now Royal Palace), 1648–55, by Jacob van Campen

3.1 Dublin, Parliament House (now Bank of Ireland), 1728–31, by Edward Lovett Pearce

3
Government buildings from the eighteenth century

Houses of parliament

THE IRISH Parliament from the late seventeenth century met in Chichester House.[1] In 1709 it was called 'very ruinous', and so in 1728 a new Parliament House was begun. The architect was Edward Lovett Pearce.[2] He was distantly related to Vanbrugh – his grandmother and Vanbrugh's mother had been daughters of Sir Dudley Carleton, the diplomat-virtuoso and acquaintance of Rubens – and his grandfather had been Lord Mayor of Dublin, his father and uncle generals. He was an army officer too. After having worked at architecture under Vanbrugh, he visited Italy in 1723–24 and got converted to Palladio – no more than ten years after Colin Campbell's and Burlington's conversion. The Dublin Parliament House is thus a building of importance in British architectural history. Its façade has two short wings and giant detached Ionic columns along the centre and the inner side of the wings. The centre of the centre is a projecting tetrastyle portico with pediment. In the middle of the block was the House of Commons, octagonal with an upper order of Ionic columns and a shallow dome of Pantheon type. The House of Lords was on the right in no prominent position. It was oblong with a narrower apse. In 1800 the Act for the Union of Great Britain and Ireland received royal assent, and the Parliament House became useless. In 1803 it was given

to the Bank of Ireland (founded in 1783). Among the conditions made by the Government for the buildings to be taken over was that the two Chambers would be subdivided, lest 'disquieting ghosts might still haunt the scenes that were consecrated by so many memories'.

The first session in the new Parliament House was 1731–32. In 1732 William Kent began to make plans for a new palace for the English Parliament.[3] It was needed. Ever since Henry VIII the House of Commons and the House of Lords and also the Courts of Justice had had to make do with St Stephen's Chapel, Westminster Hall, the Painted Chamber and whatever antiquated accommodation there was – with ale-houses and coffee-houses on the periphery.[4] Kent during the 1730s did a number of designs. They were classical, Palladian, Burlingtonian and inspired by Kent's own *Designs of Inigo Jones, with some additional Designs*, published in 1727, and by Burlington's *Fabbriche antiche*, published in 1730 and presenting Palladio's drawings of the Imperial Roman baths. Giant orders, low Pantheon domes and Venetian windows are characteristic motifs. The shape of the House of Commons in one design is a semicircle with the arms lengthened. In the light of future developments this is remarkable. However, for a whole century nothing came of all this.

3.1, 2

3.2

3.3, 4

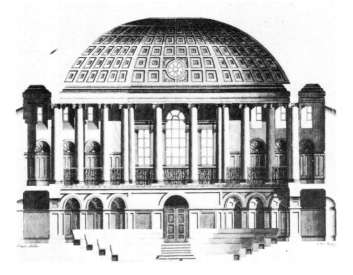

3.2 Dublin, Parliament House, 1728–31, by Edward Lovett
Pearce: House of Commons

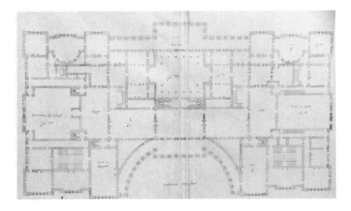

3.3 William Kent, design for Houses of Parliament for London, 1732/33: plan. The river front is at the top. *(London, Victoria and Albert Museum)*

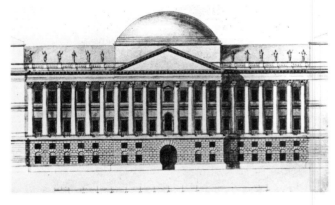

3.4 William Kent, design for Houses of Parliament for London, 1735: elevation of the central portion of the river front *(London, Sir John Soane's Museum)*

And so we must leave Britain and for a while move to America and her capitols.[5] The first is that of Virginia. In 1785 Jefferson had gone to France. His interest in, and knowledge of, architecture was proverbial. So he was asked to produce plans for the Capitol of Virginia. He consulted Clérisseau, an expert on ancient Roman architecture, who had travelled to Split with Robert Adam and published a folio on the Roman monuments of Nîmes. Jefferson knew the Maison Carrée at Nîmes too and took from it the general scheme of deep portico and demi-columns along the sides. The portico is hexastyle, of unfluted Corinthian columns. The Capitol was built in 1785–90. The resident architect was Samuel Dobie. In its plan[6] it is of no special interest.

In 1790 Washington was created as the Federal capital. Major l'Enfant's grand plan was made in 1791–92, and in 1792 a competition was opened for the Capitol and the President's House.[7] Among the designs for the Capitol submitted, the most interesting came from Dobie. It has an octastyle portico and a central rotunda with detached columns under a low dome. In the end Dr Thornton, doctor of medicine of the University of Edinburgh, won with a submission entered late. George Washington praised its 'grandeur, simplicity and convenience'.[8] It was modified by the

French architect Etienne-Sulpice Hallet and in the end had a giant portico of eight columns and a low dome. The façade motifs show French inspiration, in the unstressed parts decidedly Louis XVI. No wonder, as not only was Hallet French but Thornton also knew Paris well. The plan was interesting, with a large rotunda with detached columns immediately behind the portico and a second rotunda behind the first. The dome was of the same low Pantheon type as Dobie's and indeed Pearce's and Kent's. The House of Representatives was in the left wing, the Senate, much smaller, in the right wing. The House of Representatives had an elliptical colonnade in an oblong room, but the Senate was semicircular. This is important; for it proves a direct connection with Paris and one of the most influential of French eighteenth-century buildings, the Ecole de Chirurgie or Ecole de Médecine by Gondoin. Quatremère de Quincy in 1830 called the latter 'l'ouvrage le plus classique du 18ᵐᵉ siècle'.[9] I shall have to refer to it more than once. It had a coffered half-dome with an eye à la Pantheon. The Senate wing of the Capitol was occupied in 1800. Work was supervised first by Hallet, then by George Hadfield, the architect much later of the Washington City Hall, then by James Hoban, the architect of the White House. In 1803 Latrobe took

3.5 Richmond, Va., Virginia State Capitol, 1785–90, designed by Thomas Jefferson

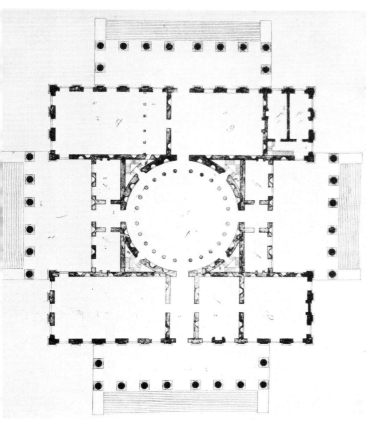

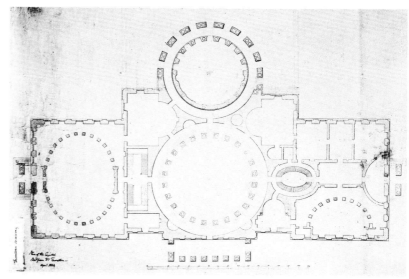

3.6–9 Designs for the U.S. Capitol, Washington, D.C. Above left and left, Samuel Dobie, 1792: elevation and plan. Above, William Thornton's modified design, c. 1794: elevation and plan

3.10 Paris, Ecole de Médecine, 1771–76, by Jacques Gondoin

3.11 Benjamin Latrobe, design for the U.S. Capitol, Washington, D.C., c. 1807–11: north elevation

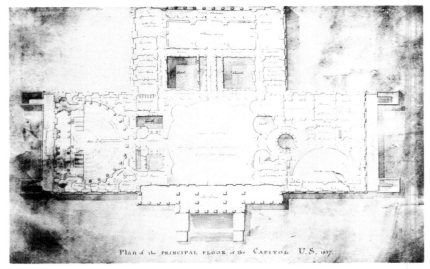

Plan of the PRINCIPAL FLOOR of the CAPITOL U.S. 1817

3.12 Benjamin Latrobe, design for the U.S. Capitol, Washington, D.C., 1817: plan of the principal floor

over. He made some internal alterations and designed a new façade with a low Greek Doric portico and a rather unorganic upper loggia of much slenderer columns. The dome remained of the Pantheon type. With Latrobe the Greek Revival entered America. He had used Doric columns already in 1800 (Philadelphia Water Works), but the Doric gained wide American acceptance only about 1830.

It is difficult to decide whether such motifs as Pantheon domes and giant colonnades were derived from the English classicism of 1720 etc. or from the French Neo-Classicism of the Gondoin generation and in particular from Peyre's *Oeuvres d'architecture* published in 1765. The Burlingtonians and Peyre of course had a common source. In the case of Kent dependence on Roman baths has already been pointed out. Peyre in his dedication to Marigny stresses his studies in Italy and especially of the baths of the Imperial palaces. His last two plates are in fact the Baths of Diocletian and of Caracalla.

So much on the sources of the early architects of the Capitol. As for the building, in 1814 the British Navy set fire to it, and Latrobe's restoration and remodelling left the Senate in its Gondoin shape, but gave the Representatives the same shape.

To complete the story I must anticipate. A substantial extension was recommended in 1850 and a competition held in the same year. Thomas U. Walter was chosen. The foundation stone was laid in 1851, the dome authorized in 1855 and completed in 1865. It is 94 feet in diameter, rises to a height of 207 feet 6 inches and has trussed shells of cast iron. Did Walter know A. Ricard de Montferrand's book *L'Eglise Cathédrale de St Isaac*, published at St Petersburg in 1845, with its plates of the iron structure of the dome? The ironwork of St Isaac's was by Baird, the engineer being Handesyde. The dome was ready by 1842. As for Washington, the latest memorable fact in the architectural history of the Capitol is the thickening to the east, carried out in 1959–60.

State capitols were a bumper crop about the 1830s.[10] They are inspired by Washington in that they tend to have a portico and a central rotunda rising into a dome. The best are the series of five by Town & Davis, starting with Connecticut (New Haven), 1827–31, without a dome, and going on to Indiana (Indianapolis), 1831–35, North Carolina (Raleigh), 1833–40, and Ohio (Columbus), 1838–57, where Town & Davis based their design on that of Henry Walters of Cincinnati.[11]

As the states of the United States, so the *cantons* of Switzerland during these years aspired to provide them-

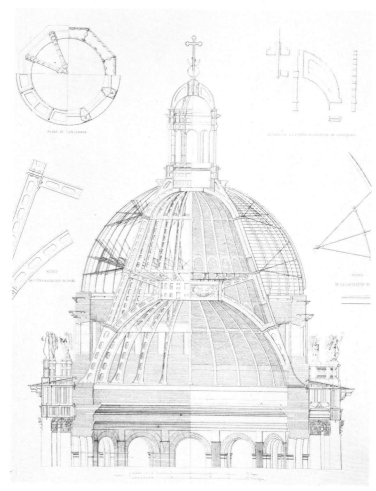

3.14 Indianapolis, former Indiana State Capitol, 1831–35, by Town & Davis

3.13 St Petersburg (Leningrad), St Isaac's Cathedral, dome completed in 1842 by A. Ricard de Montferrand: section (Montferrand, *L'Eglise Cathédrale de St Isaac*, 1845)

3.15 Columbus, Ohio State Capitol, 1838–57, by Henry Walters and Town & Davis

3.16 Washington, D.C., U.S. Capitol, enlarged 1850–63 by Thomas U. Walter

3.17 Chester, Shire Hall, 1788–1822, by Thomas Harrison

3.19 Hereford, Shire Hall, 1817–19, by Sir Robert Smirke

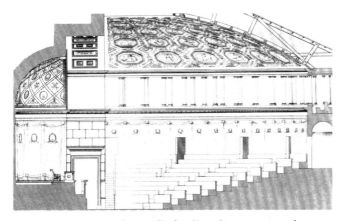

3.18 Paris, Palais Bourbon, Salle des Cinq Cents, 1795–97, by
Gisors and Leconte (Joly, *Plans, coupes* . . ., 1840). The rustication
behind the seating is hidden by curtains

3.20 Paris, Palais Bourbon, main façade, 1806–08, by Bernard
Poyet

selves with capitols: Zürich in 1832 (not executed),
Berne in 1833 (not executed), Lucerne in 1841–43. All
three followed the Gondoin scheme.[12]

In England a parallel development took place. Here
it was the counties that needed county halls or shire halls,
and some of them deserve a mention, none more than
Thomas Harrison's at Chester, part of the rebuilding of
the castle begun in 1788 but completed only in 1822. It
has a front of nineteen bays, a portico of six unfluted
3.17 Doric columns, and the main room inside is of the
Gondoin type. Harrison, whom we have met (above,
pp. 15, 17), was well aware of what was happening in
Paris. Moreover he had spent the years 1769–76 in
Rome, where Piranesi and the French *pensionnaires* must
have impressed him.[13] But the majority of the English
shire halls are later and in the Grecian taste. Examples are
3.19 Gloucester (1814–16) and Hereford (1817–19), both by
Sir Robert Smirke, the architect of the British Museum,
and Worcester (1834–35) by Charles Day.

But all this is anticipating. One other country was
concerned with the housing of its parliament and in the
very years of the capitols of Virginia and Washington:
the France of the Revolution, the Directoire and Napoleon.[14] The Assemblée Constituante intended to
commission a building in 1790. Combes suggested a vast
circular building with uncountable giant columns on the
site of the Bastille, entirely in the style of Boullée and
the Grands Prix of the eighties.[15] Another idea was to
make use of the half-built church of the Madeleine.
Legrand and Molinos' scheme had the nave surrounded
on three sides by columns and the rest a vast circle of
offices with, in the middle, the assembly hall on Gondoin's semicircular plan. Poyet wanted to make use of
the area between Louvre and Tuileries. His building
would also have been of a Grand Prix type. Vignon, the
architect of the Madeleine later on (above, pp. 16–17),
suggested an assembly hall – again semicircular – in the
Tuileries. In the end the Assemblée moved into the
oblong Salle des Machines in the Tuileries. In 1795 a
re-ordering resulted in two assemblies. The Anciens
remained in the Tuileries, but the Cinq Cents moved
into the Palais Bourbon, the large *hôtel* of the Duchesse
de Bourbon on the south side of the Seine facing the
Place de la Concorde. It was here that Gisors and Leconte
created their semicircular Salle des Cinq Cents, with   3.18
walls of smooth rustication, an upper order of columns,
a coffered semi-dome, a Pantheon eye and a coffered
apse for the President. The details have the severity of

3.21 Paris, Palais Bourbon, Salle des Séances, 1828–33, by Jules de Joly (Joly, *Plans, coupes . . .* , 1840)

6.56 Boullée and Ledoux, and Ledoux's theatre at Besançon
may indeed have inspired the architects as much as the
3.10 Ecole de Chirurgie.

The front towards the Place de la Concorde received
3.20 its monumental portico of twelve columns only in
1806–08. The architect was Poyet. The columns are
now Corinthian; for the Empire went in for grand
architectural rhetoric rather than Grecian (republican)
severity. The portico was rhetoric indeed; it leads only
to a vestibule from which a door opens into the apex
of the semicircle. Napoleon himself called it 'un para-
vent ridicule'.[16] When Jules de Joly in 1828–33 re-
3.21 modelled the interior, the new assembly hall that he
provided was again semicircular.[17] The style was still
Classical. For instance the grand Vestibule Casimir
Périer, which connected the small entrance with the
assembly hall, has a coffered tunnel vault and detached
columns, each carrying its bit of entablature.

In London in the meantime Parliament was still
housed in Westminster Palace in the same cramped and
untidy quarters as had been theirs a hundred years ago.
In 1794–96 Soane worked on designs for a new and
grand House of Lords south of Westminster Hall and a
long colonnade leading, at its north end, to a new square

House of Commons.[18] Nothing came of it. Instead, in
1820 Soane turned to new premises for the Law Courts.
They were built and will concern us later. For Parliament all Soane was allowed to do was a new royal
entrance with Scala Regia and Royal Gallery. They
3.22 were built in 1822–24 and were of great splendour. Alas,
they went up in flames when the Palace of Westminster
was burnt on 16 October 1834. A competition was held
for a new palace to give adequate accommodation.
From the point of view of the functioning of Parliament,
the fire had been a blessing in disguise. In 1831 already a
committee had been appointed to discuss the building
of a new House of Commons, preferably on another
site. Joseph Hume, the great Liberal, was the most
determined member. After the passing of the Reform
Bill in 1832 matters were even more urgent. It seems
that Hume's vision was of a semicircular room à la
Gondoin-Latrobe-Joly.[19]

The story of the designing and building of the Houses
of Parliament is common knowledge. The competition
stipulated 'that the style of the building be either Gothic
or Elizabethan'. This in iself is an interesting fact. Clearly
what was meant is that the building must not be Grecian.
Gothic could match the surviving old parts – West-

3.22 London, Houses of Parliament, Scala Regia, 1822–24, by Sir John Soane *(London, Sir John Soane's Museum)*

3.23 London, Houses of Parliament, the throne in the House of Lords, designed by A. W. N. Pugin

minster Hall, the undercroft of St Stephen's Chapel and the cloister which became the Speaker's Court. Elizabethan is more surprising. It was a recent revival[20] not yet popular, in spite of such spectacular performances as, for instance, Harlaxton, begun in 1831 to Salvin's design. But Elizabethan had the advantage, even more than Gothic, of being an indigenous style. Charles Barry won first prize with his Perpendicular design. The competition drawings were supremely attractive, all the close detail having been contributed by Augustus Welby Northmore Pugin.[21]

Whatever Barry's son and Pugin's son quarrelsomely wrote later, it was a perfect collaboration.[22] Barry's entirely is the plan, and it is a brilliant plan, far more sophisticated than any previous Houses of Parliament anywhere, with its main entrance leading through St Stephen's Hall (which replaced St Stephen's Chapel) to the polygonal central hall from which a corridor on the left led to the Commons, a corridor on the right to the Lords. Beyond the Lords were the royal quarters with the royal entrance under the Victoria Tower. Beyond the Commons was Speaker's Court, and the Speaker's house filled the north angle pavilion of the river front. Black Rod's residence more or less corresponded in the south angle pavilion. In between, all along the riverside, were the two libraries and some committee rooms.

Towards Old Palace Yard were smaller offices. Below this main storey at basement level, which is in fact ground level, wheeled traffic can run through. Beyond the plan, Barry's also is the magnificent skyline with the slim Big Ben Tower at one end, the mighty Victoria Tower near the other and the flèche above the central hall.

But all the detail is Pugin's. It is in the Perpendicular style, echoing Henry VII's Chapel opposite. The Perpendicular was the favourite phase of Gothic in the early nineteenth century. Soon, in 1840–41, Pugin and others were converted to the style of Westminster Abbey, i.e. of c. 1250–1300, which was called Second Pointed (Perpendicular being Third, Lancet First) and which went in for fewer, but bolder, less busy motifs. Jacob Burckhardt was aware of this change. He wrote in a letter of 16 August 1879 that in 1860 the approval of the building was 'nearly undivided', but since then the study of the Gothic style has made such progress that one now 'sees . . . many faults, and even a total lack of feeling'.[23]

Pugin also designed hat-racks and ink-stands and flock wallpapers and tiles and other furnishings, regardless of whether they were large or small. The result is the most splendid Neo-Gothic public building in any country. The tension between the asymmetry of the towers and spires and the symmetry of the river façade

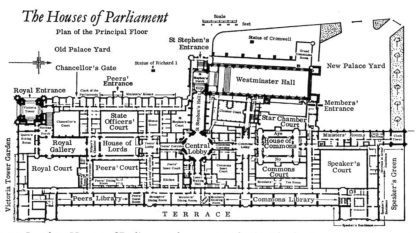

3.24, 25 London, Houses of Parliament, begun 1835, by Sir Charles Barry: river front and plan

3.26 Ottawa, Houses of Parliament, 1859–67, by Fuller & Jones

3.27 Berne, Bundeshaus: centre, 1852–57, by Friedrich Studer

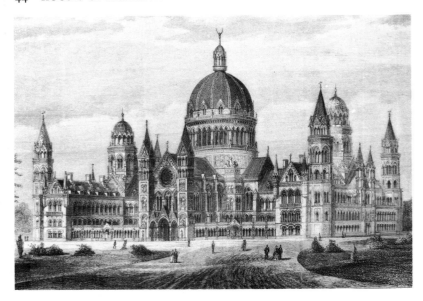

3.28 Sir George Gilbert Scott, design for the Reichstag in Berlin, 1872

3.29 Berlin, Reichstag, 1889–98, by Paul Wallot

solves itself uncannily. Remove the Perpendicular detail and you have a classical façade – but you cannot remove the Perpendicular detail. Both Pugin and Barry were aware of the tension. Pugin, one day, while passing the Palace of Westminster on a steamboat with a friend, said: 'All Grecian, Sir, Tudor details on a classic body',[24] and Bishop Barry tells us of his father that 'if a choice had been left to him without any influence of external authority or local associations, [the Classical] would have been the style of his New Palace.'[25] Did he mean Grecian like Barry's Royal Institution in Manchester of 1824–25 (now the City Art Gallery), or Italianate like his clubs, the Travellers of 1829–31 and the Reform of 1837–41? Probably the latter.

Nor was Barry alone in this preference. While the Houses of Parliament at Ottawa (by Fuller & Jones, 1859–67) are Gothic, at Berne the Bundeshaus, as built in 1852–57 to designs of Friedrich Studer, is in the Neo-Quattrocento of Munich public buildings such as the Staatsbibliothek.[26] The most highly regarded English architectural historian and critic, James Fergusson,[27] wrote this in 1862 about Berne v. London:

3.26
3.27

> Recently they have erected a Federal Palace at Berne, which is one of the best modern specimens of the Florentine style that has yet been attempted. . . . Taken as a whole, it is one of the most successful, as it is, for its situation and purposes, one of the most appropriate buildings of the present day, and forms a singular and instructive contrast with the Parliament Houses which we were erecting simultaneously and for the same identical purposes.

3.24

> Taking the outline of Barry's river façade as a basis for comparison, let us suppose a block like the centre of the Bernese Federal Palace placed at either end, where the Speaker's and Black Rod's houses now stand; between these a central block, more ornate, but of the same height as the wings, and occupying the same extent of ground as the centre division of the Parliament Houses; and then these joined by curtains four storeys in height, like those at Berne, but more ornamental in character, which their being recessed would render quite admissible. Which would have been the nobler building, or the best suited to our purposes?

The first answer that occurs is, that though so much larger in bulk, owing to the increased height, the Florentine building would have been very much cheaper – probably to the extent of one half, in so far at least as the architectural decorations of some parts are concerned.

The next reply would be, that it is more suited to our climate, having no deep undercuttings to be choked up with soot, and no delicate mouldings to be eaten away by damp and frost.

The Bernese style . . . would have produced a far more massive and a manlier building, and therefore more appropriate to its purposes, than one carried out in the elaborately elegant, but far too delicate, style employed in the Westminster design.

A few years hence, few probably will dispute that a simpler, a more massive, and more modern style would have been far better suited for our Parliament Houses than the one adopted. Whether it ought to be the one the Swiss have employed is much more doubtful. It seems, however, clear that they are nearer the truth than ourselves; and with some modifications their style might be so adapted as to make it approach more nearly to what is really right and truthful than anything which we have yet done in modern times.

In 1872 a first competition was held for a Houses of Parliament for the just united German Reich.[28] The first prize went to L. Bohnstedt of Gotha. He worked in several German towns, extensively in Russia and also in Portugal. His design for the Reichstag is decidedly classical, symmetrical, with a blocky triumphal-arch-type portal, a dome behind, and left and right of the portal long rows of detached upper giant columns à la Louvre. Second prizes went to Kayser & von Grossheim, Ende & Böckmann, Mylius & Bluntschli, all respected German firms – and to Sir George Gilbert Scott and his son John Oldrid. Scott was firmly Gothic, and, scholarly ambitions that he had, he analysed and justified his choice of style. Germany, he wrote, was most original between 'the first Otto' and Barbarossa, but she has also some good thirteenth-century Gothic work. He names – and the atrocious spelling is, we hope, the English subeditors' – Laad (= probably Laach), Auder-

3.28

3.30 Budapest, Parliament, 1882–1902, by Imre Steindl

3.31 Vienna, Parliament, 1873–83, by Theophil von Hansen

3.32 Bonn, Bundeshaus, 1930–33, by Hans Schwippert

maut (= Andernach), Limberg (= Limburg), Gelmhausen (= Gelnhausen). The list ends with Marburg and Cologne Cathedral. (Scott knew his Whewell![29]) So his design incorporates some Romanesque features, but as – he candidly admits it – he wanted pointed arches, he managed to make the total his beloved Second Pointed, i.e. thirteenth-century High Gothic. But the climax of the design has no thirteenth-century authority – a large central dome, and this also Scott defended.

Scott's dome was no doubt the inspiration of Imre Steindl's Hungarian Parliament at Budapest, built in 1882–1902.[30] But of course London must have played its part too in the choice of style. The Parliament building on the Danube is as large as that on the Thames – Budapest 950 feet, London 935 feet – but by the time it was begun the Neo-Gothic style was a matter of the past.

Even more oddly out of date was the style which Austria chose for her new Houses of Parliament in the Ringstrasse in Vienna. This palace, which was begun in 1873 to designs of Theophil von Hansen and completed in 1883,[31] is unmistakably Grecian. The façade is 530 feet long and symmetrical. The Abgeordnetenhaus (Chamber of Deputies) is semicircular. The most monumental room is the so-called Peristyle, an oblong hall surrounded by giant Corinthian columns.

Six years after the completion of the Vienna Parliament, when Berlin finally got its Reichstag in 1889–98, it was no longer Gothic nor of course Grecian nor Italianate. It was a grand well-managed Baroque. Paul Wallot was the architect, and he applied his Baroque with discretion.[32]

As for the twentieth century, the spirit of the International Modern of the 1930s with its abhorrence of rhetoric is represented by the Bundeshaus at Bonn, 1930–33, by Hans Schwippert. It started life as a *Pädagogische Akademie*, and the fact that it was not even built for its present purpose shows the change of attitude to the idea of governmental pomp. Finally, the neo-sculptural style of today, the style of wilful forms and a hankering after originality, has one of its paramount monuments in Oscar Niemeyer's Parliament at Brasilia of 1958–60, with the two houses appearing as a saucer and an inverted saucer, and between them the high, perfectly rational office-block as a twin skyscraper.

3.33 Brasilia, Parliament buildings, 1958–60, by Oscar Niemeyer

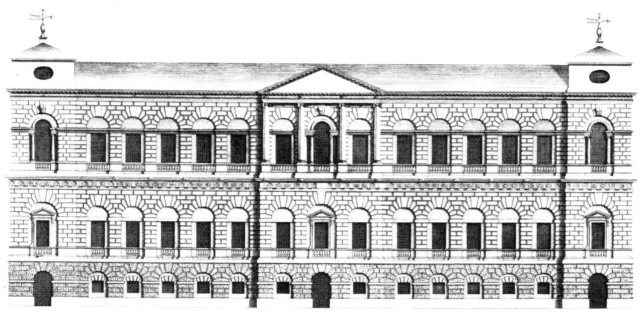

4.1 London, design for the Treasury, 1734, by William Kent

4
Government buildings from the eighteenth century
Ministries and public offices

WE HAVE seen that ideal plans of the Quattrocento when presenting town centres included a special building called 'Cancelleria'. Indeed, if the palace of Cardinal Riario, Pope Sixtus IV's nephew, in Rome is known as the Cancelleria, the reason is that it provided offices for ecclesiastical administration as well. But the Uffizi remains the first office building, even if from 1574 onward it included accommodation on the top floor for the Medici collections. Nothing major of the same kind followed, and we have to turn to the eighteenth century to be able to start on a consecutive story. The location now is England, and it is instructive to follow English ministry buildings through to 1900.

Whitehall is unique, as a street lined almost entirely by ministries. After public offices had swallowed the royal palace of Westminster, they were now going to swallow the royal palace of Whitehall. Thomas Ripley's Admiralty started it. He built it in 1723–26, a utilitarian red-brick house.[1] Pope in the *Dunciad* in 1728 said: 'See under Ripley rise a new Whitehall.'[2] The Paymaster General's Office followed, a five-bay brick house (by John Lane, 1732–33), and then Kent's Treasury of 1733–36.[3] Only the centre was built, in Kent's Burlingtonian Palladian. The building does not face Whitehall; it lies to the west behind Barry's Treasury (p. 48) and faces north, to Horse Guards Parade.

The next governmental office building established a new scale. It was built away from Whitehall, between the Strand and the river, and it was called Somerset House, because it took the place of the Lord Protector Somerset's house, that milestone in English sixteenth-century architecture. The new Somerset House was an idea of Edmund Burke; it was designed by Sir William Chambers and begun in 1776.[4] Its inner courtyard is of 350 by 310 feet, its Strand façade is chastely Jonesian, i.e. Palladian, in fact an enlarged copy of Jones's or Webb's Queen's Gallery in the old Somerset House (built in 1661–62), but the river façade of Somerset House acts a splendid drama with a rusticated basement storey originally reaching right down to the unembanked river and carrying a terrace, and above two bold accents of mighty Piranesian rusticated arches and above them transparent tetrastyle porticos with pediment. The motif repeats in the middle, but not transparent and too weak to pull the long façade together. The building housed the Navy Board, the Exchequer Office, the Privy Seal Office, the Audit Office, the Duchy of Cornwall Office, the Duchy of Lancaster Office, the Tax Office, the Stamp Office, etc., and also the Royal Society, Royal Academy and Society of Antiquaries. The offices were arranged on the left and right of long spinal corridors. The east end is by Sir Robert Smirke and serves King's College, the west

4.2 London, Somerset House, 1776–86, by Sir William Chambers

4.4 St Petersburg (Leningrad), Admiralty, 1806–15, by A. D. Zakharov

4.3 London, Board of Trade (known as the Treasury), 1845–47, by Sir Charles Barry

4.5 London, Foreign Office etc., 1868–73, by Sir George Gilbert Scott and Sir Matthew Digby Wyatt: view from St James's Park (*London, RIBA Drawings Collection*)

front is an alteration of 1876 by Pennethorne. No other country before 1800 had governmental offices the size of Chambers'. But Russia a few years later outdid London. Zakharov's Admiralty of 1806–15 is 1,374 feet – over a quarter of a mile – long.

For the next buildings London needed for ministries, Whitehall was again the site. East of Kent's Treasury, along Whitehall, Soane in 1824–25 built the Board of Trade and Privy Council, a long range of two storeys with even attached columns all along and an attic half-storey above the cornice. Barry in 1845–47 remodelled it and gave it an even giant order of attached columns and raised angle pavilions.[5] (The building, used for Cabinet offices, is still generally known as the Treasury.) The degree of relief is shallow, as it was in Gothic terms in the river front of the Houses of Parliament. High Victorian as against this Early Victorian is the neighbour of Barry's building, Sir George Gilbert Scott's Government Offices – for the Foreign Office, Home Office, etc. – of 1868–73.[6] The relief is higher, the accents are bolder and towards St James's Park the composition is totally asymmetrical with a low broad tower and quadrant to reach the projecting part of the front. This, the most successful part of the building, is however not Scott's. It is by Sir Matthew Digby Wyatt.[7] In size the Foreign Office block compares with Somerset House. It established a new scale dwarfing the Admiralty, the Horse Guards and indeed Barry's Treasury. Jacob Burckhardt[8] called it 'quite gigantic' and added that in comparison the Farnese Palace 'is a hut'.

The Foreign Office's southern neighbour, J. M. Brydon's New Government Offices of 1898–c. 1912, is yet larger. It represents – as does William Young's War Office, also of 1898 et seq. and also in Whitehall, but smaller – the English form of the universal turn from Neo-Renaissance to Neo-Baroque. The inspiration came from the late Wren of Greenwich and from Gibbs.

The internationally important French contribution to the style of governmental office building is the completion of the Louvre, begun in 1852 by Louis-T.-J. Visconti,[9] son of the Visconti whom we shall meet later (p. 116), and completed by Hector Lefuel. There had been earlier ministry buildings, the best perhaps the Ministère des Affaires Etrangères on the Quai d'Orsay, 1845–56, by Lacornée, Late Classical with two tiers of attached columns carrying entablatures, not arches. The stylistic importance of the vast additions to the Louvre is that they created – for foreign countries as well – a liking for the French Renaissance style of the mid-sixteenth to mid-seventeenth century. Admittedly, as will be pointed out in the next chapter, the enlargement of the Paris

4.7 Paris, Ministère des Affaires Etrangères, Quai d'Orsay, 1845–56, by J. Lacornée

4.6 London, New Government Offices, 1898–c. 1912, by J. M. Brydon

4.8 Paris, Louvre, everything visible except the far end of the courtyard of 1852 et seq., by L.-T.-J. Visconti and Hector Lefuel

4.9 Washington, D.C. Treasury, 1836–69, by Robert Mills

4.11 Washington, D.C. Old House Office Building (now Cannon House Office Building), 1908, by Carrère & Hastings

4.10 Washington, D.C. former State, War and Navy Office (now Old Executive Office Building), 1871–88, by A. B. Mullet

4.12 Washington, D.C. Rayburn House Office Building, 1957–63, by Harbeson, Hough, Livingston & Larson

5.11
7
Hôtel de Ville is earlier, and admittedly, as has been pointed out, the Schloss at Schwerin was designed before the beginning of the works on the Louvre. But both are exceptions, and the French Renaissance fashion, strongest in England and America, stems from the Louvre on which the American R.M. Hunt actually worked in 1854, and on which the English Professor Donaldson reported in advance to the Royal Institute of British Architects in the session 1853–54.[10] The new north and south blocks of the Louvre are each about 700 feet long. Well might Professor Donaldson speak of 'colossal operations'.

The French Renaissance fashion, most easily recognized by the pavilion roofs, reached Washington and the neighbourhood of the White House with the old Corcoran Gallery of 1858–61 by Renwick (see p. 135). It reached Washington's government buildings with the

4.10
former State, War and Navy Office, opposite the Corcoran and very much larger. This was begun in 1871 (architect A. B. Mullet) and matches in site, bulk and

4.9
plan Robert Mills's Treasury of 1836 et seq. The latter, completed by Walter, is Classical, with an endless giant colonnade between angle pavilions which have columns *in antis* and pediments. Washington has more of these Classical public office buildings, most notably Mills's

Patent Office, begun in 1836 and now the National Portrait Gallery. This has an octostyle Greek Doric portico. The Old Pension Building by General Montgomery Meigs, 1881–87, was a courageous, if belated, attempt at getting away from the Classical patterns. Here is brick, here are Renaissance windows, and here –

4.17
most memorable – is a grandiose interior boldly divided roughly into three by two screens of huge columns with gigantic Corinthian capitals.

But the Classical blight on Washington could not be remedied, and the Mills pattern was repeated, varied and developed in oversized government building after oversized government building.[11] This Classical Re-Revival began about 1900, i.e. less than ten years after the Chicago Exhibition (see p. 250) and McKim, Mead & White's Law Library of Columbia University, New York. Both

15.47
date from 1893. Peabody & Stearns' Machinery Hall at Chicago had a giant colonnade of more columns than one would care to count, and the latter architects started the sweepingly columnar Pennsylvania Station in 1906. In Washington the governmental series whose *leitmotiv* is giant colonnades set in with the Department of Agriculture by Rankin, Kellogg & Crane, 1905, followed by

4.11
the Old House Office Building of 1908 by Carrère & Hastings. The earliest with the Mills motif of the count-

4.13 Washington, D.C. 600–800 Independence Avenue, 1958–63, by Holabird, Root & Burges

4.15 Washington, D.C. James Forrestal Building, c. 1966–69, by Curtis & Davis, Fordyce & Hamby and Frank Grad & Sons

4.14 Bucarest, Ministry of Finance, 1945–47, by Radu Dudescu and Cretoin Nicolae

4.16 Berlin, Air Ministry, 1935–37, by Albert Speer

less columns was the Bureau of Engraving and Printing, 1911–14, by W. B. Olmstead (a 550-foot front), followed by Cass Gilbert's Treasury Annex of 1919.[12] In the thirties, i.e. after the Public Buildings Program had been decreed, which was in 1926, this retardataire pattern was adopted everywhere: Internal Revenue begun 1930, the huge Department of Commerce 1932, Department of Justice 1934, National Archives 1935, Department of Labor 1935, Federal Trade Commission 1937.[13]

It is worthwhile carrying on among the official Washington buildings to realize how consistently reactionary they have been until recently – so recently that even Russia had preceded in taking notice of the twentieth-century style. There is hardly a Russian building as deadly reactionary as the Rayburn Building in Washington completed in 1963.

As for the other motifs used in Washington, one could quite easily play the architectural historian's game of matching each new façade composition which appeared on the scene in Washington with its European pattern of ten or more likely twenty years back. A few examples to illustrate this. The twentieth-century style had been created by a few pioneers in Germany and Austria, France and the United States around 1900–1910.

It believed in free grouping, unrelieved blocks and absence of mouldings. In Washington they thought minor adjustments of the Eternal Columnar would do: an attic instead of a pediment (Lincoln Memorial, 1922, by Henry Bacon), giant pillars instead of giant columns (Federal Reserve, 1935–37, by Paul Cret). It was only one step from the pillars to the system by which two or three metal windows were placed one on top of the other and yet recessed and separated by vertical strips of wall (Folger Library, 1932, by Paul Cret and A. B. Trowbridge). The principle had been evolved in Germany before the First World War. One version of it, by no means late (Messel's Wertheim store in Berlin of 1896–1904, Olbrich's Tietz store at Düsseldorf 1907–09; see p. 270) had very closely set mullions and very narrow vertical window strips. This they presented in Washington at last in the later sixties (Department of Transportation, E. D. Stone, 1967–69).[14]

The grid pattern without determined stresses was no newer when Washington took to it, which was in 1958 with the Civil Service Commission, Virginia Avenue, by Helmuth, Obata & Kassabaum with Loebl, Schlossmann & Bennett. Here at least the windows indicate a direction. In the Departments of Health, etc., and Aeronautics, Independence Avenue, 1957–63 by Faulkner,

4.12

16.34, 35

4.13 Kingsbury & Stenhouse and Chatelain, Gauger & Nolan, and 600–800 Independence Avenue, 1958–63 by Holabird, Root & Burges with Carroll, Grisdale & Van Alen the grid has become totally flush – smooth marble and smooth glass.

Now, however, to finish this tale, Washington has caught up. The style of chunky concrete, created by Le Corbusier between 1947 and 1957 (Unité d'Habitation at Marseilles, Ronchamp Chapel, Maisons Jaoul in Paris, Chandigarh, Friary of La Tourette), is the style of some of the most recent buildings: in Independence

4.15 Avenue the Forrestal Building of c. 1966–69 by Curtis & Davis, Fordyce & Hamby and Frank Grad & Sons, L'Enfant Plaza by Araldo Cossutta of I. M. Pei & Partners, begun in 1965 (a commercial, not government enterprise), and the Department of Housing and Urban Development, c. 1966–68 by Marcel Breuer and Nolan, Swinburne & Associates with its four concave façades.

Finally, one paragraph on the world's largest office building: the Pentagon, completed in 1943. Here are some figures from *The Washington Guidebook* (1963) and *The World Almanac* (1968).[15] It covers 34 acres including a 5-acre circular court, and is 921 feet in length on each outer side. Inside there are ten radiating corridors and 1,900 lavatories. The daily work force is 27,000 people.

If Washington has been given such inordinate space in this chapter, the excuse is that the venue of the Mellon Lectures is Washington. All the briefer can be the end of this chapter – a glance at the Ministry of Finance at Bucarest of 1945–47 (by Radu Dudescu and Cretoin Nicolae) in order to remember that one must go behind the Iron Curtain to match the traditionalism of Washington, and a glance at the Italian Fascists and the German Nazis, though their traditionalism was less column-bound, but not for that less dead.[16]

4.17 Washington, D.C. Old Pension Office, 1881–87, by General Montgomery Meigs

5.1 Lyons, Palais de Justice, begun in 1835, by L.-P. Baltard

5
Government buildings from the eighteenth century
Town halls and law courts

IN AN earlier chapter we followed town halls from the medieval type of open ground floor and council room above (which in England incidentally survived for small buildings through the Georgian century)[1] to the scale and monumentality of the Amsterdam Town Hall. Between that and the present day any series of major town halls illustrates stylistic, not functional developments.

With law courts it is different. In the Middle Ages and even after there had been no differentiation. In Amsterdam the courts of justice were in the Town Hall; in London they were in the Palace of Westminster and more specifically Westminster Hall. Kent in 1739 put the Courts of Chancery and King's Bench on the dais of the Hall and encased them in a very pretty (and remarkably early) Rococo-Gothic envelope. He may also have designed the new Palladian extensions southwest of the Hall. They were L-shaped with a front to New Palace Yard. John Vardy built them between 1758 and 1770.[2] Further and more monumental additions were made by Soane in 1821–25.[3] It is interesting that here, a decade before the Houses of Parliament competition (see p. 41), Soane was forced to replace his own Classical façade by a Gothic one. So the conviction that the site demanded Gothic existed already before the fire.

Separate monumental buildings for law courts began in the English provinces with York, where in 1705 a Debtors' Prison had been built in a Vanbrughian style close to the castle keep. This was now, in 1773–80, enlarged by John Carr. The two additions, detached and with identical façades, served the one as a female prison, the other as assize courts. Inside are two court rooms which carry Pantheon domes. Thomas Harrison's buildings on the site of Chester Castle comprised with the Shire Hall the law courts, barracks and gaol.[4] Harrison was busy on the whole group of buildings – which also included a grand propylaea – from 1788 till 1822. They are amongst the most monumental examples of the Greek Revival, exhibiting plenty of Doric columns.[5]

In France separate buildings for law courts start in the late eighteenth century, and, being on the megalomaniac scale of Boullée and the Grands Prix of the French Academy, remained on paper. Boullée did a law courts, with colonnades of countless columns.[6] He also incidentally designed a 'Palais Municipal' or town hall, equally huge and exceedingly uninviting-looking. In 1782 P. Bernard gained first prize at the Academy with a law courts design; Cathala got second prize. They are needless to say also absurdly vast schemes; so is J. N.

5.2 London, Court of Chancery, 1821–25, by Sir John Soane
(*London, Sir John Soane's Museum*)

5.3 E.-L. Boullée, design for a 'Palais Municipal', 1792: detail
(*Paris, Bibliothèque Nationale*)

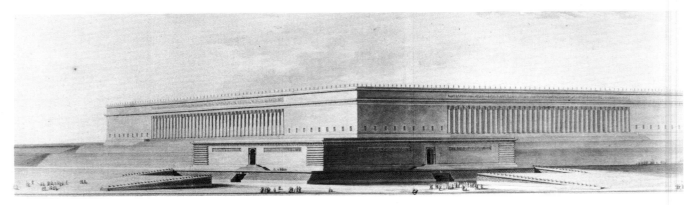

5.4 E.-L. Boullée, design for law courts (*Paris, Bibliothèque Nationale*)

Sobre's town hall of 1788, again with interminable colonnades.[7] The follower of Boullée who showed that feasible schemes could be worked out on Boullée's and the Academy's principles was J.-N.-L. Durand, whom we have already met. Durand was born in 1760 and was Professor at the Ecole Polytechnique from 1795 to 1830, and his teaching was perpetuated in his *Précis des leçons d'architecture* of 1802–09. His importance lies in the fact that he demonstrated how a rational teaching system could incorporate Boullée's crazy scale and remorseless classicism. In fact his recommended technique of designing on an underlying grid facilitated this. On the other hand Durand appears as an innovator in his *Recueil et parallèle*, published in 1801, which is a historical typology. Town halls appear in both publications – in the *Recueil* Antwerp, Amsterdam, the Senatorial Palace in Rome as remodelled by Michelangelo, and also the Gothic Brussels and Oudenaarde, in the *Précis* just one relatively small, nine-by-nine bay specimen.[8] But Durand's law courts[9] are boulléesque in scale: a spine and six apsed court-rooms all set in a square enclosure. A Greek Doric portico is present too.

The actual building nearest to the Boullée-Durand ideals is the Palais de Justice at Lyons by L.-P. Baltard, begun in 1835. The columns are Corinthian now, and the attic is typical of the Ecole des Beaux Arts style.[10] A peripteral temple above a rusticated ground floor is the Birmingham Town Hall by J. A. Hansom, started in 1832.[11] The finest and also the most original Classical building of these years in England is St George's Hall in Liverpool by H. L. Elmes, begun in 1840 and completed after Elmes's death by Cockerell.[12] It combines ingeniously a large general hall and a smaller concert hall with the Civil Court and the Crown Court – a late example of this combined type.

Leeds Town Hall of 1853–58 by Cuthbert Brodrick still continues column-happy, but it is patent that Classicism has begun to give way to the Wrenaissance. Professor Asa Briggs has told the story of the Leeds Town Hall in a masterly way.[13] For the ceremony of the laying of the first stone a 'procession of enormous length' assembled, with brass bands, and on Woodhouse Moor festivities were held in the presence of 60,000 people. At the opening Queen Victoria and Prince Albert were present, and the Loyal Address called the building 'not inferior to those stately piles which still attest the ancient opulence of the great commercial cities of Italy and Flanders'.

That is the evocative aspect of the new town halls. But there was a utilitarian aspect too, and one which the city

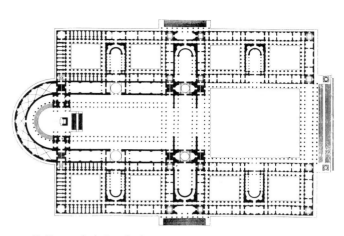

5.5 P. Bernard, design for law courts, 1782

5.7 Birmingham, Town Hall, begun in 1832, by J. A. Hansom

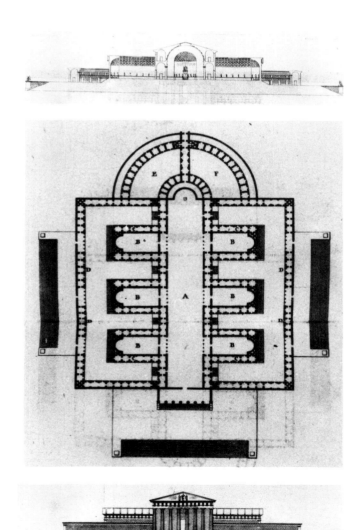

5.6 J.-N.-L. Durand, design for law courts (*Précis*, II, 1809):
section, plan and elevation

5.8 Liverpool, St George's Hall, begun in 1840, by H. L. Elmes

5.9 Leeds, Town Hall, 1853–58, by Cuthbert Brodrick

5.10 Paris, Palais de Justice, façade of 1857–68, by L.-J. Duc

5.12 Manchester, Assize Courts, 1859–64, by Alfred Waterhouse

5.11 Paris, Hôtel de Ville, 16th c., wings of 1837–46, by
E. H. Godde and J.-B.-C. Lesueur

fathers had neglected at their peril. At Leicester in the old Town Hall police accommodation had to be found, and it was only found in a place where the stench made the sergeants ill.[14]

What corresponds in France to such English town halls as that of Leeds is the part of the Paris Palais de Justice facing the rue de Harlay, added by Duc in 1857–68.[15] Here also the purity of Classicism was no longer acceptable. The attached giant columns carrying a heavy attic and the upper windows ending in segmental arches demonstrate dissolution of the Classical canons, even if they are not yet Baroque, and it is no accident that, as we have seen, Klenze did the same thing in the Befreiungshalle near Kelheim at nearly the same time, in 1850–63. Burckhardt was shocked.[16] 'The segmental arches . . . are madness' on the part of the architect, a 'présomption qui frise la folie'. The Madeleine, he continued, may be dead, but it is at least not spoiled by such ideas. Behind the incriminating façade is the grand Vestibule Harlay. Another grand sequence of rooms beginning at the main entrance was designed by A. N. Bailly for the Tribunal de Commerce in Paris (1860–65). The staircase rises in two arms in a rotunda which fulfils itself in a high dome, and behind the rotunda is the Salle d'Honneur with

columns in two tiers and a glass roof. The type of room is that of contemporary exchanges (see p. 207).[17]

Meanwhile, however, other styles had staked their claims.[18] The Paris Hôtel de Ville of François Premier's time, a big addition to which (by Louis Moreau, suggested in 1768) had not been carried out,[19] was considerably enlarged by Etienne Hippolyte Godde and J.-B.-Cicéron Lesueur in 1837–46. The enlargement became possible after the Revolution and the Empire had sanctioned the elimination of the Hôpital du Saint Esprit (see p. 141) to the left of the Hôtel de Ville and the church of St Jean behind it. The style chosen by Godde and Lesueur was that of the old centre of the building, and the French Renaissance Revival begins here. The block was now 394 by 266 feet – 25 bays to the front, two–to three-storeyed, 25 to the back, 19 to the south. The proudest display inside was the Salle des Fêtes and the staircase leading to it.[20] The Salle des Fêtes had twelve detached columns each with its own piece of projecting entablature along the long sides. It was burnt by the Commune in 1871 and rebuilt by Ballu and Deperthes.

In England after the Houses of Parliament Gothic was favoured. Alfred Waterhouse introduced it to Manchester, first in the Assize Courts of 1859–64, then

5.13 Manchester, Town Hall, 1868–77, by Alfred Waterhouse

5.15 London, Law Courts, *salle des pas perdus*, 1866–82, by
G. E. Street

5.14, 16 London, Law Courts, competition designs by Sir George
Gilbert Scott (left) and William Burges (above), 1866

5.17 Vienna, Rathaus, 1872–83, by Friedrich von Schmidt

5.13   in the Town Hall of 1868–77, which cost about £600,000.[21] Meanwhile the competition for the London Law Courts had been held in 1866. Eastlake, the historian and shrewd observer of the Gothic Revival,[22] praised Waterhouse's skill in planning and wrote that Waterhouse did not aim at the reproduction 'of any special phase or type of Gothic art'. He was 'confessedly eclectic', i.e. he used the apparatus of the Anglo-French Middle Pointed, but with 'a certain admixture of Italian Gothic in details'. In fact Waterhouse himself declared his attitude: 'The mouldings and details are thirteenth century in their general character. But wherever I thought that the particular object in view could not be best obtained by a strict obedience to precedent, I took the liberty of departing from it.' That is Waterhouse all over and contributes much to the strength and originality of his style. What also contributes is his composition of façades in 'general symmetry with variety of details'.[23] The Assize Courts no longer exist; the Manchester Town Hall does. Its façade is 306 feet long and symmetrical, with a tower 286 feet high. The interiors are impressive and seen at certain angles more than that.

Already in 1855 Gilbert Scott had submitted a large symmetrical Gothic scheme with a high middle tower for the Town Hall competition in Hamburg.[24] Symmetrical again and with a middle tower again is the Vienna Rathaus by Friedrich von Schmidt, 1872–83 – a rather mechanical performance. There can be no question; the English architects were far more at ease in the handling of Gothic forms than their Continental colleagues.
  5.17

The competition of 1866 for the London Law Courts brings that out. Street got the job; the Strand façade, symmetrical in general but not in detail, and the spectacular *salle des pas perdus* are of a high order. Sir John Summerson has recently published the competition entries by Scott, Raphael Brandon, Burges, Seddon, Waterhouse and E. M. Barry.[25] Scott is competent, symmetrical and dull, Brandon is almost entirely symmetrical and has a fantastic skyline with six spires, Seddon is massive, Burges, entirely asymmetrical, 'creates an entrancing drama', to quote Sir John Summerson. Montgomery Schuyler, America's best architectural critic, called Burges's design 'the high-water mark ... of the Gothic Revival'.[26]
  5.15 5.14 5.16

While the 1860s mark the climax of High Victorian Gothic, some Continental architects during these years were already committed body and soul to the Neo-

5.18, 19 Brussels, Palais de Justice, 1868–83, by Joseph Poelaert: façade, and staircase behind the colonnade

5.20 Rome, Palazzo di Giustizia, 1886–1910, by Guglielmo Calderini

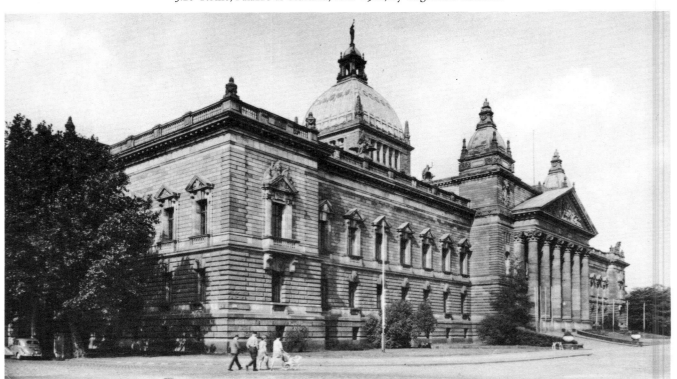

5.21 Leipzig, Supreme Court (Reichsgericht), 1887–95, by Ludwig von Hoffmann and Peter Dybwad

6.66–69   Baroque. The capital early examples are Garnier's Opéra
in Paris begun in 1861 (on which see pp. 84–86) and
5.18, 19   Joseph Poelaert's Palais de Justice in Brussels, begun in
1868 and completed in 1883 at a cost of £2½ million.
Instead of humdrum description, Verlaine's impressions
may be quoted: 'C'est babélique, et Michel-Angesque,
avec du Piranesi, et un peu, peut-on dire, de folie . . .
Extérieurement c'est un colosse, intérieurement c'est un
monstre; ce veut être immense, et ce l'est.'[27] ('There is
something of the Tower of Babel, plus Michelangelo,
with a bit of Piranesi, and a dash – one may say – of madness . . . Outside, it is a colossus, inside a monster. It wants
to be immense, and it is.')

From Poelaert to 1900 in two steps: the fussily
Baroque Palazzo di Giustizia in Rome, by Guglielmo   5.20
Calderini, 1886–1910 (length c. 610 feet), and the much
more restrained Supreme Court at Leipzig by Ludwig   5.21
von Hoffmann and Peter Dybwad, built in 1887–95.
The Supreme Court is clearly a design in opposition
against the Baroque.

Six steps from the late nineteenth century to the 1960s.
They also need no long comments. Martin Nyrop's
Copenhagen Town Hall of 1892–1905, inspired by the   5.24
Dutch and Scandinavian style of about 1600, but very
quiet in the façades and with a high, freely shaped tower;
Ragnar Østberg's Stockholm City Hall, begun in 1909   5.22

5.22 Stockholm, City Hall, 1909–23, by Ragnar Østberg

5.23 Tony Garnier, design for the Administration Centre (left) and Assembly Rooms of the Cité Industrielle, c. 1917

5.24 Copenhagen, Town Hall, 1892–1905, by Martin Nyrop

5.25 Hilversum, Town Hall, 1928–30, by W. Marinus Dudok

but finished only in 1923, with its elegant mixture of Northern Renaissance and Doge's Palace and the spiky decorative motifs typical of the 1920s; Tony Garnier's public buildings for his thesis on a Cité Industrielle, and especially the Assembly Rooms with their projecting concrete canopy designed shortly before 1917,[28] wholly twentieth-century and no longer influenced by any past style; the Hilversum Town Hall of 1928–30 by Dudok, with its free grouping of unrelieved blocks, its beautiful handling of brick, its bands of low windows, its inspiration from Frank Lloyd Wright, a milestone in the formation of the so-called International Modern of the thirties;[29] the City Hall of Ottawa by Vincent Rother, of 1956–58, in the International Modern which by then seemed to have won; and so to Chandigarh and Le Corbusier's late style.

5.23

5.25

5.27

That style, totally unexpected when it broke out with the Unité d'Habitation at Marseilles in 1947–52 and the far more radical chapel of Ronchamp in 1950–54, is not a development of the preceding International Modern but a violent reaction against it. The Law Courts at Chandigarh of 1950–57 demonstrates that. The thirties wanted maximum performance with minimum thickness of material; the Chandigarh Law Courts is cyclopean in its masses. Also it is aggressive and overpowering. These too are the dominant, the domineering qualities of the new Boston City Hall, 1962–69 by Kallmann, McKinnell & Knowles, wildly arbitrary in its motifs, oppressively top-heavy and forbidding rather than inviting.[30] It is a *tour de force*, and one marvels at the courage of the City authorities in accepting it, but it cannot be assessed in rational terms, and can it be loved?

5.28

5.26 Ottawa, City Hall, 1956–58, by Vincent Rother

5.27 Chandigarh, Law Courts, 1950–57, by Le Corbusier

5.28 Boston, City Hall, 1962–69, by Kallmann, McKinnell & Knowles

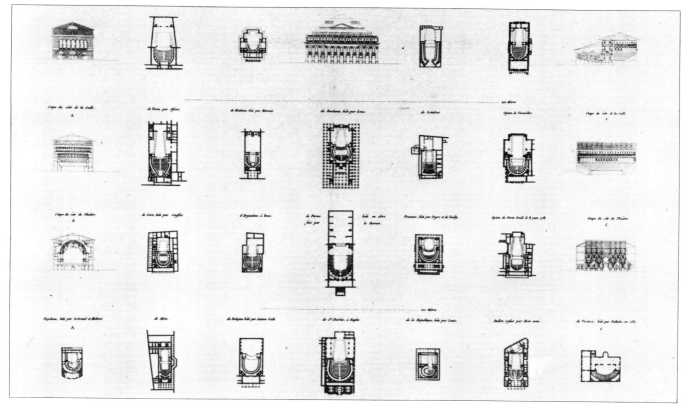

6.1 Major European theatres, 16th–18th c. (Durand, *Recueil*, 1801)

6
Theatres

WHEREAS the history of government buildings had to be followed back into the Middle Ages, the reason being architectural continuity from the twelfth to the nineteenth century, in the case of theatres there is no such reason. The story which this chapter proposes to unfold starts with the Italian Renaissance, or, technically speaking, with the change of location from the market place and the streets to the palace, and the more telling change from the multiple stage to the single stage and often also from perambulating spectators to the fixed auditorium. Now single stage and fixed auditorium were known to the fifteenth century as the ancient Roman arrangement. If the Italians of the fifteenth century were acquainted with the building and fixtures of the Roman theatre, that was due to their knowing Vitruvius' Book V, chapters III–IX.

Vitruvius wrote his *De architectura* about the year 20 BC. The book was not entirely forgotten in the Middle Ages[1] but was effectively re-discovered at St Gall by Poggio Bracciolini in 1414.[2] This is why Alberti in his *De re aedificatoria* of about 1450 could base his treatment of the theatre on Vitruvius.[3] He states that the auditorium ought to be a semicircle (*emiciclus*) with a colonnade around the top and the stage an architectural set-piece with rows of columns one above the other 'ex domorum imitatione'. But to describe is not the same

as to resuscitate. At about the same time as Alberti, Filarete was working on his *Treatise*. Of theatres he writes laconically: 'I don't know what they looked like nor what end they served.'[4]

Alberti's *De re aedificatoria* was not printed until 1485. One year later the first Vitruvius was printed, edited by Sulpizio da Veroli. Further editions appeared in Florence in 1496, in Venice in 1497, and then the first two illustrated editions: Fra Giocondo's in 1511 and Cesariano's in 1521. Cesariano has a Vitruvian plan, an auditorium with, at the back, two tiers of arched galleries modelled on the exterior, not the interior, of the Theatre of Marcellus, and a totally fanciful exterior. The standard Cinquecento edition is Daniele Barbaro's with illustrations by Palladio (1556). Only ten years earlier the first Alberti in Italian had come out (ed. Pietro Lauro, 1546) and then the standard Italian edition, Cosimo Bartoli's of 1550 with illustrations.

Vitruvius describes the auditorium as semicircular with a colonnade round the top. He writes much about acoustics, and as for the stage, he mentions the *scenae frons*, with its three doors, and the three types of scene – tragic, comic and rustic. He also knew *periacti*, i.e. tall, turnable pillars, triangular in plan. On each side part of a scene is painted and so three turns will give three sets.

In the 1480s another architectural treatise was written

63

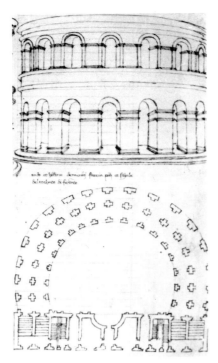

6.2 Ferento, Roman theatre, drawn by Francesco di Giorgio, *c.* 1480 (*Turin, Biblioteca Reale*)

6.3 Woodcut from the Venetian edition of Terence of 1497: a theatre

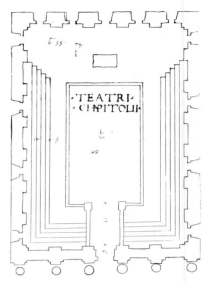

6.4 Rome, theatre on the Capitol, 1513, by G. G. Cesarini, after the 'Coner Codex' (*London, Sir John Soane's Museum*)

which includes theatres, that of Francesco di Giorgio.[5] What he says about theatres must not be taken too seriously. Corrado Maltese calls him 'extraordinarily unequal' and always 'ready to fantasticate'.[6] He shows elevations of the Roman theatres of Gubbio, Minturno and Ferento, the last-named with a plan of the semi-circular auditorium.[7] The Colosseum and the Theatre of Marcellus are also drawn.[8] When it came to inventing instead of recording, this is what Francesco suggests.[9] A city ought to have 'alcuno teatro' in which 'commedie, tragedie et altre favole . . . recitare si possino'; the auditorium ought to be an 'emicirco', to have a colonnade above the graded seats and on the stage 'triangolari facce', i.e. *periacti*; but his own theatre elevations seem to represent circular buildings.[10] In one case he actually shows the plan.[11]

It cannot be accident that in the very years of this treatise, of the first printed Alberti and the first printed Vitruvius, the first efforts were made to revive the Roman pattern, just as the Roman playwrights were revived, and especially Plautus, Terence and Seneca – all of course no strangers to the medieval reader. In fact Sulpizio da Veroli in his dedicatory letter to Cardinal Riario (the one whose palace was the Cancelleria – see below, p. 66) praised the Cardinal for having inspired the first performance of an Antique tragedy and the first 'picturatae scenae faciem', which must mean a painted backcloth on the stage.[12] Rome was indeed one of the two centres of the revival. Ferrara was the other.[13] In 1486, the year of Sulpizio's Vitruvius, Ercole I staged Plautus' *Menaechmi* in the courtyard of the palace. We are not told about the seating, but the back of the stage represented a town 'cum moenibus' (with walls). 'Super-

bae viae' are also referred to. More performances followed, that of 1491 staged inside the palace.

In Rome the *spiritus rector* seems to have been Pomponio Leto, professor at the Sapienza, a fanatic worshipper of Antiquity and a theatrical producer.[14] We know, e.g., of a performance of Seneca's *Hippolytus* in 1486. What the stage was like in such a performance cannot be said, nor anything of the auditorium. In an illustrated Terence published at Lyons in 1493 there is a background of five thin columns or posts and curtains between, in the Venice Terence of 1497 a graded semi-circular auditorium with a colonnade of square pillars running along the top – the first of a type which was to be of great importance for the Cinquecento. In the Terence the picture is called *Coliseus sive Theatrum*.

Entering the Cinquecento now, we have at once to record dates and names of High Renaissance notabilities. In 1508, at Ferrara, Pellegrino da Udine (according to a letter written by Bernardino Prosperi) staged Ariosto's *Cassaria*, and the stage showed 'una contracta et prospettiva di una terra cum case, chiesie, campanili et zardini che la persona non si può satiare a guardarla'[15] ('a street and the perspective into the countryside with houses, churches, campanili and gardens which you will never get tired of watching'). Next, in 1513, at Urbino Cardinal Bibiena's *Calandria* was performed with a stage-set by the painter Girolamo Genga. Count Castiglione, author of the *Cortigiano*, wrote of it in a letter to Lodovico Canossa: 'From the ceiling to the floor are the town walls with two big towers, done very realistically . . . The stage showed a beautiful town, with its streets, palaces, churches and towers. It was a real street, all in relief, but supported by excellent painting and well-

6.5 Sebastiano Serlio, 'tragic scene', from his *Treatise*, Book II, 1545

6.6 Architectural perspective, perhaps by Bramante *(Baltimore, Walters Art Gallery)*

6.7 Peruzzi, stage design, *c.* 1530 *(Florence, Uffizi)*

understood perspective.' Castiglione mentions in particular an octagonal temple in the middle, done in stucco relief and with painted stories, and a triumphal arch with an equestrian statue on top.[16]

In the same year 1513 on the Capitol in Rome Plautus' *Poenulus* was staged in a special theatre built for the occasion by Giovan Giorgio Cesarini.[17] The *scenae frons* showed a wall with columns, above them pilasters and five doors. In this case we are told something about the auditorium as well. It was of wood with five rows of seats arranged against three walls of an oblong structure and holding three thousand. The figure can hardly be correct. The producer was Tommaso Inghirami, pupil of Pomponio Leto, canon and Papal Librarian.

In 1514, again in Rome, Machiavelli's *Mandragola* was the play, and the artist concerned was Peruzzi. The Urbino *Calandria* of 1513 was repeated in Rome in 1518, and Peruzzi designed that set too. Vasari praised *Mandragola* for the buildings and the loggias and *Calandria* yet more specifically. This is what he wrote: 'One can hardly imagine how in such restricted space so many streets, so many palaces and so many strange temples, halls and cornices could be arranged. They were done so excellently that . . . the square did not appear painted and small, but extraordinarily large . . . Lighting was done cleverly too so that it supported the effects of perspective.'[18]

Two more performances before we can sum up and interpret. In 1519 Raphael did the decoration for Ariosto's *Suppositi*. The performances, according to a letter of Alfonso Paolucci to the Duke of Urbino, took place in the Vatican. The auditorium held two thousand and was semicircular. The stage showed the city of Ferrara in perspective.[19] Finally in 1531 Peruzzi did the stage-set for Plautus' *Bacchidae* in Rome.

Now Peruzzi is important in the history of architectural perspectives because of the Sala delle Prospettive in his Villa Farnesina, which has the first such architectural decoration without any figures. There are also plenty of drawings of urban architecture by him. However, the genre started much earlier. The possibilities of linear perspective were discovered at the time of Brunelleschi and Uccello. Mantegna's trick ceiling of the Camera degli Sposi in the palace at Mantua and Melozzo da Forlì's trick vaults of SS. Apostoli in Rome and of Loreto Cathedral with their bold *di sotto in su* date from 1468–74 and *c.* 1480 respectively. Piero della Francesca painted panels consisting only of urban perspective[20] and wrote a book on perspective (*De prospettiva pingendi*). This, probably of the eighties, was followed by Luca Pacioli's *De divina proporzione*, written in 1497 and published in 1509. Pacioli was a friend of Leonardo, but he also knew Alberti, and Alberti's *Della pittura* of 1435 makes the most of perspective. Pacioli wrote his book while in Milan, and Milan seems to have been a centre of art theory, i.e. such topics as proportion and perspective. After all both Bramante and Leonardo lived in Milan in the eighties and nineties, and Bramante's feigned choir of S. Satiro is a masterpiece of perspective. This is also where the curious paintings at Urbino and in the Walters Art Gallery at Baltimore come in.[21] An engraving of 1481 inscribed 'Bramantus fecit . . .' shows typical theatre architecture.[22] From this engraving it is only a short way to Peruzzi.

And a short way it is also from Peruzzi to his pupil Serlio. Serlio's treatise on architecture began to appear

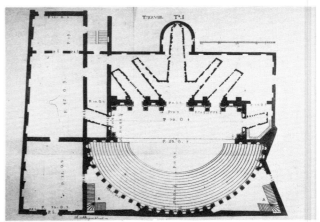

6.8–10 Vicenza, Teatro Olimpico, 1580–84, by Andrea Palladio: auditorium (left), stage by Vincenzo Scamozzi, and plan

in 1537. In 1540 he moved to France and there Book II came out in 1545. The introduction deals with 'la sottil arte della prospettiva' and the part painters have played in developing it. Mantegna, Bramante ('suscitore della bene accompagnata Architettura'), Genga, Giulio Romano and Peruzzi are mentioned. The illustrations show the semicircular auditorium similar to the theatre that he had already built in the Ca Porto in Vicenza, and three
[6.5] stage sets: 'tragica', 'comica' and 'satirica'.[23]

At the time when Serlio wrote, the change began to take place from temporary to permanent theatre structures. A permanent theatre is recorded at Ferrara with the probable date 1531,[24] and from about 1545 mentions occur more frequently: in Rome (Cancelleria) in 1545, in Mantua by Bertani in 1549, in Bologna (for an academy) in 1550, in Siena by Riccio (for another academy) in 1561, in Venice (for the Compagnia della Calza – by Palladio) in 1565, and in Florence in the Uffizi (by Buontalenti) in 1585.[25] With the 1580s we also reach the earliest surviving theatres. They are Palladio's
[6.8–10] Teatro Olimpico in Vicenza of 1580–84 with the streets in perspective by Scamozzi, and the theatre at Sab-
[6.11] bioneta, also by Scamozzi, built in 1588–90 for Duke Vespasiano Gonzaga.[26] The theatre at Sabbioneta is a separate building of Mannerist character; the auditorium

is small with semicircular seating and a colonnade at the back. The auditorium at Vicenza is similar.[27] The [6.8] auditorium of the theatre at Parma, built by Giovanni [6.12, 1] Battista Aleotti for the Farnese Duke in 1618–28,[28] has a slightly different shape. By a lengthening of the ends of the amphitheatre it became a U. In elevation it has instead of the one colonnade of Vicenza and Sabbioneta [6.8, 11] two tiers of colonnading, each bay with the opening of the type known as the Venetian or Palladio window. Parma and Sabbioneta were court enterprises, but Vicenza was built as the theatre of the Accademia degli Olimpici for members and invited guests.[29] At the time of the Olimpico Venice had already two privately built public theatres, both near S. Cassiano, one an enterprise of the Michiel, the other of the Tron family. Both were of wood and had semi-elliptical auditoria.[30]

For the French sixteenth century the date to start from is 1548. It was in that year that the Confrérie de la Passion took over the Hôtel de Bourgogne in the rue de Mauconseil near the market hall. Until then they had played in the Hôpital de la Trinité. Their name tells us that they were one of the troupes of amateurs, as a rule members of a gild or fraternity, which acted Passion plays or Mystery plays – a mystery meaning a trade or craft.[31] Drama, as is well enough known, started from

6.11 Sabbioneta, theatre, 1588–90, by Vincenzo Scamozzi

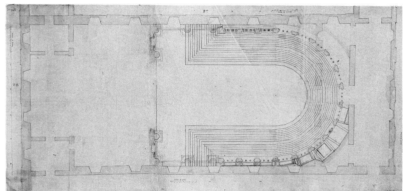

6.12, 13 Parma, Teatro Farnese, 1617–28, by G. B. Aleotti: auditorium (top) and plan

the brief dialogues or antiphons or tropes sung or spoken in church ever since the ninth (St Gall) and tenth (Aethelwold of Winchester) centuries. The length of dialogue and also the numbers of clerks involved grew, until the play moved into the open and the acting was by laymen. The Mystery plays were inordinately long – up to 80,000 lines[32] and taking up to 40 days to perform – and the scenes were acted either in individual *mansiones* (platforms or booths) set up in the market place or elsewhere in a town. In France more than in other countries the *mansiones* might be concentrated along one side of a market place or of a covered room, which meant that the spectators instead of walking around would be in a fixed position.[33]

The Hôtel de Bourgogne means to us the 'grande salle' built by the fraternity.[34] It was oblong with boxes and galleries along the long sides. As in England, performances were public. To attend you had to pay. The fee had been fixed by Parliament in 1541 at 2 sous. In 1609 Parliament decreed that the fee should be no more than 5 sous for the pit and 10 for boxes and galleries, in 1655 the figures are 15 and 20, but in the Palais Royal in 1643 they were 20 and 1 écu.[35]

The Confrérie when it moved to the Hôtel de Bourgogne was granted a monopoly by Henri II, and other troupes had to hire the theatre, in which case the first day's taking would go to the troupe, the second day's to the Confrérie. The Confrérie also made financial claims if troupes hired another place, usually one of the many *jeu-de-paume* halls.

There is no reason in this book to follow in detail the complicated history of Parisian theatres in the seventeenth century[36] – the Hôtel de Bourgogne, the Marais in the rue Vieille du Temple, the Petit Bourbon, the theatre in the Palais Cardinal, later Palais Royal, and the Salle des Machines in the Tuileries.[37] Some of the details are relatively familiar, because of the activity of Molière and his troupe. He had gone back to Paris in 1658 and died in 1673. No more than the following particulars need be given. Both the Bourgogne and the Marais were reconstructed or remodelled in the forties (Marais 1644, Bourgogne 1647). Both received two tiers of boxes (on boxes more will be said presently). In 1629 Cardinal Richelieu bought the house which goes with the present Palais Royal.[38] It was called Palais Cardinal, and it had two theatres, one small and one large. Richelieu's architect was Lemercier (who built the town of Richelieu and the adjoining mansion as well). The theatre was opened in 1641 and had two tiers of balconies and no boxes. One year later Richelieu died

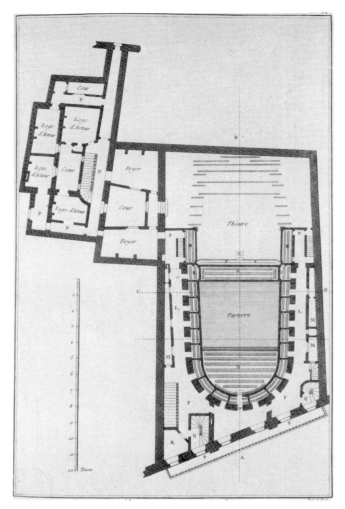

6.14 Paris, theatre of the Comédie Française, 1688–89, by François d'Orbay (Diderot and d'Alembert, *Encyclopédie*, 1772)

6.15 London, Swan Theatre, 1595 (*Utrecht, Bibliothek der Rijksuniversiteit*)

and the house went to the Queen, Anne of Austria, hence the name Palais Royal. Molière on his return first played in the Petit-Bourbon on the Quai du Louvre and then, on the demolition of the Petit-Bourbon in 1660, at the Palais Royal. At his death in 1673 his troupe had to leave. It was fused with the Marais company, and together they moved to the rue Guénégaud, between St Germain des Prés and the river. The premises had been a *jeu-de-paume*. There in 1680 out of the two companies the Comédie Française was created. Meanwhile, at the Palais Royal, the opera had replaced Molière. (The opera, an Italian growth – see below – had been established in Paris in 1661, as a privilege of the Académie Royale de Musique.) The necessary remodelling was due to François Blondel and the theatrical engineer Gaspare Vigarani, who had built the theatre at Modena. Boxes were now replacing balconies. The opera stayed on these premises until a fire destroyed them in 1763, then for a short time moved into the Salle des Machines in the Tuileries, which Vigarani had built for theatricals in 1659, giving it a stage of amazing depth – 131 feet. In 1770 the opera returned to the Palais Royal, rebuilt by Moreau-Desproux (see p. 76).

6.14 As for the Comédie Française, in 1688–89 it received its own building. The architect was d'Orbay.[39] There were a semicircular auditorium behind the parterre (which was standing space) and three tiers of boxes. The plan of the auditorium was not a U: the arms widened towards the stage. It might be described as a straight-sided bell. D'Orbay's building remained the venue of the Comédie until 1770, when the company moved into the Salle des Machines, vacated by the opera on completion of Moreau-Desproux's building. In 1782 they moved to the Odéon (pp. 76–78). For their subsequent history see p. 78.

But all this is anticipating. What happened in theatrical architecture in the second half of the seventeenth century can in any case only be understood in terms of Italian events, and these should not be tackled until a look has been had at England.

In England[40] the medieval theatre had not been essentially different from the theatre on the Continent. Drama started in the church and in the later Middle Ages moved into the open. The York, the Wakefield, the Coventry cycles of Mysteries are well enough known. In the sixteenth century performances took place at court, in the houses of noblemen and in the universities and inns of court. Choir boys, school boys, dons acted. Professional players were still regarded as mountebanks. The City in 1574 forbade theatres, for reasons of fire

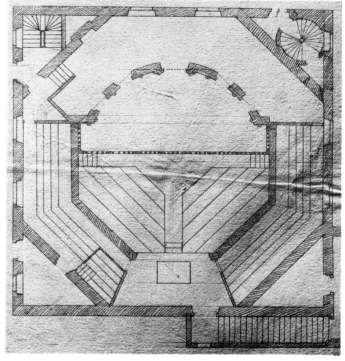

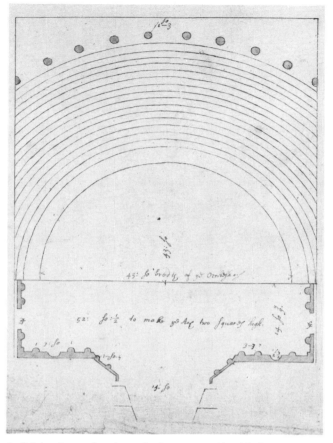

6.16, 17 London, Cockpit-in-Court, 1629, by Inigo Jones: *scenae frons* and plan (drawing by John Webb, after 1660; *Oxford, Worcester College*)

6.18 Inigo Jones, drawing referring to an unidentified theatre *(Oxford, Worcester College)*

danger, riot danger, infection danger, but essentially danger to morals, arising out of 'unchaste, uncomely and unshamefaced speeches and doings' and 'many other corruptions of youth, and other enormities' such as 'alluring of maids . . . to privy and unmeet contracts'. A preacher in a sermon in 1578 called the theatre 'a shew place of all beastly and filthie matters'.[41]

That was two years after the first theatre had been built in London – wisely outside, though close to, the City boundaries. Being the first it was simply called The Theatre. It was in Shoreditch and was built of wood as an initiative of James Burbage, who was a joiner. It was followed in 1577 by the Curtain in Moorfields, in 1587 by the Rose in Bankside on the south bank, set up by the entrepreneur Philip Henslowe, by the Swan, also in Bankside, in 1595, by the Globe *ibidem* in 1598,[42] by the Fortune north of Cripplegate in 1600, and by the Hope, again in Bankside, for which the contract of 1613 refers to 'two boxes . . . for gentlemen'.[43]

The appearance of the Elizabethan playhouse is the 'wooden O' of Shakespeare's *Henry V*, a circular or polygonal building, unroofed, with the pit filled by the groundlings and the galleries around by the better classes. The famous drawing of the Swan, while not entirely accurate, tells us enough. Most of the theatres were built

by the heads of companies, shares being held by the members. Admission was (at the Swan) 1d. for the pit, 2–3d. for the galleries. For first nights the fee might be doubled. An indoor theatre would have had patent advantages. Burbage indeed bought the refectory of the former Blackfriars, where amateur acting had already taken place, but the City in 1596 made it impossible for him to use it, although in 1609 he was allowed back. The Fortune was roofed in 1623, and the later seventeenth century was to be the time of indoor theatres. Companies were attached to noble households in a number of ways, yet could also play in public theatres on their own account. From 1597 only two companies were allowed to act – the Admiral's Men under Alleyn and the Chamberlain's Men under Burbage. In 1602 a third company was licensed: Worcester's Men. In 1604 all three became royal, i.e. the Chamberlain's became the King's, Worcester's the Queen's and the Admiral's Prince Henry's.

As in architectural history in general, so in the history of theatre buildings. Inigo Jones was the great divide. His stage-sets and costumes were under the direct influence of Italy, and so was his ideal of theatre architecture.[44] There are in the collection of Worcester College in Oxford drawings by or after him to prove

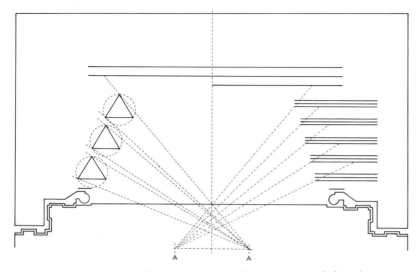

6.19 Plan of Renaissance stage showing periacti (left) and wings (right) (Streit, *Das Theater*, 1903)

6.20 Bologna, Teatro della Sala, 1639 *(Bologna, Archivio di Stato)*

6.16, 17   this. Two refer to the theatre called the Cockpit-in-Court. This was built in 1629 and consisted of an octagon set in a square. The octagon was Henry VIII's cockpit. The back of the stage, i.e. the *scenae frons*, was a concave architecture with two tiers of columns and a pediment, all in the Palladian style. Even more Palladian is another

6.18   drawing referring to an unidentified theatre. This has as its auditorium a semicircle truncated at the sides, and above it a colonnade screening a standing space, just

6.8, 10   as in Vicenza. The truncation on the other hand derives from Serlio.

Now – and again the history of architecture and the history of the theatre run parallel – while England in the person of Jones turned Palladian, Italy turned Baroque, and this Baroque was to influence most of the countries of the north. In theatrical terms the change to the Baroque expresses itself in three ways: in the creation of the opera, in the introduction of scenic wings and in the arrangement of the auditorium to accommodate the *intermezzi*. The first opera is Peri's *Dafne*, performed in Florence in 1594. Peri's *Euridice* followed in 1600 and Monteverdi's era dawned. The first theatre built for opera is the S. Cassiano in Venice of 1637. Scenic wings

6.19   gradually took the place of the *periacti*, which were still used in the late sixteenth and early seventeenth centuries. They are for example described in Daniele Barbaro's *La pratica della prospettiva* in 1568,[45] in Danti's publication of Vignola's *Le due regole della prospettiva pratica* in 1583,[46] in Buontalenti's Uffizi theatre in 1588[47] and even in Nicolo Sabbatini's *Pratica di fabricar scene* in 1638[48] and Jean Debreuil's *La Perspective pratique* in 1645. In England *periacti* seem to have been used for the first time by Inigo Jones in 1605 in a college performance in Christ Church, Oxford. In Germany Furttenbach in

1640 still has *periacti*,[49] which he, like Jones, had learned about in Italy.

But at that time, as the Baroque demanded ever more elaborate and complicated sets with central perspective, the *periacti* disappeared, and scenic wings (*telari*, now *quinte*) took their place. Giovanni Battista Aleotti is customarily credited with their invention, Giacomo Torelli with their victory. The victory was complete by the middle of the century. For Aleotti the operative buildings are the theatre of the Accademia degli Intrepidi in Ferrara, of 1606,[50] with a built scene, and then the grand Farnese Theatre in Parma, of 1617–28.[51] Torelli   6.12, 1 when he migrated to Paris in 1645 took the new type of stage there. As for England, Inigo Jones in later life was converted to wings: witness his *Salmacida Spolia*, performed in 1640. For Spain the corresponding date is earlier. Cosimo Lotti of Florence used wings in his Buen Retiro Theatre at Madrid in 1626–30.

But at Madrid not only the stage but also the auditorium had changed fundamentally. What had happened is that instead of the semicircular amphitheatre a number of different basic shapes were introduced and developed. The Buen Retiro has a U-shaped auditorium, a form which, as has already been mentioned, was used by Aleotti in Parma. An important later example is the second Tor di Nona Theatre in Rome   6.26 (1666–71, by Carlo Fontana – see below). Other varieties are the horseshoe (SS. Giovanni e Paolo, Venice, as   6.21 remodelled in 1654),[52] the bell (Teatro Comunale, Bologna), the straight-sided bell (in Paris the Salle des Machines, Tuileries, 1659,[53] Comédie Française by   6.14 d'Orbay, 1688–89) and the truncated oval or ellipse (in Rome Tor di Nona II as planned and Tor di Nona III, 1695, also by Fontana;[54] Turin 1740).

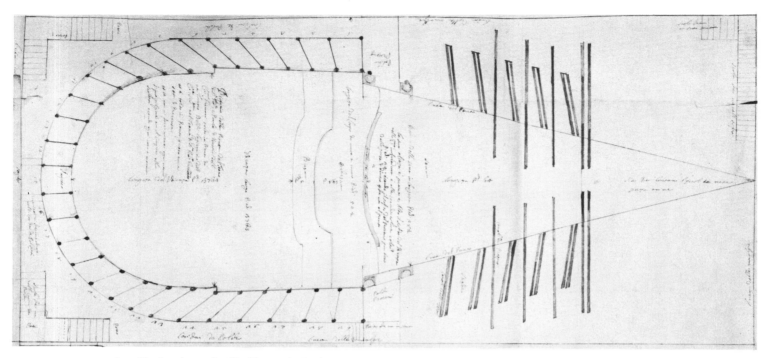

6.21 Venice, theatre by SS. Giovanni e Paolo, 1654 (drawing by Carlo Fontana; *London, Sir John Soane's Museum*)

The greatest change in the elevation of the auditoria was the introduction of boxes instead of galleries.[55] As a matter of fact they were not really an innovation. Mention of odd early cases has here and there already been made. The best description is of 1516 and refers to Autun. The reference is to '240 cellules . . . séparées au moyen de parvis intermédiaires en bois et revêtues de lambris' ('240 compartments . . . separated by wooden panelled screens'). They were for the clerics, for noblemen and council members. In the seventeenth century they were, like the galleries in England, for those who could afford to pay more. Here are a few early examples: the Aleotti drawing referring to the theatre of the Accademia degli Intrepidi (see above),[56] a temporary grandstand for a tournament in the Piazza Maggiore in Bologna of 1628[57] with three tiers, the Buen Retiro theatre of 1626–30, a grandstand for a tournament on the Prato della Valle in Padua in 1636, with 'cinque file di loggie' each for sixteen people and divided from each other by 'tramezi', the Teatro della Sala in the Palazzo del Podestà in Bologna of 1639 with five tiers of boxes, various theatres in Venice, among them that of S. Cassiano of 1637 (already mentioned as the first in the world built for opera), that of SS. Giovanni e Paolo of 1654 (also referred to before) with five tiers of boxes, that of S. Giovanni Crisostomo of 1678–79, also with five tiers of boxes, and that of S. Samuele of 1656 with seven tiers, and finally an important Roman example, the Tor di Nona Theatre,[58] already referred to for the shape of its auditorium. It was built in 1666–71 on the site of an older U-shaped theatre[59] at the inspiration of Queen Christina of Sweden who lived in Rome. It was designed by Carlo Fontana, but in spite of the ex-Queen it was a public theatre and it was financed by the box-

holders, the *palchettisti*, who would purchase one or several boxes before the theatre was built (see below). It had six tiers of boxes. Fontana remodelled it radically in 1695. The plan then was, as we have seen, a truncated ellipse – the first ever built, it seems.[60]

With these theatres the type of the Baroque was complete. No fundamental changes were going to be made for over two hundred years, except in stage machinery which was getting more and more ingenious – 'Up ye Machines' said Ben Jonson with disapproval[61] – and in the stage scenery which was becoming perspectivally more complicated, culminating in the fantastic architectures of the Galli Bibiena family. Ferdinando, born in 1657, was the first of the dynasty, and his is supposed to be the invention of 'le scene vedute per angolo'. The term comes from his *L'architettura civile*, published in Parma in 1711.[62] 'Vedute per angolo' refers to feigned architecture set up at an angle.

Strictly speaking *scenografia* is outside the scope of this book. Even so, one exception must be permitted, because it is the climax of Baroque sophistication and because it refers to Bernini. In 1637 he staged an intermezzo called *De' due teatri*. The curtain rose and the public saw a second public on the stage looking at the real public. The prologue was spoken by two actors facing the two audiences. The curtain went down, and when it rose again the feigned audience was seen to go home by moonlight and torchlight. But the end was Death on a horse, Death who 'cuts the thread of all comedies'.[63]

As regards theatre buildings, the new Italian type now began to conquer Europe. Relevant dates are the Groote Staatsschouwburg on the Keizersgracht in Amsterdam,[64] 1637, by Jacob van Campen, the architect of the Town Hall (pp. 33–34), with two tiers of boxes separated by

6.20

6.21

6.24

2.15–17

6.23 Francesco Galli Bibiena, design for a stage set with diagonal perspective *(Milan, Coll. Tordini)*

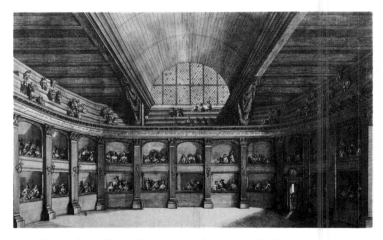

6.22 Turin, Teatro Regio, 1738–40, by Castellamonte and Alfieri; the set by Giuseppe Galli Bibiena (painting by P. D. Olivero, 1740; *Turin, Museo Civico*)

6.24 Amsterdam, Groote Staatsschouwburg, 1637, by Jacob van Campen: auditorium

giant pilasters, and an enormous gallery placed above them;[65] Santurini's Munich Opera on the Salvatorplatz, 1656, remodelled by two members of the Mauro family, Gaspare and Domenico, in 1685–86; Lodovico Ottavio Burnacini's Opera on the Cortina in Vienna, built of wood in 1665–66, with galleries rather than boxes, rebuilt in 1699 after having been burnt; also in Vienna the Opera on the Rietplatz by Francesco Galli Bibiena, 1706–08; in London Davenant's theatre of 1670–71 at the Dorset Stairs with two tiers of seven boxes, each holding twenty people,[66] and of course Wren's Theatre Royal in Drury Lane, opened in 1674, with giant pilasters (cf. Amsterdam) and a few boxes.[67] The plenitude of tiers of boxes became known in England by John James's translation in 1707 of Pozzo's *De perspectiva pictorum* (1693), which contains a theatre with five tiers of boxes, and perhaps earlier by the publication of the first treatise on theatre construction (*Trattato sopra la struttura de' teatri e scene*), published in Mantua by Carini Motta in 1676.[68]

By the late seventeenth century tiers of boxes had become the accepted form of better-class seating, and on stage, by means of scenic wings, the elaborate perspective vistas had become possible – as we have seen. The

next hundred years saw only increases in size and quality. No more than a very limited sample can here find a place. The Italian material will be presented first, the material from the other countries second.

The first theatre in Milan was built in 1598.[69] It was of wood. In 1696 it was remodelled with three tiers of boxes held by the *nobili*. A fire consumed the building in 1708 and in 1714–17 a new one was built, the Teatro Ducale. It was an enterprise of the *palchettisti* (as the Tor di Nona had been), had five tiers of boxes, and in its turn was burnt in 1776. Of 1732 is the Teatro Argentina in Rome, designed by the Marchese Teodoli with an auditorium of truncated elliptical shape. The Teatro S. Carlo in Naples by Giovanni Antonio Medrano and Angelo Caresale dated from 1737. The auditorium had a horseshoe shape and six tiers of boxes. The most ambitious building of the first half of the eighteenth century is the Turin theatre, by Conte di Castellamonte and Benedetto Alfieri, built into a wing of the palace in 1738–40 with an auditorium of truncated elliptical shape and six tiers of boxes. The boxes were again the property of those who had paid. The Turin theatre had more lavish secondary rooms than any before. The Grand Vestibule lies below the auditorium.

6.25 Vienna, Opera on the Cortina, 1665–66, by L. O. Burnacini

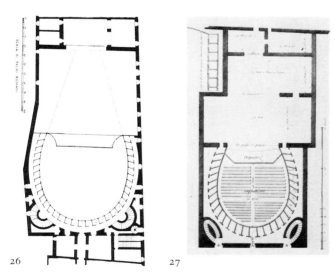

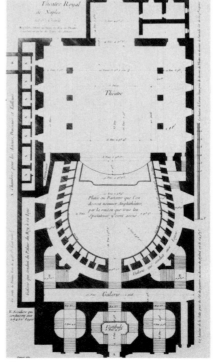

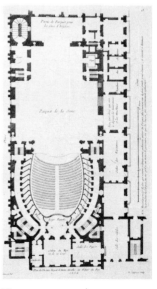

26   27

6.26 Carlo Fontana, unexecuted design for the second Tor di
Nona Theatre, Rome, 1666–71, with oval auditorium
(reconstruction by Edward Craig based on engravings by Felice
Giorgi and drawings in Sir John Soane's Museum, London)
6.27 Rome, Teatro Argentina, 1732, by the Marchese Teodoli
(Dumont, *Parallèle*, 1774 ed.)
6.28 Naples, Teatro S. Carlo, 1737, by G. A. Medrano and
Angelo Caresale (Dumont, *Parallèle*, 1774 ed.)
6.29 Turin, Teatro Regio, 1738–40, by Castellamonte and
Alfieri (Dumont, *Parallèle*, 1774 ed.)

28

29

6.30 Milan, Scala, 1776–78, by Giuseppe Piermarini

As for entrance fees at that time, Luigi Riccoboni in his *Réflexions historiques et critiques*, published in 1738,[70] tells us that a ticket costs 16 sols, a box (the whole box had to be taken) up to 10 sequins. Usually however a box was taken for a year.[71]

6.30, 31   The climax of Italian theatrical architecture is the Scala in Milan, built to Piermarini's designs in 1776–78 to replace the Teatro Ducale, and like that paid for by the box-holders. This meant incidentally that they each decorated and furnished their box and its ante-room to their taste. 'So many little drawing-rooms, the fourth walls . . . removed' is how Proust describes boxes.[72] The Scala when it was built was free-standing on three sides. The façade is surprisingly subdued – a rusticated ground floor and pilaster strips above. The auditorium has a truncated oval shape and seven tiers of boxes, a total of 266 of them. It was the largest theatre ever.[73]

6.33, 36   Of later eighteenth-century French theatres the most festive is – especially after its recent restoration – the Opéra attached to the Palace of Versailles. It is by Gabriel,[74] was built in 1763–70 and has two galleries and a few boxes. The auditorium is a truncated ellipse. However, being strictly a court theatre, its social function was different from that of the public theatres.

Court theatres in fact went on as long as the Ancien Régime lasted, and they are among the most charming we have. Examples are in Germany Celle of 1683–95, the Stadtschloss at Potsdam 1745 (by Knobelsdorff), with amphitheatrical seating and pillars in the form of palm trees, Schwetzingen 1752 (by Pigage), later added to, the Neues Palais at Potsdam 1763–69 (by Büring), Rheinsberg of 1780 and Charlottenburg of 1788–90 (both by Langhans),[75] and Wilhelmsbad near Hanau of 1780–81 (by Franz Ludwig Cancrin);[76] in Italy Caserta of 1752 (by Vanvitelli); in Czechoslovakia Český Krumlov of 1766 (a Schwarzenberg palace); in Sweden[77] Drottningholm 1764–66 (by C. F. Adelcrantz) and Gripsholm 1782 (by Erik Palmstedt), which with its semicircular amphitheatrical seating and colonnade behind and coffered semi-dome like the Ecole de Chirurgie belongs, as will soon become obvious, to Classicism rather than the Baroque; and finally in Russia[78] the Hermitage Theatre at St Petersburg 1782–85 (by Quarenghi), also with amphitheatrical seating and attached columns on the wall above (see p. 82), and Ostankino of 1792 with detached giant columns along the walls left and right.

6.35
6.34

The Berlin Opera, built by Frederick the Great to Knobelsdorff's designs in 1742, stands midway between the court and the public theatre.[79] Seats were free but

6.32

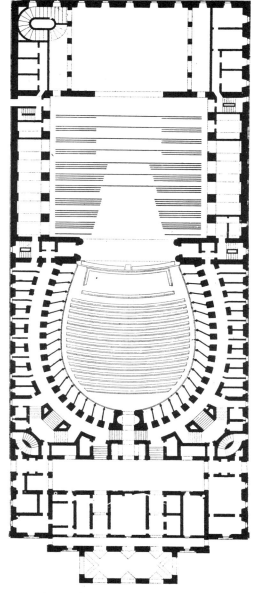

6.34 Drottningholm, court theatre, 1764–66, by C. F. Adelcrantz

6.31 Milan, Scala, 1776–78, by Giuseppe Piermarini

6.35 Český Krumlov, court theatre, 1766

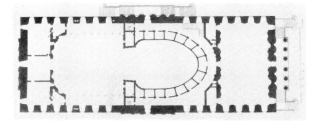

6.32 Berlin, Staatsoper, 1742, by G. W. von Knobelsdorff
(Dumont, *Parallèle*, 1774 ed.)

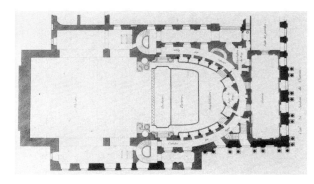

6.33, 36 (left and above) Versailles, Opéra, 1763–70, by J.-A.
Gabriel: plan (Dumont, *Parallèle*, 1774 ed.) and auditorium

6.37 Bayreuth, Residenztheater, 1744–48, by Giuseppe and Carlo Galli Bibiena; the court box late 18th c.

6.38 Munich, Residenztheater, 1750–52, by François Cuvilliés

only available by invitation. The distribution on the opening night, 10 December, was as follows: generals and other officers in the pit, the Diplomatic Corps in the ground floor boxes, civil servants on the next two tiers, then invited citizens. The first performance for admission fees was only in 1789, after Langhans had remodelled the interior very tellingly by converting the boxes into galleries. A seat on the first tier cost two thaler, on the second tier one, in all other places sixteen silbergroschen. The Berlin theatre is a detached building – a rarity at the time. In style it is Palladian, an early case for Germany. The hexastyle upper giant portico is the most telling feature. But Germany also possesses some of the finest major Rococo theatres, notably Bayreuth, of 1744–48, by Giuseppe and Carlo Galli Bibiena (the box for the court is a late eighteenth-century addition), and the Residenztheater in Munich, 1750–52, by Cuvilliés, bombed in the Second World War but rebuilt.[80]

Whereas Cuvilliés represents the French Rococo, heightened by his Bavarian milieu, the principal French theatre architects and theatres after 1750 belong to the Classicist trend[81] which had as its first monument of international significance Soufflot's Ste Geneviève, later – as we have seen – to become the Panthéon. Soufflot designed a major theatre as well, that of Lyons, begun in 1754.[82] It was the first totally detached theatre in France. The auditorium was an excessively truncated ellipse like that of Turin, and there were, also for the first time in France, spacious ancillary public rooms. The building

was destroyed by fire and rebuilt in 1828–30. The fine semicircular vestibule with detached columns dates from that time. Next in order of time came the rebuilding after a fire of the theatre in the Palais Royal, transformed into the Paris Opéra in 1764–69 by Moreau-Desproux, again with an elliptical auditorium, which could hold 2,500.[83] The façade was in a Venetian Cinquecento style, with two tiers of arcades.

But the most ambitious French theatre of the eighteenth century is Victor Louis' Grand Théâtre at Bordeaux, built in 1777–80, again totally free-standing. It has a spectacular façade with a portico of twelve detached giant columns carrying an entablature and no pediment – a motif typical of the late eighteenth century in France.[84] The auditorium was a truncated circle (or near-circle) with balconies as well as boxes, and with giant columns, of which four support the shallow dome of the ceiling. The ancillary rooms were developed far beyond those of Lyons. De Filippi said of it that it was for a long time 'le plus beau du monde'.[85]

Almost contemporary with the Bordeaux theatre was the Odéon in Paris, built for the Comédie Française and originally called Théâtre Français.[86] The architects were M.-J. Peyre and Charles de Wailly, the former Inspecteur des Bâtiments du Roi au Luxembourg, the latter Adjoint au Contrôleur de Versailles. Their first plans, of 1767–69, were for an auditorium in the form of a truncated circle and a façade with a semicircular portico (on the motif of the semicircular façade see pp. 80–84, 86).[87] Their final

6.39, 41 Bordeaux, Grand Théâtre, 1777–80, by Victor Louis: section of vestibule with concert hall above *(Bordeaux, Archives Municipales)*, and auditorium

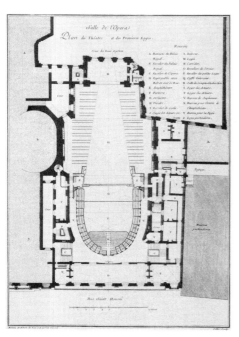

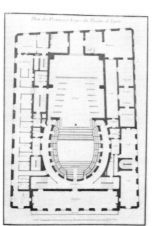

6.42 Lyons, theatre, begun in 1754, by J.-G. Soufflot (Dumont, *Parallèle*, 1774 ed.)

6.40 Paris, Opéra in the Palais Royal, 1764–69, by Moreau-Desproux (Dumont, *Parallèle*, 1774 ed.)

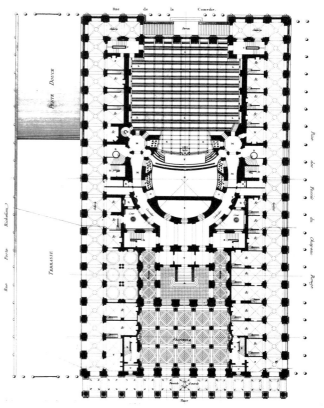

6.43 Bordeaux, Grand Théâtre, 1777–80, by Victor Louis: plan (Louis, *Salle de spectacle*, 1782)

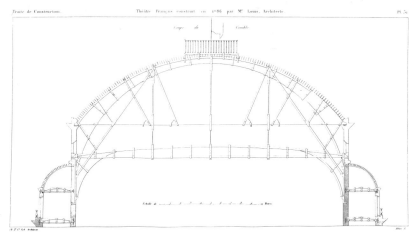

6.44 Paris, Théâtre Français in the Palais Royal, 1786–90, by
Victor Louis: iron roof structure (Eck, *Traité de construction en
poteries et fer*, 1836)

6.45 Bordeaux, Grand Théâtre, 1777–80, by Victor Louis

6.46 Paris, Odéon, 1778–82, by M.-J. Peyre and Charles de Wailly

6.46   plans were accepted in 1778. The Comédie moved in
in 1782.[88] The façade is severely blocky with a massive
giant portico of eight unfluted Doric columns carrying
once again no pediment. The top is a heavy attic above
which rises a pyramid roof. After a fire had damaged the
building in 1799 Chalgrin simplified the interior but
left the façade unchanged. The building was renamed
Théâtre de l'Egalité in 1794, and the partitions between
the boxes were removed (on the war against boxes,
more will be said presently). The name Odéon was
adopted in 1797.

In 1784 an ambitious new theatre was completed at
Nancy to the design of Mathurin-Coucy.[89] It was burnt
in 1796, redone in 1811 et seq., and altered in 1844 and
1879. Arthur Young wrote of it that it was twice as large
as the Drury Lane Theatre and five times as magnificent.
It had a portico of eight Corinthian columns, and again
a straight entablature instead of a pediment, a vestibule
with apsidal ends, a staircase with a coffered tunnel-vault,
a U-shaped auditorium, boxes on three levels and two
galleries.

In 1786–90 Louis did his next theatre: the replacement
of Moreau-Desproux's Opéra, on the right-hand side of
the entrance to the Palais Royal, which had been burnt
in 1781. Louis' theatre was on the left-hand side. It was
taken over in 1791 and called Théâtre Français by Talma
and others who had left the Comédie Française company
at the Odéon in protest against its revolutionary politics.
They soon renamed it Théâtre de la République. In 1799
after the Odéon was burnt the two companies were
reunited, and Louis's Palais Royal theatre is still the home
of the Comédie Française today.

Louis' building, like its Bordeaux predecessor, had an
auditorium in the shape of a truncated circle. The   6.83
seating arrangement was boxes, and there were giant
columns embracing two tiers of boxes. It was in this
building that an iron roof construction was first used.[90]   6.44
Louis' theatre was part of a much bigger scheme for
remodelling the whole group of Palais Royal buildings
(cf. p. 263), of which planning had begun in 1781.

But by the time of Louis' Théâtre Français opposition
had become vociferous against the whole conception as
well as the individual features of the Baroque theatre,
notably boxes. Opposition started from two different
sides, but they soon joined forces. One was social and
even political, the other aesthetic. The first rose up in
the name of equality, the second in the name of Antiquity. But in fact both were looking back to Antiquity
and to Palladio. The Roman theatre and the Teatro
Olimpico had no boxes for a privileged class. Amphi-   6.10

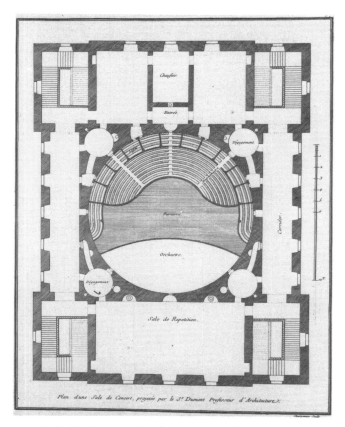

6.47 G.-P.-M. Dumont, plan for a concert hall, *c.* 1760 (*Parallèle*, ed. of *c.* 1770)

6.49 (right) Charles-Nicolas Cochin, plan for a theatre, 1765 (Patte, *Essai sur l'architecture théâtrale*, 1782)

6.48 Arnaldi, plan for a theatre (*Idea . . .*, 1762)

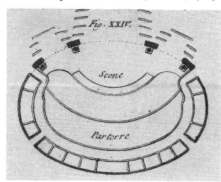

theatrical seating gave all comers the same opportunity. And the Roman theatre and the Olimpico shunned busy and showy decoration. So in the field of the theatre we shall find a true reflexion of the pre-Revolutionary and the anti-Rococo convictions. Evidence is ample.[91]

The sequence begins with two remarkable designs, which were never executed or followed up, the latter perhaps because they were so much ahead of their time. One is Levau's design of 1660 for the Louvre, the other Robert de Cotte's design of *c.* 1715 for Schleissheim, the Versailles of the Electors of Bavaria. Levau has amphitheatrical seating.[92] De Cotte has the same, with a top colonnade but also boxes.[93] The reform began seriously only a generation after de Cotte in the *oeuvre* of Piranesi, the great inspirer of the Boullée-Ledoux circle and the Grand Prix victors. His *Opere varie* of 1750 has a plate of a *Magnifico collegio*, and this includes a theatre, whose auditorium is a semicircle with the arms lengthened so as to result in a U. The colonnade at the top is also taken over. Vitruvius and Palladio must be the sources. Reformatory texts set in a little later, about 1760, with Count Algarotti's *Saggio sopra l'opera* of 1762.[94] Algarotti, whom we have already met à propos Newton (p. 13) was a man of polite accomplishments and a believer in all the Enlightenment stood for, a friend of

Frederick the Great and an admirer of English Palladianism. As for theatre buildings, he wrote that they should be fireproof, i.e. of brick or stone, and that the auditorium should be semi-elliptic, i.e. a truncated longitudinal ellipse. Boxes he still accepts, and he allows them for acoustic reasons to be of wood. The Berlin Opera is one of the few theatres he mentions with approval.[95] So this is innovation to a very moderate degree. It is different with G.-P.-M. Dumont's plan of *c.* 1760 for a concert hall. The auditorium is circular, the seating segmental. Dumont is the author of the first book of engravings of ancient Greek buildings and also of a collection of interesting though sometimes inaccurate theatre plans published *c.* 1764 with the title *Parallèle de plans des plus belles salles de spectacle d'Italie et de France.* Next in order of time is E. Arnaldi's treatise of 1762 with the telling title *Idea di un teatro . . . simile a' teatri antichi.* Here is the semicircular seating 'conforme alla dottrina di Vitruvio' but also still the system of boxes in tiers. A design by N. M. Potain submitted to Marigny (Directeur des Bâtiments under Louis XV from 1746 to 1773 and brother of Madame de Pompadour) is dated by Hautecoeur to about 1763.[96] It was for a theatre in the form of a truncated transverse ellipse set diagonally in a square. Two fronts were to have giant tetrastyle porticoes with

6.47

6.48

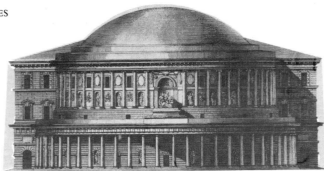

6.50 Vincenzo Ferrarese, design for a theatre (Milizia, *Trattato*, 1771)

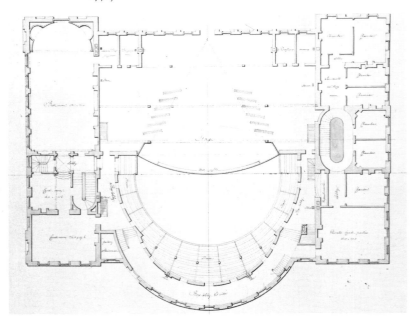

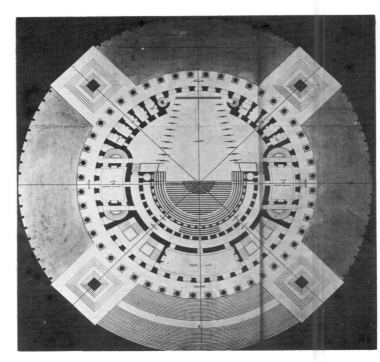

6.52 E.-L. Boullée, design for an opera house, 1781 *(Paris, Bibliothèque Nationale)*

6.51 Benjamin Latrobe, design for a combined theatre and hotel, 1797–98 *(Washington, D.C., Library of Congress)*

(already) a straight entablature. The truncated transverse ellipse was proposed again almost immediately by Charles-Nicolas Cochin in his *Projet d'une salle de spectacle* of 1765. Cochin had travelled in Italy in 1750 with Marigny and Soufflot, and his charming *Supplication aux orfèvres* of 1754 (*Mercure de France*) was one of the first French attacks on the Rococo.[97]

It has only very recently been shown that as early as 1760 Antoine (of the Monnaie) had designed a building for the Comédie Française with a semicircular front.[98] The feature turned out to have a future. We have already seen that it appeared in Peyre and de Wailly's first plans for the Odéon (p. 76). After 1760 it was, like the auditorium in the form of a truncated circle, to recur in theoretical writings, and eventually both were to be actually built.

In 1769 the Chevalier de Chaumont brought out a small book called *Exposition des principes qu'on doit suivre dans l'ordonnance des théâtres modernes*. He wants to see 'un goût pur et hardi', the grandeur of Antiquity combined with the 'commodité' of today's boxes. His specific demands are moderate: stepped-back galleries instead of tiers of boxes vertically one above the other and an exterior with a projecting façade 'à peu près circulaire'.

Francesco Milizia, protagonist in Italy in the war against the Baroque, published his *Trattato del teatro* in 1771, and here the new ideal is expressed much more peremptorily.[99] Today, he writes, the theatre is an 'ammasso di assuoli' whereas it should be a 'scuola di virtù e buon gusto'. Boxes ('cellette che diconsi palchetti') are bad for seeing and hearing as well as immoral. They make serious listening and serious plays impossible.[100] And as for the seating 'l'unica figura conveniente . . . deve essere semicircolare'. To convince his readers Milizia adds a design for a monumental theatre by Vincenzo Ferrarese. This has auditorium and stage within one circle and under one shallow dome and once again the semicircular façade to express the internal semicircle. The external semicircle has all round the curve a colonnade.

Jacques-François Blondel in the second volume of his *Cours d'architecture* – published in 1771 but representing his teaching from 1750 onwards – writes: 'Il servit bien de supprimer ce qu'on appelle *loges*.'[101] He wishes to see stepped-back galleries instead, and he proposes auditoria of circular or elliptical shape – i.e. he is not a radical. He recommends incidentally that theatres ought to be detached buildings with easy access for coaches and external arcades 'pour prendre l'air'. Of existing theatre designs he praises Dumont, Soufflot's Lyons and Gabriel's Versailles. He looks forward, as he writes, to 'Peyre et Wailly's' new Comédie Française, i.e. the Odéon.

L. S. Mercier's *Du Théâtre* was published in Amster-

6.53, 54 E.-L. Boullée, design for an opera house, 1781:
longitudinal section and exterior *(Paris, Bibliothèque Nationale)*

6.55 J.-N.-L. Durand, design for a theatre *(Précis, II, 1809)*

dam in 1773. He objects to boxes for moral reasons. They are 'an indecent custom . . . the result of our looseness of manners'.[102] Also of the seventies is A. J. Roubo's *Traité de la construction des théâtres* (1777). He introduces the motif of an ambulatory all round the auditorium semicircle, but will not give up boxes. A. E. M. Grétry in his *Mémoires . . . sur la musique* of *c.* 1789 is more radical: 'Point de loges, ni petites ni grandes, ces réduits ne servant qu'à favoriser la médisance.'

Of the eighties are two more major contributions to this paper campaign. In 1782 Pierre Patte, author of the survey of proposed monuments to Louis XV[103] and of attacks on Soufflot for static inadequacies of Ste Geneviève, i.e. the Panthéon,[104] published an *Essai sur l'architecture théâtrale*, a serious book of about 200 pages pleading for the truncated longitudinal ellipse for reasons of optics and acoustics. The book also contains detailed comments on about a dozen theatres, including the Argentina, Naples, Turin, Berlin and Moreau's Opéra (burnt a year before), and even more detailed comments on recent theatrical literature.[105]

One year earlier, in 1781, Boullée, designer of the Monument to Newton, added to his collection of large drawings destined to form a book a design for an opera house.[106] It is as megalomaniac as the Newton Monument and Boullée's other designs. The theatre is to be detached, in the middle of the Palais Royal or the Place du Carrousel, circular and surrounded by a giant colonnade of forty-eight Corinthian columns.[107] The auditorium is semicircular with a coffered semidome, again like the Ecole de Chirurgie. Boullée calls this shape 'la seule convenable à la destination d'un théâtre'. But progressive as this plan is, Boullée is not prepared to sacrifice boxes. The two top tiers are concealed in the coffering. The building, Boullée writes, was to be made fireproof by being constructed entirely of stone and brick, and fire-safe also by a large number of exits.

Among unexecuted designs, next in order of time comes one by the greatest American architect, Latrobe. Remembering his designs for the Capitol (p. 38), it cannot be a surprise that his proposed theatre for Richmond, Virginia, has a semicircular auditorium and that this auditorium projects semicircularly on the pattern of Chaumont, Antoine, the earliest Odéon plan (see p. 76) and Ferrarese. These dated from *c.* 1760–70. Latrobe's design was made in 1797–98,[108] shortly before the old theatre was destroyed by fire. The auditorium – it almost goes without saying – had a semidome. Boxes were reduced in number and largely replaced by galleries. The theatre was to be flanked by assembly rooms on the left and a hotel on the right. This also was an outstandingly novel arrangement, as will be shown in a later chapter (see pp. 172–73, 184).

Ten years later, in 1809, Durand – who contributed

52–54

6.52, 53

6.51
3.12

6.55

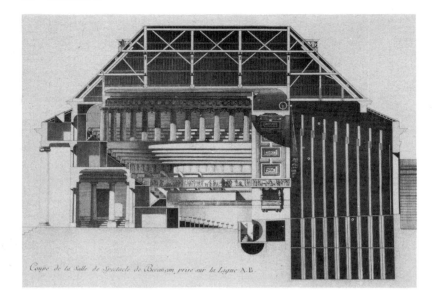

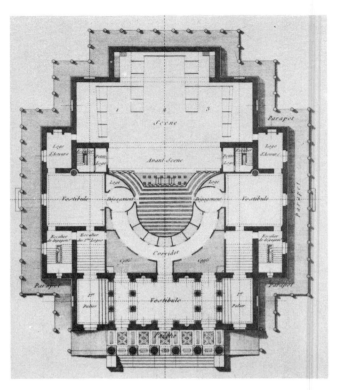

6.56–58 Besançon, theatre, 1778–84, by C.-N. Ledoux: section, façade and plan (Ledoux, *L'Architecture*, 1804)

6.55 designs for nearly all the public buildings appearing in the present book – illustrated his ideal theatre.[109] It has a semicircular front also and left and right, lying back, two square foyers. The stage-house stands up higher than the rest. The semicircle has three tiers of arcading. It indicates to the outside the semicircular auditorium, and this has receding galleries and no boxes. In his text Durand praises the theatres of Antiquity in which all could see and all could hear, whereas in today's theatre a quarter of the public sees nothing or not enough. Also the subsidiary rooms are cramped and dangerous. Durand's roof construction is of iron.[110]

One English author after so many French ones must be added. He is George Saunders, Surveyor to the County of Middlesex and author of an exceptionally interesting paper on Gothic vaults.[111] In his *Treatise on Theatres*, brought out in 1791, he combined the Classical semicircle with two tiers of galleries. This to him would be 'the most analogous to the antique that is possible for our arrangement'.[112]

6.56–58 By the 1790s, however, an actual building in France had gone much further than Saunders and Patte, even if no further than Boullée. The building is the theatre at Besançon. Its architect was Claude-Nicolas Ledoux, side by side with Boullée the most radical of the French,

which explains why many of his daring designs, like Boullée's, remained unexecuted. But the Besançon theatre was built, and built as early as 1778–84.[113] It has a portico of six columns carrying an entablature and no pediment, a sign at that moment, as we know, of advanced views,[114] and the interior has semicircular, graded amphitheatrical seating. Ledoux calls this explicitly 'the progressive form which makes humanity equal'.[115] Instead of rising vertically above one another, the different levels are stepped back; one is subdivided by low partition walls. Besançon also had a sunk orchestra, the first, it seems, to try out this Wagnerian feature. Around the back runs a colonnade, as in Palladio's theatre, but now with Greek Doric columns – in France among the earliest. There is more seating behind it.

A parallel to Besançon is Giacomo Quarenghi's small theatre in the Hermitage at St Petersburg dating from 1782–85, already referred to on p. 174. Here also there are the graded semicircular amphitheatre and the colonnade behind, and there are no boxes. In this context the designs of the Frenchman Desprez done in Stockholm need a brief mention too. Jean-Louis Desprez was born in 1743. He spent the years 1777–84 in Italy and then settled in Stockholm.[116] He was a brilliant stage designer

6.57

6.56

6.59 Paris, Théâtre Feydeau, 1788, by J.-G. Legrand and
J. Molinos: façade, drawn by Friedrich Gilly

6.60 Friedrich Gilly, design for a National Theatre in Berlin,
1797–98

6.61 Friedrich Gilly, design for a National Theatre in Berlin, 1797–98

and as an architect belonged to the Piranesi-Boullée-Grand-Prix set. He used Greek Doric and stubby Tuscan columns, occasional Egyptian motifs and also medieval motifs and designed, probably for the King's Theatre in London and probably in 1789, a semicircular, graded auditorium without boxes and with a back colonnade. The façade was to be semicircular in the Ferrarese way.[117] Other theatre designs of his are less radical.

In Paris in 1788 the Théâtre Feydeau was built, to the designs of Legrand and Molinos. In plan it is not adventurous, the auditorium being a truncated ellipse, but its façade is on a convex curve – the motif of Antoine, Peyre and Wailly, and Ferrarese fully realized for the first time.

Friedrich Gilly, designer of the Monument to Frederick the Great (pp. 15–16), was the one genius among late eighteenth-century architects in Germany. Alas he died at the age of twenty-eight in 1800. In 1797 he had visited Paris. Among his travel-sketches are the Théâtre Feydeau and the Odéon.[118] After his return to Berlin he worked intensively on designs for a National Theatre. It was not built. Had it been, it would have been the noblest of all theatres in the new vein. The exterior was to be built up in units each expressing its function. Decoration was to be used most sparingly. The principal

motifs are the low Greek Doric portico and the lunette or *thermae* windows. The auditorium – it need hardly be said specially – was to have semicircular amphitheatrical seating. At the back instead of Palladio's colonnade are – but not in all the preparatory sketches – Greek Doric columns between which one tier of boxes, semicircular in plan, is provided.

Here is the climax of the revolutionary years – in theatre design and in architecture in general. When Schinkel finally built the National Theatre, i.e. the Berlin Schauspielhaus, things had settled down both in style and in plan.[119] It is true that Schinkel to the end of his life believed in Gilly's solution. There are drawings of his of *c.* 1817 but also still of 1835,[120] which operate with segmental or semicircular seating (and with the sunk orchestra of Ledoux's Besançon), and Graf Brühl, the director of the theatre, wrote that Schinkel 'had on theatres, plays, ballet such totally different ideas from what was current that I could not hope to reach agreement'. However, he did; for Schinkel was not only an architect of sensibility and the highest competence, but also a conscientious civil servant. The result is that Schinkel's building is as perfect of its own kind as Gilly's, but that in the auditorium arrangement it is conventional, and in style it represents that Greek Revival

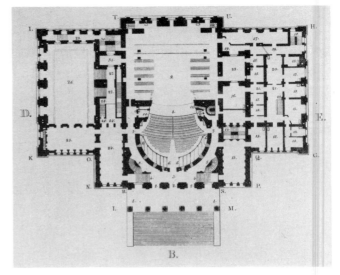

6.62, 64 Berlin, Schauspielhaus, 1818–21, by K. F. Schinkel: exterior and plan

6.63 Dresden, first Opera House, 1838–41, by Gottfried Semper (after the fire in 1869)

6.65 Dresden, second Opera House, 1869–78, by Gottfried Semper

which at the time when it was built, in 1818–21, had become the internationally accepted style for public buildings.

6.62   At the same time one might well be ready to admit that this theatre looks like a theatre. Such at any rate was Schinkel's intention – *architecture parlante*. Schinkel wrote that 'the character of a building should perfectly express itself in its exterior and the theatre could only be regarded as a theatre'.[121]

   The late eighteenth and early nineteenth centuries in England saw a number of ambitious theatres: Novosielski's King's Theatre of 1796 had five tiers of boxes; so had Holland's Drury Lane of 1794. But three tiers and ample galleries were the usual thing. Six tiers occurred only once: in Albani's remodelling of Smirke's Covent Garden in the late 1840s. Prices rose gradually. Throughout the eighteenth century the first gallery at Drury Lane cost 2s., the second 1s. In the mid-nineteenth century the prices at Covent Garden were: pit 10s. 6d., gallery 10s. 6d., 7s. 6d., 5s., unreserved 2s. 6d.[122]

   Theatres of the next forty years can be treated briefly.
6.59   The semicircular façade of the Feydeau was translated into German by Moller for Mainz in 1829[123] and by Gottfried Semper, the most important German archi-
6.63   tect of his time, for Dresden in 1838–41.[124] The style is

now Cinquecento. When a fire destroyed the Dresden theatre it was rebuilt in 1869–78 – again by Semper – 6.65 and the change of style from the Renaissance to the Baroque is striking. Semper had already reached the Baroque concept of Dresden II a decade earlier, in a design of 1858 for an Imperial Theatre for Rio de Janeiro.[125]

   But the Neo-Baroque in the theatre culminated in Paris, with Charles Garnier's glorious Opéra begun in 6.66– 1861 and completed (or left not entirely completed) in 1875.[126] The dates correspond entirely with those of Poelaert's Palais de Justice in Brussels (see p. 60). 5.18, Garnier's plan is complex and exceedingly well man- 6.67 aged. The entrance and the Grand Staircase owe some- 6.66 thing to Bordeaux. The staircase is perhaps Garnier's greatest triumph. Viollet-le-Duc realised and criticized it, Gothic rationalist that he was: 'La salle semble faite pour l'escalier et non l'escalier pour la salle.'[127] But George Augustus Sala called it 'the finest arrangement of curvilinear perspective that I have ever seen',[128] and Garnier himself wanted the staircase to be 'un endroit somptueux et mouvementé'.[129] The foyer and the auditorium are yet more splendid. The auditorium in- 6.69 cidentally is for over 2,000 people. The shape is the traditional horseshoe and there are four tiers of boxes.

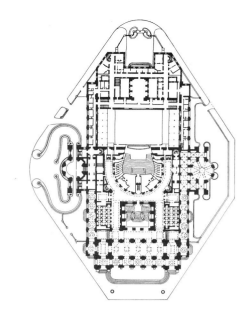

6.66–69 Paris, Opéra, 1861–75, by Charles Garnier: staircase, plan, façade and longitudinal section

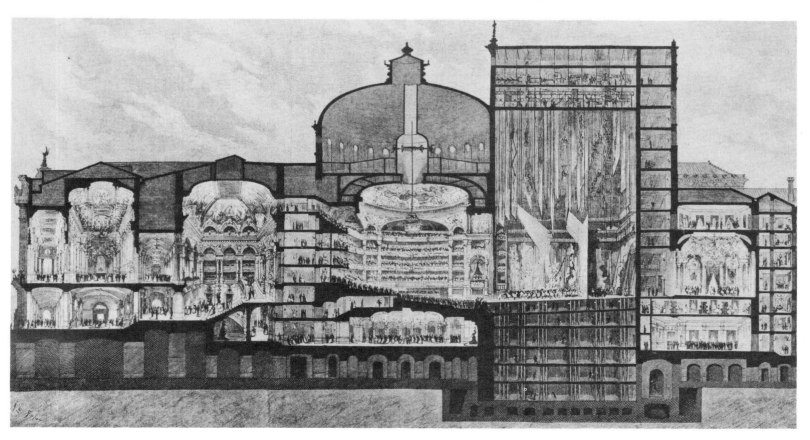

6.70 Gottfried Semper, model for a Festspielhaus for Munich, 1865/66: auditorium *(Munich, Theater-Museum)*

6.72 Gottfried Semper, model for a theatre in the Glaspalast in Munich, 1865/66 *(Herrenchiemsee, König Ludwig II-Museum)*

6.71 Gottfried Semper, model for a Festspielhaus for Munich, 1865/66 *(Herrenchiemsee, König Ludwig II-Museum)*

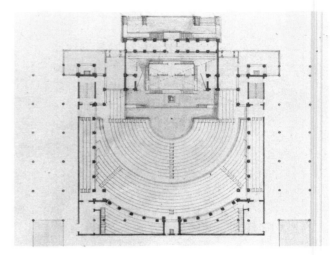

6.73 Gottfried Semper, design for a theatre in the Crystal Palace in London, 1856 *(Munich, Theater-Museum)*

The structural frame is iron, but that is nowhere allowed to show. Externally as well as internally the stylistic elements derive from the Italian, especially Genoese and Venetian, Cinquecento and from the France of Louis XIII and Louis XIV. Polychromy is widely used to heighten the impact yet further. Garnier himself waxed lyrical over his own achievement. He wrote in 1878: 'Laissez vos yeux se réjouir aux rayons dorés, laissez votre âme s'échauffer aux vibrations de la couleur et . . . retrouvez . . . l'enthousiasme de la passion.'[130] From such words it is only one step to Théophile Gautier calling the building and indeed any opera house 'une sorte de cathédrale mondaine de la civilisation'.[131]

What the Opéra conveys in the highest key, other theatres of the Victorian era also convey. The revolution of Ledoux and Gilly had not won its day, and so at the moment we have reached, i.e. about 1860, a new reformatory zeal made itself felt. In the centre now stood Richard Wagner and Gottfried Semper.[132] Wagner in 1862 in the foreword to the publication of the text of his *Ring des Nibelungen* had urged the building of a *Festspielhaus* with concealed orchestra and amphitheatrical seating. The building might be of wood, but it ought to be designed 'nur auf künstlerische Zwecke berechnet'. What this meant is patent: no social distinctions by way of seating – equality before the Wagnerian gospel. Ludwig II was convinced and in 1864 promised Wagner a large theatre built of stone. It was to stand in Munich above the river Isar, north of the Maximilianeum. Now for a while the idea of the permanent theatre developed side by side with that of a temporary theatre, to be put up in the middle of the Glaspalast, Munich's Crystal Palace, which had been built for exhibitions in 1854.[133] As a by-product of the Glaspalast design we have a plan with semicircular seating and back colonnade which was made in 1856 for the Crystal Palace in London.[134] As for the Munich projects Semper worked on both, and the King received models for them in 1865 and 1866. The Glaspalast theatre is clearly developed from Palladio, while the permanent theatre externally anticipates much of Dresden II, but internally continues the Vitruvian and Palladian features of the Crystal Palace design. Neither the temporary nor the permanent theatre was built in Munich – in 1868 Wagner entered in his Annals: 'Theater abgetan' (theatre finished, i.e. abandoned). But in the end, in 1872–76, thanks to private patronage, a grant from

6.74 Bayreuth, Festspielhaus, 1872–76, by O. Brückwald

6.76 Munich, Prinzregenten-Theater, 1900–1901, by Max Littmann

6.75 Bayreuth, Festspielhaus, 1872–76, by O. Brückwald

Ludwig and money earned by Wagner himself on concert tours, the Bayreuth Festspielhaus could be built, humble externally, of brick and half-timber, but internally realizing Wagner's demands: sunk orchestra, amphitheatrical seating, absence of boxes and galleries, and darkened auditorium. The architect was Otto Brückwald.

After a long delay a few new German theatres accepted the Wagner principles.[135] They were by Max Littmann – and his first was indeed built to be a kind of Wagner Festspielhaus: the Prinzregenten-Theater in Munich of 1900–1901. This was followed by the Schiller-Theater in Berlin of 1905–06, the Hoftheater in Weimar of 1907 and others later.[136] The great simplification in the auditorium which is so striking in these theatres is a parallel to the even more radical simplification of the stage in the designs of Adolphe Appia and Gordon Craig.[137]

In traditional buildings on the other hand two technical innovations took place, one in the auditorium, the other in the stage. In the auditorium upper galleries could by means of steel or reinforced concrete be made to project far without vertical support. They could even have their own amphitheatrical seating.[138] The first cantilevered galleries in England were those of the New English Opera House (now the Palace Theatre) in 1891. As regards the stage the innovation was the revolving stage invented in 1896 by Karl Lautenschläger.

A propos concrete it must also be noted that Perret for the Champs Elysées Theatre in 1911 used a complete concrete skeleton. The theatre had been begun by Henry van de Velde but was handed over to Perret. The details of the story are obscure.[139] For van de Velde's own architectural solution one can look at illustrations of the theatre he built for the Werkbund Exhibition at Cologne in 1914, the same exhibition which saw Gropius's famous model factory (see p. 253).

The largest and most monumental work of German Expressionism was a theatre: Poelzig's Grosses Schauspielhaus in Berlin, the brilliant conversion of a circus. The date of the remodelling was 1918–19.

The 'International Modern' followed Expressionism after a few years, and it is right and proper that Gropius's name should appear at the end of this account of the history of theatre-building; for he introduced the most recent innovation: 'theatre-in-the-round'. He called it *Total-Theater*, and drew up a design in 1927 for the revolutionary producer Erwin Piscator, with movable

6.77 Paris, Théâtre des Champs Elysées, 1911–14, by Auguste Perret: lobby

6.78 Cologne, Werkbund Exhibition Theatre, 1914, by Henry van de Velde

6.79 Berlin, Grosses Schauspielhaus, 1918–19, by Hans Poelzig

seating and stage. Gropius's aim was in his own words 'to draw the spectator into the drama'.[140]

Since then many theatres-in-the-round or nearly-in-the-round have been designed, the first being the wooden Penthouse Theatre of Washington University, Seattle, of 1939–40 by John Ashby Conway, the Teatro S. Erasmo in Milan of 1952–53 by Antonio Carminali and Carlo de Carli, and the Festival Theatre at Stratford, Ontario, of 1953–57 by Routhwaite & Fairfield. Three excellent examples are Powell & Moya's Festival Theatre at Chichester of 1961, Harry Weese's Arena Stage in Washington, D.C., also of 1961,[141] and the Octagon at Bolton in Lancashire, 1966–67, by the Borough Architect Mr G. H. Brooks.

6.82

As for external and internal appearance the style of today as against that of Gropius is demonstrated at its most ruthless in the new Teatro San Martín at Buenos Aires by M. R. Alvarez and M. O. Ruiz, 1953–60,[142] and in John Johansen's Mummers' Theatre at Oklahoma City, which the architect himself called 'brash and incisive'.[143]

One postscript and this chapter can be closed. The cinema became a serious competitor of the theatre in the course of the first third of the twentieth century, just as television became a serious (even more serious)

competitor of the cinema in the third quarter.[144] The principal inventions making the cinema possible were those of Edison in 1891 and the brothers Lumière in 1895, and then, in 1918, of sound film. The first picture theatres or picture palaces of any ambition belong to 1910–30. Gorgeousness was aimed at in America, soberer architectural values in Germany. Among the juiciest American cinemas are the Riviera at Omaha and the Avalon at Chicago, both by John Eberson and both of 1926–27, Loew's at Louisville, also by Eberson (1927–28), the Ziegfield in New York by Thomas Lamb and J. Urban (1927),[145] and the Fox, San Francisco, by Lamb (1929). By 1916 there were 25,000 cinemas in the United States. In Germany Oscar Kaufmann did the Ufa on the Nollendorf Platz in Berlin in 1910 and established himself as the cinema specialist. Poelzig did the Kapitol in Berlin in 1925 and the Deli at Breslau in 1926, Mendelsohn the Universum in Berlin in 1926, with fine, sweeping streamlining inside. A freak among cinemas of the twenties is L'Aubette at Strasbourg by Théo van Doesburg (1926–28), an extreme case of De Stijl: outside as well as inside a precarious juggling with squares of pure colours. In Britain in the thirties a jazzy modernism dominated. The most successful architect in that objectionable vein was Harry Weedon.

6.80

6.80 Berlin, Universum Cinema, 1926, by Erich Mendelsohn

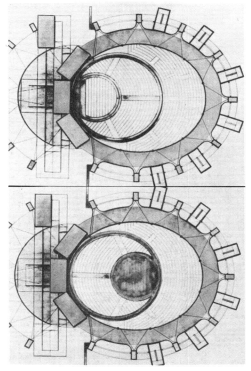

6.81 Walter Gropius, designs for *Total-Theater*, 1927, showing the movable stage in conventional (top) and central positions *(Berlin, Bauhaus-Archiv)*

6.82 Bolton, Lancs., Octagon Theatre, 1966–67, by G. H. Brooks

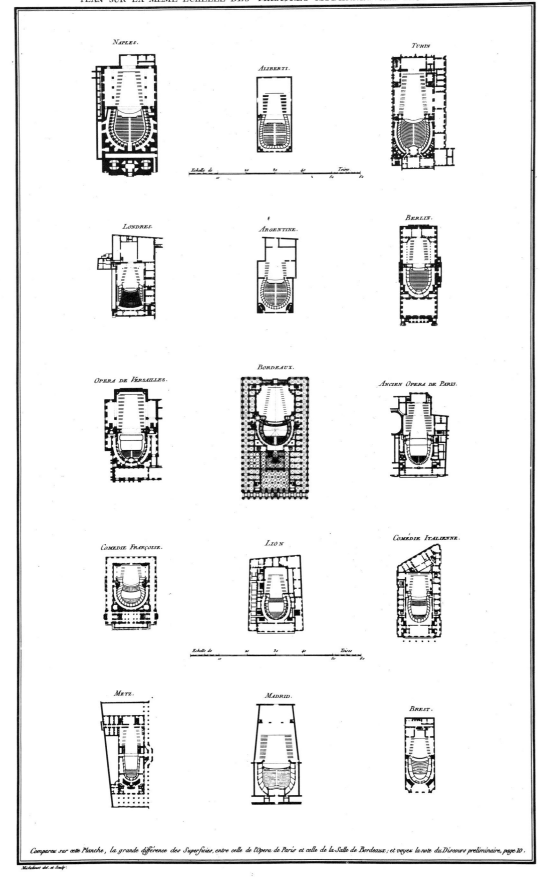

PLAN SUR LA MÊME ECHELLE DES THÉATRES MODERNES LES PLUS CONNUS.

Pl. XXII.

6.83 Comparative plans of major 18th-c. European theatres (Louis, *Salle de spectacle de Bordeaux*, 1782)

7.1 Cesena, Biblioteca Malatestiana, 1447–52

7
Libraries

WHERE should this chapter start? It is recorded that the Ptolemies' library at Alexandria had 200,000, or some say 700,000, rolls. Excavations have acquainted us with the Hellenistic library building at Pergamon and the Roman library buildings of Ephesus, Timgad and indeed Athens, all built, to quote Vitruvius, 'ad communem delectationem'[1] (for the enjoyment of all). We also know that in the troubled third and fourth centuries AD libraries closed down. 'Sepulchrorum ritu in perpetuum clausis' (sealed forever like tombs) is how Ammianus Marcellinus about 375 refers to them.

It is only after their Christian re-beginnings that we can be concerned with libraries, when the roll had changed into the codex and the papyrus into vellum. These changes belong to the third to fifth centuries. A fire in 476 destroyed the imperial library in Constantinople, said to have consisted of 120,000 volumes. As for the West, when Cassiodorus founded his monastery of Vivarium near Squillace about 530 and when Benedict founded Monte Cassino at the same time almost to the year, we know from Benedict's rule that monks were to read two hours a day in the summer and more, if they so wished, and that they would be given for this purpose 'singulos codices de bibliotheca' (individual volumes from the book-cupboard). We can also get an idea of a book cupboard from the famous late sixth-century page in the *Codex Amiatinus* showing Ezra writing the law.[2] The page is traditionally traced back to Vivarium. Another such cupboard is in one of the mosaic lunettes of the so-called Mausoleum of Galla Placidia in Ravenna of *c.* 425.

The Carolingian Renaissance included a library policy, but we know little in detail. Alcuin's Tours and the Schola Palatina must have had books. Centula (St Riquier), one of the most powerful of Charlemagne's abbeys, had about 256 volumes in 831.[3] How they were kept cannot be said. The celebrated vellum plan for St Gall dating from *c.* 820 is an ideal scheme, it must be remembered, hardly even meant for direct execution. Even so, it is worth recording that it provides for a building east of the north transept and north of the choir which is two-storeyed and has the inscription 'infra sedes scribentium, supra bibliotheca' (the scriptorium below, the library above). It need hardly be said specially that the medieval abbey, at least up to the thirteenth century, was as much producer as collector of books. The books were not all religious. Isidore of Seville's library had an inscription: 'Sunt his plura sacra, sunt mondalia plura' (there are here more sacred things, and more things of the world), though he also wrote that 'gentilium libros . . . monachus legere caveat'[4] (let the monk beware of reading worldly books); and of the

7.2

7.3

7.2 The scribe Ezra, detail from the *Codex Amiatinus*, late 6th c. *(Florence, Biblioteca Mediceo-Laurenziana)*

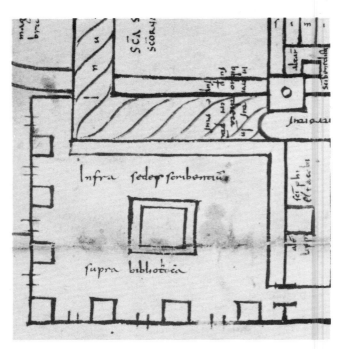

7.3 Ideal plan for the abbey of St Gall, *c.* 820, detail showing library beside the apse *(St Gallen, Stiftsbibliothek)*

great Bishop Bernward of Hildesheim his biographer writes that he collected 'copiosam bibliothecam tam divinorum quam philosophicorum codicum'[5] (an extensive library of philosophical as well as theological volumes). In the eleventh century Bobbio near Piacenza, founded by St Columbanus, had about 650 volumes, and Monte Cassino under Desiderius built a detached library building.[6]

This is perhaps the place to tabulate the number of books in monastic and cathedral libraries over the next centuries and summarize the places where they were kept.[7] Cluny in the mid-twelfth century (i.e. at the time when it was the most powerful abbey of the West) had about 500 volumes;[8] Durham at the same time had 546,[9] and in 1395 still no more than 921 volumes; Canterbury Cathedral about 1300 had about 700 volumes;[10] St Emmeram at Regensburg in 1346 250;[11] the Popes at Avignon in the end about 2,000;[12] Nicholas V in Rome in the mid-fifteenth century about 1,200;[13] Tegernsee Abbey in 1494 1,738;[14] at Cambridge the University Library in 1424 a mere 122, in the 1470s 330, in 1530 about 500 or 600,[15] in the early eighteenth century about 5,000 or 6,000,[16] Peterhouse in 1418 302, King's in 1453 174, Queens' in 1472 199; at Oxford the University Library in the mid-fifteenth century (i.e. before Duke Humphrey's gift) at least 118,[17] Merton College in the mid-sixteenth century about 500, All Souls at the same time about the same number.[18]

Books were kept in a variety of places but before the late fourteenth century rarely in places one would call a library.[19] The most usual name for the library was *armarium*.[20] Hence Geoffrey of Ste Barbe-en-Ange's 'Claustrum sine armario quasi castrum sine armentario'[21] (a monastery without a book-cupboard is like a fort without an armoury). In monasteries the books

might simply be in the choir,[22] but the most usual place was a niche in the west wall of the east cloister walk close to the transept of the church.[23] If there were more books than the niche could hold, a small vaulted room could take its place. This was especially so among the Cistercians. Aubert has listed cases for France.[24] The niche sufficed at e.g. Fontenay, Silvanès, Royaumont and Bonport. L'Escale Dieu had three smaller niches. If a room took the place of the niche it could be tunnel-vaulted (e.g. Obazine, Le Thoronet, Silvacane) or groin-vaulted (Noirlac) or rib-vaulted (Chaalis). The room was as a rule west of the sacristy (e.g. Clairvaux) or under the dormitory stair (Obazine, Noirlac, Font-froide, Silvacane). The places were the same in Cistercian abbeys in England; the niche arrangement (e.g. at Fountains, Abbey Dore and Kirkstall), two niches (at Tintern), a tunnel-vaulted book-room west of the sacristy (e.g. at Rievaulx, Byland, Tintern and Croxden), and two tunnel-vaulted book-rooms either side of the chapter-house entrance (at Furness Abbey). Another not unusual place for keeping books was above the church in the roof.[25] In all these places the books would be in cupboards – hence, *pars pro toto*, the term *armarium*.[26]

Another term which is familiar to few is carrel. It means a working niche or alcove in a library, and in the Middle Ages such niches in the cloister of a monastery were for monks ro read and write in. The best preserved example is at Gloucester (which became a cathedral only under Henry VIII). Carrels are also mentioned at St Augustine's, Canterbury, early in the fourteenth century and in the *Rites of Durham*.[27] The customary reading area was the walk closest to the church.[28]

7.4

The thirteenth century is the century of the establishment of universities, even if in Italy and Paris they had

7.4 Gloucester Cathedral, carrels (on the left) in the cloister, c. 1400

7.5 Wells Cathedral, library, c. 1425

begun earlier. Universities were needed, because, with the growth of towns and commerce, secular learning left abbey and cathedral, more and more writing was performed, administrative demands were made and thus more books became essential in more places. The Emperor Frederick II, inspired probably by the Saracens, had his own library,[29] and at the same time Louis IX had his own of over 900 volumes,[30] which at his death he left to the Blackfriars of Paris and Compiègne, the Greyfriars of Paris and the Cistercian abbey of Royaumont which he had founded. The friars were the great innovation of the thirteenth century in the monastic field; for while the Cistercians had sought out sites away from human habitation, the friars settled in towns to missionize there, and friars thus took part in the growth of the university as teachers – Albertus Magnus, Thomas Aquinas – as well as by the foundation of colleges.[31] In Oxford Gloucester Hall (Worcester College), Durham College (Trinity), Canterbury College (Christ Church), St Mary's College (Frewin Hall) and St Bernard's College (St John's) and in Cambridge Buckingham College (Magdalene) were founded as colleges for friars or monks, Gloucester Hall and Durham College as early as 1283 and 1286.

The University Library of Oxford started with some few chained volumes kept in the church of St Mary. In 1327 Bishop Cobham of Worcester made a donation of books, and a room was built for them over the Congregation House which was attached to St Mary's. However, they did not come to rest there. They were pawned, redeemed by Adam de Broome, deposited at Oriel College, recovered by students led by the Vice-Chancellor breaking in, returned to the room above the Congregation House and there at last in 1412 made available again.[32] They stayed there until Duke Humphrey's time.

For us the most important academic library of the thirteenth century is that of the Sorbonne, the college of the University of Paris founded in 1254 by Robert de Sorbon, chaplain of Louis IX. The library here at the end of the century was a detached building nineteen windows long. The books were not in cupboards but on lecterns – pairs back-to-back apparently, as there were thirty-eight lecterns – and the books were chained to them 'ad communem sociorum utilitatem'[33] (for the use of the community). There were 1,017 in 1290, over 1,700 in 1338. The Sorbonne arrangement, with the books chained to lecterns and with one window corresponding to one pair of lecterns, proved epoch-making, especially in England.[34]

As for chains, they are referred to as 'ut mos est' (customary) at Strasbourg in 1480,[35] and they were still used in the Renaissance library at Cesena in 1452 (indeed they are still there), and even in the Vatican Library in 1580 (according to Montaigne).[36] The remarkably well-preserved chained library at Zutphen in Holland is of 1561–64.[37] Cambridge dechained between about 1575 and 1620,[38] Oxford much later – at All Souls in 1752 and at Magdalen as unbelievably late as 1794[39] – and Eton took the chains off in 1719. It hardly needs saying that by the eighteenth century the Continent had almost forgotten chains. Concerning lecterns, a Continental example of the mid-fourteenth century is St Emmeram at Regensburg.[40] English examples abound. One was at the Greyfriars in London, where in 1421–22 a library 129 feet long was built and provided with 28 lecterns.[41] In the Lincoln Cathedral Library of c. 1420–25 a lectern is preserved. It is a three-seater with ends like bench-ends in churches and a top rail with pierced quatrefoils.[42] Libraries of similar proportions were built everywhere in England in the late fourteen and fifteenth centuries: Gloucester late four-

7.6 Oxford, Corpus Christi College, library, showing the stall system, *c.* 1604 and *c.* 1700

7.7 Florence, S. Marco, library, 1438, by Michelozzo

7.5 teenth century, Canterbury 1414–43, Wells *c.* 1425 (originally 162 feet long), Salisbury 1445, Durham 1446, and in such Oxford colleges as Merton 1373–78, New College *c.* 1380, Trinity 1417–31, Balliol 1431, All Souls 1438–43,[43] University 1440, Oriel 1444, and in the Cambridge colleges of Queens' 1448, Pembroke 1452, Jesus 1497, etc.

The lectern system was evidently wasteful of space, and as, with the invention of printing and the replacement of vellum by paper, books multiplied, an improvement spread which had apparently already been made occasionally in the thirteenth century. It was the adding of shelves, usually two, above the lectern. Thus spaces like alcoves were formed, and so the system goes under the name stall system. Montague James has been 7.6 able to reconstruct it as existing already *c.* 1260 at Canterbury Cathedral.[44] But its popularity was post-medieval.

Compared with the number of English fifteenth-century libraries, those of France and Germany are rare. Troyes Cathedral has a library of 1477–79 with a lierne vault on a middle pier, Rouen Cathedral a better-known one of 1477–79, Noyon Cathedral a separate building, 72 feet long, of 1507, partly timber-framed. In Germany separate buildings are as few. An example is at the Austin Friars of Erfurt. It dates from 1502–16 and is two-naved and simply vaulted. Equally rare is the English type of room, long and with windows on both sides. Professor Lehmann has Steinfeld of 1481, the Blackfriars at Brandenburg of 1497 and a few more.

The Italian Renaissance[45] changed the programme of book collecting, and it changed the architectural style of library buildings and library rooms, but it did not change the planning and the fitments of the library in any noteworthy way. Lecterns first of all remained, and chaining remained. A division into nave and aisles appeared, not until then used, but only underlining the difference between the lectern areas and the middle gangway. The first example is the library of the 7.7 Dominican friary of S. Marco in Florence, built by Michelozzo for Cosimo Medici in 1438 – Fra Angelico's and Savonarola's friary. The books included about 800 volumes collected privately by Cosimo's friend Niccolò Niccoli, benign fanatic in the new cause of Greek and Roman civilization. He left his books, incorporating Coluccio Salutati's and those of the first teacher of Greek in Italy, Manuel Chrysoloras, to the 'comune utilità di ciascuno'[46] (for the common use of everyone) – the earliest formulation of the programme of the public library. The library of S. Marco is mentioned specially in Hartmann Schedel's *Weltchronik*, published at Nuremberg in 1493.

The scheme of nave and aisles is repeated in Malatesta Novello's library at Cesena near Forlì built in 1447–52. 7.1 It is over 130 feet long, aisled, and has twenty windows left, twenty right. Malatesta Novello was the brother of the fearsome Sigismondo Malatesta of Rimini, Alberti's and Piero della Francesca's patron.

As discriminating a patron of Renaissance art and architecture as Sigismondo was Federigo da Monte-

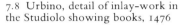

7.8 Urbino, detail of inlay-work in the Studiolo showing books, 1476

7.9 Florence, S. Lorenzo, Biblioteca Laurenziana, 1523–71, by Michelangelo

feltro of Urbino, portrayed by Piero. His library was housed in a tunnel-vaulted room in the palace. All the decoration and furnishings have gone,[47] and the books on which he spent 30,000 ducats are now in the Vatican, but his exquisite though tiny study, dated 1476, with its inlay-work in feigned perspective and its elaborate coffered ceiling, is still *in situ* (see p. 65, note 21). The Vatican acquired its humanist library under Nicholas V and Sixtus IV. Nicholas V intended to build a library 'ingens et ampla, pro communi doctorum virorum comodo' (large and spacious, for the convenience of scholars), but died too soon. However, he left 800 Latin and 400 Greek volumes.[48] When Sixtus IV died, there were 2,527, set up below the Appartamento Borgia, which in its turn is below Raphael's Stanze, along one side of the Cortile dei Papagalli. Sixtus' librarian was Platina, and Melozzo da Forlì in 1475 painted the presentation of the completed library by Platina to the Pope.

Next, Clement VII, the second Medici Pope, commissioned Michelangelo to build new premises for the second Medici Library in Florence, the Laurenziana.[49] This perturbing monument of Mannerism was built between 1523 and 1571. Its excessively high vestibule is followed by the excessively long and low aisleless library proper (about 150 feet long, less than 30 feet high), still furnished with lecterns. They are single lecterns in rows with seats attached to their backs. The books themselves were largely collected by Lorenzo the Magnificent. But the most sumptuous of Renaissance libraries is Sansovino's Marciana in Venice, begun in 1536 and completed by Scamozzi in 1581–83,[50] of which however the library proper and its vestibule occupy only less than the north half of the upper floor.[51]

As humanism spread outside Italy, so did the Renaissance. The earliest case in the field of libraries is the Corvina, the library King Matthias Corvinus collected in two vaulted rooms of his castle at Buda.[52] In the North humanism for deep-lying reasons joined forces with the Reformation. The situation called for more and larger libraries and for new emphases in the existing university and college libraries. The Reformation abolished hundreds of monasteries with much destruction of books but also transferred many to new secular receptacles. Moreover, the Reformation encouraged the reading of laymen and hence public libraries. Luther in his *An die Ratsherren aller Städte deutschen Lands* of 1524 urges them to build up 'gutte Librereyen odder Bücherheuser'.[53]

In England the Reformation had squandered the library of Oxford University and done much damage to that of Cambridge. Most of the colleges also suffered. When, with the Elizabethan Settlement, the bookcases filled up again, it became clear that the lectern system was no longer adequate. The English – not the Continental – solution was to follow the lead of Canterbury and develop the stall system. Trinity Hall, Cambridge, of about 1600 – building and fitments preserved – is the climax of the old system. The new appeared soon after the Elizabethan Settlement. For Oxford the process has

7.10 Leiden, University Library, engraving of 1610

7.11 Escorial, library, c. 1567, by Juan de Herrera

7.12 Rome, Vatican Library, 1587–88, by Domenico Fontana

been followed closely.[54] Merton got its new cases in 1589–90, New College perhaps even a few years earlier, All Souls in 1597, and then Bodley started. He found Duke Humphrey, the room above the Divinity School where the books and chiefly Duke Humphrey's gifts were, 'a greate desolate room', and he put stalls in in 1598–1600. What he added to Duke Humphrey later belongs to a different era. Other colleges followed rapidly during the final quarter of the seventeenth century,[55] and the system stayed in Oxford libraries right down to the eighteenth century. It is incidentally 7.10 well illustrated in an engraving of the University Library of Leiden, dated 1610. In 1599, at S. Agostino in Cremona, the new type of bookcases was called a 'nuova inventione'.[56]

Meanwhile, ever since the time of Queen Elizabeth's reign in England, things had taken a different course on the Continent. The new type of library is called by the German historians *Saal-System*, by the English less suggestively wall-system. It is true that what characterizes it is bookcases along the wall or walls only, but architecturally that results in the spacious amplitude of a *Saal* or hall. Only now can the room fully dominate 7.9 the fitments. One might call Michelangelo's Laurenziana the first *Saal*, but it lacks that very amplitude, and,

of course, it is not of the wall-system.[57] That and the spatial grandeur seem to have been created in the Escorial (where also, and spatially equally telling, the 7.11 staircase type called Imperial Staircase was created). The credit must go to Herrera, and the operative dates are around 1567. The room is c. 213 feet long and has only low cases. The upper parts of the walls and the tunnel-vault are painted in fresco. The first positive reaction to the Escorial Library was the new Vatican Library built 7.12 in 1587–88 across the Belvedere Court by Domenico Fontana, the favourite architect of the boldest planner among sixteenth-century Popes: Sixtus V. It is c. 235 feet long, tunnel-vaulted and painted in fresco all over. The bookcases are low and have solid wooden doors.[58] The Vaticana was quickly followed by the Ambrosiana 7.13 in Milan founded by Cardinal Federigo Borromeo – the one familiar from Manzoni's *Promessi sposi* – and built in 1603–09.[59] The main room – only c. 85 feet long – has a tunnel-vault and for the first time shelves all up the walls. Access to the upper ones can only be by ladders, and that is not only inconvenient but can be dangerous. F. A. Ebert, the distinguished Dresden librarian, in 1834 fell off a ladder to his death. A remedy however had existed ever since the Ambrosiana – a gallery or balcony halfway up. Cardinal Borromeo wanted his

7.13 Milan, Biblioteca Ambrosiana, 1603–09, by L. Buzzi, followed by A. Tesauro

7.14 Oxford, Bodleian Library, Arts End, 1610–12

7.14 library to be truly public. It should, he wrote, be open to all who came for the sake of study ('omnibus studiorum causa pateat').[60]

In England Bodley was quick in taking up the new arrangement. Arts End was added to Duke Humphrey in 1610–12 and has not only wall cases but also a gallery set on extremely slim Tuscan columns. That Bodley's creation became at once the best library of England hardly needs saying. In 1610 he even managed to obtain a promise from the Stationers' Company to give him a copy of every one of the books sanctioned by them. This so-called copyright principle, the principle of *Pflicht-exemplar* in German, had incidentally been established for the French Royal Library already by François I in 1537.[61] For Bavaria Albrecht V (1550–79) introduced it.[62] Leipzig got it in 1615, Vienna in 1621, the Royal Library of Charles II in 1662,[63] the library of the Great Elector in Berlin in 1699.[64] But the system worked properly only here and there and only now and then. Effectiveness came at last with the nineteenth century (Württemberg 1817, Prussia 1834) and for England with Panizzi, Librarian of the British Museum.

To return to architectural matters, the wall library was the standard type of the seventeenth and eighteenth centuries. Rome now received one library after another.

One can call them collegiate, though in Catholic terms: the Angelica by the church of the Austin Friars already in 1614, the Vallicelliana of the Oratorians, founded as early as 1581 (the earliest public library in Rome) but remodelled by Borromini *c.* 1640–42 with one gallery and a fine panelled wooden ceiling, the Alessandrina of 1661–62 in the Sapienza, also by Borromini and also with one gallery, but on a tripartite plan,[65] the Casanatense of 1698–1700 designed by Carlo Fontana[66] with one gallery and a tunnel-vault, and more in the eighteenth century. None of these was specially large. For the Angelica it was explicitly stated that no one, layman or ecclesiastic, was to be refused access. The library was open all weekdays, except Thursdays, both in the mornings and – for two hours – in the afternoons.[67]

The largest, most thriving, libraries were now in France, as the history of Western civilization would make one expect. The leadership in collecting and organizing was Cardinal Mazarin's and his early librarian's, Gabriel Naudé.[68] The library was first in Mazarin's house, rue de Richelieu, now part of the Bibliothèque Nationale.[69] A long gallery was specially added for it above the stables.[70] The bookcases were too high to be accessible without a balcony. At the end of 1643 Mazarin had 12,000 volumes, in 1647 45,000. The

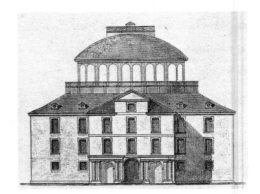

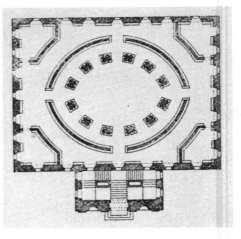

7.15–17 Wolfenbüttel, library, 1706–10, by Hermann Korb: interior (painting by A. Tacke; *Berlin, Deutsche Staatsbibliothek*), elevation and plan (E. Edwards, *Memoirs of Libraries*, 1859)

library was open every Thursday from 8 to 11 a.m. and from 2 to 5 p.m. 'à tous ceux qui y veulent aller étudier'. In this Mazarin was preceded only by the Ambrosiana and the Bodleian. When Mazarin fled in 1651 and remained absent till 1653, the library was sold. Mazarin, though now deprived of Naudé who had died in Sweden in 1653, built up a new library, and this he left to the Collège des Quatre Nations (the present Institut de France) when he died in 1661. The wall-cum-balcony principle was applied to the gallery of the Collège as well. It was nearly 215 feet long. As for numbers of books in French libraries, Pierre le Gallois in 1680[71] writes of over 50,000 volumes in the Mazarine and of 40,000 volumes and 10,000 manuscripts in the Bibliothèque du Roi. It may here be anticipated that by 1819 the latter had 350,000 and 50,000 manuscripts, the Mazarine 90,000.[72] As for other numbers picked from the literature arbitrarily, the Bibliothèque Ste Geneviève had 110,000 volumes and 2,000 manuscripts in 1819. Of the seminal building of 1843 more will be said later (p. 107). Its predecessor is known from an illustration of 1773. It was built *c.* 1726–33, or rather made cruciform by adding to an existing long gallery another across.[73]

As for English library sizes, it is enough to quote the Bodleian which in 1714 had 36,085 volumes and in 1817 about 161,000.[74] The Hofbibliothek in Vienna rose from some 9,000 volumes about 1600 to 80,000 about 1660.[75] Catherine the Great in her Western faith managed to get to St Petersburg over 100,000 volumes,[76] and the library was open to the public. The library at Wolfenbüttel (see below) had 28,415 volumes in 1661. Göttingen, founded in 1737 as the Hanoverian University and the best of the later eighteenth-century libraries in Germany, had 60,000 volumes by 1763, 200,000 by 1800 – and incidentally in Johann Matthias Gesner a librarian 'prompta adversus hospites facilitate'[77] (eager to accommodate visitors), which is more than one could say of the British Museum, opened in Montagu House in 1759 as a public library but in actual fact visited by few, the many not being in any way encouraged.[78]

Architecturally Göttingen was of no interest, but many German and even more Austrian libraries were. The following shall be singled out for a variety of reasons. First Wolfenbüttel, because Leibniz, apart from being Hanoverian librarian from 1676 to his death in 1716, was also librarian of Wolfenbüttel from 1690. He wrote a pamphlet called *Idea Leibnitiana Bibliotecae Publicae secundum Classes Scientiarum ordinandae*,[79] and in a letter of 1716 pleaded for an arrangement of the bookcases so that 'on pût arriver aux livres sans se servir d'échelle'.[80]

The library building at Wolfenbüttel was the first

7.15–1

7.18 Vienna, Hofbibliothek (now Nationalbibliothek), 1722–26, by J. B. Fischer von Erlach

7.19 Amorbach Abbey, library, 1799

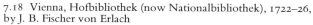
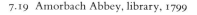

totally detached secular library ever. It was an oblong structure of 127½ by 95 feet. Set into the oblong was an oval[81] with twelve square pillars, an ambulatory, a drum with lantern lighting and a dome crowned by a large globe. This last touch makes one wonder whether Leibniz had not had something to do with the design of the whole building (which was demolished in 1887).[82] The books stood along the walls in radial alcoves and there was a gallery. Hermann Korb, the architect who built it, can hardly have known of Wren's preliminary design for Trinity, Cambridge, which was for a circular building.[83]

7.18   The Vienna Hofbibliothek of 1722–26 by Fischer von Erlach[84] is centrally planned, with a centre not circular but oval, and not as a whole simply oval as at Wolfenbüttel, but in the Austrian and South German way a longitudinal composition with the oval in the middle set transversely and west and east naves divided halfway by a screen of pairs of columns. To make libraries tripartite by screens of columns became incidentally popular in Georgian England (see e.g. Robert Adam's Kenwood) but was never done with such spatial richness. In this and in specific features the Hofbibliothek has its ancestors and progeny in monastic rather than secular libraries. Dr Adriani's book[85] illustrates eighteen, and they are by no means all. They start in the late 7.19 seventeenth century, and a belated end is Amorbach of

1799, with a gallery and all the detail Louis XVI or *Zopf*, to use the German term. The majority of the earlier examples are low with coved or vaulted ceilings. Many have not even a gallery. But the more spectacular ones are of course the higher ones, with a gallery, on brackets as at Melk of *c.* 1730 (where the placement in 7.20 one of the two pavilions jutting forward on the rock towards the Danube is unforgettable), in a curvaceous line as at St Florian of *c.* 1745–50, or on columns as at Ottobeuren in 1721–24, or even on more than life-size 7.24 atlantes as at Waldsassen about 1720–24. But the only ones to vie with the Hofbibliothek are that at Altenburg in Austria of about 1740 with its three domes and the fabulous stucco figures in the spandrels of the middle dome, and at Admont with its seven shallow domes, 7.21 the middle one singled out by columns and of greater height. It is 230 feet long. The architect was Gotthard Hayberger, and Stammel's magnificent *Four Last Things* (one of the sculptures is dated 1760), stand in it. Outside South Germany and Austria libraries similar to these can only be seen in Portugal, notably in the palace of Mafra, begun in 1717, and in Coimbra University, 7.23 begun in 1716 – both designed by João Frederico Ludovice, originally called Johann Friedrich Ludwig. Of the Mafra library Beckford wrote that he found it 'of prodigious length, not less than 300 feet, . . . but clumsily designed'.[86]

7.20 Melk Abbey, library, *c.* 1730, by Jakob Prandtauer

7.21 Admont Abbey, library, *c.* 1760, by Gotthard Hayberger

To return to Germany, in the last third of the eighteenth century North and Central German libraries are more interesting, if less splendid, than those of the South. Kassel by Simon Louis du Ry of 1769–77 is memorable for sharing its fine Classical building with portico and dome with the museum[87] (see p. 115). This had already been the case in Hellenistic Alexandria, where the whole group was called the *museion*, which fact gave us the term Museum. But that is a matter for the next chapter of this book.

Meanwhile the library at Fulda of 1771–78 with two galleries deserves a mention, because it is so handsome, and Frederick the Great's library in Berlin of 1774–84, because the exterior is a copy of Fischer von Erlach's design for the Vienna Hofburg – the great king had a curious and telling liking for looking at copied façades – and also because Frederick established his intention that this library should be public by giving it an inscription which might have been the title of this chapter. The library is presented as *nutrimentum spiritus*, and it was in fact open daily. Finally Karlsruhe must be remembered, because the new building of 1761 anticipated the great innovation of the early nineteenth century in the

separation of the stacks from the reading room.[88] It is an oblong building with the reading room in the middle, at the centre of a cross of gangways. To the left and right of the two major gangways are long very narrow rooms lined with books and each ending in a window. The origin of this arrangement is probably the English stall system which by then had of course long been given up.

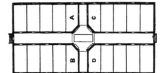

7.22 Karlsruhe, library, 1761 (E. Edwards, *Memoirs of Libraries*, 1859)

What England did instead in her finest eighteenth-century libraries was most wasteful of space and most monumental not only internally but also externally. In external monumentality Wren had set the tune at Trinity, Cambridge, as early as 1676 in the oblong library range across the end of Nevile's Court,[89] which was what the Master and the architect agreed on after the circular building first proposed (as has already been

7.23 Coimbra Abbey, library, begun 1716, by João Frederico Ludovice

7.24 Ottobeuren Abbey, library, 1721–24, probably by J. M. Fischer

7.25 Cambridge, Trinity College, library, begun 1676, by Sir Christopher Wren

7.26 Cambridge, Trinity College, library, begun 1676, by Sir Christopher Wren

7.27 Oxford, Radcliffe Camera, 1737–49, by James Gibbs

7.28 Oxford, All Souls, Codrington Library, 1715–40, by Nicholas Hawksmoor

reported) had been turned down. Wren's library is on the upper floor and still adheres to the stall system, but with a very intelligent improvement which shows full awareness of the new wall-system. Wren placed his side windows so high that his bookcases could continue along the outer wall of each stall. Externally – a typical Wren touch – the string-course between ground floor and upper floor runs actually not at the upper floor level, but at that of the window sills. One discovers the trick when one spots that the lower arcade arches to the east are filled in. The most monumental English library – that of the Queen's College, in Oxford – has nothing like that inside, but the first Oxford library of the eighteenth century, Hawksmoor's Codrington Library of All Souls, built in 1715–40, proves its architect's full conversion to the wall-system at its grandest.[90] The library is nearly 200 feet long, and Hawksmoor wanted the back wall to be covered with books bottom to top, with access by two galleries. This was not done. The wastefulness is all the more patent.[91] The same is true of the Christ Church Library designed by Dr Clarke and built in 1717–72 (the bookcases made in 1756–63). Such libraries were more like those in mansions than those in the colleges of past centuries. They received and displayed not only books, but globes, maybe astronomical apparatus, maybe paintings. Hence the delight in wide open spaces.

No library is more of a monument and more liberal with space than Gibbs's Radcliffe Camera in Oxford of 1737–49, a fully detached annexe to the Bodleian. Dr Radcliffe's money became available in 1736, but already in 1720 plans had begun to be made, and it was Hawksmoor who, inspired by Wren's first idea for Trinity, Cambridge, suggested a round building, a conceit which Gibbs took up.[92] The result is wall cases in eight radial alcoves with an upper gallery and a total, splendid, monumental waste of the whole centre.

Only one library designer was more of a waster of space than Gibbs, and he did what he did only on paper. It is hardly necessary after the chapters on National Monuments, Town Halls and Theatres to say that that designer was Boullée. As we now know,[93] Boullée in 1784 was officially asked to design new premises for the Bibliothèque du Roi and selected the area of the house of the Capuchins. The building was to be square with a cruciform plan forming four inner courtyards, a central rotunda, four ranges round the outside housing the books and a façade with twenty-one bays of giant columns, four deep, leading into a segmental entrance court with yet more columns. The cross wings were

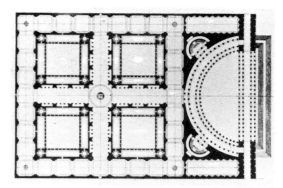

7.29 E.-L. Boullée, design for the Bibliothèque du Roi on the site of the Capuchins, 1784 *(Paris, Bibliothèque Nationale)*

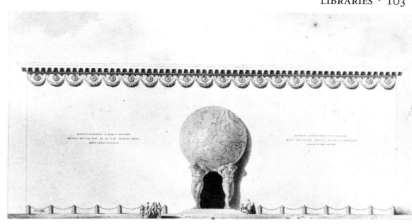

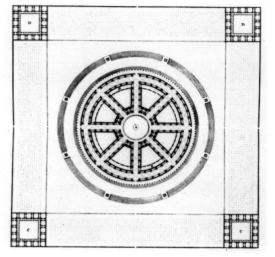

7.30 J.-N.-L. Durand, design for a library *(Précis, II, 1809)*

7.31, 32 E.-L. Boullée, designs for the Bibliothèque du Roi on the existing site, 1784: entrance façade (top) and interior *(Paris, Bibliothèque Nationale)*

probably intended for reading rooms. Statues of famous men were to stand in these, the equivalent of the library busts in Wren's Trinity Library – where he had in fact originally wanted statues, not busts, on the bookcases – and in the libraries of the English nobility and gentry.

The scheme – needless to say – proved too grandiose, and Boullée made another for the site of the existing library which had been adapted since 1724 from the Palais Mazarin.[94] Boullée suggested filling in the large courtyard by one long room, nearly 300 feet long. The books were to be displayed on the wall principle applied to absurdity. Boullée shows stepping-back levels instead of galleries, three of them, each level – to judge by the figures painted in – about 7 to 10 or 12 feet high. There was to follow above a long colonnade, as in the Antique theatre and in Palladio's theatre, but with more books between the columns, and finally a vast coffered tunnel-vault, with a long central skylight. For the façade Boullée offered different treatments – a fifteen-bay giant portico or a closed front with a Cinquecento aedicule portico or with a portal flanked by two atlantes carrying a globe (this one dated 1788).[95]

The wall-system was indeed still current in the 1780s – it had been described as a matter of course in the accepted textbook of the seventies, Jacques-François

Blondel's *Cours d'architecture* (II, 393: 'des grandes salles . . . contre les murs desquelles sont adossés . . . des armoires'), and it went on into the standard textbooks of the early years of the next century, Durand's *Recueil et parallèle* of 1801 and his *Précis des leçons* of 1802–09 (see p. 54). As in so many other building types Durand rationalized Boullée. His proposed buildings are as vast as Boullée's but appear just a little more credible. Durand's model library is a square with at the corners four subsidiary square blocks.[96] The library itself is like a wheel – a hub which is a large room with a Pantheon dome, a circular peripheric range and eight spokes. There are plenty of columns everywhere. The book-rooms have apparently wall shelving. The domed room serves the 'surveillance'. But domes were rare in library buildings and remained so for another few decades. A design for Göttingen by Johann Daniel Heumann has one and is dated 1769.[97] C. F. Adelcrantz designed one for Uppsala in 1767–70, and Jefferson, inspired by the Peyre-Boullée style and by Durand, let the library for the University of Virginia at Charlottesville have one. It dates from 1822–26, but the idea came from a suggestion of Latrobe for a lecture hall contained in a letter of 1817. Originally the rotunda had on the lower floor three oval rooms, including the chapel and the examina-

7.33 Pannonhalma Abbey, library, 1824–32, by J. Engel and J. Packh

7.34 Cambridge, University Library (now Law Library), 1837–40, by C. R. Cockerell: vault

7.35 Edinburgh, Old University Library, 1831–34, by W. H. Playfair

tion hall. After a fire in 1875 this floor was abolished and the library correspondingly heightened. The rotunda had a gallery on columns and was crowned – it need hardly be said – by a Pantheon dome.[98]

While circular libraries remained the exception, longitudinal rooms with wall-shelving and galleries were standard to the middle of the nineteenth century. Examples are the King's Library in the British Museum of 1823–24, the first range added by Robert Smirke to the old Montagu House,[99] the beautiful library of the abbey of Pannonhalma in Hungary, of 1824–32, by J. Engel and J. Packh, a long room with a segmental tunnel-vault, an apse and one gallery, the majestic addition to the Cambridge University Library by C. R. Cockerell of 1837–40 (now Law Library) with its diagonally coffered tunnel-vault, and the similar, slightly earlier (1831–34) Edinburgh University Library, designed by W. H. Playfair.[100] Victorian are the library of Grenoble designed by Questel in 1862[101] – another joint library and museum building – with three galleries and the fabulous library of the Peabody Institute at Baltimore of 1857 (by Edmund George Lind) with five tiers of galleries.

The Institute was started by George Peabody, the philanthropist millionaire, with a donation of $1,500,000.[102] He also created the Peabody estates of flats for poor people in London, and paid for the American section in the 1851 Exhibition. The Peabody Institute library is what the Americans called a free public library. Socially and not architecturally speaking, the free public library, or simply public library, is the most important nineteenth-century development in the field of libraries.[103] It originated simultaneously in America and in England, and, by the Carnegie Trust, from 1897, it was stimulated in England from America.[104] The American definition at its most idealistic was given as early as 1747 à propos the Redwood Library at Newport, Rhode Island. A public library is an institution to which 'the curious and impatient Enquirer . . . and the bewildered Ignorant might freely repair'.[105] That is more handsome than Herbert Spencer's 'They rob one man to pay for books for another man to read.'[106] Today's American definition would be something like this: It must be free, it must lend books, it must have open access to the shelves, it must have a children's department, and it ought to develop branches. To achieve all this was a gradual process, the dates differing in each individual case.[107] All the targets were achieved only close to the end of the century. As for the initial dates they are as follows.

7.36 Baltimore, Peabody Institute Library, 1857, by E. G. Lind

7.37 Quincy, Mass.: Crane Memorial Library, 1880–83, by H. H. Richardson

7.38 Boston, Public Library, 1888–92, by McKim, Mead & White

The first public library ever is supposed to have been that at Peterboro in New Hampshire, started in 1833. Legislation was brought in in Massachusetts in 1848. The Boston Public Library was opened in 1854; it is now one of the great libraries of America. Legislation followed in New Hampshire in 1849, Maine 1854, Vermont 1865, Ohio 1867. The Astor Library in New York was founded by a donation of $400,000 put into his will by J. J. Astor in 1849. Dickens in his *American Notes for General Circulation* as early as 1842 used the term 'public library' referring to Richmond, Virginia.[108] In England William Ewart, MP, was the most effective promoter. A law promulgated in 1845 allowed the raising of a local rate for a local museum. The law was extended to libraries in 1850. The Warrington Museum and Public Library is usually given the credit of having been the first in England. It was indeed opened in 1848, but it was not free. So the first is the Salford Museum and Art Gallery opened in 1850.[109] The building started as a private house and is now the nucleus of the University of Salford. The Manchester Public Library followed in 1852. All three were in the underprivileged industrial North. Liverpool, Sheffield, Birkenhead, Birmingham followed in the next four years.

Architecturally the most beautiful of the American public libraries is the one in Boston. In 1888–92 it received its noble building designed by McKim, Mead & White in a sober Cinquecento style, inspired no doubt by the Bibliothèque Ste Geneviève in Paris (on which more presently). For small libraries H. H. Richardson had by then made popular his picturesque Romanesque, a style he had discovered in France and which, though it was functionally far from ideal, allowed a great variety of grouping of parts, an art of which Richardson was a master.[110] To name only some: the Winn Memorial Library at Woburn, Mass., 1877–78, the Ames Memorial Library at North Easton, Mass., 1877–79, and the Crane Memorial Library at Quincy, Mass., 1880–83. Few if any European architects could have matched Richardson's resourcefulness in the combining of elements inside as well as outside.[111] As an example of London borough libraries, the Battersea Reference Library in Altenburg Gardens will serve, although for its date – 1924–25 – it is extremely retardataire. In spite of this it is with its low window bands and the low wall to the street very handsome in a 1900 way. The designer was T. W. A. Hayward.

As for public libraries on the Continent, Germany, thanks to the Reformation, as we have seen, had quite a

7.39 London, Battersea Reference Library, 1924–25, by T. W. A. Hayward

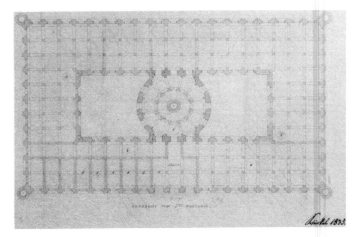

7.41, 42 K. F. Schinkel, design for the Berlin Staatsbibliothek, from his report of 1835: view and plan

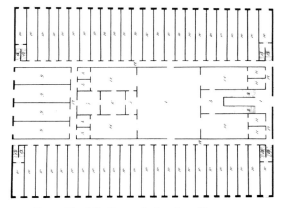

7.40 Leopoldo della Santa, design for a library, 1816

number of them. Edward Edwards[112] counted eleven by the end of the sixteenth century. But continuity into the nineteenth century was only rarely achieved. The nearest in England to this German type is Chetham's Hospital at Manchester, founded in 1653 by a textile manufacturer and combining a school with a proper public library. French public libraries Edwards called tentative in comparison with England, America and Germany.

To round off these notes on public libraries, here is what Jefferson said of them: 'Nothing of mere amusement should lumber a public library.'[113]

Now concerning the planning of library buildings to house the ever-increasing number of books, a radical change was made in the first half of the nineteenth century. The wall-system with all the books lining the walls of the reading room proved inadequate, and so the reading area was separated from the stacking area. Karlsruhe had made a start as early as 1765, as we have seen, and in fact August Hermann Francke, the Vicar of Halle, in his famous *Waisenhaus* (orphanage) had done so yet earlier, in 1727.[114] But as an object for discussion the new system only established itself with Leopoldo della Santa's *Della costruzione e del regolamento di una pubblica universale biblioteca*, published in 1816. This sug-

gests an oblong building with the public area in the middle and left and right forty-eight long narrow stackrooms like those of Karlsruhe. One year later Dr Beyerbach, City Archivist of Frankfurt, put forward a similar scheme for a new building: two storeys for stacks and each subdivided horizontally so that there would be four stacking floors only 7 feet 7 inches high, where della Santa's were 9 feet 6 inches. No ladder would therefore be necessary. The scheme was not seriously considered,[115] and the idea did not at first catch on. Christian Molbech, the Danish librarian, wrote still in 1829 that for any library specially built and intended to be more than utilitarian, the wall-system is preferable to della Santa's, which, however, he presents and illustrates.[116] And indeed Ludwig I's new library building in Munich on the Ludwigstrasse – by Gärtner, 1832–43 – was large and monumental, in the Italianate *Rundbogenstil* (its Quattrocento version, to be more precise), and had a majestic staircase and more extensive and regularly disposed stacking space than any before, but the stackrooms were still filled on the wall-system. In 1830 Schinkel was asked to design a new library for Berlin, to replace Frederick the Great's (p. 100). He made a report in 1831 and plans are dated 1832 and 1835. Another report is dated 1835.[117]

7.22

7.40

7.41, 42

7.43, 44 Paris, Bibliothèque Ste Geneviève, 1843–50, by Henri Labrouste: façade and reading room

In the centre of the oblong building was to be a domed rotunda. This, however, was not the reading room; it housed the main staircase. The stackrooms were to be aisled. The naves were kept free of books; in the aisles stood bookcases back-to-back at right angles to, and detached from, the walls. There were no cases along the walls. So from the point of view of planning Schinkel made no contribution. There were to be three floors. In his report Schinkel stresses that a library ought not to be a *Prachtgebäude*. His design, Schinkel writes, was 'zweckmässig' (functional), which implies fireproof construction. The service staircases in the four corners were to be of iron; so were the window frames, and the ceilings were to be vaulted. Externally all three windows of each bay were to be under one giant arch. The grid character is reminiscent of Schinkel's Bauakademie of 1831–35 and his Bazaar (see p. 262). Schinkel's designs were not executed. He communicated them in a letter in 1840 to the Marquis de Laborde who then mentioned them in his *De l'organisation des bibliothèques dans Paris* of 1845.

16.18

It has been said that in these designs Schinkel was reactionary in only one way: the stacking arrangements for the books. The same is true of the design of the next library of international importance, the Bibliothèque Ste Geneviève of 1843–50 as designed by Henri Labrouste. His bookcases are still set up in the stall tradition.[118] The daringly novel feature of Labrouste's building is the frankly exposed iron columns and the decorative iron arches of the vast reading room all along the first floor. The restrained Italian Renaissance façade would not make anybody expect such a revolutionary interior. César Daly, the editor of the *Revue générale de l'architecture*, in 1852 calls the library 'une oeuvre capitale' and emphasizes the great influence Labrouste was exerting on young architects.[119] Labrouste, asked by Daly to write something himself on the building, gives an engagingly bluff answer: he prefers to occupy himself with what is to be done rather than with what has been done.

7.44

7.43

Labrouste's structure inspired J. B. Herholdt in his Copenhagen University Library built in 1856–61. It is an oblong building with aisles, a gallery and a tunnel vault and it has slim iron columns.[120] Panizzi's *capolavoro*, the British Museum library, also owes much to Labrouste. Its dates are 1854–56. The grand circular reading room with its glazed dome and its 364 seats arranged radially – in the Library of Congress the arrangement is concentric – is by Sydney Smirke, but a sketch by Panizzi of 1852 exists, and he was probably

7.45

7.45 London, British Museum, reading room, 1854–56, by Sydney Smirke

inspired by a circular design by Baron Delessert, published in 1835, although this had the stacks and not the desks set radially. Also the Marquis de Laborde in his book of 1845 published a project with a circular reading room and separate stacking, and no doubt Panizzi knew that as well.[121] Panizzi was a possessed librarian. A library to him was 'not a show but an institution for the

7.45   diffusion of culture'. The dome of glass and iron,
12.39   influenced perhaps by that of the Coal Exchange (1847–49, by J. B. Bunning), has a diameter of 141 feet, as against the 143 of the Pantheon and the 139 of St Peter's. Technically, however, a yet more momentous innovation was Panizzi's iron stacks and iron floors on each level making the whole stacking area one unity subdivided by iron members vertically and horizontally.[122] The library, as everyone knows, was built into the courtyard of the British Museum, which since the beginning in Robert Smirke's Grecian halls and behind Smirke's Grecian façade had been a combined museum and library (wall-system!) building in the tradition of Alexandria, the Vatican, Kassel, etc. That it still is, is a record of English conservatism. The decision has however just been taken to remove the library, and to build a separate British Library on a site to the north.

The Bibliothèque Nationale – the name of the French Bibliothèque du Roi since 1792 – followed suit at once. In Labrouste they appointed the right architect, and so

7.46   the reading room of 1865–68 again has exposed iron columns – sixteen of them. They carry nine domes of

faience and glass. The impression is lighter and more elegant than that of the British Museum reading room, but less conducive to concentration. The stacks are again all iron. Anatole de Baudot called it 'à tous les points-de-vue' one of the most remarkable buildings,[123] Huysmans 'd'une incomparable distinction'.[124] Labrouste, incidentally, at the instigation of Merimée, spent some days in October 1867 in London to study the British Museum reading room and stackroom.[125]

The Bibliothèque Nationale now has about 7 million volumes, the British Museum about 8,500,000, the Library of Congress over 15 million. Other libraries of the first magnitude are Harvard (over 8 million), Yale (5,500,000), Chicago (nearly 4,500,000), Illinois (4,250,000), Michigan (4 million), University of California, Los Angeles (3,800,000), Bodleian (3,500,000), Stanford (3,500,000), New York Public Library (3,200,000), Cambridge (3 million).[126]

That such vast numbers of books call for new methods of storing and of transporting, of accession and issue, goes without saying. Moreover, there is now provision needed for readers' typing, for microfilm reading and for xeroxing. Also computers have begun to be installed, principally for 'information-retrieval'. Whether the computer will bring about major changes in libraries remains to be seen.

Stylistically major changes have certainly taken place. The Classical Re-Revival of the years around 1900 and the early decades of the twentieth century

7.46 Paris, Bibliothèque Nationale, reading room, 1865–68, by Henri Labrouste

7.47 Sofia, National Library, completed 1952, by I. Wassilew and D. Zolow

7.48 Cracow, Jagellon Library, 1935–37, by W. Kozyzanowski

brought the circular Low Library of Columbia University, New York, by McKim, Mead & White of 1893–97, progeny of Jefferson's Charlottesville, and the belated Central Library of Manchester by E. Vincent Harris of 1930–34 and University (Brotherton) Library of Leeds by Lanchester & Lodge of 1930–36, and yet later buildings behind the Iron Curtain such as the National Library of Bulgaria at Sofia, completed in 1952 to the designs of I. Wassilew & D. Zolow. Only Washington Federal buildings – as we have seen – can beat that in conservatism.

In other parts of the world the International Modern of the thirties has dominated since the Second World War and is dominating still. No columns, no pillars, no arches, no ornament, no contrived monumentality.

Hence, for instance, the low reading room of the Jagellon Library in Cracow by W. Kozyzanowski of 1935–37 – not all Eastern European architecture is anti-modern – and hence also the impressive pile of the Marburg University Library of 1962–68, by the Universitätsbauamt (Baudirektor Küllmer, Baurat Barth). Today's style of arbitrary, massive shapes, the very contrary of the International Modern, is shown in John Johansen's Goddard Library of Clark University, Worcester, Mass., of 1965–69. On the other hand, neither in today's nor in yesterday's trend, but of a decidedly personal character and sincere monumentality, is Philip Johnson's recent extension to the Boston Public Library – a suitable end to a chapter which began with the Italian Renaissance.

7.49 Worcester, Mass., Clark University, Robert Hutchings Goddard Library, 1965–69, by John Johansen

7.50 Marburg, University Library, 1962–68, by Küllmer & Barth

7.51 Boston, Public Library, extension, 1967–71, by Philip Johnson

8.1 Munich, Residenz, Antiquarium, 1569–71, by G. Strada, W. Egkl and F. Sustris

8
Museums[1]

ART collecting starts with the Italian Renaissance; for the Renaissance developed a sense of history, enthusiasm for the products of Classical Antiquity and whole genres of contemporary art suited to, and indeed made for, the private house: paintings with mythological subjects, paintings by Flemish artists, small bronzes and, in the North, graphic art.[2] However, furnishing must be kept separate from collecting, and if that is done, paintings and small bronzes are the former rather than the latter. Collecting proper was at first concerned with Antiquity. Ever since Ghiberti as an artist collected,[3] ever since Poggio and Niccolò Niccoli as humanists collected,[4] ever since Alfonso of Aragon and Cosimo Medici as princes and political leaders collected,[5] they collected apart from small things figures and fragments of marble to display them in courtyards, loggias and gardens. The Medici garden by the Piazza S. Marco in Florence was under the supervision of Bertoldo, and Michelangelo received his introduction to sculpture here. As for Rome, Marten van Heemskerck, who spent the years 1532–36 there, drew many *al fresco* displays of Antique pieces.[6] Already in 1471 Sixtus IV donated to the Roman people some important pieces for display on the Capitol – among others the She-wolf, the Boy extracting a thorn, and a colossal head of the Emperor Constantine.[7]

The first special setting for the display of Antiques was provided by Bramante in the Vatican. The place adjoined Innocent VIII's Belvedere Pavilion and lay beyond the far end of the Belvedere Court.[8] There is no fixed date, but the design may have been made about 1508. The display was still in the open, but in niches in a square cloister. The two most famous statues were the Apollo Belvedere and the Laocoön (found in 1506).

For the later sixteenth century several innovations are to be noted. First, the word 'museum' appears, which, it will be remembered, had already been applied in Hellenistic Alexandria to the whole cultural precinct which included the library (see p. 100).[9] Now, in 1539 Paolo Giovio for the first time writes of his collections at Como as his 'Musaeum'. In 1543 the word appeared prominently in an inscription on the building. It had an Aula Magna and smaller rooms on three sides of a colonnaded cloister. A *Musaei Joviani Descriptio* was published in 1546. Among the collections the most interesting group was portraits of famous men, poets, writers, scholars, painters, sculptors, popes, kings and other rulers – a kind of private Pantheon or Walhalla.[10] About ten years later Jacopo Strada, the goldsmith whom Titian painted in 1553, published an account of his collection of coins whose title is *Epitome Thesauri Antiquitatum . . . ex Museo Jacopi da Strada. . . .* In Samuel

8.2

8.2 Marten van Heemskerck, display of Roman sculpture in the loggia of the Villa Madama, Rome, c. 1535 *(Berlin-Dahlem, Staatliche Museen)*

8.3 The Earl of Arundel with his sculpture gallery: detail of painting by Daniel Mytens, 1618 *(Duke of Norfolk Collection)*

8.4 Sabbioneta, long gallery, 1583–90, by Vincenzo Scamozzi

von Quichelberg's *Inscriptiones vel Tituli Theatri Amplissimi* of 1565 'museum' already means a collection.[11] At the same time buildings began to be erected to house collections of statuary.[12] They are either centrally-planned rooms or long galleries. Cardinal Cesi c. 1545–50 built in his gardens an 'Antiquario' in the form of a Greek cross,[13] and the Uffizi in Florence in 1581 at the hands of Buontalenti (see above, pp. 32, 66) received their Tribuna to house works of art.[14] A few years before, beginning in 1574, Buontalenti had converted the east range of the Uffizi into a gallery for works of art, and this, according to Bocchi's *La bellezza della città di Firenze* of 1591, could be visited.[15] In fact, so frequently were galleries used to display statuary that gallery became a synonym of museum, first in France, then in Italy. A German scholar has recently followed the history of the term.[16] Here is a sequence of examples. Bernardinus, senator of Toulouse, 1440: 'ambulacrum quod nos galeriam vocamus'[17] (a passage or walk which we call a gallery). At the Château de Gaillon, visited by an Italian diplomat in 1509–10: 'una galleria sive loggia' and in it three statues.[18] Another Italian diplomat

visiting Blois: 'una galleria' decorated with busts and antlers.[19] Serlio who from 1540 lived in France designed galleries for the house of the Cardinal of Ferrara at Fontainebleau and for Ancy-le-Franc and speaks of a 'Salotto che in Francia si dice galleria' and in another place calls a gallery a 'luogo da passeggiare'.[20] Nothing here yet of works of art. The same is true of Scamozzi in 1600: 'gallerie per trattenersi a passeggio'.[21] But Scamozzi adds that galleries have recently been introduced to Rome and are used for displaying 'anticaglie di marmo'.[22]

In the Gonzaga Palace in Mantua a gallery was made about 1570. It was tunnel-vaulted and served the purpose of displaying statuary.[23] About 1580 the Villa Medici in Rome received a gallery, again for statuary.[24] In 1583–90, i.e. at the same time as the theatre (see p. 97), Vespasiano Gonzaga at Sabbioneta built his gallery for statues nearly 300 feet long.[25] But the most ambitious gallery was without doubt the Antiquarium of Albrecht V of Bavaria, built in his palace in Munich in 1569–71.[26] The plans were by Strada, the execution by Wilhelm Egkl, the interior decoration by Friedrich

6.11
8.4
8.1

8.5 Rome, Galleria Valenti Gonzaga, *c.* 1740 (painting by G.P. Pannini, 1749; *Hartford, Conn., Wadsworth Atheneum*)

Sustris. The room, destroyed in the Second World War but rebuilt, was about 200 feet long and covered with a tunnel-vault. (Above was the library: see p. 97.) It is a sign of his wealth and social status that Rubens could build a receptacle for his ancient statuary. It was described as 'like the Pantheon' and 'lighted only from the top'.[27] One of Rubens' English patrons, the Earl of Arundel, built for his collection of statuary at Arundel House in London a proper gallery known to us by a painting, probably by Daniel Mytens, which shows the Earl pointing to the gallery. It was built before 1618, and Arundel was called by Franciscus Junius the epitome in England of Castiglione's perfect courtier.[28] Peacham in *The Compleat Gentleman* praised him for having transplanted Greece to England.[29] It will be remembered that Inigo Jones was in Arundel's train when he went to Italy in 1613. Of the place where the Duke of Buckingham kept his works of art we know nothing. It was he who bought Rubens' collection of Antiques. Mazarin's famous collection of paintings was in his palace, now part of the Bibliothèque Nationale (pp. 97–98). There is an engraving by Nanteuil and van Schuppen showing

him, like Arundel, seated in his gallery,[30] the gallery built in 1645 by Mansart. Twenty years later, when Bernini was invited to design the new east front of the Louvre, his instructions included a gallery on the first floor to accommodate statues and pictures.[31]

Paintings were of course collected too, and they were usually displayed on the walls of rooms hung so closely that their framed areas formed an all-over pattern. Painted representations of such rooms, e.g. by the elder Jan Breughel and the younger David Teniers, are familiar. In the late seventeenth and the eighteenth century such a gallery proper for paintings became an almost standardized element of palace planning.[32] This applies to the town palaces of Rome – one remembers the Galleria Colonna of *c.* 1675, Ferdinando Fuga's Galleria Corsini of 1729 and the *galleria* in the villa of Cardinal Valenti Gonzaga painted by Pannini in 1749[33] – as much as to the palaces or houses of the major and minor princes of Germany. As for them here is a list: Salzdahlum (of timber) 1688–94 plus later enlargements, Rastatt 1702, Düsseldorf 1709 et seq., Pommersfelden (Schönborn) 1711–14, Belvedere in Vienna

8.6 Rome, Galleria Colonna, *c.* 1675; the building by Antonio del Grande

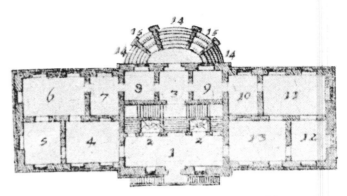

8.7 L. C. Sturm, design for a museum, 1704: ground floor. 4–8 Antiquities, 9–12 Treasury (cameos, coins, gold, precious stones, porcelain, lacquer, jewellery, rock crystal, ivory, coral)

(Prince Eugene) 1721–22, in Munich Cuvilliés' 'Reiche Zimmer' 1733, Würzburg 1736–44, Kassel (Bellevue) 1749–51, Mannheim 1751–60, Frederick the Great's Sanssouci at Potsdam, a detached building, 1756–64 (by Johann Georg Büring) – and so on through the second half of the century.[34] The galleries can be very long – Salzdahlum was longer than the Galerie des Glaces in Versailles – and they can be architecturally quite plain or as exuberantly over-decorated as Cuvilliés or as firmly articulated as Sanssouci, with its oval centre separated from the rest by detached columns close to the walls and carrying entablatures across. This tripartite arrangement is a library theme, especially in England – see p. 99.

One more aspect of eighteenth-century collecting and display must be added – a tendency to separate the types of items. The *Kunstkammer* or Cabinet of Curiosities of the later sixteenth and the seventeenth century mixed up not only sculpture and painting but also objects of natural science, specimens of rocks, corals, freaks.[35] The Enlightenment brought specialization. Already at its beginning, in 1704, Leonhard Christoph Sturm published the plan of an ideal museum,[36] and in this there are rooms for objects of natural history as well as one room on the top floor for small paintings, drawings and sculpture.[37] In Dresden a similar systematization actually took place. Porcelain went to the Japanisches Palais, statuary to the four pavilions in the Grosser Garten, arms and armour to the Jägerhof, objects of natural history to the Zwinger.[38]

All the collections mentioned so far, whether of princes or noblemen, were private. That does not mean that they could not be visited. Much visiting of country houses in England is recorded one way or another, and as for galleries in the new sense, Prince Karl Eusebius von Liechtenstein writes that 'die Forestieri und Ausländer' everywhere like to visit *Kunstgallerien*.[39] General interest was spurred on by lavish illustrated catalogues.[40] For Vienna forty volumes were projected, but they never materialized; for Paris only one volume came out in 1677, *Le Cabinet du Roi de France*, by Jean-François Félibien, the writer on art and architecture. Much later volumes on medals, tapestries, etc., followed.

The next step in the publicizing of private collections is the most characteristic one of the Enlightenment. Princes began to feel that their collections should be their subjects' as well, i.e. that museums ought to be separate buildings open to the public. The earliest document is a programme for a museum in Dresden drawn up in 1742 by Count Algarotti for Augustus III, the fanatical collector who bought among many other paintings Raphael's *Sistine Madonna* and the four great Dresden Correggios. The programme is unfortunately unillustrated.[41] Algarotti we have already met in the chapters on national monuments and theatres (see above, pp. 13, 79). He was an Italian nobleman, member of Frederick the Great's Round Table and an art agent for Frederick and for Augustus III. His taste had been formed by the mysterious Abbate Lodoli in Venice, and he was one of the earliest Italian believers in Palladio, whose 'simplicity, regularity and beauty' he considered above that of any other architect. His museum, so he writes (in a letter of 1759) was to be 'a square building with a large courtyard and in each range a Corinthian loggia and one room on either side of it. These eight galleries lead into four corner rooms, each lit by a small dome. A larger dome is above the centre of each range lighting the principal room behind the loggia.' The word 'loggia' must mean portico in this context, and the *topos* of the portico followed by a domed hall is directly derived from the Pantheon and was to be of great importance for museum buildings fifty years later, as it was also – this the previous chapters of this book have shown – for other building types. The skylighting for the central and corner rooms is explicitly referred back to the Tribuna of the Uffizi and Rubens' Rotunda. The eight galleries had normal side-light, not the high, slanting side-light which had been provided about 1700 in the Palais Royal in Paris, Philippe d'Orléans' palace.[42]

Now this lighting was also recommended by the Marquis d'Argenson, a noted *virtuoso*, as a pattern for Kassel, where in the 1770s a separate museum building went up. The attitude of the Enlightenment behind this building is brought out doubly clearly, as it was museum and library combined, and as it was from the

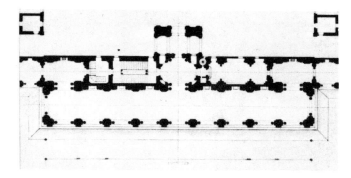

8.8 Kassel, Museum Fridericianum, 1769–77, by S. L. du Ry

8.9 Rome, Villa Albani, completed 1761, by Carlo Marchionni

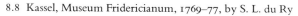

start open to the public at certain hours. The Kassel museum calls itself on its frontispiece 'Museum Fridericianum', and it was built for Landgrave Frederick II in 1769–77 on one side of the large new Friedrichsplatz next to the Landgrave's palace.[43] It is a large self-contained building with a front of nineteen bays. It is articulated by giant Ionic pilasters rising from the ground and has as its centre a portico of six unfluted giant columns carrying a pediment. The ground floor had large rooms with columns dividing them into three naves. The Antique statuary was displayed here. The left corner and the left back wing held natural science, minerals, maritime plants, butterflies, etc. In the right back wing were coins, clocks, prints, etc. On the upper floor the long front housed the library (see p. 100). The left back wing had mathematical and physical instruments and above, on the top floor, mechanical and musical instruments. On the upper floor of the right back wing, finally – and that shows that we are still at a transitional stage – the Landgrave had a private study. Above this – transitional too – were, besides arms, waxworks.

8.8   Transitional one can also call the façade of the Fridericianum. The giant pilasters look back to the Baroque, the portico forward to Neo-Classicism. And although Simon Louis du Ry was of French descent, English Palladianism was no doubt the inspiration for the portico. But Neo-Classicism was not only a new anti-Baroque architectural style: it also involved a new preference in collecting, or at least an old one which had receded into the background in Baroque collections. The revival of veneration for ancient sculpture began in Italy and was re-echoed between about 1720 and about 1760 in four museums. The earliest is Count Scipione Maffei's *Lapidario* in Verona, begun in 1744 and published under the title *Museum Veronense* in 1749.[44] The museum was open to the public from the start. The fragments were placed in a square cloister with slim unfluted Doric columns. The much higher centre portico was left over from Sammicheli's Accademia Filarmonica. It is a noble setting and one deliberately modest. This is no longer display for show but archaeological presentation. Maffei had in fact in 1723 arranged

a *lapidario* for the newly-built university of Turin. In 1739 he had visited Rome, and there the new Capitoline Museum, founded in 1734, must have inspired him. The museum was housed in the palace opposite the Palazzo dei Conservatori, and the pieces put there were transferred.[45] The collection – an interesting innovation – functioned in relation to the Accademia Capitolina, a school to draw the nude, which was also founded in 1734.[46] As there were also papal collections of paintings on the Capitol, the conjunction was profitable. So here again was a public museum. Winckelmann on 7 December 1755 writes that one can be in the collection 'in all freedom from morning to night'.[47] Less than three years after Winckelmann had written this letter he was appointed by Cardinal Albani to be his librarian and keeper of collections. In 1763 he became Superintendent of all Antiquities in Rome. Cardinal Albani had begun probably in the 1740s to build himself a villa to display his Antiques.[48] In 1761 it was ready to receive Mengs's *Parnassus*, the first ceiling painting to proclaim hostility against the Baroque and renewed faith in Raphael and ancient art. The villa is the work of Carlo Marchionni, nine bays long, two storeys high, of rather loose, by no means Neo-Classical, composition. It contains Antiquities exclusively, and it was a sign of the changed attitude that all the best pieces were now placed indoors and no longer in the open or the semi-open of cloisters or loggias.[49] Many of the statues were restored, the standard of accuracy of additions being much higher than had been customary. Both the Cardinal and Winckelmann believed in restoration on the strength of archaeological research, and Cavaceppi the restorer, who started a publication of his restorations (*Raccolta d'antiche statue*, 1768–72) with a treatise 'Dell'arte di ben restaurare le antiche sculture', was Winckelmann's friend.[50]

    The principle behind the arrangement of the statues, busts, etc., in the Villa Albani is no longer that of the Baroque which had been simply attractive decoration. Instead iconography dictates the order: emperors in the centre room on the ground floor, gods in the gallery above it. Busts of military heroes in one room, busts of poets in another. Yet other rooms are named after the

8.9

8.10 Newby Hall, Yorks., gallery, *c.* 1770, by Robert Adam

8.11 Rome, Vatican, Museo Pio-Clementino, *c.* 1773–80, by M. Simonetti and G. Camporesi

principal piece displayed in them. Later, as will be shown, chronology of styles was to be the guiding principle, as it was indeed on paper already in Winckelmann's *Geschichte der Kunst des Alterthums*, which was published in 1764. There is here the same contrast as exists between Marchionni's architecture and Mengs's *Parnassus*.

If one wants to see a real museum in the early forms of Neo-Classicism, one must leave Italy and go to England, where severe Palladianism had established itself as early as 1715–20, promoted by Colin Campbell and Lord Burlington. Robert Adam, its chief later eighteenth-century exponent, may have been lavish with his daintier decoration, but Newby Hall, begun *c.* 1767, from any Continental point of view is pure Classicism. Now at Newby Hall Mr Weddell added a sequence of three rooms for his ancient sculpture, the centre one circular and skylit, the other two oblong. That this museum should be private and attached to a country house is of course typically English. But in 1763 the younger Dance sent to one of the competitions of the Academy of Parma a design for a 'galleria pubblica' for statues, pictures, etc. It was H-shaped with the long cross-bar being the Great Gallery. The gallery has a coffered tunnel-vault. The other bars start and finish with domes, visible outside. It is all in the typical Parisian Grand Prix style, and it got the gold medal.[51]

The main stream of development leaves England behind, as it does also the Villa Albani. It runs from Algarotti's plan to Kassel and from Kassel to the Museo Pio-Clementino. This was built in the Vatican *c.* 1773–80 north and west of Bramante's octagonal Belvedere cloister, which itself was only now given its 'elegantissimo portico' (Visconti). The new rooms were in their shapes inspired by the palaces and baths of ancient Rome. They were round, polygonal and oblong, and one was called Sala a Croce Greca. In addition there was one of the most grandiose staircases of the age.[52] The museum was named after Clement XIV and Pius VI, and its designers were Michelangelo Simonetti and after him Giuseppe Camporesi.[53] The style is now throughout Neo-Classicism. The Rotunda, even if verbally anticipated by Algarotti, was to make a deep impression on later architects. The style and of course the fact that here was a museum of Classical Antiquity on the grandest scale was a demonstration of the Papacy claiming the lead in archaeological scholarship. This lead was confirmed by the collections receiving a catalogue from the pen of the most learned expert then available: Ennio Quirino Visconti.[54] It began to appear in 1782, and nothing could be more telling than the fact that Napoleon called Visconti to Paris to be the director of the Antiques of his museum. The arrangement of the sculpture in the Museo Pio-Clementino was by subject

8.12 Rome, Vatican, Museo Pio-Clementino, c. 1773–80, by M. Simonetti and G. Camporesi

8.13 Rome, Vatican, Braccio Nuovo, 1806–23, by Raffaello Stern

8.11   matter, culminating in the Rotunda as the room for the major deities. The museum after only twenty-five years proved too small, and so, in 1806–23, the Braccio
8.13   Nuovo was built, running parallel with the library across Bramante's Belvedere Court. The architect was Raffaello Stern, the style still essentially that of Simonetti and Camporesi. The centre has a dome with a skylight, and on its north side a majestic apse.

The Vatican museums were not open to the public, but it is evident from many reports and descriptions that with some introduction any gentleman could get in. The same is true of other eighteenth-century collections. In Florence the last of the Medici, Anna Maria Lodovica, widow of Jan Willem, the creator of the Düsseldorf gallery, had presented by her will the Medici collections to the city. That was in 1739. About fifty years later Pietro Leopoldo opened them to the public.[55] As for German museums Goethe, for instance, saw the Elector's gallery at Dresden[56] in 1768, when he was only nineteen, and the Mannheim[57] plaster casts in 1772. In 1777 Lessing visited the Mannheim collection, and in 1785 Schiller in the *Brief eines reisenden Dänen* – a fictitious Dane – could write of Mannheim: 'Every inhabitant of Mannheim and every stranger has the unlimited freedom to enjoy this treasure of Antiquity.'[58] Two years earlier, in 1779–83, the picture collection of the Elector of Bavaria had been assembled on the north side of the Hofgarten in a long range and the building, designed by Karl Albrecht von Lespiliez, was at once made open to the public. The timetable was all workdays 9 to 12 a.m. and 1 to 4 or 5 p.m.[59] The Hofgartengalerie was a long range with lantern lighting and it is memorable in particular for comments made on it in 1785 by one Joseph Sebastian von Rittershausen.[60] The tone is elevated and enthusiastic – noble, sublime, sacred, such are the adjectives. Ancient German painting, and especially Dürer's, is allowed vigour of expression and solemn seriousness. This is an early case of Dürer appreciation, although it must not be forgotten that Goethe had praised Dürer for his vigour in *Von deutscher Baukunst*, i.e. in 1772. Similarly, Heinse's *Düsseldorf Gallery Letters* with their fervent praise of Rubens had been published in 1776–77,[61] and now Rittershausen wrote of Rubens' sketches: 'These are miracles of the spirit which Rubens to the horror of the human soul left to posterity.' And he goes on to 'das Auf- und Niederwälzen dieser Riesengedanken', the 'brush-strokes akin to lightning', 'the flame of invention . . . thundered forth by Vulcan', and so on.

Now for a moment to Vienna and then to London. In Vienna the collections were opened properly on Mondays, Wednesdays and Fridays to anyone 'with clean shoes'. The command was issued in 1792.[62] The British Museum[63] on the other hand was public – at

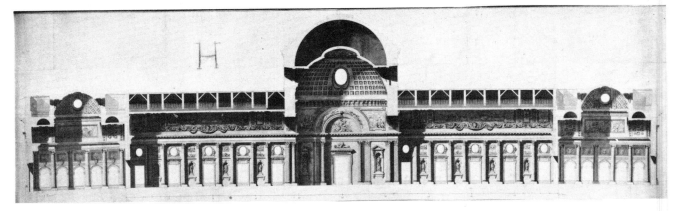

8.14 L.-F. Trouard, design for a gallery, 1753

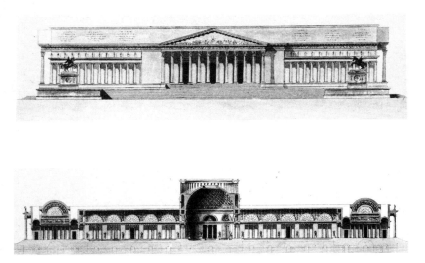

8.15, 16 Guy de Gisors (top) and J.-F. Delannoy, designs for a museum, 1778–79

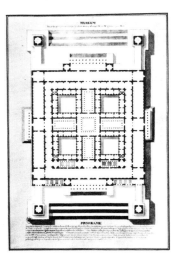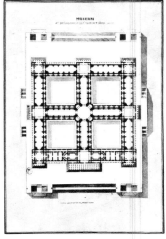

8.17, 18 Guy de Gisors (left) and J.-F. Delannoy, designs for a museum, 1778–79

least theoretically – from the start. The museum is characteristically English in that it was the one great national collection which had no regal nor princely origin – like the British Library too, and the Royal Academy. Parliament in 1753 bought for £20,000 Dr Hans Sloane's natural history collections and in 1759 put them up in Montagu House. The Hamilton Vases followed in 1772, for £8,400. But most works of art were added only after 1800 – Napoleon's Egyptian loot in 1802, the Townley Marbles bought in 1810 and 1814 for £28,000, the sculpture of Bassae in 1814 for £19,000, the Elgin Marbles in 1815 for £40,000. Entry regulations were issued at once, i.e. in 1759. Entry was by ticket only and strictly limited. Free entry to all – also on Mondays, Wednesdays and Fridays (10–4) – was only introduced in 1810. But that represents a European change of attitude for which we are not ready yet.

If Rome was one centre of the Neo-Classical movement and England another, the third was Paris, where the ideals of Piranesi – a stimulus to all who came into touch with him – had been introduced enthusiastically by the *pensionnaires* of the Ecole de France in Rome. The Académie d'Architecture set the theme of a museum several times for the Prix de Rome between 1778 and the early nineteenth century.[64] They had in fact done it twice even earlier: in 1753, with a gallery as an attachment to a palace, and in 1754 with a 'Salon des Arts'. The first prize for the gallery was given to Louis-François Trouard, and though his design is obviously Baroque, the middle rotunda with its coffered dome, the long rows of columns without any projections in the entablature and the tunnel-vaults of the galleries left and right of the rotunda are remarkable for so early a date – though a date later of course than the return of Marigny, Soufflot and Cochin from their famous Italian journey. The prize for a Salon des Arts was won by Jean-René Billandel, and his composition has as its centre a rotunda, with six niches inside. Added to this are three arms, and the interstices filled in by triple colonnading. The whole is a decidedly Baroque conceit.[65]

The task for 1778–79 was a museum for works of art and natural history plus a print-room, a cabinet of medals and a library with studies for scholars. Two first prizes were given. One of them fell to Guy de Gisors, aged sixteen, the other to Jacques-François Delannoy.

8.14

8.15,
8.16,

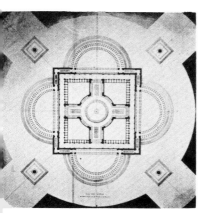

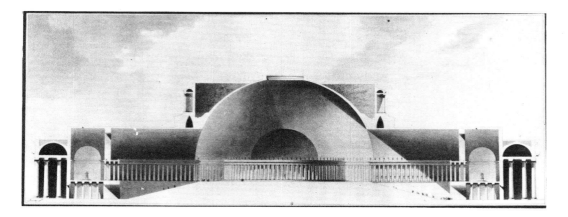

8.19–21 E.-L. Boullée, design for a museum, 1783: plan, section of central square, and elevation *(Paris, Bibliothèque Nationale)*

.17, 18 Both designs consist of a square with four courtyards, the wings separating them forming a Greek cross. The
8.15 façades have no windows at all, but multi-columned porticoes and extra colonnades wherever possible. The scale is vast, as was to be typical of all the Grands Prix to follow, and reflects the scale of Piranesi's etchings.
8.16 The rooms are mostly tunnel-vaulted, and the centres have Pantheon openings.

.19–21 With this we have reached Boullée, who designed a museum in 1783.[66] He, it will have been noticed, appeared at a crucial moment in the history of nearly all building types so far discussed, and as ever since 1747, when he was only nineteen years old, he had taught at the Ecole des Ponts et Chaussées, and as he was made a member of the Académie d'Architecture in 1762, he no doubt influenced such younger men as Gisors and Delannoy. His museum is a square with a Greek cross
8.19 set in, a rotunda at the crossing and vast semicircular porticoes in the middle of each of the four sides of the square. The rotunda was to be 'un temple de la Renommée destiné à contenir les statues des grands hommes' – i.e. a national monument in our sense. The museum proper was no doubt intended to be the four arms and the four ranges of the outer square, but how display was to be arranged Boullée does not tell. Such functional considerations left him bored. All he says is that the collections were to consist of 'les productions des sciences, des arts libéraux et d'histoire naturelle'. The building was also to provide for a library, a print-room, anatomical specimens, stuffed animals, shells, etc. Stylistically Boullée in one respect went far beyond the Grands Prix, including those after his museum. His
8.20 dome rises right from the ground and is completely
8.21 bare. Externally it does not appear at all; there is just a drum with columns around.

After 1783 the Académie asked for one more museum subject, in 1791, and it foretells its doom that what it wanted was a 'Galerie publique dans un Palais de Souverain'.[67] The time for a sovereign in France was over, though the time for public galleries was only approaching. The second prize this time, by Charles Normand, is more interesting than Claude-Matthieu Delagardette's first. Normand is well known as the author of a standard book on the Orders[68] (published in 1819 in Paris and in 1829 by Augustus Pugin Sen. in England) and of other books, e.g. the *Guide des*

8.22 Hubert Robert, 'Project for lighting the Grande Galerie of the Louvre through the roof and for dividing it without taking away the view of the length of the premises', made *c.* 1786 and shown at the Salon of 1796 *(Private Collection)*

8.23 Paris, Musée des Monuments Français, begun 1793, by Alexandre Lenoir: 'thirteenth-century room'

ornemanistes. His museum is a splendid sequence of splendid rooms, a low tunnel-vaulted entrance hall at a lower level than the rest, the large tunnel-vaulted staircase hall in which the staircase rises in one long straight flight between detached columns and ends in a coffered apse as in a gigantically enlarged version of Holkham, then further rooms on plans derived from Roman baths and a culminating Pantheon rotunda followed across the far end by the long tunnel-vaulted gallery. All this is Imperial Roman, Piranesian, Boulléean, but the exceedingly rich decoration contradicts the principles of Revolution architecture.

When this design was judged, the royal gallery in Paris had indeed been *publique* for some time. It was characteristically Marigny's initiative to display the pictures belonging to the King and to allow the public access. A petition had been presented anonymously in 1744. La Font de Saint-Yenne, the critic, repeated the request in 1746. In 1750 Marigny, who was, it will be remembered, Directeur des Bâtiments (see p. 79), made a range of rooms in the Luxembourg available. They contained Rubens' Medici Gallery, and 110 paintings and 20 drawings were exhibited; it opened twice a week, each time for three hours. Marigny's successor d'Angiviller suggested in 1775 that the Grande Galerie of the Louvre should be used, and the idea of skylighting it was contemplated. Designs were asked for from Soufflot, Clérisseau, de Wailly and two others, but none was accepted.[69] The designs are preserved.[70] In the end nothing came of it, and the rooms in the Luxembourg were closed in 1779.

Realization had to wait for the Revolution. On 27 September 1792 the Assemblée Nationale decreed that a museum should be created in the galleries of the Louvre.[71] It was to be called the Muséum Français. It was opened on 9 November 1793, and its name changed in 1796 to Musée Central des Arts. Paintings were exhibited in the Salon Carré and gradually in more and more of the Grande Galerie, ancient sculpture from 1800 on the ground floor of the Grande Galerie. The whole Grande Galerie incidentally is nearly 1,400 feet long. That the collections were open free to the public need hardly be said. The opening hours were Saturday and Sunday 9–4, the other days being for artists.[72] Guide lecturing was done among the Antiques. There was a cheap catalogue to be had, and the pictures had labels.[73]

Booty increased the size of the collections. In 1794 a hundred pictures were sent to Paris from Belgium, and more came from Italy after 1797.[74] With Napoleon's campaigns and the loot of his victories the Louvre grew to be the largest and most spectacular museum ever.[75] Moreover new acquisitions came by purchase also, thus the Borghese Antiques bought in 1808 from Napoleon's brother-in-law Camillo Borghese, and Italian Primitives – a hint at the approach of Romanticism – in 1811. The latter were bought by the brilliant Vivant Denon[76] whom Napoleon had made Director-General of the museum, which in 1804 was re-named Musée Napoléon. Denon had started as a graphic artist. In 1798–99 he accompanied Napoleon on his Egyptian campaign and published his monumental *Voyages dans la Basse et la Haute Egypte* in 1802. He made a highly successful director. From sales of engravings, plaster casts and catalogues he made an annual 30,000–35,000 francs which could be used for purchases. The popularity of the museum was indeed great. The *Décade philosophique* in 1795 called it 'the most visited of our public promenades',[77] the *Archives litéraires* reported that it had watched 'hosts of people rush' to the museum which they 'look at eagerly, on which they demand explanations and which they appreciate or condemn perspicaciously'.[78] Architectural improvements followed this success at once; for Napoleon was partial to the

8.22

8.24 Paris, Musée des Monuments Français, begun 1793, by Alexandre Lenoir: memorial to Abélard and Héloïse

8.25 Madrid, Prado, 1784–1811, by Juan de Villanueva

idea. He said:[79] 'On ne doit jamais oublier que le Louvre est le Palais des Arts.' So Percier and Fontaine redecorated the Grande Galerie in 1805–10 dividing it into six large and three small rooms. The most precious objects of the collection went into the Galerie d'Apollon. On the first floor was the Garde-Meuble, below it the Greek vases and the curiosities.[80] Below the Galerie Henri II were the archives and the library.[81] Percier and Fontaine's masterpiece in the Louvre is the monumental staircase, inspired no doubt by that of the Pio-Clementino. The Salon Carré had received skylighting shortly after 1789, but the Grande Galerie was given skylighting only in 1938, although Hubert Robert had painted it about 1786 with large skylights in the tunnel-vaults.[82] The idea came in all probability from Boullée's drawing for a National Library which, as we have seen, had just this motif. Percier and Fontaine used high side-lighting instead, as – it will be remembered – had already been done in the Palais Royal and at Kassel. This was also the method used for the Royal Academy in the Strand range of Somerset House, i.e. about 1780.

The paintings were arranged by schools, i.e. neither decoratively nor iconographically. Within the schools, however, they were not shown chronologically, which for instance the *Décade philosophique* regarded as necessary: 'Each school has its periods, even each painter has several methods. So one would wish to see the pictures hung according to the various periods of the schools and the various manners of the masters. With what pleasure would one see the gradual ascent!'

This – the principle of the future – had already been followed in 1755 by Lambert Krahe, painter and first director of the Düsseldorf gallery (in collaboration with Christian von Mechel) and a friend of Winckelmann. Mechel brought out a sumptuous volume of engravings of the gallery[83] and was on the strength of it appointed to re-arrange and catalogue the Imperial collection in

Vienna in 1779.[84] The building chosen to display them in was the Belvedere. Mechel's programme is formulated in the introduction to his catalogue. 'The purpose . . . was to use this . . . beautiful building, so suitable because of having many separate rooms, so that the arrangement should be as far as possible a visible history of art. Such a large, public collection intended for instruction more than for fleeting pleasure, is like a rich library in which those eager to learn are glad to find works of all kinds and all periods.'

It was in the Belvedere that the young Nazarenes discovered the Primitives and set out on their romantic re-conquest of the elementary and naïve in art, and of faith and truth. In terms of the history of the museum the Romantic Movement had made its one great contribution a few years earlier and in Paris. As not only the royal collections fell to the people at the Revolution but also the works of art in religious buildings, which were secularized or demolished, a second museum became necessary to store and soon to display this ecclesiastical loot. The man whose life-work was the saving of, and care for, these works of the Middle Ages was the painter Alexandre Lenoir.[85] The place where the monuments had been stored and which became the Musée des Monuments Français was the monastic premises in the rue des Petits Augustins. It was opened in 1793. By 1811 there were over 500 items, mostly funerary monuments. The rooms provided a congenial setting. Arrangement was chronological – Lenoir called 'the progress of the arts and education' his principal concern – but behind was an extensive garden known as the *jardin elysée* where works of art were used as picturesque furnishings, e.g. the monument to King Dagobert with its canopy from St Denis. There were also – just as in English eighteenth-century landscaped grounds – memorials to French celebrities. These were Molière, Boileau, La Fontaine, Descartes and, more in keeping

8.12

8.22

7.32

8.23

8.24

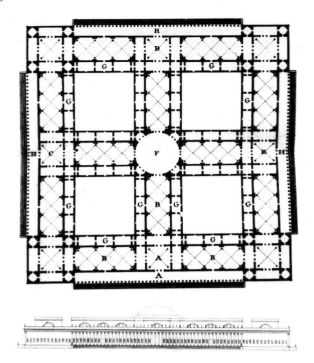

8.26, 27 J.-N.-L. Durand, design for a museum (*Précis*, 1802–09): plan and elevation

8.28 P.-A. Pâris, design for a museum, *c.* 1810 (*Besançon, Musée des Beaux-Arts*)

with the antiquarian character of the collection, Mabillon, Montfaucon, Rohault and Abélard and Héloïse. The museum was visited as enthusiastically as the Louvre. The cheap catalogue went into twelve editions between 1793 and 1816, the year in which the enterprise came to an end and all Church property was returned. To kindle a romantic passion for things medieval the Petits Augustins must have been marvellous, but they were an ominous sign all the same of the passing of the time when the unity of buildings and the works of art made for them was a matter of course. The nineteenth century was to disturb this unity and isolate the sculpture of the Middle Ages as ruthlessly as Antique sculpture had been isolated ever since collecting had begun.

While in the case of the Musée des Monuments Français the building was sympathetic to the works displayed, and while in the Vatican a sympathetic *ambiente* had been specially created, detached museum buildings designed as such were still the rarest of jobs. Only one more of the eighteenth century must be mentioned – in passing only, as it was built to display natural history, not art – the Prado, designed for the King in 1784 by Juan de Villanueva and yet another uncommonly fine example of Neo-Classicism.[86] Villanueva had been in Rome from 1759 to 1765. His is a symmetrical composition with two big end pavilions and in the centre a portico of Tuscan columns through which an apsed Temple of Science was reached. Entry was from one end by an Ionic loggia *in antis* and a skylit Pantheon rotunda. The development in terms of space management between the Museum Fridericianum and the Prado is spectacular. How much, one would like to find out, did Villanueva know of the Grands Prix?

The climax of what young architects had done in their designs for museums in the competitions is that in Durand's *Précis des leçons* of 1802–09, a book we have had to go to already for several building types. As in those cases, Durand continues Boullée but, while keeping his predecessor's passion for symmetry and massed columns, produces slightly more feasible schemes and therefore had immense influence. Everybody during Neo-Classicism seems to have had his Durand – the *Recueil* as well as the *Précis* – on his shelves. Durand's museum is a large square and set into the square a Greek cross, the four arms issuing from a central Pantheon rotunda. This is the Assembly Hall. The straight halls are one each for the three arts and in addition one for exhibitions. All the ranges are of nave and aisles, with semicircular windows high up to give the naves good lighting. The precise purposes of the rooms are not revealed. What look like cabinets may have to be explained as studios. The text for the museum also says: 'In large cities there may be several museums of which some should show the rarest products of nature, others the principal works of the arts. In less important towns one museum can serve these different purposes. To save money one might even combine the library with it.'[87] The museum, Durand continues, is like the library 'a public treasure-house', but the difference between them is that the library serves exclusively one objective, where the museum must display works of different kinds. Thus there must for instance be several entrances. Durand's design is close to Delannoy's of 1778–79. Durand himself had gained second prize in the Académie competition in 1780. He has almost exactly the same plan, but the four sides of the square have now, except for the corners, one long even colonnade each. Everything is thus less articulated and more cubic than twenty-five years before.

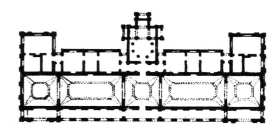

8.29–31 Dulwich Gallery, 1811–14, by Sir John Soane: plan, view and lighting

Durand was not alone in reflecting on a fine appearance for museums. Pierre-Adrien Pâris in 1809 did a design for altering the Museo Pio-Clementino, trying to regularize the sequence of rooms and remove projections and excrescences in favour of more severely cubic masses. Of probably about the same time is his drawing at Besançon of a museum 'où l'on réunit tout ce qui a rapport à l'Etude des Sciences et des Beaux Arts', including a library. He himself calls it an 'immense project'. It is indeed the most sweeping of all the designs of the period for museums. It consists of a circular courtyard connected by sixteen radial galleries – shades of the French hospital designs (see below, p. 152) – with a ring gallery from which in the main directions four short arms extend. These arms are flanked by square courtyards, and the whole is inscribed into a square with nicked-off corners. It is all utterly utopian. Pâris's design seems to have remained unnoticed. It was followed by a published one, that in Claude-Jacques Toussaint's *Traité de l'architecture*, which came out in 1812. This is patently inspired by Durand but decidedly weak in execution. Much space is taken up by rooms for an academy and even more by exhibition galleries. What is new and interesting is that Toussaint tells his readers the purposes of the individual rooms. This his predecessors, concerned solely with monumental composition, had omitted. In 1814 once again the Ecole Nationale des Beaux-Arts (as it was now called) set a museum-cum-library as its task. The first prize went to Charles-Henri Loudon and Louis-Nicholas-Marie Destouches, the second to a more interesting design by Louis-T.-J. Visconti, who became one of the most famous Parisian mid-nineteenth-century architects. All three were pupils of Percier, and all three designs are indeed Empire and no longer Revolution in style, i.e.

less radical and more ancient-Rome in the tectonic elements. A typical innovation is that now statues and even paintings are indicated in the drawings, one step beyond Toussaint's indication of at least the purposes of rooms.

The year of these designs, 1814, saw the completion of the next independent gallery building – the next after Kassel – and the competition for the next after that which was going to be a key building of the nineteenth century. The former is the Dulwich Gallery, the latter the Glyptothek in Munich. The Dulwich Gallery[88] was bequeathed to Dulwich College in 1811 by Sir Peter Bourgeois, RA, who had inherited a collection of pictures from the art dealer Noel Desenfans. He also left money for the building, to which a mausoleum for Mr and Mrs Desenfans and himself was to be added. Sir John Soane designed the gallery with five main rooms all lit on the pattern of the Royal Academy in Somerset House and cabinets along one side of the main rooms. The Mausoleum projects at the back and was flanked left and right by almshouses. The Dulwich Gallery is memorable as the first independent building erected to be a picture gallery, even if with the few appendages just named, but it harks back to the past in still being a private man's collection and administered by a private body.[89]

The Glyptothek, though built and paid for by the Crown Prince of Bavaria, the future Ludwig I, was from the beginning intended to be for the Bavarian people.[90] We know (see p. 9) that Bavaria had become a kingdom in 1806. When Ludwig was still crown prince he had said that he intended 'to make of Munich a city which would be such an honour to Germany that no traveller would leave Germany without having seen Munich'.[91] In 1808–11 Karl von

8.28

8.29–31

8.31
8.29
8.30

8.32 Haller von Hallerstein, design for the Munich Glyptothek, *c.* 1813

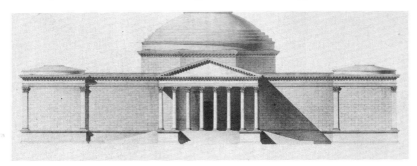

8.33 Karl von Fischer, design for the Munich Glyptothek, 1808–11

Fischer was asked to make a general plan for the city. It included a square meant to have on one side the Walhalla (see p. 18), on the other a museum. In 1812 Ludwig succeeded in buying the sculpture of the pediments of Aegina, intended for London (see pp. 18, 19). The excavators included C. R. Cockerell and the German amateur architect Karl Freiherr Haller von Hallerstein, whom we have met before.[92] In 1813 Ludwig told Haller von Hallerstein in a letter that he wanted to get designs 'from the best architects . . . for a building suitable for the display of works of sculpture'. It should be 'in the purest Grecian style with a portico of fluted columns of the Doric order'. Ludwig encouraged Haller to make and submit designs. At the same time however he had also told the Academy to start up a competition. It was made known in February 1814, the designs to be submitted by January 1815. The time was extended to January 1816. Privately Ludwig told Haller that the building ought to be equipped for festivities at night and concerts, i.e. a kitchen and confectionery department ought to be provided. The museum clearly had not yet moved far away from the palace.[93]

Meanwhile Ludwig had met Klenze. The first two meetings, as we have seen (p. 19), took place in 1814, the third in Paris in 1815. It was understood then that Klenze would join the competition. In the event Fischer, Haller and Klenze all sent in designs. Fischer's had a portico of eight Corinthian columns and a Pantheon dome derived obviously from Durand. Haller's spread out with projections and recessions, an inner courtyard and a rotunda behind it. It is rather restless in plan and elevation. Klenze offered three designs, one Grecian, one Roman, one Renaissance: nineteenth-century historicism is marching, and also

the nineteenth-century belief that Classical scholarship is a *sine qua non* of culture. Each of the three designs had a motto, one Greek from Plato, one Latin from Ovid, one Italian from Tasso.[94] Klenze's Roman design has seven giant niches and set into them screens of two columns carrying an entablature – a Roman motif indeed, but appropriated by Adam and taken up by Ledoux in his Barrière des Bonshommes, which Klenze no doubt knew. The Renaissance design had a one-storey portico of twelve Roman Doric columns and blank aedicules in the side pieces.

Klenze won, and the foundation stone was laid on 23 April 1816. Exterior and interior were complete in 1830. Already in 1816 Klenze was made Oberbaurat and a little later in the same year Hof-Bauintendant (Surintendant des Bâtiments, as the French kings called it). He now had the full confidence of the King. However, a little earlier on he had had to defend his interiors against opposition. It is an interesting story.[95] Ludwig had another *confidant*, the painter, sculptor and archaeologist Johann Martin Wagner who lived in Rome. He was asked by Ludwig in 1815 for his ideas on a museum of ancient sculpture. Wagner's two memoranda (the second of January 1816) suggest only one large room – for the sculpture of Aegina – the rest entirely small rooms, each for three or four pieces, arranged iconographically with light coming only from the north. The architectural mood inside ought to be modest – 'any ornament, anything gay in colour and glittering does damage to works of ideal art'. No floor patterns; greyish-yellowish walls. The philosophy behind all this Wagner formulated thus: 'If you visit a collection of ancient sculpture you go because of the ancient sculpture.' And more generally: 'One recognizes the merit and talent of an architect by the strict coincidence of a

8.33

8.32

8.34, 35

8.34

8.35

8.36

8.34 Leo von Klenze, 'Roman' design for the Munich Glyptothek, 1815 *(Munich, Staatliche Graphische Sammlung)*

8.35 Leo von Klenze, 'Renaissance' design for the Munich Glyptothek, 1815 *(Munich, Staatliche Graphische Sammlung)*

8.36 Munich, Glyptothek, 1815–30, by Leo von Klenze

8.37 K. F. Schinkel, design for a museum, 1800

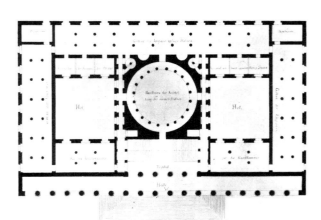

8.38 Berlin, Altes Museum, 1823–30, by K. F. Schinkel

building with its function', and 'It is my principle . . . to prefer utility to beauty in case the two cannot be united.'[96] He goes even further and writes that the 'polished marble walls and floors are an attraction only for the common rabble' (den gemeinen Pöbel).

Klenze hit back: as for north light exclusively, 'a museum is not a place for artists' training, an "akademischer Kunstzwinger", but a place in which to show a number of treasures of art to all kinds of visitors in a manner to be worthy of the objects and to create pleasure in them.' Wagner insisted yet more savagely: 'A museum is no bath-house.' But Ludwig agreed with Klenze: he also wished 'a grandiose architectural effect of whole parts of the building'.

8.36   And so the Glyptothek (the name was invented by the Court Librarian Lichtenthaler) was built. Against Ludwig's original wish the octostyle portico has Ionic not Doric columns. Klenze had succeeded in convincing him of the more festive order. The columns are unfluted, and this Klenze defended by archaeological evidence from the Heraeum at Samos and the Temple of Cybele at Sardis. The walls left and right of the portico are windowless but have blank aedicules of Renaissance rather than Greek derivation. They serve to display statues.[97] In fact the time of the unrelieved severity of Boullée, Ledoux and Gilly was over. Inside there is an entrance hall with a frieze just carrying the names of Ludwig and Klenze and also of Cornelius, the leader of the Nazarene school of German painters, whom Ludwig in 1818 called to Munich to paint frescoes in the state rooms at the back of the Glyptothek with the avowed intention of 'reviving' that technique in the north. (The locus of the revival had been the house of the Prussian Consul General Bartholdy in Rome with paintings by Cornelius, Overbeck and the other Nazarenes. They were done in 1806.) The existence of the state rooms in the Glyptothek for court occasions is a survival of the feudal past of museums and galleries. The gallery rooms were arranged chronologically, not, as Wagner still wanted, typologically. Instead display started with Egypt as 'the principal basis of Greek sculpture' and ended with one Roman room and one for works by Canova, Thorwaldsen, Schadow, Rauch and others. Schadow had, it will be remembered, co-operated with Genelli in the first designs for the national monument to Frederick the Great (see p. 15). Klenze incidentally and unfortunately also won over Wagner in refusing to have seats and labels.

The controversies at Munich were paralleled in Berlin over the preparation for, and the building of, the Altes Museum.[98] Frederick the Great, shortly before he died, had allowed artists to copy in his gallery several days a week. This was confirmed in 1788 by Friedrich Wilhelm II. In 1797 Aloys Hirt, historian of ancient architecture, who had lived in Rome in the 1780s and had become Professor of the Theoretical Part of Fine Art in Berlin in 1796, made a speech appealing to the King to build up one great collection out of all the scattered Antiques in his possession. The new king, Friedrich Wilhelm III, answered that the scheme had to be postponed, but asked Hirt meanwhile to work out a plan. This was done, and the memorandum of 1798 is in its way as revolutionary as Boullée's and Gilly's architecture and Carstens' famous letter to Heinitz.[99]

Hirt writes that works of art should not be kept in palaces but in public museums. 'May I be permitted to say that it is below the dignity of an ancient monument to be displayed as an ornament.' The rare remains which we possess 'are a heritage for the whole of mankind. . . . Only by making them public and uniting them in display can they become the object of true study, and every result obtained from this is a new gain for the common good of mankind.'

It sounds like Carstens indeed. The works of Antiquity are in Hirt's conviction 'the pattern for future times', and, moreover, 'the study of the history of modern art' is always extremely interesting. As for painting, since no Antique painting survives, 'the schools of the fifteenth and sixteenth centuries remain the precepts'. 'Genuine art can only thrive where one has patterns, and they ought to be arranged in beautiful order, and [be] easily and daily accessible to all.' So the King ought to establish a museum 'for public instruction and the noblest enjoyment'. Hence the museum should be open to artists nearly the whole week and to the public on Saturdays and Sundays from 8 to 4 (on the pattern of Revolutionary Paris). Concerning the plan, the building ought to be detached, oblong, with an inner courtyard and many small rooms, i.e. not monumental but as useful as possible – cf. Martin Wagner. The arrangement would be with the purpose of 'representing the history of art', including both the 'approach to perfection' and the decline. For this arrangement laudatory mention is made of Mechel. Antiques should be on the ground floor; paintings on the upper floor. Yet for the Antiques there is still a division suggested into Upper Gods, Lower Gods, Heroes, Athletes, Portraits – as in Paris and Rome.

Nothing came of this, except that Schinkel, as a private individual, aged only nineteen, made a design for a museum. Dating from 1800, it is entirely in the   8.37 spirit of his master Gilly and the French architecture of the Ledoux type, unrelieved on the external surfaces, without any windows to the outside, and with two inside courtyards and two rotundas. This motif appears here too early to derive from Durand; so the source is probably the Museo Pio-Clementino. No further move was made, until in 1807 Altenstein, the minister, wrote another memorandum pleading for the commercial (i.e. Mercantilist) value of art and the artist, but also adding arguments 'from a higher point of view'. The spread of art 'enhances the state of mankind'. Art makes 'mankind participate in the highest goods'. Action was only taken, however, when Napoleon's loot came back. The works which were returned were shown publicly in the Akademie der Wissenschaften every weekday, and enquiries were made whether a museum might be built on the Academy premises. Schinkel did designs, but in 1815 the Giustiniani Collection was bought and in 1821 the Solly Collection. These two new series of paintings of the highest quality (including, for example, parts of the Ghent Altar by the van Eycks) called for a special building to vie with the Glyptothek. Schinkel wrote a memorandum in January 1823, to propose the site close to palace and cathedral which was eventually chosen. Schinkel's plan was seen by the King in January and approved in April. It was engraved and published in 1825.[100] The foundation stone was laid on   8.38

8.39 Berlin, Altes Museum, 1823–30, by K. F. Schinkel

8.40 London, British Museum, 1823–47, by Sir Robert Smirke

9 July 1825, and the Altes Museum – as it was called later, when a Neues Museum had been built – was opened in 1830. The design is clearly inspired by Durand, and the Altes Museum is one of the few buildings in which the sheerness of the long colonnades so liberally put on paper by architects of the French Revolution reached reality. The eighteen fluted Ionic columns between the square angle piers are the noblest introduction to a temple of art. From Durand also comes the Pantheon rotunda in the centre which Schinkel called 'the sanctuary' of the building.[101] Thanks to the Altes Museum the Durand rotunda became a favourite motif of museums. An example is Mihály Pollack's National Museum in Budapest, begun in 1836.[102] The motif of the long colonnade is re-echoed in Sir Robert Smirke's British Museum, but here recent research has proved that, though the façade was built in the 1840s, it was designed in 1823, i.e. it can hardly have been inspired by the Altes Museum.[103] In any case with its projecting wings it is less radical than the Altes Museum. Yet behind Schinkel's unbroken colonnade is a double staircase treated in an unexpectedly picturesque way. A staircase was needed; for apart from colonnade and rotunda the exhibition rooms

are two-storeyed, on ground floor and upper floor. If Schinkel made his staircase an external as well as an internal motif, i.e. if it is visible from outside through the colonnade and a second shorter inner colonnade and yet lies further back than the exhibition rooms left and right, he must have wished to make the two-storeyed composition at once patent. Schinkel was keenly interested in cast iron, and incorporated features of English fireproof construction which he had observed during his travels in England in 1826, when he had gone to study museum buildings (see p. 277).[104]

Exhibited on the ground floor of the Altes Museum were the Antiques, on the first floor the paintings. Over display there was as much controversy as there had been a few years before at Munich. Wagner's part was played by Hirt. Hirt was sifting and cataloguing the paintings, helped in this job by the most knowledgeable young art historian of Germany, Dr Waagen. Waagen,[105] familiar in England for his travel notes on works of art in English collections, was a friend of Schinkel too. When Schinkel travelled in Italy in 1824 Waagen was with him, and at the time of the final clashes between Hirt and Schinkel, Waagen was on Schinkel's side. Hirt finally resigned from the museum Commission. The

Commission was chaired by the great Wilhelm von Humboldt, a sign of how seriously the problems of arrangement were taken. Those responsible for the principles of arrangement were, apart from Schinkel, chiefly Waagen and Freiherr von Rumohr, the other most competent art historian of the period. Rumohr did not belong to the Commission and remained an outsider. Humboldt called Rumohr's *Italienische Forschungen* 'the earliest writing on the history of art in a spirit genuinely historical and genuinely aesthetic'.[106] Waagen was made director of the museum in 1830. He was less fiery than Rumohr, but more erudite, and his directorship marks the final taking over of museums by scholars. Rumohr, for instance, stated – in opposition to the display principle of the Pio-Clementino – that an arrangement by subject-matter would be 'to seek art outside the field of art'. So Rumohr in advocating display according to history instead of iconography yet means to advocate the aesthetic value of art and the importance of aesthetics for *Bildung* in the broadest sense. Here are some passages from a memorandum by Schinkel and Waagen to confirm this: 'The principal and essential purpose is in our opinion this: to awaken in the public the sense of fine art as one of the most important branches of human civilization . . . All other purposes, concerning individual classes of the population, must be subdued to this. Among these the first is to give an opportunity to artists to manifold study; only after that comes the interest of the scholar, and finally and lastly the museum will facilitate the acquisition of information on the history of art among all and sundry.'

As for the arrangement from room to room, however, the historical point of view ruled throughout. Schinkel even designed frames in the styles of the periods of the paintings.[107] Humboldt knew that this strict adherence to history was still something exceptional and wrote: 'The gallery here is distinguished by systematically extending through all periods of painting.' Hence, he said, it was 'beneficial . . . but also necessary to fill the true and significant gaps. Many galleries, nay perhaps all, can only be regarded as aggregates, assembled by degrees without definite plan.' Later he even advocated the buying of copies for filling the gaps. Rumohr of course contradicted, because 'all the value of a painting turns round the idea of originality'.[108]

In the museum, in the end, the paintings were divided, before being displayed, into fourteen classes according to quality. Classes 10 to 14 were not to be shown. Then Rumohr suggested that these being curiosities, and also the works of the 'ganz affrösen Meister' should go into the small back rooms, and with them the 'sour tit-bits' of Crivelli, Vivarini and 'similar abnormal' pieces. The paintings of Mannerism are 'tired imitation' and 'foolish crochets'. The 'reflecting painters of the seventeenth century' are called academic. Their display should start at their highest achievements in Poussin, Lairesse and Adrian de Werff – an odd assortment indeed. The climax of the whole arrangement is to be the High Renaissance. In this all the scholars and critics were of course at one, and the most telling document of the appreciation of painting in the early nineteenth century is again the memorandum by Schinkel

and Waagen. Here are some more passages from it: 'Among all pictures those which one calls classic are undeniably the most important, i.e. those where the artist not only thinks truly and beautifully according to his subject, but is also in command of all the scientific and technical means which serve art and expresses them completely explicitly in an easy and beautiful way.' The excellence resulting from all this 'convinces everybody, artist as well as layman'. The example Schinkel and Waagen offer of this perfection is Raphael, and hence if you have ten already you should still buy the eleventh. Rumohr expresses the same view by claiming that to recognize such artists one must be 'independent of the limiting predilection for singular trends' and able 'to comprehend the essence of art purely and survey from a common point of view its often seemingly contradictory achievements'. On the strength of this principle, Rumohr could fully appreciate the Dutch of the seventeenth century and also plead for the inclusion of contemporary painters.

Schinkel and Waagen sum up their principal criteria thus: Is a work to be hung 'a good painting', that is 'a worthy representative of the time and school to which it belongs'? Once this is settled your aim should be (1) to 'display the originators of the various trends . . . as fully as possible as the true, principal and fundamental masters', (2) 'to obtain a complete idea of those great masters who are specially noteworthy for spirited variety, as for instance Rubens', (3) to show 'national painters who are at the same time great artists . . . as completely as possible', (4) 'to be sparing in pictures by masters of limited individuality . . . and who tend to repeat themselves', and (5) 'to represent only by one or two examples subordinate masters working in a peculiar trend'.

This sums up the attitude of the Humboldt period in European civilization and the spirit of Schinkel's building. At the Altes Museum for once Wackenroder's ideal had come true:[109] 'Picture Halls . . . ought to be temples, where in subdued and silent humility . . . we may admire the great artists . . . Works of art in their essence fit as little in the common flow of life as the thought of God.' What Wackenroder expressed so fervently in 1797 had already been said with equal fervour by Rittershausen in 1785: the rooms of a picture gallery should be 'as simple as possible'; for they are dedicated 'zur Seelen Vervollkommenung', 'just as churches are dedicated to prayer'.[110]

Whatever the merit – and it is outstanding – of Schinkel's Altes Museum and whatever the merits of Klenze's Glyptothek, the most influential museum building of the nineteenth century architecturally was another by Klenze, the Alte Pinakothek, designed in 1823 and 1824 and completed in 1836.[111] The Altes Museum was built to house sculpture and painting, the Glyptothek to house sculpture only. Hence in Munich a museum of painting was needed, and Pinakothek was the ancient word for such a museum.[112] The situation in London was similar. What with statuary and what with the library, there was no space in the British Museum for pictures. So after the acquisition of the Angerstein Collection in 1824 and the gift of the Beaumont Collection in 1826 a special building became necessary, and William Wilkins' National Gallery was designed and built

8.41–

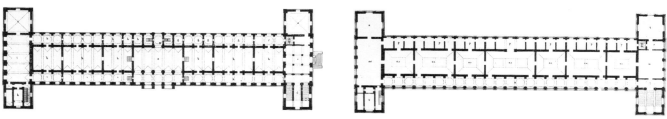

8.41–43 Munich, Alte Pinakothek, 1826–36, by Leo von Klenze: façade, and plans of ground and upper floors

between 1831 and 1838, Classical but somehow too bitty to achieve the monumentality of Smirke's design.[113] The second museum building in Berlin followed soon, the Neues Museum, designed by August Stüler, protégé of the amateur architect King Friedrich Wilhelm IV, in 1840 and completed in 1855.[114] It was to house a variety of collections – Egyptian and Northern antiquities, ethnography, medieval art, plaster casts and more. A second museum for paintings followed in 1867–76, the National-Galerie, for pictures of the nineteenth century, originally also designed by Stüler, but taken over after his death by Johann Heinrich Strack.[115] Both are still Late Classical in style, the National-Galerie even with a temple front, though with an apse at the back. Stüler was, with Klenze, the most widely renowned specialist for museums. Klenze in 1836 was asked by King Otto of Greece, a Bavarian, to design a museum for Athens. It was to house the collections of sculpture and also a school of art. It was in a pure Grecian style and remained on paper.[116] But the Hermitage at St Petersburg, also by Klenze, was built, the largest of the early museums. The dates are 1839–51, the style is Graeco-Roman. The collections are of many kinds.[117] Stüler was also called abroad. He designed the National Museum in Stockholm. It was intended for Antiques, for paintings and also for a library.[118] The building was begun in 1847 and completed in 1866. The late date explains its Renaissance style and also the arrangement of the accommodation for the pictures. Both derive from what Klenze had in the meantime done in Munich.

So we must return to the Alte Pinakothek. Klenze's first designs were made in 1822, revised designs in 1824. In 1823 Klenze had been to Northern Italy, visiting picture galleries.[119] The foundation stone was laid on 6 April 1826, the day being Raphael's birthday. Ten years later it was opened. It has none of the Grecian conventions of Glyptothek, Altes Museum and British Museum. In style it is Cinquecento, a style Klenze had already used in the Lichtenberg Palais in 1816 and was going to use more grandly, as has already been said (p. 9) in the Festsaalbau of the Royal Palace in 1832. Klenze's Königsbau of the same palace (1826–35) – this has also been pointed out – was closely dependent on the Palazzo Pitti, and King Ludwig for the decoration of the rooms in the Pinakothek specifically recommended the Pitti. Klenze disagreed: if the decoration of the rooms were made too showy, the pictures would suffer.[120] Instead of Italian Baroque Klenze wanted the Italian High Renaissance, and he won. The exterior is in a free High Renaissance, and so were the principal rooms inside. Where Klenze however did not follow any precedent of the past is in the plan of the building. The Pinakothek is twenty-five bays long from west to east but quite narrow with, in addition, wings at the ends projecting slightly to north and south. The entrance was at the east end, but this and the staircases were altered recently after war damage. The plan provided for storerooms for works not on show, for a library and print-room on the ground floor, and for public display on the upper floor. Arrangement was by schools, following on the whole a chronological system. But the most important innovation was the planning of three parallel strips all along the twenty-five bays, the middle

8.41

4
3

8.42, 43

8.42

8.43

8.44 Dresden, Gemäldegalerie, 1847–55, by Gottfried Semper

8.45 Philadelphia, Pennsylvania Academy of the Fine Arts, 1876, by Frank Furness

one of big skylit halls for large paintings, the south one for a loggia giving access to every hall, and the north one for cabinets with windows for the small paintings. This arrangement was to be immensely influential. Klenze incidentally did not invent it. Johann Georg von Dillis, successor of Mannlich as director of the King's picture collection, had proposed some time between 1816 and 1822 *Säle* and *Kabinette* with north light.[121]

Among galleries following the plan of the Pinakothek are in the first place the Neue Pinakothek in Munich (1846–52, by August von Voit) in a *Rundbogenstil* with Romanesque touches,[122] and then e.g. Stockholm (1847–66), as we have already seen, the Kunsthistorisches Hofmuseum in Vienna (1872–89, by Semper and Carl von Hasenauer: see pp. 134–35),[123] the Städelsches Kunstinstitut at Frankfurt (1876, by Oskar Sommer), and the galleries of Kassel (1871–77, by H. von Dehn Rotfelser) and Brunswick (1883–87, also by Sommer).

But the finest of this series is without doubt Gottfried Semper's Dresden Gallery, built in a Cinquecento style in 1847–55.[124] As at the Alte Pinakothek the pictures are displayed on the upper floor. The cabinets incidentally are in two tiers, the upper hidden from the outside.[125] Generally speaking Semper's gallery is in plan less functionally consistent than the Pinakothek, where all the large halls are equal in stress. Semper has instead in the middle a 'Salon Carré' with a dome, externally rather played down. The building closed the Zwinger to the north and is in its Italianate gravity a bolt against any spilling over of the flippancy of Pöppelmann's Baroque.

As for the Alte Pinakothek, nothing has yet been said about the south loggia, a lavish vaulted corridor of twenty-five bays 400 feet in length. As a motif it is clearly derived from Raphael's Logge in the Vatican.

Raphael was as we have seen considered the acme of Western painting. The Raphaelesque architecture and the arrangement of the paintings were evidence of the same conception. The decoration of the loggias (by Cornelius) has as its programme the history of painting, starting from the end bays and following Italian painting from the east and Northern painting from the west, and leading to a climax in the middle (thirteenth) bay which – it hardly needs saying – was devoted to Raphael. The north and the south bays are paired, e.g. bays 12 and 14 Michelangelo and Rubens, bays 11 and 15 Venetian painting 1470–1570 and Poussin and Le Sueur, bays 10 and 16 Correggio and Claude Lorraine and Rembrandt, bays 9 and 17 Leonardo and Dürer, bays 8 and 18 Perugino and Lucas van Leyden, bays 7 and 19 Fra Angelico and the van Eycks, and so on. Two things in the programme call for comment: that Titian does not get a separate bay and that historicism has now proceeded far enough to include Rubens, Poussin, Claude and Le Sueur. Equally interesting is the choice of artists made by Dillis for the statuary of the top balustrade of the building. Here you could find e.g. Rubens, van Dyck, Velasquez, Murillo and also Domenichino – but no longer Reni and Annibale Carracci. It is interesting to compare these names of artists with those commemorated on the Albert Memorial in London (p. 24), but it must of course not be forgotten that the Albert Memorial belongs to the 1860s, i.e. the second half of the century.

In the history of museums the second half of the nineteenth century was unquestionably the great age of new museums and galleries. Dr Wittlin says that in Great Britain in 1850 there were 59 museums, in 1914 295 more, and that Germany in the early nineteenth century saw 15 new museums, in the early twentieth century 179 new ones. America joined in vigorously.

8.46 Vienna, Kunsthistorisches Hofmuseum, 1872–89, by Gottfried Semper and Carl von Hasenauer

8.47 Munich, Bayerisches Nationalmuseum, 1894–99, by Gabriel von Seidl

8.45

The Yale Art Gallery started in 1831, the Old Corcoran in Washington (see below, p. 135) in 1859, the Metropolitan in New York and the Boston Museum of Fine Arts in 1870; Philadelphia followed in 1875, Chicago in 1879, Cincinnati in 1880, and so on. Architecturally the most memorable is that in Philadelphia, combining the gallery with the Pennsylvania Academy of the Fine Arts – vintage Furness of the grossest calibre.[126]

But by that time new museums were no longer just the homes of painting and sculpture. There were now museums of applied or decorative arts as well,[127] and museums not of art at all. The first special museum of the applied arts was the South Kensington Museum, now Victoria and Albert Museum, in London.[128] It was created in 1852 by Sir Henry Cole, member of the Executive Committee for the 1851 Exhibition and later Secretary of the Department of Practical Art. The museum was created to perpetuate the lessons of the exhibition, preserve some of its best exhibits and keep them available as models for manufacturers. Its first building was so frankly utilitarian that it was popularly called The Boilers. It dated from 1856, and its glass and iron roof has been re-erected for the Bethnal Green Museum. Extensions designed in 1862 by Captain Fowke are in an extremely pretty North Italian Quattrocento style with much terracotta.[129] Further extensions were made in 1872 and 1894. The present façade is yet later – by Sir Aston Webb, of 1899–1909 – and mixes Franco-Flemish with Wrenaissance motifs. The most important follower of the South Kensington Museum was the Österreichisches Museum für Kunst und Industrie, founded in 1863, 'on the plan of South Kensington'.[130] The building is of 1868–73 by Freiherr von Ferstel, in a rather tame Late Quattrocento. A few years later, in 1872–77, Hamburg received its Museum für Kunst und Gewerbe (by K. J. C. Zimmermann).

This was followed by the Nordiska Museet in Stockholm, 1873, which chose the so-called Northern Renaissance style, i.e. the style of Kronborg and Frederiksborg (the present building is of 1909 by Isaac Gustaf Clason). After that came Budapest (1874; present building 1896 by Ödön Lechner) and finally Berlin in 1877–81. The architects of the Berlin Kunstgewerbemuseum were Gropius & Schmieden.[131]

In France the initiative was taken earlier even than in England. Lenoir's Musée des Monuments Français focused attention on medieval art. The stimulus was felt by that fanatic collector Alexandre du Sommerard.[132] His collection went into the Hôtel de Cluny, and after Sommerard's death was made public there (1844). Less than twenty years later a society was started to promote interest in the applied arts, the Union Centrale des Arts Décoratifs which was founded in 1862.[133] They administered a museum of decorative art until in 1920 the State took it over. Of a kind different from the museums for decorative art so far mentioned was the Germanisches Nationalmuseum in Nuremberg, started in 1852 by Freiherr von Aufsess, moved into the Charterhouse in 1857 and enlarged by A. O. von Essenwein in 1866 et seq. and later. Essenwein was an architect and the director of the museum. The enlargement begun in 1866 served to house objects of painting, sculpture and the decorative arts.[134]

Epoch-making in the field of museums of applied art was the Bayerisches Nationalmuseum in Munich by Gabriel von Seidl, 1894–99;[135] for here sculpture, some painting and all the applied arts are exhibited together – incidentally chronologically, from style to style. The exterior and interior represented this concept faithfully, with picturesquely grouped Romanesque, Gothic, Northern Renaissance and Rococo features outside and inside. On the whole externally the Northern Renais-

8.47

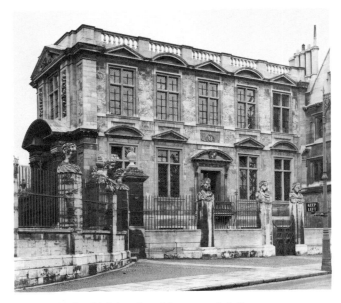

8.48 Oxford, Old Ashmolean Museum, 1678–83

8.49 Oxford, University Museum, 1855–60, by Benjamin Woodward

sance dominates, as it had already done in Gustav Gull's Schweizerisches Landesmuseum in Zürich of 1892–98. Eight years earlier than that the Kunstgewerbemuseum at Düsseldorf by Karl Hecker had been started and this also has a Northern Renaissance exterior and inside a Romanesque hall, a Gothic chapel, etc.[136] The arguments as to whether the arts should be shown together and whether rooms should have the character of the period of their exhibits need not detain us here. In the end neutral display won, as we shall see presently.

But first a glance must be cast on museums set up for the exhibiting of objects not shown for aesthetic reasons. In Paris the Jardin des Plantes, founded as a botanic garden in 1626, developed a Museum of Natural History from 1739, when Buffon was director, and this was reorganized and rationalized by the Convention in 1793. In the same year the Conservatoire des Arts et Métiers was founded and moved to the premises of the priory of St Martin des Champs to be 'a public depository of machines, models, tools, drawings, descriptions and books of all the arts and trades'.[137] The fine enlargements of 1839–47 are by Vaudoyer, an early case of the Loire Style Revival[138] (cf. Town Halls, p. 56). As for museums of natural history, they go, in at least one case, back to the seventeenth century. The case is that of the Tradescants.

John Tradescant was an enthusiastic naturalist, gardener and explorer. In 1618, for instance, he travelled to Russia. He was in the service of the Duke of Buckingham and then of Charles I. His son John (1608–62) in 1656 made a catalogue of his Museum Tradescantium. It contained birds, beasts, fishes, shells, minerals, but also utensils, instruments of war, Henry VIII's stirrups and blood that had rained in the Isle of Wight.[139] After John Jr's death a quarrel broke out between his widow and Elias Ashmole who claimed the collection. Mrs Tradescant was drowned in 1678. Ashmole had a special building erected in Oxford close to the Sheldonian Theatre, and the collection was opened in 1683.[140] The public was admitted against an entrance fee.

The next great collection of natural history, as well as coins, paintings, drawings and 'curiosities', was Dr Hans Sloane's.[141] At the time of his death the collection numbered 79,575 items.[142] Sloane who died in 1753 wanted the nation to have it so that it would be 'seen by all persons desirous of seeing . . . same'. It was finally bought for £20,000, and that was the start of the British Museum. It was from the beginning a museum-cum-library (see p. 104). Plans for a building were made in the 1750s,[143] one by Cornelius Johnston rather Baroque and un-English, three Palladian, by Gwynn, Thomas Wright and Vardy. Vardy's kept well within the tradition of Kent's plans for public buildings. It had a palatial front of eleven bays and two and a half storeys with three domes. They mark a central rotunda and two larger octagonal rooms with an ambulatory behind columns.[144] In the end the idea of a new building was given up, and the Sloane collections and the libraries of Cotton, Harley and George II went into Montagu House.

The Peale Museum in Philadelphia represents an interesting combination of arts and sciences. It was formed by the painter Charles Willson Peale, who opened his collection in 1786. It was intended to display all the natural products of America, and was housed first in Peale's studio, then in the Philosophical Hall, then in Independence Hall. Audubon admired it greatly. A painting dated 1822 shows Peale lifting the entrance curtain and revealing part of the collection. In 1797 his son Raphaelle opened a museum in Baltimore, and another son, Rembrandt, built its present premises there in 1814.[145]

One more museum of natural history belongs to the

8.48

8.50 London, Natural History Museum, 1871–81, by Alfred Waterhouse

8.25 eighteenth century: the Prado in Madrid, built, as we have seen, in 1784–1811.[146] There were, of course, also many smaller collections of natural objects, often on the verge of the *Kunstkammern*.[147] Some of them were brought together already in the late sixteenth and seventeenth centuries, e.g. Athanasius Kircher's which became the museum of the Collegio Romano in Rome. This had incidentally much Egyptian material.[148] As a rule such collections were a mixture of natural objects (especially freaks), artefacts and works of the minor arts. That of Louis XIII at Fontainebleau, according to Pierre Dan (1642), contained 'tout qu'il avait pu trouver de petites curiosités, comme médailles, antiques, argenterie, vases, figures, animaux, vêtements, et une infinité de petites gentilesses'.[149] For the mid-nineteenth century among the most memorable natural history collections of one kind or another are General Pitt-Rivers', begun in 1851, continued in the sixties and seventies, exhibited in the Bethnal Green Museum in London and given to Oxford University in 1883, Agassiz's Museum of Comparative Zoology at Harvard, begun in 1859, and the Oxford University Museum of 1855–60.[150] Architecturally this is the most interesting.

8.49

The idea of the Oxford Museum was Henry Acland's, Ruskin was keenly interested in it, and the architect was Benjamin Woodward. It is emphatically Gothic, incidentally in spite of Ruskin less Italian than Flemish, and its interior has as its centre a glazed courtyard surrounded by cloister-like arcading. This, if time is spent in studying it, turns out to be a lesson in British geology (the shafts) and British botany (the capitals). The courtyard is divided into five vessels by piers of hollow cast iron, the iron proudly exposed, and by pointed arches of iron with pretty wrought-iron leaf decoration in the spandrels. Skidmore of Coventry was responsible for this. It is interesting that Ruskin had no objection to all

8.49

this iron, especially since *The Builder* had commented on the use of 'railway materials',[151] and railways were to Ruskin the reddest of red rags. Woodward was not first in this display of iron. The Bibliothèque Ste Geneviève of 1845–50 has already been mentioned (p. 107), and the Coal Exchange in London of 1846–49 will be mentioned later (pp. 206–08).

7.44
12.39

Shortly after, in 1871–81, the biggest London museum building came into being, the Natural History Museum, a splitting-off of the appropriate collections of the British Museum, symmetrical, Romanesque with much terracotta and a splendid flying staircase inside. It makes one's admiration for Waterhouse rise by many degrees at once. The American Museum of Natural History in New York was created in 1869. The building is by J. C. Cody, Romanesque in style. The Peabody Museum of Natural History at Yale was built in 1866–76, also by Cody; Peabody donated $150,000. The Field Museum of Natural History in Chicago is named after Marshall Field, who in 1893 endowed it with $1,000,000, to which in his will he added $8,000,000. It was housed in the Fine Arts Building of the Columbian Exposition of 1893 (see p. 250), which was designed in the Classical style by Charles B. Atwood. (A new building was erected in 1911–19 by Graham, Anderson, Probst & White.) The huge Naturhistorisches Museum in Vienna was built in 1872–89, forming a pair with the art museum. Both are by Gottfried Semper and Carl von Hasenauer, the result of a collaboration that ended in violent quarrels and violent hatred. Semper's designs were made from 1869 onward. They comprised the whole Forum with the museums left and right of a vast square, and the Hofburg on the third side.[152] The style is a free Baroque developing out of Semper's former Renaissance. Carl von Lützow, the art historian, argued in 1883:[153] 'In the place where the masters of the Baroque, a Fischer von Erlach or a

8.50

8.46

8.51 Winterthur, museum, 1912–16, by
Rittmeyer & Furrer

8.52 New York, Guggenheim
Museum, 1943 and 1956–59, by
Frank Lloyd Wright

Mattielli, had pulled out all the stops any softer chords
of style would have been ineffectual.' Among natural
history museums after Vienna Berlin followed in 1883–
89, and so on to Dayton, Ohio, of 1960 by Neutra and
R. E. Alexander.[154]

As for science and technology, in spite of the early
start in Paris, nineteenth-century contributions were
few. The most interesting is that of the Smithsonian
Institution in Washington,[155] founded out of the half
a million dollar bequest of an Englishman, James
Smithson, 'for the increase and diffusion of knowledge'.
He was an illegitimate son of the Duke of Northumberland and gave the money without ever having visited
the United States. The Smithsonian encourages research
but has gradually branched out into collecting not only
objects of natural history but also of technology and the
applied arts. The building is Gothic – an odd choice –
with battlements and asymmetrically-placed turrets. It
was built in 1847–55 to a design by Renwick (who was
to do the Corcoran Museum, also in Washington:
below, p. 135). The National Museum of History and
Technology in Washington is the most recent venture
of the Smithsonian – a large, totally detached building,
still in the Washingtonian Classical Re-Revival. It was
built in 1959–64 to the last design of McKim, Mead &
White by their successors, Steinman, Cain & White.

Buffalo got a Museum of Science in 1861, but the

modern museum of this type was created with the
Deutsches Museum in Munich, by Gabriel and Emanuel
von Seidl, planned in 1903 and entirely installed in 1925.
Now others followed: e.g. the Science Museum in
London in 1908 (the building was begun in 1912) and,
to end with an oddment, the Mercer Museum at
Doylestown, Pennsylvania, built in a picturesque castle
style to Mr Mercer's design, without an architect or a
firm of builders and yet entirely in poured reinforced
concrete. The collection is of early American tools and
implements.

Oddments of thematic kinds should perhaps have a
paragraph to themselves, to mention at least a few:
Museums for the works of one artist exclusively, like
the Thorwaldsen Museum in Copenhagen of 1839–48,
that brilliant piece of Late Grecian in a highly original
form, the design of Gottlieb Bindesböll; the open-air
display of the sculpture of Gustav Vigeland in the
Frogner Park at Oslo of 1924–50, 75 acres of sculpture
of interest to the psychoanalyst at least as much as to the
historian of art; the Léger Museum at Biot of 1957–59;
and the Van Gogh Museum in Amsterdam, designed
by Rietveld shortly before his death and opened in 1974.
Another open-air museum is Skansen in Stockholm,
inaugurated in 1891 as a zoo, but also for the display of
vernacular building, since often imitated. And then
there are e.g. the Textile Museum at Lyons (founded

8.53 Humlebaek, Louisiana, 1958–59, by J. Bo and V. Wohlert

1864, recreated 1890), the Wallpaper Museum at Kassel, the Museum of Hygiene in Dresden (1927–30, by Kreis, the outcome of a hygiene exhibition held in 1911), the Museum of Timber (Siloteca) in Milan (started in 1907 and taken over by the City in 1934), and more specifically the Museums of the Motor Car in Turin (1956–60, by Amedeo Albertini), at Aalholm near Nysted in Denmark and at Beaulieu in Hampshire, the Nautical Museum at Rotterdam (by A. van der Steuer, completed in 1948), the Museum of Oceanography at Monte Carlo, the glass museums of Corning, N.Y. and St Helen's, the Museum of the American Indian in New York City, the Museum of Musical Instruments in Milan, the Museum of Bird Migration on Öland, the Bird-Cage Museum at Neheim-Hüsten in Westphalia, opened 1973, and the Forestry Museum at Gävle.[156]

Finally, a reminder of the infinite number of historical museums, general or special. For the latter one need only think of the Musée Carnavalet in Paris, established in 1866 and housed in an *hôtel* remodelled by Mansart. Historical museums are indeed often in historic houses, and tend to be more and more so as the twentieth century progresses.[157]

So to the twentieth century to end with. By far the most memorable fact is the growth of private American collections becoming public by will or grant.[158] The Corcoran Gallery of Art in Washington, already men-

tioned, came first. It was made public in 1859, and a building with a French pavilion roof was erected to a design by Renwick (known as the Old Corcoran, this is now the Renwick Gallery of the National Collection of Fine Arts). The present Corcoran Gallery is by Ernest Flagg. It dates from 1897, and an enlargement was put up for the Clark Collection in 1927. Next came the Jarves Collection bought by Yale in 1871 and the Fogg Museum of Art, established at Cambridge, Massachusetts, by Mrs Fogg in 1895.[159] The present building is of 1927, by Coolidge, Shepley, Bulfinch & Abbott.

The rest of the story is entirely twentieth-century, and one ought to distinguish between separate buildings and bequests to existing museums. To the former category belongs e.g. Fenway Court in Boston, Mrs Isabella Stewart Gardner's treasure house, 1900–1916, richly Venetian, by Willard Sears. The Pierpont Morgan Library in New York, the finest twentieth-century assembly of illuminated manuscripts, has a building by McKim. It was opened in 1906. In Washington apart from the Corcoran five museums must be referred to. The Freer Gallery of Art is specially strong in Oriental art and Whistler.[160] The gallery, which comes under the Smithsonian, was designed by Charles A. Platt and opened in 1923. The Phillips Gallery, opened in 1921, was a private house (1897, by Hornblower & Marshall) with an addition by McKim, Mead & White. Dum-

8.54 Oakland, Calif., museum, 1962–68, by Kevin Roche

barton Oaks, given by Mrs Bliss to Harvard in 1940, is a research institute and a collection mostly of early medieval and Byzantine objects. The bijou of a museum in its garden is by Philip Johnson, of 1963. But the climax in Washington is the National Gallery, designed by J. Russell Pope in 1936 et seq., and paid for by Andrew Mellon who also gave his collection. The style of the building is still the official Washington Classical Re-revival. Yet more recent is the Joseph H. Hirshhorn Museum, designed in 1969 by Skidmore, Owings & Merrill (Gordon Bunshaft) and completed in 1974.

8.52   In New York are the Frick Collection, donated in 1919 with the Neo-Renaissance house of 1914 by Carrère & Hastings, the Guggenheim of 1956–59 by Frank Lloyd Wright (of which more later) and the Whitney of 1966 by Marcel Breuer. The Walters Collection, got together by the two Walterses, father and son, is at Baltimore, the Barnes Foundation with its amazing wealth of Impressionists and Post-Impressionists instituted in 1922 is at Merion near Philadelphia, the Huntington Collection and Library of 1927 at San Marino in California.[161]

As an appendix Winterthur, the vast Henry Francis Dupont Museum of furniture, furnishings and everyday objects, mostly American; Henry Ford's Dearborn, Michigan and Greenfield Village of furniture, tools, machinery and reconstructed buildings (e.g. Edison's workshop) started in 1928 and opened in 1933; and Electra Havemeyer-Webb's Shelburne, Vermont, of

1947–52, also for Americana, including cigar-store Indians, shop signs, decoys, a pleasure steamer and a lighthouse.

As for donations and bequests to existing museums, here is a brief selection: Marquand – Metropolitan 1888 and 1890; Altman – Metropolitan 1913; John G. Johnston – Philadelphia 1917; Morgan – Metropolitan c. 1920;[162] Ringling – Sarasota 1926; Havemeyer – Metropolitan 1929; Friedsam – Metropolitan 1931; and so to the National Gallery to which the Kress (1939) and the Widener (1942) treasures were given.

Surveying now the result of so much collecting, one can say that whenever anything in the art world has become specially desirable in the last hundred years it has almost automatically aroused American ambitions to be in on it. This was true of Greco, of Rembrandt, of Vermeer (for reasons of rarity), and then of the School of Barbizon, followed by the French Impressionists and the first Post-Impressionists, i.e. Cézanne, Gauguin and van Gogh.[163]

But we are more interested in buildings than in holdings, and so many have been built, especially after the Second World War, that any selecting must be personal.[164] In fact no new principles have turned up, except that the ideal of the museum as a monument in its own right has been replaced by the ideal of the museum as the perfect place to show, enjoy and study works of art (or of history or of science). Not that this is now universally recognized. For instance there is a

8.55 Jerusalem, Israel Museum, 1959–65, by A. Mansfeld and Dora Gad, landscaping by Miller & Blum

8.56 Berkeley, Calif., University Art Museum, 1967–70, by Mario J. Ciampi & Associates

recent American vogue to make museums windowless. The arguments are that electric light is calculable and even, whereas daylight is not. Also insurance is supposed to cost more if there are windows. The argument on the other side is that fluctuation of light is a good thing resulting in longer life for the works of painting and sculpture.

8.52   Of all the new American museums, the most sensational is Frank Lloyd Wright's Guggenheim in New York designed in 1943 and built in 1956–59. Sensational it surely is, but it is also about everything a museum should not be. It is a monument, after all, and the spiral ramp which one is forced to descend makes any cross moves impossible, and cross moves at will are the spice of museum visits.[165] What else needs saying by way of criticism of new museums? Display can be handled by architects so cleverly that one's attention to it makes one forget to look at the objects displayed. A paramount example is the Castello Sforzesco in Milan by Belgioioso, Peressutti & Rogers (1954–63).[166]

8.51   Now on the positive side. Among the earliest museums in non-period forms was Winterthur in Switzerland by Rittmeyer & Furrer, and that dates from 1912–16. Vienna and Peter Behrens stand behind its style. Single-storey museums are a convincing innovation of the twentieth century. The first major example

8.57 was the Kröller-Müller Museum at Otterlo in Holland.[167] This was designed by van de Velde and built in

8.53 1937–54. But the finest example is Louisiana at Humlebaek near Copenhagen, by Jörgen Bo and Vilhelm Wohlert of 1958–59, an exquisite combination of quiet interiors and views out to trees and the sea.[168] Landscape planning as part of a museum, and in this case right in the centre of a city, is the major part of the beauty of Kevin Roche's Oakland Museum in California (1962–68). In a town the scale of landscaping is of course limited; at the Israel Museum near Jerusalem (1959–65), 8.55 where the design was due to Miller & Blum, it seems unlimited. The excellent building is by A. Mansfeld and Dora Gad.

The two mid-twentieth-century extremes in museum buildings are by the two extremes among the grand old masters of the century: the crystalline clarity of Mies van der Rohe's Berlin National-Galerie of 1962–68 and the brutalism of Le Corbusier's Museum of Western Art in Tokyo of 1957 et seq. Both have serious functional shortcomings.[169] In the Le Corbusier vein and earlier than the Tokyo museum is Affonso Eduardo Reidy's museum at Rio (1954 et seq.).

Finally, of the last ten years is Philip Johnson's series of museums ranging from the elegance and *petitesse* of the Dumbarton Oaks museum to the massive and in its ruthless way indeed monumental Kunsthalle at Bielefeld (Kaselowsky-Haus, 1966–68).[170] Ruthless monumentality seems an appropriate term also for the Anthropological Museum of Mexico City by Vásquez & Mijares (1963–65), and the brutalism which in so many chapters of this book marks what is up to date may be represented by the new Berkeley museum of 8.56 the University of California by Mario J. Ciampi & Associates (1967–70), with its ingenious if complicated plan and levels.

8.57   Otterlo, Rijksmuseum Kröller-Müller, 1937–54, by Henry van de Velde

9.1 Rome, Hospital of Santo Spirito in Sassia, 1474–82 and 1540s (fresco in the Palazzo del Commendatore of the hospital)

9
Hospitals

HOSPITAL, hospice, hostel, hotel are all derived from Latin *hospes*, the guest or the host. The multitude of words represents the multitude of functions of the medieval hospital: hospital, almshouse, asylum, orphanage, foundling home, guest-house for travellers and pilgrims, poor-house. A document of 1232 tells us that Esslingen received 'pauperes, peregrini, transeuntes, mulieres in partu agentes, parvuli a patribus et matribus derelicti, debiles et claudi, generaliter omnes'[1] (the poor, pilgrims, transients, pregnant women, abandoned children, the halt and the lame – in fact everyone). *Domus dei* is a frequent name, but *domus pauperum* even more so.[2] As in the cases of town hall, law courts, market hall and others, the development is one of diversification.

Like all the other chapters of this book, this chapter does not go back to Antiquity and the Early Christian East, i.e. in the present case the *xenodochium*.[3] In the Christian West the Rule of St Benedict, chapter 53, says that 'omnes supervenientes hospites tamquam Christus suscipiantur'[4] (every arriving guest must be welcomed as if he were Christ), and makes 'infirmum visitare' a duty of the monk. Bishop Chrodegang of Metz, who died in 766, emphasizes these duties, and his rule was accepted for the Carolingian Empire. A *capitulare* of 789 makes such forms of charity compulsory for abbeys. The Synod of Aachen of 816–17 declared it a duty of every bishop to have a hospice for the poor and for travellers, and of every canon to allocate one tenth of his income for such a purpose. Foundling hospitals and lazar houses, i.e. leper hospitals, are first mentioned in the sixth century.[5] The earliest document concerning the Hôtel-Dieu in Paris is of 829.[6] Of the same years is the famous parchment plan for the abbey of St Gall, an ideal plan rather than one to serve for actual building.[7] Here functions are already nicely separated: quarters for pilgrims and the poor ('domus peregrinorum et pauperum') south of the west apse of the church, a guest-house for superior guests north of the west apse, the infirmary for sick and old monks with its own chapel and cloister north-east of the east end.

9.2

St Gall is Benedictine; Cluniac and Cistercian houses also had their infirmary.[8] The actual day-to-day work was done in Cistercian establishments by the *conversi*, i.e. the lay brothers, and in Benedictine houses also not by the monks, but by *famuli*.[9] Gradually special lay fraternities took over looking after the sick and the poor. It is not always easy to say what order or group worked in a hospital.[10] A special case was the military orders. The earliest of them was that of St John of

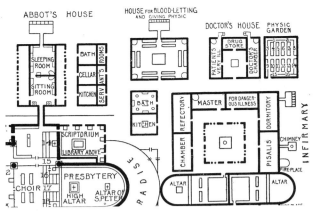

9.2 Ideal plan for the abbey of St Gall, *c.* 820: detail showing the infirmary

9.3 Ramsey, abbey guest house (now parish church), late 12th c.

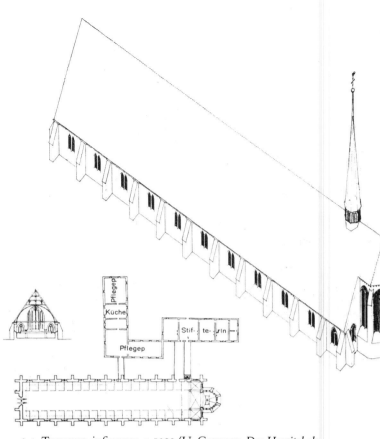

9.4 Tonnerre, infirmary, *c.* 1300 (U. Craemer, *Das Hospital als Bautyp des Mittelalters*, 1963)

Jerusalem – characteristically also called the Hospitallers. It was started at Jerusalem by merchants of Amalfi about 1070, but founded formally only after the conquest of Jerusalem in 1099 and reorganized by the Popes in 1154 and 1178. The hospital in Jerusalem was called late in the fourteenth century 'magnum et mirabile itu quod impossibile videretur'.[11] Soon other hospitals appeared under the order: at Acre, on Cyprus, in Messina, Cività Vecchia, Viterbo, Villefranche.[12] When after the Turkish conquest the order had to leave the Holy Land it annexed the island of Rhodes in 1309, and when Rhodes fell to the Turks in 1530 the Knights obtained Malta from the Emperor.[13] The next of the military orders was that of the Templars, founded in 1118 and – out of greed for its possessions – cruelly suppressed early in the fourteenth century. The third and most famous was the order of the Teutonic Knights, founded in 1190.[14] However, the Teutonic Knights, especially after they had been called in 1225 to fight the heathen Prussians, concentrated more and more on military pursuits. The Order of St John on the other hand never lost sight of their hospital duties.

But more and more lay fraternities, taking monastic vows and living under the Augustinian rule, took over. The Augustinian rule allowed social work in the world more easily than the Benedictine. Other orders were created specially for hospital service, the Lazarites looking after lepers, the Antonites after skin-diseases (Isenheim, famous for Grünewald's altar, was one of their houses), and, foremost, the Order of the Holy Spirit, an order of laymen. This had been started by Guy de Montpellier in the late twelfth century and was taken up by Pope Innocent III, who gave it privileges in 1198 and handed over to it the existing hospital of S. Maria in Sassia on the Vatican side of the Tiber. Legend had it that it was founded by the Saxon King Ina, that he retired to it and died in it in 726. It was thus known as the Saxon (i.e. Anglo-Saxon) hospice, the Schola Saxonum. The part of Rome where it stood was called the Burgus Saxonum. Hence the hospital became Santo Spirito in Sassia.[15] Santo Spirito was made the headquarters of the order, and Holy Spirit or Heiliggeist became a favourite vocable for hospitals – which, however, does not mean that all hospitals so named belonged to the order. Another complication in sorting out which premises were administered by whom is the gradual taking over of hospitals from cathedrals, from the military orders and so on by municipal councils.[16]

However, we are here more concerned with architecture than with administration. In monasteries the

9.5 Ourscamp, infirmary, early 13th c.

9.6 Angers, hospital, later 12th c.

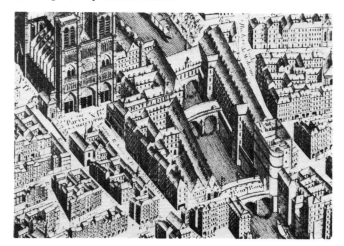

9.7 Paris, Hôtel-Dieu, 16th-c. bird's-eye view

custom was, as at St Gall, to have the guest-house west of the claustral precinct and the infirmary east. Kirkstall, the Cistercian abbey outside Leeds, can serve as an example. The infirmary was aisled and had at its east end the chapel so that the sick could see the altar and the services. It must never be forgotten that medical treatment was inadequate and communication with God more urgent than with a doctor or a medically active monk. England has a number of telling fragments of ecclesiastical infirmaries, notably those of Ely and Canterbury. At Ramsey in Huntingdonshire the large, aisled, late twelfth-century guest-house has become the parish church. Norwich, apart from the infirmary, has outside the precinct the Great Hospital, founded by a bishop in 1249. This, 200 feet long, consists again of an aisled hall and an aisleless chapel east of it.

But the best preserved hospitals of the twelfth and thirteenth centuries are in France: first Angers, founded in 1153 and built in the later twelfth century, a noble aisled hall, about 200 feet long, with Angevin rib-vaults; then Ourscamp (Oise), Cistercian, early thirteenth-century, and aisled too; and then Tonnerre (Yonne), founded in 1293, aisleless, about 330 feet long and covered by a wooden tunnel-vault.[17] Other medieval hospitals in Paris were the Quinze-Vingts,

founded by Louis IX for the blind and closed only at the end of the eighteenth century, the Trinité, founded by Philip Augustus as a hospice for travellers and famous at the end of the Middle Ages for its performances of Passion Plays (see p. 66), the Maladrerie du Tortoir, a lazar house of the fourteenth century, still preserved,[18] and the Saint Esprit, created for orphans and foundlings about the middle of the sixteenth century and swallowed up by the Hôtel de Ville (see p. 56).[19] All these served specific, not general, functions. Separation was also fairly frequent in the Middle Ages for asylums for the insane. Burdett refers to Ghent in Belgium and Bethlehem in London for the twelfth and thirteenth centuries, and to Valencia, Saragossa, Seville, Valladolid and Toledo for the fifteenth.[20] In Germany Philip the Magnanimous in 1533 founded a hospital chiefly for the insane in the secularized Cistercian abbey of Haina.

But the largest and most famous, or rather infamous, of all hospitals was not diversified – the Hôtel-Dieu in Paris.[21] It stood west of Notre Dame and in its monstrous seventeenth-century development extended across the south arm of the Seine and on to the south bank. Nothing of it survives, but we know that it had four long two-naved wards, three in a row and the fourth at right angles: the Salle St Denis, the Salle St

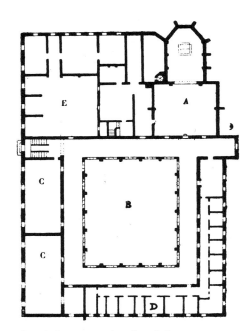

9.9 Kües, hospital, 1447: A chapel, B cloister, C common rooms, D individual rooms, E services

9.8 Beaune, Hôtel-Dieu, 1443–51

Thomas, the Infirmerie and the Salle Neuve. They were built between the late twelfth century and about 1260. The estimated total number of beds at the end of the Middle Ages is about 450, the estimated number of patients about 1,280, i.e. three patients to a bed, without discrimination of illness. Mortality figures are ghastly: 1415/16 2,057; 1416/17 1,830; 1418 5,311; 1522 2,471; 1523 3,766; 1524 5,729; 1525 2,097.[22] Other hospitals whose size is more or less known were much smaller: Nuremberg (fourteenth century) 200 patients, Nördlingen (c. 1400) 400, Augsburg (1493) 500, Ulm (1502) 209; and it must not be forgotten that such figures may include the poor, travellers and even paying guests staying for a period or for the rest of their lives.[23] 'Privatae camerae' are referred to in Cologne in the mid-twelfth century[24] and 'pensionnaires', even couples, in the Hôtel-Dieu in the thirteenth century.[25]

For the later Middle Ages it is enough to mention two hospitals for their founders and the perfection of their preservation. The hospital at Kües on the Moselle was established in 1447 by Cardinal Nicholas of Cusa, the philosopher and theologian. It was an almshouse entirely and has the unusual plan of ranges round a cloister. Nicolas Rollin, chancellor of Burgundy, built the Hôtel-Dieu at Beaune in 1443–51. The oldest ward is about 235 feet long and had originally in its sanctuary Roger van der Weyden's *Last Judgment* triptych. Even the tapestry bedcovers of the time of the completion of the building are still there. Two more ranges were

added soon so that the whole consisted of three ranges round a courtyard.

But by the mid-fifteenth century a new type of hospital premises was developing in Italy. Its first example is S. Maria Nuova in Florence, founded by Folco Portinari in 1286 'ad opus pauperum et infirmorum'.[26] In 1334 a new men's department was built, and this was cruciform, i.e. four wards radiated from a centre in which the altar was placed. The east-west arms were much shorter than the north-south arms. A second cross for women was added in 1657–60.[27] Incidentally, it is worth noting that the men were looked after by *conversi*, the women by *oblate*, i.e. lay brothers and lay sisters.

The plan scheme of S. Maria Nuova created a revolution in hospital planning, but not at once. The first hospitals following S. Maria Nuova belong to the years 1420–80. The first was the Pammatone in Genoa,[28] which was begun in 1422 and after some delays built briskly in the forties. The statute is of 1442. The purpose was formulated as service for the 'pauperes infirmos'. *Conversi* and *oblate* looked after the inmates. Pope Sixtus IV was Ligurian and we shall have ample proof of his interest in better hospitals. At the Pammatone during his rulership of the Church, i.e. c. 1475, rebuilding began. It was on the cruciform plan. The hospital also dedicated itself to foundlings – 2,820 in 1741.[29] (A new large building was begun in the 1750s to designs by Bartolommeo Orsolino. This has a palatial façade and is

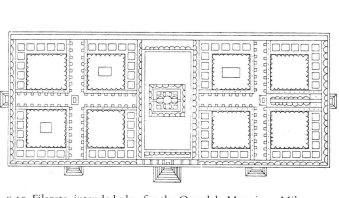

9.10 Filarete, intended plan for the Ospedale Maggiore, Milan (after his *Treatise*, early 1460s)

9.11 Milan, Ospedale Maggiore, begun 1456, by Filarete (the lower section at the far right) and others

not cruciform.) The cruciform plan of the building of the 1440s was, we are told, the result of visits to the hospitals of Florence and Siena. Florence of course means S. Maria Nuova; Siena must mean S. Maria della Scala. S. Maria della Scala survives, but the history of its buildings has not yet been unravelled.[30] It looks as if no consistent plan was adopted when the buildings went up in the first half of the fifteenth century. The justly famous frescoes by Domenico di Bartolo are in the so-called Pellegrinaccio and date from between 1440 and 1444. For the time being it remains mysterious why the architect of the Genoa hospital should have been sent to Siena. Nor was he the only one. We hear that at Brescia the new building of 1447–52 was designed 'sicut in civitate Senarum'. Little of it is preserved, but it is known that it was cruciform.[31] Pavia followed immediately, inspired probably by Brescia. But here also it is explicitly stated that the building was to be 'ad instar Florentini et Senen[sis] Hospitalium'. It was built in 1449–56 and it was indeed cruciform again.[32] Much was changed in the eighteenth century but fragments of the original building survive.

The fifties saw the start of a new cruciform hospital at Mantua (built 1450–72 and attributed to Luca Fancelli),[33] and of the most important of all Italian Renaissance hospitals, the Ospedale Maggiore in Milan. This was designed by the Florentine Filarete who, having been sent to Florence specially by Duke Francesco Sforza to look at S. Maria Nuova, used the cruciform

scheme when the Duke commissioned him in 1456 to build an unprecedentedly large hospital. Building continued very slowly into the nineteenth century.[34] The hospital was badly damaged in the Second World War but has since been restored for various purposes (university, hospitals' administration).[35] Filarete's plan is fully shown and annotated in his *Treatise*.[36] It is a rectangle, about 1,000 feet along the façade, divided into three parts: the central part consists of a large court with in the middle the chapel – a veritable church, centrally planned and with four minaret-like towers;[37] the left and right thirds each contain four wards arranged in a cross, with an altar in the crossing. Each ward was for sixty beds. Building began in the right third, and here Filarete's Tuscan Renaissance forms are easily recognized. After Filarete's departure, the executant masons returned, however, to North Italian florid Gothic. The centre court and the church are early seventeenth-century, by Ricchini. The left third is later yet. On Filarete's plan the colonnades of the ground floor were intended to be left open, for circulation of the sick as well as provisions and laundry. In his *Treatise* he describes in ingenious drawings arrangements which he intended to provide. Water was to be stored in a cistern or tank and conducted through vaulted passages with a certain fall all along the wards and ultimately down to the river. Above the passages was to be another set of passages, and these were to contain the lavatory seats. Access to the lavatories was

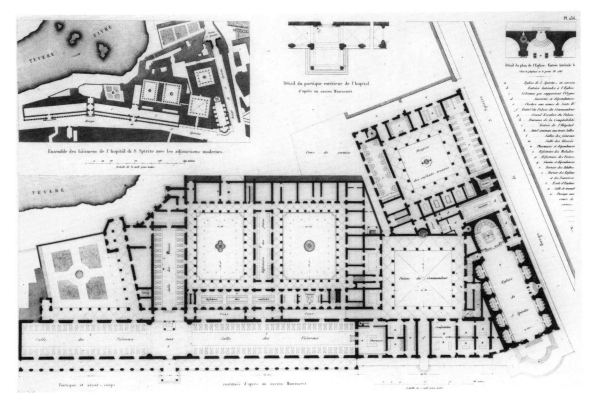

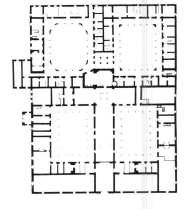

9.12 Rome, Hospital of Santo Spirito in Sassia, 1474–82 (range at bottom left) and later

9.13, 14 Santiago de Compostela, Hospital Real, 1501–11, by Enrique Egas: plan (above right) and portal (right)

to be by trapdoors between the beds. To each bed incidentally was to belong a small cupboard (*armarietto*), a chest and a flap-table. Civilization was evidently marching on.

From S. Maria Nuova and the Ospedale Maggiore the cruciform plan spread to the hospital of Santo Spirito in Sassia as rebuilt by Baccio Pontelli for Sixtus IV in 1474–82.[38] That part, just under 400 feet long, consists of two arms of the cross only, in line, and separated by what in the fully cruciform scheme would be the crossing. The dome over the crossing and the canopy over the altar were added by Palladio.[39] Enlargements took place in the seventeenth and eighteenth centuries so that in the end the site housed a short ward running at right angles to the old ones, the palace of the Commander of the order, an asylum for 500 insane persons and a foundling hospital for 800.

Direct influence from Santo Spirito is evident in the Great Hospital of the Order of St John at Valletta on Malta, built in 1575. Like Santo Spirito, it consists of a long range with another shorter range at right angles to it. The main range was originally 185 feet long, extended in 1662–63 to 504 feet. There were two superimposed wards and a basement. Patients received care that can only be called luxurious. An English naval chaplain, Henry Teonge, described it in 1675: the ward is, he writes, 'so broade that twelve men may with ease walke abreast up the midst of it; and the bedds are on each syde, standing on four yron pillars, with white curtens ... extremely neate, and kept cleane and sweete: the sick served all in sylver plate; and it contains above 200 beds ...'. (But by 1863 the wards were called dark, dismal and close.)[40] On both main floors there was a narrow window and a wall-cupboard next to each bed. On the seaward side the pairs of windows are grouped vertically within a single moulding, so that they seem to reach almost from ground level to cornice. On the landward side is an arcaded courtyard, beyond which other buildings were later added.

At the very beginning of the sixteenth century the cruciform plan appeared once in England and several times in Spain. The English case was the Savoy, built by Henry VII on the site of the Savoy Palace.[41] The earliest Spanish cases are the Hospital Real at Santiago de Compostela of 1501–11,[42] the Hospital de la Santa Cruz in Toledo of 1504–14[43] and the Hospital Real at Granada, begun also in 1504, but built slowly. All three were designed by Enrique Egas; the first and third were royal foundations, the second was founded by Cardinal Mendoza. The first two have totally Italian Quattro-

9.12

9.13,

9.15,

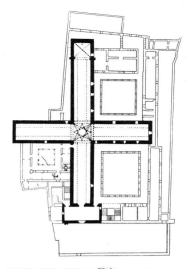

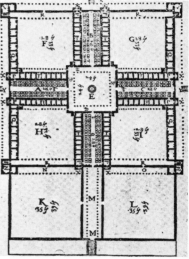

9.15, 16 Toledo, Hospital de la Santa Cruz, 1504–14, by Enrique Egas: crossing (above) and plan (above right)

9.17 (right) Philibert Delorme, design for a hospital (*Oeuvre Entière*, 2nd ed., 1626)

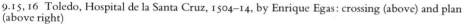

cento decoration of great elegance. Cruciform hospitals were also built in the sixteenth century at Valencia and at Seville, both begun in 1546.[44] The plan reached South America at once and Germany and France in the 1620s. Cortez built a cruciform hospital at Mexico City in 1524.[45] As for Germany, the plan appears in Furttenbach's *Architectura civilis* published in 1628 and in his *Architectura universalis* published in 1635; and as for France, the 1626 edition of Delorme's *Oeuvre entière* has a cruciform plan, and the Hôpital des Incurables in Paris of 1635–49 (by Christophe Gamard) is a combination of two crosses.[46]

The Incurables was not the only new hospital of its age in Paris. The decades of Henri IV and Louis XIII saw quite a number of new institutions, built mostly outside the ramparts. Their functions were not all the same, and in some cases they were mixed from the beginning or later on. Let us take Bicêtre as an example.[47] It started as a palace of the Duc de Berry. On its site Louis XIII built a first Hôtel des Invalides. Building began in 1634 and was left unfinished. The façade was of 33 bays. In 1656 its function was changed. It became a poorhouse. In 1660 insane persons were admitted, at the end of the seventeenth century juvenile delinquents, in 1729 other criminals. In 1836

the prison moved to the Grande Roquette, in 1837 the juveniles to the Petite Roquette (see below, p. 166). Bicêtre then became a hospice for old men too. The mixture must have been of even more ingredients; for Tenon, in his report on hospitals of 1788 (see p. 152), could write that there were 'the poor young and old, able or invalid, the mad, the imbecile, the epileptic, the . . . blind [and] all kinds of incurables',[48] and Maxime du Camp in his large work on Paris published in 1869–75 used nearly the same words: 'murderers, the debauched, the sick, the poor, the incontinent, the idiots lived pêle-mêle in the most frightful promiscuity . . .' – 'D'un seul mot, c'était un cloaque.'[49] A history of Bicêtre published in 1890 lists the variety of inmates, but states that they were classified and divided up from one another, not mixed up together in the same buildings.[50] The Salpêtrière – the name commemorates a powder magazine erected on the site in 1634 – was hardly more specialized.[51] It began in 1656 as a poorhouse and foundling hospital. In 1684 criminal women came in, and about the same time epileptics and lunatics. Tenon in 1788 wrote more or less the same as on Bicêtre: 'Old women, old men, raving lunatics, imbeciles, epileptics, paralytics, cripples, the blind and so on',[52] and the Duc de la Rochefoucauld Liancourt (Thomas Jefferson's

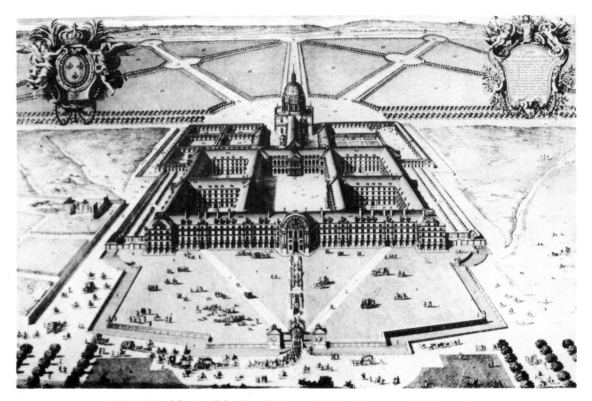

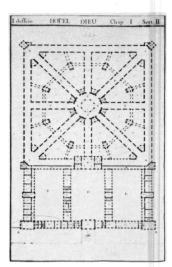

9.18 Paris, Hôtel des Invalides, founded 1670, by Libéral Bruant and Jules Hardouin-Mansart

9.19 (above right) Antoine Desgodets, design for a hospital, late 17th c.
9.20 (right) L. C. Sturm, design for a hospital (*Vollständige Anweisung*, 1720)

friend) added: 'Nulle douceur, nulle consolation, nuls remèdes.'[53] The Salpêtrière received, thanks to the munificence of Mazarin, buildings designed by Levau, who also designed the chapel of Bicêtre.

The best hospital building of the first two thirds of the seventeenth century was, in the opinion of contemporaries, the Hôpital St Louis founded by Henri IV in 1607 and designed by Claude Vellefaux. It was still praised by Tenon in 1788 and Clavereau in 1805. The Pitié started in 1612–13 as yet another poorhouse. The Charité was founded by Marie de Médicis in 1602. It was small – only 150 beds – and was considered a model hospital. Each patient had a bed to himself. It was in fact, like the St Louis, a hospital in our sense exclusively. Another specialized hospital was that created by St Vincent de Paul in 1638 for orphans and foundlings.

Only the Hôtel-Dieu remained as frightful as it had been in the Middle Ages, in spite of additions made under Henri IV by Vellefaux.[54] Cuvier could still write of it: 'Les souffrances de l'enfer doivent surpasser à peine celles de ces malheureux serrés les uns sur les autres, étouffés, brûlants, ne pouvant . . . respirer, sentant quelque fois un ou deux morts entre eux.'[55] In the 1790s Stieglitz exclaimed, 'How infinitely cruel is the way they pack four or six unfortunate patients into one bed',[56] and La Rochefoucauld Liancourt in his report

(see below, p. 152), even made it six or even eight to one bed.

Among the model foundations was the Invalides, founded in 1670 for old or disabled soldiers. The design of the hospital is by Bruant, but that of the celebrated chapel of St Louis-des-Invalides is the masterpiece of Hardouin-Mansart. The Invalides was matched by the Chelsea Hospital in London founded only twelve years later. The architect here was Wren. The Chelsea Hospital is much smaller than the Invalides.[57] Where England wanted to emulate or, better still, to outdo France, was in provision for the Navy. That is why the Greenwich Hospital, begun in 1694, became the grandest of all English palaces.

For the eighteenth century in Paris a distinguishing feature is the creation and endowment or part-endowment of new hospitals by private largesse[58] after fires had destroyed much of the Hôtel-Dieu (see below, pp. 150–51). Madame Necker in 1773 endowed a small model hospital,[59] Abbé Cochin in 1780 built a small hospice to a design (given without a fee) by C.-F. Viel,[60] Beaumont in his last years, i.e. in 1780–81, gave to the poor a million francs, and the Duc de la Rochefoucauld Liancourt was the chief donor to the Retraite of the Frères de la Charité,[61] whose building of 1781–83 was by Antoine, architect of the Monnaie. Finally Nicolas

9.18

9.21,

9.21 Greenwich, Royal Naval Hospital, founded 1694, by Sir Christopher Wren and others

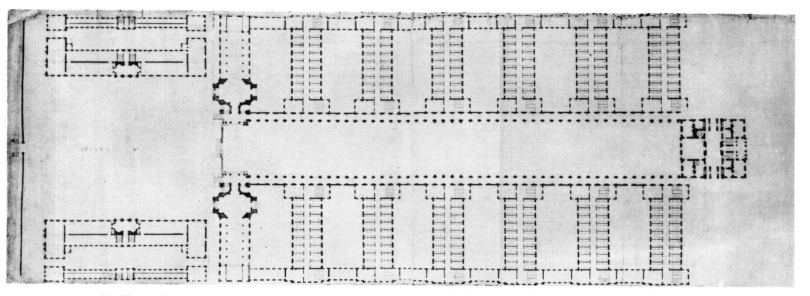

9.22 Sir Christopher Wren, unexecuted design on the pavilion principle for the Royal Naval Hospital, Greenwich, before 1702
(Oxford, All Souls College)

Beaujon, the great financier, bought up a large area by the Etoile and the Champs Elysées and founded an orphanage in 1784–85.[62] More important for the development of hospital design in the late eighteenth century than the private endowment of small new institutions, however, is a series of major buildings proposed but never executed (below, pp. 151–54).

But all this is anticipating. We must first go back to the cruciform plan and see what happened to it in the late seventeenth and early eighteenth century. For once the cruciform plan had been accepted, it could only be a matter of time for someone to hit on the idea that more spokes than four would allow more beds within the same area. The earliest of these radial plans we know about is by Antoine Desgodets, better known for his *Edifices antiques de Rome* of 1682.[63] His plan, already referred to by Tenon, was for an octagon centre and sixteen radiating wards. The centre was to carry a dome which served the purpose of sucking out used air. The lavatories were to be in the inner angles between the wards, and more wards ran along the periphery. This scheme, probably dating from the end of the seventeenth century, must have become known to Leonhard Christoph Sturm, who spent ten weeks in France in 1699. In his *Vollständige Anweisung allerhand Öffentliche Zucht- und Liebesgebäud . . . wohl anzugeben*, which has

the date 1720, is an ideal hospital, which has an octagonal church as its centre and eight radiating wards.[64] The whole formed a rectangle like the Ospedale Maggiore, and attached to the centre courtyard were three more courtyards on one side and three more on the opposite side. They are surrounded by more wards, and Sturm estimates that 1,525 patients would find space easily.

The radial plan was to have a revival over fifty years after Sturm. The cruciform plan lived on into the nineteenth century, especially for asylum buildings. Examples are Glasgow by William Stark, 1810–14,[65] Wakefield 1814–16 (by Watson & Pritchett; two crosses), Erlangen of 1814–16, and a design by Joseph Franck of 1818.[66] Asylums could have a chapter to themselves in this book, as prisons indeed do have. However, they have enough in common with hospitals to be given hospitality in this chapter. Dr D. J. Rothman could call his excellent recent book *The Discovery of the Asylum* and yet deal with prisons, poorhouses, orphanages and institutions for delinquent juveniles as well.[67]

The eighteenth century, especially in Britain, produced an unprecedented crop of hospitals, and it is not easy to select the most significant events and buildings. To illustrate quantity London is the best example. St Bartholomew's, St Thomas's and Bethlehem (Bedlam)

9.23 London, Bethlehem Hospital, 1675–76 by Robert Hooke

9.24 London Hospital, 1751–57, by Boulton Mainwaring

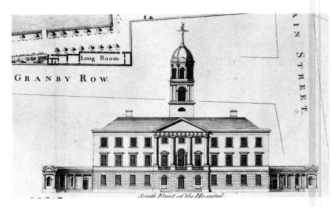

9.25 Dublin, Rotunda Hospital, 1745, by Richard Cassels

9.23 were medieval foundations. They were rebuilt in the late seventeenth and the early eighteenth centuries – Bart's by Gibbs in detached ashlar-faced blocks, starting in 1730. For the new hospitals, here are the dates:[68] Westminster 1719, Guy's 1720, St George's 1733, the London Hospital 1740, the Foundling 1742, the Middlesex 1745, St Luke's 1751.

9.24 In its appearance, the London Hospital, as designed by Boulton Mainwaring and built in 1751–57, is typical; in its size it was exceptional – twenty-three bays wide, with a pediment over the middle seven, and three storeys high. Of the London hospitals here enumerated, it will have been noticed that one was for foundling 9.23 children only; Bethlehem and St Luke's were for lunatics only. The Lying-In Hospital, founded in 1749, served another special purpose, and the same special purpose was served by the City of London Maternity of 1750 and Queen Charlotte's of 1752.[69] Mostly in the second half of the eighteenth century, the provinces began to emulate London. The list is long and includes some special-purpose foundations: Edinburgh 1729, Glasgow 1733, Royal Hampshire, Winchester 1736, Royal Infirmary, Bristol 1736, County Hospital, York 1741, Royal Infirmary, Aberdeen 1742, General Hospital, Northampton 1743, Royal Devon, Exeter 1743, Royal Salop, Shrewsbury 1745, Rotunda (Lying-In), 9.25 Dublin 1745, Royal Infirmary, Worcester 1746 (present building 1767–71 by Keek), Royal Infirmary, Liverpool 1749, Royal Victoria, Newcastle 1751, Royal Infirmary, Manchester 1752, Royal Gloucestershire, Gloucester 1755, Royal Infirmary, Chester 1761, Addenbrooke's, Cambridge 1766, Staffordshire General, Stafford 1766,

General Infirmary, Salisbury 1767, General Infirmary, Leeds 1769, Lincoln County Hospital 1769, Radcliffe, Oxford 1770, Royal Infirmary, Leicester 1771, Norfolk and Norwich 1772, Bootham, York 1772–77 (by Carr, 9.26 for the insane), General, Hereford 1776, General, Birmingham 1779 and so on to the Retreat at York of 1796, a Quaker foundation for the more humane treatment of the insane.[70] But how could a humane treatment be expected, as long as ordinary people visited Bedlam for a morning's entertainment? The founder of the Retreat was William Tuke, whose son published in 1813 a description of the Retreat and in 1815 *Practical Hints on the Construction . . . of Pauper Lunatic Asylums*. He had been preceded in France by Philippe Pinel, chief physician of Bicêtre and the Salpêtrière. His *Traité médico-philosophique de l'aliénation mentale* had come out in 1798.

Other distinguished psychiatrists pleading for the insane were Jean-Etienne-Dominique Esquirol, who died in 1840, and John Conolly, whose principal book came out in 1856 and is called *Treatment of the Insane without mechanical Restraints*.[71] The title is telling. Treatment in the early nineteenth century can hardly be distinguished from torture, even if the intention was often good: sudden dropping of the patient into cold water, and use of a circular swing that revolved with the patient a hundred times a minute.[72] Patients in chains are noted by Burdett in Spain in 1846, in Wales in 1853 (where the patient was in a shed 9 feet 4 inches by 6 feet) and in Salt Lake City as late as 1886.[73] But Dickens, who travelled in America in 1842[74] and who made a point of visiting establishments of social function, calls the State

9.27 Naples, Albergo dei Poveri, begun 1751, by Ferdinando Fuga

9.26 York, Bootham Asylum, 1772–77, by John Carr

9.28 Lyons, Hôtel-Dieu, begun 1741, by J.-G. Soufflot

Asylum in South Boston 'admirably conducted' on 'enlightened principles', the poorhouse (House of Industry), also in South Boston, 'arranged with a view to peace and comfort', and in the 'asylum for neglected and indigent boys' he looked at the inmates and says: 'A more chubby-looking . . . set of boys I never saw.' He does not comment on the external appearance of any of these American buildings. There was nothing which would have differed noticeably from comparable institutions in England.

We can take the Retreat at York as a first example. It has a centre of five bays with a pedimented doorway and six-bay wings. Bootham Park has a three-bay pediment and had originally a cupola. Worcester has seven bays and a three-bay centre. In short, these later eighteenth-century hospitals were of standard Georgian domestic forms, and it was also standard that in the early nineteenth century they took to the severe Grecian.

Diversification, as this list has shown, was still rare in England. Nor was it more frequent in Italy and France. As for Italy it must not be forgotten that the Ospedale degli Innocenti in Florence, which was begun in 1419 by Brunelleschi, was a foundling hospital. For the insane only ('ad insaniem curandum') S. Maria della Pietà was built in 1561. In the eighteenth century the most interesting special hospitals in Italy were the Alberghi dei Poveri, the largest of them in Naples and Genoa. That in Genoa – the Pammatone – has already been mentioned; that in Naples was created by Charles of Bourbon in 1751 and designed by Fuga. Building went on till 1829 and then only half was ready. The total front was to be about 1,160 feet long – as against the King's palace of Caserta, begun in the very same year and only some 830 feet long.[75] Fuga had planned a central hexagonal church and six radial halls.

Only one hospital of a comparable size was built in France, the Hôtel-Dieu at Lyons, designed by Soufflot, the architect of the Panthéon in Paris (pp. 17, 76). It was begun in 1741 and completed only in 1842. It is about 1,060 feet long. In style it is typical of its date.

The same is true of the Georgian hospitals, poorhouses and asylums in America. With their long fronts, with or without projecting wings, with or without porticoes, and with or without a cupola, they are much like country houses and, for that matter, factories (p. 276). Dr Rothman illustrates for instance the Boston House of Industry of 1821 (the one that Dickens visited) and the New York Almshouse and House of Refuge, both of 1825.[76] Houses of Refuge were for children and adolescents, orphans, foundlings and also delinquents.

Dr Rothman's survey of conditions in these institutions is so competent and so fully documented that a selected assembly of data from the States and from the late eighteenth and early nineteenth centuries elsewhere may be inserted here as a summing up. Dr Rothman's principal theory is that large and forbidding-looking piles were the visual equivalent to the faith in order of the Age of Enlightenment. Once order had been enforced, the insane would be quieter and the prisoners, including the delinquent young, would be ready for self-reformation. For prisoners old and young that meant for instance total removal from all exterior influences such as those of family and mates. Applica-

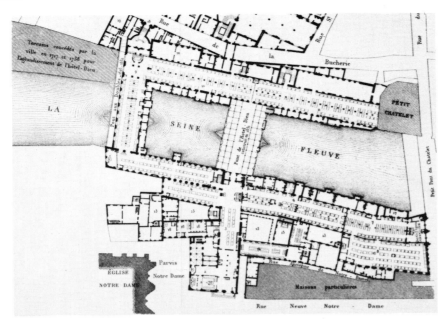

9.29 Paris, Hôtel-Dieu: plan before the fire of 1772

tion of such principles was cruel, but they were at least principles. But cruelty and misery appeared in other parts as well. For instance, as the nineteenth century proceeded, poorhouses suffered from overcrowding and hence appalling hygienic conditions. Even after 1850 American reports still state that poorhouses are 'filthy beyond description' and 'frequently swarm with vermin'. 'Common domestic animals', another report says, 'are usually more humanely provided for than the paupers.'[77] If there was no zest to improve, one reason was the widely accepted – though blatantly false – theory that the poor are poor because of their 'vicious appetites'.[78] That establishments for children and adolescents were treating them cruelly cannot surprise anyone familiar with the use of the rod in schools.[79] Physical cruelty was matched by the psychological cruelty of silence at work and at meals.

If this was done to children, how would staff treat the insane?[80] Pinel's and Tuke's books were a plea for humane treatment (see above, p. 148). Naturally private asylums run without any public control tended to be worse. Yet by 1848 half the licensed asylums were private,[81] and Lord Shaftesbury in 1859 called 'the whole system . . . utterly abominable and indefensible'.[82] Defoe had known it over a century before. In 1728 he wrote of 'these cursed houses' and 'the barbarous usage' in them and demanded 'proper visitation and inspection'.[83] Cruelty in the treatment of the insane was caused at best by wrong therapeutic ideas, at worst by sadism. Dr Rothman has examples or contemporary testimony.

To return now to hospitals proper, mortality in seventeenth- and eighteenth-century hospitals was still terrible. Chamousset in 1756 gives the figure one in four for the Hôtel-Dieu in Paris as against one in eight for the Charité.[84] He had suggested in 1754 that an insurance company ought to be created, and that people ought to pay monthly contributions according to their means.

He suggested four classes. If you are rich, older and want a suite in the hospital, you pay 5 livres or more. For 3 livres you get a room to yourself, for 40 sous a bed in a three-bed room, for 30 sous you are in a twelve-bed room, for 25 sous in a room with thirty beds.[85]

When Chamousset wrote this, a fire had destroyed one part of the Hôtel-Dieu; in 1772 another fire destroyed much of the rest. What was to be done? Should one rebuild on the site? Should one move the whole hospital? Should one reduce the number of patients by placing some, according to their complaint, in other hospitals? A spate of pamphlets, reports, committees, designs appeared from 1773 to the early years of the nineteenth century.[86]

It may be profitable to present them chronologically. The years in question are incidentally exactly the same as those of the many plans and treatises on theatre building (see pp. 80–81), a telling indication of the interest in functional design during the Age of Reason. The fire took place in the last days of December 1772. In 1773 the administration of the hospital suggested a transfer to the Plaine de Grenelle, behind the Ecole Militaire. A move had already been proposed before the first fire. It was made in 1749 by the Abbé A.-M.-D. Le Jeune, and the suggested site was the Île des Cygnes.[87] Also in 1773 or thereabouts several pamphlets were issued: by Caqué, by Penseron,[88] by Renier (printed in 1776).[89]

In 1773 Jean-Baptiste Le Roy, a scientist, suggested rebuilding on a plan which was at the time revolutionary for France. However, the project was not presented to the Académie Royale des Sciences until 1777 and only published ten years later than that.[90] The plan was worked out in collaboration with Charles-François Viel. The novelty was single-storey wards parallel to each other (unfortunately close together) running at right angles left and right of a large courtyard, at the near end of which were to be service blocks, at the far

9.29

9.30

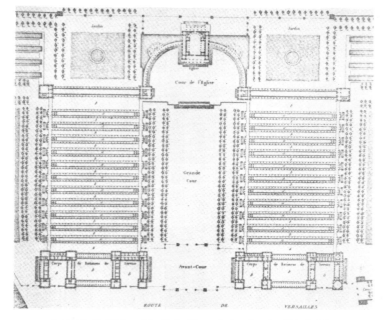

9.30 C.-F. Viel and J.-B. Le Roy, design for the Hôtel-Dieu, 1773

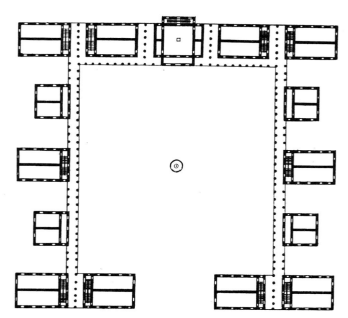

9.31 Stonehouse, near Plymouth, Royal Naval Hospital, 1756–64, by Rowehead (Durand, *Recueil*, 1801)

end the church. In his report Le Roy made the memorable statement so characteristic of the Lamettrie moment: 'A ward is, as it were, a machine for treating the sick.'[91] His wards had ample ventilation ducts in the roof; for lack of ventilation was at the time believed to be the main reason for the high mortality in the Hôtel-Dieu. Books and pamphlets dealing with ventilation had been and were published, such as Henri-Louis Duhamel de Moreau's *Différents moyens pour renouveler l'air des infirmeries*, read to the Académie des Sciences in 1748, and Claude-Léopold de Genneté's *Nouvelle construction des cheminées*, 1759. Their suggestions are based on Stephen Hales's *A Description of Ventilators* of 1743.

The principle of planning hospitals with detached pavilions left and right of a courtyard was not invented by Le Roy. It had been used in 1756–64 for the Naval Hospital at Stonehouse near Plymouth, where, however, the pavilions were very small. The effect is nearer Louis XIV's Marly than Le Roy's hospital.[92] The architect of the Naval Hospital was called Rowehead. His pioneer role was soon realized. Howard in his *Lazarettos* of 1789 and Durand in his *Recueil* illustrated Stonehouse.

Le Roy's scheme, as we have seen, was not publicly available in the seventies. What happened instead is that Louis XV ordered a transfer of the patients of the Hôtel-Dieu to St Louis and the Santé. The King died in 1774, and nothing happened. In the same year a project was published which was as bold as Le Roy's but based on another principle. Its author was the surgeon Antoine Petit, and the title of the publication is *Mémoire sur la meilleure manière de construire un hôpital des malades*. His proposed site was not the Ile des Cygnes, but the hill of Belleville, north-east of the centre of Paris.[93] The plan was a vast circle; in it, running radially from a domed centre, were six long wards. The dome served as a ventilator. The plan is not new to us. Petit must have been familiar with Desgodets' scheme.[94]

In 1775 the staff of the Hôtel-Dieu made it known that they would welcome a move to the Ile des Cygnes. However, they knew that it would cost too much. In 1776 Louis XVI gathered a Commission to examine and investigate hospitals. They suggested among other things the establishment of small hospital units in various parishes, and the new hospitals founded by private munificence (see p. 146) were small indeed.

In 1777, it must be remembered, John Howard brought out his epoch-making book on prisons. Architecturally what he suggested comes close to what was suggested in Paris for hospital buildings (see the next chapter, p. 162). Six years later, in 1783, Hugues Maret's *Mémoire sur la construction d'un hôpital*,[95] dealing specially with ventilation, appeared. Finally in 1785 the architects Claude-Philippe Coquéau and Bernard Poyet published anonymously the *Mémoire sur la nécessité de transférer et reconstruire l'Hôtel-Dieu à Paris*. Poyet was Contrôleur des Bâtiments to the City of Paris. The plan is radial like Petit's, but where Petit has six radii and 2,000 beds, Poyet proposed sixteen and 5,000 beds. For the site, the Ile des Cygnes is again suggested. Four years earlier Francesco Milizia (pp. 16, 80) brought out his *Principi di architettura civile*. In his discussion of hospitals he deprecates 'edifici grandiosi' in the large cities and like the French writers suggests building hospitals outside.[96] As for Coquéau and Poyet's plan, the King passed it to the Académie des Sciences to be examined. A committee of eight was nominated (including Lavoisier, La Place and Franklin's friend Bailly). They reported in 1786.[97] The first part of their report is severe criticism of the Hôtel-Dieu. The insane are the next-door neighbours of the surgical cases, infectious diseases are not separated and so on. We know the complaints. The Commission turned down Poyet's plan and suggested instead Le Roy's scheme, read, as will be remembered, to the Académie in 1777. The Commission also pleaded for no more than 36 beds in a ward,

9.22
9.31

.32, 34

9.34
9.32

9.19

9.33, 35

9.34

9.30

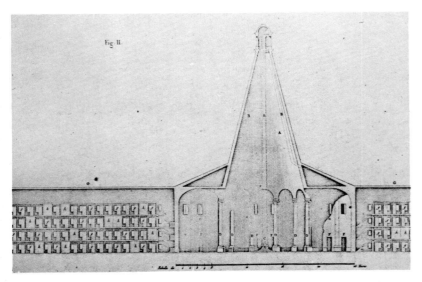

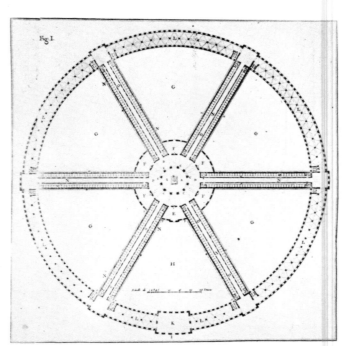

9.32, 34 Antoine Petit, design for the Hôtel-Dieu: section of the centre, and plan (*Mémoire*, 1774)

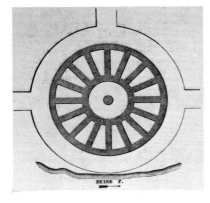

9.33, 35 Bernard Poyet, design for the Hôtel-Dieu: view and plan (*Mémoire*, 1785)

all single beds, iron bedsteads and iron window frames. The place of the Hôtel-Dieu should be taken by four hospitals each of *c.* 1,200 beds: St Louis, the Santé, the Célestins abbey and a new one beyond the Ecole Militaire. A second report, dated 1787, changed the locations of the proposed four hospitals, a third, dated 1788, made more changes.

9.36
9.30, 31
In the second report a revised plan by Poyet appears, and this is now on the Stonehouse-Le Roy pattern. Le Roy's own scheme was made public in the same year. Other plans considered by the Commission included one by Dr Iberti, which was a cross-scheme with the kitchen and not the chapel in the middle.[98] The cruciform plan had indeed been kept going, but in the St Andrew's cross variation, in Laugier's *Observations sur l'architecture* of 1765 and the Hospital of S. Luigi Gonzaga in Turin of 1794.[99]

The year 1788 saw the publication of the most valuable of the *mémoires* on hospitals. The author was J. R. Tenon, a distinguished surgeon and a member of the Académie des Sciences, and the title is *Mémoires sur les hôpitaux de Paris*. We have already more than once had opportunity to quote from it. It is an extremely well-informed[100] and well-organized book, with plenty of statistical tables, and it is written clearly and not without elegance. To be able to judge the hospital situation, Tenon even undertook a journey to England, where he found arrangements preferable to those in France. His details about the state of the Hôtel-Dieu are indeed appalling, as appalling as those given by his predecessors. The passages on the latrines are a specially unsavoury example. One of the most terrifying descriptions is that of the room where the operations took place, for in the same room lay those to be operated on next day and those operated on the day before. It must be remembered that there was not yet any means for making the patient feel less. As for overcrowding, Tenon confirms the appalling figures given by Chamousset. They had meanwhile already been confirmed by the Duc de La Rochefoucauld Liancourt (see above, pp. 145–46) in the second report to the Académie des Sciences of 1787.[101] La Rochefoucauld says six to eight in one bed, Tenon

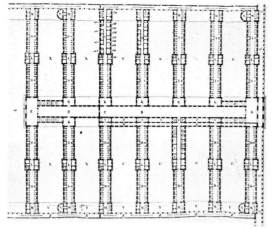

9.36 Bernard Poyet, design for a
hospital at La Roquette, first published
in 1787 (Durand, *Recueil*, 1801)

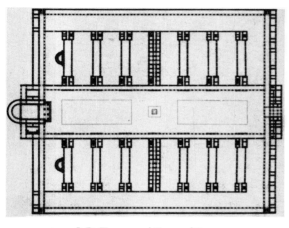

9.37 J. R. Tenon and Bernard Poyet,
design for a hospital at La Roquette
(Tenon, *Mémoires*, 1788)

9.38 J.-N.-L. Durand, design for a
hospital: elevation and plan (*Précis*, II,
1809)

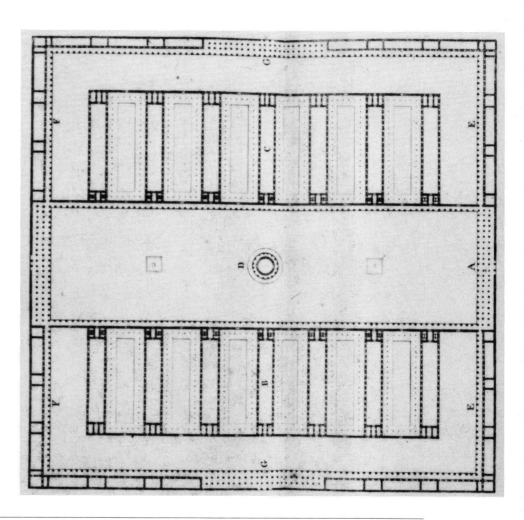

more precisely 486 in single beds, 1,230 in beds of four
to six. Chamousset's mortality figure is confirmed by
Tenon. Tenon's summing-up is that the Hôtel-Dieu is
an 'assemblage monstrueux, plus propre à prolonger les
maux, à détruire, qu'à rétablir & à conserver la santé'.[102]
The last part of the book deals with plans for replacing
the Hôtel-Dieu and includes a design for a proposed
hospital at La Roquette (a suburb of Paris) on the
Stonehouse-Le Roy principle. Tenon acknowledges
help received from Poyet.

Little remains to be studied of the last years of the
century. In England John Howard's treatise *An Account of the Principal Lazarettos in Europe* came out in
1789, twelve years after his *The State of the Prisons in
England*. The lazaretto book has remarks and plans of
lazarettos at Marseilles, Genoa, Leghorn, Spezia and
other places and a long string of remarks about the
London and some provincial hospitals. The remarks
mix praise and criticism. A few examples may illustrate
this: London Hospital: 'There are no cisterns for
water; the vaults are often offensive . . . Medical and

chirurgical patients are together . . . In a dirty room in
the cellar there is a cold and a hot bath which seem to be
seldom used.' St Bartholomew's: 'The wards . . . were
clean . . . the windows were open.' St Thomas's: 'The
wards were fresh and clean . . . there were no water
closets.' St George's: 'The kitchens . . . are underground
and were neither neat nor clean. A good cold bath, but
not used.' Bethlehem: 'There is no separation of the
calm and quiet from the noisy and turbulent, except
those who are chained in their cells. To each side of the
house there is only one vault: very offensive.' St
Luke's: 'This noble hospital was neat and clean.'[103]
Norwich: 'This spacious infirmary was neat and clean;
the beds not crowded; the wards quiet and fresh.'
Radcliffe, Oxford: 'closeness and offensiveness of four
out of the five large wards'. Leeds: 'This is one of the
best hospitals in the kingdom.'[104] Haslar near Gosport
and of course Stonehouse are also praised,[105] at Stonehouse, which he calls 'this noble hospital', specifically
the system of detached pavilions. The lazaretto book
goes back to prisons as well and indeed devotes more

Vorderanficht.

1 : 1000

Fig. 378.

9.39 Paris, Hôpital Lariboisière, 1839–54, by Gauthier: façade and longitudinal section

pages to the subject of prisons than to hospitals.

Immediately after the turn of the century Durand in his *Recueil et parallèle* (of 1801) shows on one plate[106] the Ospedale Maggiore in Milan, the Pammatone in Genoa – both, as we have seen, developed on the cross pattern – St Louis and the Incurables in Paris, and also Stonehouse and Poyet's design from his second report, captioned by Durand as the hospital 'begun at La Roquette in 1788 to designs by Poyet'. The pavilion principle of the latter two was in fact Durand's own preference, as is proved by the one hospital design he published in his *Précis des leçons*.[107] This has seven pavilions on each side of a central avenue or elongated courtyard. At the end of this he places no buildings, only arrays of massed columns in the Boullée taste.[108]

In looking back over the period of about thirty-five years, it will at once be obvious that the French plans, though no doubt caused by the terrible state of the Hôtel-Dieu and intended to be a functional advance, were cast in the forms they took because elementary geometrical plan patterns were favoured in the Boullée-Ledoux-Durand period. The first to look for the functionally – i.e. medically – best plan and leave it at that were the English, even if Stonehouse remained an exception and big Classical blocks the rule.

In fact big blocks remained the rule on the Continent as well; the Stonehouse-Le Roy-Tenon scheme was used only rarely. Examples are the Hôpital St André at Bordeaux of 1825–29 (by J. Bourguet; of 650 beds), the Hôpital Beaujon in Paris of 1837–46, and the Hôpital St Jean at Brussels of 1838–49 (by Partois). Full accept-

ance of the pavilion plan came only with the Hôpital Lariboisière in Paris, planned in 1839[109] and built in 1846–54. It is named after the Countess Lariboisière who gave the money for the building. M.-P. Gauthier was the architect. The number of beds was 905. Klasen writes that Lariboisière 'created a new epoch in hospital building',[110] Ochsner and Sturm that it is 'one of the most admirable hospital plans in the world',[111] and Husson that it presents 'all the conditions of well-being and healthiness which an establishment of this nature can provide'.[112] The hospital has a long central court with the administration at one end, the chapel and other rooms at the other and three ward pavilions on either side at right angles to the court and parallel to each other. Each pavilion has 32 beds.[113]

It is here that Florence Nightingale comes into our story.[114] She was born in 1820, a daughter of a well-to-do country gentleman. When only about twenty she was attracted to the care of the sick. In 1844 she began to visit hospitals. The Deaconesses of Kaiserswerth, established as recently as 1833, impressed her particularly, and in 1851 she went for four months to Kaiserswerth to receive a nursing training. In 1853 she became the superintendent of the Hospital for Invalid Gentlewomen in London. In the same year she visited Paris. In the next year the Crimean War broke out. Care for the British wounded and the British sick was disgraceful. Two letters to *The Times* had drawn attention to them. French arrangements were patently better. So, on the suggestion of an old friend, Sidney Herbert, later Lord Herbert of Lea, who was at that moment

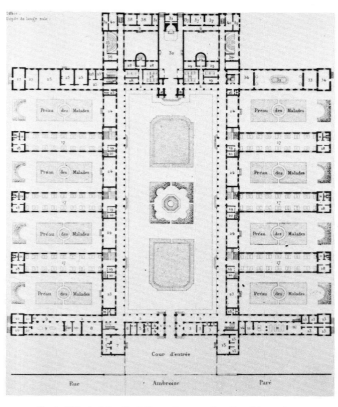

9.40 Paris, Hôpital Lariboisière, 1839–54, by Gauthier: plan

9.41 Netley, Royal Victoria Military Hospital, 1856–63

Secretary for War, she went to the Crimea taking with her thirty-eight nurses. The headquarters were a former barracks at Scutari (Üsküdar), across the Bosphorus from Constantinople. She began to act immediately with an iron energy no one had believed her capable of and with a clear head for organization. At the worst moment of cholera and dysentery the death-rate in the Scutari hospital was 42%; Florence Nightingale brought it down to 2%. In 1856, on the return of peace, she went home, debilitated by the war to such an extent that she considered herself henceforth an invalid. However, bed-ridden or not bed-ridden, she embarked on a campaign to improve conditions in English hospitals too, and she turned out a formidable adversary for those who countered her. In the centre of her campaign was the new Military Hospital at Netley in Hampshire. This vast building – it was 1,424 feet long[115] – was begun in 1856. Florence Nightingale wanted it demolished, as far as it had been built, and replaced by a building on the Lariboisière scheme. In fact she was not the first in England to believe in that scheme.[116] *The Builder* in August 1856 illustrated Netley without criticism, but then, thanks to its brilliant editor, George Godwin, woke up to the cause at once. In September it drew attention to the writings and lectures of John Roberton, an Edinburgh doctor. In a lecture he held in March 1856, he praised the existing pavilion buildings: St André in Bordeaux, St Jean in Brussels, Beaujon and Lariboisière in Paris. Florence Nightingale must have been aware of Roberton and *The Builder*. In 1857 she gave evidence to the newly appointed Royal Sanitary

Commission, in 1858 she published *Notes on Matters affecting the Health . . . of the British Army*, in 1859 *Notes on Hospitals*. Here is a sample from the latter:

It may seem a strange principle to enunciate as the very first requirement in a hospital that it should do the sick no harm. It is quite necessary nevertheless to lay down such a principle, because the actual mortality in hospitals, especially those of large crowded cities, is very much higher than any calculation founded upon the mortality of the same class of patient treated *out* of hospital would make one expect.[117]

Concerning the battle of Netley, a little more must be said. Florence Nightingale was sent the plans by Lord Panmure and appealed to Palmerston. But although she convinced him sufficiently to agree that all Netley wanted to achieve was 'to cut a dash when looked at from the Southampton river', the building went on and was completed in 1863.[118]

In style Netley is a utilitarian Italianate with a grander Italianate centre housing the chapel. Italianate is in fact, internationally speaking, the style of most hospitals.[119] Examples are Lariboisière, Pendlebury near Manchester (1872–78, by Pennington & Bridges) and the new Hôtel-Dieu in Paris (1861–78, by Diet). The Hôtel-Dieu, reduced to 650 beds, incorporates pavilions, and pavilions were indeed in the last third of the nineteenth century the sign of a progressive authority and a progressive architect. Kuhn in the hospital volume of the *Handbuch der Architektur*, i.e. in 1897, still calls the pavilion plan 'the most perfect form of hospital architecture',[120] and Guadet in his famous *Eléments et théories*

9.41

9.39

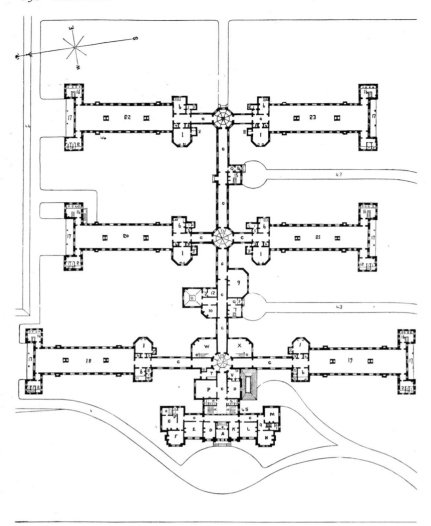

9.42 Pendlebury, Hospital for Sick Children, 1872–78, by Pennington & Bridges

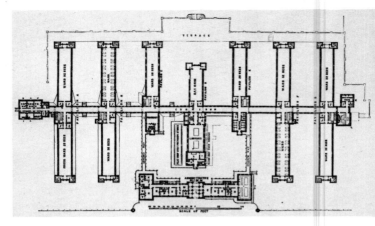

9.43 Woolwich, Herbert Hospital, begun in 1860, by Captain Galton

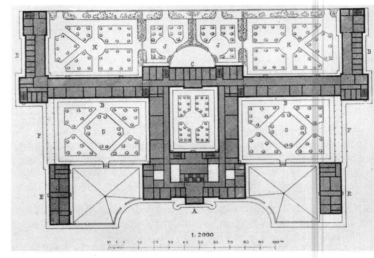

9.44 Vienna, Asylum, 1848–52, by Fellner

de l'architecture (1902) advocates pavilions too.[121] In England, Blackburn in Lancashire was the first of the pavilion schemes (1858 et seq., by James Turnbull), the Herbert Hospital at Woolwich, named after Lord Herbert of Lea, was the second (1860, by Captain Galton, R.E.). Famous American examples are Johns Hopkins at Baltimore (1876–89, by Niernsee),[122] the Free City Hospital in Boston (1861–64, by Gridley J. F. Bryant), with its oddly arranged six pavilions, and the Peter Bent Brigham Hospital, also in Boston (by Codman & Despradelle, opened 1913).

French examples are the rebuilt Hôtel-Dieu referred to above, Montpellier (1883–84, by C. Tollet, author of a standard late nineteenth-century book on hospitals),[123] and the rebuilt Hôpital Cochin in Paris (by P. L. Renaud, 1905–08). In Italy the new Pammatone of 1907–22 has pavilions. It was the replacement not of the Renaissance Pammatone but of its successor, a building of 1834–41 (by Domenico Cervetto), which belonged to the French radial type with six radiating wards. In Germany Friedrichshain in Berlin (1868, by Gropius & Schmieden) was the first hospital of the pavilion type.[124]

St Jakob in Leipzig (1871, by Nicolai) followed, and then Tempelhof, near Berlin (1875–78, by Gropius & Schmieden) and Eppendorf in Hamburg (1884 et seq., by Zimmermann & Ruppel).[125] Eppendorf did away with the spinal composition and set its more than eighty pavilions along internal streets. Important later examples in Germany are St Georg in Hamburg (1906–15, by Ruppel)[126] and the Rudolf Virchow Hospital in Berlin (1899–1906, by Ludwig von Hoffmann).

Compared with the pavilion plan the radial plan is insignificant (at least in hospitals; but see pp. 164 ff, 168). Two of the most conspicuous examples are Santerre by Vaudremer of 1862 et seq.,[127] and the Mower General Hospital at Chestnut Hill, ten miles from Philadelphia, a military hospital, built in 1862 to the design of John McArthur, Jun. Here there were fifty radial units, but the whole was of wood and one-storeyed. Beds came to 2,867.[128] That block designs carried on, in spite of the pavilion fashion, need hardly be said. Only size goes on increasing. The Kantonsspital at Zürich (1837–42, by G. A. Wegmann & L. Zeugheer) has a façade 1,784 feet long,[129] the asylum of Charenton (1838–45, by E. J.

9.45 Vienna, chapel of the Steinhof Asylum, 1904–07, by Otto Wagner

9.46 Swindon, Princess Margaret Hospital, begun in 1957, by Powell & Moya

9.47 Waiblingen, sanatorium, 1926, by Richard Döcker

Gilbert), 1,610 feet,[130] the Asylum in Vienna (1843–52, by Fellner) 755 feet, St Thomas's in London (1866–71, by Currey) 1,280 feet, and the Hôpital Tenon in Paris (1870–78, by Billon) 840 feet.

One more nineteenth-century development must have a few lines: the differentiation of hospitals to serve only one type of complaint. Foundling hospitals, asylums for the insane, lying-in hospitals had already existed before 1800; now – to take London as an example – we get the Eye Hospital in 1805, the Chest Hospital in 1814, the Ear Hospital in 1816, the Cancer Hospital in 1835, the Orthopaedic Hospital in 1838 and so on.[131]

9.45   To end with, a glance at the twentieth century. Stylistically phases follow each other much as in other building tupes. The only building of outstanding architectural quality is the monumental chapel of the Steinhof Asylum built on the then outskirts of Vienna in 1904–07, one of the masterpieces of Otto Wagner. The move of hospitals out of cities to more rural sites was a universal tendency. Parisian examples are the Incurables (to Ivry) and the Beaujon (to Clichy; see below).

Concerning planning an odd observation. Asylums begin belatedly to appreciate the pavilion principle, i.e. they begin to prefer a multitude of small buildings to one large one. The new arrangement goes under the name of 'colony'. The pioneering job was Maréville near Nancy. However, this has a complicated history.[132] It was built first in the sixteenth century as a plague house. Late in the same century it became a *maison de correction* for 'jeunes gens vicieux'. In 1714 the premises were reinstated as a woollen mill and the 'jeunes gens vicieux' were used as labour – with a fourteen-hour day, from 4 a.m. to 9 p.m. There were also a few insane youths, and they were kept in chains in casemates. In 1745 manufacturing was given up and the Frères des Ecoles chrétiennes looked after 500 youths and about 40 madmen. The premises were a group of detached buildings. They were destroyed by fire in 1794 but rebuilt as they had been. Specialization of care for the insane came only in 1838. There were 526 patients in 1842, 1,795 in the early twentieth century. So the colony layout happened by chance rather than being introduced afresh.

But pavilions and colonies were only one of two trends. The other was the very opposite. Normal hospitals, instead of spreading by pavilions, concentrated on big blocks, higher in fact that ever before. The change can also be described as that – to use Ochsner and Sturm's terms[133] – from the pre-antiseptic to the antiseptic period. The age of Florence Nightingale, apart from pleading for general cleanliness, believed the chief enemy of the sick in hospitals to be stale air. Now the recognition by Pasteur of bacteria in the passing on of diseases and the antiseptic treatment of wounds by Lister changed medicine and therefore also hospital design. The work of Pasteur and Lister belongs principally to the 1870s. It had been preceded from 1846 and 1847 onwards by the use of ether (William T. G. Morton) and chloroform (Sir James Simpson) for anaesthesia in operations. If bacteriology was right, then the need for pavilions ceased. Ochsner and Sturm could write in 1907 that the pavilion 'can no longer be used as a basis for hospital construction' and that the new tendency was for 'compact many-storeyed buildings'.[134] Similarly S. S. Goldwater in 1910 called the pavilion principle 'no longer tenable'[135] and H. Paschke looking back in 1963 could write: 'The pavilion form . . . is no longer used for new buildings.'[136] The advantage of the big block – the higher the better – lies in the saving on staff journeys and ducts, i.e. heating, lighting, cleaning and much else. The new type was created in the United States.[137] An early and still the most often illustrated example is the Columbia Presbyterian Medical Center in New York between Fort Washington Avenue, Broadway and West 165th to 168th Streets, an impressive group of twelve institutions begun in 1928 to the design of James Gamble Rogers. It has 1,499 beds. McKim, Mead & White designed the core of the Bellevue Hospital between First Avenue, East River Drive and East 25th to 30th Streets. It is continued to the north by the New York University Bellevue Medical Center of 1950 et seq. by Skidmore, Owings &

Merrill. On the same scale is also the New York Hospital Cornell Medical Center in York Avenue and East 68th to 70th Street, begun in 1933 to a design of Coolidge, Shepley, Bulfinch & Abbott. It reaches up to twenty-seven storeys and in 1971 had a total of 1,451 beds.

A first attempt at introducing the new type of hospital building to Europe was George Nelson's design for the Cité Hospitalière of Lille submitted in 1933. It was to have 27 storeys and was published with the blessings of Perret ('un de mes plus brillants élèves'), Le Corbusier, Giedion and Moser. The hospital as built in 1938–51 is by J. Walter.[138] Walter, Plousey & Cassan's new Hôpital Beaujon at Clichy, built in 1932–35, has twelve storeys. Walter had visited the United States in 1929.[139] The new Beaujon had 1,110 beds. Altogether Paris between 1920 and 1937 increased the number of available hospital beds by 9,000.[140]

For other countries two or three of the famous hospitals deserve a mention. Stockholm built the Karolinska Hospital in 1932–39 (architects E. C. Westman & Yngve Ahlbom) and the Southern Hospital in 1938–44 (architects Lederström & Imhäuser). The Bürgerspital in Basel, with a history reaching back to 1260, erected a new building (to replace one of 1840–46) in 1939–46. The designs were by Baur, Bräuning & Dürig.[141] The Princess Margaret Hospital at Swindon in Wiltshire was begun in 1957 by Powell & Moya, one of the best architectural partnerships in Britain.

Finally as a postscript the *Terrassenbau*, a speciality of Germany and Switzerland for those suffering from tuberculosis. The idea is that patients should be able to profit from fresh air all day long. The south fronts have on all floors terraces and they step back, much as they do in certain flats or tiers of small houses in the fashion of about 1965–70. The idea had first been put forward by a Swiss, Dr D. Sarasin, in 1901[142] and was taken up by the architect Richard Döcker of Stuttgart first in 1926 for a sanatorium at Waiblingen.[143]

9.48

9.46

9.47

9.47

9.48 New York, Cornell Medical Center of New York Hospital, begun in 1933, by Coolidge, Shepley, Bulfinch & Abbott

10.1 Beating hemp in Bridewell prison, from the *Harlot's Progress* by Hogarth, 1731 (detail)

10
Prisons

THIS chapter is hardly more than a postscript to the preceding one. The programmes of hospital and prison accommodation have much in common. In both cases a number of people are confined in one particular place, although they would prefer not to be, and in both cases constant supervision is necessary.

This affinity of hospital and prison explains why it is that the greatest of the prison reformers, John Howard, in his three books deals with the problems of both. The books are *The State of the Prisons*, published in 1777, *Appendix to The State of the Prisons*, published in 1788, and *An Account of the Principal Lazarettos in Europe*, published in 1789 and quoted in the hospital chapter of this book (p. 153). John Howard lived from 1726 to 1790. He was a well-to-do Bedfordshire squire of no specific promise. In 1773 he was made High Sheriff of his county and discovered for himself the state in which prisons were allowed to exist. Others knew it as well, but were too weak to act. Sterne is an example. The chapter of the *Sentimental Journey*, published in 1768, which is called 'The Captive' describes a prisoner, 'his body half wasted away', his legs in chains and his face 'pale and feverish', and leaves it at that. Only Howard knew – as against Sterne, from personal experience – what imprisonment meant. He had been a French

prisoner of war in Portugal in 1756. In 1773 he embarked on visits to the prisons of adjoining counties, and in the end he visited the prisons and hospitals of England and the Continent. He was deeply shocked and by his writing and pleading almost immediately made possible the Act of 1779, which introduced at least some improvements. It had in fact been preceded by the Popham Act of 1774, drafted before Howard was known.[1]

The state in which Howard found prisons must be seen against the background of the cruelty of legislation in every country, and particularly in England. Howard's voice must be heard *unisono* with Montesquieu's *De l'Esprit des lois* of 1748, Beccaria's *Dei delitti e delle pene* of 1764[2] and Gaetano Filangieri's *La scienza della legislazione* of 1780–88. Of these three reformers Howard quotes Beccaria.

Britain during Howard's lifetime and even twenty years after his death had about two hundred crimes avenged by capital punishment.[3] Samuel Romilly, the philanthropist and reformer and campaigner against capital punishment, said in 1810: 'There is probably no other country in the world in which so many and so great a variety of human actions are punishable with loss of life.'[4] The death sentence stood for stealing a

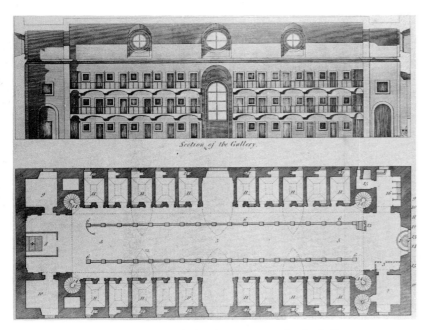

10.2 Rome, S. Michele Prison, 1703–04, by Carlo Fontana
(Howard, *Prisons*, 1777)

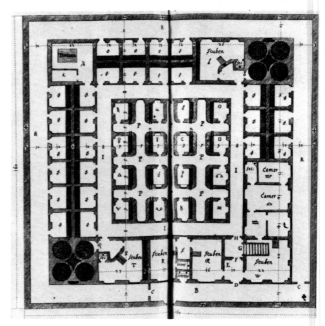

10.3 Joseph Furttenbach, design for a large prison (*Architectura universalis*, 1635)

sheep, stealing cloth from the tenter or the manu-factory, stealing mail from a mail-bag, destroying property, e.g. 'any hop-binds growing on poles in any plantation of hops'.[5] Sir William Meredith in 1777 pointed to a girl of fourteen 'lying in Newgate under sentence of being burnt alive' for hiding 'some white-washed farthings' at the suggestion of her sister and to a young married woman who stole from a counter because her children had nothing to eat after her hus-band had been taken away by a press-gang.[6] The Solicitor General in the House of Commons in 1785 stated that out of every 20 executed, 18 were under twenty-one years old.[7] Among 64 executions in that year one was for murder, all the others for offences against property.[8]

However inhuman the legislation, it must be re-membered that by no means all those condemned to death were executed. Radzinowicz gives the following figures: for 1805, capitally convicted 350, executed 68;[9] for 1810 the figures are 476 – 67;[10] and for individual crimes in 1818 e.g. horse-stealing 58 – 4, rape 11 – 2, sodomy 5 – 4, larceny over 40 shillings, 67 – 1.[11] Howard stated that in the years 1750–72 about 30 a year were executed; and he added that gaol fever, i.e. typhus, took a higher toll than that. In fact gaol fever was the worst scourge of the prison: 'Some are seen pining under diseases . . . expiring on the floor, in loathsome cells, of pestilential fevers.'[12]

Howard mentions cells here, but cells were not a matter of course. The evidence from the Middle Ages and after is ambiguous. Originally imprisonment was prior to trial, or prior to execution, or for debt, or as a cruel form of revenge. Imprisonment as a form of punishment seems to have originated in the monas-teries. The *Consuetudines* of both Cluny and Hirsau refer

to the *carcer* which is accessible only from the top by a ladder and has no door or window.[13] The Cluniacs reached their apogee in the eleventh and the early twelfth century, the Cistercians followed; the climax of their popularity and power was the latter two-thirds of the twelfth and the early thirteenth century. The Cistercian statutes of 1206 authorized abbeys to have a prison, and in an ordinance of 1229 stated that in all abbeys 'fortes et firmi carceres construantur'[14] (strong and fast prisons should be built). Of medieval secular prisons as premises, in spite of Mr Pugh's valuable work, we know little.[15] From the late Middle Ages and the Early Renaissance Graul illustrates a few dungeons at the bottom of round towers in castles or town walls.[16] At Münster in 1535 such a tower was spacious enough to be subdivided into two tiers of six radial cells for the imprisoned anabaptists.

In Italy Filarete in his *Treatise* of the early 1460s distinguishes between a small prison located in the palace and a main prison.[17] The small one is vaulted and has torture chambers above 'as required', the large one is square, 200 by 200 *braccia*, and surrounded by two walls with a moat between. The prisoners according to class or crime are in cells, those in the four corner buildings 'more sinister' and reserved for murderers, traitors and other crimes usually carrying the death penalty. Filarete's ideal city knows no death penalty but life imprisonment. The spirit of the Renaissance can be sensed in the way the 'comodita del corpo' are con-ducted into the moat so as to avoid smells, in the separation of women from men, and in the promise to wives of prisoners that after seven years they can live with their husbands. Concerning hygiene Filarete had been preceded by Alberti, who also objected to smells.[18] Whether the four rooms in each of the corner buildings represent single cells is not certain but likely. As for cells, in Italy we hear of the prison of Venice having 400 dark cells for life imprisonment[19] but do not know when they were introduced, and we also hear of the prison of the Inquisition in Portuguese Goa in the seventeenth century having 200.[20] On the other hand there is evidence used by Howard that felons were kept in dungeons, some twenty or thirty steps down and dark. The others were in rooms, many kept together, 'debtors and felons, men and women, the young beginner and the old offender'.[21] Howard wanted single cells instead, as Jonas Hanway had done before him.[22]

The building usually credited as being the first prison planned with cells and a large workroom is the prison of S. Michele in Rome, built in 1703–04 to the design of Carlo Fontana. It was built for young offenders, as a house of correction, i.e. a reformatory – 'perditis adolescentibus corrigendis' (for the correction of wayward youth), as the inscription stated. It had twenty cells to each of three storeys, ten on one side of the workroom and ten on the other. It should be noted that each cell had a lavatory. Howard illustrated the building[23] and called it large and noble.[24] It was, however, not the earliest with this rational arrangement.[25] Furttenbach in his *Architectura universalis* of 1635 has two prisons, one small, one large.[26] The accommodation for 'Maleficanten' is separate from that for citizens, and in two corners are deep holes as the worst accommodation. Debtors are not housed singly. That torture is provided for goes without saying. The most interesting single part is on Furttenbach's plate 28: a corridor with six cells either side. Yet earlier, the Malefizhaus at Bamberg was of the same type and dated from 1627,[27] and Graul illustrates the prison at Kassel dating from 1617 and consisting of cells along one side of a corridor. Graul also tells of the Carcere Nuovo in Rome of *c.* 1655, discussed and illustrated by.Howard,[28] as having cells on four floors for 68 prisoners altogether. The plan type was again the same.

As we have in this context returned to Howard, we may now go in more detail into his descriptions of prisons. Time and again prisons were found with no water, no sewers, no fresh air. In Warwick Gaol for instance he notes: 'Fourteen women, almost suffocated'. Of the same gaol he says of men felons: 'I saw thirty-two chained in a dungeon.'[29] Altogether chaining of criminals was still quite usual, although in a place where escape was almost impossible there was no need for it. Stafford: 52 men 'chained down', the women also chained. Liverpool Bridewell: 'All the men . . . in heavy irons, and seven out of eight women . . . chained to the floor'.[30]

Nor were conditions better abroad. In France, it is true, Howard finds much to praise, but they have dungeons too, 'beyond imagination horrid and dreadful'.[31] Torture chambers he found in Germany, in France and Italy, at Antwerp, Berne and Chambéry,[32] although Frederick the Great had abolished torture in 1740, and the Empress Maria Theresa in 1776. In the Liverpool Bridewell Howard saw in the men's court a pump 'to which the women are tied every week to receive discipline'.[33] Howard visited his prisons more than once, first for the book of 1777, then for the appendix and finally for the book of 1789. He is evidently anxious to be able to register improvement (the poor-house at Ipswich was 'dirty and sickly' and is now 'quite clean'),[34] but only too often he has to write 'no alteration'.

The Liverpool Bridewell has just been mentioned. The term perpetuates the Bridewell in London, a royal castle and later palace between Fleet Street and the river. In 1552 it became a prison, but in 1557 the purpose was changed to a house of correction, i.e. a confined building, intended to correct as well as punish. The remedy was work.[35] Bridewells became necessary in connection with the cessation of religious charity, the large-scale enclosures, and the movement towards a poor law.

The only country in which the principle of work for correction was taken seriously was Holland, where in Amsterdam – in the seventeenth century probably the most prosperous city of Europe – in 1596 a house of correction for men was opened, and in 1597 a house of correction for women. The former was called the Rasphuis, the latter the Spinhuis.[36] The term Spinhuis is self-explanatory; the term Rasphuis refers to the rasping with a rough saw of logs of exotic dye-wood. The rasped shavings were needed by the dye-makers. Weaving was also done by the men and net-making by the women. An inscription at the Spinhuis read: 'Courage! I don't avenge, I force you towards the good'; and indeed from early descriptions and documents one gets the impression that the Amsterdam establishments were better equipped and more humanely run than the Bridewells. Before overcrowding set in there were to be no more than two men or three women in a bed. Latrines in the bedrooms were also provided. On the other hand whipping continued to be a frequent punishment for women as well as men.[37] The Amsterdam institutions were imitated widely in the Netherlands and the towns along the North Sea and the Baltic.[38] The dates are: Leiden 1597, Leeuwarden 1598, Groningen 1601, Franeker 1608, Haarlem 1609, Enkhuizen 1612, Alkmaar 1614, Dordrecht 1614, Utrecht 1616, Antwerp 1618, Brussels 1623, Ghent 1627; Lübeck 1601, Bremen probably 1604, Hamburg 1618, Danzig 1629; Stockholm 1625.

England did not join that movement, though the Bridewells antedated the Dutch institutions. On the contrary, at the time of Howard the difference between prison and Bridewell had dimmed. The original idea had been that in Bridewells prisoners should work ten hours a day[39] – in the London Bridewell the women beat hemp – but in gaols debtors and even felons should also at least be able to work. But Howard reports that there were few Bridewells 'in which any work is done'[40] and that in some cases 'the gaol is also the Bridewell'.[41]

Architecturally the great innovation which Howard illustrates is the Maison de Force at Ackerghem outside Ghent, built in 1772–75 at the initiative of Vicomte J. P. Vilain, who called himself proudly Vilain XIV. The architects are given as Malfaison and S. J. Kluchman. It was built as a house of correction for the whole of Flanders, and the enlightened plan is only one illustration of the enlightened policy of Maria Theresa. The principle behind the building is faith in 'amélioration par éducation et travail'. At night prisoners were in

10.2

10.3

10.1

10.1

10.4

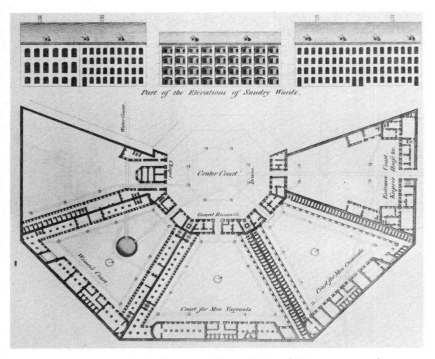

10.4 Ackerghem near Ghent, Maison de Force, 1772–75, by Malfaison and Kluchman: elevations and half plan (Howard, *Prisons*, 1777)

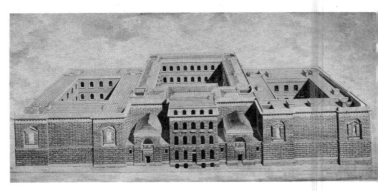

10.5 London, Newgate Prison, 1770–85, by George Dance the Younger (*London, Sir John Soane's Museum*)

10.6 C.-N. Ledoux, design for a prison for Aix-en-Provence, 1784 (*L'Architecture*, 1804)

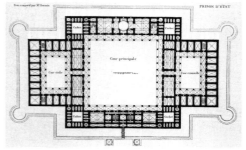

10.7, 8 Houssin, design for a state prison, *c.* 1795: plan and elevation

single cells, during the day they worked together. The plan of the building was radial; we can guess where the inspiration came from. In the *Mercure de France* in July 1765 an ideal prison was described which was octagonal with sixteen radii ingeniously arranged and a large circular courtyard in the middle, in the centre of which was to be the chapel.[42] Cells filled the radii and also the periphery. The design was by Pierre-Gabriel Bugniet, a Lyons architect. He in his turn must have been inspired by Desgodets' hospital design or just possibly Sturm's hospital design. The Ghent design incidentally is exactly contemporaneous with Petit's hospital design in his *Mémoire* (see p. 151). At Ghent eight radii were intended; when Howard saw it, four had been built.[43] The accommodation for men was in single cells, each with a bedstead, a small cupboard and a flap-table.

Howard describes the Maison de Force in detail, but curiously without any stress on the radial plan. In fact the model prisons which he designed for his books – one in 1777,[44] one in 1789[45] – are not inspired by Ghent. The

earlier one is still close in type to Newgate, which he also illustrated. The impressive thing about Newgate, which was begun in 1770 and completed after a fire in 1785, was of course aesthetic, not functional – the severity of Dance's design expressing in terms of *architecture parlante* the spiritual function of the gaol. The motifs derive from Giulio Romano and from Palladio's (or Giulio's) Palazzo Thiene in Vicenza, and the separation of part from part is already in the style of the late eighteenth century. The most *parlant* motif is the swags of fetters over the doors.[46] Ledoux's gaol for Aix is even more massive and menacing. This is of 1784, and in 1785 Milizia wrote that prisons ought to look 'tristi in ragione del loro destino . . . La malinconia si mostrerà nelle prigioni civili e l'orrore si paleserà tutto nelle più criminali' (depressing by reason of their function . . . Misery should be expressed in civil prisons and the full horror revealed in the more criminal ones). So let there be 'ombre le più forti, ingressi . . . cavernosi . . ., inscrizioni spaventosi' (deepest shade,

10.4

9.19
9.20
9.34

10.5

10.6

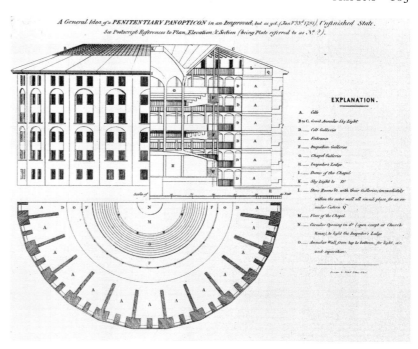

10.10 Jeremy Bentham's design for a Panopticon prison, 1791 (*Works*, IV, 1843)

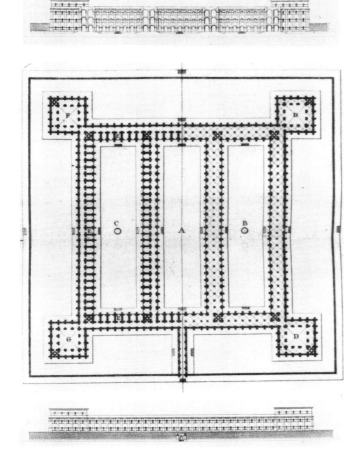

10.9 J.-N.-L. Durand, design for a prison (*Précis*, II, 1809): section, plan and elevation

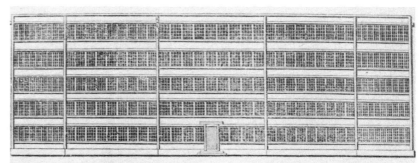

10.11 Samuel Bentham and Samuel Bunce, design for a workhouse, 1797

cavernous entrances, terrifying inscriptions). But once inside, Milizia adds, orderliness and hygiene ought to prevail.[47] Durand's prison in his *Précis de leçons* (II, 1809) is *architecture parlante* too, although in his *Recueil* (1801) the plates illustrating existing prisons include Ghent, side by side with S. Michele in Rome, Dance's Newgate and Ledoux's Aix. Even more grimly *parlant* is the prison design by which an architect called Houssin won a prize in the Paris Académie d'Architecture about 1795.[48]

By the time Houssin's design was submitted another scheme for prisons had appeared, a scheme, like the radial one, of elementary planning geometry. Jeremy Bentham published it in 1791 as the Panopticon.[49] The principle is cells along the periphery of a circle and an observation post in the middle. The idea was not his but his brother's. Sir Samuel Bentham had gone to Catherine the Great's Russia in 1780, and there, after travels which took him as far north as Archangel, as far south as the Crimea, and as far east as nearly to China,

had settled down as a lieutenant colonel and later brigadier dealing with engineering problems. The idea of the Inspection House, as it was originally called, seems to date from *c.* 1785. It could, according to Bentham, be used for schools, manufactories, hospitals and especially prisons.[50] Jeremy Bentham visited his brother in 1787. Did the Bentham brothers, one wonders, know of the Narrenturm in Vienna?[51]

Of the two patterns of prison planning, the radial Ghent pattern became widely accepted, whereas the peripheric Bentham pattern was only rarely and fragmentarily imitated. Among those built to the latter pattern, the following deserve mention. Northleach, by William Blackburn, the most important early prison designer, dated from 1789–95, i.e. from before the publication of the Panopticon. But Blackburn, who had won in 1782 the competition for a model prison under the Act of 1779, was no doubt aware of what was going on.[52] Chester by Thomas Harrison, 1793 et seq., followed Blackburn's lead. A few years later, in 1797,

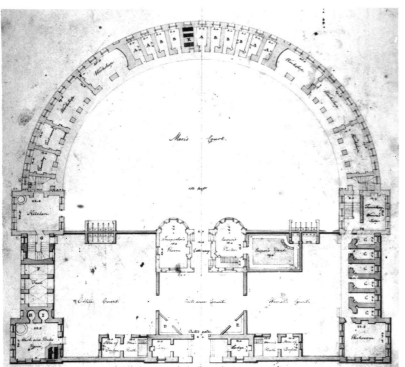

10.12–14 Richmond, Va., prison, 1785 and 1797 et seq., by Thomas Jefferson and Benjamin Latrobe: plan, internal and external elevation of semicircle, and gate (drawings by Latrobe, 1797; *Richmond, Virginia State Library*)

10.11 Samuel Bentham, back in England, published in collaboration with Samuel Bunce a workhouse with amazingly twentieth-century-looking fenestration.[53] In fact the widely spaced exposed structural members were to be of iron, as were the galleries and the staircases. In the same year Latrobe began the semicircular gaol of 10.12–14 Richmond, Virginia, for which in 1785 Jefferson had sent designs accompanied by Bugniet's plan of 1765. Jefferson's main interest in the matter was that Bugniet's design was completely cellularized, and Jefferson believed in the principle of solitary confinement, as he indeed called it.[54] The cells lay along the periphery and were on three storeys, vaulted. Each had a privy. In 1782 Soane submitted to the National Penitentiary 10.16 Competition a design for a prison for 300 women on the Panopticon principle.[55] To continue the list of 10.15 Panopticon-type designs, the Edinburgh Bridewell was built to a design of Robert and James Adam in 1791–95 as a semicircle. A full circle (or rather a sixteen-part 10.18 polygon) was the plan of the gaol at Devizes, which was built in 1808–17 by Richard Ingleman.[56] Again a semicircle was Kaiserslautern in Germany, built in 1820–23.[57] Other later Panopticon designs are Kirkdale in Lancashire of 1821, Lancaster of 1821, the Western Penitentiary at Pittsburgh of 1826, by Strickland, and a design by Abel Blouet of 1841. Indeed, it has been calculated that between 1801 and 1833 in England and Wales thirty-seven prisons were designed partially or wholly on the surveillance principle.[58]

10.4 The radial pattern of Ghent was the inspiration of many, although in early cases of the type, such as the House of Correction in Milan, built *c.* 1775, the source may well be rather the Ospedale Maggiore in the very 9.10 same city. The House of Correction has in fact a cross of four wings.[59] In 1782 Soane had also submitted a design for a prison for men: this is a demi-octagon with ranges along two of the sides and in the middle three crosses, each arm forming two parallel cell blocks. The next partisans in England of the Ghent pattern were Blackburn's Ipswich of 1785–90, mentioned in Howard's *Lazarettos* book,[60] Blackburn's Liverpool of 1787–89 and Blackburn's Dorchester of 1789–95. That after 1800 the plan was taken over for asylums has been noted in the preceding chapter. It also became the standard design, though usually only with three or four radii, for English workhouses. James Elmes published his *Hints for the Improvement of Prisons* in 1817. The most influential radial prison, however, was Millbank, built 10.19 in 1813–21 by Thomas Hardwick, John Harvey and ultimately Robert Smirke, from a design by William Williams.[61] The radii here were not straight ranges: each was a block forming a pentagon. But the most famous of the London prisons were Pentonville, of 1840–42, by Sir Joshua Jebb, Surveyor General of Prisons and author of a book called *Notes on the Construction and Ventilation of Prisons* published in 1844,[62] and Holloway, built a few years later (1849–52) by Bunning. Mayhew, who described both of these in great detail, praises the airiness of Pentonville inside and feels reminded even of the Crystal Palace. At Holloway it is the exterior he praises: 'a noble building in the castellated style', but he is horrified at the so-called refractory cells which are totally dark.[63] Some radial prisons on the Continent are: in Switzerland Geneva of

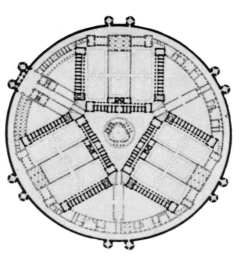

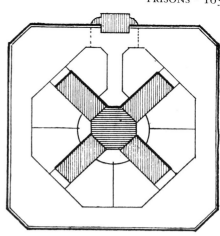

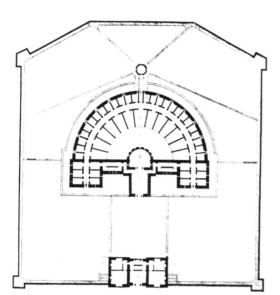

10.16 Sir John Soane, design for a
women's prison, 1782

10.17 Ipswich, prison, 1785–90, by
William Blackburn

10.15 Edinburgh, Bridewell, 1791–95,
by Robert and James Adam

10.18 Devizes, prison, 1808–17, by Richard Ingleman
(modelled from the plans of 1867 by John W. Girvan)

10.19 London, Millbank prison, 1813–21, by Thomas Hardwick and others

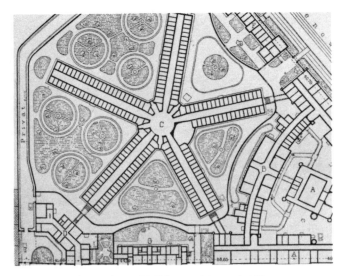

10.20 Berlin, second Moabit Prison, 1869–79, by Herrmann

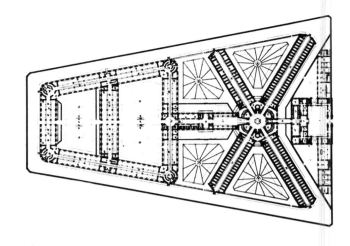

10.22 Paris, La Santé Prison, begun in 1862, by Vaudremer

10.21 Paris, La Petite Roquette Prison, 1826–30, by Hippolyte Lebas

10.23 Auburn, N.Y., prison, 1816–25

1822–25 by Vaucher-Crémieux; in Italy Japelli's Padua prison, also belonging to the twenties, Palermo of 1834–40 by Vincenzo De Martino,[64], S. Vittore in Milan of 1872–79 by Francesco Lucca,[65] and Regina Coeli in Rome of the 1870s by Contini;[66] in Belgium Brussels of 1815 et seq. (by Demesme), a Greek cross in a square;[67] in Germany Dr Julius's design, an illustration in his *Vorträge* of 1828. After 1830 in Germany Insterburg was built in 1832–38, Cologne 1834–43, Halle in 1837–41, Berlin-Moabit in 1842–46 (I) and 1869–79 (II), and so on. In France La Petite Roquette for young offenders is of 1826–30 by Lebas, six radii in a hexagon. Also for France the following must be mentioned: Baltard's *Architectonographie des prisons* of 1829, the 'immense bâtisse' of Mazas by Lecointe and Gilbert 1842 et seq.,[68] a design of 1843 by Blouet,[69] and Vaudremer's Santé of 1862 et seq. When they were ready to take over the radial plan the French sent two study teams abroad, M. de Beaumont and M. de Tocqueville in 1833, M. Demetz and Abel Blouet in 1837, and it is a telling fact that they both went to America.[70]

In fact at about this time the United States took the lead architecturally and functionally.[71] As for considerations of function, there were two systems in competition, named after two prisons, Auburn, New York, and the Eastern Penitentiary, Cherry Hill near Philadelphia.[72] Auburn was built in 1816–25 on the principle of cells for the night but for the day common work-rooms, in which however silence had to be kept. The cells from 1820 onwards had no outer windows. They received their light from the access gallery, and the gallery area, that is the core of the block, was sky-lit. Sing Sing in New York State, begun in 1826, the most widely known American prison, followed the Auburn system. The Eastern Penitentiary (Cherry Hill) was designed in 1825 on the principle of solitary confinement day and night. Work was done in the cells which were therefore larger than those of Auburn and Sing Sing. Severe critics of the separation system and of the Eastern Penitentiary were not absent, the best-known of them Dickens and Heinrich Heine. Dickens on his American journey in 1842, as we have seen (pp. 148–49) made a point of visiting hospitals, asylums and other such institutions. They included prisons.[73] He visited several and on the whole praised America's 'great wisdom, great benevolence, and exalted policy'.[74] The gaol of Kingston, Ontario, e.g., he calls 'admirable',[75] the House of Correction at Boston 'excellent'.[76]

10.20
10.21
10.22
10.23
10.24

10.24 Cherry Hill, Philadelphia, Pa., Eastern Penitentiary, designed in 1825, by John Haviland

10.26 New York, Tombs, 1834–38, by John Haviland

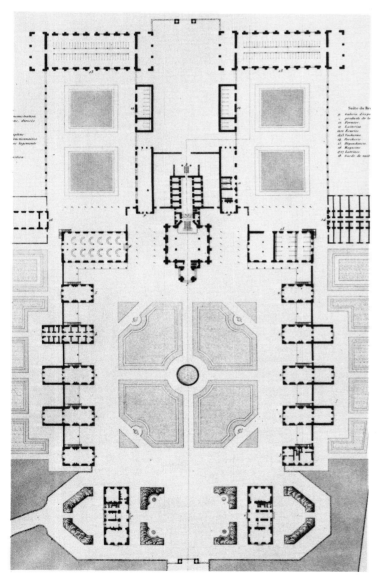

10.25 Mettray, prison colony, 1839, by Abel Blouet

10.27 Liverpool, Walton Gaol, 1848–55, by John Wightman

10.28 Manchester, Strangeways Prison, 1866–68, by Alfred Waterhouse

But the Eastern Penitentiary he calls 'hopeless, . . . cruel and wrong'. He adds: 'I believe that very few men are capable of estimating the immense amount of torture and agony which this dreadful punishment, prolonged for years, inflicts upon the sufferers.'[77] Heine was yet more savage. In his appendix to *Lutetia* he called the Pennsylvanian system 'horrible, inhuman, even unnatural', and added, 'The Bastille is a sunny garden pavilion in comparison with these small silent American hells which only a lunatic pietist could think up.'[78] Pennsylvania is indeed Quaker country, and a Society for alleviating the Miseries of the Public Prisons had been founded as early as 1787.[79] Solitude was regarded as the best way to introspection and self-improvement.[80] Dr Rothman has some telling quotations: *A Prisoner's Prayer* contains the passage 'Remove me from my old companions and surround me with virtuous associates.' In solitude the prisoner will 'reflect on the error of his ways . . . listen to the reproaches of conscience [and] the expostulations of religion'.[81] The Eastern Penitentiary was progressive incidentally concerning the equipment of the cells. Each had hot-water heating, a latrine and a tap. It can be said that it was universally accepted as the model prison of the nineteenth century.

10.24   The designer was John Haviland, a pupil of James Elmes, and the style of the building is Gothic. Gothic as a matter of fact is rare in prison design. Norman was popular in England – see Soane's design of 1782 and
10.27   also, e.g., the Walton Gaol at Liverpool, 1848–55, by John Wightman, and the Manchester (Strangeways)
10.28   Prison, 1866–68, by Waterhouse. (Internally of course such prisons are of the American iron standard. They were based on Jebb's Pentonville cell and gallery designs which followed from William Crawford and Whitworth Russell's visit to American prisons.[82]) Egyptian was accepted in the United States: Moyamensing, the Philadelphia County Prison, started Gothic by T. U. Walter in 1829 but enlarged in the Egyptian

fashion by the same architect in 1831,[83] Trenton by Haviland 1833–36, and the Tombs in New York also   10.26 by Haviland, 1834–38, a combined law courts and prison. Dickens called the Tombs 'a dismal-fronted pile of bastard Egyptian'.[84] There is no need to enlarge on the evocative suitability of Norman and Egyptian.

Nor is there a need to enlarge on prison designs in the late nineteenth and twentieth centuries. Radial plans were occasionally still used after 1900 (Stateville, Illinois by C. H. Hammond, completed 1919; Fort Leavenworth Military Disciplinary Barracks, Kansas; also prisons in Spain, according to Dr Johnston), but they were patently on the way out. Instead a new pattern came, comparable to the pavilion patterns of hospitals. Parallel single blocks were connected by a spine. The name given in America to this pattern is telephone-pole. The pioneer building – though it does not have a spine – was Mettray by Abel Blouet, 1839.   10.25 It consisted of a main building and issuing from it like elongated Palladian wings two parallel spine corridors and at right angles to them, rib-like ranges, three left and three right of both corridors.[85] Mettray was called a 'colonie agricole pénitentiaire', and the conception of colony instead of prison proved as stimulating as the plan. Concerning the latter, successor buildings are Wormwood Scrubs in London of 1874–91 by Sir Edward Ducane,[86] the Workhouse of Rummelsburg near Berlin by Blankenstein, 1877–80, and Fresnes near   10.29 Paris, 1898–1901. The architect at Fresnes was M. F. Poussin, and there are three pairs of five-storey ranges. America adopted the Fresnes plan, and there the prison of Graterford, Pennsylvania, of 1927–28, with a large central workshop and eight cell ranges, is the biggest.[87] Soledad near San Francisco is of the same type (with a spine 1,100 feet long) and so are e.g. Jackson, Michigan, of 1924–29 (with 5,700 cells), Lewisburg, Pennsylvania (1932), and Terre Haute, Indiana (1940), to name only a few.

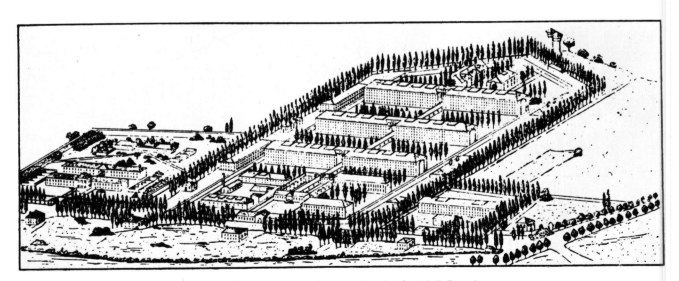

10.29 Fresnes, prison colony, 1898–1901, by M. F. Poussin

11.1 Grantham, Angel Inn (now Angel and Royal Hotel), late 15th c.

11
Hotels

WHAT IS the difference between a hotel and an inn? The hotel is nearly always larger than the inn, especially in its public spaces. The hotel has a number of public rooms, not just a tap room and some tables to eat at. But the hotel develops out of the inn, and it is this development that I shall follow. That means that no account is to be given of the *xenodochium* of Classical Antiquity and the caravanserai of the East.

Quite a number of medieval inns survive. In England the best are the Angel at Grantham, the George at Glastonbury, the Angel at Newark and the George at Norton St Philip.[1] Such inns were frequented by guests who even included royalty. Richard III signed and sealed the death warrant for the Duke of Buckingham at the Angel at Grantham. In Paris imperial ambassadors stayed at the Ange in 1500.[2] Venice in the thirteenth century had, according to the Chronicle of Martino de Canal, 'noble inns for barons and gentlemen to stay in'.[3] Italian inns in the thirteenth century had a common sleeping room and single rooms only for VIPs. In the fifteenth century they were often managed by Germans. (Enea Silvio Piccolomini says: 'hospitia faciunt theutonici'.)[4] At Borghetto near Verona in 1556 the guest had to sleep in one bed with his tutor, his host and hostess and their baby.[5] Apart from inns there were

rooms one could rent, e.g. in the Fondaco dei Tedeschi in Venice.[6] Rome in the mid-fifteenth century is said to have had 1,022 inns.[7] When the Emperor Frederick III visited Rome in 1468 his retinue lodged in inns, in the Angelo 24 men and 24 horses, in the Campana 35 plus 38, in the Corona 14 plus 22, in the San Giovanni 20 plus 32, in the Nave 20 plus 20, in the Scudo 23 plus 23, in the Sole[8] 31 plus 30, in the Spada 23 plus 20 and so on. The retinue was *c.* 600–700 in all.[9] Of the Bull (Hospitium Bovis) in Padua, Michele Savonarola in 1440 writes, 'quod nullum in Italia pulcrius vel magnificentius existat' and that it had 'curia amplissima et ornatissima', 'cameras innumeras' and stabling for 200 horses.[10] In 1361 the Duke of Brittany paid 1,000 livres for a week at an inn at St Omer. The figure must of course have included his retinue.[11] Poggio Bracciolini, the Florentine humanist and friend of Cosimo Medici, wrote to Niccolò Niccoli in 1417 of Baden, the celebrated Swiss spa, that magnificent houses for visitors stood round a square which was the centre of the spa precinct.[12] About 160 years later, in 1580, Montaigne reported from Baden that where he stayed there were 200 beds and next door 50 well-furnished rooms, and one had to pay a lot.[13]

So in the later sixteenth century, if we can trust

11.2 Scole, White Hart, 1655

11.4 London, the George Inn, Southwark, later 17th c.

11.3 Shrewsbury, Lion Hotel, assembly room, c. 1775–80

Montaigne's figures, hotel-size is reached. From the late sixteenth and early seventeenth century come three German examples, all with a great gable to crown the façade: the Ritter at Heidelberg, the Deutsches Haus at Dinkelsbühl and the Riese at Miltenberg, the latter timber-framed and dated 1590.[14] From the later seventeenth century three English inns, also statelier than before: the White Hart at Scole in Norfolk, dated 1655 and adorned with five Dutch gables, the Haycock at Wansford of about 1670,[15] and the Duke's Head at King's Lynn of 1683–89, built by Sir John Turner for visitors to the Exchange (now Customs House) also built by him. Inns, needless to say, had to have stabling. A favourite pattern was the coaching yard surrounded by galleries which gave access to the bedrooms. A famous example, though late (after 1676) and only partially preserved, is the George Inn in the London borough of Southwark.

One famous German inn, originally built c. 1635–40, was rebuilt in 1767–69: the Rotes Haus in the Zeil at Frankfurt.[16] Before 1700 it was already the best hotel in the town. It was in the Rotes Haus, e.g., that the celebrations took place when in 1690 the future Joseph I was crowned Roman King. The designer in 1767 was the City Architect, H. J. A. Liebhardt. Shortly after-

wards a top storey was added to the stables, and in 1784 a new range was built at the far end of the garden. The façade received a Louis XVI facelift about the same time. The front was then of thirteen bays and three storeys with a five-bay pediment. At the back were two thirteen-bay wings also with pediments. A monumental staircase lay at the back of the front range. Among distinguished visitors Friedrich Wilhelm I, King of Prussia, stayed in 1716, and Friedrich Wilhelm II in 1792. It ceased to be a hotel about 1800 and became the post office in 1837. It was pulled down in 1900.

The Drei Mohren at Augsburg, known to have existed already in 1344, was rebuilt by Ignaz Gunezrainer in 1722. It had an eleven-bay façade and a coaching yard at the back. On the first upper floor at the back was a large ballroom.[17] The ballroom is specially interesting from the Anglo-American point of view, because to add an assembly room to an existing inn was often the first step towards the attainment of hotel status. There are many examples: One of the finest is the Lion at Shrewsbury, where the assembly room is of c. 1775–80.[18] Forty years later the George at Lichfield (1814–18) had its assembly room as an integral part of the structure, occupying the centre of the first floor

11.5 Miltenberg, Riese Inn, 1590

11.6 Frankfurt, Rotes Haus, c. 1635–40

11.7 Frankfurt, Rotes Haus, rebuilding of 1767–84

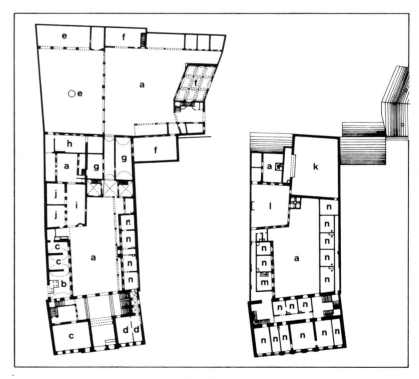

11.8, 9 (top and above) Augsburg. Drei Mohren, 1722, by Ignaz
Gunezrainer: façade, and plans of ground and first upper floors
Key a courtyards, b kitchen, c dining rooms, d sitting rooms,
e garden, f coach–house range and storerooms, g stables,
h harness room, i passage and wood-store, j rooms for women
and men servants, k ballroom, l *Rittersaal*, m chapel, n bedrooms

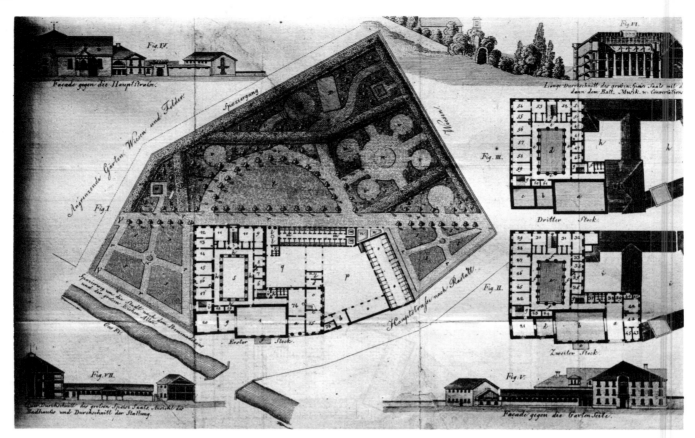

11.10 Baden-Baden, Badischer Hof, convent converted to a hotel, 1807–09, by Friedrich Weinbrenner *(Karlsruhe, Amt für Denkmalpflege)*

front. That marks the way from inn to hotel. Other inns on that momentous way are the George at Grantham (1789), the Swan at Bedford (by Henry Holland, 1794) and the Royal Clarence at Exeter (1770). The latter incidentally also called itself The Hotel.[19]

As for the use of the term 'hotel' in English, the *Oxford English Dictionary* notes the following three early occurrences – Smollett in 1766: 'The expense of living at a hotel is enormous'; R. King in *Travels & Correspondence*, 1776: 'their hotels'; and H. Arnot in *History of Edinburgh*, 1783: 'In 1763 there was no such place as a hotel; the word indeed was not known, or only intelligible to French scholars.' To these examples four more may be added: Sterne in the *Sentimental Journey*, which was published in 1768, speaks of M. Dessein or Dessin's hotel in Calais where coaches were sold. Of this hotel Johanna Schopenhauer, the philosopher's mother, who had travelled to England in 1787, wrote that it was 'one of the largest inns in the world',[20] and in 1797 the *Gentleman's Magazine* said: 'Dessin's hotel is thought to be the most extensive in Europe. It is indeed itself a town: it contains squares, alleys, gardens . . . and innumerable offices.'[21] It had a theatre and shops and its own workmen. In spite of this it got into financial difficulties, but the Government helped it on because of 'the splendour of the establishment'. Schinkel also evidently refers to Dessin when he writes in a letter of 1826 of 'a large inn' at Calais 'equipped the English way'.[22] Sterne in the *Sentimental Journey* also mentions the Hôtel de Modène in Paris and

the Hôtel Cordon Bleu in Versailles. Next William Beckford in a letter of 28 May 1782 tells that he was directed in Cologne 'to the hotel of Der Heilige Geist'.[23] A few years later Arthur Young, the agricultural publicist, wrote of the Hôtel de Henri Quatre at Nantes: 'I am in doubt whether the Hôtel de Henri Quatre is not the finest inn in Europe. Dessein's at Calais is larger, but neither built, fitted up nor furnished like this.'[24] The hotel had 60 master bedrooms, some apartments and 25 stalls for horses. Next the *Gentleman's Magazine* in 1791 reports that the Duke of Norfolk was planning a 'magnificent hotel' at Hereford,[25] and in 1802 Albany off Piccadilly, built by Chambers for Lord Melbourne in 1771–74, was sold to be converted into 'a Subscription House or Hotel'. The prospectus calls it 'a magnificent and convenient hotel' to provide accommodation for families.[26] We shall see later that an arrangement primarily for families was by no means exceptional in the first half of the nineteenth century.

But we are still in the eighteenth. In the letters and memoirs hotels are now frequently mentioned, and travel books and guide books also increase in numbers. Nicolai writes that in 1786 Berlin had 19 hotels of the first class, 3 of the second, 14 of the third.[27] Casanova in 1779 stayed in Naples at the Crocelle in Chiaia and says that 'tous les étrangers riches' stay there, and he adds (of course) that girls are easily provided.[28] Finally, Latrobe in 1797–98 designed a hotel for Richmond, Virginia.[29] It is a memorable design; for it combined a theatre with assembly rooms and a hotel. The centre, as we have seen (p. 81), was to be the theatre. To its left

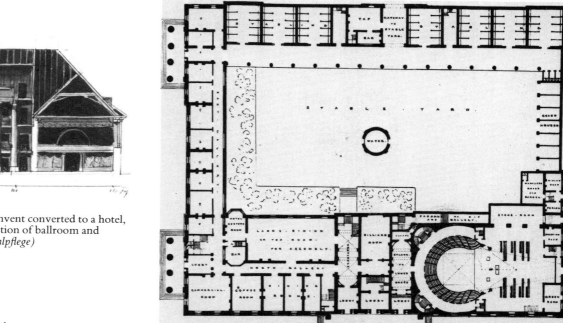

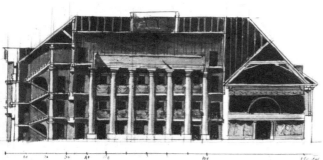

11.11 Baden-Baden, Badischer Hof, convent converted to a hotel, 1807–09, by Friedrich Weinbrenner: section of ballroom and dining room (*Karlsruhe, Amt für Denkmalpflege*)

11.12, 13 Plymouth, Royal Hotel and Athenaeum, 1811–19, by John Foulston: view, and plan of the hotel building

were the assembly rooms, to its right the hotel. This interesting arrangement will engage our special attention twice more. The hotel was intended to have, apart from the dining room, a coffee room, a sitting room, parlours and a bar.

Two more years and the nineteenth century is reached and with it almost at once indubitable hotels. The first was at Baden-Baden. The Badischer Hof[30] was originally the house of the Capuchins. It was converted by Weinbrenner in 1807–09 and is described[31] as having 'Vorhallen mit Colonnaden', large and small salons, 'especially a very large beautifully decorated ballroom . . . with balcony and a movable stage, a large tasteful dining room, surrounded by eighteen columns thirty-six feet high, with four wide galleries, in the form of an Early Christian basilica with lighting from a glazed roof',[32] library, reading room, many parlours ('Wohnzimmer'), a bathing establishment, stables and coach-house. The plan of the ground floor shows the location of these rooms, the dining room in the middle (5), the ballroom between it and the street (1), the entrance hall to the right (a), and two card-table rooms to the left of the ballroom (20, g). The bathing establishment forms the far range of the courtyard (m). It has 28 cabinets. As for bedrooms there are 12 on the ground floor, 22 on the first and 14 on the second floor. Each floor incidentally has a few lavatories: ground floor 3 plus 2, first floor 3, second floor 3.

Staying a little longer among the Germans, it is possible – largely thanks to the regular visits of Goethe – to trace the state of the *hôtellerie* in the resorts of Bohemia.[33] Karlsbad (Karlový Varý) as a resort goes back earlier than the fourteenth century, Marienbad (Mariánské Lázně) was started only in 1818. Goethe visited Karlsbad in 1795, 1806, 1808, 1809, 1810, 1811, 1812, 1818 and Marienbad in 1820, 1821, 1822, 1823. What results from the reports on Goethe's stays is that hotels existed, but that well-to-do *Kurgäste* used them only while they were looking for accommodation in specially equipped private houses.[34] This procedure is confirmed in Jean Paul's *Dr Katzenberger's Badereise*, written in 1807–08: ordinary people stay in hotels but Herr von Niess 'hired one of the prettiest little houses'.

In fact one should probably not expect much of hotels about 1800. It is worth keeping in mind that Durand in his *Recueil*, by now a familiar source for readers of this book, says of hotels that they are 'intended to receive travellers' but that they are 'in most of Europe simply private houses which offer neither more order, nor more comfort, nor more cleanliness than most farm houses'.[35]

The earliest full-scale English parallel to Weinbrenner's hotel that I have come across is the Royal Hotel at Plymouth, won in competition by Foulston in 1811 and completed in 1819.[36] It was, like Latrobe's design, a composite establishment with, apart from the hotel, an assembly room, a theatre and also an Athenaeum. Athenaeum was a favourite term during those years, meaning a literary and philosophical society or club. The London Athenaeum of 1827–30 – by Decimus Burton – is of course the best-known example. The Royal Hotel at Derby of 1837–39 (by R. Wallace)

11.14 Boston, Mass., Exchange Coffee House, 1806–09, by Asher Benjamin

11.16 St Leonards, the St Leonards (now Royal Victoria) Hotel and surrounding buildings and gardens, designed by James Burton and begun in 1828

11.15 Baltimore, Md., Barnum's City Hotel, 1825–26, by F. Small

also had an Athenaeum as part of the composition.[37] Dr Priscilla Metcalf told me of the term 'Athenaeomania' used in the *Clapham Gazette* on 25 January 1860. Foulston's hotel had its most spectacular entrance, an eight-column portico, as access to the assembly rooms, which included a dining room, 56 feet long, and above it a ballroom, 77 feet long. The entry to the hotel proper was by a four-column portico round the left corner. The hotel had its own coffee-room, bar and commercial room. On the first floor were exclusively suites of dining room, sitting-room and bedroom. The hotel had 50 bedrooms altogether. At the back were of course stables and a coach-house. The text of Foulston's publication mentions three cloakrooms. The plans however seem to show paired lavatories in basement, ground floor and first floor. The Athenaeum was separate, with a Greek Doric portico.

When Foulston started the Royal, America had already joined in the endeavours towards large and lavish inns, and her contribution was of astounding vigour from the start. The first building to be mentioned is the City Hotel in New York. This dated from 1794–96 and was really no more than two houses. Yet it had five floors and 73 rooms, which is much at so early a date.[38] Next after this a surprise and a puzzle: the Exchange Coffee House at Boston,[39] built in 1806–09. It cost $500,000. The architect was Asher Benjamin. It was seven floors high and was supposed to have a merchants' exchange on the ground floor. This central room went right up to the top and was covered with a dome, 100 feet 10 inches in diameter. In the middle of the dome was a glazed skylight. The level of the projected exchange area also had a coffee room 50 feet 6 inches long. Round the exchange ran galleries on five levels. The first was supported on twenty Doric pillars. The dining room of the hotel, 71 feet 6 inches long, was here. One

level higher was the ballroom with twelve Corinthian pillars and three domes. It was reached by a grand spiral staircase. On the two top levels was the hotel accommodation, the rooms being arranged on both sides of a corridor. There were 200 apartments. The second and third galleries had Ionic pillars, the fourth Corinthian. On the fifth was just a balustrade. The façade had a portico with six Ionic pillars, and another round the corner had nine Doric pillars. This was for carriages. The kitchen was in the basement. The ground level had a subscription library, the dining room had tables for 300, and on the fourth level was the Masonic Hall. The whole building was burnt down in 1818.

Of between 1804 and the late 1820s, Williamson in *The American Hotel* names a number of buildings. It would be easy to match them with English ones. On the American side of the Atlantic there were the Mansion House, Philadelphia, opened in 1807, in New York the Washington Hall opened in 1809, the Tammany Hotel of 1810, the Mansion House of 1821, the National of 1826, the American of 1827, the Adelphi of 1827, and many more.

In England at the same time there were for instance the Regent at Leamington of 1819, the Royal Victoria at St Leonards of 1827 (see below),[40] the Sea Hotel at Worthing of 1827, the Bedford at Brighton of 1829, the Clarendon at Leamington of 1830 (which Nathaniel Hawthorne in 1855 called 'by far the most splendid hotel I have yet seen in England'),[41] the Golden Cross and Morley's in London of 1830–33, the former designed by Tite, the latter by J. Ledwell Taylor, and so on. Charles Knight in 1843 writes à propos Long's, Warren's and Mivart's in London that they let apartments 'where families or gentlemen may take up their abode temporarily or for a continuance'.[42]

At St Leonards the hotel was the centre of James

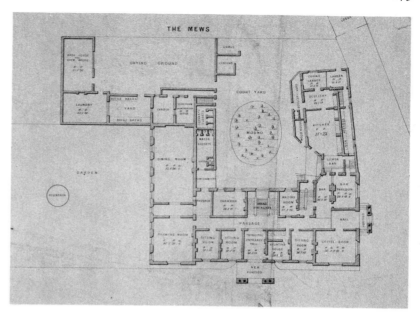

11.17, 18 Leamington, Regent Hotel, 1819: view and plan

Burton's fine, monumental composition. In front of it and in axis was the bath house with two Greek Doric porticoes, behind it and also in axis the Public Rooms, again with a Greek Doric portico. The composition was intended to have in addition a crescent of private houses. Instead two straight terraces were built – left and right of the hotel. Two more hotels made use almost at once of parts of the terraces. The main hotel was eleven bays long and two and a half storeys high. The Duchess of Kent and her daughter, the future Queen Victoria, stayed at the St Leonards Hotel in November and December 1834 and January 1835: in consequence it was at once renamed Royal Victoria. At Leamington apart from the Regent several other hotels opened (Bedford 1811, Clarendon 1824, Royal 1827), but the Regent was the most stately. It had more than 60 chambers and a dining room 58 feet long. There were three lavatories on the first floor, two on the second, one on the third. The Grecian porch was originally in a side street. The tariff was 2s. to 2s. 6d. for a single bedroom, 3s. to 4s. for a sitting room, 9s. to 12s. 6d. for a suite, 1s. 9d. to 2s. for breakfast, 3s. 6d. to 4s. for dinner.[43]

Of English hotels in general Johanna Schopenhauer in 1787 noted that they are 'very laudable indeed' and that they 'leave other countries behind, especially Germany'. Beds are good, waiters excellent, host and hostess welcoming. Matlock e.g. has 'three large beautiful inns' and the whole town of Bath is one 'huge *hôtel garni*'.[44]

But the three most monumental hotels of these years were all in the United States. The first is Barnum's City Hotel at Baltimore of 1825–26, the second the Tremont at Boston of 1827–30, the third the Astor House in New York of 1832–36. Barnum's was called by Frances Trollope who travelled in 1827–30[45] 'the most splendid in the Union', and Dickens called it 'the most com-

fortable of all the hotels in the United States'.[46] David Barnum had been keeper of the Boston Exchange Coffee House and for seven years of the Indian Queen Hotel at Baltimore. The architect of the City Hotel was F. Small. Its external appearance was humdrum, with a raised porch and steps as the only adornment. The area was 120 by 200 feet, the location at the corner of Calvert and Fayette Streets right by the Battle Monument. The house contained 'above 200 rooms or separate apartments for public accommodation' and accommodation for 'gentlemen with their families' is expressly referred to.[47]

Now the Tremont, the first American hotel built to be an architectural monument. Talbot Hamlin[48] calls it 'epoch-making', and that is not saying too much.[49] It was designed by Isaiah Rogers in 1827, when he was only twenty-eight, and it was published as a special volume in 1830.[50] The front was faced with Quincy granite. As for size, Dickens called it 'a trifle smaller than Bedford Square'.[51] One entered through a one-storeyed Greek Doric portico. Stairs led up to a domed rotunda with fluted Ionic columns. The façade left and right of the entry had six large rooms called from left to right Reading Room, Gentlemen's Drawing Room, Receiving Room, again Receiving Room, Ladies' Dining Room, Ladies' Drawing Room. At the back two wings projected at an angle. The one was the Dining Room for 200, with detached giant fluted Ionic columns and a shallow apse, the other contained nine chambers and five private parlours. The whole hotel had 170 rooms. At the far side of the yard between the two wings were eight privies, reached by a passage from the chambers and parlours. Eight bathrooms were in the basement. The public rooms were lit by gas. Free soap was provided in the bedrooms. The price per day was $2.00. The total cost had been $300,000.

11.19, 20 Boston, Mass., Tremont House, 1827–30, by Isaiah Rogers: view and plan (below)

11.21 New York, Astor House, 1832–36, by Isaiah Rogers

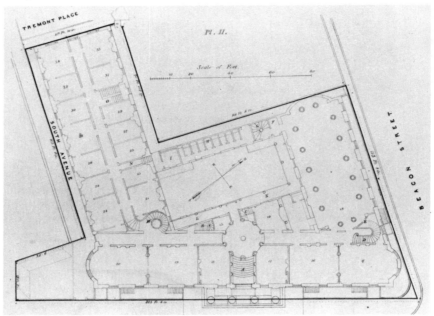

The Tremont was certainly a sensation, but it was not as single and solitary as the literature would make one expect. In Washington for instance[52] the National Hotel, completed in 1828, had 80 single and 50 double bedrooms, 12 parlours and 'a suitable number' of family lodging rooms, and Brown's Indian Queen, also completed (or enlarged) in 1828, called itself 'if not the largest in the United States, . . . nearly so'. A lithograph of c. 1837 shows it with a centre of eight bays and four storeys and wings of five bays and three storeys. It made quite a stately façade. But, of course, it had nothing of the monumentality of the Tremont.

Yet the Tremont had only a few years to enjoy its role as the prime hotel. John Jacob Astor, then approaching seventy, asked Isaiah Rogers to build him a hotel in New York to beat the Tremont in size, cost and splendour. The Astor House was built on a site opposite St Paul's churchyard, i.e. west of City Hall Park. It had a gentlemen's and a ladies' dining room, a gentlemen's and a ladies' drawing room, twenty parlours on the ground floor, suites on the first floor, 309 rooms, 17 bathrooms in the basement, and privies also on the upper floors. Lighting was by gas. The façade displayed granite, and the whole hotel cost $360,000.[53] A Frenchman in 1843 called it 'perhaps the greatest establishment of its kind in the world'.[54]

Ever since the Tremont and the Astor House the United States led the world in hotel building, and they are still leading today, though now only in certain respects. Nor was the new scale and the new standard of equipment confined to the north-east.[55] In New Orleans the (first) St Charles was opened in 1837, the (first) St Louis in 1838. The St Charles had 600 beds and a gilded dome and cost $800,000, the St Louis, which was designed by Jacques Bussière de Pouilly, cost $500,000 and had quite spectacular interiors. It was burnt in 1841, the St Charles in 1850. Of the St Louis Hamlin[56] illustrates the Pantheon-type rotunda. He also illustrates[57] the Charleston Hotel at Charleston by C. H. Reichardt, 1839, with its 150-foot-long upper loggia of giant Corinthian columns all along the façade.[58]

An early American speciality was holiday hotels, usually of wood with long verandas. The Congress Hotel at Cape May, New Jersey, was built in 1812 and burnt in 1814. It was one-storeyed and 200 feet long. The Catskill Mountain House in the State of New York was built in 1824–25. It was of wood and three storeys high. The giant upper colonnade appears in an engraving by Thomas Cole in 1828.[59] The Rockaway Marine Pavilion, New York, by Town & Davis, of 1833, was twenty-one bays long and had giant columns all along the front, a pedimented portico and a prominent cupola.

11.23 Rockaway Marine Pavilion, N.Y., 1833, by Town & Davis

11.24 Grand Hotel, Mackinac Island, Mich., 1887, by Mason & Rice

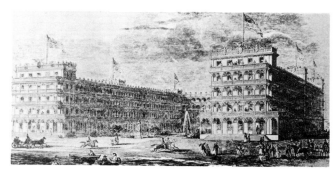

11.25 Cape May, N.J., Mount Vernon Hotel, c. 1850–53

11.22 Charleston, S. C., Charleston Hotel, 1839, by C. H. Reichardt

11.24 At least one example of the type survives, the Grand Hotel, Mackinac Island, Michigan, by Mason & Rice. It was built for 1,000 guests, and suites were rented by one of the Vanderbilts, one of the Astors, and from Chicago a Palmer and a Field.[60] The climax of all the

11.25 holiday hotels was the Mount Vernon Hotel at Cape May, opened before completion in 1853 and burnt in 1856. Only the front range and one wing had been built, the former four-storeyed and 300 feet long, the latter three-storeyed and 500 feet long. There were said to be 482 rooms for 2,100 guests. The dining room was 425 feet long. *Chambers' Journal* wrote in 1854[61] that the hotel was 'so stupendous that an Englishman has some difficulty in believing that such a structure can be a hotel. It exceeds in size anything we can even dream of as a Hotel in England.' The article also says that every bedroom had a bathroom attached, but can that statement be trusted? We have to revert to it later.

But we must first return to England and the Continent and see what happened there. One of the finest Early Victorian English hotels, and one about whose original internal arrangement we are exceptionally well

11.26 informed, is the Queen's at Cheltenham. It was designed by R. W. Jearrad, opened in 1838, and called by Granville[62] 'the first of all the hotels of English spas'. Here is the *Cheltenham Looker-On* of 21 July 1838:[63]

One of the noblest buildings of its kind in Europe, is to be opened this day: Situated at the end of one of the finest carriage drives in this or, perhaps, in any other country, upon rising ground, and commanding, consequently, the most extensive and picturesque views – in the immediate vicinity of the principal Spas, and in the very centre of gaiety and fashionable attraction – the QUEEN'S HOTEL must, of necessity, become the 'observed of all observers' – while the imposing appearance of the building itself, considered separately from its locality, cannot fail arresting the attention of the most listless and indifferent.

Then follows an illustration showing the hotel, as it still is, of thirteen bays and four storeys with a giant upper 11.26 portico of Corinthian columns and attached giant columns also to the other bays. The article then continues:

Immediately under the light and elegant portico . . . is the principal entrance, which . . . opens into the hall, a peculiarly neat and commodious vestibule, around the walls of which are a series of well-executed *basso-relievos*, models from well-known antiques except those on the centre pillars, which are adorned with copies of Thorwaldsen's beautiful designs of *Night* and *Day*. Between these two pillars is the opening of the Bar, which appears to be placed as to command all the 'exits and entrances' of the establishment. On the right hand of the Hall is the Coffee Room, measuring 50 feet in length by 26 in breadth, and occupying the entire west portion of the ground floor front. This room is lighted by seven windows, five of which look immediately down the grand approach from the High Street; the other two on to the road leading to the Montpelier Spa. The room is furnished in the most convenient and substantial manner, suitable in every respect to the purposes to which it will be appropriated, and the rank and character of the company for whose accommodation it has been provided. . . . The curtains, which have been hung with much taste, are all of crimson damask moreen, and have a very handsome appearance, harmonising well with the rich Turkey carpets covering the floor.

On the left hand of the entrance hall is a range of four rooms, occupying the eastern and southern portion of the ground floor. The corner room opening by a pair of large folding doors into that which fronts the gardens of the Hotel, . . . may be used as a double drawing or dining room; the two, when thrown into display, being capable of conveniently dining from 40 to 50 persons. Both these rooms are very handsomely furnished *en suite*, and from their retired, yet airy, situation are sure to become great favourites with the dinner parties of the establishment. Ascending the principal staircase, we arrive on the platform of the first floor, the most beautiful room of which is that forming the north western corner of the front. This room commands a look-out westward, over the roads leading to the Montpelier and the Old Wells, and northward and eastward through the greenwood vistas of the Imperial Walks and Drives, backed and surrounded by the numerous and varied buildings of the town in every direction. . . .

From this west-corner apartment, towards the centre two others open by single doors, or close by double ones, as occasion, or the wants of their occupants, may require. Immediately under the Portico, occupying the centre-front of this floor of the building, are four other handsome sitting rooms, which may be thrown into display, or effectually separated by the introduction of moveable blank doors, which being inserted into the framework of the real ones, completely disconnect one room from another. Beyond the portico eastward are two other sitting rooms fronting the road, and one overlooking the gardens of the hotel; the latter opening by large folding doors into that occupying the eastern corner of the range. There are also on this floor five sleeping rooms of lofty and spacious dimensions, beautifully and substantially furnished throughout. The whole of the sitting rooms upon this floor are fitted-up and furnished with great taste . . . in the style and fashion of Louis Quatorze. By a simple contrivance, the six sitting and two other bed rooms, constituting the eastern portion of the series, may be completely separated from communication with the other parts of the hotel, having the rooms of this suite opening into one another, or into a passage admissible only to the members of the particular family that may be in occupation of the group, and thus enjoying at the same time the quiet and retirement of a private dwelling with all the superior advantages and accommodations of a first-rate hotel.

The second floor of the hotel consists of fourteen rooms convertible into sitting or sleeping rooms, as occasion may require, and all of them commanding the most beautiful and picturesque views of Cheltenham and the surrounding hills. . . . All the front apartments on the second story of the hotel are papered to correspond, and are furnished in the same tasteful and elegant style as those on the floor below and already described. In the rear of the principal rooms occupying the centre of the building and opening from the landing on the south side of the grand staircase, are fifty rooms, suited to the accommodation of single gentlemen who prefer the retirement of the hotel department to the more public intercourse of the table d'hôte.

On the third story there are fourteen excellent bed rooms attached to the hotel, occupying the front line of the building. . . . The same arrangement obtains here as in the floors beneath, the eight rooms forming the south-eastern extremity of the series being capable of separation from the rest of the apartments on the same level. The rooms situate in the centre are agreeably shaded by the pediment which projects immediately over them, and necessarily excludes the full glare of the light of noon . . .

Having thus taken a rapid glance at the leading features of the 'grandest hotel in Europe', as George Robins hath it, we will now endeavour to take a view of the Boarding House and Table d'Hôte, a portion of the general design not a whit inferior in its appointments and accommodations to the former though in its arrangements kept wholly distinct, and occupying a separate part of the establishment, namely, the entirety of the west wing . . . The approach to the table d'hôte, from the entrance hall of the hotel, is by a passage to the right of the bar, and through the conservatory: the direct entrance is, however, opposite the new road now forming into the Old Well Lane, and having no connexion whatever with the hotel itself. The principal apartment on the ground floor [is] a dining room running east and west at the back of the building. . . . Into the dining room, and commanding the same look out, the gentlemen's drawing room opens by a pair of wide and lofty folding doors, and into this again the ladies' drawing room opens by a similar arrangement; this latter occupies the north-west corner of the building. . . . This series of apartments are fitted up and furnished *en suite*, and when thrown together display one hundred and forty feet of length, the two rooms last described being eighty-nine feet from north to south, and the dining room fifty-one feet from west to east. . . .

A separate staircase is assigned to the boarding house by which we ascend to the first floor, upon which are a suite of elegant sitting rooms, five in number, all opening into each other if required, but otherwise cut off by the system of double doors already spoken of in our notice of the hotel. These apartments are all furnished in the first style of elegance, as are also the five sleeping rooms on the same floor. On the second floor are six bed rooms, opening into each other when required, and four others having no such power of communication, and above these, on the third story, are twelve other similar bed rooms.

The points to draw special attention to in this lengthy description are the stress on suites for families and the explicit reference to rooms for single gentlemen. Single ladies apparently were not expected. Also, as against American hotels, bathrooms and lavatories are not mentioned. As for suites, it is worth recording that in London Brown's Hotel in Dover Street, opened in 1837 and enlarged by house after house to 1845, had suites only.[64] Equally in Paris the Meurice and the Bristol founded during the Restoration had suites of two to five rooms exclusively. They cost between 60 and 300 francs per day.[65] Vicomte d'Avenel, writing in 1905,[66] says that in 1830 the Meurice was praised as the most commendable hotel in Paris and that the Bristol was quite small. It had only 25 suites. He adds that in the early nineties there were no private bathrooms, whereas now – i.e. in 1905 – there are 40. In 1840 Thackeray wrote as a visitor to Paris: 'If you cannot speak a syllable of French, and love English comfort, clean rooms, breakfasts and waiters . . . don't listen to any of these commissioner fellows, but, with your best English accent, shout out boldly, Meurice, and straightaway a man will step forward to conduct you to the rue de Rivoli.'[67] English visitors were favourites at that time. After all,

11.26 Cheltenham, Queen's Hotel, 1836–38, by R. W. Jearrad

the Bristol – and all other Bristols – were called after the much-travelling Earl of Bristol, Bishop of Derry.[68]

About 1830 in other countries also hotels were established which are still flourishing, e.g. the Royal Danieli in Venice, a hotel 'in grande stile'[69] made out of a fourteenth-century palace in 1822,[70] and the Baur en Ville and the Baur au Lac in Zürich, the former opened in 1836, the latter in 1844. The Baur au Lac annexed buildings in 1852, 1877 and 1896.[71]

To revert once more to England, the Royal Western Hotel at Bristol by R. S. Pope, 1837–39, could vie with the Queen's in Cheltenham. It still stands, in the valley behind the Council House. It is of thirteen bays and four storeys and has a centre with giant Ionic columns. Pope was collaborating in this with Brunel, the great engineer, designer of the Great Western railway and the ships which had begun to run across the Atlantic in 1838. Temple Meads, the Bristol railway station, was built in 1839–40 (see p. 228).

In fact, the early railway hotels are the most interesting hotels of the early forties in England. In 1971, Christopher Monkhouse found the dining room of the Bridge House Hotel by London Bridge Station still in existence. No sooner had he discovered it than the room was demolished. It dated from between 1836 and 1840. But the buildings of the early station hotels remain at

Hull, 'in the Italian style of architecture', reticent and quite stately,[72] and at York. At Hull the hotel was completed in 1849, at York in 1853. Both were designed by J. T. Andrews. The York hotel, now called West Offices, had 55 bedrooms. When Fleetwood was at the end of the railway line from London, and for the journey to Scotland one had to exchange train for boat, Decimus Burton built the North Eastern Hotel for Sir Peter Hesketh-Fleetwood. It opened in 1841 and had a frontage of nearly 300 feet. A bedroom cost 2s. 3d. to 4s., a sitting room 3s. 4d., a table d'hôte dinner 4s.[73]

The architectural quality of the hotels by Burton and Andrews is no doubt higher than that of contemporary American hotels. *Putnam's Monthly* wrote in 1853 that hotels tend 'to look more like a penitentiary' or 'a fortress . . . than a hotel',[74] and Professor Robert Kerr wrote of American hotels about 1860 that they are 'of the ordinary barracks order',[75] and both were right. The main developments worth following in the American hotels after 1850 are those of location, those of size and those of equipment. As for location, New York is the paramount example. The march goes further and further north. The Astor House was downtown, the Fifth Avenue of 1856–59 was at Madison Square, the Windsor of 1871–73 at Fifth Avenue and 46th Street, the Buckingham of 1876 at 50th, the Plaza (not the

14.16

11.21
11.29

11.27 St Louis, Mo., Lindell Hotel, opened 1863, by Thomas Walsh

11.28 New York, St Nicholas Hotel, 1851–54, by Trench & Snook

present building) opened in 1890 between 58th and 59th Streets.[76] As for size, here are a few examples. In New York the Metropolitan opened in 1852: 29 bays, five storeys, 1,000 guests.[77] For the hotels of the next twelve years one cannot do better than quote from an article in *The Builder*[78] written by Thomas Walsh, the architect of the Lindell Hotel at St Louis.

11.27

For the last twenty years the Astor House of New York, a plain but substantial building of grey granite, costing 360,000 dollars, has been *the* hotel, when size alone was taken into account. The 'St Charles', at New Orleans; the 'Virginia' and 'Planters' of St Louis; and the 'Burnet' at Cincinnati – the latter containing some 260 rooms, and being in some respects the queen of hotels – have for fifteen or more years been among the larger hotels of the union. For the last ten years these have been excelled in the north-west by the Tremont of Chicago, which in its turn is being eclipsed by the new Sherman of the same city; which is 181 feet in front by 120 feet deep, and has six stories in front and seven in the rear, over the side walk; its cost being over 400,000 dollars. There have been many excellent houses of larger capacity, and fine specimens of architectural taste, but of less pretensions, as the Newhall at Milwaukee, the Gayosa at Memphis, the Richmond at Chicago, Barnum's in Baltimore and in St Louis &c. The large Metropolitan of New York overtopped the Astor; and the St Nicholas and Fifth Avenue, of later date, surpassed this in dimensions and modern improvements.[79] These again were all cast in the shade by the magnificent Continental of Philadelphia, which, until the Lindell of St Louis was erected, was certainly not excelled in America. The Continental is six stories in height, exclusive of basement, and presents a front of 235 feet by a depth of 194 feet. Its grand dining-room is 90 feet by 47 feet; its tea-room 65 feet by 36 feet. Its capacity is for 800 to 900 guests.

But extensive as is the Continental, the Lindell largely excels it, being seven stories high exclusive of basement. Its height from side walk to top of eave cornice is 112 feet: its south front is 272 feet; its depth, 227 feet. The east and south fronts are faced with cream coloured magnesian limestone, elaborately finished. The north and west fronts are faced with the finest stock brick, with cut stone

ornamental window trimmings. The two dining-rooms (with carving-room between), easily thrown together for dancing or other purposes, are 233 feet in length by 45 feet in width, evidently the largest in the world; that part used as the gentlemen's ordinary is alone 128 feet long by 45 feet. On the same floor, and contiguous, is a kitchen 60 feet by 46 feet, and 20 feet high. This hotel can accommodate with ease 1,200 persons.

For estimates of number of guests to number of rooms it may be useful to add that the Lindell had 525 bedrooms and incidentally 19 parlours, i.e. private sitting-rooms.

Altogether, suites played a paramount part in nineteenth-century hotels to which the twentieth has no parallel, and this predominance of suites is closely connected with the American custom of living as residents in hotels. About 1885 it was estimated that in New York hotels there were every day 200,000 transients and 100,000 residents.[80] Dickens in 1842 commented on the 'prevalent custom of married couples' to live in an hotel.[81] Over fifty years later E. I. Zeis notes the same thing.[82] But suites were of course not necessarily only for residents. Cheltenham in England, already discussed (p. 178), shows that. Cheltenham was a resort, so short stays were less likely than long. But that it was the same in London, the passage from Knight quoted on p. 174 has shown.

So much for suites. As for the single rooms, they were for gentlemen. Single ladies did not travel, or if they did, as particularly in America, they were carefully segregated in the large hotels. We have plenty of evidence for New York. William Chambers in 1854 stresses the separation of public rooms for men and for ladies and families.[83] The Metropolitan Hotel in 1852 even had a special ladies' staircase from the first floor to the ladies' reception room on the second.[84] An estimate of the fifties counted 44 women in 400 of the best New York hotel rooms.[85] The Windsor of 1871–73 was one of quite a number with separate ladies' entrance, and

11.29 New York, Fifth Avenue Hotel, 1856–59, by Griffith Thomas

this was still provided by the Manhattan Hotel in 1894–1901.

The architect of the Manhattan incidentally was Henry J. Hardenbergh, the chief hotel specialist. His favourite style was the French Renaissance. Of his hotels the Martinique in New York of 1897, the Willard in Washington and the widely familiar Plaza in New York of 1907 survive.[86] He also did the original Waldorf in 1890–93. In R. Sturgis's *Dictionary of Architecture and Building* Hardenbergh wrote on hotels and there said explicitly that 'the setting apart of rooms for . . . women is being abandoned'. In fact the Waldorf had a smoking room (the Turkish Salon) for both sexes.[87] As for equipment, Hardenbergh pleaded for one lift for every 150 guests and one bathroom at least for every two single bedrooms. But that was in 1901.[88]

So back to suites *v*. single rooms. There were of course apartment hotels with service,[89] but there were also hotels not for transients at all (in New York e.g. Murray Hill 1881–84 and Chelsea 1883–85, the latter extant and with its balconies a joy for the iron fan). The usual thing, however, was the mixture, and the three recent theses on New York hotels are full of instances, from Holt's Hotel in 1832 with 225 rooms and 25 parlours to the Fifth Avenue of 1856–59 with 530 rooms and over 100 suites, to the New Netherland of 1890–95 with 370 rooms mostly in suites, to the Empire, 1894 with 140 suites and only 24 singles,[90] and so into the twentieth century when the proportion radically changed. However, the University Arms in Cambridge, England, still advertised in 1910:[91] 'First Class for Families and Gentlemen'. Bathrooms, by the way, first multiplied by way of suites, but that development will be examined later.

As for public rooms, the scale of Tremont and Astor House was soon left behind. Just a few measurements: Windsor (1871–73), entrance hall 140 by 52 feet, dining room 105 by 50 feet; Astoria (1895–97), ballroom 93 by 96 by 40 feet.

After so much about interiors, exteriors must now be looked at. I shall concentrate on New York. Height is what one tends to look for first of all, but the consistent growth of the skyscraper must be watched among office buildings. No doubt for administrative reasons, height remained moderate for a long time. The Grand Central of 1870, with its 650 rooms, the largest hotel of its date, was 127 feet high, the Chelsea of 1883–85 140 feet,[92] the Savoy of 1890–95 and the Majestic of 1891–94 145–150 feet, the Astoria of 1895–97 214 feet, the New Netherland of 1890–93 225 feet. In the twentieth century the progress was more rapid, until the Savoy-Plaza by McKim, Mead & White, of 1927, had 36 floors and the new Waldorf-Astoria by Schulze & Weaver, 1930–31, 47 floors (i.e. it is 625 feet high).

Styles make a more entertaining record. After the noble, reticent Grecian of Tremont and Astor House, a phase of unconcealed utilitarianism ensued. The St Nicholas of 1851–54 (Trench & Snook) and the Fifth Avenue of 1856–59 (Griffith Thomas) are examples. Then styles of all kinds begin to break out. In fact, in the public rooms of the Fifth Avenue that diversification had already started lustily: entrance hall Louis XIII, but with a 'strong Middle Age character', drawing room Louis XIV, dining room Queen Anne.[93] A similar medley still infected the interiors of the Buckingham in 1875: they were, we are told, 'reminiscent of Warwick Castle, Blenheim and Chatsworth'.[94]

Now the façades of the second half of the nineteenth century. A vague slack Italianate begins at the Irving House in 1848;[95] in the Grand Hotel of 1869 it gets mixed up with French; French with pavilion roofs were the Albemarle, 1857–60, by Renwick & Auchmaty, the Gilsey of 1871, the Grand Union of 1872,[96] and – its climax – the Hardenbergh hotels already referred to, though they favour occasional borrowings from the German Renaissance (Waldorf 1890–93).[97] Queen Anne, even if taken tolerantly, is rare (Victoria 1871, Park View 1874, Murray Hill 1881–84).[98] The Roman-

11.30 Aberystwyth, former Castle Hotel (now University of Wales), 1864–65, by J. P. Seddon

11.31 Saratoga, N.Y., Grand Union Hotel, dining room

esque touches of the New Netherland (1890–93) must not be taken too seriously. Gothic never became popular in hotels, although Davis made an effort.[99] Even in England Gothic hotels are rare. The largest is of course the Midland Grand (St Pancras) in London, and of that more will be said later. Other large Gothic hotels are the former Imperial at Great Malvern by Elmslie, 1861–62 (now a girls' school), and – the most florid – the Castle Hotel at Aberystwyth (now part of the University of Wales) by Seddon, of 1864–65, with a very weird plan.[100]

The most serious of the hotel styles in America was the Italian Renaissance of McKim, Mead & White, remodellers in 1888–89 of the first Plaza, which opened in its new form in 1890.[101] The style was followed by the Holland House (opened 1891, architects Harding & Gooch) and the Savoy (completed 1895, architects Ralph & Townsend).[102]

Concerning styles it must always be remembered that the terminology was irresponsible. Here are some examples. Thomas Walsh calls the Lindell 'Italian, of the Venetian school'; *The Illustrated London News*,[103] definitely wrongly, saw in the Great Western in London 'the French of Louis XIV and after'; *The Builder* calls the Grosvenor by Victoria Station 'a modification of the Florentine Italian',[104] the New Hall Hotel at Milwaukee 'Light Italian',[105] and the Grand Hotel at Brighton simply 'Italian';[106] but a book on the Metropole at Folkestone of 1896–97 says that it combined 'all the substantialism of the Dutch Renaissance with the free classical purity of Cinquecento'.[107] That surely takes some beating.

These examples are European as well as American. But for America so far New York has been overweighted, because more research results are available. Walsh in his comments on the Lindell chiefly uses provincial hotels. What more do we know about one or

two of them? The St Charles at New Orleans 'can make up from 1,000 to 1,100 beds'.[108] George Augustus Sala called the Continental at Philadelphia (built in 1858–60) 'the most wonderful caravanserai that I have yet beheld in the United States',[109] and on American hotels in general this is his verdict: 'The American hotel is to an English hotel what an elephant is to a periwinkle . . . An American hotel is as roomy as Buckingham Palace . . . ranges of drawing rooms, suites of private rooms, vast staircases, and interminable layers of bedchambers.'[110]

That is nearly enough for the nineteenth-century hotel in American cities. All that must be added is a few data on cost, and some on construction. On equipment a good deal will have to be said later. Cost: One must remember the Tremont's $300,000 and the Astor House's $360,000. Now the Metropolitan cost $950,000,[111] the Fifth Avenue and the Grand Central (1870) over $1,000,000, the Savoy $2,500,000, the New Netherland, the Waldorf and the Astoria each about $3,000,000.[112]

In the history of hotel construction in New York the theme is the gradually increasing prevalence of iron and then steel. The 1850s were the heyday of cast-iron fronts (pp. 216–17). The Lafarge of 1855 had one and iron pillars inside. The rule almost to the end of the century remained load-bearing walls and iron framework inside. The first complete steel skeleton in New York was the Tower Building by Bradford Lee Gilbert, of 1888–90;[113] among New York hotels the first were the New Netherland, completed in 1893, and the Savoy, completed in 1895.[114]

As the city hotels grew in size and cost, so did those of the American resorts. Starting with the state of New York, at Saratoga the United States was opened in 1875 and had 800 rooms or more. The *Directory of the Principal Hotels of the World*, published in 1884, gives it 917 and calls it the largest hotel in the world. Williamson[115]

11.32 St Augustine, Fla., Ponce de Leon Hotel, opened in 1888, by Carrère & Hastings

11.33 Atlantic City, N.J., Marlborough-Blenheim Hotel, 1905, by Price & McLanahan

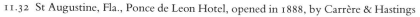

specifies 768 bedrooms and 65 suites. Baedeker[116] makes the façade 900 feet long. The Congress Hall had 1,000 beds and cost $700,000 to build, the Grand Union had 1,500 beds, a façade of 2,400 feet and cost $2,000,000.[117] The dining room was 306 feet long. Henry James in *Portraits of Places*[118] writes that the Grand Union has a piazza said to be the largest in the world, and calls this and the Congress Hall 'the two monster hotels'. Also in the state of New York, the Kaaterskill opened in 1881 and had 1,200 beds.[119] The Prospect House on Blue Mountain Lake built between 1879 and 1882 had six storeys, a front of 255 feet with a veranda along the whole length and such a veranda also along the back wing. There were 300 bedrooms, all with electric lighting. Lavatories were in an extra two-storey range.[120] The Prospect House was demolished in 1915; the fabulous Mohonk on its lake west of New Paltz still stands, begun very modestly in 1868, but in its present form built gradually up to 1911–12. It is a picturesque assembly of parts, and has very large public rooms.

For New Jersey the Mount Vernon at Cape May has already been mentioned.[121] The Stockton House, also at Cape May, had 1,000 beds;[122] in Virginia the Hygeia at Old Point Comfort had 1,000 beds, the New Atlantic at Norfolk 1,000 beds;[123] at Harrodsburg Springs, Kentucky, the hotel, built in 1842–43, had 1,000 beds;[124] and at Palm Beach in Florida the Royal Poinciana had 1,700 beds. Also in Florida, the Ponce de Leon Hotel at St Augustine, opened in 1888, was designed by Carrère & Hastings in what Walter Crane called 'a Spanish Gothic style' – in fact of course the Mission style.[125] It is 520 by 380 feet in size and built of concrete. The material had been used five years before for the Moorish Villa Zorayda by Franklin W. Smith. Smith also designed the Cordova Hotel, Carrère & Hastings the Alcazar.[126] An early hotel built in reinforced concrete is the Marlborough-Blenheim at Atlantic City, New Jersey.

The date is 1905, the architects Price & McLanahan.[127] It was at the time the largest reinforced concrete building in the world (560 by 125 feet). As for style, Price, the architect, said that 'there is more to be learnt in the Spanish, or Californian and Mexican varieties of Spanish, than any other accepted type'.[128] Yet the style of the Hotel del Coronado near San Diego, California, dated 1888 and designed by the Reid brothers, is not at all Spanish.

California got into the swing thanks to the Gold Rush, which began in 1848. San Francisco had 500 inhabitants when it started, about 25,000 in 1850, about 150,000 in 1870. Hence the two big hotels of the sixties and seventies: the Occidental, opened in 1861 with 400 rooms, and the Palace, opened in 1874. The Palace, designed by John Gaynor, had 755 rooms including suites,[129] a dining room 155 feet long and a central glazed court 144 by 48 feet with galleries around on the old Exchange Coffee House pattern.[130] It cost $5,000,000.[131] Sala calls it one of 'the most magnificent hotels on the American continent and perhaps in the whole world'.[132] Gaynor's Palace alas burned after the 1906 earthquake; but the Brown Palace at Denver, opened in 1892, is happily still with us, though with modernized decor, and it has a glazed centre and eight galleries around.[133] However, the Brown Palace is nothing if compared with the Hyatt Regency at Atlanta by John Portman, opened in 1972. It plays the Morris Lapidus game and beats Lapidus at it. The glazed court is 300 by 170 feet and 170 feet in height. There are seventeen galleries plus three storeys of suites. Deep, deep down are some incongruous public structures, and the lifts are all glass with ogee tops and bottoms and not in cages at all. The same formula was used for the Hyatt Regency at San Francisco.

Architecturally the most valuable hotel of the late nineteenth century is of course the Auditorium in

11.34 Denver, Colo., Brown Palace Hotel, opened in 1892, by F. E. Edbrooke (decoration altered)

11.35 Atlanta, Ga., Hyatt Regency Hotel, opened in 1972, by John Portman

Chicago, Adler & Sullivan's *chef d'œuvre* of 1887–89, combining the hotel with a theatre for 4,200 and an office building. The style is patently inspired by Richardson's Marshall Field Wholesale Store, built in 1885–87. The hotel part is ingeniously wrapped round two sides of the theatre. There are no more than 400 bedrooms.

11.38   In New York the first hotel to reach 1,000 rooms was the Waldorf-Astoria by Hardenbergh, the amalgam of the Waldorf of 1890–93 and the Astoria of 1895–97 back-to-back with it. The entrepreneur for the former was W. W. Astor (who however moved to London in 1890), for the latter his cousin John Jacob. Vicomte d'Avenel gives the Waldorf-Astoria a height of 272 feet, 16 visible floors and 35 lifts, and 1,500 rooms.[134] It was demolished for the Empire State Building in 1929. The Astoria had at the top single rooms for bachelors, and many suites, some let unfurnished. A suite might consist of drawing room, library, bedrooms and accommodation for servants.[135] Such suites were let semi-permanently to prominent capitalists; J. W. Gates's at the Astoria cost $20,000 per annum. The Plaza as rebuilt in 1907 boasted thirty-two resident families of high prestige.[136] Among them were A. G. Vanderbilt, George J. Gould and E. H. Harriman.[137]

Why did they choose to keep up such suites? Why were there so many residents in American hotels? And why altogether were American hotels so large? Some tentative answers may be attempted. The luxury of a hotel could not easily be matched in private houses. Even a Vanderbilt and a Gould would notice the ease with which hospitality could be arranged. And as for the less prodigiously wealthy – Paul Bourget in *Outremer* in 1895 referred to them[138] – they chose the hotel for the same reasons only felt yet more strongly. Finally, a reason for the size of the hotels was this: In Europe one could always travel from an old-fashioned well-spoken-of inn to the next inn of equal reputation and tradition. In America the roughest taverns immediately preceded the large, new hotels. In Europe also one could often travel from family friends to family friends and enjoy their hospitality. In America such a network did not exist. And also of course distances were such that most people preferred to break their journeys.[139]

And so we end with the Astor in New York of   11.37
1902–04 by Clinton & Russell with 700 rooms, the La Salle at Chicago of 1908–09 with 1,100 rooms, the Jefferson at St Louis of about the same date with 1,500 bedrooms,[140] the Stevens in Chicago (by J. A. Hola-   11.40
bird) of 1927 with 3,000 bedrooms,[141] and the Waldorf-Astoria, rebuilt on a different site in 1930–31, 47 storeys   11.38
high, with room for 2,250 guests and incorporating the ballroom from Basildon Park in England, dateable to 1776.[142] The Stevens would still be the largest hotel in   11.40

11.36 Chicago, Ill., Auditorium Building, 1887–89, by Adler & Sullivan

11.38 New York, Waldorf-Astoria Hotel: the buildings of 1890–97, by H. J. Hardenbergh, and of 1930–31, by Schultze & Weaver

11.37 New York, Hotel Astor, 1902–04, by Clinton & Russell

11.39 New York, Plaza Hotel, 1907, by H. J. Hardenbergh
11.40 (right) Chicago, Ill., Stevens (now Conrad Hilton) Hotel, 1927, by J. A. Holabird

11.41 Moscow, Hotel Rossia, 1964–67, by D. Chechulin and M. Vishnevsky

11.41 the world, were it not for the Hotel Rossia in Moscow, built in 1964–67, which boasts 3,128 rooms and suites in twelve main blocks of which one is 262 feet high.

The development of size and the development of style of American hotels is of sufficient interest to justify the pages devoted to them, but the most interesting aspect of hotel architecture in the United States is the development of equipment. Thomas Walsh, to return to the Lindell, mentions its central heating system, its 175 water-closets, running water in the bedrooms and 14 suites with bathrooms. The abundance of lavatories is as surprising as the paucity of bathrooms. There are some puzzles here. The first is that the fabulous Mount Vernon at Cape May is said to have had a bathroom to each bedroom.[143] The only parallel is at the other end of the size scale: Reichmann's Hotel in Milan, in a patrician palace in Corso Porta Romana. There, apparently about 1850, each room had a marble bath.[144] After that there is a long silence, and it seems that private bathrooms were usual only as part of a suite.

In New York the proportions between suites and bathrooms are as follows. First as a survival of the Tremont days, W. F. Baxter in *America and the Americans*, 1835, notes: 'All new erections have bathrooms'.[145] Then the Metropolitan, 1852: on the first upper floor 16 suites with bathrooms, on the second 36 with 'bathing accommodation'.[146] St Nicholas, 1851–54: on the first upper floor suites with bathrooms, on the second also,[147] and in addition on the first upper floor 37 large rooms with bathrooms. Fifth Avenue, 1856–59: more than 100 suites with bathrooms.[148] Grand Central, 1870: rooms with basins, but bathrooms only on the ground floor.[149] Windsor, 1871–73: accommodation mostly suites with bathrooms, also single rooms with bathrooms.[150] Only after that, in the nineties, was substantial progress made. Imperial, 1890: 325 rooms in suites plus 135 bathrooms.[151] Waldorf, 1890–93: 450 bedrooms, 350 bathrooms.[153] Astoria, 1895–97: 550 rooms, 415 bathrooms. In 1901 Hardenbergh[154] laid down as his rule one bathroom for every two single rooms. This was soon to be exceeded in the Hotel Astor of 1902–04, with 600 bedrooms and 400 bathrooms.[155]

In Europe things were slower. Guyer in 1885 could still write,[156] 'Bathrooms should not be totally absent in any good hotel'. He adds that 'in England in some hotels the American system of bedroom and own bathroom has been imitated'. The Savoy in London, its oldest surviving part built in 1889 to designs of T. E. Collcutt with Arthur Mackmurdo as a consultant on furniture and equipment,[157] had 67 bathrooms to over 400 rooms. The story goes that the builder asked the client whether he was catering for amphibian guests. The *Illustrated London News* notes steel joists, 'American elevators', and electric light. All rooms to the river, it says, have balconies.[158]

11.43

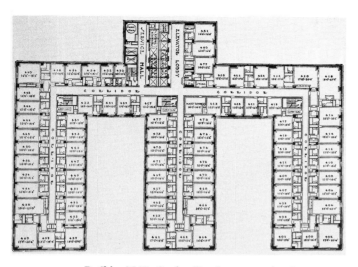

11.42 Buffalo, N.Y., Statler Hotel, 1907–11, by G. B. Post & Sons: plan of typical floor

11.43 London, Savoy Hotel, 1889, by T. E. Collcutt: original river front

The Continental delay in providing an adequate number of bathrooms was soon made up, at least in luxury hotels. In others it is not made up yet, after nearly three generations. The Ritz in Paris in 1906 had, according to Laurence Wright, a bathroom to each bedroom.[159] This is the counterpart to the Statler in Buffalo of 1907–11 by G. B. Post & Sons, which seems universally recognized as the pattern for all future bedroom and bathroom sets.[160] Williamson qualifies the claim accurately: 'the first in transient hotels'.

The Statler incidentally is one of a chain. The earliest chain, however, was according to Williamson that of Paran Stevens;[161] the most conspicuous now is the Hiltons, having spread to all parts of the globe.[162] The most familiar chains in America at the time of writing are the Sheratons, with (my count) 247 hotels, and the Holiday Inns, started in 1952 and at the time of writing with 1,398 hotels of which 75 are abroad.[163]

After bathrooms other items of technical equipment, and first central heating. Williamson's earliest case is 1846, the Eastern Exchange Hotel in Boston.[164] Next, spring mattresses: St Nicholas, New York, 1853. Gas lighting needs no documentation, as it was already an accepted possibility early in the nineteenth century, even if the Bunsen burner and the first radiators belong only to 1855. The Tremont, it will be remembered, had gas lighting in the public rooms. Williamson gives a hotel of 1835 at Boston as the first wholly gas-lit hotel.[165] Electric lighting also was introduced as soon as it had been invented. Edison developed electric bulbs in 1879–81. In 1882 the public rooms of the Gilsey in New York[166] and a hotel in Boston were electrically lit.[167] Williamson gives 1882 also for the electrically-lit Palmer House in Chicago, a grim block of thirty by thirty bays;[168] 1883 is the date for the Sagamore Hotel on Lake George, 1887–89 for the Auditorium in Chicago, 1889, as we have just seen, for the Savoy in London.

The lift also deserves a paragraph – no more, as its history is treated in detail à propos office buildings, on p. 221. Lifts began humbly for the sake of transporting luggage (Holt's Hotel, New York, 1832–33).[169] The Fifth Avenue Hotel in 1859 had two luggage lifts and one passenger lift.[170] But Beresford Hope in London in 1861 speaks of 'great central hotels with their machinery of lifts'.[171] Forty years later Henry Hardenbergh stipulated one elevator for every 150 guests.[172] A lift is English, an elevator American, while in French the term was simply *voiture*.[173] In the Fifth Avenue Hotel it is called a Vertical Screw Railway.[174] Loudon, much earlier, in his *Encyclopaedia of Cottage, Farm and Villa Architecture* of 1835[175] called it 'an ascending and descending platform'. In London the Westminster Palace (in 1860) and the Charing Cross Hotel called it an Ascending Room,[176] the Grosvenor Hotel (also in 1860) a Lifting Room.[177] In Europe 'lift' and 'elevator'

11.44 London, Paddington, Great Western Hotel, 1851–53, by P. C. Hardwick

11.45 London, Victoria, Grosvenor Hotel, 1859–60, by James Knowles

11.46 Paris, Grand Hôtel near the Opéra, opened 1862, by Alfred Armand

were for a time interchangeable terms: see Guyer's *Das Hotelwesen der Gegenwart*, published in 1885,[178] and an advertisement for the Hôtel de la Paix in Geneva in *Murray's Handbook* of 1884 referring to an 'Elevator (lift) of the most modern construction'.[179]

With some of these examples we are back in England, and England and France must now pass muster for the momentous changes of the fifties and sixties. The series – which can only be appreciated if one forgets for a while the dimensions of American hotels – begins with the Great Western, the station hotel of Paddington in London. This was built in 1851–53 to designs by P. C. Hardwick.[180] In style it is, like most of the series, Italianate, but with a French roof. It had 130 bedrooms and 20 suites, though it looks larger. The Great Northern followed in 1854–55, by Lewis Cubitt, Italianate without French motifs and not directly connected to King's Cross Station. Then Paris took over. The Grand Hôtel du Louvre in the rue de Rivoli was built to be ready for the second International Exhibition, the one following after the Crystal Palace, which took place in 1855. The hotel was designed by Armand, Hittorff, Rohault de Fleury and Pellechet. *The Illustrated London News*[181] called it 'a little town', and Professor Donaldson, praising the architectural enterprises of

Napoleon III to the skies, described it.[182] It had *c.* 700 bedrooms and covered an area 501 by 184 by 134 feet. In the middle was a spacious courtyard in a purer Classical taste. A two-arm open staircase led up to a first floor. To the outside the ground floor had all shops. On the first floor were public rooms, the salon 133 feet long, the dining room 125 feet, and suites, and there were 20 lavatories. The hotel had iron girders. In spite or because of its scale it failed and in the seventies and eighties was gradually converted into a department store (see p. 268).

Its immediate follower, however, proved a success and is still operating, the Grand Hôtel by the Opéra. This was designed by Armand and opened for the 1862 Exhibition. It had 700 bedrooms and used nearly 20,000 yards of carpeting.[183] The Hôtel du Louvre was inspired by the rue de Rivoli; this formed part of the setting for the new Opéra. The third major new hotel came for the 1878 Exhibition: the Continental, by H. Blondel.

The 1860s was a decade of much building of large hotels. It is interesting in this context that in 1865 the Ecole des Beaux-Arts set for the Grand Prix 'une vaste hôtellerie pour les voyageurs' to be located on a lake in Switzerland.[184] The data laid down comprised the following. Ground floor: Reception, etc., Vestibule, Waiting Room for arriving guests, Ladies' Room,

11.44

11.46

6.68

11.47 Scarborough, Grand Hotel, 1865–67, by Cuthbert Brodrick

11.48 London, St Pancras, former Midland Grand Hotel, 1868–76, by Sir George Gilbert Scott: main staircase

Telegraphic Office, Central hall rising to the top of the building, one Grand Staircase or more, Dining Room for 150, rooms for private dinners, Breakfast Room, Reading Room, Billiard Room, Smoking Room, Ladies' Salon. Also Washrooms, 'latrines très aérées'. The Kitchens are to be in the basement. First floor: The lake side to have suites, the other sides 'petits appartements' and lavatories. Second and third floors: 'Chambres à feu' which can be made to communicate. Stables, Coach Houses, etc., to be in subsidiary buildings. The designs submitted are criticized for artificially imposed symmetry and lack of a practical sense. Some use iron, but no one consistently.

Meanwhile in London, in the late fifties and early sixties, suddenly a number of large hotels were designed and built. The earliest of all was designed but not in fact built. Its designer was James Knowles,[185] the name was to be The International, the location in the Strand, the number of bedrooms about 230 ('besides private sitting and family rooms'). The design was published in 1858.[186] Incidentally, to show the direction in which things were moving, the description mentions specially an American bar and, as 'another American luxury', a 'hair-cutting saloon'. Knowles was luckier with his next design. The Grosvenor, by the side of Victoria Station,

11.45

was built. It was announced by a prospectus to which *The Times*[187] refers praising 'the admirable scale' of hotels 'of the American cities', and it was built in 1859–60.[188] It is of eight storeys, of which the first and second upper ones were suites, the top one servants' rooms. There was from the start a lift (called a lift), and there seem to have been two bathrooms per normal floor. As we have seen, the style is described as a modification of the Florentine Italian. That can be taken as referring to the *bifora* windows, but the roof is clearly French. A special ornament is the medallions on the façade. Queen Victoria and Prince Albert will be easily recognized, Derby, Lord John Russell and Palmerston less easily, Alexander von Humboldt only by few.

The Westminster Palace at the east end of Victoria Street followed the Grosvenor at once. The architects were A. & W. Moseley (designers of the Crystal Way – see p. 264). In fact the two hotels had been started in the same year.[189] The Westminster Palace looked larger than the Grosvenor, but the hotel accounted for only part of it. It had 286 bedrooms, 70 lavatories and fourteen bathrooms.[190] The Charing Cross Hotel by E. M. Barry and the Langham Hotel by Giles & Murray went up in 1863–65.[191] The Charing Cross had 214 bedrooms, the Langham 300. The Charing Cross had 8

11.49 London, St Pancras, former Midland Grand Hotel, 1868–76, by Sir George Gilbert Scott

11.50 Amsterdam, Amstel Hotel, 1863–66, by C. Outshoorn

11.51 Campo dei Fiori Hotel, near Varese, 1909–12, by Giuseppe Sommaruga: detail of entrance

bathrooms and 52 lavatories, the Langham 36 and about 100. Both buildings are in the free Italianate with French pavilion roofs.

11.47 The London hotels of the 1860s look distinctly joyless, and the same is true of the big new hotels in spas and seaside resorts. The most spectacular of these is the Grand Hotel at Scarborough, by Cuthbert Brodrick, built in 1865–67. So steep is the fall of the cliff that the hotel has four storeys to the town but thirteen to the sea.[192] The style is the familiar Italian-cum-French, and this is also the style of the Grand at Brighton by Whichcord, 1862–64.[193]

In the later 1870s and 1880s a second series was built: three by Trafalgar Square in Northumberland Avenue, i.e. the Victoria, opened 1876, Grand 1879, Metropole 1885. Jacob Burckhardt, the great art historian, called the Grand rather disrespectfully a 'seven-storeyed, oval stone *Wanst* rich in sculpture'.[194] A *Wanst* is a fat belly. According to Baedeker's *London* (1912 edition), these three had respectively 500 beds, 500 rooms, and 500 beds.[195] Not far away, in the Strand, the Cecil, with its 800 rooms the largest of Europe, opened in 1886. The architects were Perry & Reed.

11.48, 49 None of these hotels can be called architecturally worth while. This is different with the Midland Grand Hotel, or St Pancras Hotel, built in 1868–76. The design was by George Gilbert Scott, and he chose, and convinced his clients of, the Franco-English High Gothic – i.e. his favourite Middle Pointed, regardless of whether a medieval style suited a railway hotel. The planning is brilliant in its answer to the hotel needs and the station needs. The levels in particular are handled in a masterly way.[196] So is the skyline. The other new hotel of architectural merit is the Savoy, first opened in 1889, as we have seen, and later enlarged. The style here is a free French Renaissance, manipulated very elegantly.

Space does not allow so much detail for the other European countries, and, besides, available research is extremely patchy. Among famous city hotels the Amstel at Amsterdam dates from 1863–66 (by C. Outshoorn), the Frankfurter Hof at Frankfurt from 1872–76 (by Mylius & Bluntschli; 240 rooms), the Kaiserhof, the first modern hotel in Berlin, from 1873–76 (by Hennicke & von der Heide; 232 rooms). Burckhardt says about the Frankfurter Hof that 'the Italian Renaissance reigns to the verge of the incredible'.[197] Vienna got its first batch of modern hotels in the seventies.[198] The Grand Hotel Wien by Karl Tietz had 300 bedrooms and was completed in 1871, the Metropole by E. Schumann and L. Tischler, of 1871–73,

11.50

11.52 Copenhagen, SAS Royal Hotel, 1960, by Arne Jacobsen

11.53 Istanbul, Hilton Hotel, 1953–55, by Skidmore, Owings & Merrill and Sedad H. Eldem

11.54 Szombathély, Hotel Claudius, 1969–72, by Peter Fazakas

had about 360 'Wohnräume'.[199] It is no accident that the Vienna International Exhibition was scheduled for 1873 (see p. 248).

In Switzerland it is of course the resorts one has to watch.[200] Along the Lake of Geneva Montreux, Vevey, Ouchy were, according to Fanny Kemble, 'a continuous terrace of hotels'.[201] Lucerne and Interlaken were favourites, though now they are no longer, and a spa like St Moritz Bad has passed all its initial glamour to St Moritz Dorf.[202] At Lucerne the hotel with the longest tradition is the Schweizerhof, whose centre may be by Melchior Berri and date back to 1845–46.[203] Much was gradually added and altered, until in 1927 it had 400 beds and 100 bathrooms. The National[204] by Alphonse Pfyster, with façade by H. V. von Segesser, is of 1869 and hence has French roofs. The façade is more Baroque than those of the contemporary London hotels, and the Palace by A. Meili of 1904–06 is frankly Neo-Baroque. Art Nouveau is rare in hotels: the most sumptuous is no doubt Sommaruga's Campo dei Fiori Hotel near Varese of 1909–12.

As for the sizes of European hotels, it is worth remembering that even today hardly any come up to American scale. I take Switzerland as an example.[205] In the whole of the country only the following twenty-

two have 300 or more bedrooms. The Nova Park at Zürich has 1,000 and is very recent. So are the Geneva Intercontinental, with 785, and the Zürich International with 700. Then follow Zürich Holiday Inn, also recent, 575; Flims, Park Hotel Waldhaus 520; Territet, Grand Hôtel 500; Geneva, Président 450, and Rhône 400; St Moritz, Suvrettahaus 380; Interlaken, Grand Hôtel Victoria 360; Montreux, Palace 350; Lugano, Calypso 320; Lausanne, Palace 320; St Moritz, Palace 320; Zürich, Atlantis 320, and Airport Hilton 320; Lucerne, Grand Hôtel National 300, Palace 300, and Schweizerhof 300; St Moritz, Engadiner Kulm 300; Zürich, Dolder Grand Hotel 300; Ouchy, Beau Rivage 300.

It will have been noticed that the largest hotel at Interlaken is called after Queen Victoria. I have counted another ten Victorias. The name justifies an excursus. The English were still the best customers of luxury hotels, though not for much longer. The Hotel d'Angleterre at Baden Baden is to Gérard de Nerval who writes in 1860 the most beautiful in the place.[206] Angleterres also exist or existed at Geneva, at Ouchy, at St Petersburg.[207] At St Petersburg the Angleterre offered 'large suites' as well as 'bedrooms for single gentlemen'. Yet another Angleterre was by tradition the first hotel of Copenhagen. The first hotel at Spa was the Britannique.

Venice had a Regina d'Inghilterra (listed already by Murray in 1874).[208] The best hotels of Nice are in the Promenade des Anglais. In Rome I found an Inghilterra, a Londra, an Isole Britanniche.[209] Naples had an Isole Britanniche too.[210] But there was also an Albergo Nuova York, and in Rome an America, and so one appreciates William Morris's relief to find himself in Florence in an old-fashioned hotel and not one where he would 'form part of the furniture of a gigantic Yankee hutch'.[211]

The twentieth century has brought more changes, both stylistically and functionally. As for style, historicism began to disappear between the end of the nineteenth century and the First World War. One can watch in the Adlon in Berlin (1907 by Gause & Leibnitz)[212] and the Regina in Munich (1908 by Stöhr, architect and builder) how historicism is made less and less of, and the style of the twentieth century dawns. Among the European centres of radical innovation during those years was Vienna. Otto Wagner, professor at the Academy, published a book in 1896 which he called *Moderne Architektur* and which contained denouncements of historicism and academicism. His buildings from 1898 onwards were beacons of light. One of his faithful, the architectural journalist Joseph Lux, wrote an article in *Der Architekt* in 1909 dealing with hotel architecture.[213] This is what he lays down: 'The hotel must satisfy three demands.' It must function, 'machine-like, like a perfectly constructed apparatus; it must be up to the standard of wagons-lits, and it must, as regards hygiene and cleanliness, fulfil clinical demands.' He then sums up: 'What is needed is 'a synthesis of hospital, wagons-lits and machinery'. 'Maybe,' he adds, 'maybe that in fifty years we will reach such excellent hotels.'

Fifty years – that would be 1959. Lux was not far out. Of 1960 is the SAS's Royal Hotel in Copenhagen by Arne Jacobsen, the International Modern in its greatest purity, and of 1953–55 is the Hilton at Istanbul by Skidmore, Owings & Merrill with Sedat H. Eldem representing to perfection a compositional type which can now be found in countries all over the world. But the new restlessness of the sixties and the playing with oddly-shaped pre-cast concrete members is also represented, e.g. by the Hotel Claudius at Szombathély in Hungary (1969–72, architect Peter Fazakas).

Functionally the changes in hotel building are mostly post-Second World War. They are all the consequence of the greater mobility by car, coach and charter flight. So the classes which made the Isle of Man tick comfortably now go to the Costa Brava or the Costa del Sol, with the effect that whole coasts, and not only in Spain, are developed for hotels and blocks of flats until nature is entirely shut out. Copacabana was probably the first such desperate twentieth-century sea-front.

While this urge to spend holidays far from home has led to a multiplication of hotels,[214] the other three innovations do damage to existing hotels. One is camping, more and more taken up by young families including the professional and academic classes, partly for cheapness and partly for informality – a blessing without any doubt for children and hence also for their parents. The second is holiday camps, where you have a cabin to yourself and free access to ample public rooms and entertainments. Butlin's in England are the most familiar. They are ideal for the gregarious and those who are longing to be gregarious.

The third innovation, of architectural significance, is the motel, i.e. a 'motor hotel' on a highway away from the city centre and initially consisting of units, not of bedroom and bathroom, but of bedroom, bathroom and garage. So the motel tends to be low and stretching out. A paragraph or two on its history may make a final flourish for this chapter. That invention and early development were all American need hardly be mentioned. The first motel ever is said to have been at Douglas, Arizona, in 1913. The units were still called cabins.[215] In 1925 in California a chain was projected. The prototype was built at San Luis Obispo in 1926.[216] The real start, however, was during the thirties. The usual name was 'motor court'. The initial *raison d'être* was the depression.[217] In the late twenties there were about 600. By 1939 *c.* 13,500, by 1946 *c.* 20,000, by 1953 nearly 50,000.[218] In 1955 it was estimated that of Americans going on holiday and stopping en route 59 per cent stop at motels and 36 per cent at hotels, but when they reach their destination 25 per cent stay at hotels and only 10 per cent at motels.[219] The first Swiss motel is said to have been built at or near Interlaken and opened about 1955,[220] the first English one – at least the first to be published – was the Dover Stage by L. Erdi, 1956–57.[221] Not that all motels look like the Dover Stage. How sordid motels can be some will remember from *Lolita*.[222]

11.52

11.53

11.54

11.55

11.55 Minehead, Butlin's Holiday Camp

12.1 Milan, so-called Banco Mediceo, *c.* 1455–60, probably by Michelozzo
(from Filarete's *Treatise*; *Florence, Biblioteca Nazionale Centrale*)

12
Exchanges and banks

BANKING begins with the discovery that a written promise to pay can take the place of a cash payment, or, in other words, banking originates in the need for credit. But as he who gives you credit or he who accepts your promise to pay will need an extra inducement to take the risk, the charging of interest is at the beginning of banking too. Now the charging of interest was condemned by the church as usury; the first bankers in Christian society were the Syrians and then, more and more exclusively, the Jews. At the start of Christian lending are monastic establishments helping land-owners on the principle of *mort-gage*, the security being the land itself. With the development of towns and of literacy, first in Italy then also in the North, Christian pawnbrokers-cum-money-lenders took over from the Jews. We call them Lombards, although they did not all stem from Lombardy. They achieved a position of international power by establishing themselves as the collectors of Papal revenues (Peter's Pence) which involved conversion of currency and was bound to lead into banking. The other medieval source of banking was the great fairs, especially those of Champagne. Trading initially of goods against goods quickly expanded to goods against money, and when bills of exchange took the place of money banking was estab-lished. The term incidentally comes from the benches (*banchi*) and the trestle table of the banker. When he turned out to be insolvent, his bench was broken up (*banca rotta*). In the thirteenth century, apart from the transactions of the Lombards and the transactions at the fairs, the order of Templars did banking so successfully that it was destroyed by Philip IV of France and Pope Clement V in 1307–11, largely for reasons of King's and Pope's envy and greed.

However, none of all these can really be called bankers as a professional term. The banker is a four-teenth-century creation, and a Mediterranean creation, although even then banking was not an exclusive occu-pation but a concomitant of trading. The merchant-banker is the first professional banker. An instructive example is Marchesa Origo's *The Merchant of Prato*,[1] dealing with Francesco Datini who died in 1410 and who had branches under *fattori* in Florence, Pisa, Genoa and also Avignon and Barcelona, Valencia and Palma de Mayorca.

It is in Datini's time that we find the first premises specially designed and built for merchants and bankers, i.e. the first exchanges. The earliest dates are 1382 for the Loggia dei Mercanti at Bologna and 1383 for the *lonja* or Taula de Canvi ('exchange table') at Barcelona.[2] The

12.2 Valencia, Silk Exchange, 1483

12.3 Bruges, Place de la Bourse (Sanderus, *Flandria Illustrata*, 1641–44)

building at Bologna was open on the ground floor like the town halls we have met in a previous chapter and the market halls we shall meet in a future chapter.[3] The building at Barcelona was a room with aisles and outer windows. More exchanges followed quickly; for the merchants and the bankers needed a covered place for their work. At Barcelona the room was called the Casa de Contratación.[4] The dates are Perpignan 1397 (with an open ground floor), Palma 1426, Valencia 1483.

The fourteenth and fifteenth centuries are the great centuries of Italian merchant-bankers,[5] the best-known of them all being Cosimo de' Medici, his son Piero and his grandson Lorenzo the Magnificent.[6] Benedetto Dei in 1469 said of them 'fanno merchantia per tutti i luoghi del mondo'.[7] They were of course not alone in the field. In the fourteenth century the leading Florentine bankers were the Bardi and the Peruzzi.[8] Now these names are familiar to anyone interested in the history of painting. The Bardi Chapel and the Peruzzi Chapel in S. Croce in Florence were painted by Giotto. It is indeed a fact worth recording and speculating upon that these early capitalists were the leading patrons of art. As for architecture, Cosimo de' Medici built the Palazzo Medici employing Michelozzo, Giovanni Rucellai built the Palazzo Rucellai employing Alberti, Filippo Strozzi built the Palazzo Strozzi employing Cronaca, Andrea Pazzi built the Pazzi Chapel in the cloister of S. Croce employing Brunelleschi. The name Pazzi is remembered primarily for the Pazzi conspiracy of 1478, which ended in the murder of Giuliano de' Medici, Lorenzo's younger brother. The conspiracy is a telling reminder of

the fact that banking, trading and manufacturing in the age of Alberti and Botticelli were not as peaceable occupations as they are now. The cause of the conspiracy was partly commercial competition, partly the anti-Medici policy of Sixtus IV. To continue the roll-call of merchant-banker patrons of art: the leading banker of Rome at the beginning of the sixteenth century was Agostino Chigi, and he built the Villa Farnesina employing Peruzzi and Raphael. Raphael also painted portraits of another Roman banker, Bindo Altoviti.

Now for the Medici connections. Lorenzo was married to a Tornabuoni, and the Tornabuonis commissioned Ghirlandajo to paint the choir of S. Maria Novella. The other great cycle of Ghirlandajo's frescoes is in the Sassetti Chapel in S. Trinita, and Francesco Sassetti was the manager of the Medici Bank from 1464 to 1490. Ghirlandajo also painted Sassetti's portrait with his grandson (now in the Metropolitan Museum in New York). The Medici representative in Rome was Giovanni Tornabuoni. In Milan it was Pigallo Portinari, married to a Baroncelli, and the Baroncelli Chapel, in the choir of S. Croce, was painted by Taddeo Gaddi several generations before. Another Portinari, Tommaso, represented the Medici interest at Bruges. Here the artists employed were Flemings, as indeed Giovanni Arnolfini, a silk merchant from Lucca, had done before – see the van Eyck double portrait in the National Gallery in London. Tommaso Portinari commissioned the famous altarpiece by van der Goes for the hospital of S. Maria Nuova in Florence. The hospital has already engaged our attention (p. 142).

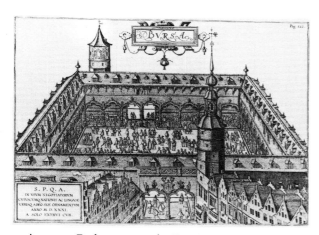

12.4 Antwerp, Exchange, 1531, by Dominicus van Waghemakere

12.5 Florence, Palazzo Medici Riccardi, begun 1444, by Michelozzo

Banking in the fourteenth, fifteenth and sixteenth centuries was an extremely risky business. For the biggest loans went to princes, and they often did not or could not repay. As Edward III had ruined the Bardi and the Peruzzi,[9] so Charles the Bold's death ruined the Milan house of the Medici.

But we are not concerned in this chapter with a history of banking nor a history of merchant-bankers as patrons of the arts, however striking an illustration the latter history is of the theme of Early Capitalism as a substructure of art. What this chapter must try to elucidate is banking premises, and the first question is: Did they exist in the fifteenth century? The answer must be: to a very limited degree, yes. In Bruges the merchants, and that – as we have seen – included the bankers, met in a square known as the Place de la Bourse from a house of the van der Beursse family.[10] Hence the German term *Börse* and the French *bourse*. In that square were the factories, the term used in the old sense (a factor being a commercial agent), or, to use another term, the *fondaci* (p. 237), of the Italian traders by 'nations' and also of the Northern Hanseatic traders. The community coherence by town or country of origin dictated the premises just as it did in early universities. The Fondaco dei Turchi and the Fondaco dei Tedeschi in Venice are better known – and also bigger – than their opposite numbers in Bruges. In the illustration the four-bay house without a gable was the van der Beursse house and became the Venetian factory. To its left was the Genoese factory. The Florentine factory is the one with the pinnacles.

With the commercial decline of Bruges and the triumphal progress of Antwerp, premises for merchants and bankers had to be found or provided in Antwerp, and so in 1531 Dominicus van Waghemakere built the first exchange of the North 'for the use of traders of all nations and all languages'. The architectural scheme was totally different from that of the Spanish *lonjas*: an open space surrounded by cloisters, the details still in the elaborate, flamboyant Latest Gothic. The building must have created a sensation; for Guicciardini in his *Descrizione di tutti i Paesi Bassi*, published in 1567, calls is 'veramente bella'.[11]

The Hanseatic merchants who did some banking too, although never on the scale of the Italians, built themselves a house in Antwerp also, in 1564–68. It provided lodgings and warehousing space and for that reason will be mentioned again in later chapters (see pp. 213, 237).

But the *fondaci* and the *bourses* served general trading purposes. Were there also premises in existence for banking in particular? Or to give the question its briefest form: Where did Cosimo and Lorenzo de' Medici bank? The answer of course is: in their palatial town house. But beyond that commonsensical statement the evidence is scanty.[12] On the first floor towards the back garden was a room called Camera della Tasca. *Tasca* is a purse or a money bag, and in an inventory of the palace dated 1492 there is a mention of 'uno chassone di nocie anticho dove sta la tascha del bancho' (an ancient walnut coffer containing the money bag of the bank). So one must imagine negotiations taking place in any room of the palace, but some space set aside for storing of money and probably of certain goods, and also some space for clerks keeping the books.

For book-keeping during the fifteenth century had become a technique requiring considerable skill. The first manual of double-entry book-keeping is Book III of Luca Pacioli's *Summa de arithmetica, geometria, proportioni et proportionalita*, published in 1494. But Pacioli did not invent the 'partita doppia'.[13] It had existed in Venice in the early fifteenth century[14] and even earlier in the Banco di S. Giorgio in Genoa. This was founded in 1408 by Marshal Boucicaut, the French Governor, and Dauphin-Meunier calls it the first public bank in Europe.[15] To return to double-entry book-keeping, the Bardi and the Peruzzi did not know it. Pacioli is better known for his *De divina proporzione*. He knew Alberti and Piero della Francesca but lived mostly in Milan, where he must have been familiar with Bramante and Leonardo.

Milan must also be the next item for this chapter; for while for the Medici Palace in Florence we found ourselves reduced to guesswork, we are in a better position in the case of the Medici premises in Milan. The building, described by Filarete,[16] is in the literature usually called the Banco Mediceo. That is, as we shall see, misleading. It was another Medici palace, and in it lived the Milan representative of the Medici company, Pigallo Portinari, brother of Tommaso. Francesco Sforza had become ruler of Milan in 1450 and, being a friend of the Medici, gave them a building in 1455. The building was made little use of; the Medici, Filarete says, erected a building on the site 'quasi come di nuovo fatto'. There 'Pigallo Portinari reggie e guida tutto el traffico che hanno a Milano' (controls and directs all the business that they have in Milan). Filarete has drawn the façade of the palace. Its designer was probably Michelozzo, who had designed the Medici Palace in Florence and no doubt also Pigallo Portinari's Chapel in S. Eustorgio in Milan.[17] Filarete's description of the palace is remarkably detailed. Yet efforts to reconstruct the plan have so far been vain. Even so, certain facts of great interest in our context are patent. On the ground floor the most important rooms were the winter dining room, 21 by 13 braccia, and the study, 13 by 10 braccia. The great hall, 41 by 13 braccia, was on the upper floor, and – like the façade – was decorated 'allanticha'. Store rooms are referred to under the terms *fondaco* and *maghazzino* and one room specifically as the 'fondaco per i panni', i.e. for cloth. In addition the room above the study is described as the one 'dove stanno a scrivere e apparare le ragioni del banco' – 'where they write and keep the affairs of the bank'. So here we have the first office of a banker. We shall presently come across another, and now, in accordance with the political and commercial developments, north of the Alps.

For Early Capitalism had its representatives in the North as well as in the Mediterranean border countries. For England one need only name the de la Poles of Hull, later Dukes of Suffolk, and for France Jacques Coeur of Bourges, *argentier* of Charles VII – the arch-capitalist of the French fifteenth century.[18] His interests extended to mining and shipping. He lent Charles VII 200,000 écus for the conquest of Normandy and rode into Rouen with the King.[19] His house at Bourges built in the 1440s and 50s still exists. It was not yet complete when Jacques Coeur's wealth and enterprises were destroyed. He died an exile on Chios. The house is the stateliest French town-house of the century, but too little is known of the functions of the rooms. The only evidence which might be of interest in our context is a room on the top floor of one of the three towers which was entered by a door with an exceptionally elaborate lock.[20] That room was probably the treasury.

As for the sixteenth century, the most powerful enterprise of merchant-banking was conducted in the North. It goes without saying that this was the enterprise of the Fuggers of Augsburg and especially of Jakob Fugger *der Reiche* (1459–1526) and his nephew Anton (1493–1560).[21] The Fuggers had branches in Nuremberg, Frankfurt and Cologne, in Leipzig, Breslau (Wroclaw) and Vienna, in Venice, Milan and Rome, in Lyons and Spain, and also in smaller places where their industrial interests called for offices, i.e. at Fuggerau near Villach, at Neusuhl, Schwaz and Hall. These interests were chiefly in the mining of metals, and they stretched from the Spanish mercury and silver (the income of the three great Orders of Santiago, Calatrava and Alcantara made over to the Fuggers by Charles V as security for loans of money) to Slovakia and Hungary and the Tyrol (silver, copper, lead). Politics plays as large a part in the Fugger business as in that of their Italian fifteenth-century predecessors. The Fuggers were pro-Habsburg and pro-Catholic. Charles V's succession to his grandfather Maximilian was won by Fugger money, and Jakob was certain enough of his indispensability to write to Charles V in 1523: 'It is known and obvious that Your Majesty could not have obtained the crown without us.'[22] As for the Fuggers' Catholic policy, this caused violent abuse by Hutten and severe censure by Luther.

The house of the Fuggers in Augsburg fronts the Maximilianstrasse. It was built in the 1490s and enlarged in 1512–15. The façade in the end was of 26 bays, over 300 feet in length. The architect was Burckhard Engelberger, and Hans Burgkmair, the leading Augsburg painter of the Early Renaissance, painted the façade. A small inner courtyard, called the Damenhof, had a cloister of very elementary Ionic columns, nothing like as authentically *all'antica* as the Fugger Chapel in St Anna which was begun in 1509 and is the earliest German ensemble in the new Italian fashion. The most famous piece of Fugger architecture, the Fuggerei, was built a little later, c. 1516–23, as almshouses, larger than any other.[23]

Now, as in the case of the Banco Mediceo, we ought to find out what offices existed in the house of the Fuggers. Here however we are once again unlucky, for the famous description of the offices quoted in much of the more popular Fugger literature is a nineteenth-century fabrication.[24] The cupboard in the Fugger Museum at Augsburg is not much more useful. It was knocked together out of old parts in the nineteenth century. Yet one feature in particular is likely to represent something genuine of the early sixteenth century. It is the twice eight upper drawers and twice five lower drawers. The drawers are labelled with the names of places and such indications as *Conti*, *Quietanze*, *Ricordi*. There are also the dates 1507 and 1528. The reason why one might be inclined to trust the drawers is that such business cupboards did exist in the time of Jakob, as we

12.6 Bourges, House of Jacques Coeur, 1442–53

12.7 Matthäus Schwarz in his office, from the *Trachtenbuch* (*Brunswick, Herzog Anton Ulrich-Museum*)

shall presently see. The evidence is connected with Matthäus Schwarz, Jakob's chief book-keeper.[25]

We know much of him. He was born in 1497, went to Venice in 1514, after having looked in vain in Milan and Genoa for someone who would be able to teach him book-keeping. Fresh from the technique he had finally learned in Venice (where Jakob had also been trained) he returned to Augsburg in 1516 and was engaged by Jakob Fugger. But in his work for the firm he realized at once that he knew nothing. However, he now applied himself to learning, and so in 1518 he wrote a book on book-keeping. He proposed – one understands why – not to publish it. Three copies exist of between 1550 and 1565. Here is one passage from the book: Book-keeping – and he means double-entry book-keeping – 'is a serviceable, tidy, orderly, just, entertaining, beautiful . . . art'. It was 'invented by the Italians, but this rich-making art is little liked by the Germans'. And here is a second much briefer entry: 'Interest is polite usury, finance is polite thieving.'[26] In a book commissioned by Schwarz and known as the *Trachtenbuch* – it is kept in

the Brunswick Landemuseum – is an illustration showing Schwarz at his desk with a ledger, Jakob Fugger standing by him, and behind them a tall cupboard with the drawers labelled Rome, Venice, Budapest, Cracow, Milan, Innsbruck, Nuremberg, Antwerp and Lisbon, i.e. the same type of arrangement as on the cupboard at Augsburg.

The Fuggers were not the only German millionaires. The story of the Welsers is just as spectacular, and there were the Tuchers in Nuremberg.[27] We do not know more about their premises than about those of the Fuggers. But we have a substitute: a large woodcut called *Eigentliche Abbildung dess gantzen Gewerbs der löblichen Kaufmannschafft*. It is by Jost Amman, a Swiss who lived at Nuremberg. He was born in 1539 and died in 1591.[28] We know incidentally of a journey he made to Augsburg in connection with illustrations to Fugger's *Buch der Gestüten*. Also, Amman knew Marx Fugger. The woodcut has at the top rows of coats of arms of mercantile cities. The centre is a big allegorical fountain. The lower third has four interior scenes much

12.8 Jost Amman, woodcut of merchants and their activities, later 16th c. *(London, British Museum)*

like *mansiones* in the early theatre. Between the two left and the two right ones sits the merchant himself and at the bottom are more scenes and also some allegorical figures. Above the merchant's throne is a niche, and in this he keeps his 'Secret-Buch'. The woodcut has in fact ample captions. Bottom centre is Fortune on a ball (the motif of Dürer's famous engraving). A man behind her represents Integritas. To the right of Fortune two men demonstrate 'Taciturnitas'. Balancing them on the left are two Turks, inscribed 'Linguarum Peritia' (knowledge of languages) and illustrating the need for foreign languages in business. To the left of them follows the 'Vertreter des Cassier', the cashier's deputy. He enters in a book 'Ein- und Ausgaben' (income and expenditure). More or less above him is another clerk entering into a book each day what happens in trade. Further left are packers unpacking goods. On the right-hand side are men counting money and putting it into bags, and behind them packers packing goods and despatching them to the Fair, and yet another clerk transferring entries from the journal into the 'Haupt-Buch', putting 'Den Debitor zu linken Hand/Den Creditor im Gegenstand' (the debtor on the left, the creditor on the opposite side). In fact in the long title of the woodcut there is a reference to the 'löblichen, schönen, uralten

Kunst des Buchhaltens' – the laudable, beautiful, very ancient art of book-keeping. Matthäus Schwarz had not lived in vain. Finally, the *mansiones*. They show from left to right the weighing of goods, a meeting of three men concerning some mining matters, the 'Gross Schreibstuben' (great office) containing the cash-box, and two men concerned with 'Kleinodien und edle Stein' (precious objects and gems).

It is a great pity that we have no similar Italian or Spanish document; for in the fifteenth and sixteenth centuries interesting developments had taken place in the Mediterranean countries. We hear of a bank at Barcelona established in 1401; in Italy the Casa di S. Giorgio in Genoa, started in 1408,[29] has already been mentioned. Of particular importance within the banking bodies of the fifteenth century was the establishment of the so-called *Monti di Pietà* by the Franciscans. They were established to serve the smaller man by means of small loans. If the Franciscans could do that, it demonstrates that the taking of interest was no longer considered usury. But that story is full of contradictions. On the one hand Accurius, teaching Roman Law in France in the early and mid-thirteenth century, and Bartolo di Sassoferrato, who taught law at Perugia in the fourteenth, tried to justify lending with interest. On the

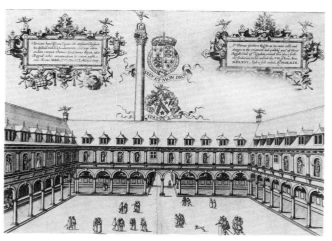

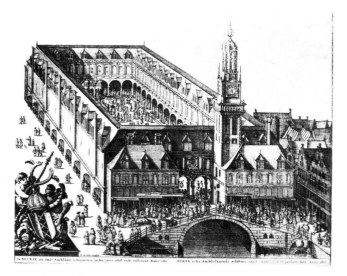

12.9 Amsterdam, Exchange, 1608–11, by Hendrik de Keyser

12.10 (above right) London, Royal Exchange, 1566
12.11 (right) London, the second Royal Exchange, 1667–71, by
Edward Jarman

other hand S. Bernardino of Siena, who died in 1444, still preached passionately against it: 'Usury is an infectious disease. Yet no one blushes, no one fears it, no one even among Christians seems to know its gravity. . . . Such men are honoured by all, one gets up in their presence . . . they contract noble marriages [and] one buries them in the churchyards, even in churches with more pomp than others.'[30] The first Monte di Pietà was started in 1428 at Arcevia near Sinigaglia. Others followed in the 1460s at Perugia, Orvieto, Gubbio and Assisi.

Secular public banks came into their own only in the late sixteenth century. We know of the Banco della Piazza di Rialto in Venice founded in 1587,[31] the Papal Banco di Santo Spirito in Rome, founded in 1591[32] and the Banco di S. Ambrogio in Milan founded in 1593. Shortly after, the North caught up with Italy, and now one after another public banks were created; in Rotterdam in 1599 (rebuilt in 1635),[33] in Amsterdam in 1609 (called Wisselbank and located in the Town Hall, see p. 34), in Middelburg in 1616 (also Wisselbank), in Hamburg in 1616, in Delft in 1621, in Nuremberg in 1621, and so on.

It will be noticed that among these places none is in the Southern Netherlands, and indeed, owing to the Wars

of Religion, the Southern Netherlands, including Antwerp, lost their commercial leadership. It passed to London and to Amsterdam. A sign of this development is the foundation of exchanges in London in 1566 and in Amsterdam in 1608–11, the latter designed by Hendrik de Keyser. The London Royal Exchange[34] was due to Sir Thomas Gresham, agent of the Queen at Antwerp and a far-sighted economist (who for instance first conceived the idea of an equalization fund to secure the balance of the pound). The plan of the Royal Exchange and that of the Amsterdam Beurs followed that of Antwerp with the open courtyard and cloister,[35] and when in the Fire of London in 1666 the Royal Exchange was burnt, it was rebuilt on the same plan in 1667–71. The architect was Edward Jarman. Due to him was the clumsy treatment of the façade with its triumphal arch motif expressed by a middle archway and pairs of giant columns left and right, carrying segmental pediments, and the over-sized tower above.

London needed a new exchange; for trade was expanding rapidly. London banking in the seventeenth century was the goldsmiths' preserve. Sir Francis Child and Sir Richard Hoare were the first to move from the goldsmith's trade into banking as their principal occupation. Pennant[36] calls Francis Child 'the first regular

12.12 Liverpool, Bank of England, branch office, 1845–48, by C. R. Cockerell

12.14 London, Westminster Bank, Lothbury, 1838: banking hall by Sir William Tite

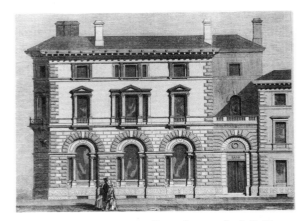

12.13 Manchester, Heywood's Bank, 1849, by J. E. Gregan

12.15 London, Bank of England, the first premises, 1732–34, by George Samson (London, Sir John Soane's Museum)

banker' and 'the father of the profession'. The public bank, as against these private banks, only appeared in 1694 with the establishment of the Bank of England.[37] The Bank of England started as a private enterprise, lending the central government £1,000,000.[38] In 1697 it was granted the monopoly of joint-stock banking. In 1707 it became the principal agent for exchequer bills, in 1717 it was the agent for issuing a government loan, and so it became gradually but quite rapidly the banker for the government, including the treasury. In the late eighteenth century private banks stopped issuing notes of their own, using Bank of England notes instead. In 1833 at last the notes of the Bank of England became legal tender. Private banks did go on, however, and were used in a way not different from today, though they did not yet have branch offices.[39] Branch offices seem to have started in the early nineteenth century.[40] Routine banking transactions also did not differ from today; this is evident for instance in the article *Banque* of Diderot and d'Alembert's *Encyclopédie* which began to appear in 1751. The article starts with some banking terms, and among them are such familiar terms as *ouvrir un compte* and *avoir du crédit en banque*.[41]

The headquarters of Georgian and even Early Victorian banks were exactly like private houses, with the business rooms on the ground floor left and right of the entrance and the manager's living quarters above. Examples are Hoare's Bank in Fleet Street, a seven-bay house of three storeys, designed by Charles Parker and begun in 1829,[42] and the Westminster Bank in Lothbury, also of seven bays, built in 1838 and demolished in 1908. The façade was designed by C. R. Cockerell. He also did the sombrely impressive branch buildings of the Bank of England at Bristol, Liverpool and Manchester in 1845–48 and insurance buildings for the Westminster Fire Office in King Street in 1829–30, the Westminster Insurance Co. in the Strand in 1832 (a rehearsal for the Bank of England branches), the Sun Fire Office in 1841–42 and the Liverpool, London & Globe Insurance in 1855–57. They will be mentioned in connection with office buildings (pp. 213–14). As for the Westminster Bank, the façade is typical Cockerell, with the massive, rusticated giant angle pilasters carrying sculpture and the deeply recessed doorway and windows. But more important than the façade is what lay behind. For here is our first case of a domed hall. It was not *the* first case, as will be shown presently. The type soon became standard. In the Westminster Bank the feature was by Tite, not Cockerell. Of Tite also more later. Again in London, four years after the Westminster

12.12

13.4

12.14

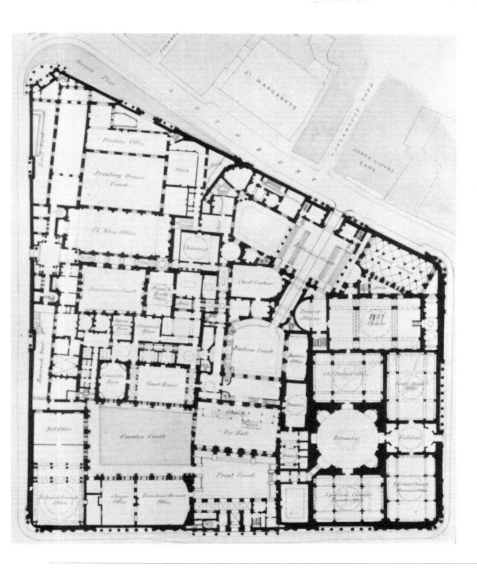

12.17 London, Bank of England, Rotunda, 1765–70, by Sir Robert Taylor

12.18 London, Bank of England, Tivoli Corner, by Sir John Soane

12.16 London, Bank of England, 1788–1834, by Sir John Soane: plan

Bank, in 1842, a large hall, oblong, with tall columns, a big coving and skylights was built by a biscuit manufacturer as the Hall of Commerce. It then became for a short time the Stock Exchange and later was taken over by various banks.[43] As an example from the provinces Sir Benjamin Heywood's Bank in St Ann's Square, Manchester, of 1849 still has an entirely domestic character, though the appearance is no longer Georgian but Italianate. In fact, Zola in *L'Argent*, published in 1891 but dealing with the sixties lets Gundermann, his Jewish millionaire, live on the premises of the bank.[44]

12.13

Back to London and now to the Bank of England which had started in Mercers' Hall, soon moved to Grocers' Hall, and then, in 1724, to the private house of Sir John Houblon, head of the bank. In 1732 they decided to build, and the result was a house of seven bays and two and a half storeys with upper giant columns and pilasters. The formulae were Palladian; the architect was George Samson. The exterior thus was like a private house, but inside was a banking hall of 73 by about 39 feet. Soon enlargement became necessary, and so, in 1765–70, Sir Robert Taylor provided new rooms. The principal features were a rotunda of about 60 feet diameter, and radiating from it four vaulted halls, each 65 by 45 feet with aisles and glazed

12.15

12.17

domes. There was no bank building anywhere as ambitious as this. Even so, further enlargements followed in 1774. So the ground was well prepared when Soane was appointed architect to the bank in 1788.

From 1788 to 1823 Soane added hall after hall, and courtyards too. Soane's exteriors were forbidding, without windows, though with some columnar features, especially the Lothbury entrance with six attached giant columns *in antis* and the Tivoli corner at the junction of Lothbury and Princes Street. The area covered – three acres – was more than that of any other bank, be it before or after. In fact, the sizes of Soane's halls were a matter of sheer prestige. They were patently much larger than the transactions taking place in them can have demanded. Their names tell us what their functions were: Bank Stock Office, Accounts Office, Consols Office, $3\frac{1}{2}\%$ Consols Transfer Office, Discount Office, £5 Note Office and so on. In plan they were mostly oblong with a dome over the middle square, an oblong bay to its left and another to its right and narrow aisles. The counters separated the aisles from the 'nave'. The style of the rooms was so original and so characterful that, apart from Gilly (pp. 15, 83) and Boullée and Ledoux, there was no architect anywhere on the same elevated level. That these halls were pulled down in

12.19, 20

12.18

12.16

12.16, 19

12.19, 21 London, Bank of England, Stock Office, 1791–92, and Rotunda, 1796, by Sir John Soane (London, Sir John Soane's Museum)

12.20 C.-N. Ledoux, design for the Caisse d'Escompte, 1788 (L'Architecture, 1804)

12.22 Friedrich Gilly, design for an exchange for Berlin, c. 1799

1921–37 to make space for the conventional grandeur of a big superstructure by Sir Herbert Baker is one of the worst acts of vandalism committed in Britain in our century.

12.19   Style and features were set by Soane from the start, i.e. from the Bank Stock Office of 1791–92. The dome with large simple windows along the drum stands on pendentives. The pendentives lead down to the points where two of the arches meet which determine the centre square. The arches are segmental, the pendentives horizontally ribbed and adorned with just one patera. The piers from which the pendentives rise are fluted pilasters with no proper capitals to mark the junction between pier and arch. The middle bays of the aisles are as high as the elongations of the 'nave', the corner pieces of the aisles are much lower. It is without any doubt an Early Christian, Early Byzantine scheme, but the expression achieved by it is all Soane's. His intention was to deny mass. The piers without capitals, the segmental arches, the totally unmoulded arches into the corner pieces of the aisles, the ribbed pendentives all seem to be of membrane thinness. The motifs and the effects are more or less the same even thirty years later. The drums may have slender columns or single or paired caryatids, the arches for the dome may be semi-circular instead of

segmental, the pier mouldings may continue into the arches without even a band to separate them. With the scale of its halls and the forbidding silence of its outer walls, the Bank of England remained right into the twentieth century the noblest of all bank buildings.

France followed England in 1716 and started a state bank, the Banque Générale, in Paris. But as under the régime of John Law it issued far more notes – the infamous *assignats* – than could be justified, it came to a catastrophic end in 1720. The shock kept France from new attempts until in 1776 the Caisse d'Escompte was established. It is for this that Ledoux in 1788 designed his 12.20 severe and monumental building, and, at least in connection with it, that for the Grand Prix of the Académie d'Architecture in 1790 a national bank was set as a subject. The plan of Bergognon's scheme is entirely in the 12.23, 2 Boullée tradition, vast, symmetrical and regardless of function. The façade is more convincing, with its total absence of windows and its low, long entrance arcade leading into a high, oblong banking hall with giant columns and a coffered tunnel vault.

In the event the Banque de France was founded in 1800 and operated from makeshift quarters of inadequate size in the Hôtel de Toulouse right down to the 1920s and 1930s when extensive additions were built.[45]

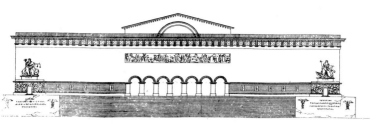

12.23, 24 Bergognon, design for a national bank, 1790: elevation and section

12.25 Paris, Halle au Blé, 1763–68, by Lecamus de Mézières, the dome 1808–13 by Bélanger

Other nations created official issuing banks earlier: Sweden in 1668, Denmark and Norway in 1736, Frederick the Great's Prussia in 1756, Catherine the Great's Russia in 1768. Austria followed in 1816.

But whereas France lagged behind in this respect, it was leading in the late eighteenth and early nineteenth centuries in regard to exchanges. The history of exchanges continued like this. We had left them at the moment of the second London building, the one of 1667–71 (by Jarman). Their chief planning motif, the open courtyard surrounded by a cloister, was not abandoned even then. It was carried on e.g. at Lille in 1652–53, at Rotterdam in 1720, at Cologne in 1727, at Bordeaux[46] in 1736 and also in the first London Corn Exchange (1750) and the first London Coal Exchange (c. 1755). The growing specialization even within the limited field of exchanges ought to be noticed. For Berlin at the very end of the eighteenth century Gilly designed an exchange. It was to be built in the north-east corner of the Lustgarten. The style is internationally up-to-date, a rotunda with tetrastyle portico and a Pantheon dome, and at right angles two wings of which one was to be a coffee-house.[47]

When in 1838–44 the present Royal Exchange in London, designed by Tite, replaced Jarman's building,

the plan type remained claustral – a remarkable sign of conservatism. In 1880 the courtyard was glazed over.[48] The Classicism of Tite's design is rather undisciplined.[49]

Not one of the exchanges mentioned in the preceding paragraphs is architecturally outstanding. We rise, however, to that level when we turn to the Paris Halle au Blé or Corn Exchange, which was designed by Lecamus de Mézières and built in 1763–68. It stood on the site of the present Bourse de Commerce (by P. Blondel) and was pulled down in 1885.[50] The building was circular. So was, incidentally, Thomas Cooley's Dublin Exchange, built in 1769–79; this had a tetrastyle portico of Corinthian columns and a rotunda with giant demi-columns.[51] The Halle au Blé had no rotunda: the courtyard was open. It was closed in 1783 by a wooden dome designed by Legrand & Molinos – the joiner was A. J. Roubo – and after that had been consumed by fire, by an iron and glass dome by Bélanger in 1808–13. It is this dome that can be called epoch-making. Bélanger had already in 1783 proposed these two materials for the dome. We do not know what this design looked like; we only know a memorandum of fifteen years later.

To return to the evolution of general exchanges, an entirely different scheme had been devised over a hundred years before Bélanger's dome and had begun

12.11
12.22
12.40
12.25

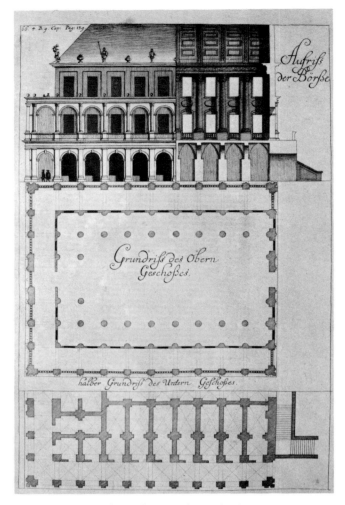

12.26 L. C. Sturm, design for an exchange (*Vollständige Anweisung*, 1699)

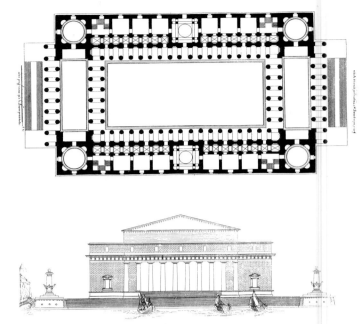

12.27, 28 P. Bernard, design for an exchange, 1782: plan (top) and elevation

12.29 J.-N.-L. Durand, design for an exchange (*Précis*, II, 1809)

to make converts in the late eighteenth century. The new scheme seems to appear for the first time in Leonhard Christoph Sturm's edition of Nikolaus Goldmann's *Vollständige Anweisung zur Civilbaukunst* of 1699. The courtyard is given up and replaced by an oblong hall rising through two floors. The exterior has arcading in two tiers. The model is evidently Palladio's Basilica at Vicenza, and Sturm says so, calling the Basilica an exchange. The plan, as prophetic as Sturm's hospital plan discussed earlier on (p. 146), did not catch on for a long time. The acceptance may have had something to do with Boullée; for it is in the circle of his followers that the first examples appear. They are these: a Grand Prix design by Bernard of 1782, another by Tardieu of 1786, Thomas de Thomon's Exchange at St Petersburg of 1804–16[52] – built and preserved in all its glory – and a design by Durand published in 1809 in his *Précis*.[53] The base on which de Thomon's exchange stands is faced with colossal blocks of granite. The colonnade is of slender Tuscan columns carrying not arches but a straight entablature. The body of the building rises above it and has to the front a lunette window. The great hall inside is tunnel-vaulted. Thomon must have known Bernard's and Tardieu's designs. Tardieu and Thomon in their turn are the sources of Durand's

design. In his text Durand says that a bourse is also called a *loge* (the Spanish *lonja*!) or a *change* (the English exchange!), and that in Antiquity the trade of the exchange was carried on in basilicas.[54] In modern times, he continues, exchanges sometimes have cloisters. His references are to London and Amsterdam, Jarman's London being credited to Inigo Jones. The first London Stock Exchange preceded St Petersburg by a few years.[55] It was built on an awkward site in 1801–02. The architect was James Peacock, and the interior showed at once that he was a pupil of the younger Dance. The room was divided into nave and aisles by square pillars carrying unmoulded arches and a glazed clerestory.[56]

We can now go to Paris again and look at the Bourse designed by Brongniart and built in 1808–26. It is surrounded on all sides by Corinthian columns – the choice of Corinthian instead of the severer Doric or Tuscan is typical of the change from Revolution to Empire. The large size is due to the building housing the Tribunal de Commerce as well as the exchange.

For banks the severe Grecian had the preference in these years, the style probably intended to express security. It is enough to name the following, all American: Latrobe's Bank of Pennsylvania at Philadelphia of 1798 with Ionic hexastyle porticoes, a low brick dome with

12.30, 31 Tardieu, design for an exchange, 1782: elevation (top) and section

12.32 London, Stock Exchange, 1801–02, by James Peacock

12.33 Paris, Bourse, 1808–26, by A. T. Brongniart (engraved after Brongniart)

12.34 St Petersburg (Leningrad), Exchange, 1804–16, by Thomas de Thomon

12.35 Philadelphia, Pa., Bank of Pennsylvania, 1798, by Benjamin Latrobe

12.37 London, National Provincial Bank, Bishopsgate, 1865, by John Gibson

12.36 Philadelphia, Pa., Second Bank of the United States, begun 1818, by William Strickland

12.38 Hamburg, Exchange, 1837–41, by Wimmel & Forsmann

12.36 lantern, and at the back the Stockholders' Room with two apses,[57] Strickland's Branch Bank of the United States in Philadelphia of 1818 et seq., with two mighty octastyle Doric porticoes and a tunnel-vaulted banking hall with giant Ionic columns,[58] William Kelly's Branch Bank of the United States at Erie, Pennsylvania, of 1839 with a hexastyle Doric portico,[59] and the State Bank at Shawneetown in Illinois, also of 1839, with a Greek Doric portico of – oh horror! – five columns.[60]

The rest of this chapter is with one or two exceptions a matter of stylistic development. Functionally only two changes have to be noted. One is the emergence of the Savings Bank, i.e. the little man's bank to protect his savings. The seventeenth and eighteenth centuries made a few efforts,[61] but all the rest is nineteenth-century, and mostly the time about 1810–40. The other functional innovation is the splitting up of the one exchange into special exchanges. It is once more that process of diversification which this book has to draw attention to time and again. Corn exchanges, wool exchanges, coal exchanges and even – at Leipzig – a booksellers' exchange.[62] The style of the Leipzig building was the German Renaissance.

12.13 So over to style, to examine it in all kinds of exchanges and in banks. The Heywood bank in Manchester had already marked the move from Grecian to Italianate.

More ambitious by far is the mid-nineteenth-century headquarters building of the National Provincial Bank in Bishopsgate, by John Gibson, of 1865.[63] The single-storeyed entrance pavilion and the banking hall with its three glass domes on crowded red columns have recently been saved from demolition. Externally and internally there is rich Italianate decoration. Much more correct and restrained – to quote an Italianate exchange – is Wimmel & Forsmann's Hamburg Exchange of 1837–41.[64] Italianate also must be called two other exchanges: the Coal Exchange in London of 1846–49 and the Corn Exchange in Leeds of 1861–63, the former by J. B. Bunning, the latter by Cuthbert Brodrick – both no doubt inspired by the Halle au Blé. The Leeds Corn Exchange is oval outside and inside,[65] the London Coal Exchange was circular, at least inside.[66] 'Was', for it has been totally and senselessly destroyed. The exterior was in a debased Classical, but the interior was glass, tiles and iron – the London parallel to the Bibliothèque Ste Geneviève in Paris. The Coal Exchange had three tiers of iron balconies and a glass and iron dome. The lower iron supports had rope mouldings, and so had the balcony railings. The dome ribs were of elegant slenderness. Sang painted the panels of allegorical figures, of arabesques, of towns and collieries, miners and colliers, and below the dome were very large tree ferns, painted

12.37

12.38

12.39
12.41

12.25

12.39
7.44

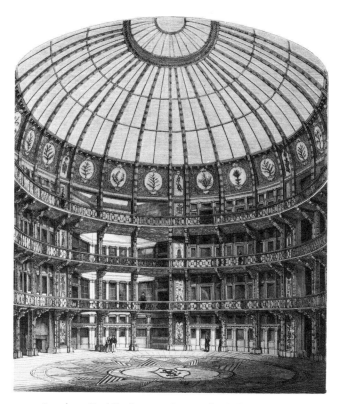

12.39 London, Coal Exchange, 1846–49, by J. B. Bunning

12.41 Leeds, Corn Exchange, 1861–63, by Cuthbert Brodrick

12.40 London, the third Royal Exchange, 1838–44, by Sir William Tite; the glass roof of 1880

12.42 Vienna, Exchange, 1869–77, by Theophil von Hansen

12.43 Pittsburgh, Pa., the second Mellon Bank, 1871

12.44 Zürich, Schweizerische Kreditanstalt, 1873–76, by J. F. Wanner

12.45 Frankfurt, Exchange, 1874–79, by H. Burnitz and O. Sommer

12.46 Frankfurt, the first Exchange, 1839, by F. A. Stüler: exterior (top) and interior

by Melhado from specimens in the British Museum.

Around the middle of the nineteenth century cast iron was adopted for office buildings, especially frequently in America (the next chapter will deal with office buildings). As for banks, Haviland in 1829–30 gave the Miners' Bank at Pottsville in Pennsylvania an iron façade,[67] and Montgomery Schuyler mentioned the Continental Bank in New York by Leopold Eidlitz as having a 'frame work of iron supports' and that building dated from 1856–57.[68] As a later example of a bank with a cast-iron front we might look to the Mellon Bank in Smithfield Street, Pittsburgh, of 1871.

The Leeds Corn Exchange is not of special structural interest, but it deserves notice for its robust yet exceptionally sober design. The building has two boldly convex porches. The walls have big diamond rustication from bottom to top, the hall inside semi-elliptical as well as semicircular ribs. There is only one balcony, and the externally truncated-looking dome is only partially glazed.[69]

The Early Victorian Italianate developed into the High Victorian free Cinquecento and ultimately into a verbose Baroque. Free Cinquecento would fit the Vienna Exchange, 1869–77 by Theophil Freiherr von Hansen. The great hall, 185 by 83 feet and 72 feet high,

with two tiers of demi-columns, must have been very impressive indeed.[70] For an interior one cannot do better than to leave the description to Zola. The Banque Universelle has, Zola writes, a sumptuous banking hall and from there 'un escalier d'honneur conduisait à la salle du conseil, rouge et or, d'une splendeur de salle d'opéra'. And externally the façade 'se dressait fleurie d'ornements, tenant du temple et du café-concert'.[71] For other exteriors one might choose the Schweizerische Kreditanstalt in Zürich of 1873–76 by J. F. Wanner, on the way evidently towards the Baroque,[72] and, even more Baroque, the Frankfurt Börse by H. Burnitz and O. Sommer, 1874–79.[73]

But not all the inspiration came from Italy. At Lyons René Bardel built the Bourse in 1857 in the French Renaissance with orders of pilasters, pavilion roofs and a hall with arched gallery and clerestory lighting.[74] In Paris both the older parts of the Crédit Lyonnais (W. O. W. Bouweins de Boijen, 1878–1913) and the Comptoir d'Escompte (E. J. Corroyer, 1880–89) are Louis XIII, whereas the early twentieth-century parts of the Crédit Lyonnais are Louis XVI to Empire.[75] The architectural story is one of patient adding. In Munich the Bayerische Hypotheken- und Wechselbank (Schmidt, 1895–98) is Rococo, in New York the

12.47 Munich, Bayerische Hypotheken- und Wechselbank, 1895–98, by Schmidt

12.48 Paris, Crédit Lyonnais, Grande Coupole, 1908, by W. O. W. Bouweins de Boijen

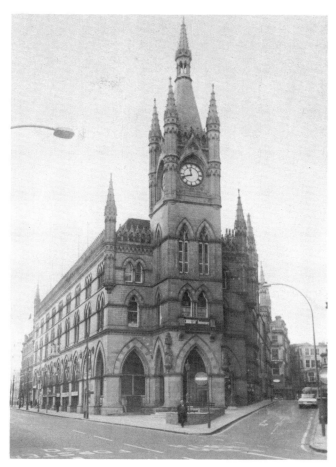

12.50 Bradford, Wool Exchange, 1864–67, by Lockwood & Mawson

12.51 Bremen, Exchange, 1861–64, by Heinrich Müller

12.49 Paris, Crédit Lyonnais, vestibule, 1913, by W. O. W. Bouweins de Boijen

12.52, 53 Amsterdam, Exchange, 1898–1903, by H. P. Berlage

Produce Exchange (Bowling Green; G. B. Post, 1881–85) was *Rundbogen all'italiana*,[76] in Sheffield the Corn Exchange was Tudor Gothic (M. E. Hadfield & Son, 1881, recently pulled down).[77]

Gothic for exchanges and banks was not association-ally a very convincing choice, as ever since Pugin and Ruskin Gothic had had connotations of religion and of good honest medieval craft. Three examples are suffi-cient: first the Exchange at Frankfurt, preceding the present one. This was won in competition by Stüler in 1839. It had a perfectly harmless Classical exterior with large, round-arched windows on the ground floor but inside nave and aisles like a *lonja*, except that it is vaulted by English fan vaults.[78] The other two Gothic exchanges are of the sixties: the Bremen Exchange by Heinrich Müller of 1861–64,[79] and the Bradford Wool Exchange (more and more sub-divisions!) by Lockwood & Maw-son, of 1864–67.[80] The exterior has medallions of appropriate celebrities, e.g. Arkwright and Sir Titus Salt as textile manufacturers, Stephenson, Watt and Jacquard as inventors and engineers, Palmerston and Gladstone as politicians, and so on. The good council members of Bradford, having decided on Gothic, were rash enough to invite Ruskin in 1859 to talk to them about the proposed building. They got a memorable speech insisting on the moral responsibilities of anyone employing the Gothic style. He said:[81]

My good Yorkshire friends, you asked me down here among your hills that I might talk to you about this Exchange you are going to build: but earnestly and seriously asking you to pardon me, I am going to do nothing of the kind. I cannot talk or at least can say very little about this same Exchange. I must talk of quite other things . . . I cannot speak to purpose of anything about which I don't care; and most simply and sorrowfully I have to tell you that I do *not* care about this Exchange of yours . . . in a word . . . because *you* don't; and you know perfectly well I cannot make you. Look at the essential conditions of the case, which you, as business men, know perfectly well, though perhaps you think I forget them. You are going to spend £30,000, which to you collectively, is nothing; the buying of a new coat, is, as to the cost of it, a much more important matter of consideration to me, than building a new Exchange is to you. But you think you may as well have the right thing for your money. You know there are a great many odd styles of architecture about; you don't want to do anything ridiculous; you hear of me, among others, as a respectable architectural man-milliner; and you send for me that I may tell you the leading fashion; and what is, in our shops, for the moment, the newest and sweetest thing in pin-nacles. . . . Now, pardon me for telling you frankly, you cannot have good architecture merely by asking people's advice on occa-sion. All good architecture is the expression of national life and character; and it is produced by a prevalent and eager national taste, or desire for beauty.

And so on to morality as the genuine basis of taste, to

12.46

12.51
12.50

12.54, 55 Vienna, Postal Savings Bank, 1904–06, by Otto Wagner: detail of the exterior, and banking hall

12.56 Budapest, Postal Savings Bank, 1899–1902, by Ödön Lechner: detail

12.57 Buenos Aires, Bank of London and South America, 1960–66, by Clorindo Testa and others

competition as a vice, to the treatment of operatives and to too much profit for the manufacturer. Catastrophe will be upon Bradford if manufacturers go on worshipping the idol of profit.

Ruskin from 1849 and William Morris from 1877 went round England preaching their gospel of truth and honesty in architecture and design, as they had been practised in work of the Middle Ages. Among those outside England whom they convinced was Berlage in Holland.[82] His Exchange at Amsterdam was built from 1898 to 1903 and stands indeed mid-way between the historicism of the nineteenth and the originality and simplicity of the first half of the twentieth century. The elements and motifs of the building are patently derived from Holland's so-called Renaissance, i.e. the sixteenth and early seventeenth centuries. But the tower is blockier, and the window details as well as the details of piers and arches are blunter than in any of the real Renaissance buildings. The capitals in particular are of primeval directness. The hall is oblong with aisles and two upper galleries, and the roof is iron and glass.

Contemporary with Berlage's Beurs is Ödön Lechner's Postal Savings Bank in Budapest of 1899–1902, with curvaceous windows and panels between them and an undulating roof line of a boldness which can only be compared with Gaudí's.[83] If Lechner at his best

stands for Art Nouveau, Otto Wagner's Postal Savings Bank in Vienna of 1904–06 represents the actual turn to the new style for the new century.[84] The exterior is faced with thin marble slabs and, to make it obvious that they are a facing only, they are pegged to the wall by aluminium bolts. The vestibule has a staircase with cubic posts and aluminium balusters, and the banking hall has exposed iron posts and a glass roof, three-centred in section.

From this hall it was only one step into the so-called International Modern of Gropius's factory at Alfeld (p. 281) and its followers in cubic glass and iron structure. A mature example by one of the best firms of architects of America, Skidmore, Owings & Merrill, is the Manufacturers' Hanover Trust Company in Fifth Avenue of 1953–54.[85] Here is perfection, and, as is the fate of classic achievement, it cannot last long – the Italian High Renaissance less than twenty years, from Leonardo's *Last Supper* to about 1515 – and so today's architectural style is the aggressive denial of perfection, because perfection is denounced as dull and impersonal. Let the example for this chapter be the Bank of London and South America at Buenos Aires of 1960–66 by Clorindo Testa, Santiago Sanchez Elia, Federigo Peralta Ramos and Alfredo Agostini.[86] Looking at the building one wonders how that collaboration has worked.

12.58 New York, Manufacturers' Hanover Trust Company, 1953–54, by Skidmore, Owings & Merrill

13.1 London, St Katharine Dock, begun 1827, by Philip Hardwick: D warehouse

13
Warehouses and office buildings

IN THIS chapter office buildings and warehouses are treated together. Office buildings were built either to provide premises for one firm or organization or for a number of firms not known beforehand. A warehouse is a less precise term. We speak of bonded warehouses where goods lie for trans-shipment and hence are exempt from duty. Such were or are the warehouses along London's docks (e.g. West India by William Jessop and others 1800 et seq., London by Daniel Asher Alexander 1802 et seq., St Katharine's by Philip Hardwick 1827 et seq.)[1] and such also was Schinkel's Packhof in Berlin (1829–32).[2] But as a rule warehouse refers to the storage space of one firm which more often than not has office space in the same building. A very large early warehouse is that of the Swedish East India Company at Göteborg, designed by C. Harleman about 1740. It is nineteen bays long and four storeys high with a pediment over the centre.[3]

The story of warehouses is essentially one of the nineteenth and twentieth centuries, although one could argue that town halls in the sixteenth and seventeenth centuries – Antwerp of 1561–65, Amsterdam of 1648–55 – were to a large extent office buildings, that the Uffizi in Florence of 1560–74 are called Uffizi because they were an office building, and that the great cloth halls of the Netherlands – beginning with Ypres in the thirteenth century – were warehouses. As it is the cloth halls are treated in this book as market halls, which is just as justifiable (below, p. 236). Also partially warehouses (and also treated as market halls here) were such trading establishments as the Fondaco dei Tedeschi in Venice of 1500, the Steelyard of the Hanseatic League in London, rebuilt after the great Fire in 1667 and again in 1751, and Cornelis Floris's Hanseatic building in Antwerp of 1564–68 (see p. 195). These *fondaci* also served as dwellings for the merchants and the factors or agents.

The consecutive story starts in London in the early nineteenth century with the County Fire Office of 1819, designed in Nash's Regent Street Classical by Robert Abraham. It is taken seriously, or else it would not have qualified for the *point-de-vue* at the north end of the lowest stretch of Regent Street.[4] Next in order of date are three insurance offices by C. R. Cockerell and hence more original than Abraham's: the Westminster Fire Office of 1829–30 in King Street, Covent Garden,[5] the Westminster Insurance Co. of 1832 in the Strand and the Sun Fire Office of 1841–42 in Threadneedle Street, next to the Bank of England and the Royal Exchange. The Westminster Insurance Office is a dress rehearsal

213

13.2 Berlin, Packhof, 1829–32, by K. F. Schinkel *(Berlin, Staatliche Museen)*

13.3 London, County Fire Office, 1819, by Robert Abraham

13.4 London, Sun Fire Assurance Office, 1841–42, by C. R. Cockerell

12.12 for the Bank of England branch buildings (see p. 200), and, as it is twelve years earlier, the freedom in the composition of Grecian elements is very remarkable.[6]

13.4 The Sun Fire Office is yet bolder, with its stilted segmental arches to the ground floor windows, its rows of pilasters and columns linking the top two storeys, and its angle cut diagonally and provided with columns and with windows on first and second floors decorated in a way not following precedent. Nicholas Taylor calls it an 'exuberant advertisement'.[7]

Of warehouses the most monumental of before 1850

13.5 was Milne Buildings in Mosley Street, Manchester.[8] Neither its architect nor its date is recorded. About 1840 is the most likely date. It was twenty-one bays long and had two superimposed giant orders of attached columns for the pedimented angle pavilions, pilasters otherwise. Dr A. Granville, writing about 1840,[9] may well have thought of this building when he wrote of Manchester: 'We find now houses of business externally decorated with columns, and porticoes, and frescoes, and pediments, and, in fact, ornamented like palaces.' The largest of the Manchester warehouses followed a little

later: Watt's in Portland Street by Piccadilly. This is about 300 feet long and nearly 100 feet high. The architects were Travis & Mangnall; the date of erection was 1851.

So far the buildings mentioned were put up and used by one firm only, but by 1850 buildings also existed which were erected to be let as office suites to whoever came along and was ready to pay the rent. About this innovation, as far as London was concerned, we are fully informed. The source is a lecture which Edward I'Anson delivered to the RIBA in 1864.[10] He told his audience that within his recollection 'merchants dwelt in the City over their counting houses and next to their warehouses', but that thirty years ago, i.e. in the 1830s, 'certain houses [were] let out in separate floors and used as offices'. I'Anson then continued: 'The first building which I remember to have been erected for that special purpose was a stack of office buildings in Clement's Lane at the end nearest to Lombard Street.' This dated from about 1823 and was by an architect called Voysey. The first building I'Anson himself designed as an office building, and quite a large one, was in Moorgate Street.

13.5 Manchester, Milne Buildings, c. 1840

13.6 London, Royal Exchange Buildings, 1842–44, by Edward I'Anson

13.7 London, 5–9 Aldermanbury, c. 1845

13.6   This was built about 1837.[11] Five years later he did the Royal Exchange Buildings, and this also was designed 'with special reference to being let as offices'. Further on, I'Anson delivered to the RIBA in 1864.[10] He told his Corbett, another 'modern office building' in Mincing Lane by Arthur Green (of about 1845–46), Longbourne Chambers in Fenchurch Street by James S. Scott and one or two others. It will be noticed that the architects of these buildings are all little-known or unknown. The first flight still kept away from such commercial speculations.

Two postscripts to I'Anson's lecture deserve to be added. The first is to record that the same development took place in New York but some years later. Russell Sturgis wrote in 1902 that 'prior to 1858, except in a few commercial cities like New York, office buildings were usually converted dwellings', and called the building for letting divers offices 'a unit building'.[12] To elucidate the prehistory and the early history of office buildings in France and Germany too little is still known.[13] The second postscript to I'Anson's lecture is that in the discussion Professor Donaldson complained that iron

fronts had not been touched upon, and I'Anson himself reminded his audience that 'a large amount of window space [is] of the first importance'.

This second postscript leads on into the next stage of the development. The demand for maximum glazing was best satisfied by using iron, but this was not to everybody's taste. For factories, as we shall see later (p. 277), iron framing had been introduced before 1800. John Rennie, the great engineer, realized the advantages of iron for warehouses as early as 1807. He recommended to the Navy the use of fireproof construction 'upon the plan of the cotton and flax mills lately erected at Derby, Leeds, Manchester and Glasgow'.[14]

But there is all the difference between accepting a new material for factories and naval stores and accepting it for City façades. So a building like 5–9 Aldermanbury   13.7 of c. 1845 has masonry verticals, and so have the by now famous Jayne Building of 1849–52 in Philadelphia by   13.8 William Johnston, and the equally famous Oriel   13.9 Chambers in Liverpool by Peter Ellis of 1864. However, the oriels which gave the building its name were done all in metal, and at the back and even more at the back of

13.8 Philadelphia, Pa., Jayne Building, 1849–52, by William Johnston

13.9 Liverpool, Oriel Chambers, 1864, by Peter Ellis

13.10 Liverpool, 16 Cook Street, 1866, by Peter Ellis

13.10 Ellis' No. 16 Cook Street proper curtain walling was introduced.[15]

As for iron and glass façades, the United States and Britain seem to have introduced them at about the same time, the United States winning by a few years. In 1829–30, as we have seen (p. 208), Haviland gave the Miners' Bank at Pottsville in Pennsylvania an iron façade, and in 1837 Pierre Lorillard used giant cast-iron piers for a narrow warehouse in Gold Street in New York.[16] *The Builder* in 1847 mentioned 'a block of three story buildings... in the course of erection in Cincinnatti, the entire fronts of which are of cast iron'.[17] In the later forties Daniel Badger and James Bogardus had foundries downtown in New York.[18] Both may well have been inspired by *Metallurgic Architecture*, the book which the somewhat dotty William Vose Pickett had brought out in 1844.[19] Anyway, both Badger and Bogardus turned to casting iron members for façades. Bogardus (1800–74) is the more interesting of the two. He was an inventor, chiefly of machines in connection with engraving. In 1839 he even gained a prize from the British government. He displayed cast-iron architectural members for the first time in his own factory building of 1848–49. The oldest example to survive in any form is

13.11 Laing's, which stood at the corner of Washington Street and Murray Street, New York, built in 1848.[20] Two years later, Bogardus (and partially Badger) built the new premises of the Baltimore *Sun* at Baltimore (architect Hatfield of New York), and this also had a cast-iron front and much iron inside.[21] Semper in his *Wissenschaft, Industrie und Kunst*, published in 1852,[22] wrote of American buildings: 'Often the whole front

consists of richly ornamented cast iron.' Prime examples are Bogardus's often illustrated buildings for Harper's of 1854, i.e. built one year before the equally often illustrated Jamaica Street warehouse in Glasgow (1855–56, by John Baird Sen.),[23] Badger's Gilroy Building of 1854 with two orders of giant pilasters, one of two, one of three tiers, and two buildings which were stores, and will therefore be mentioned again later (pp. 267, 270), but which belong to the story of cast iron: Badger's happily surviving Haughwout Building of 1857 at Broadway and Broome Street (architect J. P. Gaynor),[24] and the Stewart Building of 1859–62 (by John Kellum). In the United States iron fronts became popular everywhere.[25] Sigfried Giedion drew attention to the St Louis waterfront mostly of the 1870s,[26] which is alas no longer. An early Chicago example was No. 1 South Water Street of 1856,[27] an early Massachusetts example the Foster Block at Worcester of 1854 by Elbridge Bryden,[28] an early Wisconsin example the Iron Block at Milwaukee of 1861,[29] an early Rhode Island example the Lyceum Building at Providence of 1865,[30] an early Virginia example the Branch Building at Richmond of 1866, designed by G. H. Johnson,[31] an early New Orleans example the Bank of America, also of 1866, by Gallico & Esterbrook.[32] Badger's *Illustrations of Iron Architecture* brought out in 1865 contains a long list of examples.[33] A little later were a building at Troy, New York, of 1870,[34] the Mellon Bank at Pittsburgh of 1871 (see p. 208), and the Hale Building at Salem, Mass., of 1873.[35] Yet later and very attractive is a very American-looking iron façade in England – Messrs Arighi, Bianchi & Co. at Macclesfield of 1882–83.[36]

13.13

13.14

13.12

13.15

13.11 New York, Laing Stores, 1848, by James Bogardus

13.13 New York, Harper's, 1854, by James Bogardus

13.12 New York, Haughwout Building, 1857, by J. P. Gaynor; ironwork by Daniel Badger

13.14 Glasgow, Gardner Warehouse in Jamaica Street, 1855–56, by John Baird Sen.

13.15 Macclesfield, Arighi Bianchi, 1882–83

13.16 Chicago, Home Insurance Building, 1883–85, by William Le Baron Jenney

13.17 Chicago, Tacoma Building, 1886–89, by Holabird & Roche

13.18 Chicago, Marshall Field Wholesale Warehouse, 1885–87, by H. H. Richardson

Parallel with the takeover of iron in façades was its takeover inside buildings. Cast-iron columns had been used in churches and theatres ever since Georgian days. The English mills (i.e. factories) of the Industrial Revolution were the first to be consistent: iron supports and iron beams (see p. 277). Iron supports appear in Nash's Brighton Pavilion of 1816 et seq. and in Mills's Patent Office in Washington of 1839 et seq. The Théâtre Français and the Bibliothèque Ste Geneviève in Paris and the Coal Exchange in London have all been discussed in their appropriate places (pp. 78, 107, 206). In France churches also made use of iron. The churches by Boileau in Paris, especially St Eugène of 1854–55 and the later St Augustin of 1872, are well known. Not everybody appreciated them. Charles Garnier, the architect of the Opéra, wrote in 1869 that to visualize iron as the building material of the future 'is a great error': 'le fer est un moyen, il ne serait jamais un principe'.[37] Five-and-twenty years earlier a Scotsman had been less prejudiced and closer to recognize what the future would have in store. John Robison, secretary of the Edinburgh Royal Society, had written to Loudon in 1833: 'The introduction of iron into building operations will no doubt spread rapidly ... Rich and poor will, by degrees, find themselves enclosed in iron cages.'[38] In office buildings and warehouses iron columns and beams indeed gradually took over. Often the façades remained masonry or brick and the iron framing was independent. Only when the façade wall is carried separately for each floor on the iron beams can one speak of a true skeleton structure. In office buildings this stage was reached in Chicago with William Le Baron Jenney's Home Insurance Building of 1883–85 and Holabird & Roche's Tacoma Building of 1886–89,[39] of which more will be said presently.

13.16
13.17

The Tacoma Building in its exterior is patently on the way out of historicism. But a glance at that development must wait until we have looked at the forms which historicism took in the later nineteenth century. A few examples must be enough, and it is architecturally irrelevant whether the upper floors are offices or flats: 127 Breite Strasse, Cologne, for the Venetian *palazzo*, the Provident Life and Trust Company in Philadelphia by Frank Furness of 1879 for Gothic at its most robust and wildest – what Goodhart-Rendel used to call rogue-architecture – the offices of Charles Lecomte in the rue d'Uzès by E. Guillaume of 1879 too, but Beaux-Arts-Classical at its most civilized,[40] the New York Insurance Company at Budapest by Alois Hauszmann of 1891–95 for a rather dissolute Baroque,[41] Norman Shaw's New Zealand Chambers, once in Leadenhall Street, London, of 1872–73 as a rare attempt at applying the new elegant domestic style to commercial premises, the Marshall Field Wholesale Store of 1885–87 at Chicago for Richardson's Romanesque, the Auditorium of 1887–89, also in Chicago, for Sullivan's Richardsonian applied to a combined office building, theatre and hotel (see above, p. 184),[42] Martin Dülfer's *Allgemeine Zeitung* in Munich of 1901 for Art Nouveau, and J. M. van der Meij's Scheepvaarthuis at Amsterdam of 1912–16 for Expressionism or a kind of angular Gaudí.

13.17

13.22

13.19

13.21

13.20

13.18
11.36

13.23

13.24

The next step after this was into the twentieth-century style. But, as has been indicated, that step had already been taken some years earlier in Chicago, and to see it in its context one has to remember the early history of the skyscraper. Many have been the attempts to define the skyscraper. For the purpose of this book it is enough to say that a building must be distinguished by some height above those surrounding it to give the impression of scraping the sky. The skyscraper in this sense

13.19 Paris, 3 rue d'Uzès, 1879, by E. Guillaume

13.20 London, New Zealand
Chambers, 1872–73, by Richard
Norman Shaw

13.21 Budapest, New York Insurance
Company Building, 1891–95, by Alois
Hauszmann

13.22 Philadelphia, Provident Life and
Trust Company, 1879, by Frank Furness

13.23 Munich, offices of the *Allgemeine Zeitung*,
1901, by Martin Dülfer

13.24 Amsterdam, Scheepvaarthuis, 1912–16,
by J. M. van der Meij: entrance

13.25 New York, Western Union Building, 1873–75, by G. B. Post

13.26 Buffalo, Guaranty Building, 1894, by Louis H. Sullivan

began in New York where land was costly and ground on which to build solid rock. Here are a few buildings and their heights: Equitable 1868–70 by Gilman and Kendall and G. B. Post, 130 feet, Western Union Building, Broadway and Dey Street by G. B. Post, 1873–75, 230 feet, Tribune, Park Row, by R. M. Hunt, 1873–75, 260 feet, Washington Building, No. 1 Broadway, 1882–85 by E. Kendall, 250 feet, Manhattan Life Insurance, 64 Broadway, by Napoleon Le Brun, 1893–95, 348 feet, World (or Pulitzer), Park Row, by Post, 1889–90, 360 feet, Park Row Building, by R. H. Robertson, 1896–99, 382 feet.[43] And Leroy Buffington had in 1888 already designed a free-standing tower block of 425 feet. This is a fact, even if it has nothing to do with the invention of the skyscraper, and even if Buffington did occasionally backdate drawings done some years later. The style of the tower of 1888 is Richardsonian, the technique is that of the Chicago of after 1883–85. This latter is a crucial date. For until then skyscrapers were of normal masonry construction, or at least had combined internal iron columns and beams, such as factories had had since before 1800, with load-bearing outer walls, and clearly one could not go on for ever building higher without a change in technique: for walls, at ground level, were tending to become more and more massive.

So in Chicago, as has already been said, William Le Baron Jenney discovered in his Home Insurance Building of 1883–85 that the system of iron framing could be extended to the outer walls so that the walling material for each floor stood on the iron and its weight was never more than what the framework of one tier could carry. Jenney revealed the new principle in an article in the *Sanitary Engineer* in December 1885 (XIII, 32–33). It has never been given up since. Aesthetically the Home Insurance is desperately weak. Externally the iron framing does not tell at all – as it had done in Bogardus's and other iron fronts: it is hidden behind heavy masonry. Holabird & Roche, pupils of Jenney, accepted in their Tacoma Building of 1886–89 the skeleton construction and designed the exterior so that it conveys in its fenestration the sense of identical units of measurement. Solids and voids, however, were still in balance in the façade. Sullivan in 1890, in the Wainwright Building at St Louis, and in 1894, in the Guaranty Building at Buffalo, presented a far more sensitive version of the unit exterior and enriched it by feathery ornament in the broad cornice and the panels above the windows. Burnham & Root, on the other hand, in the Monadnock Building of 1889–92, refused all ornament but also refused total iron framing. The building, in spite of its

13.27 Chicago, Monadnock Building, 1889–92, by Burnham & Root

13.28 Chicago, Marquette Building, 1894, by Holabird & Roche

13.28 size, is in essentials of brick construction.[44] In Holabird & Roche's Marquette Building of 1894 the ultimate purity was finally achieved.

One year later Paul Bourget, the French *romancier* and critic, wrote this of the skyscrapers of Chicago: 'The simple power of necessity is to a certain degree a principle of beauty; and these structures so plainly manifest this necessity that you feel a strange emotion in contemplating them.'[45]

Among the premises of the skyscraper, the most important has so far remained unmentioned: the lift or, in American, the elevator. Its development must be outlined before we can enter the twentieth century.[46] Lifts are older than most people think. In the Colosseum in Regent's Park in London, in 1823, was 'a moving apartment . . . raised by machinery' to take six to eight people to a platform from which to view the panorama which was the *raison d'être* of the building. Such lifts were operated by steam, but in or about 1845 hydraulic machinery was evolved, probably by Sir William Thompson. It took long to be accepted. Shortly afterwards Elisha Otis, who ran a factory making bedsteads, designed a lift for use in his own factory. For this he invented a catch which would prevent the cabin from crashing, should the rope break. He showed his lift in the New York Crystal Palace exhibition of 1853. The term elevator goes back to that year. The Haughwout Building of 1857 (see pp. 216, 267) had the earliest of all passenger lifts; the Fifth Avenue Hotel of 1859 (p. 187) the second.

13.12

In 1867 Leon Edoux demonstrated a hydraulic lift in the Paris Exhibition (p. 246). This system was taken up in England in 1870 by Richard Waygood, the first to build passenger lifts in England. In New York by the end of the sixties the New York Life, the National Park Bank and the Equitable had lifts, the Boreel Building of 1877–79 had a group of four, the Produce Exchange by Post, 1881–84, a battery of nine. In 1880 in London the General Hydraulic Company was founded, but in the same year Werner von Siemens built the first electric lift. The first New York electric lift appeared in the Demarest Building in 1889, the first London one in the Crystal Palace in 1890. For the rest of the story a few bald facts are all that is needed: 1883 the first paternoster (i.e. a never-ending chain of one-man cabins), 1892 the first push-button mechanism, in a Vanderbilt house in New York, 1895 the first escalator patent, 1900 an Otis escalator at the Paris Exhibition,[47] 1903 Otis introduces gearless action, 1908 self-closing gates. The Woolworth Building has 26 lifts, the Empire State 58.

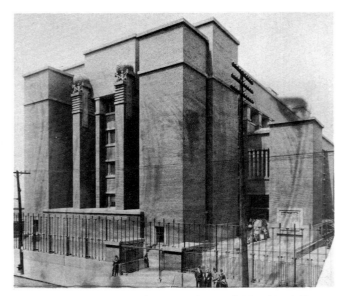

13.29 Buffalo, Larkin Building, 1904, by Frank Lloyd Wright

13.31 Berlin, Telschow Building, 1927–28, by Luckhardt & Anker

13.30 Breslau (Wroclaw), office building in the Junkernstrasse, 1911, by Hans Poelzig

Back now to the twentieth century, its records and its styles. As for records of heights: in New York the Singer Building by E. Flagg, 1906–08, 612 feet; Metropolitan Life by N. Le Brun & Sons, 1909, c. 700 feet; Woolworth by Cass Gilbert, 1911–13, almost 800 feet; Chrysler by William van Allen, 1929–32, 808 feet; Empire State by Shreve, Lamb & Harmon, 1930–31, 1,250 feet; World Trade Center by Minoru Yamasaki, 1964–75, 1,350 feet; Sears Tower, Chicago by Bruce J. Graham of Skidmore, Owings & Merrill, 1972–75, 1,454 feet.

13.29 Now to style. The International Modern was heralded by Frank Lloyd Wright in his Larkin Building at Buffalo in 1904, a blocky block with, in the four corners, windowless staircase enclosures, and inside a large skylit centre like that of a Continental department store, and like such a store surrounded by galleries. The building is said to have been the first to be air-conditioned.

When the International Modern began to spread, the Chicago of the nineties and the early twentieth century was one of its inspirations. But, curiously, skyscrapers took long to adopt that strictly functional style. The first examples were Raymond Hood's McGraw-Hill Building of 1931 in New York and Howe & Lescaze's vastly superior Philadelphia Savings Fund Building of 1932 in Philadelphia.

But at that time the long horizontal window bands of Howe & Lescaze were no longer quite such a novelty in Europe and especially in Central Europe. Hans Poelzig's office building in the Junkernstrasse at Breslau dating from 1911 seems to be the first. The Telschow Building in Berlin of 1927–28 by Luckhardt & Anker is a perfect example. Side by side with overstressed horizontals appeared overstressed verticals, e.g. in Peter Behrens' Mannesmann Building at Düsseldorf of 1911–12 (with reminiscences of Schinkel) and in Fritz Höger's Chile- 13.30 13.31 13.32

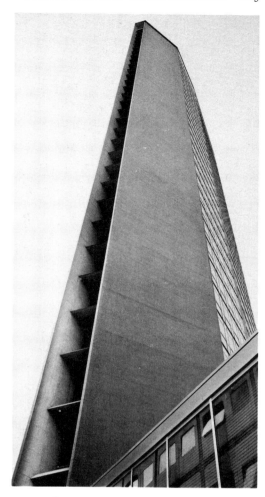

13.34 Milan, Pirelli Building, 1955–56,
by Gio Ponti and Pier Luigi Nervi

13.32 Hamburg, Chilehaus, 1922–23, by Fritz Höger

13.33 Frankfurt, headquarters of I. G. Farben, 1928–30, by Hans Poelzig

13.35 New York, Lever House,
1950–52, by Gordon Bunshaft of
Skidmore, Owings & Merrill

13.33

13.36

haus at Hamburg of 1922–23 (fully fledged Expressionism).[48] Among the largest of office buildings in the International Modern are Poelzig's headquarters of I.G. Farben at Frankfurt of 1928–30 and Eero Saarinen's Administration Block of the Research Laboratories for General Motors at Warren near Detroit, the former with horizontal window bands used in moderation, the latter a radical curtain-walling job.

13.35

Both these buildings are low, but most of today's office buildings rise high. The only one of these which can be called epoch-making is Skidmore, Owings & Merrill's Lever House in New York of 1950–52 (designer Gordon Bunshaft). For it was here that the scheme was created by which the high, curtain-walled slab stands on a low podium which continues the street's building-line. In Lever House the podium is of two storeys and has a generous inner courtyard with some planting.

One postscript and this chapter is at an end. Reinforced concrete has become a serious competitor of steel.[49] This was first noticed in factories in the 1890s (see p. 288), in buildings like hotels and department stores shortly after 1900, and then in exhibition halls (p. 254), and of course in office buildings. Even high office buildings, i.e. skyscrapers, are occasionally framed in concrete. Two examples are Ingall's Building in Cincinnati of 1902 by Elzner & Anderson (16 floors, 210 feet)[50] and Monolith Building in New York of 1907 by Howells & Stokes (12 floors, c. 145 feet).[51] But that strikes one as a substitute. Concrete for skyscrapers made its own contribution only when the bold cantilevering was used of which the material is capable and which bridges (by Maillart) had been the first to take advantage of. The best-known example is Nervi's core of Gio Ponti's Pirelli Building in Milan, built in 1955–56. The height is c. 410 feet.

13.34

13.36 Warren, Mich., General Motors Research Area, begun 1948, by Eero Saarinen

14.1 London, Euston Propylaea, 1835–39, by Philip Hardwick

14
Railway stations

THE building of railway stations presupposes the existence of railways. A railway for the purpose of this book is a means of transport on special track for the conveying of passengers as well as goods and with traction by a machine. Before there were railways in this sense, the three elements had been introduced separately. It is a long and complicated story, and here it is enough just to set out events and dates: Trucks in mines in Germany running on wooden planks: illustrated about 1535 (*Der Ursprung gemeyner Berckrecht*),[1] and described in Agricola's *De re metallica* in 1556. In England the first record is at Barnard Castle in the mid-sixteenth century.[2] Trucks on tracks pulled by horses are recorded at Wollaton *c.* 1605. This system spread through the seventeenth century. One of the most elaborate was the Tanfield Tramway, *c.* 1671. In the eighteenth century iron was brought in to fortify the track and the wheels, e.g. by Ralph Allen of Bath who owned the Combe Down quarry. The first cast-iron rails were made at Coalbrookdale in 1767; the first edge-rails are of 1788. The first horse-drawn public freight railway was the Surrey Iron Railway, Croydon–Wandsworth 1803, the first public passenger railway Swansea–Mumbles 1807, the first steam engine suited to be movable Richard Trevithick's Steam Carriage of 1801 and various experiments with the locomotive on tracks, 1801–05.[3] The next locomotives were Blenkinsop and Murray's improved locomotive (at Middleton Colliery near Leeds) 1812, Blackett and Hedley's *Puffing Billy* 1814, George Stephenson's *Blücher* 1814 and *Locomotion* 1825. The latter served on the Stockton–Darlington railway from 1825. The railway, designed by George Stephenson,[4] was 27 miles long; it served mainly for the transport of goods and only very occasionally passengers.[5] Of 1826 are Walter Hancock's steam omnibuses in London from the City to Paddington.[6]

George Stephenson also designed the first real railway in the sense defined above: Liverpool to Manchester, opened on 15 September 1830. The line was 34 miles long. In 1831 already over 1,000 passengers per day travelled. Speed varied from *c.* 15 to *c.* 30 miles per hour. The locomotive was the *Rocket*. Fanny Kemble wrote: 'No fairy tale was ever half so wonderful', and 'When I closed my eyes the sensation of flying was . . . strange beyond description.'[7]

By 1845 there were over 2,000 miles of railway in England, by the end of 1850 over 6,000. In the 1830s other countries began to build railways as well. The relevant dates are America 1829, France 1831, Belgium 1835, Germany 1835, Austria 1837, Russia 1837, Italy

14.2 Liverpool, Crown Street Station, 1830

14.3 Monkwearmouth, station, 1848, by John Dobson

14.4 Chester, General Station, 1847–48, by Francis Thompson

1839, Holland 1839.[8] The first Belgian railway (Brussels to Malines, 1835) was built by John Cockerill. The first locomotives on the first two German railways (Nuremberg to Fürth 1835 and Leipzig to Dresden 1837–39) and the first locomotives to reach America were British-made. The earliest German railway even had an English engine driver, and his wages were higher than the line manager's salary.[9] Of the greatest railway engineers Robert Stephenson worked in Belgium and Sweden, John Locke in Holland, France (Paris–Le Havre, Cherbourg–Nantes) and Spain (Barcelona–Mataró), Brunel in Italy.

The earliest of all railway stations is Liverpool Road at Manchester, the Manchester terminal of the Liverpool–Manchester railway which, as has been said, started operations in 1830. The station is very modest indeed; a five-bay house of two storeys with a tripartite entrance and a tripartite window over. Part of the platform also survives.[10] Crown Street, the Liverpool terminal, was hardly more ornamental, a two-storeyed block along the line, the rails being covered by a timber roof. This remained in fact the most frequent arrangement in the early years. It can be seen for instance at the handsome station of Cambridge (by Sancton Wood, 1845).[11] An amplification of this scheme placed two

14.2

blocks along and left and right of the line. One example is Oxford (1852) which nobody would have called handsome in its first state.[12] Another example was Swindon (1841–42).[13] The third and most important type is that of most terminal stations, i.e. the main block across the lines at their end and two wings connected with it and taking the place of the two buildings of the preceding type. The earliest example was Nine Elms in London by Tite, 1837–38.[14]

In the rest of this chapter nothing will be said of gauges, of locomotives and of trains – say the start of sleeping cars (USA 1865, Compagnie des Wagons Lits 1876), of underground railways (London 1863), or of international express trains (Orient Express 1888), or of the introduction of electric traction (Siemens & Halske 1879, Baltimore & Ohio Railroad 1895, Trelleborg–Narvik 1895).[15] As for stations, little changed functionally in the course of the century, but stylistically change followed change. The station is therefore a suitable type to sum up the chronology of styles imitated, as we have found it more or less fragmentarily in the foregoing chapters.

We have to start with the Grecian and at once its climax: the Euston screen whose centre was viciously demolished as recently as 1962.[16] It ought to have been

14.1

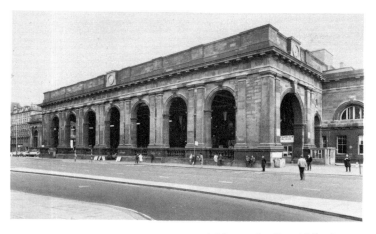

14.5, 6 Newcastle, Central Station, 1846–55, by John Dobson: façade and main shed

14.7 Newmarket, old station, 1848

14.8 London, London Bridge Station, 1844–45, by Henry Roberts

re-erected in the pedestrian square in front of the new station, whose necessity and appropriateness no one denies. The screen was by Philip Hardwick and dated from 1835–39. Four lodges flanked two carriage entrances, and in the middle rose the massive ceremonial entrance 'on the purest principle of Grecian Doric'.[17] On the other hand the functionalist is bound to deny that Hardwick worked on the purest principle of functionalism. This display of solemn monumentality is a screen; it is no more. That is: the rails and the necessary building alongside of them were not even in axis with the propylea. However, while the functionalist must therefore call it a sham, it receives its ultimate justification from its evocative quality. Victorian historicism can only be appreciated if one is ready to admit the associational values of buildings. Styles were chosen for what they would evoke. Robert Stephenson's railway all the way from London to Birmingham at a break-neck speed of up to 30 miles an hour was considered one of the greatest achievements of the human mind. Hence only the greatest of all architectural styles could express it.

At the Birmingham end of the line, in Curzon Street, the terminal feature – happily still preserved – is Ionic. Strictly Classical also are the excellent stations of Amsterdam–Willemspoort (1843),[18] Huddersfield (1847, by J. P. Pritchett) and Monkwearmouth (1848, by John Dobson). Strictly Palladian was Döpersberg (Wuppertal, 1846–50).[19] Somewhat looser, still Classical, but with a crowded giant order is Newcastle (by John Dobson, 1846–55). Newcastle has the earliest roof covering all the platforms. Here and at York they are curved in plan. Newcastle is exceedingly long; so is Derby by Francis Thompson (1839–41),[20] which is more discreetly Classical, and so is Chester (1847–48), also by Thompson, whose Classical now turned free Cinquecento.[21] In the regal Newmarket Station (1848) – the station for the Newmarket races – Classical has turned Baroque.[22]

But the more usual successors of the Classical work are the several varieties of the Italianate. The palazzo type is relatively rare (London Bridge by Henry Roberts, 1844–45, with an asymmetrically placed campanile). Much more frequent is the *Rundbogenstil* in any guise from Early Christian to Quattrocento. Early Christian to Italian Romanesque appeared in Munich (Friedrich Bürklein, 1849)[23] – understandably, considering the Ludwigstrasse – and also at Karlsruhe (Friedrich Eisenlohr, 1842).[24] It appeared surprisingly early at Providence, Rhode Island, by Thomas Tefft of 1848, the first

14.3

14.5, 6

14.4

14.7

14.8

14.9 New Haven, Conn., station, 1848–50, by Henry Austin *(Yale University Library)*

14.10 Leipzig, Thüringer Bahnhof, 1840–44, by E. Pötsch

major American station.[25] The style is strikingly Bavarian. Close to the Tuscan Quattrocento is Kassel (Gottlob Engelhardt, 1852–61).[26] *Rundbogen* all over, but no style known to man, must be the verdict on Budapest (1846).[27]

Freaks did indeed appear very early, though very rarely. Thus in Loudon's *Architectural Magazine* in 1836,[28] one W. J. Short proposed an Egyptian railway station, because the style is massive with few bold details and no expensive workmanship. But the ultimate was 14.9 New Haven by Henry Austin (1848–49), no longer with us. It had two towers of different height and details with *Rundbögen* and outrageous roofs. The middle erection on the roof is even a piece of Chinesery. A freak perhaps one might also call the Moorish-looking Plaza de Armas station at Seville (1898–1901), by José Santos Silva.[29]

Now this has a façade with, as its centre, a vast lunette window. The window of course indicates the shed and is thus a sign that we have here a railway station. These lunette windows represent one early solution of the design problems of the terminal station. The other is arcading of some sort between two towers. The latter started earlier and seems to have been favoured in 14.10 Germany: Leipzig, first Thüringer Bahnhof, 1840–44 by Eduard Pötsch,[30] Leipzig, Bayerischer Bahnhof, 1841–42,[31] Berlin, first Hamburger Bahnhof, 1842,[32] second Hamburger Bahnhof, 1845–47 by Holz & Arnold,[33] Rotterdam, 1845, Gothic not *Rundbogen*, Zürich, 1847 by G. A. Wegmann,[34] Salem, Massachusetts, 1847, by G. J. F. Bryant.[35] The motif ends with a splendid flourish in the giant triumphal arch of Brussels, Midi in 1863–69 by Auguste Payen.[36]

The lunette, the most functional façade motif, seems to have been created by François Duquesney for the 14.11 Gare de l'Est in Paris in 1847–52. The first Montparnasse, 1850–52, by Victor Lenoir, had two lunettes to represent a twin-vaulted shed and a clock-turret between.[37] Montparnasse was the direct pattern for Lewis Cubitt's 14.12 King's Cross in London, begun in 1851 and completed

in 1852. It is one of the most demonstratively functional buildings of its age – the very opposite of Euston. Hardwick wanted to conjure up greatness, Cubitt told you in a few words that this is a station. The twin sheds are the distinguishing feature; so they must appear externally; covered approaches for carriages and carts are needed; so is a clock. No ornament, no decoration. Cubitt himself said that what he wanted to achieve at King's Cross was 'fitness for its purpose and the characteristic expression of that purpose'.[38]

Among the many later stations with the lunette, two deserve to be singled out; the Anhalter Bahnhof in Berlin (by Franz Schwechten & Wiedenfeld, 1872–80),[39] because it has much of the peremptoriness of King's Cross, and the Gare du Nord in Paris (by Hittorff, 14.14 1861–65), because it is one of the most complete extant examples of the Beaux Arts style at its grandest. Jacob Burckhardt, faithful believer in the pure Italian Renaissance, called it 'a scandal' and 'one of the greatest architectural infamies of our century'.[40]

From here the way was wide open into the later nineteenth century Baroque. But another route was from the free Cinquecento of such buildings as the Potsdamer Bahnhof in Berlin (1868–72 by Weise, Döbner & Sillich),[41] Mannheim (1871–76 by Helbing),[42] the Eastern Station at Budapest (1881–84 by Gyula Roch- 14.13 litz and – more Baroque – Zürich (1865–71 by J. F. 14.19 Wanner).

Nothing has so far been said about medieval styles. Yet they were used right from the start, though much more rarely. Isambard Kingdom Brunel built the original Bristol station in 1839–40, a terminal station in 14.16 Tudor Gothic with a wooden false-hammerbeam roof to the shed.[43] Even earlier and a folly in appearance was the Gothic station at Brunswick for the line to 14.15 Wolfenbüttel. It dated from 1838.[44] 1845 was the date of the Gothic station of Rotterdam already referred to, 1848 of the Tudor Gothic first station at Shrewsbury (by T. M. Penson), 1859–65 the large fancifully Gothic

14.11 Paris, Gare de l'Est, 1847–52, by François Duquesney

14.12 London, King's Cross Station, 1851–52, by Lewis Cubitt

14.14 Paris, Gare du Nord, 1861–65, by J.-I. Hittorff

14.13 Budapest, Eastern Station, 1881–84, by Rochlitz

14.15 Brunswick, station, 1838

14.16 Bristol, Temple Meads Station, 1839–40, by Isambard Kingdom Brunel: former train-shed

14.17 London, St Pancras Station, the train-shed, 1868–69, by W. H. Barlow

station Vienna Nord (by Theodor Hoffmann).[45] Only a few years separate Vienna Nord from St Pancras in London, 1868–76, by Sir George Gilbert Scott and the engineer W. H. Barlow.[46] St Pancras is Franco-English thirteenth-century Gothic, brilliantly composed and of a plan which gives their due to the station hotel (see p. 190) and the ticket-offices and other railway necessities. The train-shed spans in one sweep 243 feet – the largest span ever until then achieved by man. Among train-sheds it was only excelled twenty years later by Pennsylvania Station at Jersey City, 1888 (252 feet), Reading Station, Philadelphia, 1891–93 (256 feet), and the second Broad Street, Philadelphia (300 feet); but the Galerie des Machines of the 1889 exhibition had of course left all these far behind (see p. 249).[47] Scott was not a functionalist; so his terminal building hides the grandiose shed. Nor was he an evocationalist; so his High Gothic can by no flight of imagination be associated with the idea of a railway station. Scott used his style simply because to him this was the best of all styles.[48]

Another medieval style appeared in the late nineteenth-century stations in America. It is the Neo-Romanesque of Richardson – of his Marshall Field Wholesale Store as well as his branch libraries. For the Romanesque in railway architecture there was also only

a marginal associational justification. It is a strong, massive, unembellished style, and that, according to Richardson, meant a style suitable to America. Examples among stations were Michigan Central at Detroit of 1882–83 by C. L. W. Eidlitz, Grand Central at Chicago of 1888–90, and Union at St Louis of 1891–96.[49]

Other styles made only occasional appearances, e.g. the Moorish of Seville (but with the shed lunette à la Gare de l'Est, on which see above, p. 228), and the French Renaissance, mostly demonstrated by no more than pavilion roofs. The best known of these is the first Grand Central in New York of 1869–71 by Isaac C. Buckhout and J. B. Snook.[50] A few years earlier E. M. Barry in London also used pavilion roofs, at Charing Cross (1862–64) and Cannon Street (1863–66).[51] Paddington was built yet earlier (1852–54 by Brunel and Sir Matthew Digby Wyatt) but can hardly be called French Renaissance.[52] (For the station hotel, see p. 188.) In Paris St Lazare is in a free Louis XIII (1886–89 by Just Lisch);[53] Amsterdam in 1881–89 chose the equivalent of the French Renaissance, i.e. their own national so-called Renaissance. The architect was the best the country had: P. J. H. Cuijpers.

Neo-Baroque at its latest and wildest appears at the Brignole Station in Genoa in 1902–05 by Ottino,[54]

14.19 Zürich, station, 1865–71, by J. F. Wanner

14.18 Amsterdam, Amstel Station, 1881–89, by P. J. H. Cuijpers

14.20 New York, first Grand Central Station, 1869–71, by I. C. Buckhout and J. B. Snook

14.21 Milan, Central Station, 1912 and 1925–31, by Ulisse Stacchino

14.22 Washington, D.C., Union Station, 1903–07, by
D. H. Burnham & Co.

14.23 St Louis, Mo., Union Station, 1891–96, by T. C. Link and
E. A. Cameron

14.24 Karlsruhe, station, 1906–13, by August Stürzenacker

and with more than a dash of early Otto Wagner and
early d'Aronco (see p. 9) at Milan Central, which was
won in competition by Ulisse Stacchini in 1912 and
built in 1925–31, by which time station architects, be
they modernists or traditionalists, did totally different
things.[55]

The traditionalists had the field to themselves in the
United States.[56] The most ambitious buildings were
Grand Central II in New York, 1903–13 by Read & Stern
and Warren & Wetmore, Union Station in Washington,
1903–07 by D. H. Burnham & Co., and Pennsylvania,
also in New York, 1906–10 by McKim, Mead & White,[57]
recently demolished. Their style can be called the
Classical Re-Revival. While the choice of style represented the same defeat as the buildings of the Chicago
Exhibition of 1893 (see p. 250), they bore witness to a
functional change or at least a radical change of accent.
Until then the most monumental element of the station
had been the train-shed: it now became the concourse,
and the rail part of the building was kept low and purely
utilitarian. As for the concourses, they are at their most
majestic when they are reminiscent of the baths of the
Roman Emperors. The earliest of the monumental concourses were St Louis, 1891–96 by Theodore Link and
E. A. Cameron, externally, as we have seen, Richardsonian but internally provided with a vast tunnel-vaulted
concourse (with Richardsonian and Sullivanian details)
and Illinois Central at Chicago, 1892–93 by Bradford
Lee Gilbert, where the concourse is vaulted too. Also
tunnel-vaulted but yet grander were Union Station in
Washington, Grand Central in New York, and Pennsylvania in New York, all three of the first decade of our
century.

So much for the revivalists. The modern style can be
watched equally well in station buildings. Karlsruhe,
1906–13 by August Stürzenacker, with its broken gable
and the splendid sheerness of its concourse is no longer
derived from any period style.[58] In the same year 1906
the Leipzig station by Lossow & Kühne was begun. It
was completed in 1915 and has remained the largest of all
stations. The two concourses at ground level are as large
as those of America, but the upper concourse with access
to the platforms is yet more monumental.[59] This latter
concourse incidentally is of reinforced concrete, a
material which, owing to the wide cantilevers of which
it is capable, lends itself especially well to platform
roofs.[60] The Helsinki station of 1910–20, by Eliel
Saarinen, is much bolder in its plan, with the asymmetrically set tower, and bolder also in the forms used.[61]
The concourse is patently inspired by the Vienna Seces-
sion. One year after Helsinki the Stuttgart station was
begun. The architects were Bonatz & Scholer, and the

14.25 Leipzig, Hauptbahnhof, 1906–15, by Lossow & Kühne

14.26 Basel, Badischer Bahnhof, 1912–13, by Curjel & Moser

14.27 Helsinki, station, 1910–20, by Eliel Saarinen

14.28 Florence, station, 1934–36, by Giovanni Michelucci

building was ready in 1928.[62] Here also an asymmetrically-set tower is the climax of the composition. The heavy rustication used throughout gives the building something of the elementary character of the Völkerschlachtsdenkmal (see p. 25). The Badischer Bahnhof at Basel, 1912–13 by Curjel & Moser, has nothing of the aggressiveness of Stuttgart and rather follows Karlsruhe, but with a touch of the Classicism of 1800 which Karlsruhe had not found necessary.

Stations took long to get acclimatized to the International Modern, and nothing outstanding was produced between the two wars, except for Michelucci's Florence station of 1934–36.[63] Other inter-war examples are Reims, 1930–34 by Le Marec & Limousin with concrete segmental tunnel-vaulting,[64] Versailles–Chantiers of 1931–33, by A. Ventre, with an elegant concrete concourse,[65] Düsseldorf 1931–34 by Krüger & Behnes,[66] the excellent small Underground stations of London, designed by Charles Holden and built from 1932 on,[67] and two suburban stations of Amsterdam by H. G. J. Schelling of 1939.[68] The best European station of the last half-century is the Stazione Termini in Rome, begun to a Fascist design in 1938 and completed to a different design in 1951. The architects were first Mazzoni, then Montuori with the engineer Leo Calini.[69] The upper parts of the façade, about 760 feet long, are entirely plain with long bands of low windows, but the concourse projects far forward and has an undulating concrete roof, its double curve carrying on the outline of an adjoining piece of the Agger Servianus wall which the station was under obligation to protect.

The Second World War destroyed hundreds of stations, and they were rebuilt mostly in the International Modern. Brutalist concrete elements are rare (Naples, 1960–63 by the architects to the railway company; Almelo, Holland, 1964 by Koen van der Gaast).[70] One elevational scheme to be met in a number of major stations is a long, totally flat, usually entirely or largely curtain-walled front much like that of any office building (Rotterdam Centraal, 1956–57 by S. van Ravenstijn; Munich, 1955–63 by Heinrich Gerbel; Saarbrücken, 1963–71 by Friedrich Reutler, Paris Montparnasse, 1958–69 by Beaudoin, Cassan, de Marien & Saubot).[71] As for new stations of character one might name Heidelberg, 1953–55 by Conradi & Dutschmann,[72] Solingen, 1956–57 by B. Humpert,[73] and Eindhoven, 1956 by van der Gaast, but every critic will make his own choice.

As a postscript to railway stations a reminder must be added about the terminal buildings for motor-coaches and for air travel. As regards the former, one outstanding example is Nervi's bus station by the George Washington Bridge in New York (1960–63).

Of important aerodrome buildings there are more than can be referred to here. In whatever country, they all seem to be forever growing. Cranes or scaffolding never leave the premises. The architectural results, however, are indifferent. Thinking back one will find that very few have left visual memories. St Louis is Yamasaki at his rare best or rather Helmuth, Yamasaki & Leinweber (completed in 1956), TWA New York (1959–62) is Eero Saarinen at his worst, though the sensational features may have been done under pressure from the clients eager to advertise themselves. Dulles near Washington is Saarinen at his best (1958–63).

14.29 Rome, Stazione Termini, completed 1951, by Eugenio Montuori and Leo Calini

15.1 Paris, Halles Centrales, 1853–58, by Victor Baltard

15
Market halls, conservatories and exhibition buildings

IRON was first used structurally for fire resistance. Hence it appeared specially early in the roofs of theatres, conflagrations in theatres, often with loss of life, being of gruesome frequency. The introduction of the iron roof took place in Louis' Théâtre Français in 1786 (p. 78). It shows Napoleon's foresight that in 1806 he wanted an iron roof for the monument which became the Madeleine (p. 17). Other churches did indeed soon make use of iron, mostly for their roofs (Southwark Cathedral in London, roof 1822–25, Rouen, spire 1823–76,[1] Mainz Cathedral, east dome 1827, Chartres Cathedral, roof 1836–38). Factories, as will be discussed in another chapter, began in England to use cast-iron columns and soon also cast-iron beams. The dates are in the 1790s (pp. 276–77). Cast-iron columns and beams had the additional advantage of easy assembly. This, as we have seen, recommended them to Bogardus and Badger from 1848 for the elements of façades as well (see p. 216). But for façades iron had a further advantage. The members could be thinner than members of wood or stone, and that allowed more light to enter. In fact the combination of glass and iron is one of the most characteristic features of quite a number of nineteenth-century building types. The first glass and iron dome was Bélanger's of 1809–11 at the Halle au Blé (see p. 203). Sir G. S.

Mackenzie in 1815 and Loudon in 1817 followed with designs for domed conservatories. Now for conservatories and indeed for exchanges such as the Halle au Blé iron had yet another quality superior to all other materials: the possibility of wide spans without intermediate supports.[2] Hence iron conquered the architecture of market halls and exhibition buildings, of train-sheds and of factories.

Market halls and exhibition buildings – the latter included as the continuation of conservatories – will be treated in this chapter. Train-sheds and stations were dealt with in the preceding chapter, factories will be in the last. All these types were essentially created in the eighteenth and early nineteenth centuries – all except the market hall. The market hall is a joint building for a large number of individual shops. In this form it takes us right back to the Forum of Trajan, with about 150 shops on various levels selling wine, grain and oil.[3] It also takes us back to the oriental bazaar. The so-called Cotton Market in Jerusalem, dating from 1329, is covered by a vault with closely set pointed transverse arches. In the Western Middle Ages, as we have seen (p. 27 ff.), town hall and market hall were often one, the former above, the latter below and open along the sides. An example with exceptionally many individual shops

235

15.2 Jerusalem, Cotton Market, 1329   15.3 Bruges, Halles, *c.* 1240 to late 15th c.

15.4 Ypres, Cloth Hall, *c.* 1200 and later

which has also already been discussed is Thorn (p. 29).[4] Similar was Bruges, the city being one of the most prosperous this side of the Alps and the Pyrenees.[5] The Halles were begun *c.* 1240, the crazy tower heightened late in the fifteenth century and originally completed by a spire.[6] On the ground floor of the Halles, the mercers, the spicers, the butchers sold their wares. But we also hear of sweets and saddles and knives. Festivities took place on the upper floor. For the cloth trade, the most important wholesale trade of Bruges, a separate cloth hall, the Waterhalle, was also built in the thirteenth century. It stood at right angles to the Halles on the east side of the Grand' Place and was about 245 feet long. The Town Hall was yet another separate building. It was erected on part of the castle site.

The Netherlands was the great country for *halles*.[7] Most of them, however, were not general market halls, but specialized in cloth or meat. The largest – and one of the earliest – was indeed a cloth hall: that of Ypres, built from about 1200 to 1620 but mostly in the thirteenth century.[8] However, the Ypres Cloth Hall, in spite of its name, comprised in a secondary fashion town hall, law courts, prison and chapel.[9] It is *c.* 435 feet long and two storeys high. At Ghent[10] Cloth Hall, Town Hall and Meat Hall are three separate buildings.

The Belfry dates from the late thirteenth to the late fourteenth century and was originally detached. It is *c.* 310 feet high and was to have been higher. The Cloth Hall is by Symon van Assche and was started in 1425. The Meat Hall lies at some distance from the other two, was started in 1417 and is 223 feet long. At Louvain also the three buildings were separate. The Cloth Hall begun in 1317 was 200 feet long. The Courtrai Cloth Hall, much altered, is 272 feet long. At Malines Cloth Hall and Town Hall shared a building. So they did at Gouda and Middelburg (p. 30).

Other countries of course built market halls too, though not on the scale of the Netherlands. In France, for instance,[11] we still have the market hall at Crémieu (Isère), stone outside, all timber inside, including the arcades between nave and aisles and of course the roof. Enlart refers to a lost inscription with the date 1317. Other examples are St Pierre-sur-Dives (Calvados) of the thirteenth to fourteenth century and Cordes (Tarn) of the fourteenth century with stone arcade piers. The type is still the same in Richelieu's town of Richelieu in the 1630s.

Another type, also appearing early on, is the open market area surrounded by booths or shops often connected with the area by a cloister. Comparison with a

15.5 St Pierre-sur-Dives, market hall, 13th–14th c.

15.6 Richelieu, market hall, c. 1630

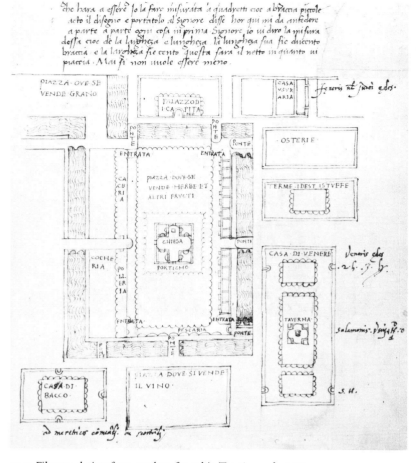

15.7 Filarete, design for a market, from his *Treatise*, early 1460s
(*Florence, Biblioteca Nazionale Centrale*)

monastic cloister was made by Joinville à propos Saumur, which was first built by Henry II of England. The Halles of Paris combined the two types. We are told by Félibien (the seventeenth-century French art historian whom we already met on p. 114) that there was a large enclosure, but inside there were two detached buildings.

15.7   Filarete's ideal market belongs to the claustral type as well.[12] The centre is an oblong area for the stands and booths surrounded by arcading on columns. Behind the arcades on the west side are the meat and poultry halls, with the slaughter-house behind them, and on the south side is the fish market. A canal runs round the entire market to carry away the refuse. Beyond the canal on the north are the corn market, the Palazzo del Capitano and the exchange ('casa usuraria'), on the east side inns, a bath house and a brothel ('casa di Venere'), on the south side the wine market and tavern ('casa di Bacco'). Francesco di Giorgio's *Trattato*, written about 1480, has both the 'foro per il mercato . . . di portici circundato' (an open space for the market, surrounded by porticoes), 'case dei mercatanti' with 'fine and spacious rooms', including 'banchi da far conti', and store rooms for goods referred to as *fondaco* (see p. 196).[13]

The term *fondaco* is ambiguous. The famous *fondachi* are the two in Venice, the Fondaco dei Turchi, of the thirteenth century in the Veneto-Byzantine style, and the Fondaco dei Tedeschi, rebuilt after a fire in 1505. The latter has a courtyard with a cloister and three upper galleries.[14] A *fondaco*, one can perhaps say, is a warehouse, a wholesale market and living accommodation. This combination was more or less the same for the monumental Hansa building at Antwerp by Floris, almost on the scale of the Town Hall (see p. 32). The date is 1564–68, i.e. nearly exactly the date of the Town Hall. It was 230 by 200 feet in size, with a façade of 31 bays and in a style close to that of the Town Hall. The combination was also similar for the Steelyard in London, also a Hanseatic establishment. It lay east of Dowgate Wharf, i.e. where Cannon Street Station now is. It was finally closed down in 1597.[15]

15.8

In Italy the market was of quite a different type right through the sixteenth century. It is the *loggia*. In Florence the Mercato Vecchio was where the Piazza Vittorio Emanuele now extends. Along its west side ran the fish market, nine bays long, of 1567, by Vasari. The Mercato Nuovo was built in 1547–48 by Giovanni Battista del Tasso, a one-storeyed loggia. The same type is Vasari's long Loggia dei Mercati at Arezzo of 1573–81.

15.10

15.8 Antwerp, House of the Hansa, 1564–68, by Cornelis Floris

15.9 Venice, Fondaco dei Tedeschi, after 1505 (engraving by Raphael Custos, 1616, destroyed)

For two hundred years there is now nothing of significance to report, and after that the development is concentrated in the great metropolises.[16] The need for numbers of separate market halls was a matter of the sizes of cities, and the need for buildings instead of open markets a matter of sanitary improvements in marketing victuals. The populations of Paris and London about 1660–70 had been half a million: by about 1800 Paris had only grown to 650,000, London to 787,000. Paris reached a million about 1850, London already about 1820. Maxime du Camp in his *Paris, ses origines, ses fonctions, sa vie*[17] wrote: 'En 1848, Paris allait devenir inhabitable. Sa population, singulièrement accrue, et remuée par le mouvement incessant des chemins de fer . . . étouffait dans les ruelles putrides . . . où elle était parquée. Tout souffrait de cet état de choses, l'hygiène, la sécurité, la rapidité des communications et la moralité publique.' (In 1848 Paris had almost become uninhabitable. Its population had increased at an unprecedented rate, and was stirred up by the constant movement of the railways; . . . it stifled in the putrid alleys . . . where it was penned up. Everything suffered from this situation – hygiene, security, communications, and public morality.)

The new market halls of Paris about 1770 were – according to J.-F. Blondel's *Cours d'architecture civile*[18] – totally inadequate. They lacked 'une ordonnance d'Architecture qui, quoique rustique, annonçât par sa décoration, l'opulence de cette grande ville'. Buildings with porticoes ought to surround the open areas. Durand, who published the *Précis* of his lectures in 1802–09,[19] was even more outspoken. Existing markets are 'mesquines'; they degrade our towns.[20] Durand's own design is square with a central courtyard. It has three storeys and is all arcaded. Marketing takes place below, grain storing above.

But when Durand's *Précis* came out, the Napoleonic campaign for better markets had already started, and the initiative went on after his fall. The new markets were built between 1800 and the 1850s. Baltard's Halles in Paris (demolished in 1971) were the climax, but the beginning was equally grand – only it remained unexecuted: an Emulation Prize of the Académie d'Architecture for 1784 given to La Clothe, a pupil of Mique.[21] It was a vast affair in the Boullée style, totally symmetrical with five square buildings with cloisters and four exedras. What followed after and is entirely realistic is first Parisian, Napoleonic and diffuse, then English, of the years of George IV and William IV, and the work of one man. The Napoleonic and post-Napoleonic markets are listed by Hautecoeur. They were as a rule built on the open courtyard type and with arcading. Some buildings used outer arcading as well.[22] The largest of the markets were St Martin by the younger Peyre (1811–16)[23] and St Germain by J.-B. Blondel (1813–16). Iron came in only slowly. The earliest French iron roofs over market halls do not seem to be earlier than the thirties.[24]

Architecturally superior to the Paris markets is Alexander Paris's granite Quincy Market in Boston of 1824–26 with its Tuscan portico,[25] and superior to the Quincy Market is Japelli's meat market of 1821 at Padua, worthy of the same architect's Caffè Pedrocchi of 1816–31 and as Grecian.[26] Inside it has a Gondoin semi-dome. But for markets in general, certainly from the late twenties to the late thirties, England could boast the most brilliant architect: Charles Fowler (1791–1867).[27] He made his name with the conservatory of Syon House, built for the Duke of Northumberland in 1827–33 and provided with a steep glass and iron dome 38 feet in diameter. In 1827 also the Duke of Bedford commissioned him to build the Covent Garden Market to regularize the messy market dealings in the Piazza which had been first authorized in 1670. Fowler's market was completed in 1830.[28] With its long ranges on an E-plan whose rib strokes, however, are longer

15.13

15.10

15.14

15.11

15.12

15.10 Arezzo, Loggia dei Mercati, 1573–81, by Vasari

15.11 Paris, Marché St Germain, 1813–16, by J.-B. Blondel

15.12 Padua, former meat market, 1821, by Giuseppe Japelli

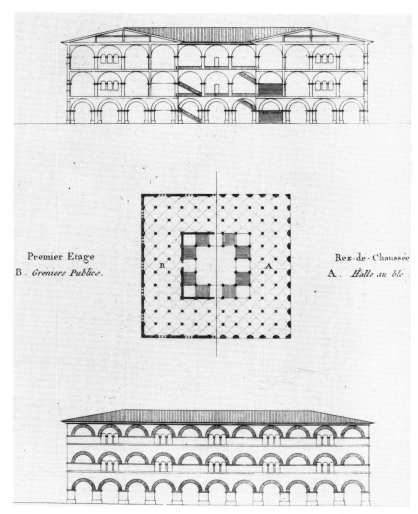

15.13 J.-N.-L. Durand, design for a market (*Précis*, II, 1809)

15.14 La Clothe, design for a market, 1784

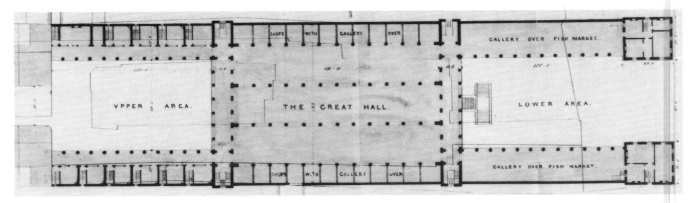

15.15 London, Hungerford Market, 1830–33, by Charles Fowler (the Strand is to the left, the river to the right)

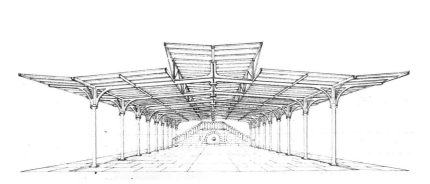

15.16 London, Hungerford Market, butterfly roof of the fish market, 1835, by Charles Fowler *(London, RIBA Drawings Collection)*

15.17 Paris, Jardin des Plantes, conservatory, 1833–36, by Mirbel & Rohault *fils*

than the spine stroke, and its consistent colonnading, it is evidently influenced by the Parisian markets. The motifs are Grecian, and iron is used only subsidiarily. At the time of writing the market, no longer used, is being freed from later accretions.

15.15, 16   On the strength of Covent Garden Fowler was appointed in 1829 to design the Hungerford Market[29] and this was built in 1830–33. It made use of the proximity of the river and the rise of the bank up to the Strand. The buildings consisted of a great hall on the Strand level with an open courtyard north of it and Hungerford Street connecting the courtyard with the Strand; a lower courtyard south of the Strand was at river level. The hall was basilican and had galleries on arches over the aisles. Galleries and aisles were for shops. Below the hall were vaults. The upper courtyard had colonnading round all four sides and larger shops on the west and east sides. The lower courtyard was designated as a fish market and had colonnading as well. A monumental staircase led up to the hall. Pubs were at strategic points, e.g. the south ends of the west and east porticoes of the lower courtyard. In 1835 Fowler was asked to design a roof for the lower courtyard. He designed an ingenious 15.16   cast-iron double butterfly structure to stand detached

from the walls and incorporate a clerestory. The Hungerford Market turned out a failure. The hall became a lecture hall in 1851 and was burnt in 1854, and in 1862 the railway bought the whole site and built Charing Cross Station on it.[30]

In the twenty years between the completion of the Hungerford Market and the start on Charing Cross Station, much of great importance in the field of iron and glass architecture took place (see also the preceding chapter, on railway stations). We must examine the new structures independent of whether they were market halls or conservatories or indeed that new type, the exhibition building.

The first conservatories of glass and iron had appeared in 1815 and 1817.[31] Glass, of course, was necessary anyway; so until then conservatories had been of glass and stone, the openings being round-headed or straight-headed. The grandest is that of Versailles of 1684–86, about 920 feet long. Others are at Kew, by Chambers of 1761, at the Jardin des Plantes in Paris, by Molinos of 1795 (with arches on columns – i.e. really Neo-Quattrocento) and at Carlton House in London, by 15.18 Hopper of 1807 (with glass and stone fan-vaults). Of iron and glass conservatories, 1827 was the date of W.

15.19 Chatsworth, Great Conservatory, 1837–40, by Joseph Paxton

15.18 London, Carlton House, conservatory, 1807, by Thomas Hopper

15.20 Kew Gardens, Palm Stove, 1844–48, by Richard Turner and Decimus Burton

and D. Bailey's conservatory at Bretton Hall, Yorkshire, with a diameter of 100 feet, 1827–33 of Fowler's Syon House conservatory, 1833–36 of C. F. Brisseau de Mirbel & C. Rohault *fils*'s new conservatory in the Paris Jardin des Plantes.[32] As early as 1831 Loudon had proposed for the Birmingham Horticultural Society a conservatory of 200-foot diameter.[33]

Paxton's great Chatsworth Conservatory was built in 1837–40.[34] It was 277 feet long and 67 feet high. Queen Victoria visited it on 1 December 1842. In her Journal she called it 'the most stupendous and extraordinary creation imaginable', and Paxton (3 December) 'quite a genius; for [she added] he plans out all the buildings, as well as laying out his [i.e. the Duke of Devonshire's] gardens'.[35] It was followed after a few years by Richard Turner and Decimus Burton's Palm Stove at Kew, 362 feet long and 62 feet high.[36]

So far England had been leading, France following. With Hector Horeau France for a few years took the lead.[37] Horeau (1801–72) was the Nervi of his age, in full mastery of a new material and eminently resourceful in its treatment. What, however, distinguished him from Nervi, is that Nervi is kindness itself and a sage, whereas Horeau was a fighter, a radical – aggressive and incapable of diplomacy. Hence of all his great schemes so little was built. The *Gazette des architectes et du bâtiment*, of which Viollet-le-Duc *fils* and Baudot were to be editors,[38] called Horeau 'l'homme du progrès par excellence', Huysmans in 1883 called him 'le plus audacieux architecte de notre temps', but also 'désespéré',[39] Jeanne Doin in 1914 a 'figure éffacée'.[40]

Now Horeau was always interested in what went on outside France. He travelled before he settled down to England, Italy and Egypt and later to Germany, Russia, Sweden, Finland. No doubt one of his principal concerns was already iron and its structural capacities.[41] Unfortunately we lack precise information about dates during his early years, and he may well, like Buffington (p. 220), have succumbed at some time to the temptation of antedating, or indeed he may have misremembered dates in the direction in which he wished them to lie. He exhibited in the Salons of 1833, 1837, 1841 and 1842. In 1836 he made a design for an exhibition building at the entrance to the Champs Elysées.

For there was a tradition in France, not matched in England, of holding exhibitions of national industry every so often. The first had been held in 1798, a date a good deal later incidentally than the first exhibition on

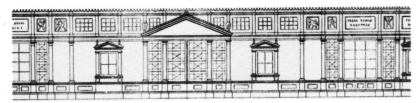

15.21 Paris, building for the Exhibition of 1849, by Louis Moreau

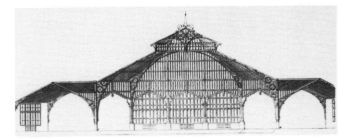

15.22 Lyons, conservatory, 1847, by Hector Horeau

15.23 Hector Horeau, design for the Paris Halles Centrales, 1845

15.24 J. B. A. Couder, design for an exhibition building, 1840

the premises of the Society of Arts in London which was opened in 1761.[42] Further exhibitions took place in 1801, 1802, 1806, 1819, 1823, 1827, 1834, 1839 and 1844.[43] They were held in various places, including the Champ de Mars, the Louvre courtyard, the Louvre building itself, the Place de la Concorde and the area facing the Invalides and the Champs Elysées. The latter area was the choice for 1839, 1844 and 1849. The structures were large, somewhat like the markets, and if ornamental details occurred they were Classical. The only permanent building stood on the site of the Grand Palais and the Petit Palais and was pulled down in 1898. Perhaps it is worth recording that as late as 1840 an architect, J. B. A. Couder, had still proposed a building entirely in the Boullée style.[44]

Of Horeau's style up to 1844 we know nothing. Vapereau tells of designs published or otherwise made known.[45] Next in order of time comes his design for the Opéra, made in 1843–45 (see above, p. 84, note 126). It shows no step forward in matters of iron and glass. But in 1845 Horeau made designs for the much-needed central market hall and perhaps in the same year, and at any rate, according to his own statement, before 1848, for an exhibition building.[46]

From 1847 onwards we are on safer ground. Of 1847 was the Conservatory at Lyons, with a raised centre and two ambulatories around it. Also of 1847 was the publication – alas unillustrated – of a 'Château des Fleurs' in Paris. Next followed the Jardin d'Hiver in the Avenue des Champs Elysées in Paris, which, however –

against Jeanne Doin's attribution – is not by Horeau.[47] The *Revue générale de l'architecture et des travaux publics* at the time raised the question of its designer. Was it Charpentier? In any case the engineer Hippolyte Menadier claimed it emphatically. Horeau is not mentioned. Nor is he in a hostile review of the building published by Semper (who had fled to Paris in 1848) in the *Zeitschrift für praktische Baukunst* in 1849.[48] This is what he wrote: 'It will take long before iron is mastered technically so perfectly that it can claim validity and appreciation as an artistic element . . . side by side with stone, brick and wood. I have not met a single example of a monumental building with exposed, artistically adequate iron construction.' Only railway stations does he find satisfactory. The ironwork of the Bibliothèque Ste Geneviève he calls 'unhappy', as it makes any feeling for seclusion impossible. The end of the article is that the Jardin d'Hiver is to him 'an enormous glass box of shapeless plan with a façade' (by Charpentier) 'beneath contempt'.

Meanwhile a battle royal had begun about the Halles Centrales. Victor Baltard had been commissioned in 1843 to submit a sketch. He delivered it in 1845, and it was accepted. Horeau, uninvited, made a counter-proposal, a brilliant design under one large vaulted roof of glass and iron, spanning about 300 feet. It was turned down, and Baltard was re-appointed. The foundation stone was laid in 1851, but what was built was demolished, and a new design demanded. This was made by Baltard in collaboration with F. Collet.

15.25 Paris, Halles Centrales, begun 1853, by Victor Baltard

Baltard's original design had been monumental and conventional.[49] The new design, profiting from iron and glass structures designed late in the forties, was iron and glass predominantly and introduced a plan more suited to a market hall than Horeau's.[50] The point about Baltard's plan is that it consisted of pavilions – fourteen in number – connected by tunnel-vaulted avenues. The parts were all glazed and each pavilion served one type (or some types) of produce. The building was begun in 1853. It was opened in 1858. By 1870 ten of the pavilions were ready. George Augustus Sala in 1879–80 called it 'an Exposition Universelle of victuals'.[51]

In 1971 alas the building was razed to the ground. It had been hailed by Viollet-le-Duc for frankly exposing materials selected as the most sensible for a building of such a function.[52] About thirty years later Huysmans called the Halles 'une des gloires du Paris moderne'.[53] Zola was of the same opinion. The future, he writes, lies with iron and glass. In 1873 in the *Ventre de Paris* Claude Lantier says, pointing to the Halles and such adjoining buildings as St Eustache: 'Ceci tuera cela, le fer tuera la pierre, les temps sont proches' – the Halles being, in spite of their 'élégance' and their 'puissance de moteur mécanique', only a timid 'révélation du XXe siècle'.[54] He might not have said the same if he had known the Horeau story of the Great Exhibition building.

We have indeed to leave markets; we will return to them only once more, much later. In 1849 another industrial exhibition was held in Paris. Horeau's design, which was not executed, is known. It is the one he claims to have done before the revolution of 1848. It was a nave with double aisles below one vast, low-pitched roof, the whole about 280 feet wide. In making it known the *Revue générale*[55] called the accepted design by Moreau 'dispandieux et désordonné'. After his failure in Paris, Horeau in 1850 submitted the same design to the jury for the exhibition in London, which led to Paxton's Crystal Palace.

The prehistory of the Crystal Palace[56] is by now so widely known that a few paragraphs will be sufficient here. Prince Albert in 1847 accepted the Presidency of the Society of Arts. This, on the example of France, though on a much smaller scale, held exhibitions of manufactures in 1847, 1848 and 1849. Henry Cole, an enterprising, energetic, young civil servant also keenly interested in design and craft, approached Prince Albert late in 1848 with a view to a much more ambitious exhibition. Albert was captivated but suggested something yet more ambitious: make the exhibition international. Cole and Matthew Digby Wyatt were sent to Paris in May and June 1849. Wyatt reported. Grants were asked for and came in. Opposition also grew. A Royal Commission was established on which sat Peel, Gladstone, William Cubitt, the large-scale builder, John Scott Russell, the engineer, and Barry, the architect (e.g. of the Houses of Parliament). This board appointed an Executive Committee with Robert Stephenson as chairman and Matthew Digby Wyatt as secretary. Early in 1850 a Building Committee was appointed

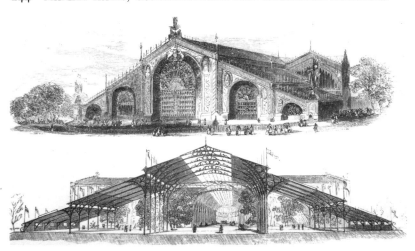

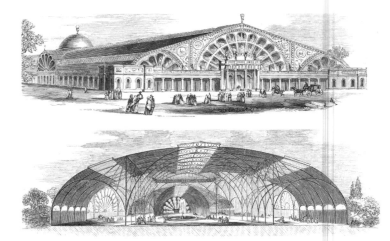

15.26 Hector Horeau, design submitted for the Paris Exhibition of 1849 and the London Exhibition of 1851, probably dating back to before 1848

15.28, 29 Richard Turner, design for the Crystal Palace, 1850

15.27 Building Committee design for the Crystal Palace, London, 1850

15.30 Joseph Paxton, first design for the Crystal Palace, London, 1850 (*London, Victoria and Albert Museum*)

The members included the architects C. R. Cockerell and Donaldson, the engineer Brunel and William Cubitt. The site in Hyde Park was agreed upon. Then a competition was held. Two hundred and forty-five submissions came in. Among honorary mentions were Henry Ashton,[57] Bunning (of the Coal Exchange), J. P. Cluysenaar of Brussels, J. T. Knowles (of the Grosvenor Hotel), 'A lady with great diffidence', G. L. F. Laves (Court Architect of Hanover),˙ A. Rosengarten (of Hamburg), J. P. Seddon and Thomas Worthington (of Manchester). A yet higher distinction was conferred on Thomas Bellamy, Henard of Paris, Horeau, P. Sprenger of Vienna and Richard Turner of Dublin. In the end the first prize went to Horeau and Turner, both proposing glass and iron structures. Turner, it will be remembered, was the engineer for the Kew Palm Stove. Horeau and Turner were not the only ones, by the way, to choose iron for the structure. Laves's scheme, aesthetically poor, proposed railway rails for its structure.[58] However, neither Horeau nor Turner was commissioned. The Building Committee did its own design – a mongrel affair of a long, aisled nave with *Rundbögen* everywhere. The façade was rather like that of a railway station, but at the far end rose a mighty glass and iron dome, 200 feet in diameter. This was Brunel's contribution.

When the official design became known, Paxton entered the stage – Paxton famous for his Chatsworth Conservatory. He was not satisfied and tried to find out whether a design of his might still be considered. Privately he got an encouraging answer and began to develop his ideas. W. H. Barlow, the engineer and much later designer of the St Pancras train-shed, helped him on calculations of strength. The doodle survives which Paxton made on 11 June 1850, and which shows to perfection what he was after. On 20 June he took his final plans to London, on 24 June he showed them to Prince Albert. On 6 July he presented them to all and sundry by publishing them in *The Illustrated London News*. On 15 July they were accepted by the Committee. On 30 July the contractors started earth-moving. Then the framework went up. Glazing could start in mid-December. The building was complete in January 1851, and the exhibition could open as intended on 1 May. The building was 1,848 feet long and 408 feet wide. The length is a little more than that of the Palace of Versailles, the height to the top of the transept was 108 feet, i.e. a little higher than Westminster Abbey. The height made it possible to preserve some trees inside. To make the building entirely an affair of iron and glass was itself not new, and predecessors were not only conservatories – indeed, C. H. Gregory called the building 'a great metropolitan conservatory' – but also, as we have seen, the prize-winning competition entries by Horeau and Turner. At a meeting of the Institution of Civil Engineers on 14 January at which Matthew Digby Wyatt described the building and its erection, Turner took part in the discussion.[59]

What justifies Paxton's fame as one of the great architectural designers of the nineteenth century is that in designing and detailing his building he virtually created the method of pre-fabrication – i.e. members to

15.31 London, Crystal Palace, 1850–51, by Joseph Paxton

standard sizes, production of these on manufacturers' premises and only assembly on the site. So the Crystal Palace could be built in six months. It was designed on a 24-foot module and used about 3,300 iron columns, 2,150 iron girders, 372 roof beams, 24 miles of gutter, 250 miles of sash bar and 293,635 glass panels. The result was something unrelievedly stark – the first design starker even than the final one. The exhibition was a tremendous success. Over six million people visited it. The public, including the Queen, loved it. Thackeray rhymed enthusiastically: 'A blazing arch', 'A palace as for fairy prince', . . . and so on;[60] but Wilhelm Liebknecht, the German socialist, saw the exhibition differently: 'The proletariat of Paris mourned at the graves of the heroes of the July revolution . . . whereas the bourgeoisie, pleased with the silence of the church-yard, sucked wondrous vigour [out of the exhibition] and opened up to an extraordinary *floraison*. From all countries and zones the bourgeoisie made their pilgrimage to London and the Crystal Palace.'[61]

However controversial the Crystal Palace was, those concerned with exhibitions learned the lesson at once.[62] The Crystal Palace of New York was erected in 1853 on the site of the present Public Library. The architects were Carstensen & Gildemeister. The building had the form of a Greek cross with lower triangles to connect the arms of the cross. Inside there were aisles and galleries. The dome over the crossing was 100 feet in diameter and 123 feet in height.[63] Next in order of time came the Glaspalast of Munich, built in 1854.[64] The architect was August von Voit, and the oblong building

was about 765 feet long. Not everyone liked it. Klenze, it was said, spat whenever he had to pass it.[65]

In 1852 re-erection of the London Crystal Palace at Sydenham started. It was completed in 1854. The design was somewhat altered. It was slightly shorter, but had three transepts and two water towers, 284 feet high and twelve-sided, designed by Brunel. The water of the towers mainly served the copious fountains. In usable area the Sydenham building far surpassed the original Crystal Palace. Among the permanent displays one feature is eminently typical of Victorian historicism. There was a whole series of courts, each representing one style: Greek, Roman, Pompeian, Byzantine, Romanesque, Gothic,[66] Renaissance, Chinese, Moorish, Egyptian, and for full measure distant prehistory was represented too, in the shape of life-size models of dinosaurs by a lake in the park. On 31 December 1853, on the premises of the model-maker, dinner for twenty-two was served inside the iguanodon.

Among all these designs, one stands out, Bogardus's project for the Crystal Palace in New York of 1853. Its chief interest is its circular centre tower, 300 feet high, from which the roof of the body of the building is suspended by iron chains forming catenary curves. The principle is that of suspension bridges, and Hittorff had made use of it already in 1838–39 for the Rotonde des Panoramas in Paris. His design was exhibited in 1841.[67]

Then the majestic march of the great international exhibitions started: Paris 1855, London 1862, Paris 1867, Vienna 1873, Philadelphia 1876, Paris 1878, Paris 1889, Chicago 1893, Paris 1900 – and so on into the

15.33 James Bogardus, design for the New York Crystal Palace of 1853

15.32 New York, Crystal Palace, 1853, by Carstensen & Gildemeister

15.34 London, Exhibition of 1862, by Captain Fowke

twentieth century. Not one of the main buildings had the uncompromising radicalism of Paxton's Crystal Palace. But the areas grew far beyond that of Paxton's building: 1851 about 20 acres, 1855 about 24, 1862 about 23, 1867 about 37, 1873 about 40, 1876 about 75, 1878 about 55, 1889 about 52, 1893 200, 1900 about 113. The number of visitors also grew steadily.[68]

The Paris Exhibition building of 1855 appears much less single-minded than the London one of 1851. The size was 835 by 360 feet. The façades were of limestone, and only the aisled interior, 115 feet high in the centre, displayed iron and glass. The envelope was designed by J. M. V. Viel, the interior by Barrault & Bridel. Viel's style might be called a free Cinquecento.[69]

In 1862 in London[70] an interesting plan was proposed by E. J. Payne and the geographer George Maw. It was in concentric ellipses with a dome over the middle. What was put up instead, to a design of Captain Fowke, is unremarkable. Horeau once again sent in his scheme of 1849 and 1851. Only the decoration was changed.[71] Paris in 1867 took up the Payne-Maw scheme and developed it with great logic.[72] The idea of Frédéric Le Play, mining engineer and author of books dealing with social reform,[73] Commissaire Général to the exhibition (as he had been for that of 1855) and indeed its *spiritus rector*, was that the concentric ovals – actually the plan is oblong with semicircular ends – should be used for objects by types or classes (there were 95 classes), while taken in sections at right angles from the periphery to the central gardens they represent the nations. So in one way you could see all the products of one class, in the other all objects exhibited, say, by Italy or the United States. The system was

ingenious and at first sounds convincing. Where it breaks down is that not all the nations are equally strong in every class.[74] The ellipse was about 650 by 330 feet. Théophile Gautier praised the building; 'En cherchant l'utile, on a, sans le vouloir, rencontré le beau.'[75] Viollet-le-Duc was cooler.[76] He was happy with the exhibition as such. 'It has', he wrote, 'far surpassed what even the most favourably inclined could hope for', but when it came to the building he called it 'la boîte elliptique' and added that it does not claim attention.

In connection with the 1867 exhibition, Horeau made a last attempt at having his scheme of 1849–1851–1862 accepted. He was again unsuccessful. This time his building was to be 2,050 by 656 feet and the nave was to have a 197–foot span and an apse at its far end.[77] In the years between he had still been unrecognized. So he decided to leave France and settle in England where so much more seemed to go on in the field of metallic construction. Little is known of his English years. In 1859 he held an exhibition of his projects.[78] It took place in the Hanover Square Rooms, and lectures were also announced, in English as well as in French. There were 36 exhibits, and they included designs for the exhibitions of 1836, 1851 and 1855, designs for purifying sewers and designs for a government building between Westminster and Somerset House, for a bridge (but, he says, don't give it a name like Waterloo which commemorates slaughter), for an arts palace and school in the grounds of Gore House in Kensington, for a city hotel, for the Paris Opéra, and also for a mansion recently built in Surrey, a railway station in Surrey and a house, also recently built, near Primrose Hill in London. The house in London, not yet identified, was

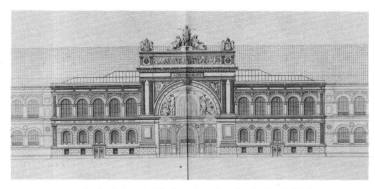

15.35 Paris, Palais de l'Industrie, 1855, by J. M. V. Viel

15.36 Hector Horeau, design for the Paris Exhibition of 1867

15.37 Paris, Exhibition of 1867, by F. Le Play

15.38 Vienna, Exhibition of 1873, by van der Nüll & Siccardsburg and Carl von Hasenauer (painting by J. Lange; *Vienna, Museum der Stadt Wien*)

15.39 Philadelphia, Centennial Exhibition, 1876

15.41 Paris, Exhibition of 1878, detail of the main building, by Léopold Hardy

15.40 Gustave Eiffel, design for the Paris Exhibition of 1878

15.42 Paris, Exhibition of 1889, central building by J.-A. Bouvard

remarkably original.[79] Horeau's last years brought no recognition either. Late designs of his were for a market hall (Cebada Square) in Madrid (1868), a theatre at Cairo (1870) and the Paris Hôtel de Ville (1871).[80] In 1868 he was given space by Viollet-le-Duc and Baudot for a paper in the *Gazette des architectes* to write about improvements for Paris:[81] they cover a wide range, and, cranky as their presentation tends to be, they are prophetic of the twentieth century: *pissotières* in all public buildings, cremation instead of interment, the removal of prisons, hospitals, barracks from Inner Paris, abolition of the death penalty, and the laying out of a *ceinture jardinée*, that is a green belt. No wonder that with so many revolutionary ideas he joined the Commune in 1870. After the collapse he was arrested and kept in prison for five months. He died in 1872.

15.38 So much on, and à propos of, the exhibition of 1867. The next was that of 1873 in Vienna. The idea was by van der Nüll and Siccardsburg, the architecture by Hasenauer. The idea was novel: a long rectangle with a central rotunda and to its left and right a long spinal avenue from which issue thirty-two rib-pavilions. The rotunda had been designed by Scott Russell, the British engineer, and had an external diameter of about 355 feet and a height of 275. Apart from this principal building

there were others, e.g. the Machinery Hall which was a long and narrow structure of about 2,625 by 165 feet, and also many small buildings. Philadelphia in 1876 is noteworthy for the consistent use of pavilions and also for attempts to reconcile the historicist leanings of the age with abundant glazing by choosing an Elizabethan or Jacobean motif, the Elizabethan style having gone in for 'more window than wall'.[82] 15.39

Then followed Paris in 1878. Eiffel had made a design for it, but this was not executed. The building, designed by Léopold Hardy, had three ranges, a shorter one of about 985 feet opposite the Ecole Militaire and two long wings towards the Seine, about 2,380 feet long. In addition the Trocadéro was built across the river (to designs by Davioud and Barrault). The Machinery Hall spanned 121 feet. The style, especially in such features as the main entrance pavilion and the Vestibule 15.41 d'Iéna inside it, is wild and dissolute or 'magnificent and fantastical' as Henry James put it,[83] the opposite extreme from the Crystal Palace, but an illustration of the universal late nineteenth-century temptations into a super-Baroque. 15.40

The exhibition halls of the 1889 exhibition, again in 15.42, 43 Paris, were as wild, but what has secured for this exhibition greater fame than for any other Parisian one is

15.43 Paris, Exhibition of 1889, central building by J.-A. Bouvard

15.44 Paris, Exhibition of 1889, the Eiffel Tower

15.45 Paris, Exhibition of 1889, Galerie des Machines by Dutert and Contamin

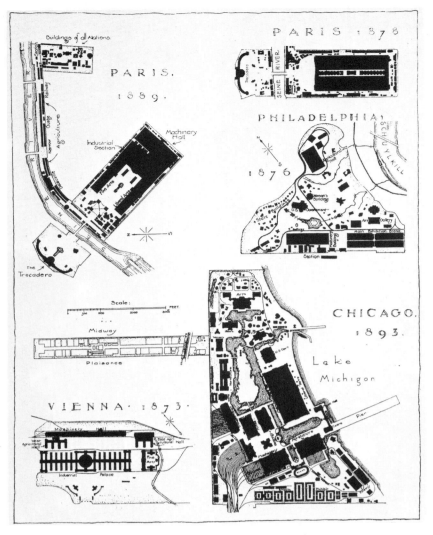

15.46 Plans of exhibitions, 1873–93, to scale

15.47 Chicago, Ill., World's Columbian Exposition, 1893, Machinery Hall by Peabody & Stearns

15.48 St Louis, Mo., Louisiana Purchase Exhibition, 1904, Festival Hall by Cass Gilbert

15.44
15.45
the Eiffel Tower, 984 feet high, and the Galerie des Machines (by Dutert and Contamin) with the largest span ever to have been achieved until then: 364 feet 2 inches.[84] The length of the Galerie was about 1,380 feet. As for the Eiffel Tower – built to serve as an entrance archway to the exhibition – its reception was by no means all enthusiasm. It is true that Eugène Melchior de Vogüé praised it for its 'search . . . to find its own form of beauty',[85] but vituperation prevailed. An address signed by Garnier, Gounod, Dumas, Sardou, Maupassant, Lecomte de Lisle, Sully Prudhomme and others called the tower 'a disgrace to Paris', 'hideous beyond repair' and 'dizzily ridiculous'.[86] The main building of the exhibition had a span of about 170 feet, and again there were plenty of small buildings around, e.g. 'The History of the Human Habitation', designed by Garnier as forty-four separate houses.[87]

The World's Columbian Exposition held in Chicago in 1893 had nothing as flamboyant as what the French thought necessary for an international exhibition, but the general plan of the centre with a long *cour d'honneur* and a domed building in the *point de vue* was lifted

straight from Paris by Daniel Burnham, Chief of Construction.[88]

Architecturally the Chicago exhibition was the triumph of Beaux-Arts Classicism and the death knell for the Chicago School (p. 220) and for Sullivan's style. The two largest buildings were the Manufactures and Liberal Arts Building and the Machinery Hall, the former by G. B. Post, the latter by Peabody & Stearns. The former was about 1,700 by 780 feet, which made it the largest building in the world. It had a span of about 367 feet, a very little more than that of the Galerie des Machines of 1889, and in height was about 62 feet more than the Galerie. Among architects at Chicago the Classicists were C. B. Atwood (triumphal arch and flanking colonnades, also Fine Arts Building, the latter 500 by 320 feet), R. M. Hunt (Administration Building), Van Brunt & Howe (Electricity Building) and McKim, Mead & White (Agriculture Building). The sculptor Augustus St Gaudens (of General Sherman fame) called Atwood's Palace of Art 'the best thing done since the Parthenon'.[89] Sullivan, as is familiar, foretold that all this Classicism would set the clock of

15.47

15.49 Paris, Exhibition of 1900, entrance from the Place de la Concorde by R. Binet

15.52 Paris, Exhibition of 1900, Palais des Illusions by Eugène A. Hénard

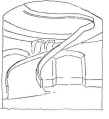

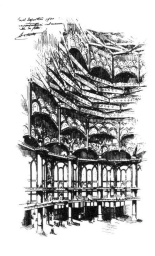

15.50 Paris, Exhibition of 1900, Petit Palais, staircase by François Hennebique (E. Schild, *Zwischen Glaspalast und Palais des Illusions*, 1967)

15.51 A. de Baudot, design for the Paris Exhibition of 1900

15.53 Paris, Exhibition of 1900, Grand Palais by H. Deglane

American architecture back by fifty years. Indeed the only forward-looking building was Sullivan's Transportation Building.[90]

The next international exhibition to be held in America was the Louisiana Purchase Exhibition at St Louis in 1904.[91] It covered 1,272 acres – twice the area of the Chicago exhibition. The style was a gaudy Baroque, especially spectacular the Festival Hall by Cass Gilbert. From Chicago St Louis took over the obsession with long colonnades – the motif which was soon to become the pet of the architects of the new Federal buildings of Washington (pp. 50–51). St Louis, apart from the big buildings – 1,600 feet, 1,300 feet, 1,200 feet, 1,000 feet, etc., in length – had uncountable small buildings. Those who tried to count gave the figure 1,576. The large number of small pavilions was to be characteristic of the great exhibitions of the twentieth century.

The first of them took place in the very year 1900, in Paris.[92] It is the exhibition for which the Grand Palais and the Petit Palais were built, the former by H. Deglane, the latter by C. Girault. These two are Baroque though tempered in the Beaux-Arts way by the long rows of giant columns which the United States had made their own. Internally, of course, iron had to appear. Hautecoeur writes neatly: 'La galerie des machines inserée dans un musée'.[93] The Petit Palais holds another structural surprise. Hennebique, chief French promoter of reinforced concrete, provided two large cantilevered spiral staircases inside. For these were the years when concrete came into its own. Professor Peter Collins has told the early story of concrete exhaustively.[94] Anatole de Baudot, Viollet-le-Duc's most faithful pupil, whose St Jean-de-Montmartre begun in 1894 used reinforced brick and cement, submitted a scheme for a vast 'salle des fêtes' with equally idiosyncratic features. It was not accepted. In the end Baudot did the restaurant, but that had metal domes.

However, in spite of such instances of awareness of new materials, from the structural point of view the exhibition – coming only eleven years after the Eiffel Tower and the Galerie des Machines – was a disappointment. The exteriors and interiors seem a frantic whipping up of the Baroque of 1878 and 1889 to yet more extreme performances. Iron as a rule was necessary but

15.54 Breslau (Wroclaw), market hall, 1906–08, by Heinrich Küster

15.56 Reims, market hall, 1928–30, by E. Maigrot

15.55 Leipzig, market hall, 1927–29, by H. Ritter

15.57 Breslau (Wroclaw), Centenary Hall, 1911–13, by Max Berg

tended to be hidden under stucco, and Guadet had the impudence to try and justify this by referring to the gypsum indigenous to the Paris area.[95] Others felt and resented the banishment of the structural members. Muthesius for instance wrote of 'buildings without rhyme or reason, without taste and devoid of any higher goal',[96] and Hautecoeur of 'gigantesques pâtisseries'[97] – in medieval, in French Renaissance, in Louis XV. Among the most spectacular buildings[98] were the group of the Château d'Eau by J. B. Paulin and behind it the Palais de l'Electricité by E. A. Henard, both incidentally of concrete,[99] and the portal from the Place de la Concorde by René Binet. The latter was planned quite ingeniously. It was three-legged so that the public came in under one arch and was then at once distributed half left and half right to go through the sets of turnstiles. Very few pavilions refused to join the riot. Among them the only larger one was the Palais des Congrès by Charles F. Mewès, a quiet disciplined design in a free Louis XVI. The other pavilions to be singled out for architectural character were S. Bing's seven-room house, all Art Nouveau, and Sauvage's Pavillon Loïe Fuller, even purer Art Nouveau and certainly more challenging. The whole façade was given the form of a curtain, all of course in stucco.[100] Guimard of Métro

15.49

fame had a separate *pavillon* too, and this contained items from the Castel Béranger, i.e. Art Nouveau again.[101]

Beyond these adventurous pavilions and beyond the exuberance of the largest buildings it should not be forgotten that the exhibition also still had plenty of pavilions in period styles, especially on the Quai des Nations. A picturesque bogus Vieux-Paris had also been put up. Among the national pavilions the Finnish was the most interesting – by Eliel Saarinen, still in a folksy style, but undeniably original.[102]

For the twentieth century much needs saying about exhibitions, little about conservatories and market halls. As for market halls, one point must be made, and it applies to exhibitions as well. Reinforced concrete took the place of steel, having the advantage of combining the crushing strength of stone with the tensile strength of iron. Just four important examples: Breslau (Wroclaw) 1906–08 by Heinrich Küster with concrete parabolic arches of 62-foot span,[103] Leipzig 1927–29 by H. Ritter with two low, ribbed domes, Reims 1928–30 by E. Maigrot with a tunnel vault, and Algeciras 1933 by Torroja with a shallow dome and a Pantheon oculus.

Back to exhibitions. In this field the difference from the nineteenth century is that innovation appeared more

15.54

15.55
15.56

15.59 Darmstadt, Exhibition of 1901, Ernst Ludwig Haus by J. M. Olbrich

15.58 Cologne, Werkbund Exhibition of 1914, Glashaus by Bruno Taut

15.60 Paris, Exhibition of 1925, Pavillon de l'Esprit Nouveau by Le Corbusier

often in specialized than in international universal exhibitions. The following need to be mentioned. The start of the century, 1901, saw the famous exhibition on the Mathildenhöhe at Darmstadt sponsored by the Grand Duke of Hesse, Ernst Ludwig. It was the first exhibition in which whole, solidly built houses were shown. They were radical in style – no period motif anywhere. And they were to be occupied after the closure of the exhibition. Among the designers were Peter Behrens and Joseph Maria Olbrich. Olbrich also designed the one larger building which was for studios and for community purposes. This has no echoes of past styles either.[104]

In 1913 at Breslau, as a memorial of the centenary of the defeat of Napoleon, Max Berg (with R. Konwiarz and the engineer Trauer) did the Centenary Hall, the first building to make full use of the possibilities of arcuated concrete.[105] The hall has a dome 213 feet in diameter resting on four segmental arches 135 feet in span.[106] One year later, in 1914, the exhibition held at Cologne by the Deutscher Werkbund,[107] then only seven years old, contained two buildings of international importance: Gropius' now famous model factory, or rather machinery hall and administration range, with its two spiral staircases in glass cylinders, and Bruno Taut's Glashaus, a polygon with walls of thick glass bricks, a pointed dome constructed on the space-frame principle and a metal and glass staircase inside. Next, after the war, the Paris exhibition of 1925 was dedicated to the *arts décoratifs et industriels modernes*. It was for this exhibition that Le Corbusier built his Pavillon de l'Esprit Nouveau in the white unrelieved forms of his early villas and with a tree growing inside. 1927 is the year of the Werkbund exhibition at the Weissenhof near Stuttgart, consisting of a number of permanent houses by such architects as Behrens, Gropius, Hilberseimer, Mies van der Rohe, Poelzig, Scharoun, Schneck, Taut, Oud, Stam, Le Corbusier, Bourgeois. Mies van der Rohe was responsible for the German pavilion at the international exhibition of 1929 in Barcelona. It was a masterpiece of open planning – spaces flowing into each other – and with its supports of stainless steel and its slabs of travertine, green marble, grey, green and black glass and onyx proved once for all that the so-called International Modern, maligned at the time as cigar-boxy and barracks-like, was capable of conveying a sense of opulence. Next the Stockholm exhibition of 1930 where Asplund showed how elegant the International Modern could be. It was a step forward beyond the cubic style of the Corbusier villas towards

15.61 Barcelona, Exhibition of 1929, German pavilion by Ludwig Mies van der Rohe

15.63 Stockholm, Exhibition of 1930, by Gunnar Asplund

15.62 New York, World's Fair, 1939

15.64 Turin, Salone Agnelli, 1948–49, by Pier Luigi Nervi

transparency and the principle of maximum performance with a minimum of mass. In 1937 Paris came back. This time the title was 'Arts et techniques appliqués à la vie moderne'. This was the exhibition for which the Trocadéro was pulled down and replaced by the Palais de Chaillot. Of the pavilions what stuck in one's mind more than anything else was the Soviet and the Nazi buildings remarkably similar in mood and grimly facing one another.[108] New York held two international exhibitions both called World's Fair – in 1939 and in 1964–65.

Of exhibition buildings of the last twenty-five years priority must be given to Nervi's brilliant halls at Turin, of highly original concrete construction. They went up in 1948, 1950 and 1961 and covered areas of 240 by 309, 213 by 240, and 262 by 328 feet. Even larger is the span of the Centre National des Industries et des Techniques at the Rond Point de la Défense in Paris, 1957–58 by Camelot, de Mailly and Zehrfuss with Jean Prouvé.

This is an equilateral triangle, about 710 feet along each side. It is covered by a hyperbolic paraboloid roof resting on three points. Ten years before, the hyperbolic paraboloid (alias collapsed-tent) roof had been introduced into the exhibition repertoire by Le Corbusier in the small Philips pavilion at the international exhibition of Brussels (1958). Pavilions at exhibitions tend to display gimmicks. The Philips pavilion was so small that it did not call for this kind of roof. Exhibitions of course tend to exhibitionism, and so Egon Eiermann's German building in Brussels, clean, clear and crisp, was quite a relief. In some cases, however, it is not easy to draw the line between what is innovation and what is gimmick. A case in point was Habitat, the monster housing scheme by Moshe Safdie at the international Montreal Expo in 1967. What was built – 156 flats on nine floors – is only a fragment. The original project was for 5,000 on twenty floors. Only at such a figure, the architect explained, would the scheme be economic.

15.65 Paris, Exhibition of 1937, showing pavilions of Germany (left) and Russia (right)

15.67 Paris–Nanterre, Exhibition Hall at the Rond-Point de la Défense, 1957–58, by Camelot, de Mailly and Zehrfuss with Jean Prouvé

15.66 Brussels, Exhibition of 1958, Philips Pavilion by Le Corbusier

15.68 Osaka, Exhibition of 1970

The block was built up of pre-cast concrete units, each weighing 70–90 tons. They were assembled to achieve a maximum appearance of disorder. Yet one cannot call the whole a gimmick; for the architect described as his intention to create 'the rhythms and variety of urban experience essential to community experience'. That this is desirable is left as an axiom. Even if one were to accept it, one might still wonder whether in the architect's mind the axiom or the vision of the huge crag came first. Equally ambiguous between innovation and intended visual shock was Frei Otto's German pavilion with its suspended roofs and divers peaks.[109] The United States pavilion was one of the largest so far of Buckminster Fuller's geodesic domes.[110] It had a diameter of 254 feet and was 200 feet high. The dome of the Union Tank Car Company at Baton Rouge (1958) has a diameter of 384 feet and a height of 116 feet. The principle of the Fuller domes of space-frame construction is by now familiar. In the context of this chapter Fuller's Climatron at St Louis is of interest, as it is a conservatory. Its diameter is 175 feet, and it was built in 1960.

Finally Osaka 1970. The plan in the *Architectural Review* lists 107 buildings. The general impression was chaotic. The British pavilion by Powell & Moya had a suspended roof once more, but here it carefully avoided the sensational. The suspended roof was altogether much in evidence, and no doubt it is the riotous forms of the buildings which in such an exhibition secures success with the millions of visitors.

Is a summing-up needed to the more than a hundred years of exhibitions from the Crystal Palace to Osaka? The Duke of Wellington provided us with his summing-up of 1851 a week after the opening of the Crystal Palace, and it is as valid as it was then: 'Whether the show will be of any use to anybody may be questioned, but of that I am certain, nothing can be more successful.'[111]

15.69 Montreal, Expo, 1967

15.71 Montreal, Expo, 1967, American pavilion by Buckminster Fuller

15.70 Montreal, Expo, 1967, Habitat by Moshe Safdie

15.72 Montreal, Expo, 1967, German pavilion by Frei Otto

16.1 Antoine Watteau, sign board of the art dealer Gersaint, c. 1720 (Berlin–Dahlem, Staatliche Museen)

16
Shops, stores
and department stores

THE development of the design of shops moved in very slow steps. There is no essential difference between the shops of the Forum of Trajan (early second century AD) or of Ostia (mid-second century) and the shop painted by Ambrogio Lorenzetti in 1338–39 in his fresco of *Life under a good Regimen*. And just as in Imperial Rome a row of shops extended left and right of the entrance to a house of several storeys, so it was still in the High Renaissance – in Bramante's House of Raphael.[1] Even the counter which acts as a bar between street and shop is the same as in Imperial Rome. When shops became larger a counter would bisect the shop in the longitudinal direction. The shop of Gersaint, the art dealer on the Pont Notre Dame, was of this kind, as we know from Watteau's exquisite sign board. It could be a shop of today. So planning-wise the shop is not of interest to the art historian. But technologically and stylistically it is. First the glazing of the shop front. Until the later seventeenth century the shop had been open to the street. Glazing seems to have started in Holland in the later seventeenth century. Examples of glazing appear for instance in Gerrit Adriansz Berckheyde's view of the Market Square of Haarlem in the Detroit Institute of Arts and in Job Berckheyde's *Baker's Shop* at Oberlin College. The corresponding date for France was given

me as *c.* 1700 by Michel Gallet in a letter. He calls the best eighteenth-century shop fronts in Paris that on the Quai d'Orléans and that on the Quai des Carmes (now des Célestins) of *c.* 1760 and *c.* 1775 respectively.

As for London, in an engraving of Bishopsgate dated 1736 an open and a glazed shop appear side by side. The glazed one of course has the close grid of glazing bars typical of the eighteenth century. But gradually, in the early nineteenth century larger panes came in. Dickens in *Sketches by Boz* (1836) speaks of the sudden passion for plate glass as a phenomenon of six or eight years ago. In Charles Knight's *London*, vol. V, published in 1843, we read of a shop in Ludgate Hill that glass united ground floor and first floor, and of a shop in St Paul's Churchyard that there was 'an uninterrupted mass of glass from the ceiling to the ground, no horizontal bars being seen'.[2] However, the Georgian shop window glazing remained ubiquitous right down to 1840. Tallis's famous *London Street Views* of 1838–39 show such shops filling the ground floor of buildings all over the centre of London. Karl Philipp Moritz,[3] the impecunious visitor from Germany, wrote in 1782 of the Strand that 'one shop jostles another'.[4] Georgian shop fronts are often a door between two windows, and the windows are often segmentally convex.[5] Quite a num-

16.2

16.3

16.1

16.4
16.5

16.6

16.3 Rome, House of Raphael, 1514, by Bramante

16.2 Ambrogio Lorenzetti, detail from *The Good Regimen in the City*, 1338–39, showing a shop (*Siena, Palazzo Pubblico*)

16.4 G. A. Berckheyde, detail from *View of the Groote Kerk in Haarlem*, 1695, showing shops (*The Detroit Institute of Arts*)

16.7 ber of Georgian shop fronts survive, the best known in London being Fribourg & Treyer in Haymarket and the row of smaller premises along Woburn Walk (1822). Many more such shop fronts can still be found all over the provinces. *The Buildings of England* tries to record them. The type which replaced them divides part from part by means of columns. As early as 1709 Addison in the *Tatler* refers to the Corinthian columns of a shop.[6]

16.8 John Buonarotti Papworth, who designed many shop fronts in the second and third decades of the nineteenth century, went in for this type. However, Georgian glazing would have made nonsense of it. So its rise to full success was only made possible by the introduction

16.10 of plate glass for the windows. Miss Eldridge in an excellent paper[7] states that in 1828 panes were about 4 feet long and never more than 5. The size began to increase about 1840.[8] Tallis's edition of 1847 speaks of 'vast sheets of plate glass'. The duty on glass was repealed in 1845. By 1850 sheets 7–8 feet by 3–4 feet were

16.9 available. Asprey's in London still have the arrangement of *c.* 1860, Benson, also in Bond Street, that of 1866.[9] Jacob Burckhardt, the great Swiss Renaissance scholar, noted in a letter of 1879 that these 'giant panes of glass' had still been a rarity in 1860.[10] Many complained that visually the plate-glass shop window resulted in the

painful impression of the masonry of the upper floors being supported entirely by glass. In fact quite often the upper floors were supported by concealed iron stanchions, the whole arrangement having the purpose of emphasizing the integrity of the glass front. Miss Eldridge quotes a shop in Regent Street illustrated in Elmes's *Metropolitan Improvements* of 1827, and a shop in Oxford Street of 1845. For the United States the year of the first iron shop front is 1835, if one can trust Davis's statement.[11]

As for styles used, Paris shop fronts have different motifs but are at one with London in the refusal of embellishments. Krafft and Ransonnette in 1801–02 have quite a number of these.[12] The most interesting is the Cour Batave in the rue St Denis, designed by Sobre and Happe in 1791 for some Dutch speculators. The front to the street was 22 bays long and had a small cupola. Behind the front was a large courtyard. Shops faced on to the street and also to the courtyard. There were flats above the shops. While the Empire Style was popular in France, Greek Revival was popular in England.[13] Gothick and later Gothic were never popular. L. and J. Taylor in 1792 have one example,[14] Whittock in 1840 a few more.[15] The climax is[16] the façade of the Grover & Baker Sewing Machine Co.'s

16.11,

16.13

16.5 Job Berckheyde, *The Bakery Shop*, *c.* 1680 *(Oberlin College, Ohio, Allen Memorial Art Museum)*

16.6 London, view of Bishopsgate in 1736

16.7 London, Woburn Walk, 1822

16.8 J. B. Papworth, design for a shop front in Piccadilly, London *(London, RIBA Drawings Collection)*

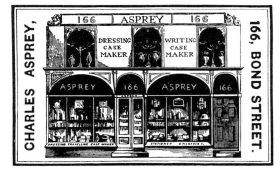

16.9 London, Asprey's, Old Bond Street, *c.* 1860

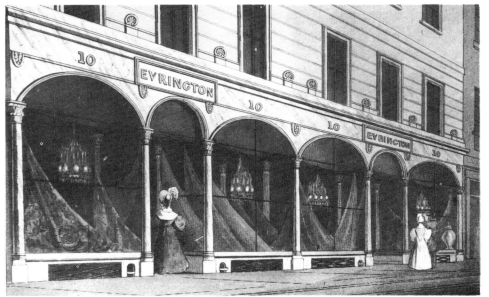

16.10 London, shop front (Whittock, *On the Construction and Decoration of the Shop Fronts of London*, 1840)

16.11 Paris, Cour Batave, 1791, by Sobre and Happe

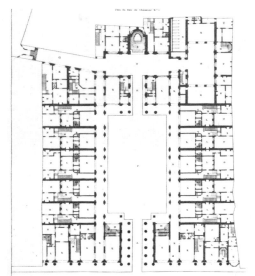

16.12 Paris, Cour Batave, 1791, by Sobre and Happe

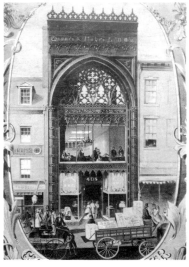

16.13 New York, Grover & Baker, c. 1850

16.14 Philadelphia, Oakford's Hat Store, c. 1855–60

premises in New York, of c. 1850.[17] Rarer still than Gothic were Egyptian and Moorish, the former in T. King's *Shop Fronts* of the 1830s,[18] the latter in Whittock, i.e. illustrated in 1840.[19] Papworth has one shop with Chinoiserie motifs, but that was for Sparrow's, the tea merchants. It was done in 1802, though a drawing of it is dated 1822.[20] Elizabethan, as we have seen in other chapters, had a vogue in the Early Victorian decades. Examples among shop fronts are Fortnum & Mason's – very debased – as illustrated by Whittock in 1840[21] and – even more debased – a shop in the Regent Street Quadrant as illustrated in the *Companion to the Almanac* for 1841, where it is called 'Renaissance or Elizabethan'.[22] *The Builder* in 1851 tells of a shop which it calls 'elegant though bizarre', in that it has Elizabethan and Gothic touches.[23] Elizabethan bordering on Jacobean in its decoration is the interior of Oakford's Hat Store in Philadelphia, of c. 1855–60.[24]

The French equivalent to English Elizabethan is François I. Normand in his *Paris Moderne* (1843)[25] has examples, later by some years than the famous 'House of François I', re-erected in Paris, whose François I features are genuine but not *in situ*.[26] Italianate in a variety similar to that of Early Victorian England is illustrated by Hautecoeur.[27] Louis XV or Rococo appears twice in Whittock.[28] Finally mixed motifs. Osler's shop in Oxford Street by Owen Jones had minor Louis XV on the walls but a glass roof inspired by such medieval timber roofs as that of S. Zeno in Verona.[29] The shop was built in 1858–60.

There is no point in following the shop through the rest of the nineteenth century and into the twentieth. It is sufficient to point to two shops, both emphatically post-historicist – yet one distant by fifty years from the other. The early one is for the twentieth-century style remarkably early: Adolf Loos's shop for Goldman &

16.14

16.15

16.16

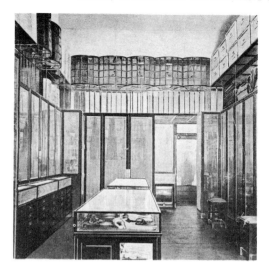

16.16 Vienna, Goldman & Salatsch,
1898, by Adolf Loos

16.17 San Francisco, Calif.,
V. C. Morris's Gift Shop (now Helga
Howie Boutique), 1948–49, by Frank
Lloyd Wright

16.15 Owen Jones, design for Messrs Osler's shop in London, 1858

16.17 Salatsch in Vienna, of 1898. The other is of 1948–49 and was designed by Frank Lloyd Wright. V. C. Morris's Gift Shop in San Francisco has the perverse peculiarity of a total lack of shop windows. Yet because nobody else was doing it, the silent entrance ready to suck you in might in the end be the best advertisement.

So far we have only looked at single shops. Now we must expand. In the Middle Ages one trade kept to one street. Hence our Milk Streets and Bread Streets and Cordwainer Streets and rues de la Lingerie and de la Ferronnerie. That represents gild-controlled trading. Under liberated making and selling, shops of various appeals tend to congregate in one place. Shops also tend to multiply. One can see in Tallis how shops lined all the streets of inner London. Could things be made more convenient and more comfortable for the customer? Yes – he can for instance be protected from rain. Hence the medieval arcaded streets of Italy, of Southern

France, of Innsbruck and Berne.[30] Yet more convenient and comfortable is the street reserved for walkers and entirely roofed over. Such are the oriental bazaars. The Grand Bazaar of Istanbul covers an area of nearly 2,000,000 square feet. The nearest thing in the Western World – if that term is accepted – is GUM, the bazaar of Moscow, consisting of sixteen blocks separated from each other by three lengthwise streets and three shorter cross streets.[31] GUM replaced a whole district of shacks where goods were sold. It was designed by Pomeranzev and built in 1888–93. The features were all taken from arcades, but we cannot turn to Western arcades without having cast a glance on Western bazaars.

16.21

The bazaar was really no more than a fashion in nomenclature, and it was almost entirely confined to England. Dr Geist[32] lists fifteen in London. What the term indicates is that goods of more than one kind were sold, although women's dresses, dress materials, acces-

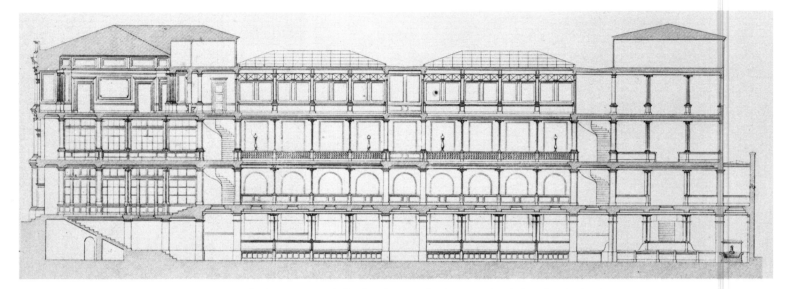

16.18 K. F. Schinkel, design for a *Kaufhaus*, 1827 *(Berlin, National-Galerie)*

16.19 Paris, Galeries du Commerce et de l'Industrie, 1838, by Grisart & Froelicher: longitudinal section

sories and millinery seem to have been the staple trade. In England the term had a vogue in the first third of the nineteenth century. The Soho Bazaar in the northwest corner of Soho Square came first. It was started in 1816 and operated on two levels like the exchanges. Then came the Queen's Bazaar in Oxford Street of about 1820–25 and the Pantheon in Oxford Street. The Pantheon had been built in 1772 by James Wyatt as a swagger place of entertainment, a winter 'Ranelagh'. Later it became a theatre and in 1834 in the hands of Sydney Smirke a bazaar.[33] Similarly the Pantechnicon of 1830 in Motcombe Street was known as a bazaar. It sold larger items: furniture and carriages. There are French examples too. Normand illustrates one called Bazar de l'Industrie,[34] on the Boulevard Montmartre. The architect was Lelong, the date of erection 1830. The same type on a larger scale, but not called bazaar, was the Galeries du Commerce et de l'Industrie, Boulevard Bonne Nouvelle. The architects were Grisart & Froelicher, the date 1838.[35] The Galeries had shops on all floors. It is probably in relation to such bazaars that one should look at Schinkel's drawing of 1827 called 'Kaufhaus'.[36] The word *Kaufhaus* can mean different things. Today it means a department store, but what Schinkel had in mind was a bazaar, with many small

shops belonging to different owners. Schinkel's Kaufhaus was to be built at the east end of Unter den Linden in Berlin. It was in Schinkel's most original, unhistoricist style and was to consist of three ranges round a large area open to the street. There were to be two main selling floors and two mezzanines for dwellings. (The large windows hide the existence of the mezzanines.) Additional inspiration may have come from arcades Schinkel had seen in Paris in 1826.

For those were the classic years of arcades – *passages*, as the French called them, *Passagen* in German, *gallerie* in Italian. The arcade is a roofed street for pedestrians. Its origin is in London, where Thomas Gresham's Royal Exchange had stalls to let to artisans or tradesmen. Its plan, as we have seen (p. 199) was of four ranges with cloister walks. Stalls on the ground floor faced the outside, on the upper floor the cloister. Nearer in appearance to the future arcades was the New Exchange running south from the Strand, built in 1608 by the Earl of Salisbury, and the Exeter Exchange built in 1676 and running parallel with, and north of, the Strand, further west. They were both on two levels too. Inigo Jones made a design for the New Exchange – his earliest – but it was not accepted. The New Exchange might well have been called an arcade. It stands at the begin-

16.20 London, the Pantheon converted into a bazaar, 1834, by Sydney Smirke

16.21 Moscow, GUM, 1888–93, by A. N. Pomeranzev

ning of the type, but, as history would have it, the type was brought to fruition in Paris, not in London. The story has been told exhaustively by Dr Geist. The origin in Paris was the Palais Royal (see pp. 67, 76, 78)[37] originally Richelieu's, then Anne of Austria's (hence royal), then the Duc d'Orléans', brother of Louis XIV, then Philippe Egalité's. The gardens at the back had always been public. Philippe Egalité in 1781–86 surrounded them by colonnades. His architect was Louis who, it will be remembered, built the Théâtre Français in 1786–90 as part of the Palais Royal (p. 78). The intention had been to add a cross wing between palace and garden. This part of the scheme was however not built. Instead wooden stalls in three rows were put up and remained till 1828. Their purpose was to add to the income of Philippe. They were called the Galeries de Bois. Balzac in *Illusions perdues* describes them as stinking and of ill repute, the place of business of booksellers, fashion magazines and prostitutes. In 1829 they were finally replaced by the Galerie d'Orléans. But other arcades must be referred to first. Dr Geist has a plan of roofed Paris arcades from 1790 to 1860.[38] There were twenty of them, the majority of before *c.* 1830. The earliest was the Passage Feydeau, discovered by Dr Geist. It was built in 1790 and demolished in 1824.

It was close to the Théâtre Feydeau of 1791 (see p. 83), and the rue des Colonnes of 1797–98 with its strange Revolutionary pillars. Next followed the Passage du Caire running west from the rue St Denis. This dated from 1798–99.[39] In 1800 followed the Passage des Panoramas close to the Feydeau group. It led north to the two panoramas. (The panorama was an English invention.)

Louis Montigny in his *Le Provincial à Paris* published in 1824–25 tells what shops had gone into the arcades: a café, shops for *confitures*, fruit, shoes, gloves, stationery, Marquis chocolate, a joiner, a goldsmith, delicatessen, sheet music, tobacco and toys.

The Passage Delorme of 1808 led from the rue de Rivoli to the rue St Honoré. The roof was partly sheets of glass (from the start?). The Passage Montesquieu was built in 1811 west of the Palais Royal. In the twenties arcades multiplied. The Passage de l'Opéra of 1822–23 was a pair of parallel arcades. They were covered by pitched glass roofs. After that Pont Neuf 1823, Lafitte 1824, Vivienne 1824, Cerf 1824, Saucède 1825, Choiseul 1825, Colbert 1826 and so on. Of noteworthy elements the Passage Vivienne has transverse arches with wreaths *à l'antique* supporting the pitched glass roof, the Passage Colbert had as its climax a rotunda with a glass dome.

16.22

16.22 Paris, Galerie d'Orléans, 1828–30

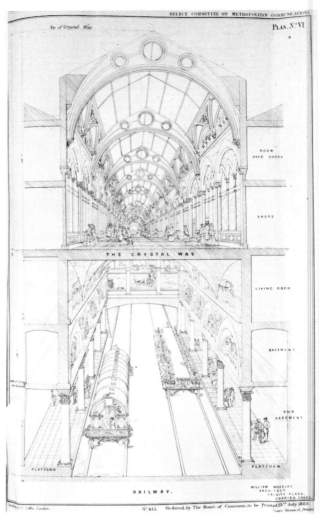

16.23 William Moseley, design for the Crystal Way, 1855

16.22 Colbert also had a pitched glass roof; so has Choiseul. But the Galerie d'Orléans was the first to be covered by a glass tunnel vault. The date is 1828–30, and the motif was epoch-making.

London has fewer arcades, but two very fine ones: the Royal Opera Arcade built in 1816–18 by Nash and Repton behind the old opera house in the Haymarket, vaulted and with a small glass dome over each bay, and the Burlington Arcade, built in 1818–19 to a design of Samuel Ware who called it 'after the principle of . . . Exeter Change'.[40] There were 72 shops including (in 1828) milliners, hosiers, glovers, shoemakers, hairdressers, hatters, tobacconists, jewellers, a goldsmith, an optician, a wine merchant and a book-seller. The arcade had a pitched glass roof on transverse arches, as the Passage Vivienne had six years later.[41] Whereas the Royal Opera Arcade and the Burlington Arcade survive, the third of the great London arcades, the Lowther Arcade, was demolished in 1902. It belonged to the so-called West Strand Improvements and was built in 1829–31 by H. E. Kendall. It was eleven bays long with transverse arches and glass domes. Other early arcades of note were at Bordeaux (1831–34, well preserved), Bristol (1824–25 by Foster), Glasgow (1827 by Baird), Milan (Galleria De Cristoforis, 1831–32 by Pizzala, not preserved), Newcastle (1831–32 by Dobson, recently shamefully demolished), Philadelphia (1825–27 by Haviland, Grecian), and Providence, Rhode Island (1827–29 by Russell Warren, two tiers of galleries).

About 1850 the scale went up. A sign of the new adventurousness is the Great Victorian Way, planned in 1855 by Paxton for London and never executed. In the same year William Moseley made a similar scheme called the Crystal Way. They made their plans as part 16.23 of evidence submitted to the Select Committee on Metropolitan Improvements. Both suggested a loop-line for trains, close to what the London Underground actually did less than ten years later. Moseley's plan appeared a month before Paxton's. Moseley suggested a two-storey arcade, the lower for trains, the upper with a pitched glass roof on transverse arches for pedestrians. The upper arcade was to be lined with shops. The Crystal Way was to be about two miles long. Paxton's Victorian Way was planned with a length of ten miles. The arcade was to be 108 feet high and provided with a glass roof. Its width was to be that of the original transept of the Crystal Palace. The arcade was for carriages and pedestrians. Shops lined it on both sides. Deliveries ('wagons') were forbidden between 9 a.m.

16.24, 25 Milan, Galleria Vittorio Emanuele II, 1865–67, by Giuseppe Mengoni: interior (above) and dome (above right)
16.26 Cleveland, Ohio, Cleveland Arcade, 1888–90, by John Eisenmann and G. H. Smith

and 9 p.m. The railway – with separate lines for local and for express trains – was to be in separate tunnels. Express trains would take 5–6 minutes from the Bank to Regent Circus and 8 from the Bank to the end of a branch line in Belgravia.[42]

While the Victorian Way and the Crystal Way remained dreams, the largest arcade ever designed – the Galleria Vittorio Emanuele II in Milan – became reality, thanks to the spirit of enterprise of a thriving Milan plus English finance.[43] The Galleria – for most tourists *the* Galleria – is as busy as it was when it was new a hundred years ago. It was designed by Giuseppe Mengoni and built in 1865–67. The beginning, it must be remembered, was only six years after the liberation of Milan and four years after the coronation of Victor Emanuel. It is cross-shaped with longer north-south than east-west arms. The south arm opens to the Piazza del Duomo in a triumphal arch added in 1877. The arms are 96 feet high, and they meet in an octagon 137 feet 3 inches high and 128 feet in diameter. The arms have glass tunnel-vaults, the crossing a glass dome. The style may be called a variation on the Certosa di Pavia and such-like buildings of the Lombard Early Cinquecento. The Galleria was followed immediately by the Kaisergalerie in Berlin in 1871–73 – note that it was called a

Galerie, not a *Passage* – and the Galleria Umberto I in Naples in 1887–91. But by then the great vogue was slackening, although the finest arcade of America, that in Cleveland, Ohio, was built as late as 1888–90.

The Cleveland Arcade belongs to a different type. It has a pitched glass roof and four upper tiers of iron galleries reached by prominent staircases in the middle axis.[44] The sources to which John Eisenmann and George H. Smith went were neither in London nor in Paris. They seem to be the Barton Arcade in Manchester of 1871 with three iron galleries, the Lancaster Arcade of *c.* 1873 close to the Barton Arcade with two iron galleries, and probably also the Sailors' Home in Liverpool of 1846–48 with five iron galleries. In its own way the Cleveland Arcade is as much a climax as the Galleria.

Now to return to the real subject of this chapter – the shop and the store – it must be remembered that however grand and thrilling arcades are, they consist of individual, single shops each selling its own special wares. The phase of transition from shop to store is the shop selling a multitude of goods, though goods somewhat more specialized than the real department store.

To trace it to its source we have to go to Revolutionary France and to the *magasins de nouveautés*.[45] These

16.24, 25

16.25

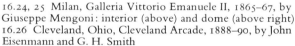

16.26

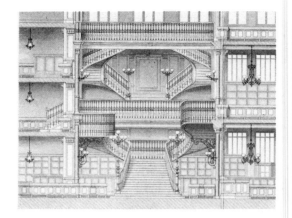

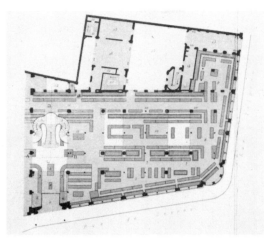

16.27, 28 Paris, Bon Marché, 1869–72, by M. A. Laplanche: portal in rue de Sèvres, main staircase, and ground plan

were large shops which sold fabrics and such accessories as millinery, lingerie, shoes, and soon also made-up dresses. They appeared in France when the Revolution had freed trade – with one exception: the store for which the banker Kromm received a privilege from Louis XV.[46] All the others date from the end of the eighteenth century to the 1830s. Jarry in his book *Les Magasins de nouveautés* mentions Le Petit Dunquerque on the Quai Conti, of which L. S. Mercier in the *Tableau de Paris*, i.e. in 1781–88, wrote that it 'étincelle de tous ces bijoux frivoles que l'opulence paie [et] que la fatuité convoite'. Jarry also mentions Pygmalion in the rue St Denis as founded in 1793.[47] Famous by 1817, he says, were La Fille mal-gardée, Le Diable boîteux, Au Masque de fer, and Les Deux Magots. Anatole France's mother shopped at the Deux Magots. These old names were taken over – nobody has explained why – from popular plays. The Trois Quartiers was founded in 1829; the Petit St Thomas in rue du Bac (where Boucicaut, who was to found the Bon Marché, worked) existed in 1830 and is mentioned by Anatole France; the Grand Condé was well known in 1833.[48] Now a page of the advertisements of the opening of the Belle Jardinière in 1824 refers explicitly to *prix fixes*. Balzac's *César Birotteau* meets his future wife at the

Petit Matelot on the Ile St Louis where she is a salesgirl in the linen department. He at once buys six shirts, and Balzac also refers to the *prix fixes* and to advertisements as 'séductions commerciales'.[49] *César Birotteau* was published in 1837, but the meeting of the two young people took place about 1800. As we shall see, fixed prices were to be one of the key features of selling in the future. In the early 1840s the Ville de Paris started and developed until it had a staff of 150. Jarry's illustrations of the Belle Jardinière and Ville de St Denis show them to be the size of department stores.[50] Mid-century must be the Grand Colbert; for it had windows of plate glass up to and including the mezzanine above the ground floor.[51] This was to be a standard motif of department stores. Another was the glazed roof of a central hall. Haute-coeur tells us that it appeared timidly in the Ville de Paris, and more assuredly in the Villes de France (1847).[52]

In England a similar development took place from the 1830s.[53] Kendall Milne in Manchester had started in 1831 and was called The Bazaar. The goods were visibly priced. So they were from 1841 at Bainbridge's in Newcastle, founded in 1830, and so they were at the Pantechnicon in Motcombe Street in London and a little later at Hyam's in Liverpool (where David Lewis

16.29 Paris, Bon Marché, section of staircase, 1876, by L.-C. Boileau

was an apprentice). Permission to exchange, bargain lines and the sending of patterns also existed.

At least two Parisian establishments which were not *magasins de nouveautés* appear to be significant architecturally. As we have seen (p. 262), Normand in *Paris moderne* illustrated the Bazaar de l'Industrie of 1830 and the Galeries du Commerce et de l'Industrie of 1838, and they look much like department stores. So too does the cast-iron palace of E. V. Haughwout & Co. in New York, at the corner of Broadway and Broome Street, built in 1857 and still standing. It was designed by J. P. Gaynor and manufactured by Daniel Badger (see above, p. 216). Inside it had a large glazed well – a common feature of nineteenth-century department stores – and the earliest of all passenger lifts, installed by Elisha Otis. Haughwout, like Tiffany's and Asprey's, sold elegant goods for the home, such as china, glass and statuary, some imported and some made on the upper floors of his store, which also provided warehouse space.

Now for the true department store. The year of its creation is known; its definition offers no problem. A department store is a store which consists of a multitude of departments – selling, as William Whiteley is alleged to have said, everything from pins to elephants. The first department store was the Bon Marché, created

in 1852 by Aristide Boucicaut. He was born in 1810 and died in 1877. As we have seen, he had been a salesman in the Petit St Thomas, a *magasin de nouveautés* in the rue du Bac. The origin of the Bon Marché was a shop of 1820, a few hundred yards to the south in the rue du Bac, selling *mercerie*. Boucicaut went into partnership with another when it came to enlarging and indeed to establishing the idea of the department store. That was in 1852. From 1863 he was alone. In 1869 he commissioned a purpose-built *grand magasin* on a lavish scale from M. A. Laplanche. By then other purpose-built department stores existed (of which more presently), but the story of the Bon Marché should be followed through. In the new store the curvaceous staircase was the climax. The windows were large but not excessively so, and no use was made of iron.[54] The building was at the corner of rue de Sèvres and rue Velpeau. Enlargement began almost at once. Louis-Charles Boileau (son of Louis-Auguste, the architect of the church of St Eugène with its bold use of exposed iron inside) extended the store in 1873 and 1876. The engineer was at first Moisant, then Eiffel. In the end the Bon Marché occupied the whole block bounded by rue de Sèvres, rue de Babylone, rue du Bac and rue Velpeau. In the *Encyclopédie d'architecture* Boileau wrote about the build-

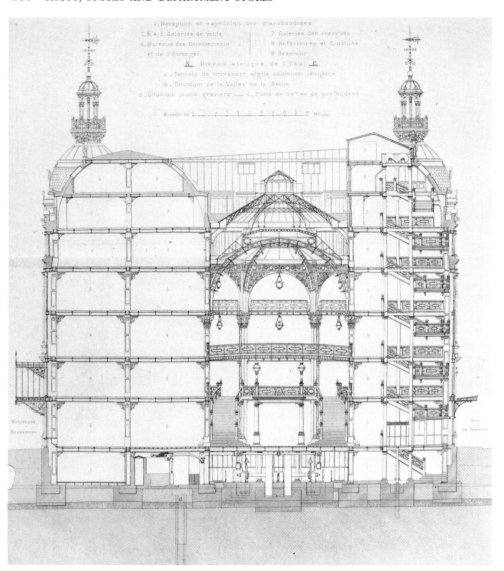

16.30, 31 Paris, Printemps, 1882–83, by Paul Sédille: section and façade

16.29

ing, first in 1876 and then in 1880.[55] He praises the 'concert lumineux' of glass and iron and stresses the fact that his building is 'une immense cage métallique' and that the stone piers are 'étrangers à l'ensemble' and wholly self-supporting. He praises Labrouste ('si grand') and Viollet-le-Duc's *Entretiens* and incidentally also Lebas ('grand artiste'). The store flourished. Sales amounted to nearly half a million francs in 1852, 5 million in 1860, 21 million in 1869, 67 million in 1877, 150 million in 1893. What made the Bon Marché such a success was the principles which Boucicaut followed. They were fixed prices, clearly displayed, permission to exchange purchases, and small profit to secure quick turnover.

When Boucicaut died, his widow took over. Both of them had been charitable on a splendid scale. The store was virtually made over to its employees. An insurance for employees and a retirement fund were created, and in addition to grants for staff, Madame Boucicaut gave 150,000 francs to the Institut Pasteur and created a new hospital of 570 beds, the Hôpital Boucicaut.

Two years after the creation of the Bon Marché, in 1854–55, the Grand Magasin du Louvre, an enterprise of two adventurous businessmen, Chauchard and Heriot, had opened, taking over some of the shops on the periphery of the Hôtel du Louvre (see p. 188). Gradually the store ate up the hotel. In 1867 followed two new buildings for stores. The Belle Jardinière, a *magasin de nouveautés*, as we have seen, was rebuilt next to the Pont Neuf after its former premises had been expropriated in 1866 for the new building of the Hôtel-Dieu. The architect was Blondel. The fenestration is that which now became standard: ground floor and mezzanine are of one composition, and so are first and second floors.[56] The other new store building of 1867 was the Magasins Réunis in the Place de la République by Davioud, the architect of the Trocadéro. Here the ground floor had large windows, and the first and second floor windows were tied together.[57] The Printemps came next, its promoter being Jules Jaluzot. A fire destroyed his premises, and in 1882 a new building was begun at the Carrefour du Havre. It was designed

11.46

16.32

16.30

16.32 Paris, Belle Jardinière, 1867 by Blondel

16.34 Chicago, Ill., Carson, Pirie, Scott (formerly Schlesinger & Mayer), 1899–1904, by Louis H. Sullivan

16.33 London, Selfridge's, begun 1908, by R. Frank Atkinson with D. H. Burnham (consultant)

16.27 by Sédille. The skeleton was iron, the outer walling stone, but with the typical large glazed areas, subdivided by iron mullions, and with exposed iron girders.[58] Finally came the Samaritaine, started by Ernest Cognacq on a small scale in 1867.[59] Its growth was amazing, the sales figures being 830,000 francs in 1874, 2 million in 1877, 6 million in 1882, 25 million in 1890, 1,700 million in 1931. The famous Art Nouveau store of 1905 was by Zola's friend Frantz Jourdain, but the present main façades are by Sauvage, of 1927. The interior is, of course, again iron. Cognacq and his wife were public benefactors like the Boucicauts. Testimony is the Cognacq-Jay Museum.

If one wants to evoke the impression of such stores as the Bon Marché and the Printemps, one ought to read some pages of Zola's *Au Bonheur des Dames*, published in 1883:[60] 'The high door . . . was all of glass, surrounded by intricate decorations overloaded with gilding, and reaching to the mezzanine. Two allegorical figures . . . their bare breasts exposed were unrolling an inscription: Au Bonheur des Dames . . .'. A new exten-

sion, opened as the action of the book takes place, is described like this: The architect was 'a young man in love with modernity'. 'He had made use of stone only for the basement and the corner pillars' and for the rest all was iron – an 'ossature en fer' – except for the ceiling vaulting which was of brick (see p. 276). 'It was a cathedral of modern business, strong and yet light.' Inside, the lifts were 'clad with velvet', but the main route to the upper floor was the 'iron staircase with double spirals in bold curves'. Bridges ran across high up, and the detail of the ironwork is compared with lace. The summing up is 'a temple to Woman, making a legion of shop assistants burn incense before her'.

Zola's theme is of course the store killing the small shops. The theme is as topical today as it was a hundred years ago, except that now the shop is starved not only by the department store but also, as we shall see, by the chain store and by the supermarket.

For the moment the architecture of the department store in countries other than France must be given some attention. For the United States the facts have been

16.35 Berlin, Wertheim, 1896–1904, by Alfred Messel: view from the Leipziger Platz

16.36 Düsseldorf, Leonhard Tietz, 1907–09, by J. M. Olbrich

16.37 Berlin, Hermann Tietz, 1898, by Sehring & Lachmann

assembled, but no story of anything like the interest of the Parisian story emerges.[61] The first New York department store was A. T. Stewart & Co. Stewart, like his European counterparts, started with dry goods. That was in 1823. In 1848 he was able to build for himself a marble palace. In 1859 he moved his store north and built a whole block bounded by Broadway, Fourth Avenue, and East 9th and 10th Streets. The new building, by John Kellum, had one of the most ambitious iron frontages of New York. It survived until 1956 as part of Wanamaker's (see below). Stewart's has already been mentioned in the context of cast iron (p. 216).

The years 1870–1910 saw a spectacular growth in the American department store business. John Wanamaker had started in Philadelphia in 1861 with one small shop. After ten years his store had a façade to 6th Street 180 feet long. A new building followed in 1875–76 and a yet newer one in 1902–10. In 1896 he bought Stewart's in New York and in 1903 built a fifteen-storey neighbour. The other most familiar East Coast department stores are Macy's and Bloomingdale's in New York. The former started small in 1858, the latter in 1872. Neither has any architectural merit. In Chicago the first were Potter Palmer and Marshall Field, in competition and then in partnership. In 1865 the firm was Field,

Palmer & Leiter, in 1868 Field, Leiter & Co. In 1881 Leiter left. Much of the firm's trade was wholesale, and for this the great Richardson in 1885–87 built one of his most monumental masterworks. Richardson's architectural heir was Louis Sullivan, whose last major work, the Schlesinger & Mayer store – later Carson, Pirie, Scott – is as well lit as any contemporary German example (see below), but with the system of steel structure proudly displayed. It was built in 1899–1904 and is the apotheosis of the Chicago School (p. 220). The steel skeleton is faced on the upper floors with terracotta tiles, but on the two lowest ones with cast iron sumptuously and closely covered in Sullivan's feathery leaf ornament.[62]

16.34

In Britain one need not go farther back than 1900. In London Harrods started small in groceries in 1849, but the present building is of 1901–05 by Stevens & Hunt. The style is French Renaissance with plenty of buff terracotta. Whiteleys began small in dry goods in 1863. Today's building with its long row of upper giant columns is by Belcher & Joass, of 1908–12.[63] In 1908 also Gordon Selfridge started his columnar showpiece in Oxford Street. He had been a junior partner in Marshall Field's, and he got Daniel Burnham of Chicago as architectural consultant. The result is gorgeously im-

16.33

16.38 Brussels, Innovation, 1900–1901, by Victor Horta

16.39 Zürich, Jelmoli, 1899, by Stadler & Usteri

perialistic. Outside London Lewis's of the Midlands deserves a few lines.[64] David Lewis had opened a small shop in Liverpool in 1858. The main goods were at first men's clothing. The Liverpool store is of 1912–18, and stores were also opened in Manchester in 1877 (new building 1912–18), in Birmingham in 1885 (new building 1926–29) and in Leeds (1929–32).[65]

Architecturally more interesting is Germany. It is enough to draw attention to four or five buildings. The first must be Wertheim in the Leipziger Strasse in Berlin, 1896–1904, by Messel. In the end the façade was 985 feet long. The oldest part has granite pillars and all glass in between; but far more influential was the end pavilion towards the Leipziger Platz with its closely set giant mullions. Four by two bays; each bay of three plus three lights. The closely set giant mullions were taken up by Olbrich for Leonhard Tietz in Düsseldorf in 1907–09.[66] Hermann Tietz also built two stores of importance: in Munich, by Hellmann & Littmann, 1904–05, more historicist outside but of reinforced concrete and with an impressive central hall,[67] and in the Leipziger Strasse in Berlin, the earliest of all and the most daring – so daring in fact that it was only rarely imitated. The architects were Sehring & Lachmann, and their design is of 1898. Fifteen years later, Alfred

Wiener in the *Werkbund-Jahrbuch* for 1913[68] wrote that here 'every support, every pier is banished from the façade and placed inside the building. Only the gigantic glass areas, 26 metres [85 feet] long and 17.05 metres [56 feet] high, remained in the front.' So here was the fully mature curtain wall. It was matched by Jelmoli in Zürich (Stadler & Usteri, 1899), Saintenoy's Old England store in Brussels of 1899–1902, and Horta's L'Innovation, also in Brussels, of 1900–1901.[69] Finally in Germany, Erich Mendelsohn, constitutionally an Expressionist, took the formula of Sullivan's Chicago store and turned it into Expressionism, for instance in the Schocken Store at Stuttgart of 1926.

A further development beyond the department store was the chain store. Thomas Lipton opened a grocery shop in Glasgow in 1872. In 1898 there were 245 shops.[70] Marks & Spencer started small in 1884 and in 1960 had 240 shops.[71] More recently they have become international. Thoroughly international is Woolworth's,[72] which was founded on the principle of low-cost goods. F. W. Woolworth in 1879 opened a shop at Lancaster, Pennsylvania, in which nothing cost more than 5 cents. A second shop at Utica, New York, was opened in the same year. Then shops followed one another rapidly. An attempt at diversification was made – 5 and 25 cents

16.35

16.36

16.37

16.39

16.38

16.40

– but that was not a success. From 1890 the terms of reference were 5 and 10 cents, which proved a wise move. There were 12 shops then, in 1899 54, in 1909 238. Woolworth's could then afford to build the highest skyscraper ever. The Woolworth Building (see p. 222) was designed by Cass Gilbert – in the Gothic style, which was evocatively not a convincing choice – and built in 1912–13. In 1919 there were 1,081 shops. In 1909 the invasion of Britain had begun – Liverpool being the bridge-head – and twenty years later there were 766 Woolworths in Britain. In Germany, where the attack took place in 1936, there were 82 in 1941. An instructive parallel to the chain store, first in America, then extending to Europe, is the chain of hotels (p. 187).

Of recent innovations in selling, three must be remembered: the shopping precinct, the supermarket, the suburban branches of stores. All three were caused by the motor car. The shopping precinct is an area of shops with only pedestrian front access. It may be a cluster of streets or passages, or it may be an arcade minus its roof.[73] The first of the latter was the Lijnbaan

in Rotterdam, 1951–53, by van den Broek & Bakema. The Yorkdale Shopping Plaza outside Toronto is typical of the large shopping centre on the edge of a town or in the country. Opened in 1964, it occupies 72 acres and includes four major as well as some 120 smaller stores. There is parking space for 6,736 cars. As for suburban branches of department stores, in the eastern United States Arnold Constable by 1956 had four, Bloomingdale's by 1959 also four.[74]

That leaves the supermarket. A supermarket is a self-service store originally mainly for groceries but soon also for other commodities of the right format. We find them in towns but also on sites like those of suburban branches of department stores or outer shopping centres. The first supermarket was, according to tradition, King Kullen in New York, which opened in 1930. Big Bear in New York is of 1932. Self-service is supposed to have been a Los Angeles innovation of *c.* 1930. M. F. Roggero in Carbonara's *Architettura pratica* (1962) writes that 40% of Americans shop in 10,000 supermarkets; for frozen goods the figure is 54.7$\frac{1}{2}$.[75]

16.40 Stuttgart, Schocken, 1926, by Erich Mendelsohn

16.41 Rotterdam, Lijnbaan, 1951–53, by van den Broek & Bakema

16.42 Yorkdale Shopping Plaza, near Toronto, opened 1964

17.1 Sèvres, Royal Porcelain Factory, 1753–56, by Lindet *(Sceaux, Musée de l'Ile de France)*

17
Factories

A FACTORY for the purpose of this book is a building of some size in which products are made in some quantity. It is not necessary, according to this definition, for the products to be made with the help of machines, although they mostly are. The word as used today is an illogical reduction of manufactory with the *manu* forgotten about. But factory without *manu* has also a different derivation. The factor was a commercial agent, and the factory thus a 'trading station', i.e. a building for storage, wholesale trade and dwellings. In this sense the factory is the same as the *fondaco* (p. 237).

It may well be argued that the earliest factories were the workshops of some printers. Anton Koberger of Nuremberg, who brought out Schedel's *Weltchronik* in 1493, had, according to Neudörffer (who wrote in 1547), twenty-four presses and more than a hundred compositors, printers, correctors, etc.[1] Similarly, Christopher Plantin in Antwerp in the second half of the sixteenth century employed about a hundred and at times more.[2]

Blondel in his *Cours d'architecture* of 1771[3] calls the factory *manufacture* and has no more to say about factories than that they should look simple and solid, and that they should be built on the periphery of a town by a river. Milizia in his *Principi di architettura civile*

of 1785[4] cribs from Blondel as he often does: *manufattorie* should be simple but proud, and they should be away from towns.[5] As for terminology in England, the word manufactory occurs in 1796 and 1797, the term factory in 1803.[6]

In France the royal workshops for furnishing were called Manufacture des Meubles de la Couronne. They were created by Colbert in 1667 and became the pattern of royal or altogether governmental workshops.[7] The most famous part was the Gobelins, the royal tapestry works,[8] named after the Gobelin family of Reims, who had moved in the fifteenth century to Paris as dyers. They were not tapestry makers: in 1597 Henri IV settled Flemish tapestry makers in the Jesuit house in the Faubourg St Antoine and when the Jesuits returned in 1603 the tapestry makers moved into the house of the Gobelin family. In 1662 Louis XIV – or rather Colbert – bought the house. A famous engraving by Sébastien Le Clerc shows Colbert visiting the Gobelins. He is seen in the long gallery of the house. But the premises would not justify the inclusion in this chapter. Nor would the premises of the Savonnerie, nor indeed those at Meissen where in 1708 Johann Friedrich Böttger had invented porcelain ('Dresden China') – or rather re-invented it after the Chinese. State porcelain

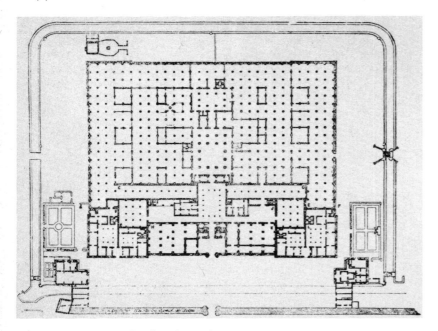

17.2 Seville, tobacco factory, 1728–70

17.4 Linz, wool mill, 1722–26, by J. M. Prunner

17.3 Derby, Lumbe's silk mill, 1717

works were the craze of princes, be their territory large or small. Here is a list just for Germany: Vienna 1717 (Imperial 1744), Höchst 1746, Nymphenburg 1747 (to Nymphenburg 1761), Fürstenberg 1748, Berlin 1751 (Royal 1763) Frankenthal 1755, Ludwigsburg 1758, and more later. Capo di Monte near Naples started in 1743, Sèvres in 1753,[9] Buen Retiro in Madrid in 1759, Copenhagen in 1772.

17.1 The premises at Sèvres were on a new scale, and in a palatial style, with a middle and two end pavilions, altogether about 425 feet long and of four floors. The architect was Lindet.[10] The Marquis d'Argenson wrote in 1755:[11] 'C'est un bâtiment immense, et presque aussi grand que l'Hôtel des Invalides.' That is an exaggeration, and Sèvres was in fact by no means unique in its size. As a matter of fact the prejudice must at once be contradicted that large factory buildings became possible only after the introduction of power-driven machinery. It is sufficient to present some illustrations. First from Spain the Fábrica de Cristalos at La Granja nearly 660 feet long,[12] and the Fábrica de Tabacos at 17.2 Seville (where Carmen worked), built in 1728–70, c. 615 by 480 feet in size.[13]

Some early privately built and run mills deserve attention too. The earliest and most important is the Vanrobais manufactory of fine cloth.[14] The van Robais were clothmakers at Middelburg in Holland: Colbert in 1665 succeeded in luring Josse van Robais to France. He went to Abbeville and settled with fifty of his Dutch workmen. The premises, largely still extant, are a palatial centre range of thirteen bays and two storeys, which was the van Robais dwelling, plus lower monumental wings 300 feet long and further detached buildings. The main building was erected in 1709–13.

Only a few years later Lumbe's silk mill at Derby was built.[15] The mill was 110 feet long and five storeys high. The water-wheel had a diameter of 23 feet. In 1730 about 300 were employed. Lumbe had spied on the Italian technique and was – so the story goes – poisoned by an Italian woman. His brother took over but committed suicide after a few years.

Of 1722–26 was the wool mill at Linz in Austria by 17.4 Johann Michael Prunner, architect of the pilgrimage church of Paura. The factory was of four ranges round a courtyard, the façade 28 bays long. The privilege of making woollens went back to 1672. The State took

17.5 Monschau, Rotes Haus, 1756, by J. B. Scheibler

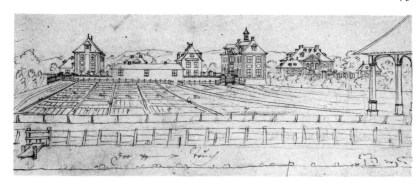

17.6 Basel, Emanuel Ryhiner factory (drawing by E. Büchel, 1751; *Basel, Staatsarchiv*)

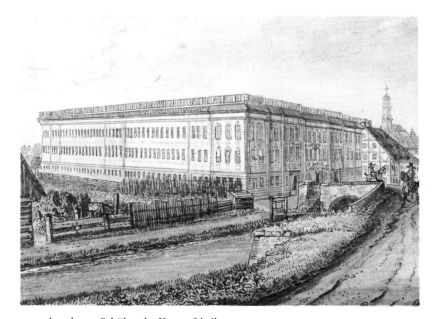

17.7 Augsburg, Schülersche Kattunfabrik, 1770–72

over the premises in 1754. In the last quarter of the eighteenth century the management was remarkably progressive. They employed a doctor, arranged for free hospital treatment and for a pension fund. The buildings were demolished in 1969 – a scandalous story.[16]

17.6 In 1731 at Basel, Emanuel Ryhiner built new additional premises to his and his brother's textile printing works which had been started in 1716. The main buildings looked more like a country house than a factory. It was in these new buildings that Oberkampf's father acquired his experience.[17]

17.5 1756 is the date of Johann Bernhard Scheibler's Rotes Haus at Monschau, south of Aachen, allegedly employing 4,000, the vast majority working at home. The building is of eight bays and three storeys, plus two more in the roof. A six-bay pediment acts as a distinguishing feature. An addition became necessary in 1786, and whereas the original building was factory, warehouse and dwelling in one, the addition was factory only. Another factory was built outside the town in 1793, and that was of three storeys and nineteen bays.

17.7 A few years later the Schülersche Kattunfabrik at Augsburg followed (1770–72).[18]

Of these early mills the one at Derby is the most important; for it stands at the beginning of a series of Derbyshire mills which were for a few decades the structurally most advanced buildings in the world. The decades in question are among the earliest of the Industrial Revolution. It is just as well to remember the most important innovations and inventions.[19] As will be noticed they all refer to iron smelting or construction or to yarn spinning and cloth weaving: 1709 Abraham Darby: coke instead of wood for smelting – 1733 J. Kay's fly-shuttle – 1746 Benjamin Huntsman's crucible process for melting steel – 1760 R. Kay's shuttle drop box – 1764–67 Hargreaves' spinning jenny – 1765 Watt's condenser for steam engines – 1769–75 Arkwright's water frame – 1774–79 Crompton's spinning mule – 1775–81 the Coalbrookdale Bridge, the earliest of all iron bridges, designed by T. F. Pritchard and cast by Abraham Darby – 1781 Watt's steam boiler – 1783 Cort's puddling – 1785 Cartwright's power loom – 1799 Jacquard's loom. The unprecedented industrial progress which these innovations made possible can be measured in the following figures. In 1765 England's output of coal was about 5 million tons, in 1785 over

17.8 Cromford, Masson Mill, 1783

17.9 Marple, Samuel Oldknow's Mellor Mill, 1790

10.[20] In 1813 England had 2,000 power looms, in 1829 45,000, in 1835 96,679, in 1850 about 250,000.[21]

Among the inventor-manufacturers Richard Arkwright in 1769 (or 1770? or 1771?) went into partnership with Jedadiah Strutt.[22] The partnership was dissolved in 1781, and it was after that date that William Strutt, Jedadiah's son, began to experiment with the structural use of iron.[23] Iron colonnettes had been used long before: the earliest case seems to be the colonnettes supporting galleries which were put into the House of Commons in 1706[24] – but that is another matter.

Strutt's reason to investigate the possibilities of iron as a structural material for factories was the appalling frequency of fires in factories. A particularly sensational one was that of the Albion Mill in London in 1791.[25] It had only been built in 1783–86. The design was by Samuel Wyatt. It was of brick, seven by eleven bays, six storeys high and timber-framed inside. Boulton & Watt provided a steam engine. The size of the Albion Mill was not outstanding. Here are a few comparable mills in Derbyshire and Cheshire. At Cromford, for Arkwright, 1771, the earliest cotton spinning mill, a second Cromford mill, also Arkwright's, 1776, and a third, Masson Mill, 1783, six storeys, brick, with odd fenestration of the centrepiece.[26] At Macclesfield, Frost & Sons, 1785, silk, thirteen bays and four storeys; Styal, Quarry Bank Mill, Samuel Grey of Belfast, silk, 1784; Calver Mill, Curbar, 1785, stone, six storeys; Marple, Samuel Oldknow, 1790, five storeys, twenty-five bays, not preserved.[27] By 1790 Jedadiah Strutt owned a cotton mill at Milford built in 1780, one at Derby of c. 1785, and two at Belper, South Mill of 1776–78 and North Mill of 1784–86 (later replaced by fireproof structures in 1812 and 1804 respectively). After 1790 his son built for him at Derby and Belper the first fireproof mills, of which more below.[28]

Mill buildings were as a rule severely utilitarian, except for a cupola. One can understand Sir Uvedale Price, the most brilliant interpreter of the Picturesque, complaining of the 'dis-beautifying' effect of the factories in the Derbyshire dales.[29] Worse than the aesthetic aspects were the social. At Cromford Arkwright employed 200 operatives, chiefly children, working in shifts, day and night.[30] In the churchyard of Linley are the graves of 163 children who had worked in the Castle Mill with its pretty Gothic trim.[31]

Some saw the cruelty of it all. Dr Aikin in his *A Description of the Country from thirty to forty miles round Manchester* of 1795[32] says of the 'children of very tender age' that they are collected from the workhouses of London and work 'unknown, unprotected and forgotten'. He also complains that the children 'work by day and night, one set getting out of bed when another goes into the same'. Robert Owen in his *A New View of Society* (1813–14)[33] praised Mr Dale, who founded the Lanark spinning mill, for his benevolence to the children, but he added that to make the necessary profit for housing the children well, feeding them well and clothing them well they had to work from six in the morning to seven at night, and so they turned out sickly, feeble, deformed and hardly literate. Wordsworth called the mill children slaves 'to whom release comes not',[34] and Blake, appalled by Malthus's *Principle of Population*, wrote: 'And when . . . children sicken, let them die; there are enough born, even too many.'[35] Of the shoddy mill of Batley Carr Sir George Head in 1835 writes that 'a single whiff of air' inside the mill 'was almost more than could be endured'.[36] These conditions were known by all, and it is therefore more than can be endured to read the hypocrites such as Dr Ure who assured his readers that British factories are viewed by foreigners with 'jealous adminiration', that the workmen get 'good, unfailing wages, besides a healthy workshop' and moreover 'abundant food, raiment, and domestic accommodation'.[37]

In 1792–93, one year after the burning of the Albion Mill, William Strutt, who was an engineer, built for his father at Derby the first fireproof mill. It is not preserved, but we know that it had iron instead of wood

17.10 K. F. Schinkel, sketch of mills in Manchester, 1826

17.11 Ditherington, near Shrewsbury, Marshall, Benyon & Bage flour mill, 1796–97

pillars and floors on shallow brick arches, and that it was six-storeyed and 115 feet long. A water-wheel and a Boulton & Watt engine operated the machinery. Next, in 1793–95, William Strutt built the West Mill at Belper. It is still standing. It has six storeys, is 190 feet long and has, like its predecessor, iron pillars or rather colonnettes and brick-arch floors. But the beams in both mills are timber – usually fir and about 12 by 12 inches thick.

17.11 The change to iron beams was made not by William Strutt but by Charles Bage of Shrewsbury, novelist as well as an inventing and calculating amateur. The mill where the change took place was Marshall, Benyon & Bage's flour mill at Ditherington outside Shrewsbury. This also survives, and in a remarkably good state. John Marshall was a Leeds man and had built there a timber-framed five-storey mill in 1794–95.[38] At Ditherington construction began in 1796. The Boulton & Watt engine was installed in 1797. The building is 177 feet long. With its iron colonnettes and beams it was the first iron-frame structure ever, though the outer walls are still load-bearing. The last step to full skeleton construction was made for warehouses (in France) in the 1860s (see pp. 286–88), for factories in the seventies and for skyscrapers in the eighties (see p. 220).

After the introduction of complete inner iron framing the idea was adopted widely everywhere in Britain. Here are the data assembled by Professor A. W. Skempton:[39] Philips & Lee, Salford, 1799–1801 by Boulton & Watt, seven storeys, 238 feet long. The building was destroyed in 1940. It marks two further innovations. Its columns were hollow cylinders and served for central heating, and in 1805 Murdoch installed gas lighting. Of the first years of the new century were (or are) Leeds, Meadow Lane 1802–03 (157 feet), Shrewsbury, Castle Fields 1803–04 (208 feet), Belper, North Mill 1803–04 (123 feet, five storeys), Glasgow, Houldsworth 1804–06 (224 feet) and so on to Sedgwick Mill at Manchester of 1818, which has eight storeys.

The number of these long and high unadorned blocks was indeed changing the scenery of certain parts of Britain. For visitors from the Continent the sight was amazing. The best evidence we have is Schinkel's. He travelled in 1826, officially to study museums.[40] His companion on the journey was Beuth, a high civil servant in the Prussian Board of Finance and a great promoter of Prussian trades. The journey started in London, where Schinkel noted the iron beams of the British Museum, brand-new at the time,[41] and the roof construction of Maudsley's premises with iron roof on hollow columns used for drainage and with brick vaults.[42] He visited Bramah's showrooms and mentions the chain pier at Brighton built on the suspension-bridge principle.[43] Going north he passes Derbyshire. At Belper he calls Strutt's mill 'the most beautiful in England' but was not allowed inside.[44] In the Black Country he is impressed by the multitude of factories, their chimneys 'thousands of smoking obelisks 80 to 180 feet tall',[45] and he makes a sketch to go with that remark. He went as far north as New Lanark, which will be referred to later and where he comments on spartan schools.[46] But it is naturally in Lancashire that factories impressed him most. A sketch again illustrates what he has to say: Factories everywhere, pretty villas of the manufacturers,[47] and in Manchester mills of 17.10 seven or eight storeys, as long as forty bays, i.e. as long as the Royal Palace in Berlin.[48] Beuth had written the same to Schinkel on a previous journey – in 1823: factories of eight and nine storeys with iron columns and iron beams and thin outer walls.[49] He writes: 'The miracles of the new age are the machine and the buildings for it called factories.'[50] On his way back south Schinkel took a more westerly route and observed the Iron Bridge at Coalbrookdale and the Conway suspension bridge opened a few days before his coming,[51] and in the Stroud Valley he visited two textile mills better built, he writes, than they are in Lancashire.[52] The columns here are 14 to 16 feet tall.[53] Of conditions of labour Schinkel noticed nothing. That is both understandable and pardonable.

But it is not in a case such as that of Dr Granville who

17.12 New Lanark, Robert Owen's mill

17.12 in his book *The Spas of England*[54] admired at Manchester the 'stupendous cotton mills . . . belonging to Messrs Birley & Co. in which a thousand people are employed' and went out of his way to add that the women and children 'looked healthy and happy' and not 'miserable and slavish as a great philanthropist has stated'. Robert Owen,[55] whom Granville of course meant, thought otherwise when it came to organizing his New Lanark mill. He had been manager of a Manchester mill at the age of twenty-one and, at the age of twenty-eight, bought with a partner the New Lanark Mill. He left England for America in 1824 and there established New Harmony in Indiana. It was not a success, but New Lanark was, especially from the point of view of propaganda for a fundamentally different treatment of the workers. He had about 180 in 1800. His most incisive argument, set forth in his *A new View of Society* (1813–14), is that all good and successful manufacturers see to it that machines are kept well repaired, clean and altogether in good order. But what you do for 'your inanimate machines', you don't do for 'your living machines'. If you did it would repay you a hundredfold. But what is it that is needed to improve the 'delicate complex living mechanism' of the worker?[56] The answer was given partly at New Lanark – and visitors

(including the Russian Tsar) flocked to see the settlement – partly only on paper. The 'ties between employers and employed' must not be 'what immediate gain can each derive from the other'.[57] Hence reduced hours, education of the children, co-operative housing, unemployment relief and the fostering of trade unions. On paper Owen set out the ideal industrial settlement.[58] The settlement or village should be for about 800–1,200 people. It is a large rectangle set in arable land. In the middle are three detached buildings: church, school and canteen. The four ranges on the four sides of the rectangle leave the corners open. In the ranges are mostly flats or bed-sitting-rooms, but also children's dormitories, an inn, an infirmary and stores.[59]

17.15

Owen was not alone. Other manufacturers felt as philanthropic. An example is John Wood, a Bradford mill-owner. About 1830–35 he had some 600 workers, mostly girls. He provided a school and a schoolmaster, weekly visits of a doctor, ten hours work and no more for children, and good ventilation in the mill. Owen probably had inspired him.[60] He certainly inspired Carlyle. But Carlyle never made up his mind. He wavered between admiration of industry and detestation of capitalism: 'The humming of Manchester at 5.30 a.m. is as sublime as a Niagara.'[61] But 'My starving

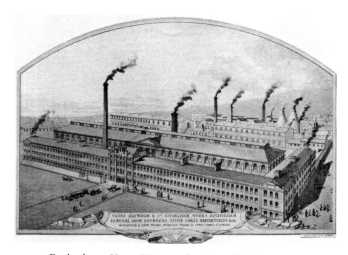

17.13 Rotherham, Yates, Haywood & Co. Effingham Works, c. 1860

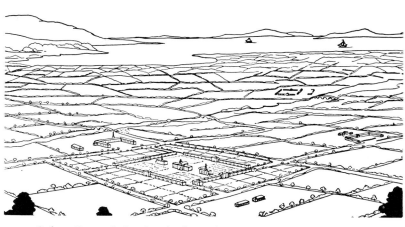

17.15 Robert Owen, design for a 'Village of Cooperation', 1816

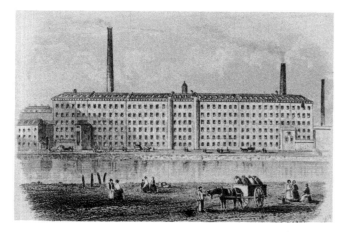

17.14 Preston, Swainson, Birley & Co. Fishwick Mill, c. 1830

17.16 Saltaire, Sir Titus Salt's mill and part of the town, begun 1851

workers?', says the rich millowner, 'Did not I hire them fairly in the Market? Did I not pay them to the last sixpence the sum covenanted for? What have I to do with them more?'[62] No – answered Carlyle, 'Cash payment is not the sole relation of human beings', and English liberalism is 'no more than liberty to die by starvation'.[63] But, as we have seen, some millowners were not like Carlyle's. Disraeli invented two: Mr Millward in *Coningsby* (1844) and Mr Trafford in *Sybil* (1847). Mr Trafford, whose employees numbered more than 2,000, believed that between the employer and the employed 'there should be other ties than payment of wages and the receipt of wages'. He built workers' houses, a whole village with church, school and baths.[64] Mr Millward also is generous to his men and women. By the way, Disraeli, being the observant man he was, describes Mr Trafford's mill in detail, and every detail is familiar to us: hollow cylindrical iron columns 18 feet high and used for drainage and 'groined arches' for the ceilings.

The state of development which Carlyle and Disraeli record tallies with the first English factory village, Colonel Ackroyd's Copley near Halifax begun in 1847,[65] and the much more generously planned second: Saltaire near Leeds, begun in 1851, which had twenty

17.16

years later 820 houses besides Institute, school, Congregational church and public park.[66] The mill is 550 feet long and six storeys high and was designed by Fairbairn the engineer and Lockwood & Mawson the architects. The chimney is 250 feet high. The warehouses running north are 330 feet long. The employees numbered 4,000. That there were cast-iron columns (highly ornamented incidentally), cast-iron beams and hollow brick arches goes without saying. Not as big as Saltaire but also imposing was Orrell's Mill (Travis Brook Mill) at Stockport built in 1837–38: it is six storeys high and 29 bays long and has two projecting wings.[67] Much larger than Orrell's Mill were the Fishwick Mill of Swainson, Birley & Co. at Preston of c. 1830: 42 bays, seven storeys, the centre with two castellated turrets and the usual cupola (not preserved); the Effingham Works of Yates, Haywood & Co. at Rotherham of c. 1860: 73 bays, three storeys (preserved); and the Houldsworth Mill at Reddish of 1865: 45 bays, four storeys (also preserved).

17.14

17.13

17.17

No more need be said about English factories of the nineteenth century. For other countries all that can here be offered is samples, not so much for lack of space as for lack of comprehensive research. For the United States research is at least partially done. John Coolidge's *Mill*

17.17 Reddish, Houldsworth Mills, 1865: central block

17.18 Cohoes, N.Y., Harmony Mill No. 3, 1867–72

17.19 Lawrence, Mass., Bay State Mills, 1846

and Mansion[68] is a pattern for all work yet to be done, but it deals with Lowell, Massachusetts, only, even if other places are used for comparison. In addition there is the *New England Textile Mill Survey*, a selection from the *Historic American Buildings Survey*.[69] The first mills with spinning machinery dated from *c.* 1790 (Beverly, Massachusetts, 1787, Lowell 1790).[70] The first successful power loom was set up by Francis Cabot Lowell in 1814 at Waltham, Massachusetts.[71] The mill was built of brick, six storeyed, with a cupola. A second building was provided in 1818, a third in 1820. However, most early mills were smaller, but they added up. By 1810 there were 54 in Massachusetts, 26 in Rhode Island, 14 in Connecticut and 12 in the State of New York.[72] More often than in England the manufacturers provided housing at once. In the centre of John Coolidge's book is the Merrimack Manufacturing Company. It was started in 1822. The first building was ready in 1823, two more in 1826, and yet two more immediately after.[73] The five were identical, 150 feet long, of four floors.[74] In 1847–48 the type was once more repeated but on a gigantic scale – five floors and forty-one bays with a central seven-bay projection and a cupola.[75] The new mill was built with iron columns, but on the whole iron was introduced late. The pub-lished *New England Textile Mill Survey* registers iron columns for the first time in 1846–47.[76] Of other mills in the *Survey* Lippitt Mill, Rhode Island, is the first: 1810.[77] An example of growth similar to Lowell is Cohoes in the state of New York.[78] Harmony Mill was built in 1836–37, four-storeyed but not large, No. 1 was added behind in 1851–53, No. 2 (larger) south-east of both in 1857–66. Finally No. 3 followed in 1867–72. It was called Mastodon Mill and was 1,185 feet long and five storeys high. Housing was also erected, and, as at Lowell, quite a number of other mills gathered around. Finally the mill which called itself the largest in the world: the Bay State Mills at Lawrence, Massachusetts, built in 1846. This is a rectangle of 1,000 by 400 feet. The three main mills are in a row, nine storeys high and each 200 feet long. There were 956 male and 911 female employees.[79] But 'the largest textile mill in the world', according to the *Survey*, was the Amoskeag Mill at Manchester, New Hampshire.[80] In 1915 it produced 50 miles of cloth per hour, but also made locomotives, fire engines and machinery.

To return for a moment to Lowell. Between 1825 and 1840 nine competitors to the Merrimack Company established themselves.[81] In 1841 Dickens visited Lowell. Like Granville in Manchester he found the factory

17.20 Manchester, N.H., Amoskeag Millyard, begun 1838

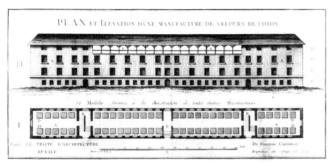

17.21 Rouen, building for the Royal Textile Mills, 1791, by F. Coitereaux

17.22 Le Creusot, Royal Foundry, 1779–85

girls not at all 'degraded brutes' but healthy and well dressed and the mills clean, comfortable and provided with plenty of fresh air.[82] Virtulon Rich saw a different industrial America. Pittsburgh, he wrote in 1832,[83] is the Manchester of the West, dirty and smoky, with many tall chimneys. Chevalier in 1839 says the same ('flakes of soot', 'dense black smoke'),[84] and such impressions could be multiplied. Industrialization marched faster in America than on the European Continent.

For France, at the present stage of research it is safer to confine oneself to a few items.[85] The first is a rare treatise: F. Coitereaux, *Traité sur la construction des manufactures*, 1791. It contains the description of Coitereaux's rebuilding of the Royal Textile Mills in the Faubourg St Sever in Rouen. He mentions that he has also built factories in Lyon and the Dauphiné. The Rouen factory is nineteen bays long and four storeys high. The exterior is deliberately plain; for the function 'n'oblige pas à des beautés'.[86] Coitereaux pleads for the use of *pisé* (rammed earth) – the age of iron framing was not to dawn in France for some time to come.

From the almost unknown to the internationally known: Schneider Creusot.[87] However, the brothers Schneider came in only in 1836, whereas our principal interest belongs to the last quarter of the eighteenth century. Coal extraction, iron works and also glass works had existed in this neighbourhood ever since the sixteenth century. Efforts to develop made from about 1760 took note of English innovations such as smelting by coke as introduced by Abraham Darby. In 1771 a meeting was held at which among others William Lord Stewart, captain in the Zweibrücken army, was present. Others interested were Gensonne, author of a book on iron foundries, and Brigadier Marchant. The latter went to England in 1773 or 1774 and met English manufacturers, and in 1775 William Wilkinson, younger brother of the more famous John Wilkinson, went to France. In 1779 Louis XVI wanted a great foundry to be built. The site chosen was Le Creusot, and put in charge were Ignace de Wendel, Touffaire and Wilkinson. Wendel was the royal commissar, Touffaire was an engineer; the architects were the brothers Raimbaud. In 1785 production could begin. The King was patron and the largest shareholder. The dedication tablet calls the Le Creusot foundry 'la première de ce genre en France et suivant la méthode apportée d'Angleterre par M. William Wilkinson'. We know what the building looked like. The main range had only two storeys. There was a pedimented centre and two projecting quads left and right. When Arthur Young travelled in

17.23 St Gobain, view of the glassworks, c. 1820

17.24 Jouy, Oberkampf's textile printing works in 1803 (detail of a painting by L. L. Boilly; *Private Collection*)

17.25 Chaux (Arc-et-Senans), gatehouse to the Royal Salt Works, 1776, by C.-N. Ledoux

France in 1789[88] he found Le Creusot with 500 or 600 employees. From 1784, a glass works was built up of which the Queen was patron. Its premises were four ranges round a courtyard, 400 by 320 feet. These years were the climax. About thirty years later England appeared once more at Le Creusot. Aaron Manby, Black Country ironmaster, in 1819 founded engineering works at Charenton near Paris[89] and in 1826 bought Le Creusot and joined it to his company. The enterprise failed and the Schneiders came in.

17.23   Almost as familiar as Le Creusot is St Gobain near Laon.[90] The glass works received their patent in 1665. They settled at St Gobain in 1692. The objective was to replace Venetian mirrors. The enterprise was successful, and the mirrors of the Galerie des Glaces in Versailles were made by the new factory. Workers' housing was built concurrently with the factory premises. In the late eighteenth century the employees numbered about 1,000. There were (and are) subsidiary works, and the headquarters is now at Neuilly, north of the Bois de Boulogne – a long curtain-wall job of seven storeys.

And one more famous name: Oberkampf's factory at Jouy producing printed linens known as *toiles de Jouy*.[91] Oberkampf was born near Ansbach in 1738. His father had worked at Ryhiner's textile printing works in Basel – mentioned at the beginning of this chapter. The son went to Paris in 1758, to Jouy in 1766. Jouy was built up to produce printed cotton. It became a *manufacture royale* in 1783, and Oberkampf was

knighted in 1787. The main building (pulled down in 1864) was 342 feet long and of three storeys.[92] The pillars were still of wood. An additional building went up in 1805 and was raised to five floors in 1818. There were in the early nineteenth century about 1,300 employees. Napoleon visited Jouy in 1805, and Oberkampf received the *Légion d'honneur*.   17.24

From about the same years date Ledoux's plans for Chaux (or Arc-et-Senans).[93] He was made Inspector of the Royal Salt Works in 1771 and must shortly after have begun to think in terms of new premises containing in a geometrical pattern the works, the director's house and numerous employees' houses. His first scheme was a square in a square, a favourite piece of planning also with Boullée and his successors.[94] But Ledoux quickly changed his scheme, first to an oval, then to a circle. Finally the circle was reduced to a semi-circle. According to that plan building began. The gate-   17.26 house is dated 1776. It is severely Neo-Classical with a   17.25 giant Tuscan portico carrying an entablature, not a pediment, and with, inside, romantic (or Berninian) imitation rocks and imitation frozen brine – even this rendered in stone. At the top of the semi-circle was the director's house with a portico of alternately blocked Tuscan giant columns carrying a pediment. The source here was Giulio Romano and Palladio. Left and right of the director's house were the works, and the semi-circle itself had the employees' houses, each of nine bays and one storey but with a raised centre. Hardly anything of

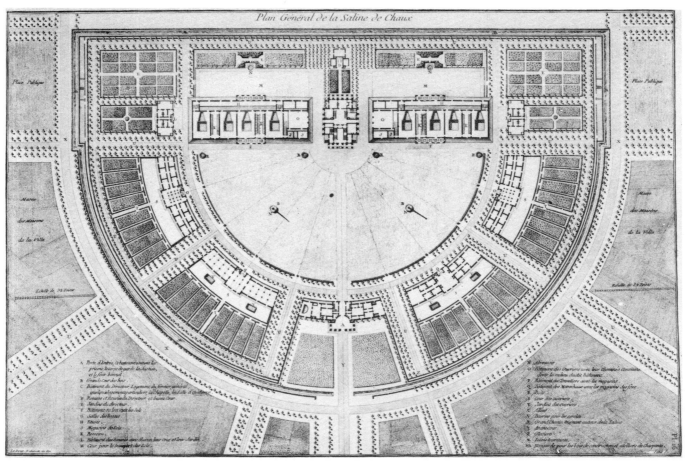

17.26 C.-N. Ledoux, plan of the Royal Salt Works of Chaux, *c.* 1775 (*L'Architecture*, 1804)

what had been built survives. The demolition took place this century between the two wars. Long after building had stopped, Ledoux worked on on paper and gradually transformed a real group of utilitarian buildings into a Utopian city with a church the size of a cathedral, a vast square market area, public baths, again in terms of a vast square, an exchange, a hospice and domestic as well as public buildings, mostly of vague function. Among the latter was a house 'consacrée au culte des valeurs morales', a temple 'consacré à l'amour' (a brothel), a temple of conciliation, the Panarétéon and the 'asile de la félicité'. The details are weird, and the shapes of many of the dwellings weirder still.

While contemplating Ledoux's Utopia the mind moves back to Robert Owen and forward to Fourier. Charles Fourier, born in 1772, i.e. thirty-six years after Ledoux, called his Utopian unit a 'Phalanstère'.[95] It was most convincingly presented in his *Le nouveau monde industriel* which came out in 1829. The Phalanstère was intended for 1,600–1,800 people. The plan proposed was for one large monumental building with wings and six more symmetrically arranged buildings. Fourier believed in collective living (each building for about 30 families) and especially in collective education, to remove any pernicious parental influence. Fourier never found a philanthropist to finance his scheme. J.-B. André Godin was such a philanthropist. At Guise where he had started a foundry in 1846, he employed 1,200, and he provided housing, co-operative shopping,

17.29

schools and a nursery school, a theatre, a library, baths, a park, vegetable plots, pensions and insurance.[96] He died in 1888 and left in his will the factory and 3,500,000 francs to his workers.

After France Germany. Here we have at once one of the most interesting surviving factory buildings of the European Continent. It is situated at Ratingen, north-east of Düsseldorf,[97] and calls itself proudly the first mechanized cotton spinning mill on the Continent. It was founded and developed by Johann Gottfried Brügelmann. He came from Elberfeld where his father had started a small factory. At the age of twenty, in 1770, he moved to Basel, no doubt because of Ryhiner's. His ambition was to compete with England and also – this is specially said – with Rouen, which must mean the Royal Textile Mills. He obtained by indirect and probably direct spying at Arkwright's Cromford mills pieces of machinery, and indeed named his factory Cromford. He leased the site in 1783 and began two buildings at once, one of four storeys and five bays, the other of two storeys and eight bays. They were designed by Hofbaumeister Flügel. The factory went into action in 1784 and soon employed nearly 100 workers. Like all others of the early millowners, Brügelmann employed children as well.[98] In 1785 the Elector Palatine visited the factory. An additional brick building was put up in 1796, and there were also a paper mill, dye works and an iron works. By 1802, the year of his death, Brügelmann employed between 400 and 500. His house

17.28
17.27

17.27, 28 Ratingen, Cromford textile mill, 1783–84, by Flügel

17.29 Guise, industrial settlement, begun 1846

17.30 Bielefeld, Ravensberger Spinnerei, 1854

was built in 1787 and had an English garden attached to it. Shortly before he died he tried a partnership with Johannes Lenssen at Rheydt. Lenssen in 1824 planned a 'mechanische Fabrik', the machinery mostly to be bought in England. It included a steam engine.[99]

There are no doubt more early factories in Germany, but the Denkmalpflege, the equivalent of the English Royal Commission on Historic Monuments, is only now beginning to study them.[100] One which has recently been studied is the iron foundry (*Giesshalle*) at Sayn near Koblenz. It was started in 1769–70 and the main range was put up in 1824–30 to the design of Carl Ludwig Althaus. It is of iron and glass, about 115 feet long, and consists of nave and aisles with an 'east end' curiously reminiscent of S. Croce in Florence. The 'west front' with Gothic intersecting tracery does not survive. The foundry served military needs primarily, but *Kunstguss* was also done.[101] Two other factories which I have come across are the Spinnerei Reutte of 1845, just across the Austrian border (now Reutter Textilwerke; with the pillars and beams still of timber), and the Ravensberger Spinnerei at Bielefeld of 1854.

For Belgium I want to refer to one factory in particular, although, under the direction of M. Maurice Culot, early factories are gradually being collected and

verbally and photographically recorded.[102] The most interesting building of which M. Culot informed me is Le Grand Hornu.[103] It is situated in the Borinage district between Mons and Valenciennes. It was begun in 1822, the architect being Bruno Renard, a pupil of Percier and Fontaine in Paris and the restorer of Tournai Cathedral. The works are built round an oval courtyard about 460 by 260 feet, inspired probably by Ledoux, and workers' cottages were built concurrently – a very early case, and here depending presumably on Robert Owen. In 1830 there were about 250 of them. The factory has stone, not yet iron, pillars but already brick vaults. Another early industrial establishment in Belgium is the coal-mining premises of Bois du Luc, dating from 1838.

As for Italy, Milan with its tradition of silk manufacture turned early to wool and later also to cotton. Wool was introduced by a Swiss, Jakob Tieffen, in 1704. The factory was of 'ample dimensions'. The promoters of cotton at the end of the eighteenth century were foreigners too: G. A. Kramer and F. Schmutz. Factories were in Milan itself and in Monza.[104]

It will have been noticed that nearly all the factories illustrated or discussed have an unmistakable utilitarian look. Only at the beginning were a few Georgian

17.31 Reutte, Tirol, spinning mill, 1845

17.32 Leeds, John Marshall's Temple Mill, 1838–40, by Ignatius Bonomi

17.34 Le Grand Hornu, begun 1822, by Bruno Renard

17.35 Glasgow, Templeton carpet factory, 1889–92, by William Leiper

17.33 Fécamp, Bénédictine manufactory, 1893–1900, by C. Albert

17.36 Newton Abbot, engine house and station on the atmospheric railway, 1847

17.37 Sanssouci, near Potsdam, engine house, 1841–42, by Ludwig Persius

17.38 Noisiel-sur-Marne, Menier chocolate factory, 1871–72, by Jules Saulnier: iron skeleton

motifs other than the ubiquitous clock cupola admitted. For the nineteenth century the cases of historicism in motifs are rare but not entirely lacking. John Marshall's Temple Mill in Leeds of 1838–40 (by Ignatius Bonomi) is Egyptian, modelled on the temple of Edfu. The building, which is single-storeyed, has iron columns and shallow brick arches with circular skylights in each bay. In order to maintain the humidity necessary for flax-spinning, the roof was originally covered with turf. To keep the turf down sheep were kept. The roof drained internally through the iron columns.[105] French Gothic to Early Renaissance is the manufactory of Bénédictine liqueur at Fécamp. The style is screwed up to a pitch so high that a date before the late nineteenth century would be out of the question. The date is indeed 1893–1900. The architect was C. Albert, and the building combines factory and offices.

Gothic in Britain is Messrs Doulton's pottery works on the south bank of the Thames in London – Second Pointed, the phase favoured by Pugin, Scott, Street and many others. The designer was R. Stark Wilkinson of Oxford and the date is 1878. Messrs Templeton's carpet factory in Glasgow is modelled on the Doge's Palace in Venice, a tribute to Ruskin – the associational justification being eastern trade. The building was designed by William Leiper and built in 1889–92.

The Italianate option was taken in many places. It was favoured for instance for waterworks and pumping stations. Their campanile chimneys are often met and easily recognized. Priscilla Metcalf quotes Cassell's *Greater London* on the Crossness Pumping Station near London of 1865: 'The Crossness Works are perfectly wonderful . . . nearly all noted foreigners . . . visit them.'[106] Italianate also are the engine houses of the atmospheric railways, e.g. that of Newton Abbot on the Exeter-Plymouth line, built in 1847.[107] But the engine house of Sanssouci outside Potsdam, by Schinkel's pupil Persius, is Moorish. It dated from 1841–42.[108] Equally ambitious are the engine houses of Klein Glienicke and Babelsberg, both also close to Potsdam and also designed by Persius. They date from between 1840 and Persius's premature death in 1845. Glienicke is in the style of Schinkel's Charlottenhof, i.e. Classical, with Italianate touches and boldly asymmetrical, Babelsberg is castellated and again asymmetrical.

That must be enough on the theme of historicism in factories. We can now turn to the way in which historicism was defeated. Examples come from France and then from America and Germany. The innovations are structural in the first two, stylistic in the third. The great structural innovations in France were the iron and later the steel frame and, from the end of the century, reinforced concrete. This new material and its possibilities have already been discussed (pp. 224, 254). As for iron and steel the decisive step was to carry the skeleton right into the façade so that load-bearing walls were avoided, and an iron beam would have to carry only the weight of one floor. The earliest cases in France are a warehouse at the St Ouen Docks in Paris, *c.* 1864–65 (see p. 215, n. 14), and the often illustrated

17.39 Tourcoing, Charles Six spinning mill, 1895, by François Hennebique

17.42 Detroit, Mich., Packard factory, Building 10, 1905, by Albert Kahn

17.40 Paris, Esders sewing workshop, 1919, by Auguste Perret

17.43 Berlin, AEG turbine factory, begun 1908, by Peter Behrens

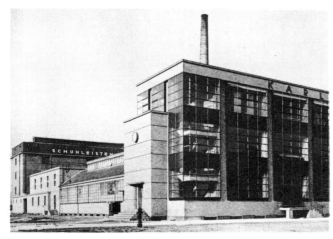

17.41 Alfeld, Fagus shoe factory, 1910–11, by Gropius & Meyer

17.44 Rotterdam, van Nelle tobacco factory, 1927–29, by Brinkmann & van der Vlucht

17.38 factory of Menier chocolate at Noisiel-sur-Marne by Jules Saulnier. Its date is 1871–72, which means that the step taken in Chicago was taken here about twelve years earlier (see p. 220). Saulnier's façade incidentally has its (brick-filled) steel frame set lozenge-wise, which is a motif recently taken up again but in concrete.[109]

So to concrete. The man who made reinforced con-
17.39 crete a practical proposition was François Henne-
bique.[110] By him is the famous Charles Six spinning mill at Tourcoing which was built in 1895. Many factories followed, and soon outside France as well.[111] The most important specialist in concrete factory design was Albert Kahn of Detroit,[112] and his first
17.42 factory in reinforced concrete Packard's No. 10 build-ing of 1905. All these factories were on the post-and-beam or trabeated system. Maillart in his Tavenasa Bridge of 1905 showed how boldly and originally concrete arches could be designed. Perret, the most successful concrete designer in France, kept as a rule to
17.40 the trabeated, but in the great hall of the sewing work-shops of Esders in 1919 he introduced parabolic arches.

By 1919 the battle for serious yet appropriate archi-tecture for factories had been won, and it was won in Germany.[113] The two masterpieces are by now familiar
17.43 to everybody: the turbine factory by Peter Behrens for
17.41 the AEG in Berlin and the shoe-last factory by Gropius at Alfeld, the former begun in 1908, the latter in 1910. The former aspires to monumentality without the slightest touch of academic historicism, the latter

started the International Modern with its beautifully proportioned glass wall. But the turbine factory and the shoe-last factory were not the only documents. Behrens built more factories for the AEG, Poelzig in
17.45 1911–12 built a chemical factory at Luban near Poznan, and Albert Marx in 1912 the excellent central heating plant at Nauheim.[114] As for the ten years after the First World War, they saw a brief emergence of Expressionism and then the victory of rationalism and functionalism. The way runs straight from Alfeld to,
17.44 say, Brinkmann & van der Vlucht's van Nelle factory at Rotterdam of 1927–29, and then to the standard
17.47 American type of today: strictly cubic, but low and windowless. But there is another way one can follow: from Art Nouveau to Expressionism and from there to
17.45 today. Poelzig's Luban factory with its lunette win-dows, and Mendelsohn's more radical hat factory at Luckenwalde of 1921–23 attack us with sharp angles, very much the kind of angles architects of the 1960s were addicted to, especially where their material was concrete. But in concrete a far more positive develop-ment – because primarily structural and not arbitrarily formal – is that connected with Pier Luigi Nervi. The tobacco factory at Bologna of 1952 is characteristic of
17.46 his work. The shuttering boxes of which the ceilings consist were patented by Nervi.

No further architectural event needs comment.[115] What the effects of automation will be remains to be seen.

17.45 Luban, chemical works, 1911–12, by Hans Poelzig

17.46 Bologna, State Tobacco Factory, 1949–52, by Pier Luigi Nervi

17.47 Felixstowe, Sangamo Weston meter factory, 1963–64, by Johns, Slater, Haward

CONCLUSION

WE HAVE reached the end of this book. Looking back at it the reader will have noticed that in it three stories have been interwoven: one following functions, one materials and one styles.

The functional story is one of diversification, starting already in the Middle Ages, when the market hall may break away from the town hall, and may itself split up into a corn hall and a cloth hall, and when the law courts as well as the exchange begin to require extra buildings. Then in the later sixteenth century government offices first received a building of their own: the Uffizi (pp. 31–32). But the top storey of the Uffizi became the Medici art gallery, and special museum buildings began to be segregated from the palaces of which they and also the major libraries had formed part. The Fridericianum in Kassel (1769–77; pp. 100, 115) is an early case of independent library combined with independent museum, the British Museum is an absurdly late one (1823–56; pp. 107–08, 127). That museums and libraries became public is one aspect of the rise of the middle class into prosperity and into faith in *Bildung* – the Humboldt ideal. Wolfenbüttel (1706–10) was the first independent separate library building (pp. 98–99), Dulwich (1811–14) the first independent picture gallery (p. 123). The clerestory lighting there was an innovation too, the result of functional thought.

With Dulwich we are in the nineteenth century, and universal diversification belongs to the nineteenth century – for good reasons. In the wake of the Industrial Revolution the nineteenth century saw an unprecedented growth of population and especially of urban population. Hence not only did the scale of all public buildings increase enormously, but beyond a certain level of scale diversification was bound to become the remedy: separate buildings for government offices – the Home Office, the Foreign Office, the Treasury, the Pentagon, etc. – a children's hospital, an eye hospital, a chest hospital, etc., and also an asylum and a poorhouse – a museum of the decorative arts, a natural history museum, a science museum, a folk museum, etc. – a corn exchange, a coal exchange, a wool exchange, etc. – special buildings where firms can rent office space – and so on. All these new types required close investigation

on function, whether new function or altered function – new the railway station, the exhibition building and the department store, altered the factory; new the motel, altered the hotel; new the bank building, altered the prison. For all these modifications and innovations plans must be studied. The story of the cross plan and its descendant the radial plan begins in the fifteenth-century hospital (see pp. 142 ff., 147) and then goes on in prisons. In both these types humanitarian and hygienic considerations ran parallel. There are few types as fruitful as the hospital, if one wants to see how functional thought, i.e. medical convictions and discoveries, is reflected in plans and elevations: the pavilion plan instead of the cruciform plan (pp. 150–51, 154 ff.), and the big blocks of today owing to antisepsis (p. 158). Similarly in theatres, the type with tiers of boxes and the purely amphitheatrical type represent social differences – the amphitheatrical type spelling out equality, the other distinction by status and by money (pp. 71–72, 78 ff.)

The second story in the chapters of this book is that of new materials or new uses of existing materials: cast iron and glass as new uses, steel and concrete as new materials. The iron story in particular has a way of turning up in many types: the internal skeleton of English factories from the 1790s onwards (p. 277), the roof members of Louis' Théâtre Français of 1786–90 (p. 78) and those stipulated by Napoleon for the Madeleine (pp. 16–17), the iron and glass dome of the Halle au Blé of 1808–13 (p. 203) and the iron and glass vault of the Galerie d'Orléans of 1828–30 (p. 264). Then iron-and-glass becomes accepted, and is therefore exposed. Some key facts about iron preceded its main discussion in the chapter starting with market halls (pp. 240 ff.). Here a summary may be useful. Exposed iron appeared internally in the Bibliothèque Ste Geneviève of 1843–50 (ill. 7.44), the Coal Exchange in London of 1846–49 (12.39), and e.g. (prettily decorated) in Woodward's Oxford Museum of 1855–60 (8.49). Externally it appeared in the Laing Building in New York of 1848 (13.11), in many successors in New York and other American cities, and also of course in the Crystal Palace of 1851 (15.31), in the Jamaica street warehouse,

Glasgow in 1855–56 (13.14), and in Saulnier's factory at Noisiel of 1871–72, where it was combined with brick, not glass (17.38). The nearly all-glass wall appeared at the back of a Liverpool office building of the 1860s (13.10), and c. 1900 notably in Hermann Tietz's department store in the Friedrichstrasse in Berlin and Innovation in Brussels (16.37, 38). The story of the Chicago School and the development of iron and steel skeleton construction is too familiar to be retold once again. It begins in the 1880s (pp. 218, 220). The highest steel structure until 1930 was the Eiffel Tower of 1889 (15.44), the widest steel span the Galerie des Machines of 1889: 364 feet 2 inches (15.45). But Buckminster Fuller's geodesic domes leave the late nineteenth century far behind. The largest up to date has a diameter of 384 feet (Union Tank Car Company, 1958). The largest dome in the world, just completed, is the Louisiana Superdome at New Orleans, 680 feet in diameter, with a lamella roof. This is of course a trifle when compared with the spans of some suspension bridges: George Washington, New York (1931) 3,500 feet; Golden Gate, San Francisco (1937) 4,200 feet; Mackinac Straits, Michigan (1957) 3,800 feet; Verrazano Narrows, New York (1964) 4,260 feet. The greatest span on the continent of Europe is the Tajo Bridge of 1966, 3,320 feet; the greatest British spans are the Firth of Forth Road Bridge of 1964, 3,300 feet, and the Severn Bridge of 1966, 3,240 feet.

A totally new building material was reinforced concrete. Hennebique, concrete pioneer, used it for factories from 1894 onwards (e.g. the Charles Six spinning mill at Tourcoing of 1895, 17.39). In 1900 he did the boldly cantilevered staircases in the Petit Palais in Paris (15.50), and in 1911–14 Perret gave the Théâtre des Champs-Elysées a complete concrete skeleton (p. 87). As against this trabeated use of concrete, Maillart in his bridges of 1905 and after pioneered arcuated concrete. The finest concrete building of before the First World War is Max Berg's Centenary Hall at Breslau (Wroclaw) of 1911–13 with a span of 213 feet (p. 253). The span of Nervi's Palazzo dello Sport in Rome of 1958, however, is about 300 feet. Roofs of hyperbolic paraboloid form were introduced by Matthew Nowicki's Arena at Raleigh, North Carolina, of 1952–53, and have since found many successors, notably the French Palais des Expositions at the Rond Point de la Défense in Paris of 1957–58, which has spans of 780 feet (p. 254). Another structural technique which has recently been talked about a great deal is the suspended roof as demonstrated by Frei Otto (p. 256). It is worth pointing out that as early as 1853 Bogardus had proposed for the New York exhibition of that year a central tower from which the roofs were to be suspended (p. 245 and ill. 15.33).

So much for structure, materials and function. One result of looking at these wherever they have appeared in the history of building types is that there are more events to note in the late eighteenth, the nineteenth and the early twentieth centuries than in all preceding centuries put together. Now when it comes to style that will be so even more patently; for the nineteenth century is the period *par excellence* of historicism, and historicism means the use of different styles by the same architect, or at the same time, in some sequence. This situation is familiar and serves all laymen as the most characteristic feature of these hundred to a hundred and fifty years. But it was brought up at the very beginning of this book, the type being palaces of royalty (pp. 9–10). The sequence there had been Greek Revival, Quattrocento Revival, Cinquecento Revival, French Renaissance and French Baroque. The Scottish Baronial style and the castle style came in in this series out of order. Such irregularities will be found also where other types are concerned, and that shall now, in conclusion, be examined.

At the start must be placed the Georgian Classical and the Ancien Régime Classical. It characterized architecture in Britain from about 1715 and architecture in France from about 1760. Other countries joined soon. The result was stylistically remarkably uniform. Certain typical motifs were used all over Europe and North America. The two favourites were the Pantheon dome and the half-dome, i.e. the Pantheon dome cut in half vertically. The former Houses of Parliament in Dublin about 1730 had both (3.2); domes are the climax of Kent's projects for the Houses of Parliament in London (3.4), the museum in Robert Adam's Newby Hall begun c. 1767 (8.10), Sir Robert Taylor's rotunda in the Bank of England of 1765 and Soane's of 1796 in the same building (12.17, 21), the Assize Courts in York of 1773–80 (p. 53), the Museo Pio-Clementino of c. 1773–80 (8.11), several of the grandiose Boullée schemes (e.g. 8.20), many of the Grand Prix designs in Paris, Dobie's and Thornton's designs of 1792–94 for the Capitol at Washington (pp. 36–37), Latrobe's designs for the Capitol of 1814 et seq. (p. 38), several of Durand's model types, the library of the University of Virginia, Gilly's design for an exchange (12.22), the Glyptothek in Munich as designed by Karl von Fischer (8.33), Schinkel's Altes Museum (8.38), and so on to Isaiah Rogers' Tremont House hotel in Boston of 1827 et seq. (p. 175), and Pollack's National Museum at Budapest begun in 1836 (p. 127).

The half-dome owed its popularity to Gondoin's Ecole de Médecine of 1771–76 (3.10), but Kent had already introduced it in his design of 1732 for the Houses of Parliament (3.3). Descendants of Gondoin are Ledoux in the theatre of Besançon of 1778 et seq. (6.56), Harrison at Chester in 1788 et seq. (3.17), Boullée's design for an opera house of 1781 (6.53), Palmstedt's Gripsholm theatre of 1782 (p. 74), Gisors in the Palais Bourbon in 1795–97 (3.18), Latrobe in Washington in the Capitol in 1814 et seq. (p. 38), and so on.

The buildings containing rotundas or demi-rotundas were as a rule Palladian, but when the Greek Revival replaced Palladianism, Greek Doric columns were often sufficient to demonstrate the claim – inside as in the Besançon theatre (6.56) or outside as at Budapest.

The Greek Revival was the last universally accepted style for over a hundred years. Greek Doric columns are the sole adornment in Genelli's and then Gilly's designs for a monument to Frederick the Great (1787 and 1797 respectively: 1.8, 9), in Klenze's Walhalla above Regensburg (begun 1821: 1.18) and Playfair's Calton Hill monument in Edinburgh (begun 1822: 1.28), and so on, including the splendid (and so unfunctional) Edinburgh Royal High School of 1825–29 by

Thomas Hamilton (not mentioned in this book).

But the very uniformity of the Greek Revival bred opposition. It took several forms: a movement towards Baroque exaggeration, a movement towards unbounded liberty and a movement towards the cancellation of all adornment. To the first tendency belong Basevi's Fitzwilliam Museum in Cambridge with its crowded giant columns and heavy attic, French Beaux-Arts in inspiration (begun 1837), Cockerell's Ashmolean Museum in Oxford (begun 1841), in the treatment of giant columns carrying projecting pieces of entablature and short arches much more original, Cockerell's commercial buildings of the forties (e.g. 12.12), Hittorff's magnificent Gare du Nord (1861–65: 14.14) and Duc's façade of the Palais de Justice (1857–68: 5.10). The Palais de Justice has segmental instead of round arches, a telling sign of anti-Classical ambition. Klenze used them in his late Befreiungshalle near Kelheim (1842–63: 1.20). The path into unbounded liberty – or should one say licence? – was trod by few, the boldest being Greek Thomson in his churches of the fifties and sixties. In his domestic buildings, however, his inspiration was the Schinkel of the Berlin Schauspielhaus (1818–21: 6.62). The bands of narrow upright windows and square pillars tell of Schinkel's thoughts in the direction of unadorned *Sachlichkeit*. Had he lived longer – he died in 1841 – he might have concentrated more and more on this style which, as it is, was realized only in the Bauakademie begun in 1831. It was, however, proposed also for a *Kaufhaus* or bazaar in 1827 (16.18) and the Royal Library in 1835 (7.42). As it was, this style of Schinkel found no immediate successors, just as Soane's equally personal style of the banking halls of the Bank of England (12.19, 21) found none.

Heralding the historicism of the nineteenth century is one exceptional sheet by Gandy done to Soane's instruction in 1818, demonstrating to the Church Commissioners that one and the same church can be clad in divers Classical and divers Gothic and indeed in a kind of Norman garb. The Continental counterpart is the *oeuvre* of Klenze in Munich, Grecian preferably (8.36) but also competent in the Italian Renaissance (8.35) and even in a kind of Neo-Byzantine. Chapter and verse are to follow presently, but first the absence of the Neo-Gothic from Klenze's buildings requires a few words.

For the Gothic Revival was the only serious competitor of the Greek Revival in the early nineteenth century. However, it plays only a lesser part in this book, because the Gothic Revival started in the eighteenth century as a country-house variety (Strawberry Hill, begun 1748, Fonthill, begun 1796) and then became an ecclesiastical variety, gradually dominating more and more over the Grecian. As a style for major public buildings it became fully accepted only with Barry and Pugin's Houses of Parliament, begun in 1835 (3.23, 24). Between this and the Law Courts in London, built in 1866–82 (5.15), lie the great decades of the Gothic Revival in England. Milestones were the Oxford Museum by Woodward (1855–60: 8.49), Waterhouse's Assize Courts (1859–64) and Town Hall (1868–77), both in Manchester (5.12, 13), Seddon's hotel at Aberystwyth (1864–65: 11.30) and Scott's St

Pancras Station and Hotel (begun 1868: 11.48, 49). On the Continent the situation was different. The Frankfurt Exchange of 1839 with its fan vault is a rarity (12.46). The most monumental Neo-Gothic buildings are the Vienna Town Hall of 1872–83 (5.17) and the Budapest Houses of Parliament of 1882–1902 (3.30), both symmetrical, which the Houses of Parliament and the Manchester Town Hall had not been. Renaissance derivatives were much more frequent on the Continent than Gothic derivatives. Neo-Renaissance appeared in many guises. Quattrocento arcading à la Foundling Hospital in Florence was already used by Ledoux. Klenze used a very subdued Italian Renaissance as early as 1816 (Palais Leuchtenberg, Munich, for Eugène Beauharnais) and a pure Florentine Palazzo-Pitti Quattrocento for the Königsbau in Munich (1826–35: p. 8). The Festsaalbau, a few years later (1832–42: p. 8), is, on the other hand, Cinquecento and not at all pure.

It is this style, known at the time as the Free or Mixed Renaissance, which ruled in the second third of the century – see e.g. Semper's second as against his first Dresden Opera (1869 *v.* 1838: 6.63, 65) and his Dresden Gallery (8.44). Another division of Neo-Renaissance, used today by American and English scholars, is the palazzo versus the villa style. But the villa style was almost exclusively domestic – take Osborne of 1845–49 as an example (p. 8). The palazzo style on the other hand proved suitable for commercial premises in cities, more closed if Florentine, more open if Venetian. The Sansovino style saw a fruitful revival in America between *c.* 1850 and *c.* 1875, the members of the façades all of cast iron, as we have seen (p. 217). A Cinquecento contrast between France and England and also Early-Neo-Quattrocento and High-Neo-Quattrocento is provided by Lacornée's Foreign Office in Paris of 1845–56 (4.7) and Scott's (and M. D. Wyatt's) Foreign Office in London of 1868–73 (4.5), one symmetrical, the other asymmetrical; one reserved, the other exuberant. On the way from the Neo-Cinquecento to the Neo-Baroque stands the Leeds Town Hall of 1853–58 (5.9) with its Wrenaissance motifs. But Victorian historicism never moved direct. Two more sources of inspiration must be examined before we are ready for the Neo-Baroque.

First the *Rundbogenstil*, to use its German name, Germany being its centre. It can be Neo-Early Christian, Neo-Byzantine, or Neo-Italian Romanesque. In England the few examples are all churches, but a subspecies was Neo-Norman, and this was suitable e.g. for gaols (Liverpool, 1848–55: 10.27). In Germany the *Rundbogenstil* was even used for railway stations (e.g. Munich, by Bürklein, completed 1849). Later Neo-Romanesque is rare, and the examples are scattered: Waterhouse's Natural History Museum of 1871–81 (8.50) is the best in England. Internationally important is only what America did with the Romanesque. H. H. Richardson, meditating on a style sufficiently solid and powerful to represent ascending America, found the Romanesque suitable and made use of it for big as well as small buildings – the Marshall Field Wholesale Warehouse of 1885–87 (13.18), Sullivan's inspiration for the Auditorium of 1887–89 (11.36) – as well as the libraries of minor Massachusetts towns in the 1870s and 80s (e.g. 7.37). So, in the Romanesque Revival America played the most important part. It also did in the French Renaissance Revival. This had set in with the wings of the Paris Hôtel de Ville of 1837–46 (5.11), but was universally noticed only with the completion after 1852 of the Louvre by Visconti and Lefuel for Napoleon III (4.8). Richard Morris Hunt worked on the Louvre and used its style for rich men's mansions in New York and elsewhere, but only once is a great American mansion on the scale of English Victorian country palaces: Biltmore, 1890–95, in a kind of Louis XII. The hallmark of the Neo-French Renaissance is the so-called pavilion roof. Renwick's Old Corcoran of 1859 (p. 135) faces the old State, War and Navy Office of 1871–88 (4.10). Both have pavilion roofs. The old Grand Central Station in New York was begun in 1869 (14.20), the Grosvenor Hotel in London, the best in London in that style, already in 1859 (11.45). Out of all order that could be expected is the French Renaissance Palace at Schwerin (p. 9). It was begun in 1843, and the style is handled so competently that the palace cannot be treated simply as a freak.

Yet freaks there were. The American freak of all freaks was the New Haven railway station of 1848–50 (14.9). For Britain one is tempted to propose Greek Thomson's steeples. For England Marshall's Mill at Leeds, in Egyptian style, must rank high (17.32). The year of its beginning, 1838, is the year of the completion of the equally Egyptian Tombs in New York (10.26). For France the Bénédictine headquarters at Fécamp of 1893–1900, in a very fancy Louis XII, belong in this category as well (17.33). So does, of course, Neuschwanstein, started in 1868 (p. 10). And might not the Spanish Mission style of California and the Southern States find its niche here (Ponce de Leon Hotel, 1888, by Carrère & Hastings: 11.32) – or was it too widely accepted?

Back anyway to the main stream. It is the stream from Free or Mixed Renaissance to Baroque. Of the two internationally outstanding Neo-Baroque buildings the dates are remarkably early – 1861 for the beginning of the Paris Opéra (6.66–69), 1868 for the Brussels Palais de Justice (5.18, 19). One may add to these the buildings for the Paris Exhibitions of 1878, 1889 and 1900 (pp. 248–51), King Ludwig II's private Versailles, Herrenchiemsee, begun in 1878 (p. 10), the Printemps store in Paris, begun in 1882 (16.30, 31), Selfridge's store in London, begun in 1908 (16.33), d'Aronco's wild design of 1884 for the monument to Victor Emanuel II (1.1), and the equally wild Milan railway station begun in 1912 (14.21).

But 1912 is a very late date for this kind of exuberance. The new ministries in Whitehall, one begun in 1898 (4.6), the other in 1900, are indebted to Wren and Gibbs and are consequently in a very muted Baroque, and in the United States the buildings of the Chicago Exhibition of 1893 (15.47) and then McKim, Mead & White's Classical Re-Revival were winning victory after victory. Pennsylvania Station in New York, begun in 1906, with its long colonnade is one reminder, the endless colonnades of the Washington ministries of the 1930s and after by a number of faceless architects is another. On the Continent the paramount monument is that to Victor Emanuel II by Count Sacconi, begun in 1885 (1.36).

The move into the twentieth century seems at first one of self-denial. In Fascist Italy and Nazi Germany it was indeed. Columns became square pillars and window mouldings and window pediments were shaved off (4.16). The cubic insistence of the Lenin and Atatürk Monuments belongs here as well (1.34, 35).

But in the architecturally leading areas the moves were more positive. About 1890–1900 there was a great difference between the progressives in Europe and in America. In both areas the programme was to get out of historicism into a new style for a new century. But in Europe the first step was Art Nouveau, while in America Art had little to contribute. Art Nouveau on the whole was a domestic phenomenon, but some public buildings participated: Horta's Maison du Peuple in Brussels, begun in 1896 (not referred to in this book) and his Innovation of 1900–1901 (16.38), Lechner's Budapest savings bank of 1899–1902 (12.56) and Sommaruga's Campo dei Fiori Hotel of 1909–12 (11.51). One way rarely made use of led from Art Nouveau into the short-lived architectural Expressionism. Two examples are all this book has to offer: the Scheepvaarthuis in Amsterdam of 1912–16 (13.24) and the Chilehaus in Hamburg of 1922–23 (13.32). It was a blind alley.

The royal road took architecture in another direction. Otto Wagner in Vienna had started before 1898 in an Austrian Baroque. In 1898 he, aided and abetted by his pupil Olbrich, designed the Stadtbahn stations in an excellent Art Nouveau. Olbrich then did the main building of the Darmstadt exhibition of 1901 just as originally but more powerfully, with sharply cut in, entirely plain horizontal windows, and in 1904 Wagner's Vienna Postal Savings Bank shed not only historicism but also all embellishments (12.54, 55). The new style was achieved.

Chicago however had achieved it earlier – in fact as early as Holabird & Roche's Marquette Building, i.e. in 1894 (13.28). Sullivan, Art Nouveau in his ornament but not in his architecture, followed with the Carson, Pirie, Scott store in 1899–1904 (16.34), and Sullivan's pupil, Frank Lloyd Wright, followed him with the Larkin Building in 1904 (13.29). On the Continent the new style was developed decisively between 1900 and the First World War: by Hoffmann in Vienna, by Perret in Paris, and then by Loos and Tony Garnier, the latter a fanatic of concrete. Their works, once again, are untainted by any historicism. So are the factories of Peter Behrens (17.43), starting in 1907, and Gropius & Meyer's Fagus Factory begun in 1910 (17.41). But there is an historically important difference between the factories of Gropius and his master Behrens. The Fagus-Werke is uncompromisingly cubic and displays a curtain wall. With such qualities and motifs it and the model factory of the Cologne Werkbund exhibition of 1914 mark the establishment of what about fifteen years later Henry-Russell Hitchcock and Philip Johnson christened the International Modern. Its climax lay between about 1925 and about 1945–50. Examples are Mendelsohn's Schocken store at Chemnitz of 1928–29, Luckhardt & Anker's Telschow Building in Berlin of 1927–28 (13.31), the van Nelle factory in Rotterdam of 1927–29 (17.44), Mies van der Rohe's exquisite pavilion at the Barcelona exhibition of 1929 (15.61), and after the Second World War the General Motors Research Area at Warren, Michigan, begun 1948, by Saarinen (13.36), Lever House in New York, 1950–52, by Skidmore, Owings & Merrill (13.35), Louisiana, the museum outside Copenhagen, of 1958–59 (8.53), the Israel Museum at Jerusalem of 1959–65 (8.55), and Jacobsen's SAS Royal Hotel in Copenhagen of 1960 (11.52).

But the historian is obliged to brand the most recent of these as conservative or retardataire or reactionary, for in the late forties Le Corbusier had come out with buildings of a totally different character: no longer light but heavy, i.e. neglecting the International Modern demand for maximum performance with a minimum of material, and also not self-effacing but de-monstratively personal, and not crisp but massive. The key buildings – not in this book – are the Unité d'Habitation in Marseilles begun in 1947, the pil-grimage chapel at Ronchamp of 1950 and the Maisons Jaoul begun in 1954. In this book only the following appear: the Boston City Hall, begun in 1963 (5.28), the Bank of London and South America in Buenos Aires, begun in 1960 (12.57), the Goddard Library of Clark University, begun in 1965 by John Johansen (7.49), and the University Art Museum at Berkeley, California, begun in 1967 (8.56). In the same spirit but not in Le Corbusier terms are Frank Lloyd Wright's Gug-genheim Museum of 1943–59 (8.52) and Moshe Safdie's Habitat at the Montreal exhibition of 1967 (15.70).

Where have we reached then? I said at the beginning of this concluding chapter that the bulk of the examples would be taken from the nineteenth century and that the distinguishing feature would be historicism. Why is that so? Why all these styles, in sequence or at the same moment? Much has been said by many historians,

including myself, to explain historicism. Their answers were varied and, in my opinion, of only fragmentary validity. My own answer is this: every building creates associations in the mind of the beholder, whether the architect wanted it or not. The Victorian architect wanted it. Nineteenth-century architecture is evocative architecture. Hence for instance the preference for Gothic in churches. Buildings for education were designed to evoke the Age of Pericles or the learning of the cloister. Banks and offices liked to allude to the Renaissance palazzo – i.e. to evoke Lorenzo the Magnificent. The gaol of course had to have the motifs of the medieval castle. And so on – but also in reverse. The greatness of the Crystal Palace is that there was nothing it could evoke.

Now if the importance of evocation is granted, what part does evocation play in the anti-period styles of the twentieth century? There are none of the familiar period motifs to guide us. We have to rely on more direct evocation. But can we? Can we trust our own evocation as valid for others? The attempt may be worth while to end this book with. As for the International Modern, it conveys clarity, precision, technological daring, and a total denial of superfluity, but it also conveys neutrality. The style of the Boston City Hall and John Johansen's library is the opposite. Motifs may recur as they do in any valid style, but their combination allows for much demonstration of per-sonality, too much where a certain anonymity is a reasonable demand. However, the motifs speak as evocatively as any of Mies van der Rohe and Arne Jacobsen. Only they evoke aggression and a cyclopean brute force. Or am I wrong in assuming that such will be the reaction of the naïve beholder and the unbiased critic?

BIBLIOGRAPHIES
AND NOTES

General bibliography

J.-F. Blondel, *Cours d'architecture civile*, II, Paris 1771

P. Carbonara, *Architettura pratica*, 4 vols., Turin 1954–62

D. Donghi, *Manuale dell' architetto*, 3 vols., Turin 1925–30

J.-N.-L. Durand, *Recueil et parallèle des édifices de tous genres, anciens et modernes*, Paris 1801
Précis des leçons d'architecture données à l'Ecole Polytechnique, 2 vols., Paris 1802–09

Handbuch der Architektur, ed. J. Durm, Teil IV, 13 vols., Darmstadt 1880 et seq.

C. Gourlier and others, *Choix d'édifices publics projetés et construits en France depuis le commencement du XIXᵉ siècle*, Paris 1825–50

J. Guadet, *Eléments et théorie de l'architecture*, Paris 1902–04

T. Hamlin, *Forms and Functions of Twentieth-century Architecture*, 1952

L. Klasen, *Grundriss-Vorbilder in Gebäuden aller Art*, 15 pts., Leipzig 1884–96

Dictionary of Architecture, ed. Wyatt Papworth, 8 vols. plus 3 vols. of plates, London (Architectural Publication Society) 1853–92

P. Planat, *Cours de construction civile*, 2 ser., Paris 1880–83
Encyclopédie de l'architecture et de la construction, 6 vols., Paris 1888–95

L. Reynaud, *Traité d'architecture*, 2 vols., Paris 1850–58

Wasmuths Lexikon der Baukunst, 4 vols., Berlin 1929–32

Abbreviations used in the specialized bibliographies and notes

Arch. Hist.   *Architectural History*
Arch. Rev.   *Architectural Review*
BSHAF   *Bulletin de la société de l'histoire de l'art français*
Enc. d'arch.   *Encyclopédie d'architecture*
Enc. spett.   *Enciclopedia dello spettacolo*
Gaz. des arch.   *Gazette des architectes et du bâtiment*

Gaz. des b.-a.   *Gazette des beaux-arts*
Jb. d. Kais. Deutschen Archaeol. Inst.   *Jahrbuch des Kaiserlichen Deutschen Archaeologischen Instituts*
Jb. d. Preuss. Kunstsamml.   *Jahrbuch der Preussischen Kunstsammlungen*
JRIBA   *Journal of the Royal Institute of British Architects*
JSAH   *Journal of the Society of Architectural Historians*
Mitt. d. Kais. Deutschen Archaeol. Inst.   *Mitteilungen des Kaiserlichen Deutschen Archaeologischen Instituts*
Münchner Jb. d. Bild. Kunst.   *Münchner Jahrbuch der Bildenden Kunst*
Précis   *Précis des leçons d'architecture données à l'Ecole Polytechnique*
Recueil   *Recueil et parallèle des édifices de tous genres, anciens et modernes*
Rev. gén. de l'arch.   *Revue générale de l'architecture et des travaux publics*
Trans. RIBA   *Transactions of the Royal Institute of British Architects*
Zs. f. Bild. Kunst.   *Zeitschrift für Bildende Kunst*
Zs. f. Kunstgesch.   *Zeitschrift für Kunstgeschichte*

Introduction

NOTES

p.9 1. *Architecture and Society. Selected essays of Henry van Brunt*, ed. W. A. Coles, Cambridge, Mass. 1969, 165. From 'On the Present Condition and Prospects of Architecture', published in 1886.

2. *G. A. Demmler, 1804–1886. Die Autobiographie eines grossen Baumeisters*, ed. B. Mertelmeyer, Schwerin n.d.

10 3. W. Blunt, *The Dream King: Ludwig II of Bavaria*, London 1970. The chapter on Ludwig and the Arts is by M. Petzet. In German the most recent contribution is N. Knopp, 'Gestalt und Sinn der Schlösser König Ludwigs II.', in *Argo – Festschrift für Kurt Badt*, ed. M. Gosebruch and L. Dittmann, Cologne 1970, 340–53.

1 National monuments and monuments to genius

BIBLIOGRAPHY

Handbuch der Architektur (ed. J. Durm), Teil IV, Halbband 8, Hefte 2a and 2b (*Denkmäler*, by A. Hofmann), Stuttgart 1906. – H. Schrade, *Das deutsche Nationaldenkmal*, Munich 1934. – A. Neumeyer, 'Monuments to "Genius" in German Classicism', *Journal of the Warburg Institute*, II, 1938–39, 159–63. – L. Ettlinger, 'Denkmal und Romantik', in *Festschrift für Herbert von Einem*, Berlin 1965. – T. Nipperdey, 'Nationalidee und Nationaldenkmal', *Historische Zeitschrift*, CCVI, 1968, 529–85.

NOTES

p.11 1. *Karl der Grosse; Lebenswerk und Nachleben*, II, *Das geistige Leben*, Düsseldorf 1965, 23. It is really a reliquary in the form of a triumphal arch.

12 2. U. Keller, *Reitermonumente absolutistischer Fürsten*, Munich and Zürich 1971, I have not used.

3. Handel was also still alive when in 1738 his statue by Rysbrack was erected in Vauxhall Gardens (T. Hodgkinson, *Bulletin of the Victoria and Albert Museum*, I, London 1964, no. 4).

4. English priority was accepted abroad. Professor Neumeyer has found a reference in A. W. G. Becker, *Vom Kostüm an Denkmälern*, 1776. It would be desirable, Becker wrote, that 'as in England' scholars, artists and other men of merit should be honoured by monuments, 'which is rare here' (A. Neumeyer, 'Monuments to "Genius" in German Classicism', *Journal of the Warburg Institute*, II, 1938–39, 159). Rare in France too, he may have added, or so at least Pierre Patte writes in his *Monuments érigés à la gloire de Louis XV*, Paris 1767, 71: 'Ce sont les grands hommes qui font, dans tous les temps, la gloire d'un état.' Yet, he continues, we honour by monuments only our kings, not our 'hommes célèbres' (p. 93). He does not refer to England, but to the bronze statue of Erasmus erected in 1622 at Rotterdam (p. 86). He might have re-

ferred to a yet older statue. In 1580 in the courtyard of the Basel Town Hall a statue was erected commemorating Munatius Plancus, the presumed founder of Basel (*Denkmäler im 19. Jahrhundert*, ed. H. E. Mittig and V. Plagemann, Munich 1972, 23 and 319).

A few years after Patte's plea, in 1774, d'Angiviller, Directeur Général des Bâtiments, set out on just such a scheme. He commissioned statues of famous Frenchmen ·to 'ranimer la vertu et les sentiments patriotiques' (W. Graf Kalnein and M. Levey, *Art and Architecture of the Eighteenth Century in France* (Pelican History of Art), Harmondsworth 1973, 155–56). They were La Fontaine, Poussin, Cassini, Buffon, Montaigne, Molière, Vauban, Turenne, du Guesclin and Racine, and they were intended to be displayed in the Louvre, when the Louvre had become a public museum (see p. 120). Among the selected sculptors were Pajou and Caffieri.

So much for French Worthies. In the same years Italian Worthies were being looked after by the Venetian patrician Andrea Memmo. (See F. Haskell, *Patrons and Painters*, London 1963, 354–58.) O. Ronchi, *Guida Storico-Artistico di Padova e Dintorni*, Padua 1923, has a complete list. More recent is Neri Pozza and others, *Padova: Guida ai Monumenti e alle Opere d'Arte*, Padua 1971.) He was Provveditore of Padua and saw to it that the marshy and untidy Prato della Valle was laid out with an elliptical centre for holding fairs and a moat round it. The layout was to include a large number of statues of men noteworthy in Padua. He started in 1775; by 1777 19 statues were *in situ*, by 1786 53. There are now 87. The quality is poor. One statue by Canova is one of the exceptions. Canova himself incidentally received a statue too, although he was still alive (1796). The donor was on the whole more interesting than the statues. Memmo must have pleaded with great conviction all over Europe. Statues were given e.g. by the Duke of Gloucester (1776), the King of Poland, the King of Sweden, Pope Pius VI, the Elector of Saxony, the Duke of Parma and the monks of Montecassino.

5. Samuel Clark and William Wollaston were theologians much appreciated by the Queen. For the Hermitage see M. I. Webb, *Michael Rysbrack, Sculptor*, London 1954, 147 ff. The story of the busts, as it appears in Mrs Webb's book, is more complicated than it appears in my précis. Also it would be worth while to follow the story of the library bust from the 1730s onwards. To have busts of great men on the bookcases in private libraries was an English speciality.

6. See Haskell, op. cit., 287–92. E. Croft-Murray, *Decorative Painting in England, 1537–1837*, II, London 1970, 239–42.

13 7. On Boullée see J.-M. Pérouse de Montclos, *Etienne-Louis Boullée, 1728–1799. De l'architecture classique à l'architecture révolutionnaire*, Paris 1969 (English translation 1974, not used by me). Also H. Rosenau, *Boullée's Treatise on Architecture*, London 1953, and for our specific purpose the brilliant book by A. M. Vogt, *Boullées Newton Denkmal; Sakralbau und Kugelidee*,

Basel and Stuttgart 1969.

8. The term megalomania was first used in this context by Henri Lemonnier in *L'Architecte*, V, 1910, 92 ff. On the Grands Prix see H. Rosenau in 'The Engravings of the *Grands Prix* of the French Academy of Architecture', *Arch. Hist.*, III, 1960.

For megalomania of the Boullée type one of the patterns was Piranesi's *Ampio e magnifico Collegio* of 1750, another Robert Mylne's submission to the Concorso Clementino of the Accademia di San Luca in Rome (1758), which asked for an 'Edificio pubblico monumentale per l'esibizione dei busti di Uomini Celebri'. Cf. J. Harris, 'Robert Mylne at the Academy of St Luke', *Arch Rev.*, CXXX, 1961, 341–42, and most recently G. Teyssot, *Città e utopia nell'illuminismo inglese: George Dance il giovane*, Rome 1974.

9. In 1972 the funeral decoration for Gustavus III of Sweden in the Riddarholm Church at Stockholm included at gallery level rows of cypress trees, and the vault was converted into a starry sky. (A. Lindblom, *Svenska Kunsthistoria*, Stockholm 1946, III, 655.)

10. A. Bernard and G. Wildenstein, *La Tour*, Paris 1928, 52 and pl. 53.

11. *Principes mathématiques de la philosophie naturelle*.

14 12. See Henry Chadwick, 'Origen, Celsus, and the Resurrection of the Body', *Harvard Theological Review*, XLI, 1948, 83 ff. and A.-J. Festugière, 'De la Doctrine Origéniste du corps glorieux sphéroïde', *Revue des sciences philosophiques et théologiques*, XLIII, 1959, 81 ff. Professor Chadwick kindly referred me to these articles. I had come across the matter in his *The Early Church*, Harmondsworth 1967, 106. Alberti was partial to the sphere too. In his *De re aedificatoria* of c. 1450 he writes (bk. VII, chap. IV): 'Rotundis naturam in primis delectari . . . in promptu est', and when (chap. III) he wants to praise the round temple of Vesta he calls it – very oddly indeed – 'ad pilae similitudinem' – round as a ball. The two passages can be found in Latin and Italian in the edition of G. Orlandi and P. Portoghesi (Il Polifilo, Milan 1966, 547 and 549) and in English in the reprint of Leoni's edition of 1726 (London 1955, 137 and 138).

13. See e.g. O. Sirén, *China and Gardens of Europe*, New York 1950, 125 ff. The National Gallery at Dublin has Hubert Robert's *Apotheosis of Rousseau* painted in 1794.

14. L. Grote, *Führer durch den Wörlitzer Park*, Dessau 1929, 22.

15. See *Denkmäler im 19. Jahrhundert*, op. cit., 186–89 and ill. 401. On Luther monuments also T. Nipperdey, 'Nationalidee und Nationaldenkmal', *Historische Zeitschrift*, CCVI, 1968, 557.

16. On the designs for the monument see K. Muckle, *Das Denkmal König Friedrich des Grossen*, Berlin 1894, H. Schmitz, 'Die Entwürfe für das Denkmal Friedrichs des Grossen', *Zs. f. Bild. Kunst*, N.F. XX, 1909, 206 ff., and more recently A. Oncken's excellent *Friedrich Gilly*, Berlin 1935. Also Nipperdey, op. cit., 534–40.

17. *Berlinsche Blätter*, 1787, 162. See C. F. Hartlaub, 'Denkmalsromantik der Freiheitskriege', *Zs. f. Bild. Kunst*, N.F. XXVIII, 1916. Quoted from Neumeyer,

op. cit.

15 18. Rosenau, 'Engravings of the *Grands Prix*', op. cit., 26 and pl. 34.

19. Genelli incidentally in the same year also made a Gothick design to commemorate Herder. See Neumeyer, op. cit.

20. E. Bassi, *Giannantonio Selva, architetto italiano*, Padua 1936, 82.

21. Another design by Harrison was a Doric triumphal arch. See J. M. Crook in *Country Life*, CIL, 1971, 1091.

22. The middle interstice is wider than the others – a survival from the Baroque and unacceptable of course for a strict Grecian.

23. K. Lankheit, 'Ein Entwurf Gottfried Schadows zum Friedrich-Monument', *Festschrift für Gert von der Osten*, Cologne 1970, 189 ff.

24. The same term – 'Sanctuary of the Nation' – had been used a year before by A. F. Kraus (Nipperdey, op. cit., 537).

16 25. *Dizionario delle arti del disegno*, I, 166. I am quoting from the Bassano 1822 ed. In another of his books, the *Principi di architettura civile*, 1781 (I quote from the 2nd ed., Bassano 1785, 345 ff.), Milizia pleaded for the erection of monuments 'alla gloria degli uomini più utili al pubblico' as an 'omaggio solenne'. On Milizia see also E. Brües, 'Die Schriften des Francesco Milizia', *Jahrbuch für Aesthetik und allgemeine Kunstwissenschaft*, VI, 1961, and Etta Arntzen's still unpublished thesis (Columbia University, New York 1970).

26. Unfortunately I cannot re-trace this reference.

27. *The Architecture of Country Houses*, New York 1850, 27.

28. *Sammlung architektonischer Entwürfe von Schinkel*, 2nd ed., Berlin 1873, 21 and pls. 163–68. (The first edition was published in 1819–40.)

29. On Napoleon's monuments the literature is extensive. It may, however, be enough here to refer to M.-L. Biver, *Le Paris de Napoléon*, Paris 1963, and more generally to vols. III, IV and V (Paris 1952–55) of Louis Hautecoeur's *Histoire de l'architecture classique en France*.

17 30. Two versions of the statue exist: one in marble at Apsley House, London, of 1802–10, and one in bronze in the courtyard of the Brera, Milan, of 1809. Napoleon did not like it. To David he said he wanted 'une image conforme à son génie'. (R. Cantinelli, *J.-L. David*, Paris 1930, 69.)

31. T. W. Gaehtgens, *Napoleons Arc de Triomphe* (Abhandlungen der Akademie der Wissenschaften in Göttingen, Philosophisch-historische Klasse, 3 Folge, no. 90), Göttingen 1974, contains much valuable material. In my opinion Professor Gaehtgens underplays the influence of Cellerier's Champ de Mars arch.

The Revolution and its aftermath had produced a number of ephemeral triumphal arches, more severe than Chalgrin's. Hautecoeur (op. cit., V, 1953) illustrates them: One of 1790 by Cellerier (121), one of 1793 (124) and another of 1795 (131). See also C. Simond (i.e. P. A. van Clemputte): *La Vie parisienne à travers le XIXe siècle*, I, 1900, 201 and 273 for two more.

32. See M. Petzet, *Soufflots Sainte Geneviève und der französische Kirchenbau des 18. Jahrhunderts*, Berlin 1961.

33. The building went back to cult in

1806, back to the Pantheon function in 1830, back to cult again in 1852, and finally back to Pantheon in 1885.

34. Crook, op. cit. (above, n. 21), 1090–91.

35. A. Freiherr von Wolzogen, *Aus Schinkels Nachlass*, Berlin 1862–63, III, 232.

36. Quoted from H. Beenken, *Schöpferische Bauideen der deutschen Romantik*, Mainz 1952, 67–68.

18 37. O. Hederer, *Karl von Fischer; Leben und Werk*, Munich 1960.

38. W. von Pölnitz, *Ludwig I von Bayern und Johann Martin von Wagner*, 1929.

39. H. Beenken, op. cit. The sketches were burnt in the Second World War. I have not seen a recent PhD thesis on Haller von Hallerstein by K. Frässle, Freiburg University 1971.

19 40. O. Hederer, *Leo von Klenze*, Munich 1964, 303.

20 41. L. Ettlinger, 'Denkmal und Romantik', *Festschrift für Herbert von Einem*, Berlin 1965.

42. ibid.

43. K. Eggert, *Friedrich von Gärtner*, Munich 1963, 120 ff.

21 44. Dorothy Stroud published it recently in her *George Dance, Architect*, London 1973, 245 and ill. 76a.

45. Nearest to its style is a German design for a Schiller Monument produced in 1807, two years after Schiller's death, by Johann Gottfried Klinsky. For particulars see *Denkmäler im 19. Jahrhundert*, op. cit. (above, n. 4), 143 and 367. The memorial has a low Doric portico with an entirely Ledolcian elementary pediment (cf. Aix prison, my ill. 10.6) and a round tower behind.

46. J. Jefferson Miller, 'The Designs for the Washington Monument in Baltimore', *JSAH*, XXIV, 1964.

47. The Washington initiative came shortly after a New York initiative. The New York Washington Monument Association was founded in 1832. In 1843 Calvin Pollard suggested a Gothic pile 425 feet high. The design was influenced by the Edinburgh Scott Memorial. Robert Kerr of London suggested a three-storeyed rotunda, Minard Lafever a 500-foot obelisk. See J. Landy, 'The Washington Monument Project in New York', *JSAH*, XXVIII, 1969, 291 ff.

48. Henry van Brunt compares the 555 feet with the 520 of the Pyramid of Cheops, the 518 of St Peter's and the 501 of Cologne Cathedral. See *Architecture and Society, Selected Essays of Henry van Brunt*, ed. W. A. Coles, Cambridge, Mass. 1969.

49. *Form and Function*, ed. H. A. Small, University of California Press 1947.

22 50. Van Brunt, op. cit., 195 ff.

24 51. *Handbook to the Prince Consort National Memorial*, London 1872 and many later impressions.

52. On the plinth of Rauch's monument to Frederick the Great some great men in cultural pursuits were represented too, but only 20 out of a total of 105 (Nipperdey, op. cit., 539).

53. *Denkmäler im 19. Jahrhundert*, op. cit., has a whole chapter (by J. Gamer) on monuments to Goethe and Schiller: 141–62 and 56 illustrations on 365 ff.

26 54. *Building News*, 18 May 1888.

55. On monuments to Wilhelm I see O. Kuntzemüller, *Die Denkmäler Kaiser Wilhelm des Grossen*, Bremen 1902, on Bismarck monuments *Handbuch der Architektur*, Teil IV, Halbband 8, Heft 2b (A. Hofmann, *Denkmäler*) Stuttgart 1906, and *Denkmäler im 19. Jahrhundert*, op. cit., 217–52, a whole chapter (by V. Plagemann) with illustrations of towers on 419, 428–33 and 436–39. Of the leading architects, another purveyor of national monuments was Wilhelm Kreis (*Handbuch*, op. cit., 650, 651, 661, 674, 679, 680).

56. It should not be forgotten that already in 1814 Ernst Moritz Arndt, fanatical patriot, had pleaded for such a monument to be erected on the battlefield as 'a colossus, a pyramid, a Cologne Cathedral' (*Entwurf einer Teutschen Gesellschaft*, Frankfurt 1814). I found this passage quoted in G. Eimer, *Caspar David Friedrich und die Gotik*, Hamburg 1963, 20. Also in 1814 Weinbrenner pleaded for a National-Denkmal to the victory (Nipperdey, op. cit., 560). In the same year the building of a memorial church was suggested by Karl Sieveking, historian and politician (ibid., 546) and by Görres, more famous politician (ibid., 550), and in 1815 one De Witte proposed a whole chain of Gothic temples (G. Germann, *Gothic Revival in Europe and Britain*, London 1972, 91). Also in 1814–15 Schinkel was commissioned by the King of Prussia to design a memorial church. The designs – Gothic of course – are familiar (see Wolzogen, op. cit., III, 198–99, and G. F. Koch, 'Schinkels architektonische Entwürfe im gotischen Stil', *Zs. f. Kunstgesch.*, XXXII, 1969, 282–300). Inside against the piers statues of scholars, artists and others of non-military achievements were to be placed. In the end all that was done in Prussia was Schinkel's Kreuzberg monument to those fallen in the war of 1813. It was put up in 1818–21, a Gothic tabernacle of cast iron, 65 feet high. That was inadequate if seen against the Bavarian monumentality.

57. *Handbuch*, op. cit., 2b, 673.

2 Government buildings from the late twelfth to the late seventeenth century

NOTES

p.27 1. See F. Kirschen, *Antike Rathäuser*, Berlin 1941.

2. J. Paul, *Die mittelalterlichen Kommunalpaläste in Italien*, PhD thesis, Freiburg im Breisgau University 1963.

3. ibid., 46 and 135 ff.

4. ibid., 49 and 147 ff. Also *Storia di Milano*, Milan (Fondazione Treccani) III, 1954, 520; IV, 1954, 186, 372 ff., 516 ff., V, 1955, 259, 716 ff.

28 5. Ill. e.g. in J. Evans, *Art in Medieval France*, Oxford 1948, pl. 239, and in O. Stiehl, *Das deutsche Rathaus im Mittelalter*, Leipzig 1905, and K. Gruber, *Das deutsche Rathaus*, Munich 1943. More recent are R. Delling, *Deutsche Rathäuser*, Frankfurt 1958, and W. Kiewert, *Deutsche Rathäuser*, Dresden (1961).

For Northern France and Belgium see C. Enlart, *Hôtels de ville et beffrois du nord de la France*, Paris n.d., and M. Battard, *Beffrois, halles, hôtels de ville dans le nord de la France et la Belgique*, Arras 1948. For good illustrations of French and German town halls see also still A. Verdier and F. Cattois, *Architecture civile et domestique au moyen-âge et à la Renaissance*, 2 vols., 1855–57.

6. Paul, op. cit., 78 ff. and 207 ff.

7. ibid., 33.

8. ibid., 91 ff. and 208 ff., also J. Paul, *Der Palazzo Vecchio in Florenz*, Florence 1968.

9. Paul, *Mittelalterliche Kommunalpaläste*, op. cit., 93 and 264 ff.

29 10. A. Lensi, *Palazzo Vecchio*, Milan and Rome 1929, 12 and 114.

11. Apart from the books by Stiehl and Gruber already referred to, see C. Steinbrecht, *Die Baukunst des deutschen Ritterordens in Preussen*, I, *Thorn*, Berlin 1885, and K. Gruber, *Das Rathaus in Thorn*, *Deutsche Kunst und Denkmalpflege*, 1940–41, 50 ff. Also R. Heuer, *Thorn*, Berlin 1931.

12. At Plauen in Upper Saxony in the second half of the fifteenth century the upper floor was already arranged as a corridor with offices on both sides (see *Wasmuths Lexikon der Baukunst*, Berlin 1929–32, I, 686). The same arrangement appears on the top floor of the town hall at Leipzig of 1556 et seq. (see *Beschreibende Darstellung der älteren Bau- und Kunstdenkmäler des Königreichs Sachsen*, XXIV, 1896, 310).

13. Stiehl, op. cit., 109, also Steinbrecht, op. cit. The German words are 'rathus, Kaufhaus, dinghus, Cromen [from Kramer], Brodbenke, Buden, wage und andir gemeche'.

30 14. Battard, op. cit., and Enlart, op. cit.

15. For Dutch town halls see *Duizend Jaar Bouwen in Nederland*, ed. S. J. Fockema Andreae, E. H. Ter Kuile and M. D. Ozinga, Amsterdam 1958, 351–59.

16. M. de Stabenrath, *Le Palais de Justice de Rouen*, Rouen 1842; E. Spalikowski, *Le Palais de Justice de Rouen*, Rouen 1939; P. Chirol, 'Le Palais de Justice', *Congrès archéologique*, LXXXIX, 1926, 158 ff. I owe information on Rouen to M. C. Simonnet, Conservateur, Bibliothèque Municipale, Rouen.

17. As regards the nineteenth-century restoration, Ruskin of all people found himself justified in praising it. This is what he wrote in 1849: 'My experience has furnished me . . . with only one instance, that of the Palais de Justice at Rouen, in which the utmost degree of fidelity which is possible has been achieved.' (*The Seven Lamps of Architecture*, chap. VI, § 18)

18. Le Roux de Lincy, *Histoire de l'Hôtel de Ville de Paris*, Paris 1846. Briefer, but with fine plates, is V. Calliat and Le Roux de Lincy, *Hôtel de Ville de Paris*, Paris 1844.

19. Their parts in the design have never been satisfactorily cleared up.

31 20. ed. J. R. Spencer, 2 vols., New Haven, Conn. 1965. Vol. I, ills. 3–4 after p. xxxviii, vol. II, fol. 73r.

21. G. L. Hersey, *Alfonso II and the Artistic Renewal of Naples*, New Haven, Conn. 1969.

22. Francesco di Giorgio Martini, *Trattati di architettura, ingegneria e arte militare*, ed. C. Maltese, Milan 1967, II, 364. See also R. Papini, *Francesco di Giorgio architetto*, Florence 1946.

23. Maltese, op. cit., p. 350 and pl. 206.

24. ibid., 335 ff., deals with the lavatories.

32 25. U. Borini, 'Come sorse la fabbrica degli Uffizi', *Rivista Storica degli Archivi Toscani*, V, 1933, 1–40.

26. F. Prims, *Het Stadhuis van Antwerpen*, Antwerp 1930. I want to thank Dr Willekens, Director of the Antwerp Library, for help in the interpretation of the inventory, and also Dr Jan van Roey.

27. R. Coope, *Salomon de Brosse*, London 1972, 155–77 and 268–73. I want to thank Dr Coope for having helped me over the functions of the various rooms of the Palais. See also below, p. 161, n. 31.

33 28. K. Freemantle, *The Baroque Town Hall of Amsterdam*, Utrecht 1959, an exemplary monograph.

3 Government buildings from the eighteenth century: houses of parliament
NOTES

p.35 1. F. G. Hall, *The Bank of Ireland*, Dublin 1949; the architectural part by C. P. Curran, 425 ff.

2. H. Colvin and M. Craig, *Architectural Drawings in the Library of Elton Hall by Sir John Vanbrugh and Sir Edward Lovett Pearce* (Roxburghe Club), London 1964; and the Knight of Glin, 'Summerhill', in *The Country Seat*, London 1970.

3. F. Kimball, 'William Kent's Designs for the Houses of Parliament, 1730–1740', *JRIBA*, 3rd ser., XXXIX, 1931–32, 733–55 and 800–07. Also *JRIBA*, 3rd ser., XLVI, 1938–39, 228–31, and M. Jourdain, *The Work of William Kent*, London 1948, illustrations on pp. 101 ff.

4. On the appearance of the Palace of Westminster in the eighteenth century, see H. Colvin, 'Views of the Old Palace of Westminster', *Arch. Hist.*, IX, 1966.

36 5. J. H. and P. Price, *Executive Mansions and Capitols of America*, New York 1969. Professor H.-R. Hitchcock and Mr W. Seale are working on a book about American capitols.

6. The wings are of 1904–06, and the open staircase up to the portico did not exist originally either.

7. Glenn Brown, *History of the United States Capitol*, Washington, D.C. 1900–02.

8. ibid., 8.

9. *Histoire de la vie et des ouvrages des plus célèbres architectes*, 2 vols., Paris 1830, II, 332. Dr Robin Middleton drew my attention to this passage.

38 10. T. Hamlin, *Greek Revival Architecture in America*, Oxford 1944.

11. For Ohio a book exists, however only in typescript: A. L. Cummings, *Ohio's Capitols at Columbus, 1810–1861*, 1948. In 1800 the Legislature met in a log-house, with the Athenaeum below and a bar above. The Public Square three years before building began still had clover, pigs and a wooden fence. The terms of the competition in 1838 stipulated the Greek Doric. The history of the building brings in a number of architects and not-quite-architects: W. R. West, Nathan B. Kelly and at the end Isaiah Rogers (1858–61). James Fergusson, the widely recognized English architectural critic, called the Ohio Capitol in 1862 'the most admired after that of Washington' (*History of the Modern Styles of Architecture*, 442), and

William Dean Howell (*Harper's Magazine*, CXXIX, 1914, 597) praised 'the noble rotunda' and the grandeur of the whole interior.

40 12. J. Gantner and A. Reinle, *Kunstgeschichte der Schweiz*, IV, Frauenfeld 1962, 85.

13. See now J. M. Crook in *Country Life*, CIL, 1971, 876 ff., 944 ff., 1038 ff., 1539.

14. For the following see L. Hautecoeur, *Histoire de l'architecture classique en France*, V, Paris 1953, 116 ff., 135 ff., 207 ff. Also F. Boyer, 'Projet de salles pour les assemblées révolutionnaires à Paris', *BSHAF*, 1933, 170 ff.; 'Les Tuileries sous le Directoire', *BSHAF*, 1934, 242 ff.; 'Le Conseil des Cinq Cents au Palais Bourbon', *BSHAF*, 1935, 59 ff.; 'Le Palais Bourbon sous le Premier Empire', *BSHAF*, 1938, 91 ff. In addition M.-L. Biver, *Paris sous Napoléon*, Paris 1963, and J. Marchand, *Le Palais Bourbon*, Paris 1962.

15. H. Rosenau, 'The Engravings of the Grands Prix of the French Academy of Architecture', *Arch. Hist.*, III, 1960.

41 16. Marchand, op. cit., 107.

17. J. de Joly, *Plans, coupes et élévations du Palais de la Chambre des Députés*, Paris 1840. After the remodelling the Senate moved to the Luxembourg, where Gisors did the necessary alterations.

18. A. T. Bolton, *The Works of Sir John Soane*, London n.d.; D. Stroud, *The Architecture of Sir John Soane*, London 1961; J. Summerson, *Sir John Soane*, London 1952.

19. See G. H. Weitzman, 'The Utilitarians and the Houses of Parliament', *JSAH*, XX, 1961, 99 ff.

20. Mark Girouard, 'Attitudes to Elizabethan Architecture, 1600–1900', in *Concerning Architecture*, ed. J. Summerson, London 1968.

42 21. A. Barry, *The Life and Work of Sir Charles Barry, R.A., F.R.S.*, London 1867; B. Ferrey, *Recollections of Augustus Welby Northmore Pugin and his father Augustus Pugin*, London 1861; P. Stanton, *Pugin*, PhD thesis, University of London 1950 and *Pugin*, London 1971. Also M. Trappes Lomax, *Pugin*, London 1932, and A. Gordon Clark, 'A. W. N. Pugin' in *Victorian Architecture*, ed. P. Ferriday, London 1963.

22. E. W. Pugin, *Who was the Art Architect of the Houses of Parliament*, London 1867 ('art architect' is an immensely characteristic Victorian term); A. Barry, *The Architect of the Palace of Westminster*, London 1868; E. W. Pugin, *Notes on the reply of the Rev. Alfred Barry to the 'Infatuated Statements' made by E. W. Pugin*, London 1868.

23. *Briefe an einen Architekten, 1870–1889*, 6th ed., Munich 1913.

44 24. Ferrey, op. cit., 248.

25. Barry, *Life and Work*, op. cit., 90.

26. The Bundeshaus was considerably enlarged in 1888–1900. See H. Markwalder in *Berner Zeitschrift für Geschichte und Heimatkunde*, 1948, 133 ff.

27. On Fergusson see now my book, *Some Architectural Writers of the Nineteenth Century*, Oxford 1972, 238–51.

28. The German *Reichstag* from 1663 to 1806 had met in the town hall at Regensburg and in 1848–49 in the church of St Paul at Frankfurt. For the competition of 1872 see in English *The Architect*, VII,

1872, 316–17 and 328–30, and VIII, 1872, 36, 48 and 55.

46 29. W. Whewell, *Architectural Notes on German Churches*, first published in 1830.

30. F. Merenyi, *Cento Anni di Architettura ungarese, 1867–1965*, Rome 1965.

31. *Die Wiener Ringstrasse*, ed. R. Wagner-Rieger, I, Vienna, Cologne and Graz 1969, Objekt 144.

32. M. Rapsilber, *Das Reichstagsgebäude*, Berlin (1895).

4 Government buildings from the eighteenth century: ministries and public offices
NOTES

p.47 1. C. Hussey in *Country Life*, LIV, 1923, 684 ff. and 718 ff.

2. Bk. III, II, 327.

3. 'Drawings by William Kent for the Houses of Parliament, 1739', *JRIBA*, 3rd ser., XLVI, 1938–39, 228–31; *Survey of London*, XIV, London 1931; M. Jourdain, *The Work of William Kent*, London 1948; and H. M. Colvin, *A Biographical Dictionary of English Architects*, London 1954.

4. J. Harris, *Sir William Chambers*, London 1970, 96–106.

48 5. For Barry's and Soane's buildings, see *Survey of London*, XIV.

6. The *Handbuch der Architektur*, Teil IV, Halbband 7, Heft 1 (*Gebäude für Ministerien*, by A. Kortüm), Darmstadt 1887, is informative. See pp. 96–97. It makes the total cost of the building £250,000.

7. So Scott acknowledged. He wrote that the 'idea as to its grouping and outline' was suggested to him 'by a sketch of Mr Digby Wyatt's' (*Personal and Professional Recollections*, London 1879, 200). Wyatt in any case did the courtyard of the India Office inside the block.

8. *Briefe an einen Architekten, 1870–1889*, 6th ed., Munich 1913, 8 August 1879.

9. L. Hautecoeur, *Le Louvre et les Tuileries*, 2 vols., Paris 1924. Also C. Gourlier, *Choix d'édifices publics projetés et construits en France depuis le commencement du XIX⁰ siècle*, Paris 1825–50, and of course Hautecoeur's *Histoire de l'architecture classique en France*, V and VI, Paris 1953, 1955.

50 10. *Trans. RIBA*, 1853–54, 83–86.

11. H. N. Jacobsen and F. D. Lethbridge, *Guide to the Architecture of Washington*, New York etc. 1965. I have to thank Mr Lethbridge for much help with the Washington government buildings. One should consult in addition H. P. Caemmerer, *Washington the National Capital*, Washington, D.C. 1932, and Caemmerer's *Manual on the Origin and Development of Washington*, Washington, D.C. 1939.

51 12. The earliest of all was actually built for another purpose: the Central Library of 1902 by Ackerman & Ross, rather Beaux Arts in the interpretation. The first giant colonnade is the Union Trust by Wood, Dunn & Deming of 1906. Of the same type are the City Post Office of 1914 (by Graham & Burnham) with a colonnade of fourteen giant columns, and the Chamber of Commerce by Cass Gilbert of 1925; and of course Henry Bacon's Lincoln Memorial of 1922 belongs here as well.

13. The architects were: Internal Revenue, Louis Simon; Department of Commerce, York & Sawyer; Department of Justice, Zuntzinger, Boris, Medary; National Archives, Russell Pope; Department of Labor, Arthur Brown; Federal Trade Commission, Bennett, Parsons, Frost.

14. A variant of greater interest is the Museum of History and Technology with seemingly windowless walls in two alternating planes, but in fact the windows done in long narrow vertical strips placed at right angles to the planes and filling the step between front and back plane. It was designed in 1957–63 by McKim, Mead & White and Mills, Petticord & Mills.

52 15. J. and K. Walker, *The Washington Guidebook*, New York 1963, and *The World Almanac*, New York 1968.

16. *Il nuovo Stile Littorio*, Milan and Rome 1936. – *Das Bauen im neuen Reich*, 2 vols., Bayreuth 1938–42.

5 Government buildings from the eighteenth century: town halls and law courts

NOTES

p.53 1. High Wycombe 1757, Uxbridge 1789, Keswick 1813, etc., etc.

2. M. Jourdain, *The Work of William Kent*, London 1948, H. M. Colvin, *A Biographical Dictionary of English Architects*, London 1954, 'Drawings by William Kent for the Houses of Parliament, 1739', *JRIBA*, 3rd ser., XLVI, 1938–39, 228–31. Ill. in Colvin, 'Views of the Old Palace of Westminster', *Arch. Hist.*, IX, 1961, fig. 53.

3. A. T. Bolton, *The Works of Sir John Soane*, London (1924), 95 ff.; D. Stroud, *The Architecture of Sir John Soane*, London 1961.

4. The latter has been demolished.

5. J. M. Crook in *Country Life*, CIL, 1971, 876 ff., 944 ff., 1088 ff., 1539.

6. J.-M. Pérouse de Montclos, *Etienne-Louis Boullée, 1728–1799. De l'architecture classique à l'architecture révolutionnaire*, Paris 1969 (English translation 1974, not used by me); H. Rosenau, *Boullée's Treatise on Architecture*, London 1953.

54 7. H. Rosenau, 'The Engravings of the *Grands Prix* of the French Academy of Architecture', *Arch. Hist.*, III, 1960.

8. *Recueil*, Paris 1801, pl. 17; *Précis*, II, Paris 1809, pl. 7.

9. *Précis*, op. cit., pl. 6.

10. L. Hautecoeur, *Histoire de l'architecture classique en France*, VI, Paris 1955, 152 ff. For other French law courts of the same phase see his pp. 171 (Reims, by Caristie, 1841) and 192–94 (e.g. Montpellier, 1846).

11. D. Evinson, *Joseph Hansom*, MA thesis, University of London 1966, ch. 2. Also 'A Descriptive Account . . . of the Birmingham New Town Hall', *Architectural Magazine*, 1835, and J. Hansom, *Statement of Facts Relative to the Birmingham Town Hall*, Birmingham 1834.

12. J. A. Picton, *Memorials of Liverpool*, 2nd ed., 1875; P. Fleetwood-Hesketh, *Murray's Lancashire Architectural Guide*, London 1955; N. Pevsner, *South Lancashire* (The Buildings of England), Harmondsworth 1969, 155–57.

13. A. Briggs, *Victorian Cities*, London 1963, Penguin ed., Harmondsworth 1968, 166 and 174. Also D. Linstrum, *Historical Architecture of Leeds*, Newcastle 1969, 54–57.

56 14. I am quoting this from G. L. Hamilton, *The Transformation of the Town Hall in England in the nineteenth century*, MA report, University of London 1971.

15. Hautecoeur, op. cit., VII, 1957, 128 ff.

16. *Briefe an einen Architekten, 1870–1889*, Munich 1913, 22 August 1880.

17. Hautecoeur, op. cit., VII, 1957, 141 ff.

18. Including the Egyptian of Davis's Tombs (i.e. law courts and gaol) in New York of 1834–38: see p. 168 and ill. 10.26.

19. See G. Bardet, *Naissance et méconnaissance de l'urbanisme*, Paris 1951, 295–314. Moreau's project included a new river front and a new large courtyard. I owe this reference to Dr Helen Rosenau, *Social Purpose in Architecture*, London 1970, 31 and 49.

20. V. Calliat and Le Roux de Lincy, *Histoire de l'Hôtel de Ville de Paris*, Paris 1844.

58 21. Pevsner, op. cit., 280–82.

22. C. L. Eastlake, *A History of the Gothic Revival in England*, London 1872, 312 ff. and 401, also 426–27.

23. *Building News*, V, 1859, 365. The quotation from Waterhouse is from his description to the RIBA of the Manchester Assize Courts: see *JRIBA*, 12 June 1863, 31–40. I owe this reference to Dr Stuart Allen Smith.

24. *Builder*, XIV, 1856, 63. See also H. J. Brandt, *Das Hamburger Rathaus*, Hamburg 1957. I have not seen Charlotte Kranz, *Studien zu dem deutschen Rathaus des Kaiserreichs, Gestaltung und Programm*, PhD thesis, University of Tübingen 1971.

25. *Victorian Architecture*, New York and London 1970, 77 ff. Also *JRIBA*, January 1970, and M. H. Port, 'The New Law Courts Competition', *Arch. Hist.*, XI, 1968, 75 ff.

26. M. Schuyler, *American Architecture*, ed. W. H. Jordy and R. Coe, Cambridge, Mass. 1961, I, 122.

60 27. P. Saintenoy, 'Joseph Poelaert', *Bulletin Classe des Beaux-Arts*, Académie Royale de Belgique, XXV, 1943, 150.

62 28. C. Pawlowski, *Tony Garnier*, Paris (Centre de Recherche d'Urbanisme) 1967.

29. *William M. Dudok*, Amsterdam and Bussum 1954, 52–69.

30. G. M. Fitch in *Arch. Rev.*, CXLVII, 1970, 399–411. Also *Architectural Forum*, CXXX, 1969, 39–54, and *Architectural Record*, CXLV, 1969, 144–58.

6 Theatres

BIBLIOGRAPHY

An enormous amount has been written on the history of the theatre. But 'the theatre' includes scenery, the actors and the public, performances, stage machinery and more. We are concerned only with theatre buildings, but even so the reference books and papers are legion. The following is a selection.

General

Enciclopedia dello spettacolo, 10 vols., Rome (Fondazione Cini) 1954–66. Invaluable. – A. Nicoll, *The Development of the Theatre*, London 1927; 5th ed. 1966. – *Handbuch der Architektur*, ed. J. Durm, Teil IV, Halbband 6, Heft 5 (*Theater*, by M. Semper), Stuttgart 1904. – *Wasmuths Lexikon der Baukunst*, IV, Berlin 1932. – M. Berthold, *Weltgeschichte des Theaters*, Stuttgart 1968. – A. Streit, *Das Theater*, Vienna 1903. – M. Hammitsch, *Der moderne Theaterbau*, Berlin 1907. – G. R. Kernodle, *From Art to Theatre*, Chicago 1944 (with long bibliography). – H. Kindermann, *Theatergeschichte Europas*, 2nd ed., Salzburg 1966–72. So far 4 vols.; only marginally architectural.

G.-P.-M. Dumont, *Parallèle de plans des plus belles salles de spectacles d'Italie et de France*, Paris c. 1764 etc. (reprint New York 1968). – *Encyclopédie ou dictionnaire raisonné des sciences*, ed. D. Diderot and J. d'Alembert, vol. X of the plates, Paris 1772. Excellent plans of thirteen, mostly important theatres (though see below, n. 105). – A. Donnet, *Architectonographie des Théâtres de Paris*, ed. J. A. Kaufmann, Paris 1857. – J. de Filippi and C. Contant, *Parallèle des principaux théâtres modernes de l'Europe*, Paris 1860. – A. Gosset, *Traité de la construction des théâtres*, Paris 1886.

Finally Simon Tidworth, *Theatres, an illustrated history*, London 1973. It is my fault that the book came too late to my notice. All that I can do is to recommend it to my readers. It is excellent in presentation, very knowledgeable, and amongst the illustrations there is a good deal which is rarely shown. As a matter of fact in several cases the author's choice has been my choice as well. Especially interesting are the designs by Robert Adam and by Soane, pp. 131 and 120, and the fantastic design by the Brothers Luckhardt (p. 200) which reminds one of Finsterlin.

Middle Ages and Renaissance

H. H. Borcherdt, *Das europäische Theater im Mittelalter und in der Renaissance*, Leipzig 1935 (paperback Hamburg 1969); with bibliography. – E. K. Chambers, *The Medieval Stage*, 2 vols., Oxford 1925–55. – G. Cohen, *Le drame en France au moyen-âge*, Paris 1928. – P. Toschi, *Il teatro del medioevo*, Milan 1936. – G. W. G. Wickham, *The Medieval Theatre*, London 1974 (too recent for me to use).

Renaissance and Baroque

R. Klein, *Le lieu théâtral à la renaissance*, Paris 1964. – G. Schöne, *Die Entwicklung der Perspektivbühne von Serlio bis Galli-Bibiena* (Theatergeschichtliche Forschungen, XLIII), Leipzig 1933.

Baroque

M. Baur-Heinhold, *Baroque Theatre*, London 1967. – H. Tintelnot, *Die Entwicklungsgeschichte der barocken Bühnendekoration in ihren Wechselbeziehungen zur bildenden Kunst*, PhD thesis, Berlin University 1938, and *Barocke Theater und barocke Kunst*, Berlin 1939.

Eighteenth century in France

M. Steinhauser and D. Rabreau, 'Le théâtre de l'Odéon de Charles De Wailly et Marie-Joseph Peyre, 1767–1782', *Revue de l'art*, no. 16, 1973, 9–50, goes far beyond its monographic title.

Nineteenth century

E. O. Sachs, *Modern Opera Houses and Theatres*, 3 vols., London 1896–98. – F. B. Biermann, *Die Pläne für Reform des Theaterbaues*, Berlin 1928.

Great Britain

G. W. G. Wickham, *Early English Stages, 1300–1660*, London 1970. – G. E. Bentley, *The Jacobean and Caroline Stage*, 7 vols., Oxford 1941–68. – R. Leacroft, *The Development of the English Playhouse*, London 1973, reached me alas too late for me to make full use of his results. His text is as good or nearly as good as his isometric drawings. There are over sixty of them, and they are all to the same scale. The drawings and descriptions of stage machinery are of the greatest value, and the book has also many useful references to such matters as boxes and upper galleries and entrance fees. Mr Leacroft ends his book about 1900 with the cantilevered galleries of the New English Opera House of 1891 by Collcutt and Holloway (engineers Neade and Riley) and Her Majesty's Theatre of 1897 by C. J. Phipps. It is a pity he did not include the Craig revolution.

NOTES

p.63 1. For instance Alcuin, a scholar from England called by Charlemagne to live and work in France and Germany, knew him. See *Karl der Grosse, Lebenswerk und Nachleben*, Düsseldorf 1965, II (*Das geistige Leben*), 23.

2. I have not seen A. Klein and H. Zerner, 'Vitruve et le théâtre de la Renaissance', in *Le Lieu théâtral à la Renaissance*, Colloque international du centre national de la recherche scientifique, 1964.

3. Bk. VIII, chap. 7. The most recent edition is by G. Orlandi and P. Portoghesi, Milan (Il Polifilo) 1966. See also *Enc. spett.*, I, Rome 1954, 227 ff. A reprint of Leoni's English Alberti of 1726 taken from the 2nd and 3rd eds. came out in London in 1955. On Alberti see F. A. Yates, *Theatre of the World*, London 1969.

4. *Treatise on Architecture, being the treatise by Antonio Averlino, known as Filarete*, ed. J. R. Spencer, New Haven, Conn. 1965, I, 151. In the same book Filarete discusses amphitheatres and circuses. Yet more recent is the edition by L. Grassi, Milan (Il Polifilo) 1972.

5. Biblioteca Reale, Turin, Cod. Saluzzo 148. The treatise has recently been edited: *Trattati di architettura, ingegneria e arte militare*, ed. C. Maltese, 2 vols., Milan (Il Polifilo) 1967.

64 6. ibid., I, 276.

7. ibid., pls. 130, 131.

8. ibid., pls. 129, 130.

9. ibid., II, 365, I, 54–55; pls. I, 23 and 37.

10. ibid., I, 256, 259–60; pls. I, 23 and 37.

11. ibid., I, pl. 23.

12. 'Tu etiam primus picturatae scenae faciem quom Pomponiani commediam agerent: nostro saeculo ostendisti.' See J. Burckhardt, *Die Kultur der Renaissance in Italien*, Leipzig ed. of 1919, II, 235, also I, 239 and 329.

13. E. Povoledo in *Enc. spett.*, V, 173–85.

14. I have not seen M. Dietrich's paper on Pomponio Leto, in *Vierteljahrsschrift für Theaterwissenschaft*, III, no. 3, 1951.

15. G. Schöne, *Die Entwicklung der Perspektivbühne von Serlio bis Galli-Bibiena* (Theatergeschichtliche Forschungen, XLIII), Leipzig 1933. Also E. Povoledo in *Enc. spett.*, VII, 1820–21.

16. Quoted from A. M. Nagler, *A Source Book of Theatrical History*, New York 1952, 71. Also H. H. Borcherdt, *Das europäische Theater im Mittelalter und in der Renaissance*, Leipzig 1935, 95, and E. Povoledo in *Enc. spett.*, V, 1034–35.

A polygonal building appears in the middle of the background of Raphael's *Sposalizio* of 1504, painted in imitation of Perugino's picture of 1480–82 in the Sistine Chapel in Rome, where the building is indeed octagonal. As we shall see, Raphael designed for the theatre as well. He also painted the portraits of people involved with the theatre – Cardinal Bibiena, Castiglione, and Tommaso Inghirami.

65 17. P. Toschi, *Le origini del teatro italiano*, Rome 1955, 122 ff. The report is by G. Palliolo. For more detail see F. Cruciani, *Il teatro del Campidoglio e le feste romane nel 1513*, Milan (Il Polifilo) 1968. My thanks are due to Mr Edward Craig for information on this theatre, for the illustration, and for his great kindness in reading and commenting on the text of this chapter.

18. G. Vasari, *Vite . . .*, ed. G. Milanesi, 9 vols., Florence 1878–85, IV, 600. Also Nagler, op. cit., 72.

19. A curtain is here mentioned for the first time. See Schöne, op. cit., 45. The Duke of Urbino is Lorenzo de'Medici, one of the two dukes who have their monuments in Michelangelo's Medici Chapel. On Raphael see above, n. 16.

20. P. Sanpaolesi, 'Le prospettive antitectoniche di Urbino, di Filadelfia e di Berlino', *Bolletino d'arte*, 1949, no. 4. The panel in East Berlin is now assigned to Laurana.

21. R. Krautheimer, 'The tragic and comic scenes of the Renaissance: the Baltimore and Urbino panels', *Gaz. des b.-a.*, pt. 6, XXXIII, 1948, 327 ff. Also P. Murray, 'Bramante milanese', *Arte Lombarda*, VII, 1962, no. 1. In this context the wooden inlay panels with tricks of perspective at the Ducal Palace in Urbino (Studiolo) of *c.* 1476 and in S. Maria in Organo in Verona (choir and vestry) of 1499 must find mention. For the Studiolo see below, p. 95, n. 47.

22. Bramante's drawing was engraved by Bernardo Prevedari. Only two prints exist, in the Print Rooms of Berlin and London. See F. Graf Wolff Metternich, 'Der Kupferstich Bernardos de Prevedari', *Römische Jahrbuch für Kunstgeschichte*, XI, 1967–68, 9–108.

66 23. Often illustrated, e.g. Nagler, op. cit., 73–78. For Serlio see also Schöne, op. cit., 11 ff.

24. E. Povoledo in *Enc. spett.*, V, 177.

25. ibid., IX, 763 (by E. Povoledo). But the glory of Florence was operas with *intermezzi*, masques and the like and their elaborate and ingenious stage machinery. See A. M. Nagler, *Theatre Festivals of the Medici*, New York 1965.

26. Plan in V. Mariani, *Storia della scenografia italiana*, Florence 1930, pl. 24. Views in A. Puerari, *Sabbioneta*, Milan 1955. Also T. Buzzi, 'Il teatro all' antica di Vincenzo Scamozzi in Sabbioneta', *Dedalo*, VIII, 1928, 488–524.

27. The Palladio literature is too extensive even to begin quoting here. On the Teatro Olimpico in particular: L. Puppi, *Il Teatro Olimpico*, Venice 1963; G. Zorzi, *Le ville e i teatri di Andrea Palladio*, Vicenza 1969, 232 ff. Also L. Magagnato, 'The Genesis of the Teatro Olimpico', *Journal of the Warburg and Courtauld Institutes*, XIV, 1951, 209 ff.

28. P. Donati, *Descrizione del Gran Teatro Farnesiano*, Parma 1817. Also G. Lombardi, 'Il Teatro Farnesiano di Parma', *Archivio storico per le provincie parmensi*, n.s. IX, 1909, 1–52.

29. M. Maylender, *Storia delle accademie d'Italia*, Bologna (1929), IV, 109 ff.

30. *Enc. spett.*, IX, 1530 ff. (M. T. Muraro) and 761 (E. Povoledo).

31. On the early French theatres see G. Cohen, *Histoire de la mise-en-scène dans le théâtre religieux français du moyen-âge*, Paris 1951 (1st ed. 1926). Also G. Cohen, *Le Drame en France au moyen-âge*, Paris 1928.

67 32. *Le Mystère des apôtres* by Arnould Gréban (d. 1471).

33. Memling's *Passion of Christ* in Turin (Galleria Sabauda) places each scene in a kind of *mansio*. Real *mansiones* can be seen in an illustration of a mystery play given at Valenciennes in 1547 (Paris, Bibliothèque Nationale, MS fr. 12536, fol. 2 bis), reproduced e.g. in Nagler, *Source Book*, op. cit., 47 ff. Also G. Altmann, R. Frend, K. Macgowan and W. Melnitz, *Pictorial History of World Theatre*, Berkeley and Los Angeles 1953, fig. 56. H. Rey-Flaud, *Le Cercle magique*, Paris 1973, came out too late for me to do more than refer to it in this note. The author endeavours to prove that the *mansiones* seen one after the other were rare, that Valenciennes cannot be taken as proof and that as a rule the Mystery play was performed as theatre 'in the round'.

34. S. W. Deierkauf-Holsboer, *Le Théâtre de l'Hôtel de Bourgogne*, Paris 1963. Also for the Hôtel de Bourgogne and the Paris theatres to *c.* 1630 see W. Wiley, *The Early Public Theatre in France*, Cambridge, Mass. 1960.

35. The figures are taken from E. Rigal, *Le Théâtre français avant la période classique*, Paris 1901, 156 ff., and S. W. Deierkauf-Holsboer, *L'Histoire de la mise-en-scène dans le théâtre français de 1600 à 1657*, Paris 1933.

36. For this history see E. Povoledo in *Enc. spett.*, IX, 763 ff. (*Teatro*) and VII, 1618 ff. (*Parigi*). See also n. 81 below, and the following in order of publication: A. Babeau, 'Le Théâtre des Tuileries sous Louis XIV, Louis XV et Louis XVI', *Bulletin de la société de l'histoire de Paris*, 1895; Rigal, op. cit.; F. Loliée, *La Comédie française; histoire de la maison de Molière de 1658 à 1907*, Paris 1907; Deierkauf-Holsboer, *Histoire de la mise-en-scène*, op. cit.; H. Leclerc, *Les Origines italiennes de l'architecture théâtrale moderne*, Paris 1946; S. W. Deierkauf-Holsboer, *Le Théâtre du Marais*, 2 vols., Paris 1954; G. Cohen, *Etudes d'histoire du théâtre en France*, Paris 1956; Wiley, op. cit.; G. Montgrédien, *La Vie quotidienne des comédiens au temps de Molière*, Paris 1966.

37. See the plans of the Hôtel de Bourgogne in Deierkauf-Holsboer, *Histoire de*

la mise-en-scène, op. cit., 44; of the Marais in Deierkauf-Holsboer, *Théâtre du Marais*, op. cit., pl. VII, and D. C. Mullin, *The Development of the Playhouse*, Berkeley 1970, 25; of the Palais Royal in *Handbuch der Architektur*, Teil IV, Halbband 6, Heft 5 (*Theater*, by M. Semper), Stuttgart 1904, 31, and Deierkauf-Holsboer, *Histoire de la mise-en-scène*, op. cit., 51; of the Tuileries in *Handbuch der Architektur*, 32, *Enc. spett.*, IX, 1680, and Mullin, 46. Also interior views of the Petit Bourbon in Mullin, 27, and Deierkauf-Holsboer, *Histoire de la mise-en-scène*, 49.

38. V. Champier and G. R. Sandoz, *Le Palais Royal*, Paris 1900.

68 39. N. Bourdel, 'L'Etablissement et la construction de l'hôtel des Comédiens français rue des Fossés-St-Germain-des-Prés', *Revue de l'histoire du théâtre*, II, 1955, 145–72.

40. The literature on the theatre in Shakespeare's time is almost unlimited. I name only, in chronological order: W. W. Greg, *Henslowe's Diary*, London 1904; E. K. Chambers, *The Elizabethan Stage*, 4 vols., Oxford 1923, a classic; W. J. Lawrence, *The Physical Conditions of the Elizabethan Playhouse*, Cambridge, Mass. 1927; and A. Harbage, *Shakespeare's Audience*, New York 1941. An excellent, fairly recent summary is M. M. Reese, *Shakespeare, his World and his Work*, London 1953, 97–344. Of great interest because controversial is Yates, op. cit. (above, n. 3), 92 ff.

69 41. Quoted from Yates, op. cit., 94.

42. C. W. Hodges, *Shakespeare's Second Globe*, Oxford 1973, came too late for its arguments to be presented here.

43. R. Leacroft, *The Development of the English Playhouse*, London 1973, 33. Mr Leacroft also records that the Banqueting Hall of 1606 had 'well secured boxes all round'.

44. S. Orgel and R. Strong, *Inigo Jones: the Theatre of the Stuart Court*, London, New York and California 1973; J. Harris, S. Orgel and R. Strong, *The King's Arcadia: Inigo Jones and the Stuart Court Theatre* (catalogue, Arts Council of Great Britain), 1973, no. 194; *Survey of London*, XIII, London 1930, 62–63; G. E. Bentley, *The Jacobean and Caroline Stage*, VI, London 1968, 267–88; Harry R. Beard in *Enc. spett.*, VI, 793–96; D. F. Rowan, 'The Cockpit-in-Court', in *The Elizabethan Theatre*, ed. D. Galloway, Ottawa 1969; also Leclerc, op. cit., pls. 24, 25; and I. Mackintosh, 'Inigo Jones – theatre architect', *Tabs*, no. 100, September 1973 (vol. XXXI, no. 3). I owe this last reference to Mr R. A. Sayce, Librarian of Worcester College, Oxford.

70 45. Schöne, op. cit., 16–17.

46. ibid., 21.

47. ibid., 45.

48. ibid., 42. Also Nagler, *Source Book*, op. cit., 87 ff.

49. J. Furttenbach, *Architectura recreationis*, Augsburg 1640, 59 and pl. 22. He still described them in 1663. See M. Berthold, *Weltgeschichte des Theaters*, Stuttgart 1968, 405, and M. Barthélemy in *Enc. spett.*, V, 778.

50. Maylender, op. cit.; Schöne, op. cit.

51. Schöne, op. cit. The most important paper is F. Rapp, 'Ein Theaterbauplan des

Giovanni Battista Aleotti', *Neues Archiv für Theatergeschichte*, II, 1930, 79–125. Dr K. Boetzkes of Cologne also drew my attention to F. Rapp, 'Notes on little-known Materials for the History of the Theatre', *The Theatre Annual*, 1944, 60 ff.

52. Also Mantua 1735, Argentina in Rome 1732, S. Carlo in Naples 1737.

53. For the plan see e.g. *Encyclopédie ou dictionnaire raisonné des sciences*, ed. D. Diderot and J. d'Alembert, Planches, X, Paris 1772. (On the theatres illustrated in that volume, see below, n. 105.)

54. ibid.

71 55. E. Povoledo in *Enc. spett.*, VII, 1502 ff. Also J. J. Lynch, *Box, Pit and Gallery*, Berkeley, Calif. 1953.

56. 'Theaterbauplan', op. cit. (n. 51).

57. *Enc. spett.*, II, pl. 117. Also still C. Ricci, *I teatri di Bologna nei secoli XVII e XVIII*, Milan 1888.

58. F. Giorgi, *Descrizione istorica del teatro di Tor di Nona*, Rome 1795.

59. I owe this information to Mr Edward Craig.

60. E. Coudenhove-Erthal, *Carlo Fontana*, Vienna 1930, 83 ff. Also P. Bjurström, *Feast and Theatre in Queen Christina's Rome*, Stockholm 1966; and the annotated catalogue by A. Ravà, *I teatri di Roma*, Rome 1953. Bjurström has an excellent survey of the early theatres with boxes. He refers for a precursor to a passage in Vasari about a theatre of 1549 in the Palazzo Colonna (Vasari, op. cit. (above, n. 18), VI, 583) with 'gradi' for the audience and 'stanze' for the cardinals. Bjurström has also published a paper called 'Giacomo Torelli and Baroque Stage Design', *Acta Universitätis Upsaliensis, Figura*, n.s. II, 1961.

61. *Collected Works*, e.d. C. H. Herford and P. Simpson, Oxford 1925–52, VIII, 403.

62. V. Mariani in *Enc. spett.*, II, 473. Also Schöne, op. cit., 66 ff.

63. Quoted from C. E. Tanfani in *Enc. spett.*, II, 374. Bernini told Chantelou of his intermezzo.

64. B. Hunningher, 'De Amsterdamsche Schouwburg van 1637', *Nederlands Kunsthistorisch Jaarboek*, IX, 1958, 109–71.

72 65. The stage was reactionary: it had a built scene for religious drama. Mr Edward Craig pointed out this contrast.

66. Leacroft, op. cit., 87.

67. *Wren Society*, XII, 1935, 19 and pl. 23. More recently R. Leacroft, 'Wren's Drury Lane', *Arch. Rev.*, July 1951. B. Dobbs, *Drury Lane, Three Centuries of the Theatre Royal*, London 1972, reached me only after this chapter had been written.

Leacroft (*Development*, op. cit.) quotes prices. Davenant in his own house charged 5s. a seat (p. 78); at Killigrew's playhouse in 1660, Pepys tells us, gallery places cost 1s. 6d. At the Theatre Royal, Drury Lane a box seat cost 4s., pit 2s. 6d., middle gallery 1s. 6d., upper gallery 1s.

68. Recently republished, edited by Edward Craig: Milan (Il Polifilo) 1972. The book also contains comparative material, including plans of some major Italian and French theatres of the late sixteenth to early eighteenth centuries.

69. *Storia di Milano*, XII, Milan (Fondazione Treccani) 1959, 890 ff., also 824.

74 70. See Nagler, *Source Book*, op. cit.

71. Horace Walpole says in England they were usually taken for a month. See Lynch, op. cit., 200. Lynch gives as English prices for tickets to the gallery 1s. to 2s. (ibid., 203). For prices see also n. 67, above.

72. *The Guermantes Way*, pt. I, London 1949, 43–44. Steinhauser and Rabreau (below, n. 81) quote from G. M. Monginot, *Exposition des principes qu'on doit suivre dans l'ordonnance des théâtres modernes*, Paris 1769, 87–88: 'Les Italiens veulent garder l'incognito' and to be 'chez eux' (p. 38).

73. Other much publicized Italian Settecento theatres are the Teatro Filarmonico at Verona by Francesco Galli Bibiena, opened in 1732 and reconstructed in 1754 by Del Pozzo after a fire (see T. Lenotti, *I teatri di Verona*, Verona 1949), the Fenice at Venice (not the present interior) by Selva, 1790–92, with a horse-shoe auditorium and five tiers of boxes, the Teatro Nuovo (Teatro Verdi) in Trieste, also by Selva, 1788–1801, also horse-shoe in plan (see E. Bassi, *Giannantonio Selva*, Padua 1936, 57 ff. and 66 ff.) and the theatre at Imola by Cosimo Morelli, 1779–80, a transverse truncated ellipse (see *Pianta e spaccato del nuovo teatro d'Imola*, Rome 1780).

74. But see A. Gruber, 'L'Opéra de Versailles, est-il l'oeuvre de Gabriel?', *Revue de l'art*, no. 13, 1971, 87–97.

75. H. A. Frenzel, *Brandenburgisch-Preussische Schlosstheater*, Berlin 1959, also for the Neues Palais and Rheinsberg.

76. *Wilhelmsbad und sein Theater*, Wilhelmsbad 1969. Also *Bauwelt*, 19 October 1970 (restoration by Ferdinand Kramer).

77. A. Beifer, *Court Theatres of Drottningholm and Gripsholm*, Malmö 1933. I have not seen this and am quoting from Mullin, op. cit.

78. G. K. Loukomski, *Les Théâtres anciens et modernes*, Paris 1934. The dates come from *Enc. spett.*, VI, 1378, and the large *Soviet Encyclopedia*, 2nd ed.

79. H. Felting, *Die Geschichte der deutschen Staatsoper*, East Berlin 1955. Also E. Meffert, *Das Haus der Staatsoper*, Berlin 1942 and *Dramaturgische Blätter* (Deutsche Staatsoper Berlin), February 1968. This information was given me by Mr Erdmann H. Treitschke.

Of the same type and scale as the court theatres are the monastic theatre of Lambach in Austria of the second half of the eighteenth century and the civic theatre of Hvar in Yugoslavia, probably of 1803. The Hvar theatre is on the upper floor above the Arsenal (or was it a dry-dock?). The inscribed date 1612 must refer to the building: it can't refer to the theatre. See M. Baur-Heinhold, *Baroque Theatre*, London 1967, pl. 109 and p. 163. I owe the information on Hvar to my friend Professor Alfred Albini.

76 80. J. Lechner and H. Steinmetz, *Das alte Residenztheater zu München*, Munich 1958.

81. D. Rabreau, 'Le Théâtre et la Place Greslin de Mathurin Coucy à Nantes', *Congrès archéologique de Haute-Bretagne*, Paris 1968, 89–135, goes far beyond its title. It surveys many publications on theatre building, plan types and characteristic motifs. Brilliant and recent – indeed too recent for me to have made full use of

it – is M. Steinhauser and D. Rabreau, 'Le Théâtre de l'Odéon de Charles De Wailly et Marie-Joseph Peyre, 1767–1782', *Revue de l'art*, no. 16, 1973. Apart from the buildings and projects mentioned by me, it discusses projects for sites including those of the Hôtel de Conti, the Hôtel de Soissons (later used for the Halle au Blé – see p. 203) and the Carrousel. M. Rabreau is particularly enlightening on the financial aspects, Dr Stainhauser on the sequence of the plans for the Odéon by Peyre and de Wailly.

On Parisian theatres in general see L. H. Lecomte, *Histoire des théâtres de Paris*, 10 vols., 1905–12, and of course E. Povoledo in *Enc. spett.*, VII (*Parigi*).

82. Many illustrations in G.-P.-M. Dumont, *Parallèle de plans des plus belles salles de spectacles d'Italie et de France*, Paris c. 1764 (reprint New York 1968).

83. It was on the right-hand side of the Palais Royal and not, like Louis' theatre, on the left. See also below, n. 90.

84. L.-N. [Victor] Louis, *Salle de spectacle de Bordeaux*, Paris 1782; J. d'Welles, *Le Grand Théâtre de Bordeaux*, Paris 1949. For the motif of the portico without a pediment see below, n. 114.

85. J. de Filippi and C. Contant, *Parallèle des principaux théâtres modernes de l'Europe*, 2 vols., Paris 1860.

86. Steinhauser and Rabreau, op. cit.

87. Steinhauser and Rabreau, op. cit., reached me too late for me to incorporate the following points of interest. The truncated circle plan occurs also in 1760 in Antoine's design for the Comédie Française (their fig. 65), in 1767 in J.-F. de Neufforge's *Recueil élémentaire d'architecture* (fig. 66), in 1769 in Damun's plan for the Comédie Française on its old site (p. 35 and fig. 60), and in 1772 in Damun's unpublished *Prospectus d'un nouveau théâtre tracé sur les principes des Grecs et des Romains* (p. 35). Neufforge has also a plan with a semicircular façade (fig. 62).

Damun was Contrôleur des Travaux of the City of Paris. M. Rabreau also attributes to him a plan of 1759 for the Comédie Française on the site of the Hôtel de Soissons (fig. 5). Damun is discussed in L. Hautecoeur, *Histoire de l'architecture classique en France*, IV, Paris 1952, 439, where there is also much else on eighteenth-century theatres: pp. 430–54.

78 88. On the intricate moves of the Comédie Française see C. Alasseur, *La Comédie française au XVIIIe siècle*, Paris 1967, and J. Lough, *Paris Theatre Audiences in the seventeenth and eighteenth centuries*, 2nd ed., Oxford 1965.

89. Rabreau, op. cit.

90. Though Hautecoeur, op. cit., IV, 1952, 449, says that Moreau-Desproux's Opéra had an iron roof as well. Louis used a method of construction invented by Ango in 1782. In England – leaving for a later chapter the use of iron in industrial building (p. 277) – Thomas Hardwick used iron for the roof of Inigo Jones's St Paul's, Covent Garden, when he reconstructed the church in 1795–98. Another early use of iron was recently brought to light by John Harris: Richard Payne Knight, the amateur of architecture and collector of antiquities, bought No. 3

Soho Square, London, in 1808 and installed a library vaulted with three domes. The domes were of iron. (See J. Harris, 'C. R. Cockerell's Ichnographia Domestica', *Arch. Hist.*, XIV, 1971, 20 and fig. 15 b.) Foulston used iron construction in the Theatre Royal at Plymouth in 1811–19. In Germany Ludwig Catel as early as 1803 suggested an iron roof for the future Berlin National Theatre (see my *Pioneers of Modern Design*, Harmondsworth ed. of 1960, 118–19), and in 1825 Heinrich Hübsch published a book called *Entwurf zu einem Theater mit eiserner Dachrüstung*.

79 91. All the following is based on F. B. Biermann, *Die Pläne für Reform des Theaterbaues*, Berlin 1928, an excellent book, and as far as was still possible on Steinhauser and Rabreau, op. cit. Hautecoeur, op. cit., 436, draws attention to the fact that as early as 1733 Count Giovanni Montanari published a *Discourse* on the Teatro Olimpico.

92. L. Hautecoeur, *Le Louvre et les Tuileries de Louis XIV*, Paris 1927, 109 and pl. 16.

93. There were in fact to be two theatres at Schleissheim, a small one on the ground floor with a gallery instead of boxes, and the opera on the *piano nobile* with boxes. The shape was a lengthened U. (See M. Hauttmann, 'Die Entwürfe Robert de Cottes für Schloss Schleissheim', *Münchner Jb. d. Bild. Kunst*, VI, 1911, 256–76.)

94. Quoted here from the translation and edition by R. Northcott, London 1917, especially pp. 43 ff. On Algarotti see A. Gabrielli in *Critica d'arte*, III, 1939 and in *Essays in Honour of Hans Tietze*, New York 1958, 309 ff. Also F. Haskell, *Patrons and Painters*, London 1963, chap. XIV.

95. But he also praises Tomaso Temanza and Count Girolamo del Pozzo, both as admirers of Palladio. On del Pozzo see below, n. 97.

96. 'Projet d'une salle de spectacle par N. M. Potain', *BSHAF*, 1924, 30, and *L'Architecture*, 10 February 1924.

80 97. Count Girolamo del Pozzo's *Sui teatri degli antichi e su l'idea d'un teatro adatto all'uso moderno* of 1768 is mentioned by Hautecoeur (*Architecture classique*, op. cit., 436), but I have not seen it.

98. By Mlle Monique Mosser: Steinhauser and Rabreau, op. cit., 9 (n. 3), 36 and fig. 65. The design was formerly attributed to Soufflot.

99. I am quoting from the 3rd ed., Venice 1773. The first came out in Rome and is rare.

100. ibid., 83 ff.

101. *Cours d'architecture ou traité de la décoration, distribution et construction des bâtiments*, II, Paris 1771, 263–70. On Blondel see R. Middleton, 'J.-F. Blondel and the *Cours d'architecture*', *JSAH*, XVIII, 1959.

81 102. p. 336.

103. *Monuments érigés en France à la gloire de Louis XV*, Paris 1764–71.

104. *Mémoires de la construction de la coupole projettée pout couronner la nouvelle église de Sainte Geneviève à Paris*, Paris 1770.

105. In this context it may also be recorded that in Diderot and d'Alembert's *Encyclopédie*, op. cit., the following theatres are illustrated: Turin, Lyons, Argen-

tina in Rome, Tor di Nona in Rome, S. Carlo in Naples, d'Orbay's Comédie Française, Parma, Tuileries, Montpellier, Metz, Moreau-Desproux's Opéra, La Guépière's Stuttgart and some projects by Dumont. A number of the plates are the same as those in Dumont's *Parallèle*, op. cit. (above, n. 82), and therefore share their occasional inaccuracy. This is particularly true of the Italian theatres. (Dumont's inaccuracy was pointed out to me by Mr Edward Craig.) Stage machinery is illustrated in the *Encyclopédie* in far greater detail and with far more accuracy.

106. J. M. Pérouse de Montclos, *Etienne-Louis Boullée, 1728–1799. De l'architecture classique à l'architecture révolutionnaire*, Paris 1969 (English translation 1974), 149 ff., also 127.

107. Bélanger, incidentally, took this up. In 1781 (probably) he designed a theatre with a semicircular front. See Pérouse de Montclos, op. cit., 151. A circular Odeum, i.e. concert hall, by L.-P. Baltard was published in 1811 (see H. Rosenau, *Social Purpose in Architecture*, London 1970, 35).

108. T. Hamlin, *Benjamin Henry Latrobe*, New York 1955, 86–87, 117–20 and pls. IX and X.

82 109. J.-N.-L. Durand, *Précis*, II, Paris 1809, pl. 16.

110. ibid., 63.

111. This was delivered in 1811 and published in 1814. See P. Frankl, *The Gothic*, Princeton 1960, 499 ff., and my *Some Architectural Writers of the Nineteenth Century*, Oxford 1972, 21.

112. Two English early nineteenth-century theatres must at least be granted the hospitality of a footnote. One is Foulston's at Plymouth, of 1811–19, combined like Latrobe's with a hotel, and published in his *The Public Buildings erected in the West of England . . .*, 1838. The other is Benjamin Wyatt's new Drury Lane of 1811–12 – see his *Observations on the Principles of Design for the Theatre Royal, Drury Lane . . .*, London 1813. In 1809 Samuel Ware published *Remarks on Theatres and on the Propriety of vaulting them with Brick and Stone*. He was interested in medieval vaults as well.

113. M. Raval and J.-C. Moreux, *Claude-Nicolas Ledoux*, Paris 1945, and H. Leclerc, 'Au Théâtre de Besançon', *Revue de l'histoire du théâtre*, 1958, no. 2. Dr Monika Steinhauser told me about this paper.

114. Cf. e.g. Potain's theatre design of 1763 (pp. 79–80), the Hôtel de Hallwyl by Ledoux of 1766, the Monnaie by Antoine begun in 1768, the Hôtel de Brunoy by Boullée of 1774–79, and the Hôtel de Salm by Rousseau of 1782–86. Also at least one foreign example: the cathedral of Vác in Hungary, by Isidore Canevale, 1767–72.

115. *L'Architecture considérée sous le rapport de l'art . . .*, I, Paris 1804, 3. However, Ledoux did not wholly condemn boxes. On this, see his controversy with Poyet (on whom see below, p. 151): Steinhauser and Rabreau, op. cit. (above, n. 81), 37.

116. N. G. Wollin, *Desprez en Italie*, Malmö 1935, and *Desprez en Suède*, Stockholm 1939.

83 117. Wollin, *Desprez en Suède*, op. cit., 114–16.

118. For Gilly's sketch of the interior of

the Odeon before the fire, see A. Oncken, *Friedrich Gilly*, Berlin 1935, pl. 41.

119. *Sammlung architektonischer Entwürfe von Schinkel*, ed. Schinkel and Berger, pt. II, Berlin 1826.

120. Biermann, op. cit., 29 ff. and 47.

84 121. *Aus Schinkels Nachlass*, ed. A. Freiherr von Wolzogen, Berlin 1862–64, III, 172. The remark is of 15 January 1810.

122. Leacroft, op. cit. (above, n. 43), 173 and 225.

123. H. G. Sperlich, *Georg Moller*, Darmstadt 1959.

124. M. Semper, *Gottfried Semper*, Berlin 1880, and an extensive literature including G. Semper, *Das Hoftheater in Dresden*, Brunswick 1849.

125. Ill. D. and M. Petzet, *Die Richard Wagner-Bühne König Ludwig II*, Munich 1970, fig. 735.

126. M. Steinhauser, *Die Architektur der Pariser Oper*, Munich 1969 – an exemplary monograph. Specially interesting is the chapter on the iconography of the building. Dr Steinhauser also discusses and illustrates the competition designs by E. M. Barry of London and by Viollet-le-Duc. In figs. 80–111 she shows other competition designs, and it is a telling fact that so many of them have the semicircular front of Mainz and Dresden, as does one by Horeau of 1843–45 (figs. 174–75). On Horeau see below, pp. 245, 246.

127. ibid., 104.

128. *Paris herself again*, London 1878, 77.

129. Steinhauser, op. cit., 133.

86 130. ibid., 168.

131. *Le Moniteur*, 13 May 1863.

132. For the following see M. Semper's volume of the *Handbuch der Architektur*, op. cit., and by the same *Das Münchner Festspielhaus, Gottfried Semper und Richard Wagner*, Hamburg 1906. A recent brief summary by H. Habel is on pp. 298–315 of Petzet, op. cit. See also Dr Hoffmann's contribution to the symposium, *Die deutsche Stadt im neunzehnten Jahrhundert*, Munich (Fritz Thyssen Stiftung) 1972.

133. Petzet, op. cit., figs. 761–65.

134. ibid., 311. The Sydenham theatre was to be a reconstruction of an 'antique theatre'. Semper was actively interested in the history of the theatre. In 1836 he helped Ludwig Tieck on a reconstruction of a Shakespearean theatre. See S. Tidworth, *Theatres*, London 1973, 154–55.

87 135. On these successors see Habel in Petzet, op. cit.

136. e.g. Stuttgart: see M. Littmann, *Das Königliche Hoftheater in Stuttgart*, Darmstadt 1912.

137. Appia first made his ideas known in 1895 (*La Mise-en-scène du drame wagnérien*) and 1899 (*Die Musik und die Inszenierung*) and could first demonstrate them in a private theatre in Paris in 1903. Hermann Graf Keyserling, the philosopher, reported on the event. Among those who were impressed were Mahler, Max Reinhardt and Jacques Dalcroze of Hellerau, where Appia was allowed to experiment in the theatre just then. The Hellerau theatre was built in 1911–12 by Heinrich Tessenow. Gordon Craig was ten years younger than Appia but had moved from actor to designer already in 1897. The two journals he brought out are *The Page*

(1898–1901) and *The Mask* (1908–29); the book that made him known, *The Art of the Theatre*, was published in 1905 with a preface by Graf Kessler. Craig's theories and realizations were developed independently of Appia. In connection with Appia and Craig see M. Krüger, *Über Bühne und bildende Kunst*, Munich 1912. The book also gives its due to the *Stilbühne* by Peter Behrens, the famous architect. This was discussed by K. E. Osthaus in *Westfälisches Kunstblatt*, 1909, and in *Kunstgewerbeblatt*, December 1910 and February 1911. See also P. Behrens, *Feste des Lebens und der Kunst*, 1900–1901, and Jutta Boehe, *Jugendstil im Theater (Die Darmstädter Künstlerkolonie und Peter Behrens)*, Vienna University, Institut für Theaterwissenschaft, 1969, though I have not see the latter.

138. Two examples of many are the Schauspielhaus in Dresden, 1911–12 by Lossow & Kühne, with two deep amphitheatrical galleries, and the theatre at Turin, rebuilt by Morbelli & Morozzi after a fire in 1936, also with two deep galleries, though with boxes lower down as well.

139. For van de Velde's version see his *Geschichte meines Lebens*, ed. H. Curjel, Munich 1962, 328–35. According to this, the idea to use reinforced concrete instead of steel had been van de Velde's.

88 140. Quoted from S. Giedion, *Walter Gropius, Work and Teamwork*, London 1954. For more detail H. W. Wingler, *Das Bauhaus*, Brunswick 1962 (English translation Cambridge, Mass. 1969); also Gropius himself in *Apollo in the Democracy*, New York 1968, 152–63. *Die Bühne im Bauhaus*, Munich 1925, deals with the stage rather than the auditorium. In 1930 Gropius designed a theatre on the same principles for Kharkov (Wingler, op. cit.). Gropius's *Total-Theater* had incidentally been preceded by the *Projektionstheater* in revolutionary Russia (R. Fülöp-Miller and J. Gregor, *The Russian Theatre*, London, Bombay and Sydney 1930, 71; German translation 1927).

141. On experimental theatres in the United States see R. Leacroft in *JRIBA*, LXX, 1963, 145 ff. and 195 ff. Also I. Joseph, *Theatre in the Round*, London 1967. After 1970 are the theatres of Tufts University, Mass., by Hugh Hardy and Earl Flensburgh, and Evry near Paris. Dr Hoffmann, op. cit., draws attention to pioneer cases of theatre-in-the-round: the Politeama in Florence in 1861 and a performance in the round of *Measure for Measure* in the Cirque d'Eté in Paris in 1898.

142. *Teatro Municipal General San Martín*, Buenos Aires 1959.

143. *Time*, 31 May 1971.

144. H. Schliepmann, *Lichtspieltheater*, Berlin 1914; A. S. Meloy, *Theatres and Motion Picture Houses*, New York 1916; P. Zucker, *Theater und Lichtspielhäuser*, Berlin 1926, 128 ff. (this illustrates four German cinemas of 1912); P. M. Shand, *Modern Theatres and Cinemas*, London 1930; P. Bode, *Kinos*, Munich 1957; D. Sharp, *The Picture Palace*, London 1969.

145. This was built for *Follies* and became a cinema only later. For lush cinemas of the twenties see also W. Hawkins Ferry,

The Buildings of Detroit, Detroit 1968, 323 ff. – one of 'rococo elaborateness', one reminiscent of 'prehistoric Central America'.

7 Libraries

BIBLIOGRAPHY

The literature on libraries is immense, or at least at a first glance seems immense. But that is due to an ambiguity. You speak of the Library of Congress, but you also say: 'I have not got a single book on horses in my library.' So a library can mean a building to house books, but it can also mean, and usually does, an accumulation of books however they are housed. This chapter as all the others of this book deals with the buildings; the overwhelming majority of library literature deals with the books. Few books are devoted to the buildings, in all the others one has to pick out the pages or chapters on the buildings. With this proviso, here is a summary of useful books.

Handbooks

The best are German. F. Milkau and G. Leyh, *Handbuch der Bibliothekswissenschaft*, 2nd ed., Wiesbaden 1952 et seq. For us is the part of vol. II (1961) called 'Das Haus und seine Einrichtung', by G. Leyh, 843 ff., and also the whole of vol. III (1955–57), 'Geschichte der Bibliotheken', for many occasional references to buildings – K. Löffler and J. Kirchner, *Lexikon des gesamten Buchwesens*, 3 vols., Leipzig 1935–37, and more recent, J. Kirchner, *Lexikon des Buchwesens*, 4 vols., Stuttgart 1952–56. Two of the volumes are a *Bilderatlas*, and of them vol. II (1956) has illustrations of buildings on pp. 516 ff. – V. Gardthausen, *Handbuch der wissenschaftlichen Bibliothekskunde*, 2 vols., Leipzig 1920. Mostly lists of literature. – J. Vorstius, *Grundzüge der Bibliotheksgeschichte*, Leipzig 1935. Very brief, almost telegraphese, but excellent. – The *Enciclopedia Italiana*, VI, Rome and Milan 1930, 942 ff., can also be recommended.

History

The best book is again German: A. Hessel, *Geschichte der Bibliotheken*, Göttingen 1925. Old but still indispensable two English books: J. W. Clark, *The Care of Books*, Cambridge 1901, and even E. Edwards, *Memoirs of Libraries*, 2 vols., London 1859. More recent J. Müller, 'Bibliothek', in *Reallexikon zur deutschen Kunstgeschichte*, II, Stuttgart and Waldsee 1948, and E. Mehl, *Deutsche Bibliotheksgeschichte* (*Deutsche Philologie im Aufriss*, ed. W. Stammler), Berlin etc. 1951.

Buildings

There is, as has already been said, disappointingly little. I have published a brief summary in *Arch. Rev.*, CXXX, 1961, 241 ff., and have used for the present book A. Thompson, *Library Buildings of Britain and Europe*, London 1963. This is mostly about the twentieth century, but the historical survey is good. A. Masson, *Le Décor des bibliothèques du moyen-âge à la révolution*, Geneva 1972, reached me too late for me to profit from it. It is particularly useful for France in the Middle

Ages. R. Willis and J. W. Clark, *The Architectural History of the University of Cambridge*, III, Cambridge 1886, 387–471, treats both Cambridge and Oxford and other places as well. W. Schürmeyer, *Bibliotheksräume aus fünf Jahrhunderten*, Frankfurt 1929, is mostly illustrations. E. Lehmann: see 'Middle Ages' below. G. Adriani: see 'Baroque' below. The part of the *Handbuch der Architektur* devoted to libraries, by A. Kortüm and E. Schmitt (Teil IV, Halbband 6, Heft 4, Darmstadt 1893) has only three or four pages of history; the rest is about nineteenth-century buildings, i.e. buildings still topical in 1893.

Antiquity

Pauly's *Real-Enzyklopädie der klassischen Altertumswissenschaft*, ed. G. Wissowa, Halbband V, Stuttgart 1897, col. 406–24 by K. Dziatzko. – J. W. Thompson, *Ancient Libraries*, Berkeley 1940. – L. Crema, *L'architettura romana* (*Enciclopedia classica*, sect. III, vol. XII, pt. 1) 1959, 367ff.

Middle Ages

J. W. Thompson, *The Medieval Library*, 2nd ed., Chicago 1957. Quite bulky but with little on the buildings and totally unillustrated. – F. Wormald, 'The Monastic Library', in *The English Library before 1700*, ed. F. Wormald and C. E. Wright, London 1958. Not at all bulky: concentrated nourishment. – T. Gottlieb, *Über mittelalterliche Bibliotheken*, Leipzig 1890. – K. O. Meinsma, *Middeleeuwsche Bibliotheken*, Amsterdam 1902. Not used by me. – J. de Ghellinck, *Les Bibliothèques médiévales*, Paris 1939. Not used by me either. – A. Masson: see 'Buildings' above. – W. Wattenbach, *Das Schriftwesen im Mittelalter*, 3rd ed., Leipzig 1896. First published in 1871; a classic. – C. Löffler, *Deutsche Klosterbibliotheken*, 2nd ed., Bonn and Leipzig 1922. – E. Lehmann, *Die Bibliotheksräume der deutschen Klöster im Mittelalter*, Berlin 1957. – E. A. Savage, *Old English Libraries*, London 1911. – B. H. Streeter, *The Chained Library*, London 1931. – A. N. L. Munby, *Cambridge College Libraries*, Cambridge 1960. – P. Morgan, *Oxford Libraries outside the Bodleian*, Oxford 1973. – A. Franklin, *Les anciennes bibliothèques de Paris*, 3 vols., Paris 1866 et seq. (part of the *Histoire générale de Paris*).

Italian Renaissance

J. F. O'Gorman, *The Architecture of the Monastic Libraries in Italy, 1300–1600*, New York 1972.

Baroque

G. Adriani, *Die Klosterbibliotheken des Spätbarock in Österreich und Süddeutschland*, Graz, Leipzig and Vienna 1935. Reviewed by H. Keller in *Zs. f. Kunstgesch.*, N.F. VII, 329 ff. Also, outstandingly illustrated, M. Baur-Heinhold, *Schöne alte Bibliotheken*, Munich 1972. I was unable to make use of O. Feger, *Geist und Glanz oberschwäbischer Bibliotheken*, Biberach a. d. Reis n. d. (recent).

Twentieth century

P. J. Turner, *Library Buildings, their Planning and Equipment*, Montreal 1929.

Bibliotheksbauten in der Bundesrepublik Deutschland, ed. G. Liebers, Frankfurt 1968.

NOTES

p.91 1. *Rombergs Zeitschrift für praktische Baukunst*, 1852, cols. 79ff. and pls. VIII–X.
2. On the *Codex Amiatinus* see R. L. S. Bruce-Mitford, 'The Art of the Codex Amiatinus', *Journal of the British Archaeological Association*, 3rd ser., XXXII, 1969, 1–25.
3. J. W. Thompson, *The Medieval Library*, 2nd ed., Chicago 1957, 64, 246.
4. E. Mehl, *Deutsche Bibliotheksgeschichte* (*Deutsche Philologie im Aufriss*, ed. W. Stammler), Berlin etc. 1951.
5. Quoted from A. Hessel, *Geschichte der Bibliotheken*, Göttingen 1925, 18 and 28.
92 6. Thompson, op. cit., 174–75.
7. G. Becker, *Catalogi bibliothecarum antiqui*, Bonn 1885.
8. ibid., 130.
9. ibid.
10. ibid., 373.
11. E. Lehmann, *Die Bibliotheksräume der deutschen Klöster im Mittelalter*, Berlin 1957, 15. But Mehl, op. cit., 321, says that the Munich State Library still possesses about 1,000 volumes from St Emmeram.
12. J. Vorstius, *Grundzüge der Bibliotheksgeschichte*, Leipzig 1935, 10. Charles V of France incidentally had 973 volumes at the same time (ibid., 10).
13. ibid., 13.
14. ibid., 14.
15. J. C. T. Oates, 'The Libraries of Cambridge 1570–1700', in *The English Library before 1700*, ed. F. Wormald and C. E. Wright, London 1958. Also R. Willis and J. W. Clark, *The Architectural History of the University of Cambridge*, III, Cambridge 1886, 402–03.
16. C. Sayle, *Annals of the University Library*, Cambridge 1916, 91.
17. This figure was cited by Mr Graham Pollard.
18. N. R. Ker, 'Oxford College Libraries in the sixteenth Century' (Sanders Lectures, 1955), *Bodleian Library Record*, VI, 1959, 471.
19. D. Knowles, *The Monastic Orders in England, 940–1216*, Cambridge 1939, 2nd ed. 1963, 522–27, and *The Religious Orders in England*, II, Cambridge 1961, 331–53.
20. Thus e.g. in the Cistercian *Consuetudines*: see M. Aubert, *L'Architecture cistercienne en France*, 2 vols., Paris 1947, II, 39. The English term could be 'almery' (F. Wormald, 'The Monastic Library', in *The English Library*, op. cit., 18).
21. About 1170; Vorstius, op. cit., 7.
22. Wormald, op. cit., 16–17.
23. ibid., 18–19.
24. Aubert, op. cit., II, 22–44.
25. Notre Dame, Paris (W. Wattenbach, *Das Schriftwesen im Mittelalter*, 3rd ed., Leipzig 1896, 619); Seville Cathedral (ibid., 620); Tegernsee (Hessel, op. cit., 32). Professor Lehmann (op. cit.) also describes as a German speciality libraries above the Lady Chapel, which was east of the chapter house. This was so e.g. at Hirsau. At Hirsau incidentally some Late Gothic bookcases are preserved. At Maulbronn (c. 1520) books were kept above the north transept.
26. Meaux in the East Riding had in the armarium four psalters and 320 volumes in alphabetical order. See W. H. St John Hope, *Fountains Abbey*, Leeds 1900, 74.
27. Wormald, op. cit., 18.
28. Aubert, op. cit., II, 22 and 44.
93 29. See the letter of c. 1232 to the University of Bologna accompanying a gift of translations of Aristotle. The operative passage is 'librorum volumina armarium locupletant' (F. Milkau and G. Leyh, *Handbuch der Bibliothekswissenschaft*, 2nd ed., III, Wiesbaden 1955–57, 459).
30. Hessel, op. cit., 39.
31. J. F. O'Gorman (*The Architecture of the Monastic Libraries in Italy, 1300–1600*, New York 1972) quotes K. W. Humphreys, *The Book-Provisions of the medieval Friars, 1215–1400*, Amsterdam 1964, a book I have not used.
32. Pollard, op. cit.
33. Lehmann, op. cit., 8; Wattenbach, op. cit., 607.
34. Professor Lehmann (op. cit., 7) has pointed out that no lecterns are mentioned for St Victor in Paris about 1120–30, nor by Humbert de Romans about 1255–60.
35. Lehmann, op. cit., 15.
36. *Journal du voyage en Italie*, ed. M. Rat, Paris 1942, 113: a large number of books attached to 'plusieurs rangs de pupitres'.
37. A very good illustration is in R. Hootz, *Die Niederlande*, Munich 1971, 347.
38. Willis and Clark, op. cit., 429 ff.: Peterhouse 1574, Pembroke 1617, Caius 1620.
39. P. Morgan, *Oxford Libraries outside the Bodleian*, Oxford 1973.
40. Lehmann, op. cit., 15.
41. E. Edwards, *Memoirs of Libraries*, II, London 1859, 669. As a Franciscan achievement the *Registrum librorum Angliae*, the cumulative catalogue of the holdings of 160 houses, deserves a line.
42. J. W. Clark, *The Care of Books*, Cambridge 1901, 117–21.
94 43. E. Craster, *The History of All Souls College Library*, London 1971.
44. M. R. James, *The Ancient Libraries of Canterbury and Dover*, Cambridge 1903.
45. O'Gorman, op. cit.
46. Hessel, op. cit., 51.
95 47. P. Rotondi, *Il Palazzo Ducale di Urbino*, 2 vols., Urbino 1950–51, I, 383 ff. The paintings of kneeling patrons and seated female figures of the Liberal Arts (of which two are in the National Gallery in London and two were formerly in Berlin) are now thought by some to have come not from the library at Urbino but from Federigo's Studiolo at Gubbio: see Cecil H. Clough, 'Federigo da Montefeltro's Private Study in his ducal palace at Gubbio', *Apollo*, LXXXVI, 1967, 278–87.
48. Hessel, op. cit., 54.
49. See most recently J. S. Ackerman, *The Architecture of Michelangelo*, 2 vols., London 1952.
50. Scamozzi did the south half and, in 1591–93, the ante-room to the library proper for the display of 'anticaglie'. F. Barbieri, *Vincenzo Scamozzi*, Verona and Vicenza 1956, 127 ff. and 140.
51. For the plan see most recently M. Tafuri, *Jacopo Sansovino e l'architettura del '500 a Venezia*, Padua 1969, 47.
52. A. de Hevesy, *La Bibliothèque du roi*

Matthias Corvin, Paris 1923. Also C. Csapodi, *Corvinian Library: History and Stock*, Budapest 1973 (not used by me).

53. Hessel, op. cit., 64.

96 54. J. N. L. Myres, 'Oxford Libraries in the Seventeenth and Eighteenth centuries', in *The English Library*, op. cit., 236 ff. Also Ker, op. cit., 459 ff.

55. B. H. Streeter (*The Chained Library*, London 1931) was wrong in dating the Magdalen fitments c.1480, and the usual date for the Hereford Cathedral Library fitments is wrong too.

56. D. Guttierez, 'La Biblioteca Agostiniana di Cremona', *Analecta Augustiniana*, XXIV, 1961, 313 ff. Quoted from O'Gorman, op. cit.

57. Later still and yet not of the wall-system is Joseph Furttenbach's design for a library in his *Architectura recreationis*, Augsburg 1640, 57 and pl. 18.

58. E. Müntz and P. Fabre, *La Bibliothèque du Vatican au XVe siècle*, Paris 1887. I. Cavini, *La Biblioteca Vaticana*, Rome 1892.

59. A. Paredi, *Storia dell'Ambrosiana*, Milan 1967.

97 60. P. le Gallois in his *Traité des plus belles bibliothèques de l'Europe* published in 1680 writes of the Ambrosiana: 'elle est publique, c'est-à-dire on y peut aller étudier certains jours de la semaine' (p. 99). Lady Mary Wortley Montagu confirmed this in a letter of 25 September 1739 (Everyman ed., 274): 'All strangers have free access.'

61. Milkau and Leyh, op. cit. (above, n. 29), 1st ed., I, 1931, 805 ff. and 2nd ed., I, 1952, 1000–05.

62. Hessel, op. cit., 67.

63. ibid., 81. The instrument was the Licensing Act which was replaced in 1709 by the Copyright Act.

64. ibid., 86.

65. P. Portoghesi, *Borromini nella cultura europea*, Rome 1964, 81 and 160; and of course other Borromini literature.

66. E. Coudenhove-Erthal, *Carlo Fontana*, Vienna 1930, 81.

67. For the Angelica see A. Giorgetti Vichi, *Alma Roma*, IX, 1968. For the Alexandrina see C. Ferrari and F. Pintor, *La Biblioteca Universitaria Alexandrina*, Rome 1960. For the Vallicelliana see E. Pinto in *Miscellanea della Reale società di Storia patria*, Rome 1932. For the Casanatense see L. de Gregori in *Accademie e Biblioteche d'Italia*, II, 1928–29. For the Alexandrina I have to thank the Director for information, and for the Angelica Dr Marta Frizzeri.

68. Whose *Advis pour dresser une bibliothèque* of 1627 is a classic.

69. A. Franklin, *Histoire de la Bibliothèque Mazarine*, 2nd ed., Paris 1901.

70. A case of converting stables into a library existed in Germany. The Duke of Braunschweig-Lüneburg put his books into the *Marstall* at Wolfenbüttel in 1649. See H. Reuther, 'Das Gebäude der Herzog August Bibliothek zu Wolfenbüttel', in *Leibniz, sein Leben, sein Wirken, seine Welt*, ed. W. Totok and C. Haase, Hanover 1966, 349.

98 71. *Traité*, op. cit., 121 ff.

72. L. C. F. Petit-Radel, *Recherches sur les bibliothèques anciennes et modernes*, Paris 1819, 345 ff.

73. A. Franklin, *Les anciennes bibliothèques de Paris*, I, Paris 1866, 79 ff. The illustration

is also in Edwards, op. cit., II, 672.

74. *The Bodleian Quarterly*, I, 1914–16, 260. Richard Bentley in his *A Proposal to build a Royal Library and establish it by Act of Parliament*, published in 1697, suggests that the library should set itself 200,000 volumes as the target.

75. Hessel, op. cit., 66; *Handbuch der Architektur*, Teil IV, Halbband 6, Heft 4, Darmstadt 1893 (the section on libraries, by A. Kortüm and E. Schmitt), 44.

76. Hessel, op. cit., 87.

77. ibid., 93.

78. J. M. Crook, *The British Museum*, London 1972. Brief but excellent. For more detail see A. Esdaile, *The British Museum Library*, London 1946, 51 ff. Isaac d'Israeli writes that it took a day or even two days to get the volumes you had asked for.

79. *Opera Omnia*, ed. L. Dutens, V, Geneva 1768, 209 ff. My thanks go to Anke Hölzer of the Niedersächsische Landesbibliothek for help in locating this pamphlet.

80. Reuther, op. cit., 356.

99 81. A similar design – an oblong with semicircular ends – in the Grünes Schloss at Weimar was converted into a library in 1760–65.

82. Reuther, op. cit., 349–60. Also O. von Heinemann, *Die herzogliche Bibliothek zu Wolfenbüttel*, Wolfenbüttel, 2nd ed. 1894. The corner areas outside the oval were stack rooms. They are called *repositorium* in 1782 (p. 344). On Wolfenbüttel see also above, n. 70.

83. Wren Society, V, 1928, 32 ff. and pls. 18–21. Also S. Lang, 'By Hawksmoor out of Gibbs', *Arch. Rev.*, CV, 1949, 183 ff.

84. W. Buchowiecki, 'Der Barockbau der ehemaligen Hofbibliothek in Wien', *Museion*, N.F. I, 1957, 46 ff. and 140 ff.

85. G. Adriani, *Die Klosterbibliotheken des Spätbarock in Österreich und Süddeutschland*, Graz, Leipzig and Vienna 1935.

86. *Italy, with Sketches of Spain and Portugal*, Paris 1834, 229.

100 87. Ill. J.-N.-L. Durand, *Recueil*, Paris 1801, pl. 18.

88. E. Gutmann, *Zeitschrift für Geschichte der Architektur*, Beiheft V, 1911, 74–75. Twenty years later Francesco Milizia, whom we have met in the history of theatre building (p. 80), recommended in his *Principi di architettura civile* (1781 – I quote from the 2nd ed., Bassano 1785, II, 268) that the ground floor of a detached library should be 'magazzini per libri'. The library itself, he writes, can be round ('una gran rotunda'), with cases between detached columns.

89. P. Gaskell and R. Robson, *The Library of Trinity College, Cambridge*, Cambridge 1971.

102 90. Cole, Horace Walpole's friend, the Cambridge antiquary, called the wall-system still 'à la moderne' in 1742 à propos the Fellows' Library of Clare College. I am quoting from Willis and Clark, op. cit., 453.

91. Myres, op. cit. (above, n. 54).

92. Lang, op. cit.

93. J.-M. Pérouse de Montclos, *Etienne-Louis Boullée 1728–1799. De l'architecture classique à l'architecture révolutionnaire*, Paris 1969, 165 ff. (English translation 1974, not used by me). Also still H. Rosenau,

Boullée's Treatise on Architecture, London 1953.

103 94. The premises of the Bibliothèque Nationale were and are a maze (see L. Hautecoeur, *Histoire de l'architecture classique en France*, II, pt. 2, Paris 1948, 48–51). Joseph Gwilt in 1842 (*Encyclopaedia of Architecture*, London 1842, 793) called it 'little more than a warehouse for holding the books'. Largely the area and to a limited extent the premises are those of the Palais Mazarin. At the southeast end it included the Hôtel Tuboeuf and north of it the two-storeyed Galerie Mazarine of 1645, and along the rue de Richelieu further north-west Mazarin's stables and above them his library (see p. 97). The northernmost part of the area became after Mazarin's death the Hôtel de Nevers.

95. In 1787 the Académie d'Architecture in its competition for the Grand Prix voted an emulation prize to the architect J.-B.-L.-F. Lefebure for a library entirely à la Boullée, with an endless front colonnade, a circular reading room or assembly room with a Pantheon dome and long narrow ranges presumably for the books. Grand Prix designs are rarely explicit as to the function of rooms. See H. Rosenau, 'The Engravings of the *Grands Prix* of the French Academy of Architecture', *Arch. Hist.*, III, 1960.

96. J.-N.-L. Durand, *Précis*, II, Paris 1809, 54 and pl. 10.

97. Milkau and Leyh, op. cit. (above, n. 29), II, 1961, 877.

98. W. B. O'Neal, *Jefferson's Buildings at the University of Virginia. The Rotunda*, Charlottesville 1960. Also F. D. Nichols, *Thomas Jefferson's Architectural Drawings*, Boston and Charlottesville 1961, 8 ff. At the time of writing, the original arrangement is being restored.

104 99. It has cast-iron girders.

100. Ill. P. J. Turner, *Library Buildings, their Planning and Equipment*, Montreal 1929, 15.

101. *Handbuch der Architektur*, op. cit., 59; Hautecoeur, op. cit., VII, 1957, 140–42.

102. Two more examples of American prodigality benefiting libraries: Walter L. Newberry of Chicago (d. 1868) left $ 2,500,000 for the Newberry Library, and John Crerar of Chicago (d. 1889) $ 3,400,000 for the Crerar Library.

103. E. Edwards, *Free Town Libraries*, London 1869; T. Greenwood, *Free Public Libraries*, London 1886; W. I. Fletcher, *Public Libraries in America*, Boston 1894; H. B. Adams, *Public Libraries and popular Education*, Albany 1900; W. S. Learned, *The American Public Library*, New York 1924; A. E. Bostwick, *The American Public Library*, 4th ed., New York 1929; J. L. Wheeler and A. M. Gibbens, *The American Public Library Buildings*, New York 1941.

104. T. W. Koch, *A Book of Carnegie Libraries*, New York 1917. Koch gives the following figures. Up to 1907 Carnegie had given 1,636 libraries, 1,014 of them in the United States. The total cost of the 1,636 was $45,000,000.

105. Fletcher, op. cit., 12.

106. ibid., 14.

107. Boston, Mass., in the 1880s had

eleven branches, Bradford seven, Bristol five, Birmingham five. The figures come from Greenwood, op. cit., who also tells us that Leeds had twenty-two. Berlin as early as 1850 had four *Volksbibliotheken*, an immediate effect of Friedrich von Raumer's visit to America (Hessel, op. cit., 125).

105 108. Penguin ed. (ed. J. S. Whitley and A. Goldman), Harmondsworth 1972, 181.

109. *Daily Despatch*, 21 December 1905. I have to thank Miss D. N. Pearce, the City Librarian of Salford, for this information.

110. H.-R. Hitchcock, *H. H. Richardson and his Times*, rev. ed., Hamden 1963.

111. Massachusetts is the state richest in small-town libraries. Fletcher, op. cit., i.e. in 1894, counted 212.

106 112. op. cit., 224 ff.

113. W. B. O'Neal, *Jefferson's Fine Art Library*, Charlottesville 1956, 32.

114. Milkau and Leyh, op. cit., II, 879.

115. P. Pesche, 'Die Entwicklung des neueren Bibliotheksbaues', in *Aufsätze Fritz Milkau gewidmet*, Leipzig 1921, 264 ff. Also Milkau and Leyh, op. cit., II, 1961, 878 ff. So Dr J. F. O'Gorman in his *The Architecture of Frank Furness* (exhibition catalogue, Philadelphia Museum of Art, 1973) is in error when he calls the separation of stack room from reading room in the library of the University of Pennsylvania in Philadelphia, built in 1887–91, an innovation (p. 61).

116. *Om offentlige Bibliotheker*, Copenhagen 1829 (in German *Über Bibliothekswissenschaft*, 1833), 19 ff. G. Leyh in 'Das Haus und seine Einrichtung' (Milkau and Leyh, op. cit., II, 1961, 845 ff.) also mentions Zoller with the date 1846 as one who appreciated della Santa.

117. P. O. Rave, *Karl Friedrich Schinkel, Lebenswerk* (the so-called *Schinkelwerk*): *Bauten in Berlin*, III, Berlin 1962, 24–37. Also G. Leigh, 'Schinkels Entwurf für einen Neubau der Königlichen Bibliothek in Berlin', *Zentralblatt für Bibliothekwesen*, XLIX, 1931, 113–19.

107 118. *Rev. gén. de l'arch.*, X, 1852 and XI, 1853. On Labrouste there is now a thesis: R. Plouin, *Henry Labrouste, sa vie, son oeuvre (1801–1875)*, University of Paris 1965 (not used by me).

119. ibid., X, 380.

120. T. Faber, *A History of Danish Architecture*, n.d., 121–28. Also K. Millech and K. Fisker, *Danske Arkitekturstrǿminger, 1850–1950*, Copenhagen 1951, 101–06.

108 121. Marquis L. de Laborde, *De l'organisation des bibliothèques dans Paris*, Paris 1845, Letter VIII: 'De la construction des bibliothèques'. The letter was translated into German and published in *Rombergs Zeitschrift für praktische Baukunst*, op. cit. (above, n. 1). A review with five plates of Laborde's book came out in the *Rev. gén. de l'arch.*, VIII, 1849, 415–37.

122. Not entirely an innovation; for Walter, the architect of the Capitol in Washington, had used iron book-shelving in 1851–53.

123. *Gaz. des arch.*, III, 1865, 107. See also C. Beutler, 'St Eugène und die Bibliothèque Nationale', in *Miscellanea pro Arte* (Schnitzler Festschrift), Düsseldorf 1965, 315–26.

124. *L'Art moderne*, Paris 1883. I quote from 2nd ed., 1902, 242.

125. I owe this information to Dr Robin Middleton. Horeau (see below, pp. 241 ff.) tells us that he designed a library in 1837, but we don't know what it looked like (G. Vapereau, *Dictionnaire universel des contemporains*, 3rd ed., Paris 1865, 902).

126. These figures provided for me by the Library Association must of course be used with a pinch of salt. For instance: are volumes counted or titles? Also the largest of all libraries is said to be the Lenin State Library at Moscow with 25 million volumes. Surely that must mean that they keep a number of copies of the same title. Elmer D. Johnson, *History of Libraries in the Western World*, 2nd ed., Matuchen, N.J. 1970 (mimeographed), 172, makes it 'over 22 million catalogued items'. In fact the book *Libraries in the USSR*, ed. S. Francis, London 1971, says that the Lenin State Library was increased in the last thirty years 'by 14 million copies'.

8 Museums

BIBLIOGRAPHY

Dr H. Seling, *Die Entstehung des Kunstmuseums*, PhD thesis, Freiburg University, 1953, also printed in an abridged form in *Arch. Rev.*, CXLI, 1967, 103 ff. – A. S. Wittlin, *The Museum, its history and its tasks in education*, London 1949, 2nd ed. 1970 (much rearranged and rewritten), 3rd ed. 1974; I had to use the first edition. – *Handbuch der Architektur*, Teil IV, Halbband 6, Heft 4, Darmstadt 1893 (the section on museums, by H. Wagner). – *The Directory of Museums*, ed. K. Hudson and A. Nicholls, London 1975. – M. D. Levin, *Twentieth Century Museum Architecture*, PhD thesis, University of London 1974, came so late too late for me to make use of it. – V. Plagemann, *Das deutsche Kunstmuseum 1790–1870*, Munich 1967. – V. Scherer, *Deutsche Museen*, 1913. – L. Brieger, *Die grossen Kunstsammler*, 1931. – D. and E. Rigby, *Lock, Stock and Barrel*, Philadelphia, New York and London 1944. – F. H. Taylor, *The Taste of Angels*, London 1948.

NOTES

p.111 1. This chapter is really by Dr Helmut Seling as far as p. 126, and only after that by me. Dr Seling delivered a PhD thesis at Freiburg University in 1953, entitled *Die Entstehung des Kunstmuseums*. All I did was to shorten it considerably with a loss of hundreds of details hidden in footnotes and translate it. In this shortened form *The Architectural Review* published it in 1967 (CXLI, 103 ff.). The chapter as it is now presented is much longer than it was there.

2. The most important book on Renaissance art collecting is still J. Burckhardt, *Die Kultur der Renaissance in Italien*, first published in 1860 (and here quoted from the 5th ed., 1896). In addition see J. Burckhardt's 'Die Sammler' in *Nachgelassene Beiträge zur Kunstgeschichte von Italien*, Basel 1898, and M. Wackernagel, *Der Lebensraum des Künstlers in der florentinischen Renaissance*, Leipzig 1938. The various papers of Adolf Michaelis are indispensable for any study of the collecting of Antique statuary.

3. Burckhardt, 'Sammler', op. cit., 331, also J. von Schlosser, *Die Kunstliteratur*, Vienna 1924, 90.

4. Burckhardt, ibid., 331–32, also 203.

5. ibid., 330; E. Müntz, *Les Collections des Médicis*, Paris 1888; and M. L. Gothein, *Geschichte der Gartenkunst*, Jena 1926, I, for the Medici statuary garden.

6. C. Hülsen and H. Egger, *Die römischen Skizzenbücher von Marten van Heemskerck*, Berlin 1913.

7. A. Michaelis, 'La Collezione Capitolina di Antichità', *Mitt. d. Kais. Deutschen Archaeol. Inst.*, VI, 1891, 11 ff. Also H. Siebenhüner, *Das Kapitol in Rome*, Munich 1954.

8. J. S. Ackerman, *The Cortile del Belvedere*, Vatican City 1954, 18 and 32 ff. Ackerman calls it 'the first museum building since antiquity'.

9. For the term *Mouseion* see Pauly-Wissowa, *Real-Enzyklopädie der classischen Altertumswissenschaft*, XXXI, 1933, 797 ff. Also C. Daremberg. E. Saglio and E. Pottier, *Dictionnaire des antiquités grècques et romaines*, III, Paris 1904, 2071 ff. On the Mouseion itself G. F. C. Parthey, *Das alexandrinische Museum*, Berlin 1838.

10. P. O. Rave, 'Das Museo Giovio zu Como', *Miscellanea Bibliothecae Hertzianae*, Munich 1961, 275–84.

11. R. Berliner, 'Zur älteren Geschichte der allgemeinen Museumskunde in Deutschland', *Münchner Jb. d. Bild. Kunst*, N.F. V, 1928, 330. Quichelberg was Fugger librarian from c. 1550 to 1553, became ducal librarian (and ducal physician) in Munich in 1553 and went to Italy in 1563. See B. J. Belsiger, *The Kunst- und Wunderkammern . . . 1565–1750*, unpublished thesis, University of Pittsburgh 1970. Chiefly but by no means entirely a catalogue.

112 12. The statues incidentally were now handed over to restorers, i.e. fragments were less appreciated. For the Vatican see A. Michaelis, 'Geschichte des Statuenhofes im vatikanischen Belvedere', *Jb. d. Kais. Deutschen Archaeol. Inst.*, V, 1890, 5 ff. For Lorenzetto, whom Vasari calls the first restorer, see the *Vite*, ed. G. Milanesi, 9 vols., Florence 1878–85, IV, 579 ff. For the Farnese Collection see Burckhardt, 'Sammler', op. cit., 493–94.

13. P. Gnoli, 'Il Giardino e l'Antiquario del Cardinale Cesi', *Mitt. d. Kais. Deutschen Archaeol. Inst., Röm. Abt.*, XX, 1905, 267 ff.

14. Vasari, op. cit., IX, 480. Also H. Huth, 'Museum and Gallery', *Beiträge für Georg Swarzenski*, Berlin and Chicago 1951, 238 ff.

15. He says that those in charge were 'cortesi . . . a chi vuol vedere'. Quoted from A. S. Wittlin, *The Museum, its history and its tasks in education*, London 1949, 111.

16. W. Prinz, *Die Entstehung der Galerie in Frankreich und Italien*, Berlin 1970.

17. Ducange, *Glossary of Medieval Latin*, 1883–87, quoted from Prinz, op. cit., 7.

18. R. Weiss, 'The Castle of Gaillon in 1509–1510', *Journal of the Warburg and Courtauld Institutes*, XVI, 1953, 7; quoted from Prinz, op. cit., 8.

19. Prinz, op. cit., 8–9.

20. In the edition of 1619, VII, chap. 18, p. 42 and chap. 24, p. 56; quoted from Prinz, op. cit., 10.

21. V. Scamozzi, *Idea*, Venice 1615, pt. I, bk. 2, chap. 18, p. 305; quoted from Prinz, op. cit., 10.

22. Prinz, op. cit., 11.

23. ibid., 26–27.

24. ibid., 49.

25. C. Yriarte, 'Sabbioneta, la petite Athènes', *Gaz. des b.-a.*, 3rd per., XIX, 1893, 1 ff. and 201 ff. Also A. Puerari, *Sabbioneta*, Milan 1955, fig. 55 ff.

26. O. Hartig, 'Die Kunsttätigkeit in München unter Wilhelm IV und Albrecht V', *Münchner Jb. d. Bild. Kunst*, X, 1933, 147 ff.

113 27. By Roger de Piles and Sandrart. Quoted from M. Rooses, *Rubens*, Philadelphia and London 1904, 150–51.

28. Quoted from F. H. Taylor, *The Taste of Angels*, London 1948, 225.

29. Quoted from Wittlin, op. cit., 47.

30. Ill. ibid., pl. XIII, also D. and E. Rigby, *Lock, Stock and Barrel*, Philadelphia, New York and London 1944, 199. See also R. A. Weigert, 'Le Palais Mazarin', *Art de France*, 1962, II, 147 ff., and A. Braham and P. Smith, *François Mansart*, London 1974, I, 70–74 and 223–34.

31. Braham and Smith, op. cit., 129.

32. In *The Builder's Dictionary*, 2 vols., London 1734, there are under the heading 'Disposition of Pictures' thirteen rules as to what should be where. Rule X says: 'Histories, grave Stories and the best Works become Galleries, where any one may walk and exercise their Senses in viewing, examining, delighting, judging and censuring.'
Dr J. Dobai's *Die Kunstliteratur des Klassizismus und der Romantik in England, I: 1700–1750*, Bern 1974, has on p. 375 à propos Sir Henry Wotton some valuable references to galleries as display areas for paintings. See Wotton's *Elements*, 1624, 99; also, even earlier, Ben Jonson, *The Poetaster*, 1602 ('no pictures in the hall nor in the dining room but in the gallery only'); and Zeiller's *Wörterbuch*, 1632. For this and more see H. Huth, 'Museum and Gallery', *Beiträge für Georg Swarzenski*, Berlin and Chicago 1951, 238–45.

33. In the Wadsworth Atheneum at Hartford, Conn. See H. Olsen, 'Et malet Galleri af Pannini', *Kunstmuseets Årsskrift*, 1951. Olsen calls Pannini's a 'free representation' of the gallery.

114 34. A. Fink, 'Die Baumeister von Salzdahlum', *Zeitschrift für Kunstwissenschaft*, IV, 1950, 183–96. Also A. Fink, *Geschichte des Herzog Anton Ulrich-Museums in Braunschweig*, Brunswick 1954; R. Klapheck, *Die Baukunst am Niederrhein II*, for Düsseldorf, where the gallery was a detached building of three ranges; G. Peters, *Das Rastatter Schloss*, Karlsruhe 1925; K. Lohmeyer, *Schönbornschlösser*, Heidelberg 1927; B. Grimschitz, *Johann Lucas von Hildebrandt*, Vienna 1932; H. Kreisel, *Amtlicher Führer der Residenz in München*, Munich 1937; R. Sedlmaier and R. Pfister, *Die fürstbischöfliche Residenz zu Würzburg*, Munich 1923; O. Gerland, *Charles and Simon Louis du Ry*, Stuttgart 1895; F. Walther, *Das Mannheimer Schloss*, Karlsruhe 1922 and *Bauwerke der Kurfürstenzeit in Mannheim*, Augsburg 1928; E. Henschel-Simon, *Die Bildergalerie Friedrichs des Grossen*, Berlin 1930. To such cases others must be added, where an older building was adjusted to take paintings. Such are the Grande Galerie in the Louvre, used for the Academy exhibitions, the

Stallburg in Vienna of 1558 et seq. used for the Imperial Gallery since before 1684, and the Stallhof in Dresden of 1586–88, adapted in 1722–25. *Stall* means stables, and one may remember that Mazarin's long library was above the stables (p. 97), and that at Wolfenbüttel a library was made in 1649 by adapting the stables (p. 97, n. 70).

35. J. von Schlosser, *Die Kunst- und Wunderkammern der Spätrenaissance*, Leipzig 1908; Belsiger, op cit.; Major, *Unvergreiffliches Bedenken von Kunst und Naturalien-Kammern*, 1674, mentioned by Mundt (below, n. 127) but unknown to me.

36. *Der geöffnete Ritterplatz*, Hamburg 1704; anonymous. See Berliner, op. cit. (n. 11), 336.

37. On the first floor are historical exhibits, ethnography, religious monuments, natural history, skeletons, stuffed animals and shells; on the second floor paintings, sculpture, drawings, mathematical and astronomical instruments, models of buildings, machinery, maps and globes.

38. G. Klemm, *Zur Geschichte der Sammlungen für Wissenschaft und Kunst in Deutschland*, Zerbst 1838.

39. V. Fleischer, *Fürst Karl Eusebius von Liechtenstein als Bauherr und Künstler*, Vienna and Leipzig 1910, 197.

40. See C. H. von Heinecken, *Idée générale d'une collection complète d'estampes*, 1771; also M. Stübel, 'Deutsche Galeriewerke und Kataloge des 18. Jahrhunderts', *Monatschrift für Bücherfreunde und Graphiksammler*, I, 1925, 247 ff. and 301 ff.

41. H. Posse, 'Die Briefe des Grafen Francesco Algarotti an den sächsischen Hof', *Jb. d. Preuss. Kunstsamml.* LII, 1931, Beiheft.

42. On the Palais Royal see V. Champier and G. R. Sandoz, *Le Palais Royal*, 2 vols., Paris 1900.

115 43. A. Holtmeyer, *Die Bau- und Kunstdenkmäler im Regierungsbezirk Kassel*, IV, Marburg 1923.

44. G. Rodenwaldt, 'Goethes Besuch im Museum Maffeianum zu Verona', 102nd *Winckelmannsprogramm der Archaeologischen Gesellschaft zu Berlin*, Berlin 1942.

45. C. Justi, *Winckelmann, sein Leben, seine Werke und seine Zeitgenossen*, Leipzig 1866–72; A. Michaelis, 'Storia della collezione capitolina', *Mitt. d. Kais. Deutschen Archaeol. Inst.*, Röm. Abt., VI, 1891, 3 ff.

46. N. Pevsner, *Academies of Art, past and present*, Cambridge 1940.

47. The collection of the King of Naples' excavations of Herculaneum and Pompeii housed in the palace of Portici (1743–47) and the Farnese collections housed inadequately in the palace of Capodimonte were on the other hand far from easily accessible: Justi, op. cit., 173 ff. and 203 ff.

48. Justi, op. cit. There are also eighteen drawings by P.-A. Pâris in the library at Besançon.

49. I have not used J. Gans, *Carlo Marchionni*, Cologne and Graz 1967.
The hemicyclical so-called Coffee-House contains ancient sculpture too, but also landscape paintings. The ante-room to the Coffee-House proper is the Egyptian Cabinet.

50. Winckelmann had in fact in 1756 written a paper called *Von der Wiederher-*

stellung und Ergänzung der Werke der Alten, but never published it. Justi, op. cit., II, 72. On Cavaceppi see Justi, 307.

116 51. Designs are in the Soane Museum in London. See D. Stroud, *George Dance, Architect, 1741–1825*, London 1971, 70–71. The plan is illustrated in G. Teyssot, *Città e utopia nell'illuminismo inglese: George Dance il giovane*, Rome 1974.

52. What Burckhardt called 'die herrliche Doppeltreppe'.

53. G. B. and E. Q. Visconti, *Il Museo Pio-Clementino, illustrato e descritto*, ed. N. Bettoni, Milan 1818. Also a series of engravings by Vincenzo Feoli and a series of watercolours in the Staatliche Museen in Berlin, perhaps by Volpato. Milizia disapproved of the design (as he also disapproved of Marchionni) and praised instead a design made in Rome by Thomas Harrison and especially its central dome 'in guisa del Pantheon'. Harrison was in Rome from 1769 to 1776, designed for Clement XIV, but saw nothing executed. I am quoting from E. Brües, 'Die Schriften des Francesco Milizia', *Jahrbuch für Aesthetik und allgemeine Kunstwissenschaft*, VI, 1961, 69–113. Dr Brüess refers to a paper by L. Pirotta in the *Strenna dei Romanisti*, April 1960, which I have not seen. On Harrison see most recently J. M. Crook in *Country Life*, CIL, 1970, 876 ff., 944 ff., 1038 ff., 1539.

54. G. Sforza, 'Ennio Quirino Visconti e la sua famiglia', *Atti della Società ligure di storia patria*, LI, 1923, 1–234.

117 55. Information kindly supplied by Dr Emma Michelotti. Catalogues were published in 1759, 1779, 1790.

56. *Dichtung und Wahrheit*, pt. II, chap. 8.

57. ibid., pt. III, chap. 11.

58. *Rheinische Thalia*, Heft I, 176–84.

59. P. Böttger, *Die Alte Pinakothek in München*, Munich 1972, 55–56.

60. *Die vornehmsten Merkwürdigkeiten der Residenzstadt München für Liebhaber der bildenden Künste*. See Böttger, op. cit., 117–25.

61. In the *Teutscher Merkur*.

62. A. Stix, *Die Aufstellung der ehedem Kaiserlichen Galerie in Wien im 18. Jahrhundert*, Vienna 1929.

63. J. M. Crook, *The British Museum*, Harmondsworth 1972. Also E. Miller, *A Brief History of the British Museum*, London 1970 (not used by me).

118 64. Grand Prix designs for 1774 to 1795 were published by H. Rosenau in 'The Engravings of the *Grands Prix* of the French Academy of Architecture', *Arch. Hist.*, III, 1960.

65. The archivist of the Ecole des Beaux-Arts kindly pointed out to me the designs by Trouard and Billandel.

119 66. Pérouse de Montclos, op. cit., 163–64.

67. Not in Dr Rosenau's paper (op. cit.).

68. *Nouveau parallèle des ordres de l'architecture.*

120 69. For the Paris collections at the time of the Revolution and the Empire see F. Benoît, *L'Art français dans la Révolution et l'Empire*, Paris 1897; C. Saunier, *Les Conquêtes artistiques de la Révolution et de l'Empire*, Paris 1902; A. Lemaitre, *Le Louvre, monument et musée*, Paris 1878; M.-L. Biver, *Le Paris de Napoléon*, Paris 1963, 297 ff.; and C. Aulanier, *La Grande Galerie*, Paris 1949.

70. Archives Nationales, Paris: Série o'1670, nos. 78–254. Information given by Dr Christiane Aulanier.

71. Benoît, op. cit., 111.

72. ibid., 117.

73. Dr Crook (*British Museum*, op. cit., 63) lists for early labelling the Plater-Museum at Basel, 1663, and the Aldrovandi Museum at Bologna, 1688.

74. Saunier, op. cit., 29 ff.; Lemaitre, op. cit., 281 ff.

75. Saunier, op. cit., 69 ff.

76. P. Lelièvre, *Vivant Denon*, Paris 1940. Also J. Chatelain, *Dominique Vivant Denon et le Louvre de Napoléon*, Paris 1973 (not used by me).

77. Issue for 1 February.

78. Saunier, op. cit., 23; Benoît, op. cit., 133.

121 79. Biver, op. cit., 297.

80. Still!

81. Biver, op. cit.

82. Y. Christ, *Le Louvre et les Tuileries*, Paris 1949, 145 ff., and Aulanier, op. cit. The date of Hubert Robert's design was established as *c.* 1786 in the catalogue of the exhibition *French Painting 1774–1830* shown in Paris, Detroit and New York in 1975 (p. 591 and pl. 79). Robert was made custodian of the paintings of the Royal Museum in 1784. Cochin supports skylighting in a memorandum of 1786. D'Angiviller, Directeur des Bâtiments wants 'elevated openings . . . at the top of the vault'. His statement is later than 1786 but undated. Several versions exist of Robert's scheme for the Grande Galerie, including the sketch in the Louvre, probably the earliest, of *c.* 1786 (in the exhibition), the painting shown at the Salon of 1796 (which I reproduce), and a variant on that painting (ill. Crook, *British Museum*, op. cit., pl. 5).

83. N. de Pigage, *La Galerie électorale de Düsseldorf*, Basel 1778. For Düsseldorf altogether see Klapheck, op. cit. (n. 34).

84. For Vienna see A. Stix, op. cit. (n. 62).

85. *Inventaire des richesses d'art de la France: Archive du Musée des monuments français*, Paris 1883. Also Benoît, op. cit.

122 86. F. Chueca and C. de Miguel, *La vida e las obras del arquitecto Juan de Villanueva*, Madrid 1949, 285 ff., and F. Chueca Goitia, *El Museo del Prado*, Madrid 1952.

87. So London is a less important city.

123 88. A. T. Bolton, *The Works of Sir John Soane*, n.d., 76 ff. Also D. Stroud, *The Architecture of Sir John Soane*, London 1961, 110, figs. 156 ff.

89. On English private picture and sculpture galleries built specially as such see C. Hussey in *Country Life*, CXXIII, 1958, 202 ff. The earliest is the sculpture gallery at Castle Howard of 1802. The next are Brocklesby for sculpture, by Tatham, of 1807, and Attingham for paintings, by Nash, also of 1807. Nash's is memorable for having an iron and glass coving. Nash also did the picture gallery of Buckingham Palace (1825–30). Specially famous were Thomas Hope's exhibition galleries of the first years of the nineteenth century in his house in Duchess Street. On this see D. Watkin, *Thomas Hope and the neo-classical Idea*, London 1968. I have not used F. Herrmann, ed., *The English as Collectors*, London 1972.

90. From this point to about 1870 the best source is V. Plagemann, *Das deutsche Kunstmuseum*, Munich 1967. On the Glyptothek in particular see pp. 43–64. In addition L. von Klenze and L. Schorn, *Beschreibung der Glyptothek*, Munich 1837 and L. von Klenze, *Sammlung architektonischer Entwürfe*, Munich 1830. Also O. Hederer, *Leo von Klenze*, Munich 1964; O. Hederer, *Karl von Fischer*, Munich 1960, 101 ff.; H. Kiener, 'Hallers Entwürfe zur Glyptothek und Walhalla', *Münchner Jb. d. Bild. Kunst*, XIII, 1923, 102 ff.; W. Freiherr von Pölnitz, *Ludwig I von Bayern und Johann Martin von Wagner*, Munich 1929; C. T. Heigel, 'Briefe des Kronprinzen Ludwig an Karl Theodor Haller von Hallerstein', *Zs. f. Bild. Kunst*, XVIII, 1863, 161 ff., 194 ff., 221 ff.

91. Quoted from Böttger, op. cit. (above, n. 59), 13.

124 92. A PhD thesis on Haller von Hallerstein by K. Frässle, Freiburg University 1971, I have not seen.

93. The Salon Carré in the Louvre was incidentally used for the wedding of Napoleon and Marie-Louise in 1810. The paintings had to be removed. (Biver, op. cit., 300.)

94. Böttger, op. cit., 95.

95. On this story Pölnitz, op. cit., 231 ff., is best.

126 96. What English reader would not remember the start of Francis Bacon's *Essay of Building*? 'Houses are built to live in, and not to look on; therefore let use be preferred before uniformity except where both may be had.'

97. The aedicules continue on the east and west sides. Among the artists of the statues specially interesting for English readers are Gibson and Tenerani. See Plagemann, op. cit., 388.

98. P. O. Rave, *Karl Friedrich Schinkel, Lebenswerk: Bauten in Berlin*, I and II, Berlin 1941 and 1948; also *Zs. f. Kunstgesch.*, IV, 1935, 171 (review of S. Spiero, 'Schinkels Altes Museum' in *Jb. d. Preuss. Kunstsamml.*, LV, 1934, Beiheft): F. Stock in *Jb. d. Preuss. Kunstsamml.*, XXXV, 1914, Beiheft; XLVI, 1925, Beiheft; XLIX, 1928, Beiheft; LI, 1930; LIII, 1932; LIV, 1933; LVIII, 1937, Beiheft; LXIV, 1943, Beiheft. Also P. Seidel, ibid., XLIX, 1928. In Plagemann, op. cit., the Altes Museum is dealt with on pp. 38 ff. and 66 ff.

99. This is translated in my *Academies of Art*, op. cit., 194–97.

100. *Sammlung architektonischer Entwürfe von Schinkel*, ed. Schinkel and Berger, pt. VI, Berlin 1825, pls. 37 ff.; also pt. XVII, 1831, pls. 103 ff.

127 101. Plagemann, op. cit., 26.

102. A. Zádor, *Pollack Mihály*, Budapest 1960, 336 ff.

103. Crook, *British Museum*, op. cit., 115–28. This supersedes my paper, 'The British Museum; some unsolved problems of its architectural history', *Arch. Rev.*, CXIII, 1953, 179 ff. Also (F. G. Kenyon), *The Buildings of the British Museum*, London 1914, and Miller, op. cit. (above, n. 63).

104. In 1811 he designed a cast-iron monument to Queen Luise at Gransee, in 1813 he designed with the King the Iron Cross, the famous Prussian military decoration, and in 1819–20 the Gothic iron monument on the Kreuzberg in Berlin. Moreover, the *palais* for Prince Albrecht of 1830–33 has an iron staircase. See H. G. Pundt, *Schinkel's Berlin*, Cambridge, Mass. 1973, 217, 204, 205, 209, 219.

105. W. Waetzoldt, *Deutsche Kunsthistoriker von Passavant bis Justi*, Leipzig 1924, 29 ff.

128 106. Stock, op. cit., LVIII, 1937, Beiheft, 6. See also W. Waetzoldt, *Deutsche Kunsthistoriker von Sandrart bis Rumohr*, Leipzig 1924, 292 ff.

107. J. Sievers, *Karl Friedrich Schinkel, Lebenswerk: Die Möbel*, Berlin 1950, figs. 207–17.

108. Böttger, op. cit., 59.

109. W. H. Wackenroder, *Herzensergiessungen*, Berlin 1797, 79–80.

110. Böttger, op. cit., 173. Cornelius, needless to say, agreed: Museums are for 'spiritual elevation' (ibid., 169).

111. Böttger, op. cit., contains most of the relevant material.

112. Pliny: 'Pictores . . . quorum tabulae pinacothecas emplent.' Quoted from Wittlin, op. cit., 4.

129 113. G. Martin, 'Wilkins and the National Gallery', *Burlington Magazine*, CXIII, 1971, 318–29.

114. Plagemann, op. cit., 117 ff. and 395.

115. Dr M. Kühn referred me to the following progress reports: G. Erbkam in *Zeitschrift für Bauwesen*, XIX, 1869, 265–82, 413–16; XX, 1870, 217–18; XXI, 1871, 243–46; and in *Deutsche Bauzeitung*, X, 1876, 183–84, 193–95.

116. Plagemann, op. cit., 90 ff.

117. ibid., 109 ff. and 395.

118. ibid., 145 ff.

119. Böttger, op. cit., 29.

120. ibid., 166 ff.

130 121. ibid., 22.

122. Destroyed in the Second World War. Cf. Plagemann, op. cit., 127 ff. A monograph by W. Mittlmaier had not yet come out at the time of writing.

123. The name of the museum is eminently characteristic of the date. This was to be not a museum of art but a museum of the history of art – final triumph of historicism.

124. Plagemann, op. cit., 131 ff. and 398.

125. Klenze had suggested two tiers of cabinets for the Athens museum.

131 126. J. F. O'Gorman, *The Architecture of Frank Furness* (exhibition catalogue, Philadelphia Museum of Art), 1973.

127. B. Mundt, *Die deutschen Kunstgewerbemuseen im neunzehnten Jahrhundert*, Munich 1974 – published since I wrote this chapter – contains disappointingly little on the topic of this book. On opening days and hours see pp. 194–96, on entrance fees p. 197. Mentioned and not known to me is G. Semper, *Ideales Museum für Metalltechnik*, written in London in 1852. The manuscript is at the Österreichisches Museum in Vienna.

128. C. H. Gibbs Smith and K. Dougharty, *The History of the Victoria and Albert Museum*, London 1952. Also C. R. Richards, *Industrial Art and the Museum*, New York 1927, 44 ff. A major book on the history of the V. & A. by S. Barry and J. Physick is in hand.

129. The glazed faience staircase is of 1868–76, and it is certainly worth recording that the dining room was commis-

sioned from William Morris as early as 1867.

130. Richards, op. cit., 71.

131. *Das Kunstgewerbe-Museum zu Berlin (Festschrift zur Eröffnung)*, 1881. The original initiative goes back to Peter Beuth, civil servant in the Prussian Treasury, and founder of the Gewerbeschule in 1821. In the same year Schinkel began to publish model sheets for manufacturers and artisans. As in Vienna the chief impetus for a museum came from London. The Crown Princess, daughter of Queen Victoria, took a special interest, and the final outcome was the Kunstgewerbemuseum.

132. R. Middleton, *Viollet-le-Duc and the rational Gothic Tradition*, PhD thesis, Cambridge 1958. Also Hautecoeur, *Architecture classique*, op. cit., VI, 1955, 281.

133. Richards, op. cit., 35 ff.

134. *Anzeiger des Germanischen Museums*, 1926 and 1927.

135. G. Himmelheber, 'Gabriel Seidls Bau des Bayrischen Nationalmuseums', *Münchner Jb. d. bild. Kunst*, 1972. Also W. Lübbeke in *Die deutsche Stadt im neunzehnten Jahrhundert*, Munich (Fritz Thyssen Stiftung) 1974.

136. I learned this from M. Bringmann, *Studien zum neuromanischen Architektur in Deutschland*, PhD thesis, Heidelberg University 1968, 203.

137. C. R. Richards, *The Industrial Museum*, New York 1925, 7.

138. Hautecoeur, *Architecture classique*, op. cit., VI, 1955, 265–66 and ill. 226.

139. Rigby, op. cit. (above, n. 30).

140. The original Ashmolean building is now a museum of the history of science. Part of Tradescant's collection is shown in the present Ashmolean Museum.

141. G. de Beer, *Sir Hans Sloane and the British Museum*, London 1953. Also Crook, op. cit. (above, n. 63), 42–48, and Rigby, op. cit., 245.

142. Rigby, op. cit., 245 ff., makes the number nearly 200,000.

143. Crook, op. cit., 49–51.

144. Vardy's design is dated 1754 and was published in *Arch. Rev.*, CXLII, 1967, 5, by 'N.T.' (Nicholas Taylor).

145. Mr W. H. Hunter, Director of the Peale Museum, in a letter of August 1974 cleared up certain points for me and contributed certain details. The painting of Charles Willson Peale is in the Pennsylvania Academy of the Fine Arts. See W. H. Hunter, *The Story of America's Oldest Museum Building*, Baltimore 1964. On the Philadelphia years see C. Coleman Sellers, *Charles Willson Peale*, Philadelphia 1969.

146. Chueca Goitia, op. cit. (above, n. 86).

147. Belsiger, op. cit. (above, n. 11).

148. *De Sepibus Romani Collegii S.J. Museum*, Amsterdam 1678.

149. *Le Trésor des merveilles de la maison royale de Fontainebleau*, Paris 1642.

150. P. Ferriday, 'The Oxford Museum', *Arch. Rev.*, CXXXII, 1962, 408 ff. Also G. L. Hersey, *Early Victorian Gothic*, Baltimore and London 1972, 191–98.

151. XIII, 1855, 291.

152. A. Lhotsky, *Die Baugeschichte der Museen und der neuen Burg (Festschrift des Kunsthistorischen Museums)*, Vienna 1941, pt. I.

153. ibid., 92.

154. R. Alloi, *Musei*, Milan 1962, 389 ff.

155. J. M. Goode, *The Smithsonian Institution* (mimeographed), 1971.

156. I owe the information on the Milan Siloteca to Signorina Anna Rosato of the Biblioteca Comunale, Milan.

Other museums with odd exhibits, listed in *The Directory of Museums* (ed. K. Hudson and A. Nicholls, London 1975), include the following: in Budapest and Tokyo, fire-fighting; in Newcastle-on-Tyne, bagpipes; in Teheran, crime; in Vienna, dogs; in Wethersfield, Conn., ladies' caps. There is also a museum of the American china trade at Milton, Mass.

157. Over 400 in the United States. See L. V. Coleman, *Historic House Museums*, Washington 1933.

158. W. G. Constable, *Art Collecting in the United States*, London etc. 1964, is excellent. A. B. Saarinen, *The Proud Possessors*, New York 1958, is chattier but can also be recommended.

159. M. E. Gilman, 'The Fogg Museum of Art', *Art in America*, October 1944, 215–22.

160. Freer bought the Peacock Room in 1904.

161. The darling of the visitors is Gainsborough's *Blue Boy*, bought in 1921 for £620,000.

162. The estimate (Saarinen, op. cit., 62) is that Morgan in less than twenty years spent $600,000,000 on his collections.

163. Havemeyer had 38 Degas, Ryerson in Chicago 16 Monets (Constable, op. cit., 77, 80).

164. Alloi, op. cit.; M. Brawne, *The new Museum*, London 1965. Also P. Carbonara, *Architettura pratica*, 4 vols., Turin 1954–62, III, 2, 1401–1504.

165. Klenze knew that, when he designed the loggia of the Alte Pinakothek with doors from it to every one of the big halls and doors from the big halls into every second or third cabinet.

166. Alloi, op. cit., 235 ff. Pioneer work for the best modern display is Franco Albini's in the Palazzo Bianco in Genoa, 1950. See Alloi, 175 ff.

167. ibid., 167 ff.

168. ibid., 93 ff.

169. For the Berlin National-Galerie they have been pointed out and discussed by J. Posener in 'Absolute Architecture', *Neue Rundschau*, I, 1973, 79–95. As for Japan, several brutalist museums were built in the last fifteen years, following immediately after Le Corbusier's in Tokyo. For these see Alloi, op. cit.

170. Utica 1960, Fort Worth 1961, Lincoln, Nebraska, 1963. See *Philip Johnson – Architecture 1949–1965*, London etc. 1966.

9 Hospitals

BIBLIOGRAPHY

General

F. O. Kuhn in *Handbuch der Architektur*, Teil IV, Halbband 5, Heft 1 (*Krankenhäuser* – 969 pages of which over 300 deal with history), Stuttgart 1897; A. Husson, *Etude sur les hôpitaux*, Paris 1862; C. Tollet, *De l'Assistance publique et des hôpitaux jusqu'au XIXe siècle*, Paris 1889; H. C. Burdett, *Hospitals and Asylums of the World*, 4 vols. in 6 and a portfolio of plans, London 1891–93; K. D. Young, *On the Evolution of Hospital Design*, London 1910, brief; P. J. Stone, 'Elements of the Hospital', *Arch. Rev.*, CXXXVII, 1965, 413 ff., brief; D. Leistikow, *Ten Centuries of European Hospital Architecture* (sponsored by Messrs C. H. Boehringer), Ingelheim 1967, popular and handsomely illustrated. Announced at the time of writing is J. D. Thompson and G. Goldin, *The Hospital, a Social and Architectural History*, New Haven, Conn. 1975.

Britain

C. Dainton, *The Story of England's Hospitals*, London 1961; F. N. L. Poynter, ed., *The Evolution of Hospitals in Britain*, London 1964; B. Abel-Smith, *The Hospitals*, London 1964; A. G. L. Ives, *British Hospitals*, London 1948; R. M. Clay, *The Medieval Hospitals of England*, London 1909.

France

J. R. Tenon, *Mémoires sur les hôpitaux de Paris*, Paris 1788; N. M. Clavereau, *Mémoire sur les hôpitaux civils de Paris*, Paris 1805 (not used by me); M. Möring, *Collection de documents pour servir à l'histoire des hôpitaux de Paris*, 4 vols., Paris 1881–87 (not used by me); H. Thoillier, *L'Hôpital français*, Paris 1943; L. Pasteur Vallery-Radot, *Deux Siècles d'histoire hôpitalière*, London, Paris and New York 1947, and by the same author *Un Siècle d'histoire hôpitalière*, London, Paris and New York 1948.

Germany

D. Jetter, *Geschichte des Hospitals, I: Westdeutschland von den Anfängen bis 1850*, Sudhoffs Archiv für Geschichte der Medizin, Beiheft 5, Wiesbaden 1966 (with a bibliography of 815 titles); S. Reicke, *Das deutsche Spital und sein Recht im Mittelalter*, Stuttgart 1932.

Middle Ages

U. Craemer, *Das Hospital als Bautyp des Mittelalters*, Cologne 1963; Reicke (see above, Germany); E. Grunsky, *Doppelgeschossige Johanniterkirchen und verwandte Bauten*, PhD thesis, Tübingen University 1970.

Eighteenth Century

Various publications by Dr H. Rosenau: 'Antoine Petit und sein Zentralplan für das Hôtel-Dieu in Paris', *Zs. f. Kunstgesch.*, XXVII, 1964, 228 ff., 'The Functional and the Ideal in late eighteenth-century French Architecture', *Arch. Rev.*, CXL, 1966, 253 ff., and *Social Purpose in Architecture, Paris and London compared, 1760–1800*, London 1970.

Nineteenth Century

C. Tollet, *Les Hôpitaux modernes au XIXᵉ siècle*, Paris 1894; A. J. Ochsner and M. J. Sturm, *The Organization, Construction and Management of Hospitals*, Chicago 1907.

Twentieth Century

Architectural Forum, December 1928; *Architecture d'aujourd'hui*, 9th ser., V, December 1934; H. Ritter, *Der Krankenhaus-*

bau der Gegenwart, Stuttgart 1932; C. Butler and A. Erdman, *Hospital Planning*, New York 1946; L. Pasteur Vallery-Radot, *Un Siècle* (see above, France); G. Birch-Lindgren, *Modern Hospital Planning*, Stockholm 1951; H. Paschke, *Das neue Krankenhaus*, Jena 1963.

NOTES

p.139 1. S. Reicke, *Das deutsche Spital und sein Recht im Mittelalter*, Stuttgart 1932, 281. E. Grunsky quotes for Wesel in 1298 'in usu infirmorum, pauperum et peregrinorum' (*Doppelgeschossige Johanniterkirchen und verwandte Bauten*, PhD thesis, Tübingen University 1970, 117). The Bürgerspital at Basel is called in 1378 'domus ubi peregrini vel miseri suscipiuntur' (*Das Bürgerspital Basel, 1260–1946*, Basel n.d.). Yet another quotation is found in C. Lallemand, *Histoire de la Charité*, 5 vols., Paris 1902–12, II, 117 ff.: the hospital was for 'pauperes et pellegrini' and also to cure the sick stricken 'infirmitatibus, vulneribus et languoribus'.
2. Reicke, op. cit., 29, 31, 50, 121, 123.
3. For Byzantine hospitals see D. J. Constantelos, *Byzantine Philanthropy and Social Welfare*, New Brunswick, N.J. 1968. Also G. Schreiber, *Gemeinschaften des Mittelalters*, Münster 1948.
4. Reicke, op. cit., 13.
5. *Handbuch der Architektur*, Teil IV, Halbband 5, Heft 1 (*Krankenhäuser*, by F. O. Kuhn), Stuttgart 1897, 1–5.
6. E. Coyecque, *L'Hôtel-Dieu à Paris au moyen-âge*, Paris 1891, I, 21 ff. M. Möring, *Collection de documents pour servir à l'histoire des hôpitaux de Paris*, 4 vols., Paris 1881–87, is a collection of documents on the Hôtel-Dieu.
7. H. Reinhardt, *Der St Galler Klosterplan*, St Gall 1962; also 'Studien zum St Galler Klosterplan', *Mitteilungen zu Vaterländischen Geschichte*, St Gall, XLII, 1968.
8. For the Cluniacs see *Udalrici Consuetudines Cluniacenses*, bk. III, chap. 25–26, and *Sancti Wilhelmi Consuetudines Hirsaugienses*, bk. I, chap. 55–57, both in J. P. Migne, *Patrologia latina*, CXLIX, Paris 1853, cols. 767–69, and CL, 1856, cols. 1122–32. For the Cistercians see M. Aubert, *L'Architecture cistercienne en France*, Paris 1947, II, 148–52.
9. Migne, op. cit., for instance CL, 1856, col. 1127.
10. See the survey in Reicke, op. cit.
140 11. A. Gabriel, *La Cité de Rhodes, 1310–1522*, Paris 1921.
12. M. Ellul in *Bulletin of the Malta Cultural Institute*, XXV, October and November 1972.
13. The hospital on Rhodes was begun immediately. It was not yet completed in 1356. In 1394 we are told it was 'cum medicis semper paratis' (Gabriel, op. cit., 14). Much later material has been accumulated by Dr Grunsky (op. cit.). His thesis is first and foremost proof of a prodigious amount of reading. It deals with far more than what the title promises, with two-storeyed churches other than those of the Hospitallers, with centrally planned churches, Hospitallers' and otherwise, with certain churches of the Order of the Holy Spirit, with churches built *ad instar* of the Holy Sepulchre, with cemetery chapels, with two-storeyed Lady chapels, and with churches with west galleries.
14. Of the extensive literature I name only one classic and one recent book: J. Vogt, *Geschichte des Deutschen Ritterordens*, 2 vols., 1857–59, and M. Tumler, *Der Deutsche Orden*, 1955.
15. P. De Angelis, *L'Ospedale di Santo Spirito in Sassia*, 2 vols., Rome 1959.
16. Innocent III in 1198 had stated explicitly that hospitals were *loci publici*. Two examples to stand for many: at Mainz the hospital arranged by the canons of the cathedral was handed over in the mid-thirteenth century to the Order of the Holy Spirit (Grunsky, op. cit., 162 ff.), and at Basel the famous Bürgerspital was served by a community of *conversi* and *beguinen* (*Bürgerspital*, op. cit.).
141 17. All these are illustrated not only in the books listed in the bibliography at the beginning of these notes, but also in A. Verdier and F. Cattois, *Architecture civile et domestique du moyen-âge et de la renaissance*, I, Paris 1855.
18. C. Tollet, *De l'Assistance publique et des hôpitaux jusqu'au XIXe siècle*, Paris 1889, 50.
19. More in L. Pasteur Vallery-Radot, *Deux Siècles d'histoire hôpitalière*, London, Paris and New York 1947, 14, 15, 21, 22 ff.
20. H. C. Burdett, *Hospitals and Asylums of the World*, I, London 1891, 54–55.
21. Coyecque, op. cit.
142 22. Figures from ibid., 73 and 117 ff. For the eighteenth century the figure of 2 in 9 is given by K. D. Young, *On the Evolution of Hospital Design*, London 1910.
23. Reicke, op. cit., 298.
24. ibid., 201.
25. Coyecque, op. cit., 62. In Germany the corresponding term is *Pfründner*.
26. U. Procacci, *Lo Spedale di S. Maria Nuova*, Florence 1961. Also W. and W. Paatz, *Die Kirchen von Florenz*, Frankfurt 1952, IV, 5 ff.
27. D. Jetter tries to trace the origin of the cross plan for hospitals to the Islamic Near East: 'Das Mailänder Ospedale Maggiore und der kreuzförmige Krankenhausgrundriss', *Sudhoffs Archiv für Geschichte der Medizin*, XLIV, 1960, 64 ff. Professor Oleg Grabar kindly provided me with some bibliographical references and comments. For the Nuri and Kaimari Hospitals at Damascus, see E. Herzfeld, 'Damascus', *Ars Islamica*, IX, 1942; for the Mansurian or rather Qala'un Hospital at Cairo, now destroyed, see K. A. C. Creswell, *Muslim Architecture in Egypt*, II, Oxford 1959, 204 ff., plan on p. 207. Dr Jetter stresses the *liwan* or *iwan* cross, but about this question Professor Grabar writes: 'on the question of the *iwan* cross, total confusion reigns, and what you can read in Herzfeld or Creswell (op. cit., 104–34) . . . does not seem to me to correspond to reality. My own feeling . . . is the following. Some time in the twelfth century . . . the *iwan*, known at least since Oelmann (*Bonner Jahrbücher*, CXXVII, 1922) became a passe-partout monumental unit used singly or in groups of two, three and four for any number of functions, one of which was the hospital.'
28. P. Cassiano Carpaneto, *Pammatone – cinque secoli di vita ospedaliera*, Genoa 1953.
29. ibid., 179.
143 30. I am extremely grateful to John Fleming and Hugh Honour for having travelled to Siena for no other reason than to visit the hospital. They also gave me the titles of the following two books which, however, I have not seen: *I regi spedali riuniti di S. Maria della Scala*, Milan 1913, and G. Sanesi, *L'origine dell'ospedale di Siena*, Siena 1898.
31. A. Peroni, 'L'architettura e la scultura nei secoli XV e XVI', *Storia di Brescia*, II, Brescia 1961, 682 ff. I owe this reference to Dr Renzo Bresciani.
32. C. Saletti, 'La fabbrica quattrocentesca dell'Ospedale di S. Matteo in Pavia', *Arte Lombarda*, V, 1960, 48–55. I am grateful to Professor Peroni for information on Pavia.
33. See E. Marani, *Mantova; Le arti*, II, Mantua 1961, 68 ff.
34. D. Jetter, 'Das Mailänder Ospedale Maggiore', op. cit., 64 ff. Also G. C. Bascapè, 'Il progresso dell'assistenza ospedaliera nel secolo XV e gli ospedali a crociera', *Tecnica ospedaliera*, 1936, fasc. 1–2, pp. 1–15, and *L'Ospedale Maggiore di Milano*, Rome 1934, 475 ff. (both not used by me); also *Storia di Milano*, Milan (Fondazione Treccani) VIII, 1957, 405 ff.
35. John Fleming kindly referred me for the present state of the building to G. Lopez and S. Severgnini, *Milano in mano*, 1968 ed.
36. *Treatise on Architecture, being the treatise by Antonio Averlino, known as Filarete*, ed. J. R. Spencer, New Haven, Conn. 1965, I, 137 ff. Fully annotated is the yet more recent edition published in the Il Polifilo series and edited by L. Grassi, Milan 1972. Also still *Antonio Averlino Filaretes Tractat über die Baukunst*, ed. W. von Oettingen, *Quellenschriften für Kunstgeschichte*, N.F. III, Vienna 1890, 332–69. On Filarete personally see still M. Lazzaroni and A. Muñoz, *Filarete, scultore e architetto del XV secolo*, Rome 1908.
37. On the pattern of Michelozzo's Portinari Chapel at S. Eustorgio in Milan.
144 38. P. De Angelis, op. cit.
39. R. Pane, *Andrea Palladio*, Turin 1961, 114–15.
40. L. F. Q. Hughes, *The Building of Malta*, London ed. of 1967, 153–56. I am grateful to Professor Hughes for help over Malta. See also A. Critien, *Holy Infirmary Sketches*, Malta 1946, and A. Critien, *The Borgo Holy Infirmary*, Malta 1950. For the *Bulletin of the Malta Cultural Institute* see above, n. 12.
41. R. M. Clay, *The Medieval Hospitals of England*, London 1909.
42. But completed only in the eighteenth century.
43. Only two courts were executed.
145 44. D. Jetter, 'Hospitalgebäude in Spanien', *Sudhoffs Archiv für Geschichte der Medizin*, XLIV, 1960, 239 ff. Also Grunsky, op. cit., 326 ff., and F. Chueca Goitia, *Architectura del siglo XVI* (*Ars Hispaniae*, XI), Madrid 1953, 41 ff.
45. For the plan see *Hospital Care in the United States*, New York 1947, 427. See also G. Kubler and M. Soria, *Art and Architecture in Spain and Portugal and their American Dominions, 1500 to 1800* (Pelican History of Art), Harmondsworth 1959, 63.
46. For this and other seventeenth-century hospitals of Paris see Vallery-

Radot, op. cit. (above, n. 19). Also D. Jetter, 'Frankreichs Bemühen um bessere Hospitäler', *Sudhoffs Archiv für Geschichte der Medizin*, XLIX, 1965, 147 ff., and H. Rosenau, *Social Purpose in Architecture*, London 1970.

47. Vallery-Radot, op. cit., 101–05.

48. ibid., 102.

49. *Paris, ses organes, ses fonctions et sa vie . . .*, 6 vols., Paris 1869–75.

50. P. Bru, *Histoire de Bicêtre*, Paris 1890. I have to thank Mr Robin Evans for this point, and also for his kindness in reading and commenting on the text of this chapter in typescript.

51. Vallery-Radot, op. cit., 109–16. Also L. Boucher, *La Salpêtrière, son histoire de 1656 à 1790*, Paris 1883.

52. Vallery-Radot, op. cit., 114.

146 53. ibid. F.-A.-F. Duc de la Rochefoucauld Liancourt was a believer in social reform and hence a member of the Etats Généraux and the Constitutante and president of the Assemblée Nationale. He fled to England, where he was received by Young, and then to America. In Paris he was a friend of Jefferson, and he visited Jefferson at Monticello. He wrote up his American travels in *Travels through the United States*.

54. The enlargements consisted of a bridge across the southern arm of the Seine (1651), a ward across the same arm (1634) and wards on the south bank, parallel with the old buildings (1651 and 1717). See my ill. 9.29.

55. Vallery-Radot, op. cit., 52.

56. C. L. Stieglitz, *Enzyklopädie der bürgerlichen Baukunst*, Leipzig 1792–98, II, 749. His information might have come from Chamousset, on whom see p. 150 and n. 84.

57. When the hospital opened in 1689 it accommodated 476 non-commissioned officers and men.

58. Vallery-Radot, op. cit., 33.

59. ibid., 137 ff.

60. ibid., 151 ff.

61. ibid., 157 ff.

147 62. Vallery-Radot, op. cit., 163 ff.

63. Rosenau, op. cit., 62; also Jetter, 'Frankreichs Bemühen', op. cit., and W. Herrmann, 'Antoine Desgodets and the Académie Royale d'Architecture', *Art Bulletin*, XL, 1958, 23 ff. Dr Herrmann reports that Desgodets was working on a treatise of which he read in advance some chapters to the Academy. They dealt with building types, an arrangement alien to preceding treatises. Dr Herrmann quotes in this context J. Duportal, 'Le Cours d'architecture de Desgodets', *Revue de l'art ancien et moderne*, XXXVI, 1914–19, 153 ff.

64. See D. Jetter, *Geschichte des Hospitals, I: Westdeutschland von den Anfängen bis 1850*, Sudhoffs Archiv für Geschichte der Medizin, Beiheft 5, Wiesbaden 1966, 87, and R. Herrlinger, 'Utopische Krankenhaus-Pläne', *Das Krankenhaus*, LIV, 1962, 344 ff.

65. Stark had already in 1807 published *Remarks on the Construction of public Hospitals for the Care of the Mentally Deranged*. In 1809 Robert Read published *Observations on the Structure of Hospitals for the Treatment of Lunatics*. His proposed design also has a cruciform plan.

66. See Jetter, op. cit. (above, n. 64),

215 ff., and Rosenau, op. cit. A late-comer is the University College Hospital in London, 1897–1904, by Waterhouse. This is cruciform, but the cross is set diagonally. Hardly more than a curiosity are circular wards with the beds set radially. Burdett (op. cit., IV, 142 ff. and pls. 22–24) illustrates Hastings, Burnley and Antwerp (eight such wards). To these can be added New End, Hampstead, London, which by the way was begun as a workhouse. The radial wards are of 1883.

67. J. J. Rothman, *The Discovery of the Asylum*, Boston and Toronto 1971. On asylums see A. Funk in *Handbuch der Architektur*, Teil IV, Halbband 5, Heft 2, Stuttgart 1891; Burdett, op. cit., I, 1–106, also II; D. Jetter, 'Das ideale Irrenhaus im Spiegel historische Baupläne', *Confinia Psychiatrica*, V, 1962, 1 ff.; W. Parry Jones, *The Trade in Lunacy*, London 1972, on private asylums; and even more recent K. Jones, *A History of the Mental Health Services*, London 1972. D. S. Gardner, *The Design of Sanity*, MA essay, Columbia University, New York 1972, is chiefly on the New York State Lunatic Asylum at Utica. G. Grob, *Mental Institutions in America*, New York 1973, arrived too late to be used here; and I overlooked M. Foucault, *Histoire de la folie*, Paris 1961 (English translation *Madness and Civilisation*, London 1967).

148 68. Cf. J. Summerson, *Georgian London*, Penguin ed., Harmondsworth 1962, and F. N. L. Poynter, ed., *The Evolution of Hospitals in Britain*, London 1964, C. Dainton, *The Story of England's Hospitals*, London 1961, and B. Abel-Smith, *The Hospitals*, London 1964.

69. This is the place to remind oneself that already about 1450 Alberti, in his *De re aedificatoria*, bk. V, chap. 8, had pleaded for the separation of foundling children from the sick, the sick in general from those suffering from leprosy, the curably from the incurably sick, and all these from the *decrepiti* and the *mantecatti*. See the edition by G. Orlandi, Milan (Il Polifilo) 1966, I, 366–68.

70. The Derbyshire General Infirmary came somewhat later. It was built in 1806–10. It is of three floors and had a centre of five bays and slightly projecting wings of three. Glover (*History and Gazetteer of the County of Derby*, Derby 1833, 529) says that its 'building was arranged by William Strutt Esq.' (see below, p. 276), to designs by Mr Browne. Glover praised among other features the 'water closets' and summed up: 'it is furnished with every convenience'. The great Schinkel agreed. When he travelled in England in 1826 he wrote this of the Derby Infirmary: 'the famous infirmary, beautiful, convenient in every respect, with a superb staircase, the treads faced with lead'. He refers also to air heating, lavatories, baths and laundry and sums up: 'All is very intelligently arranged.' (*Aus Schinkels Nachlass*, ed. A. Freiherr von Wolzogen, Berlin 1862–63, III, 79.)

71. When Conolly started in 1839 he could still describe horrors he had seen, e.g. women 'chained to their bedsteads, naked . . . in the month of December'. The edition of Conolly's *Treatment of the Insane* by R. Hunter and I. Macalpine, London

1973, appeared too late to be made use of here.

72. Burdett, op. cit., I, 63–64.

73. ibid., 71–75. See also the quotation from Dorothy Lynde Dix in n. 117 below.

74. *American Notes for General Circulation*, London 1842: Penguin ed., Harmondsworth 1972, 95, 97 and 99.

149 75. A. Venditti, *Architettura neo-classica a Napoli*, n.d.; also R. Pane, *Ferdinando Fuga*, Naples 1956, and V. Golzio, *Seicento e Settecento* (Storia dell'arte classica e italiana), Turin 1960, 996.

76. Rothman, op. cit. (above, n. 67). In Gardner's essay (above, n. 67) there are similar illustrations, e.g. the New York State Asylum of 1838–47 at Utica, with a Greek Doric portico, Mills's asylum at Columbia, S.C., of 1821–25 with a huge portico of unfluted Doric columns (ill. also T. Hamlin, *Greek Revival Architecture in America*, Oxford 1944, pl. xii), Strickland's Naval Asylum at Philadelphia of 1826–29 with a portico of unfluted Ionic columns, and the asylum of 1816–19 at Bloomingdale outside New York.

150 77. Rothman, op. cit., 288, 287, 198. For conditions in one particular – English – workhouse see I. Anstruther, *The Scandal of the Andover Workhouse*, London 1973. The book is painful to read.

78. Rothman, op. cit., 169, also 162.

Drink as the cause of crime and sickness had been illustrated by Hogarth (*Gin Lane*). George Cruikshank's *Worship of Bacchus* of 1864 (Tate Gallery, London) has as its background in the left half breweries, in the right half a gaol, a workhouse, a house of correction and also a hospital and a lunatic asylum. In Hogarth's time it was gin that did it, whereas beer was wholesome. Now the demon is beer.

79. Dr Rothman (ibid., 230–34) quotes one month's punishments from the diary for 1825 of the first manager of the New York House of Refuge: leg iron 1, ball and chain 2, one-day prison 2, whip 4, cat 4. Rattan was available everywhere for strokes on the hand, the soles of the feet and the buttocks covered or bare.

80. Gardner, op. cit., is surely too optimistic.

81. Parry-Jones, op. cit.

82. ibid.

83. ibid.

84. C. H. Piarron de Chamousset, *Oeuvres complètes*, Paris 1783, 139 ff. and table on 169.

85. ibid., 29 ff.

86. J. R. Tenon, *Mémoires sur les hôpitaux de Paris*, Paris 1788; A. Husson, *Etude sur les hôpitaux*, Paris 1862, 26–35; *Handbuch der Architektur*, op. cit., Heft 1, 73 ff.; Jetter, 'Frankreichs Bemühen', op. cit. (above, n. 46), 147 ff. Also four publications by H. Rosenau: 'Antoine Petit und sein Zentralplan für das Hôtel-Dieu in Paris', *Zs. f. Kunstgesch.*, XXVII, 1964, 228 ff., 'The Functional and the Ideal in late eighteenth-century French Architecture', *Arch. Rev.*, CXL, 1966, 253 ff., *Stil und Überlieferung in der Kunst des Abendlandes* (International Congress), Bonn 1967, I, 226 ff., and *Social Purpose*, op. cit., 51 ff.

87. Tenon, op. cit., IV. The Ile des Cygnes lay between the Pont des Invalides and the Pont de l'Alma. It was united with

the left bank in 1773.

88. For these two *Handbuch der Architektur*, op. cit., 73–74, quotes *Récit de ce qui s'est passé tendant à la construction d'un nouvel Hôtel-Dieu*, Paris 1773. I have not seen this. Jetter, 'Frankreichs Bemühen', op. cit., includes Penseron.

89. *Projet d'un hôpital des malades.*

90. *Précis d'un ouvrage sur les hôpitaux*, Paris 1787. (In *Histoire de l'Académie des Sciences*, 1789, year 1787. I have to thank Dr Rosenau for this reference.)

151 91. Quoted from L. Klasen, *Grundriss-Vorbilder in Gebäuden aller Art*, 15 pts., Leipzig 1884–96, pt. IV, 315.

92. Tenon (op. cit.) does indeed refer to Marly to indicate what hospital plan he favours.

93. The Parc des Buttes Chaumont is in the *quartier* of Belleville.

94. It is less likely that he knew Sturm (above, p. 147 and ill. 9.20), and totally unlikely that he knew Fuga's radial scheme of 1751 for the Albergo dei Poveri in Naples (above, p. 149).

A circular asylum was by the way built in Vienna in 1783. It was known as the Narrenturm and had five floors and a round inner courtyard. A corridor ran around this, and beyond it were single cells each having an outside window and a lavatory. The building was centrally heated. (For illustrations see e.g. H. Tietze, *Alt Wien in Wort und Bild*, Vienna 1924, 122.)

95. Dijon 1783 – see *Handbuch der Architektur*, op. cit., 79 ff.

96. Bassano 1781. I quote from the 2nd ed., Bassano 1785, 286 ff.

97. *Second Rapport des Commissionnaires chargés par l'Académie des projets relatifs à l'établissement des quatre hôpitaux.*

152 98. Description in Husson, op. cit., 29.

99. But Laugier also presents a scheme with eight radii.

100. Tenon quotes, e.g., Humezovsky, *Medizinisch-Chirurgische Betrachtungen*, Vienna 1783, a book I have not seen.

101. Vallery-Radot, op. cit., 34 ff.

153 102. Tenon, op. cit., p. II.

103. J. Howard, *An Account of the Principal Lazarettos in Europe*, London 1789: all the quotations up to this are from pp. 131–40.

104. ibid., 154, 171, 192.

105. ibid., 180, 187.

154 106. J.-N.-L. Durand, *Recueil*, Paris 1801, pl. 29. On his other plate of hospitals, pl. 30, the centrepiece is the vast lazaretto of Milan, while the oriental caravanserai is represented by five examples.

107. II, Paris 1809, pl. 18.

108. Dr Rosenau in *Social Purpose*, op. cit., also publishes a pavilion scheme which appeared in 1805 in N. M. Clavereau's *Mémoire sur les hôpitaux civils de Paris*.

109. L. P. Vallery-Radot, *Un Siècle d'histoire hôpitalière*, London, Paris and New York 1948, 19 and 47 ff.

110. op. cit., IV, 326.

111. A. J. Ochsner and M. J. Sturm, *The Organization, Construction and Management of Hospitals*, Chicago 1907.

112. op. cit., 9. Similarly L. Degess, *Der Bau der Krankenhäuser*, Munich 1862, 190.

113. On the pavilion plan see Cassagne, *Les Hôpitaux sans étages et à pavillons isolés*, Paris 1878.

114. E. T. Cook, *The Life and Work of Florence Nightingale*, 2 vols., London 1913; C. Woodham-Smith, *Florence Nightingale*, London 1950.

155 115. It *was*, not is; for demolition began in 1966, and now all that remains is the chapel and the dome which adjoins the chapel.

116. A. King, 'Hospital Planning; revised thoughts on the Origin of the Pavilion-Principle in England', *Medical History*, X, 1966, 360 ff.

117. Florence Nightingale's outrageous statement had been anticipated a hundred years before by Sir John Pringle in his *Observations on the Diseases of the Army* written in 1752. His words were: 'Hospitals are the chief cause of mortality in the army.' (Burdett, op. cit., IV, 33.)

An American forerunner of Florence Nightingale and successor of Howard was Dorothea Lynde Dix (1802–87), who reported passionately on the state she found asylum patients in: 'Chained, naked, beaten with rods and lashed into obedience'. See *Dictionary of American Biography* and Rothman, op. cit. (above, n. 67), 132 ff.

118. The architect, according to Nicholas Taylor, was called Mennie.

119. Butterfield's Royal Hampshire Hospital at Winchester of 1863–68 is, needless to say, Gothic. It is in this a great exception. See P. Thompson, *William Butterfield*, London 1972, 112–17.

120. p. 497.

156 121. III, 507. Burdett, op. cit., IV, 101–64, is all about hospitals on the pavilion scheme.

122. Called epoch-making still in 1947: see *Hospital Care*, op. cit. (above, n. 45), 474 ff.

123. *De l'Assistance publique et des hôpitaux jusqu'au XIXe siècle*, Paris 1889 (see above, n. 18).

124. D. Leistikow (*Ten Centuries of European Hospital Architecture*, Ingelheim 1967, 85) reports however a design of 1820 for the Catharinenhospital at Stuttgart which had three parallel ribs at the back of the main block. It was submitted by Giovanni Salucci. See, according to Jetter, op. cit. (above, n. 64), W. Speidel, *Giovanni Salucci*, dissertation, Technische Hochschule, published Stuttgart 1936.

125. *Handbuch der Architektur*, op. cit., 791–93; plan after p. 790.

126. A. H. Murken, 'Aus der Hamburger Krankenhausgeschichte', *Historia Hospitalium*, VII, 1972, 25–43, especially 33 ff. Also *Handbuch der Architektur*, op. cit., 790–98.

127. L. Hautecoeur, *Histoire de l'architecture classique en France*, VII, Paris 1957, 361–62.

128. *Handbuch der Architektur*, op. cit., 279 ff.

129. *Rev. gén. de l'arch.*, VIII, 1849, pls. 28–34.

157 130. *Die Kunstdenkmäler der Schweiz*, X (*Zürich Stadt*, I), Basel 1939, 371–72.

131. The dates are taken from Dainton, op. cit. (above, n. 68), 93 ff. In Paris, according to the *Handbuch der Architektur*, op. cit., 153, the first children's hospital was started in 1802.

132. C. Pfister, *Histoire de Nancy*, 3 vols., 1902–09, III, 305–09 and 809–12. I thank the Municipal Library at Nancy for help.

158 133. op. cit., 479 ff.

134. ibid., 26.

135. Quoted from I. Rosenfield, *Hospital Architecture and Beyond*, New York, Toronto, etc. 1969, 26.

136. Paschke, op. cit., 3.

137. *Hospital Care*, op. cit. (above, n. 45); Rosenfield, op. cit.

138. P. Carbonara, *Architettura pratica*, 4 vols., Turin 1954–62. George Nelson also designed the 11-storey Franco-American Memorial Hospital at St Lô in Normandy. It was opened in 1956.

139. Vallery-Radot, *Un Siècle*, op. cit. (above, n. 109), 173 ff.

140. ibid., 38.

141. *Das Bürgerspital Basel*, op. cit. (above, n. 1).

142. H. Schmieden, *Krankenhausbau in neuer Zeit*, Kirchheim 1930, 7.

143. R. Döcker, *Der Terrassentyp*, Stuttgart 1929.

10 Prisons

BIBLIOGRAPHY

Not much of a general nature exists. The best by far is H. J. Graul, *Der Strafvollzugsbau einst und heute*, Düsseldorf 1965. In English, T. A. Markus, 'The Pattern of the Law', *Arch. Rev.*, CXVI, 1954, 251 ff. is the most useful. One might also consult the relevant pages of the *Handbook of Correctional Institution Design and Construction*, U.S. Bureau of Prisons, 1949, and the relevant chapter in D. J. Rothman, *The Discovery of the Asylum*, Boston and Toronto 1971. Though nearly 150 years old, N. H. Julius's *Vorträge über die Gefängnis-Kunde*, Berlin 1828, is still indispensable, being more detailed concerning the history of prisons than Markus. In the *Handbuch der Architektur* the relevant volume is Teil IV, Halbband 7, Heft 1 (and in it *Gerichtshäuser, Straf- und Besserungsanstalten*, by T. von Landauer, E. Schmitt and H. Wagner), Darmstadt 1887, 253–402. Useful also is the one chapter in H. Rosenau, *Social Purpose in Architecture*, London 1970, 77 ff. I personally have benefited most from Norman B. Johnston's PhD thesis, *The Development of Radial Prisons*, University of Pennsylvania 1958, and I am glad to be able to report that Dr Johnston has recently brought out a brief summary of prison architecture under the title *The Human Cage*, New York 1973. The book appeared after this chapter was written. I have not been able to see O. F. Lewis, *The Development of American Prisons*, Albany 1922, or E. Bumke, *Das Gefängniswesen*, Berlin 1928. Announced at the time of writing is *Prison Architecture*, by the United Nations Social Defense Research Institute, London 1975, with many illustrations.

NOTES

p.159 1. My thanks to Mr Robin Evans for pointing out this fact. He had the great kindness to read my text in typescript.

2. French translation 1766, English translation 1768.

3. L. Radzinowicz, *A History of English Criminal Law, I, The Movement for Reform*, London 1948.

4. ibid., 3–4. Blackstone in the 1760s set

the figure at 160, Sir Thomas Fowell Buxton in 1819 at 223. In 1822 the death penalty was abolished for a hundred offences. Dickens in his *American Notes for General Circulation*, London 1842, could still say more or less the same a whole generation after Romilly: 'England . . . in the reign of the Third King George, in respect of her criminal code and her prison regulations [was] one of the most bloody-minded and barbarous countries on the earth.' (Penguin edition, ed. J. S. Whitley and A. Goldman, Harmondsworth 1972, 101.)

160 5. Radzinowicz, op. cit., 656.
6. ibid., 474–75. The sentence was of course not carried out: the last execution by burning in England was in the seventeenth century.
7. ibid., 14.
8. ibid., 151.
9. ibid., 153.
10. ibid.
11. ibid., 154–55.
12. J. Howard, *The State of the Prisons*, London 1777, 7.
13. *Udalrici Consuetudines Cluniacenses*, in J. P. Migne, *Patrologia latina*, CXLIX, Paris 1853, col. 736; *Sancti Wilhelmi Consuetudines Hirsaugienses*, ibid., CL, 1856, col. 1047.
14. M. Aubert, *L'Architecture cistercienne en France*, Paris 1947, II, 73. The most usual location was under the dormitory staircase. More evidence of monastic prisons in O. Lehmann-Brockhaus, *Lateinische Schriftquellen zur Kunst in England, Wales und Schottland vom Jahre 901 bis zum Jahre 1307*, 5 vols., Munich 1955–60 (references under *carcer* in vol. II of the Index).
15. R. B. Pugh, *Imprisonment in medieval England*, Cambridge 1968. Also for a major Continental city R. Davidsohn, *Geschichte von Florenz*, IV, pt. 1, Berlin 1922, 336–50.
16. H. J. Graul, *Der Strafvollzugsbau einst und heute*, Düsseldorf 1963, 16 ff.
17. *Treatise on Architecture, being the treatise by Antonio Averlino, known as Filarete*, ed. J. R. Spencer, New Haven, Conn. 1965, I, 125 and II, 281. Also, more recent, the edition by L. Grassi, Milan (Il Polifilo) 1972.
18. Alberti also differentiates between 'huomini rozzi', who should be restricted, 'insolventi', and 'odiosi criminali', only the latter to be 'sepolti nelle tenebre'. (*L'Architettura*, V, 13, ed. G. Orlandi and P. Portoghesi, Milan (Il Polifilo) 1966, I, 396–99.)

161 19. William Beckford in a letter of 4 August 1780 mentions indeed that the tribunal 'sometimes by way of clemency, . . . condemns its victims to perpetual imprisonment in close, stifling cells'. (*Italy, with sketches of Spain and Portugal*, Paris 1834, 59.)
20. F. A. K. Krauss, *Im Kerker*, Freiburg 1895, 342.
21. *Prisons*, 1777, op. cit.
22. *The Defects of Police, the Cause of Immorality*, 1775. Hanway's argument was that solitude leads to reflection and may lead to self-improvement.
23. *Prisons*, 1777, op. cit., pl. by p. 51.
24. *Appendix to the State of the Prisons*, London 1788, 48.
25. Graul, op. cit. Also E. Rosenfeld, *Zur Geschichte der ältesten Zuchthäuser*, Stuttgart 1933.
26. J. Furttenbach, *Architectura universalis*, Ulm 1635, 71–76 and pls. 27–29.
27. Graul, op. cit.
28. ibid., 111 ff. and pl. 11.
29. *Prisons*, 1791 ed., 158.
30. ibid., 173, 206.
31. *Prisons*, 1777, op. cit., 87. J.-F. Blondel in his *Cours d'architecture civile*, II, Paris 1771, 456, says: 'Nos prisons sont infects, nos cachots font horreur.' Remember, he adds, that 'les prisonniers sont des hommes'.
Dr Roselyn Coope showed me that the original plans of 1618 for the Palais de Justice at Rennes (see her book *Salomon de Brosse*, London 1972, figs. 196–99 and my ill. 2.14) have on the one hand 'cachots noirs', on the other such humane features as a dayroom for the prisoners with adjoining privies and a room for prisoners' visitors.
32. *Appendix*, 1788, op. cit., 39, 64, 66, 67, 68, 70 and 79.
33. ibid., 181.
34. *An Account of the Principal Lazarettos in Europe*, London 1789, 155.
35. For a good comment on prison *v.* house of correction, see N. H. Julius, *Vorträge über die Gefängnis-Kunde*, Berlin 1828. Graul (op. cit., 28) quotes Abraham a Sancta Clara who says that such houses of correction should 'durch Arbeit . . . zu einem ehrbaren und züchtigen Wandel . . . bringen'.
36. T. Sellin, *Pioneering in Penology*, Philadelphia 1944. Also G. Radbruch, 'Die ersten Zuchthäuser', in *Elegantiae Juris Criminalis*, 2nd ed., Basel 1950, 116–29.
37. Let it not be forgotten that whipping and torture still went on in the nineteenth century. In that far too little known book, W. Langewiesche's *Wolfs, Geschichten um ein Bürgerhaus*, Munich and Leipzig 1919 (on which see below, p. 284, n. 99 and 100), it is said that in Hanover in 1826 thumbscrews and the iron maiden were used (267–68) and that about 1850 in the Waldheim prison in Saxony in one year nearly 25,000 cuts with the rod and the cane were administered (373).
38. Sellin, op. cit., 102 ff.
39. *Prisons*, 1777, op. cit., 68–77. On workhouses there is now N. Longmate, *The Workhouse*, London 1974 – too recent for me to have made use of it.
40. *Prisons*, 1777, op. cit., 10.
41. ibid., 16, 69.
162 42. pt. I, 183–85. Bugniet's design is discussed and illustrated in H. C. Rice, Jr., 'A French Source of Jefferson's Plan for a Prison at Richmond', *JSAH*, XII, 1953, no. 4, 28 ff. Bugniet's description, plan, elevations and section are in the Bibliothèque de la Ville de Lyon.
43. Only in the 1830s was the building complete. It could then house 2,600 persons.
44. *Prisons*, 1777, op. cit., by p. 48.
45. *Lazarettos*, op. cit., pl. 20.
46. H. D. Kalman, 'Newgate Prison', *Arch. Hist.*, XII, 1969, 50 ff. Even more monumental than Newgate are the Debtors' Prison at York, built as early as 1705 and Vanbrughian in style, and its counterpart of 1773–80, the Female Prison by Carr (see also above, p. 53).

163 47. F. Milizia, *Principi di architettura civile*, 2nd ed., Bassano 1785, II, 227 ff. *Architecture parlante* is not entirely a thing of the past. Here is a passage from Paul Valéry's *Eupalinos ou l'Architecte* (1923): 'Les demeures de la justice doivent parler aux yeux de la rigueur et de l'équité de nos lois.' (*Oeuvres*, Pleiade ed., II, Paris 1960, 94.)
48. H. Rosenau, 'The Engravings of the *Grands Prix* of the French Academy of Architecture', *Arch. Hist.*, III, 1960, figs. 116 and 117. The name Houssin is otherwise unknown, and Dr Rosenau suggests the designer may have been J. A. Coussin.
49. R. Evans, 'Bentham's Panopticon', *Architectural Association Quarterly*, Spring 1971 – an excellent study.
50. *The Collected Works of Jeremy Bentham*, ed. J. H. Burns, *Correspondence*, III (ed. I. R. Christie), London 1971, 502–03, 511 ff.
51. Circular also, as we have seen, was the arrangement of the cells of the Anabaptists at Münster in 1535, but the pedigree here was different. On the Narrenturm see above, p. 151, n. 94.
52. Other prisons by Blackburn are listed in H. M. Colvin, *A Biographical Dictionary of English Architects*, London 1954, 78. Not referred to are Oxford 1786–89, Limerick 1787, Gloucester 1788–91, and Exeter completed 1792. Blackburn had died in 1790.
164 53. Evans, op. cit., 25.
54. Rice, op. cit. (see above, n. 42). Also T. Hamlin, *Benjamin Henry Latrobe*, New York 1955, 92 and 120.
55. H. Rosenau, *Social Purpose in Architecture*, London 1970, 84, 85 (ill.). The design appears in Soane's *Designs for Public and Private Buildings* of 1828 – as Dorothy Stroud kindly told me, not in the first edition of 1826.
56. Mr John W. Girvan first told me about this prison. The illustration is from a model made by him. See also *Victoria County History, Wiltshire*, V. 1957, 186–89.
57. *Wiebekings Bürgerliche Baukunde*, Munich 1821–26, IV, 508–15 and pl. 148.
58. By Robin Evans in his PhD thesis, *Prison Design 1750–1842* (Architectural Association, London 1975). Mr Evans told me this: I have not seen his thesis. For illustrations see Evans, 'Bentham's Panopticon', op. cit. Yet later examples are the Maison de Force et de Correction at Rennes (a hexagon by A. Normand, 1870s) and Arnhem in Holland (a circle, *c.* 1880). They are illustrated in *Gerichtshäuser, Straf- und Besserungsausstalten*, by T. von Landauer, E. Schmitt and H. Wagner, *Handbuch der Architektur*, Teil IV, Halbband 7, Heft 1, Darmstadt 1887, 376–77 and 271. Dr Norman B. Johnston refers to three prisons of Panopticon type of the 1880s in Holland and to the Isle of Pines in Cuba, built as late as the early twentieth century (*The Development of Radial Prisons*, PhD thesis, University of Pennsylvania 1958, 21–22). Also early twentieth-century is Joliet in Illinois. There the centre is a circular dining hall; it is surrounded by eight panopticons. By 1930 three were built. See A. Hopkins, *Prisons and Prison Building*, New York 1930, 38 ff.

59. The arrangement inside allowed for 120 single cells and workrooms on the ground floor. The sick and the adolescents were kept separate from the men and women. See Graul, op. cit., 33.

60. p. 155.

61. I owe Williams' name to Mr Robin Evans.

62. His ideal plan is again the cross of Filarete.

63. H. Mayhew and J. Binny, *The Criminal Prisons of London and Scenes of Prison Life*, London 1862, 113 ff., 535. Refractory cells: Millbank 258, Pentonville 135. On p. 247 is an illustration of the fetter room. As for punishments altogether, the following are listed for one year at Millbank: cat 2, birch 4, bread and water 543, dark cell 52, refractory cell 304. Mayhew distinguishes between convict prisons (e.g. Millbank and Pentonville), correctional prisons (e.g. Cold Bath of 1794 and Holloway) and detentional prisons (e.g. Newgate).

For Holloway see now J. Camp, *Holloway Prison, the Place and the People*, Newton Abbot 1974 (too recent for me to have used it).

166 64. Dr Piera Casile told me the name of the architect.

65. Signorina Anna Rosato of the Biblioteca Comunale kindly told me about this. See F. Ragioni, *Milano, 1810–1943*, Milan 1947, 376.

66. Dr Volker Hoffmann gave me the reference to M. Armellini, *Le chiese di Roma*, II, Rome 1842, 804.

67. *Wiebekings . . . Baukunde*, op. cit., IV, 514 and pl. 148.

68. The phrase comes from Victor Hugo's *Histoire d'un crime*, in his description of Napoléon le Petit's *coup d'état* (*Collected Works, Histoire*, I, 1907, 356–61).

69. Ill. Hopkins, op. cit., 47.

70. The *Rapports à M. le Comte de Montalivet . . . sur les pénitenciers des Etats–Unis*, Paris 1837, by M. Demetz and A. Blouet, are models of their kind. Dr Johnston in his thesis (op. cit., above, n. 58) lists the triumphs of the radial system in Holland, Denmark, Sweden and Norway, the appointment of commissions and various study journeys.

71. The first notable American prison was in Walnut Street, Philadelphia. It dated from 1790 and was of seventeen bays, with a three-bay pediment and a cupola, i.e. of the general Georgian type also used, as we have seen, for hospitals, poorhouses, etc. (above, p. 149). For illustrations of Walnut Street see Graul, op. cit., 22, 26, and D. J. Rothman, *The Discovery of the Asylum*, Boston and Toronto 1971, 54.

72. Ill. in Demetz and Blouet's *Rapports*, op. cit., pls. 1, 23, 28 and 29.

73. *American Notes for General Circulation*, London 1842, chap. VII. I am quoting from the Penguin ed., op. cit. (above, n. 4).

74. ibid., 101.

75. ibid., 249.

76. ibid., 103.

168 77. ibid., 146.

78. *Sämtliche Werke*, ed. E. Elster, Leipzig and Vienna 1887 etc., VI, 312. Professor Windfuhr kindly provided me with this bibliographical reference. In Langewiesche, op. cit. (above, n. 37), 373, there

is a reference too to 'das entsetzliche amerikanische Zellensystem'.

79. A. Ten Eyck Gardner, 'A Philadelphia Masterpiece', *Bulletin of the Metropolitan Museum of Art*, New York, XIV, 1955–56, 103 ff.

80. This had been the argument of Jonas Hanway in England in 1775: see above, n. 22.

81. Rothman, op. cit., 83 and 85.

82. N. Johnston, *The Human Cage*, New York 1973, 33–34.

83. Ill. M. Whiffen, *American Architecture since 1780*, Cambridge, Mass. 1969, 49.

84. American Notes, op. cit., 131.

85. Graul, op. cit., 103 and ill. 57. Also L. Hautecoeur, *Histoire de l'architecture classique en France*, VI, Paris 1955, 93 (n.) and 224.

86. See A. Hasluck, *Royal Engineer; a Life of Sir Edmund DuCane*, London 1973 (not used by me).

87. *Handbook of Correctional Institution Design and Construction*, U.S. Bureau of Prisons, 1949. Also Johnston, op. cit. (above, n. 58), and Graul, op. cit.

11 Hotels

BIBLIOGRAPHY

There is no comprehensive architectural history of the hotel. The best history in general is F. Rauers, *Kulturgeschichte der Gaststätte*, 2 vols., Berlin 1942, even though it is irritatingly thin on dates of buildings and has no plans. For America indispensable is J. Williamson, *The American Hotel*, New York 1930. Moreover it is now fortified by three theses written at Pennsylvania State University under Professor Winston Weisman. They deal exclusively with New York hotels, as follows (in chronological order): V. L. Glasgow, *The Hotels of New York City prior to the American Civil War*, 1970; F. J. Kaplan, *The Architecture of New York City Hotels from 1860 until 1885*, 1970; and L. S. Dubin, *The Hotels of New York City, 1885–1900*, 1969. For England Christopher Monkhouse is working on a PhD at the University of London and he has already found evidence about English hotels much earlier than the first discussed by me. But his discoveries must remain his. In the meantime there is (not used by me) D. Taylor and D. Bush, *The Golden Age of the British Hotel*, London 1974.

NOTES

p.169 1. A. E. Richardson and H. B. Eberlein, *The English Inn, past and present*, London 1925.

2. Larousse *Dictionnaire de Paris*, Paris 1964.

3. Quoted from *Enciclopedia italiana*, II, Rome and Milan 1929, 140–41.

4. ibid., 141. It is confirmed more than once by E. Zaniboni, *Alberghi italiani e viaggiatori stranieri, secoli XIII–XVIII*, Naples 1921, and by U. Gnoli, *Alberghi e osterie di Roma nella rinascenza*, Rome 1940, 15–16. On the common sleeping room vs. single rooms see Zaniboni, 23–24.

5. Zaniboni, op. cit., 34.

6. ibid., 75.

7. Gnoli, op. cit., 16.

8. The Sole still existed in Gregorovius's

time, i.e. in the third quarter of the nineteenth century, and he called it grandiose and severe (Gnoli, op. cit., 133).

9. Zaniboni, op. cit., 120. Gnoli, op. cit., 69. In 1676 Duke Christian von Eisenberg still had a retinue of 76 on a visit to Venice (Zaniboni, 63).

10. 'Commentariolus de Laudibus Patavis', in *Rerum Italicarum Scriptores*, XXIV, 1738 (ed. L. A. Muratori).

11. Vicomte G. d'Avenel, *Le Mécanisme de la vie moderne*, V, Paris 1905, 4.

12. T. von Liebenau, *Das Gasthofs- und Wirtschaftswesen der Schweiz in älterer Zeit*, Zürich 1891, 289.

13. ibid., 294.

170 14. All three are illustrated in M. Hoffmann, *2000 Jahre Gaststätte*, Frankfurt 1954. See also F. Rauers, *Kulturgeschichte der Gaststätte*, Berlin 1942.

15. Or was this a private house, as Sir A. E. Richardson, *The Old Inns of England*, 6th ed., London 1952, suggests?

16. Rauers, op. cit., 340, 385. Also *Archiv für Frankfurter Geschichte und Kunst*, N.F. IX, 1882, 380, and X, 1883, 114 and 131, and *Die Baudenkmäler von Frankfurt*, III, Frankfurt 1914, 123–36. The name Rotes Haus goes back to 1329.

17. Rauers, op. cit., 177, 398–99, 446.

18. A square assembly room was added to Wetherburn's Tavern in Williamsburg in 1752. At Williamsburg the Apollo, the assembly room of the Raleigh Tavern, was also an addition. The splendid assembly room of Gadsby's City Hotel at Alexandria, Virginia, of 1793 is now in the Metropolitan Museum in New York.

172 19. I wish to stress the fact that of English hotels of the later eighteenth and early nineteenth centuries Christopher Monkhouse has found much new evidence. As his PhD thesis (University of London) had not yet been presented I could not make use of it.

20. *Reise durch England und Schottland*, Leipzig 1813. I am quoting from the 2nd ed., 1818, 104–05. In her *Jugendleben und Wanderbilder* she wrote the same. Dessin is 'truly colossal'. She added, 'I have never seen its like.' I am quoting from the Danzig ed. of 1884, 157.

The librarian of the Bibliothèque Municipale at Calais in a letter kindly added to this information that the hotel (called Hôtel d'Angleterre, in the rue Royale) was by 1768 famous and very large, that in 1772–74 M. Dessin added a theatre and that Louis XVIII, George IV, Louis Philippe and Napoleon III stayed at the hotel. It closed in the late nineteenth century; the buildings were hit by bombs and partly demolished in 1940.

21. LXVII, pt. 1, 451.

22. 'auf Englischem Fuss'. A. Freiherr von Wolzogen, *Aus Schinkels Nachlass*, Berlin 1862–63, II, 155.

23. *Italy, with Sketches of Spain and Portugal*; I am quoting from the Paris 1834 ed., 134. Also in 1782 Beckford uses the word hotel referring to Naples (p. 124), and in 1787 referring to Falmouth (p. 177).

When Thomas Jefferson arrived in Paris in 1784 he stayed first in the Hôtel d'Orléans, rue de Richelieu, and then in another Hôtel d'Orléans, rue des Petits Augustins (D. Malone, *Jefferson and his Time*, II, Boston 1951, 5).

24. A. Young, *Travels in France during the years 1787, 1788 and 1789*, ed. C. Maxwell, Cambridge 1929, 116.

25. LXI, pt. 2, 860.

26. *Survey of London*, XXXII, London 1963, 373.

27. M. Hoffmann, *Geschichte des deutschen Hotels*, Heidenheim 1961, 147.

28. I am quoting from *Enciclopedia italiana*, op. cit., 143. Of the Crocelle in 1805 Elisa von der Recke wrote, 'So much good taste, so much elegance, so much cleanliness' as she had not found elsewhere (Zaniboni, op. cit., 162).

29. T. Hamlin, *Benjamin Henry Latrobe*, New York 1955, 86 ff. and pls. ix and x.

173 30. I have to thank Dr Monika Steinhauser for first telling me of this hotel.

31. J. L. Klüber, *Beschreibung von Baden bei Rastatt und seiner Umgebung*, Tübingen 1810, 125 ff. and pl. II. The *Beschreibung* is incidentally referred to in Rauers, op. cit., 882.

32. U. von Hase in her contribution to the Thyssen symposium, *Die deutsche Stadt im neunzehnten Jahrhundert*, Munich (Fritz Thyssen Stiftung) 1974, 131, prints a description made in 1810 of the Gesellschaftshaus built at Wiesbaden in 1803. Wiesbaden became one of the leading spas of Germany. The Gesellschaftshaus had a hall 127 by 67 feet with 28 columns and a coffered vault. The designer was Johann Christian Fais.

33. J. Urdizil, *Goethe in Böhmen*, 2nd ed., Zürich 1965, where also much other literature is quoted. I only want to refer to three books not specializing in Goethe: K. Ludwig, *Altes Karlsbad*, Karlsbad 1920; V. Karell, *Karlsbad im Wandel der Jahrhunderte*, Marburg 1958; and *Unser Marienbad*, ed. F. Arnold, Marburg 1958.

34. Examples of hotels are at Karlsbad the Posthof, the Drei Mohren and the Goldenes Schiff, at Marienbad the Klinger and Weimar. Goethe and the Levetzows took rooms in the Klebelsberg Palais.

35. II, Paris 1809, 180.

36. J. Foulston, *The Public Buildings erected in the West of England*, London 1838. Also F. Jenkins, 'John Foulston and his Public Buildings in Plymouth, Stonehouse and Devonport', *JSAH*, XXVII, 1968, 124 ff.

174 37. Mr Monkhouse quoted to me another hotel-cum-Athenaeum. The design was exhibited as by H. Duesbury at the Royal Academy in 1839.

38. J. Williamson, *The American Hotel*, New York 1930, 10; V. L. Glasgow, *The Hotels of New York City prior to the American Civil War*, thesis, Pennsylvania State University 1970, 27. Also L. Dorsey and J. Devine, *Fare thee well*, New York 1964, 36.

39. Most of my information on the Exchange Coffee House comes from an article published in *Omnium Gatherum*, Boston 1810, 3–9, to which my attention was drawn by Mr Leonard Lee Bacon. It also lists people who had offices in the building, and says that the hotel apartments were for travellers and also 'resident boarders'. The article as a summing-up calls the building 'the most elegant, convenient and useful on the continent'. See also C. H. Snow, *A History of Boston*, Boston 1825, which adds further details and corrects a mistake in *Omnium Gath-*

erum – which gives 100 feet as the dome's circumference, not diameter (Snow, p. 530). Also P. Metcalf, 'Courtyard Hotels', *Arch. Rev.*, CXLVI, 1969, 156, and Williamson, op. cit., 11.

40. Useful information on seaside hotels, as well as on the Royal Victoria Hotel, is to be found in J. Manwaring Baines, *Burton's St Leonards*, Hastings 1952. On the development of Hastings, St Leonards and the hotel, there is now Christopher Monkhouse in *Country Life*, 14, 21 and 28 February 1974. Mr Monkhouse shows that the drawings for the hotel complex are signed 'J. Burton'.

41. But he added, 'though not equal in splendor or convenience to many in America'. (*The English Notebooks*, ed. R. Stewart, New York and London 1941, 120.) Why he said that we shall see presently.

42. *London*, IV, London 1843, 310 ff.

175 43. I wish to thank Mr F. J. Cridlan for much help over the Regent Hotel and Mr H. S. Tallamy for general help over Leamington.

44. Schopenhauer, *Reise*, op. cit. (above, n. 20), I, 251–55, 185 ff., II, 15 ff.

45. *Domestic Manners of the Americans*, Vintage Books ed., New York 1960, 214.

46. *American Notes for General Circulation*, London 1842. I am quoting from the Penguin edition, ed. J. S. Whitley and A. Goldman, Harmondsworth 1972, 184.

47. Thanks to help from Mr Ronald Rey I could read *Niles' Register*, 7 May and 19 September 1825, *Annals of Baltimore*, 1825, 251–52, and *Balto-American*, 1 January 1827, 5.

48. *Greek Revival Architecture in America*, Oxford 1944, 112 ff.

49. But he also calls it 'the first modern hotel in America', and that statement must now be modified.

50. W. H. Eliot, *A Description of Tremont House*, Boston 1830.

51. *American Notes*, op. cit., 74. Dickens, though critical of much in the United States, is complimentary to nearly all hotels: Barnum's in Baltimore has already been mentioned. The Richmond he calls 'very large and elegant' (181), Harrisburg 'a snug hotel' (184), Pittsburgh 'most excellent' (200), Galt House, Louisville 'splendid' (211), Planters' House, St Louis 'excellent' (218), Neil House, Columbus 'very large, unfinished' (235), Lebanon 'great' (256), West Point 'most excellent' (261).

176 52. So Mr D. D. Reiff informed me, with cuttings from the *National Graphic and Literary Register*, 19 September and 2 October 1828, and 26 January 1829.

53. According to Thomas Walsh in *The Builder*, XXI, 1863, 92 ff. (cf. my p. 180). But Williamson, op. cit., 32, says $400,000. For the Astor House see Glasgow, op. cit., 31–32 and 71–76. Mr Glasgow in his thesis also discusses Holt's Hotel of 1832–33 (with 165 bedrooms and 25 parlours, a dining room the same size as that of the Astor House (100 feet in length), six floors, a central cupola, and the first luggage lift in New York), and the North American Hotel, also of 1832.

54. Glasgow, op. cit., 18.

55. For nearly all the following pages see Williamson, op. cit.

56. *Greek Revival*, op. cit., 224. For the St Charles see also Glasgow, op. cit., 22.

57. Hamlin, *Greek Revival*, op. cit., pl. 27.

58. B. St J. Ravenel, *Architects of Charleston*, 2nd ed., Charleston, S.C. 1964, 177–79.

59. R. van Zant, *The Catskill Mountain House*, New Brunswick, N.J. 1966. Mr D. D. Reiff and Mr H. Schaefer told me about this book.

177 60. H. Huth, *Nature and the Americans*, University of California 1957, 146.

61. Quoted from Williamson, op. cit., 244.

62. *The Spas of England*, London 1841, 314.

63. I am grateful to Mr B. Swadling, Borough Librarian of Cheltenham, for a Xerox copy of the article.

64. The part of Brown's in Albemarle Street followed much later. See E. Vale, 'The Story of Brown's Hotel', *Blackmansbury*, VIII, 1971, 45–60. In this context it is worth remembering that Club Chambers in Lower Regent Street (by Decimus Burton) was built in 1838 and contained unfurnished 'bed-sitters' exclusively – 77 of them. Originally there were also refreshment and reading rooms. Club Chambers provided what the clubs – multiplying just then – provided inadequately. See e.g. P. Metcalf, *Victorian London*, London 1972, 30.

65. L. Hautecoeur, *Histoire de l'architecture classique en France*, VII, Paris 1957, 323.

178 66. Vicomte d'Avenel, *Mécanisme*, op. cit. (above, n. 11), 15–16.

67. Mr Titmarsh in *The Paris Sketch Book*, London 1840, 22.

179 68. In the *Schweizer Hotelführer* for 1973 I counted fifteen Bristols, and I may well have overlooked some. Both Vienna and Berlin had well-known Bristols. Theodor Fontane shows in *Der Stechlin*, published in 1891, that he did not know this derivation. Old Stechlin says (chap. 32), 'All [hotels] must be called Bristol . . . Why Bristol?' It is after all 'a place of the second order'.

69. Zaniboni, op. cit. (above, n. 4), 81.

70. R. B. Ludy, *Historic Hotels of the World*, Philadelphia 1927, 202.

71. I owe this information to Dr P. Guyer, City Archivist.

72. *Builder*, VIII, 1850, 106; *Illustrated London News*, XXV, 1854, 396. It had originally a central hall of 60 by 60 feet, skylit and with galleries.

73. I wish to thank Mr D. B. Timms, Borough Librarian, for this information.

74. Glasgow, op. cit., 39.

75. In the 3rd ed. of James Fergusson's *History of the modern Styles of Architecture*, London 1891.

180 76. Glasgow, op. cit., and two other theses at Pennsylvania State University: F. J. Kaplan, *The Architecture of New York City Hotels from 1860 until 1885*, 1970, and L. S. Dubin, *The Hotels of New York City, 1885–1900*, 1969.

77. Glasgow, op. cit., 35. Also Dorsey and Devine, op. cit., 50. The architects were Trench & Snook.

78. XXI, 1863, 92 ff.

79. This, according to Glasgow (op. cit., 104–12 and 119–26), is not correct. The St Nicholas (1851–54) had 22 bays plus an addition of 12, 6 floors and 500 rooms and

100 suites, the Fifth Avenue (1856–59) had 14 bays, 6 floors and 530 rooms (i.e. 800 guests).

80. Dubin, op. cit., 37.

81. *American Notes*, op. cit. (above, n. 46), 287.

82. *The New Metropolis*, 1899. Quoted from N. Silver, *Lost New York*, (Boston) 1967, 64.

83. *Things as they are in America.* Quoted from Glasgow, op. cit., 20.

84. ibid., 91.

85. Kaplan, op. cit., 64.

181 86. M. Schuyler, 'The Work of Henry Janeway Hardenbergh', *Arch. Rev.*, VI, 1897, 375 ff. Hardenbergh's early Dakota Apartment Building was built in 1884.

87. Dubin, op. cit., 228.

88. R. Sturgis, *Dictionary of Architecture and Building*, New York 1901–02, II, cols. 410–13.

89. e.g. the Victoria of 1870 by R. M. Hunt (Kaplan, op. cit.). For much later examples see *Architectural Forum*, Apartment Hotel Number, XLI, 1924.

90. Glasgow, op. cit., 28–29; ibid., 120–21; Dubin, op. cit., 191; ibid., 119.

91. Bradshaw's *Railway Guide,* April, reprint Newton Abbot 1968.

92. Kaplan, op. cit., 9 ff., 41 ff.

93. Glasgow, op. cit., 122–25.

94. Dorsey and Devine, op. cit., 95.

95. Glasgow, op. cit., ill. p. 219.

96. Kaplan, op. cit.

97. Dubin, op. cit.

182 98. Kaplan, op. cit.

99. R. Hale Newton, *Town & Davis Architects*, New York 1942, fig. 36 (design for a hotel on Constitution Island).

100. *Building News*, 1866.

101. They were commissioned in 1888 to 'redecorate and replan' an apartment hotel by Carl Pfeiffer, built before 1884; their building was of red brick. See *Real Estate and Guide*, 1 December 1888. I owe this reference to Mr Stanley Baron.

102. Dubin, op. cit. All the hotels so far mentioned were intended to be expensive and luxurious. But efforts at cheap hotels for New York deserve at least a note. D. O. Mills's People's Hotel No. I was designed by Ernest Flagg (of the Singer Building and the Naval Academy at Annapolis) and built in 1896–97. It had 1,500 cubicles and a night cost of 20 cents. One bathroom went with 52 cubicles. Hotel No. II opened one year later. It had 600 cubicles. (Dubin, op. cit., 178 ff.)

103. 18 December 1852.

104. *Builder*, XVIII, 1860, 755.

105. ibid., XVI, 1858, 668.

106. ibid., XX, 1862, 914.

107. Quoted in L. R. Jones, *Metropole Folkestone, the old . . . the new*, Folkestone 1969, 19.

108. *Builder*, IX, 1851, 602.

109. Quoted from Ludy, op. cit. (above, n. 70), 235.

110. *Temple Bar Magazine*, II, 1866. Quoted from Williamson, op. cit., 49.

111. Thus Glasgow, op. cit. But Dubin, op. cit., says about $500,000, which seems more likely.

112. Dubin, op. cit., 251 ff.

113. Chicago had been earlier. See below, pp. 218–20.

114. Mrs Dubin commented on this statement as follows: Both had steel frames, the New Netherland perhaps a skeleton, probably a cage. The Savoy is more likely to have had a true skeleton. The only hotel of those years certain to have had a true steel skeleton is Hardenbergh's Manhattan of 1896.

115. op. cit., 91.

183 116. ed. of 1909.

117. ibid.

118. London 1885, 325.

119. Van Zant, op. cit. (above, n. 59), 231. Also Ludy, op. cit., 227.

120. I owe these facts to D. D. Reiff, who also referred me to H. K. Hochschild, *An Adirondack Resort in the nineteenth Century*, Adirondack Museum 1962.

121. *The Story of Mohonk*, 4th ed. 1911.

122. Baedeker, op. cit., 181.

123. *Directory . . .*, 1884, 63 and 67.

124. R. Newcomb, *Architecture in Old Kentucky*, Urbana 1953, 128 ff.

125. W. Crane, *An Artist's Reminiscences*, London 1907, 395. Mrs Lesley Freudenheim gave me the Crane quotation.

126. Baedeker, op. cit., 617.

127. P. Collins, *Concrete*, London 1959, 87. Professor Collins writes that the first hotel in reinforced concrete was Hennebique's Imperial Palace at Nice, dating from 1900.

128. *American Architect*, LXXXIX, 1906, 119.

129. But F. von Hellwald, *Amerika in Wort und Bild*, Leipzig (c. 1883), I, 741, says 1,200 guests.

130. Kaplan, op. cit., 18, mentions the Windsor in New York as also having a hall from ground level to top and galleries. The date is 1871–73, the architect John Sexton.

131. The hotel was rebuilt after 1906. That building survives at New Montgomery and Market Streets. See R. Olmsted and T. H. Watkins, *Here to-day*, San Francisco 1928, 86, and D. Gebhard and others, *A Guide to Architecture in San Francisco and Northern California*, Santa Barbara and Salt Lake City 1973, 67.

132. Ludy, op. cit., 235. Incidentally the Union Hotel in Vienna by A. Prokop, 1873, seems to have been built on the same principle. See L. Klasen, *Grundriss-Vorbilder in Gebäuden aller Art*, 15 pts., Leipzig 1884–96, pt. II, 140–41.

133. Here are a few addenda to the Brown Palace at Denver, taken from their brochure. Height 10 storeys, triangular shape, each side 810 feet, cost $1,600,000 plus £400,000 for the furnishings. In 1959 a 22-storey tower was added at the side.

184 134. op. cit., V, 50–56.

135. Dubin, op. cit., 66 ff. and 88 ff.

136. ibid., 111.

137. Dorsey and Devine, op. cit., 139.

138. Paris 1895, 99.

139. Another reason was that people lived in hotels while their houses were being built; though this was of course never widespread. See, for instance, Mrs Louisine W. Havemeyer's *Sixteen to Sixty: Memoirs of a Collector*, New York (p.p.) 1961. The Havemeyers lived at the Plaza. I owe this observation and reference to Mr Stanley Baron.

140. Baedeker, op. cit., 410.

141. A plan is in *Wasmuths Lexikon der Baukunst*, Berlin 1929–32, III, 163.

142. E. Hungerford, *The Story of the Waldorf-Astoria*, New York 1925, 158; Williamson, op. cit., 295; H. B. Lent, *The Waldorf-Astoria*, New York 1934. Also J. R. McCarthy, *Peacock Alley*, New York and London 1931.

186 143. Williamson, op. cit., 245.

144. *Storia di Milano*, Milan (Fondazione Treccani) 1960, XIV, 760. The volume deals with 1815–59. The hotel is also mentioned by Zaniboni, op. cit. (above, n. 4), and Rauers, op. cit. (above, n. 14), I.

145. Quoted from Glasgow, op. cit., 22.

146. ibid., 93, 95.

147. ibid., 106, 107, 112.

148. ibid., 121–22.

149. Kaplan, op. cit., 12.

150. ibid., 20.

151. Dubin, op. cit., 139.

152. ibid., 208.

153. Hungerford, op. cit., 259.

154. In Sturgis, op. cit. (above, n. 88), 413.

155. As for the provinces, Williamson (op. cit., 61) quotes the Victoria Hotel at Kansas City, opened in 1888, with 240 suites of bedroom, parlour and bathroom, and the Arlington in Boston in 1894, also entirely a family hotel. On the other hand F. von Hellwald, writing about 1885 (op. cit., 155), tells us that the American monster hotels have 'hot and cold baths in every bedroom'. Did he mean basins? And Paul Bourget writes in 1895 (*Outremer*, 33): 'You can count the bedrooms which have not their private dressing room with bathroom.'

156. op. cit., 145.

157. *The Illustrated London News*, 26 October 1889, 534–35, gives the architect as W. Young. The many bathrooms are called 'a new idea'. See also Stanley Jackson, *The Savoy*, London 1954.

158. The river front was refaced in 1910.

187 159. *Clean and Decent*, London 1960, 234.

160. See the special hotel issue of *Arch. Rev.*, XIX, 1913, 104. The issue is mostly about recent American hotels. Plans of the standard bedroom-bathroom combination are on pp. 37 and 38. W. Hawkins Ferry (*The Buildings of Detroit*, Detroit 1960, 212) reports that the Statler of Detroit (also by Post) dated from 1914 and had 800 bedrooms all with bathrooms. As for other hotels, the Touraine in Boston of 1897 by Winston & Wetherel and the Vanderbilt in New York, by Warren & Wetmore, hotel specialists, had the standard arrangement. (I have to thank Miss Cederholm of the Boston Public Library for information on the Touraine. In style it was a sumptuous Louis XII.)

161. Williamson, op. cit., 153.

162. C. H. Hilton, *Be My Guest*, Englewood Cliffs, Calif. 1957.

163. K. Wilson, *The Holiday Inn Story*, Memphis, Tenn. 1971.

164. Williamson, op. cit., 63. Glasgow, op. cit., 35 (Metropolitan 1852, only public rooms). Kaplan, op. cit., 62 (Grand Central 1870, first in New York for guest rooms).

165. op. cit., 24.

166. Kaplan, op. cit., 63.

167. Williamson, op. cit., 66, 168.

168. op. cit., 68, also Hellwald, op. cit. (above, n. 129), 570.

169. Glasgow, op. cit., 28.

170. ibid., 41, 121.

171. *The English Cathedral in the nineteenth century*, 128–29.

172. In Sturgis, op. cit. (above, n. 88), quoted from Dubin, op. cit., 264.

173. *Rev. gén. de l'arch.*, XVII, 1859, 276.

174. Glasgow, op. cit., 126.

175. ed. of 1842, 703.

176. *Illustrated London News*, 25 February 1860; *Builder*, XXII, 1864, 878. The same term still in an advertisement for the London Savoy in 1891.

177. *Illustrated London News*, 7 June 1860.

188 178. op. cit., 148.

179. Other early lifts were in the Galt House at Louisville, Ky., the Occidental in San Francisco, Calif., the Monongahela in Pittsburgh, Pa., the Maxwell House in Nashville, Tenn., the St Charles in New Orleans, La., and the Congress at Saratoga, N.Y. See *Otis Elevator Company; the first one hundred years*, 1953, 9.

180. *Civil Engineer*, XIV, 1851, 355.

181. 27 October 1855, 406.

182. *Trans. RIBA*, 1854–55, 27 ff.: 'I cannot recall any period since the time of the Roman Emperors when works of such magnitude, magnificence and essential utility were executed.'

183. *Rev. gén. de l'arch.*, XX, 1862, 284.

184. *Gaz. des arch.*, III, 1865, 145–51.

189 185. P. Metcalf, *The Rise of James Knowles, Victorian Architect and Editor*, PhD thesis, University of London 1971.

186. *Illustrated London News*, 3 April, 349–50. Also *Building News*, IV, 1858, 320.

187. 18 October 1858.

188. *Builder*, XVIII, 1860, 755 and XIX, 1861, 375.

189. *Trans. RIBA*, 1861–62, 111 ff.; *Builder*, XX, 1862, 165.

190. Andrew Carnegie stayed at the Westminster – see his *An American Four-in-Hand in Britain*, London 1889, 18.

191. *Builder*, XXII, 1864, 876 and 930; XXI, 1863, 531, and XXIII, 1865, 433.

190 192. *Scarborough Gazette*, 25 July and 1 August 1867.

193. Builder, XX, 1862, 914–15.

194. *Briefe an einen Architekten*, Munich 1913, 4 August 1879.

195. Baedeker, op. cit., also mentions the size for the following: Strand Palace 500 rooms, Royal Palace Hotel 350 beds, Great Central (Marylebone) 700 beds, Russell 500 rooms, De Keyser's Royal (in the City) 400 rooms.

196. J. Simmons, *St Pancras Station*, London 1968.

197. op. cit., 51 (4 September 1877).

198. I am grateful to Professor Wagner-Rieger for much of the following information.

191 199. *Allgemeine Bauzeitung*, XXXVI, 1871, 244–46 and XLIV, 1879, 91. Also Klasen, op. cit. (above, n. 132), 142–43.

200. Professor Peter Mayer gave me some information on Swiss hotels.

201. *Further Records*, London 1878, 178.

202. The five leading hotels at St Moritz Bad had together 1,450 beds, the four (still) leading hotels at Dorf have 1,430. That includes the Suvrettahaus. (Baedeker's *Switzerland*, 1927 ed.)

203. J. Gantner and A. Reinle, *Kunstgeschichte der Schweiz*, IV, Frauenfeld 1962, 111. Also P. Planat, *Encyclopédie de l'architecture et de la construction*, 6 vols., Paris 1888–95, V, 157.

204. Gantner and Reinle, ibid.

205. My source is the *Schweizer Hotelführer*, 1973.

206. *Souvenirs d'Allemagne*, Paris 1960, 39.

207. The last-named is listed in Murray's *Handbook* in 1874.

192 208. Murray also carried an advertisement for the Angleterre in Berlin, 'residence of Her British Majesty's Messengers'.

209. Zaniboni, op. cit. (above, n. 4), 139 ff.

210. ibid. For Bristols see above, p. 179. The *Schweizer Hotelführer* for 1973 has also Alexandra, Ascot, Derby, Windsor.

211. P. Henderson, *The Letters of William Morris*, London 1950, 57.

Finally, a postscript to names. Zaniboni, op. cit., has plenty of English ones: Torre di Londra in Verona (eighteenth century; p. 36), in Venice the Regina d'Inghilterra (78), Villa di Londra (134), Albergo d'Inghilterra (139), Isole Britanniche (139), and Londra (139); in Naples the Vittoria, Grande Bretagne and Villa di Londra (165). And there also are in Rome an Ecu de France, a Petit Paris and a Petit Louvre (133, 130), and an Albergo d'America in Rome and a Washington and a New York in Naples (139, 165, 167).

212. 400 beds, 250 bathrooms.

213. Quoted from O. A. Graf, *Die vergessene Wagnerschule*, Vienna 1969.

214. The British Hotels, Restaurants and Caterers Association tells me that in London between 1968 and 1973 thirteen hotels of 400 rooms or more were opened.

215. P. Carbonara, *Architettura pratica*, Turin 1954–62, vol. II, 209 ff.

216. G. Baker and B. Funaro, *Motels*, New York 1955, 1.

217. *Motels, Hotels, Restaurants and Bars (Architectural Forum)*, 1953, 2nd ed. 1956, 29 ff.

218. Baker and Funaro, op. cit., 3. C. Vernon Kane, *Motor Courts*, New York (1954).

219. Baker and Funaro, op. cit., 2.

220. A. Koch, *Hotelbauten, Motels, Ferienhäuser*, Stuttgart 1958, 288 ff.

221. G. Aloi, *Alberghi, Motel, Ristoranti*, Milan 1961, 257–58.

222. V. Nabokov, *Lolita*, London 1955, pt. II, chap. I, 143–45.

12 Exchanges and banks

BIBLIOGRAPHY

For exchanges the bibliography is easy. Dr K. H. Schreyl's *Zur Geschichte der Baugattung Börse*, PhD thesis, Berlin 1963, covers the field excellently in hardly more than thirty pages. The notes at the end are a full introduction to other existing literature.

The situation concerning banking is the very reverse. What can here be given of general books and papers is from the architectural point of view quite inadequate. The best introduction to the whole field is M. Palyi and P. Quittner, *Enzyklopädisches Lexikon für das Geld-, Bank- und Börsenwesen*, 2 vols., Frankfurt 1958. – A brief but satisfying history of banking is A. Dauphin-Meunier, *Histoire de la banque*, Paris 1951. Yet briefer but also profitable are the entries in the *Enciclopedia italiana*, VI, Rome and Milan 1930, 33 ff.,

and the *Encyclopaedia Britannica*, 1970 ed, III, 92 ff.

NOTES

p.193 1. Iris Origo, *The Merchant of Prato*, London 1957, also Penguin ed., Harmondsworth 1963.

2. J. Ainaud, J. Gudiol and F.-P. Verrié, *La ciudad de Barcelona (Catálogo Monumental de España)*, Madrid 1947, I, 322.

194 3. The type continued into the later Cinquecento, with the Loggia dei Banchi in Genoa, attributed to Alessi and built in 1570–96.

4. Origo, op. cit., 126.

5. A. Doren, *Studien zur florentinischen Wirtschaftsgeschichte*, 2 vols., Leipzig 1901–08. A Doren, *Italienische Wirtschaftsgeschichte*, Jena 1934. R. Davidsohn, *Geschichte von Florenz*, 4 vols., Berlin 1896–1908, especially vol. IV, pts. 1, 2 and 3. R. de Roover, *Money, Banking and Credit in Mediaeval Bruges*, Cambridge, Mass. 1948. F. Edler de Roover, *Glossary of Mediaeval Terms of Business*, Cambridge, Mass. 1937.

For Italian bankers and merchants in England see J. Hatcher, *English Tin Production and Trade before 1550*, Oxford 1973, and G. D. Ramsey, 'The undoing of the Italian mercantile colony in sixteenth-century London', in *Textile History and Economic History (Essays in Honour of Miss Julia de Lacy Mann)*, ed. N. B. Harte and K. G. Ponting, Manchester 1973, 22–52 – neither used by me.

6. R. de Roover, *The Rise and Decline of the Medici Bank*, Cambridge, Mass. 1963. Also, briefer: R. de Roover, *The Medici Bank*, New York and London 1948. On other Florentine bankers and their relation to the arts see several papers in A. Warburg, *Gesammelte Schriften*, I, Leipzig and Berlin 1932.

7. Quoted from Roover, 1948, op. cit., 3.

8. One example for many: At Michaelmas 1326 Hugh le Despenser Jun. deposited £5,735 with the Peruzzi.

195 9. Doren, *Studien*, op. cit., I, 355. The sum involved was for the Bardi 550,000 gold florins, for the Peruzzi 351,000 (Davidsohn, op. cit., IV, pt. 1, 304).

In Lucca the most important bankers were the Riccardi, and their most famous client was Edward I of England. See M. C. Prestwich, *War, Politics and Finance under Edward I*, London 1972, and R. W. Kaeuper, *Bankers to the Crown*, Princeton 1973.

10. So Guicciardini says, in his *Descrizione di tutti i Paesi Bassi*, Antwerp 1567. See H. van Werveke, 'Les Origines des bourses commerciales', *Revue belge de philologie et de l'histoire*, XV, 1936, 133 ff.

11. op. cit., 67.

12. R. Hadfield, 'Some Unknown Descriptions of the Medici Palace in 1459', *Art Bulletin*, LII, 1970, 232 ff., has nothing; W. A. Bulse, 'Die ursprüngliche innere Aufteilung des Palazzo Medici', *Mitteilungen des Kunsthistorischen Instituts in Florenz*, XIV, 1970, 369 ff., a little.

196 13. V. Vianello, *Luca Pacioli nella storia della ragioneria*, Messina 1896. Also R. Gene Brown and K. S. Johnston, *Pacioli on Accounting*, New York 1963, and B. Penndorf, *Abhandlung über die Buchhaltung*, Stuttgart 1933. For Venice the Mastro of Giacomo Badoer dates from 1436–39.

14. Mastro of the Fraternità dei Soranzo – see Vianello, op. cit., 134–35.

15. A. Dauphin-Meunier, *Histoire de la banque*, Paris 1951, 262.

16. *Treatise on Architecture, being the Treatise by Antonio Averlino, known as Filarete*, ed. J. R. Spencer, New Haven, Conn. 1965, I, 325–27. Even more recent is the edition by L. Grassi, Milan (Il Polifilo) 1972.

17. O. Morisani, *Michelozzo architetto*, Turin 1951, 71 ff.

18. M. Hazé, *Notices pittoresques sur les antiquites . . . de Bourges*, Bourges and Paris 1834; P. Clément, *Jacques Coeur et Charles VII*, 2 vols., Paris 1853; H. Prutz, *Geschichte eines patriotischen Kaufmanns aus dem 15. Jahrhundert*, Berlin 1911, especially 251–327.

19. Dauphin-Meunier, op. cit., 190–96.

20. Ill. Hazé, op. cit., pl. 35.

21. For the Fuggers in general the best book is still R. Ehrenberg, *Das Zeitalter der Fugger*, 2 vols., Jena 1896. Also G. Freiherr von Pölnitz, *Die Fugger*, 2nd ed., Frankfurt 1960, and the same author's *Anton Fugger, Studien zur Fuggergeschichte*, nos. 13, 17, 20, 23, Tübingen 1958 etc. (so far 3 vols.). Briefer: E. Herring, *Die Fugger*, Leipzig 1939; G. Strieder, *Jakob Fugger der Reiche*, Leipzig (1926); W. Winker, *Jakob Fugger der Reiche*, Munich 1940. For the purposes of the present book, however, we have now N. Lieb, *Die Fugger und die Kunst*, 2 vols., Tübingen 1952–58.

22. Quoted from Ehrenberg, op. cit., I, 111–12.

23. Not, as some people want to make it appear, as a workers' estate. The houses were 'for certain poor and needy citizens and inhabitants . . . who don't publicly ask for alms'. (Lieb, op. cit., 1952, 250 ff.).

24. Professor Lieb gave me chapter and verse. The first appearance of the description is in 1879, in the *Bildercyclus Die Fugger und ihre Zeit*. This was followed in 1900 by A. Hauber, *Das Haus Fugger*. See also Professor Lieb himself on this matter (op. cit., 305 and 331).

197 25. H. Bechtel, *Matthäus Schwarz*, 1935. I was not able to use this book. Instead I had access to A. Weitnauer, *Venezianischer Handel der Fugger; nach der Musterbuchhaltung des Matthäus Schwarz*, Munich and Leipzig 1931.

26. Weitnauer, op. cit., 134 and 8.

27. J. M. von Welser, *Die Welser*, 2 vols., 1917. Also, and for the Tucher, the Hochstetter and others, see Dauphin-Meunier, op. cit., 216–22.

28. Thieme-Becker, *Künstlerlexikon*, I, Leipzig 1907.

198 29. And re-started in 1587. Frankfurt had something similar, the Wessil (i.e. *Wechsel* or *cambio*) of 1402.

199 30. Quoted from Dauphin-Meunier, op. cit., 179–80.

31. Another bank followed in Venice in 1619. This was called Banco del Giro and fused with the Rialto bank in 1638.

32. E. Ponti, *Il Banco di Santo Spirito*, Rome 1951. The architects involved in the building are the younger Antonio da Sangallo and Borromini. For Borromini see most recently *Studi sul Borromini (Atti del Convegno promosso dell'Academia Nazionale di San Luca)*, Rome 1967, 379.

33. The new building was still small. Its signboard read *Asylum Egentium*, and indeed it was called *Bank van Leening*, i.e. it was a kind of Monte di Pietà. Stockholm started in 1657, Copenhagen in 1736. My thanks are due to Dr Loose of the State Archives for Hamburg, to M. J. van Lieborg Jun. for Rotterdam, to Miss E. Hertz of the Municipal Library for Nuremberg, to G. Pettersson of the Municipal Library for Stockholm, to Miss Steffensen of the City Library for Copenhagen and the Deputy Mayor and Town Clerk of Delft. Incidentally the Nuremberg bank (located again in the Town Hall) was called *Bancho Publico*, that is *all'italiana*.

34. J. E. White, *History of the three Royal Exchanges*, London 1896.

35. The same plan type was used at Seville, where the exchange was built in 1582–99 to Juan de Herrera's design (G. Kubler and M. Soria, *Art and Architecture in Spain and Portugal and their American Dominions, 1500–1800* (Pelican History of Art), Harmondsworth 1959, 14 and pl. 5).

Serlio in his Book VII, first published in 1575, illustrates the plan of an exchange. It has no connection with the existing plan types for such a building. There is a five-bay colonnade to the street, and the *Sala* is on the upper floor. (*Tutte le opere d'architettura*, Venice 1584, bk. VII, 116–17.) On this see now M. N. Rosenfeld, 'Sebastiano Serlio's Drawings in the Nationalbibliothek in Vienna for his Seventh Book on Architecture', *Art Bulletin*, LVI, 1974, 407–08.

36. *Some Account of London*, London 1793, 413. I am quoting from the third edition.

200 37. For England after the foundation of the Bank of England there is now P. L. Cottrell and B. L. Anderson, *Money and Banking in England, 1694–1934*, Newton Abbot 1974, though I have not seen it.

38. Of the large literature on the Bank it is sufficient to refer here to Sir John Clapham, *The Bank of England, a History*, 2 vols., Cambridge 1944, and H. R. Steele and F. R. Yerbury, *The Old Bank of England*, London 1930.

39. R. D. Richards (*The early History of Banking in England*, London 1929, 195) writes that by 1826 there were 780 private banks in the country and 60 in London.

40. See e.g. T. E. Gregory, *The Westminster Bank*, London 1936. I have not been able to trace early cases of branch banks. That they multiplied in the nineteenth century and after is familiar. The Crédit Lyonnais had 307 provincial branches in 1913 and 1,494 in 1962 (see *Un Siècle d'économie française, 1863–1963* – below, n. 75). I counted in the telephone book for Inner London 157 branches of Lloyds Bank.

41. Geneva 1772, II, 60.

42. H. P. R. Hoare, *Hoare's Bank, 1672–1932*, London 1932, 50 ff.

201 43. See Gregory, op. cit., II, 55–57.

44. Chap. 3. This is the text: 'Gundermann occupait . . . un immense hôtel, . . . assez grand pour son innombrable famille. . . . Et, à part deux de ses gendres qui n'habitaient pas l'hôtel, tous les autres avaient leurs appartements, dans les ailes de gauche et de droite, ouvertes sur le jardin; tandis que le bâtiment central était pris entièrement par l'installation des vastes bureaux de la banque.'

45. For the Hôtel de Toulouse in the pre-bank centuries see F. Laudet, *L'Hôtel de Toulouse*, Paris 1932. Also A. Blunt, *François Mansart*, London 1941, 34. For the earliest years of the bank see M. Marion, 'La Fondation de la Banque de France', in *History of the Principal Public Banks*, The Hague 1934. A brief but useful account is in Dauphin-Meunier, op. cit., 65 ff. and 386 ff.

203 46. For Bordeaux in the sixteenth century see P. Roudié, 'L'Ancienne bourse des marchands de Bordeaux', *Revue de l'art*, no. 20, 1973, 78 ff.

47. A. Oncken, *Friedrich Gilly*, Berlin 1935, 92 and pl. 75.

48. At Bordeaux this had already been done in 1803. See K. H. Schreyl, *Zur Geschichte der Baugattung Börse*, PhD thesis, Berlin 1963, n. 121.

49. Cockerell's design, which was not accepted, is far more coherent and dramatic.

50. L. Hautecoeur, *Histoire de l'architecture classique en France*, IV, Paris 1952, 171–72, and V, 1953, 223–25; M. L. Biver, *Le Paris de Napoléon*, Paris 1963, 123–24; and now in much greater detail, D. Wiebenson, 'The Two Domes of the Halle au Blé in Paris', *Art Bulletin*, LV, 1973, 262–79. Also J. Stern, *A l'Ombre de Sophie Arnould*, Paris 1930, II, 202. Of older publications see L. Bruyère, *Etudes relatives à l'art des constructions*, Paris 1823–28, I, Recueil II. C. L. G. Eck. *Traité de construction en poteries et fer*, Paris 1836, pl. 36. M. E. Isabelle, *Les Edifices circulaires et les dômes*, Paris 1843, 142–45, and pls. 77–78.

It was incidentally at the Halle au Blé that in 1786 Thomas Jefferson was introduced by Trumbull to Maria Cosway. See e.g. M. D. Peterson, *Thomas Jefferson and the New Nation*, Oxford and New York 1970, 347.

51. The Exchange is now the City Hall. The façade is illustrated e.g. in Sir John Summerson's *Architecture in Britain, 1530–1830* (Pelican History of Art), 5th ed., Harmondsworth 1969, pl. 178. For details see E. McFarland, 'James Gandon and the Royal Exchange Competition', *Journal of the Society of Antiquaries of Ireland*, CII, pt. 1, 1972, 38–42, and J. A. Culliton, 'The City Hall of Dublin', *Dublin Historical Record*, XVI, no. 3, March 1961.

204 52. Published in 1806 in Thomon's *Recueil de plans et façades des principaux monumens construits a Saint-Pétersbourg*.

53. II, Paris 1809, 60 and pl. 14.

54. In Francesco Milizia's *Principi di architettura civile*, 2nd ed., Bassano 1785, the *borsa* is immediately preceded by the *tribunale* (p. 271), which is like a Roman basilica. Milizia refers explicitly to Palladio.

55. C. Duguid, *The Story of the Stock Exchange*, London 1901.

56. Classicism also characterizes, or characterized, the exchanges of the same decade at Trieste and Manchester. Trieste, by Antonio Mollari, 1802–06 (C. Meeks, *Italian Architecture, 1750–1914*, New Haven, Conn. 1966, 153–54), had a giant Tuscan portico. Manchester, by Thomas Harrison, 1806–09 (J. Aston, *A Picture of Manchester*, Manchester 1816, 204–12), had a semicircular end articulated by thin

giant Greek Doric demi-columns. The room behind had a demi-dome.

206 57. T. Hamlin, *Benjamin Henry Latrobe*, New York 1955, 153–57. The bank was not unknown in England. In Disraeli's *Sybil*, i.e. in 1845, an American says: 'I'll give you a cheque at sight on the Pennsylvania Bank.' (Penguin ed., Harmondsworth 1954, 338.) Another bank by Latrobe was his last work: the Louisiana State Bank, 405 Royal Street, New Orleans. It had a centrally-planned vaulted hall with three lunette penetrations and the supports totally devoid of capitals (see Hamlin, 526–27). New Orleans incidentally also had an exchange in the Latrobe style, with a central rotunda. The date is 1835; the architects were Dakin & Dakin. It was demolished in 1960 (Hamlin, 227).

58. T. Hamlin, *Greek Revival Architecture in America*, Oxford 1944, 75 ff., pl. xx and fig. 8 on p. 277.

59. ibid., 277 and pl. lxxviii.

60. ibid., 302. Ill. W. Andrews, *Architecture in Chicago and Mid-America*, New York 1968, 13.

61. See *Encyclopaedia Britannica*, 1970 ed., XIX, 1108–09, and *Enciclopedia italiana*, IX, Rome and Milan 1931, 316 ff. (*Cassa di Risparmio*).

62. For the Buchhändlerbörse see *Leipzig und seine Bauten*, Leipzig 1892, 461.

63. *Builder*, XXIII, 1865, 834–35, 901–03, 909.

64. Schreyl, op. cit., 58 ff.

65. D. Linstrum, *Historic Architecture of Leeds*, Newcastle 1969, 58–59.

66. H.-R. Hitchcock, *Early Victorian Architecture in Britain*, New Haven, Conn. 1954, 320–34 and pls. X 14–24.

208 67. A. Gilchrist, 'John Haviland before 1816', *JSAH*, XX, 1961, 137.

68. M. Schuyler, *American Architecture*, ed. W. H. Jordy and R. Coe, Cambridge, Mass. 1961, I, 163.

69. For Manchester the Berlin firm of Hennicke & von der Hude designed an exchange in the Renaissance style with a vast elliptical hall: ill. *Builder*, 14 December 1865.

70. *Die Wiener Ringstrasse*, ed. R. Wagner-Rieger, I, Vienna, Cologne and Graz 1969, 146–47 and ill. pl. 106 a–e. Also *Handbuch der Architektur*, Teil IV, Halbband 2, Heft 2 (*Börsengebäude*, by H. Auer), Stuttgart 1902, 288.

71. *L'Argent*, chap. 8. The book has also splendid descriptions of the Bourse in feverish action. Here is one from chap. 10: 'Les quatre travées, en forme de croix, fermées par des grilles, sorte d'étoile à quatre branches ayant pour centre la corbeille, étaient le lieu sacré interdit au public; et, entre les branches, en avant, il y avait d'un côté un autre compartiment, où se trouvaient les commis du comptant, que dominaient les trois coteurs, assis sur de hautes chaises, devant leurs immenses registres; tandis que, de l'autre côté, un compartiment plus petit, ouvert celui-là, nommé "la guitare" à cause de sa forme sans doute, permettait aux employés et aux spéculateurs de se mettre en contact direct avec les agents. Derrière, dans l'angle formé par deux autres branches, se tenait, en pleine foule, le marché des rentes françaises, où chaque agent était repré-

senté, ainsi qu'au marché du comptant, par un commis spécial, ayant son carnet distinct; car les agents de change, autour de la corbeille, ne s'occupent exclusivement que des marchés à terme, tout entiers à la grande besogne effrénée du jeu.'

72. J. Gantner and A. Reinle, *Kunstgeschichte der Schweiz*, IV, Frauenfeld 1962, 100.

73. *Handbuch der Architektur*, op. cit., 285. Also *Frankfurt und seine Bauten*, Frankfurt (Architekten- und Ingenieur-Verein) 1886, and *Börse und Banken in Frankfurt am Main*, ed. E. Mushake and L. M. A. Mushake.

74. Hautecoeur, op. cit., VII, 1957, 88–89 and 157–59.

75. The Crédit Lyonnais sent me excellent documentation: *Notice sur le Crédit Lyonnais*, Paris 1913; *Un Siècle d'économie française, 1863–1963*; *Bulletin trimestriel*, special number on the internal remodelling, Paris 1971.

The Banque Nationale de Paris (or Banque pour le Commerce et l'Industrie), successor of the Comptoir National d'Escompte, was as helpful.

210 76. Ill. e.g. in *The Rise of an American Architecture*, ed. E. Kaufmann, Jr., New York, Washington and London 1970, 134, ill. 3–26.

77. *Builder*, XLI, 1881, 615.

78. Like the retrochoir of Peterborough Cathedral.

79. Müller also did the exchange at Königsberg (Kaliningrad), in 1875.

80. Norman Shaw in 1864 did a design for Bradford – see S. Muthesius, *The High Victorian Movement in Architecture*, London and Boston, Mass. 1972, 129–31. The style Shaw chose (being only thirty-three years of age) was Gothic.

81. *The Crown of Wild Olive*, Library Edition, ed. E. T. Cook and A. Wetherburn, XVIII, 433 ff.

212 82. P. Singelenberg, *H. P. Berlage, Idea and Style*, Utrecht 1972. Also by the same author *H. P. Berlage*, Amsterdam 1969, and still J. Gratama, *Dr H. P. Berlage, Bouwmeester*, Rotterdam 1925.

83. J. Kismarty-Lechner, *Lechner Ödön*, Budapest 1961.

84. H. Geretsegger and M. Peinter, *Otto Wagner*, Salzburg 1964 (English translation London 1970).

85. *Architecture of Skidmore, Owings & Merrill, 1950–1962*, London 1963.

86. F. Bullrich, *Arquitectura Latinoamericana*, Buenos Aires 1969.

13 Warehouses and office buildings

BIBLIOGRAPHY

There is no worthwhile general literature on warehouses and office buildings. The nearest one gets to it in English is Henry-Russell Hitchcock's two standard works, *Early Victorian Architecture in Britain*, 2 vols., New Haven, Conn. 1954, and *Architecture, Nineteenth and Twentieth Centuries* (Pelican History of Art), 3rd ed., Harmondsworth 1968; and in German the *Handbuch der Architektur*, Teil IV, Halbband 2, Heft 2 (*Geschäfts- und Kaufhäuser . . .*, by K. Zaar and A. L. Zaar), Stuttgart 1902, L. Klasen, *Grundriss-Vorbilder in Gebäuden aller Art*, Leipzig 1884–96, pt. VI, and *Wasmuths Lexikon der Baukunst*,

Berlin 1929–32, I (*Bürohaus*).

On skyscrapers on the other hand there is a vast literature. It may be enough here to refer to the following: Henry-Russell Hitchcock's Pelican History of Art volume, already mentioned, and C. W. Condit, *American Building Art: the Nineteenth Century*, New York 1960. Also F. Mujica, *History of the Skyscraper*, New York 1930. – In addition a number of papers by Professor Winston Weisman, including 'New York and the problem of the first skyscraper', *JSAH*, XII, no. 1, March 1953, 13 ff., *Art Bulletin*, XXXVI, 1954 (see below, n. 16), and 'A New View of Skyscraper History', in *The Rise of an American Architecture*, ed. E. Kaufmann, Jr., New York 1970, 115–60. – In a language other than English: W. Gerling, *Das amerikanische Hochhaus*, Würzburg 1949. – For Chicago the best book is C. W. Condit, *The Rise of the Skyscraper*, Chicago 1952. – On Buffington see E. M. Upjohn, 'Buffington and the Skyscraper', *Art Bulletin*, XVII, 1935, and three papers by H. Morrison, D. Tselos and M. B. Christison in *Art Bulletin*, XXVI, 1944, 1–24.

NOTES

p.213 1. See J. Summerson, *Georgian London*, Penguin ed. Harmondsworth 1962, 259; also J. Pudney, *London's Docks*, London 1975.

2. H. G. Pundt, *Schinkel's Berlin*, Cambridge, Mass. 1973, 144 and 158 ff.

3. Ill. T. Paulsson, *Scandinavian Architecture*, London 1958, pl. 71.

4. The present building is an echo of the original one.

5. According to Howard Colvin (*Biographical Dictionary of English Architects*, London 1954), measured drawings appeared in *The Architect and Building News*, 1 March 1935.

214 6. *Survey of London*, XVIII, London 1937, pl. 111.

7. *Monuments of Commerce* (drawings in the collection of the RIBA), London 1969, 12.

8. To Manchester's shame it was pulled down in 1972.

9. *The Spas of England*, London 1841, II, 17.

10. 'Some Notice of Office Buildings in the City of London', *Trans. RIBA*, 1864–65, 31–36.

215 11. When I'Anson was only about 25. He lived from 1812 to 1888.

12. R. Sturgis, *A Dictionary of Architecture and Building*, New York 1901–02, III, cols. 11 and 12.

13. L. Hautecoeur (*Histoire de l'architecture classique en France*, Paris 1943–57) is not enlightening, and for Germany *Wasmuths Lexikon der Baukunst* (I, Berlin 1929, 686) names as the first *Bürohaus* the Dovenhof in Hamburg (by Martin Haller), of as late as 1885–86. The definition applied is a good one: letting was by the square metre.

14. H. R. Johnson and A. W. Skempton, 'William Strutt's Cotton Mills', *Transactions of the Newcomen Society*, XXX, 1955–57, 180. The Navy took up the suggestion only fifty years later. The boat-store at the Sheerness dockyard looks indeed more like 1958 than its real date, 1858. For an illustration see e.g. my

Pioneers of Modern Design, Harmondsworth 1970 ed., and for much more A. W. Skempton, 'The Boat Store, Sheerness', *Transactions of the Newcomen Society*, XXXII, 1959–60, 57–78. Also E. de Maré and A. W. Skempton, 'The Sheerness Boat Store', *JRIBA*, June 1961. In another paper Professor Skempton has a paragraph on a warehouse along the St Ouen Docks in Paris which was designed by the engineer Hippolyte Fontaine and built *c*. 1864–65. This had exposed iron framing (*The Guild Engineer*, X, 1959, 47).

216 15. See my *South Lancashire* (The Buildings of England), Harmondsworth 1969, 177 and 171. The development of commercial frontages to give more and more window area without taking advantage of iron is exemplarily traced for America and England by Professor H.-R. Hitchcock in *Architecture, Nineteenth and Twentieth Centuries* (Pelican History of Art), 3rd ed., Harmondsworth 1968, 233–38.

16. T. Hamlin, *Greek Revival Architecture in America*, Oxford 1944, 150. Ill. e.g. in my *Pioneers*, op. cit. (p. 120), where there is altogether some treatment of the story of structural iron. The best treatment is in C. W. Condit, *American Building Art: the Nineteenth Century*, New York 1960. Pottsville is on pp. 27–28, Lorillard pp. 28–29. For New York refer also to W. R. Weisman, 'Commercial Palaces of New York, 1845–1875', *Art Bulletin*, XXXVI, 1954, 285–302, especially 290 and 293 ff.

17. V, 464.
18. Condit, op. cit., 30–33.
19. On Pickett see P. Collins in *Arch. Rev.*, CXXX, 1961, 267–68, and *Changing Ideals in Modern Architecture*, London 1965, 133–38.
20. J. F. O'Gorman, 'A Bogardus Original', *Arch. Rev.*, CXLVII, 1970, 155–56, and W. R. Weisman, 'Mid-nineteenth-century Commercial Building by James Bogardus', *Monumentum*, IX, 1973, 63–76. The building has been dismantled, and despite setbacks should be re-erected on the South Street Seaport site. One can only hope that the re-erection will indeed take place.
21. *The Sun*, 3 March and 26 June 1851, also 24 April 1852. I owe these references to Professor Phoebe Stanton, but I also want to thank Eleanor Lyne of the Enoch Pratt Library at Baltimore.
22. Brunswick 1852, 23.
23. A. Gomme and D. Walker, *Architecture of Glasgow*, London 1968, 115.
24. A bouquet to Margot Gayle for creating the Friends of Cast-Iron Architecture and fighting its battles. She has at last published a book on New York's cast-iron office, store and warehouse fronts: *Cast Iron Architecture in New York*, New York 1974 (photographs by E. V. Gillon, Jr.).
25. More American buildings outside New York with cast-iron fronts were kindly communicated to me by Margot Gayle. The comments are hers too. The buildings are the following:
Buffalo, N.Y. – Tucker Building, 410 Main St. Built 1888. Six-storey, entire iron front.
Chicago, Ill. – There are no longer any total iron façades left, but there were a lot at one time. There was the 5-storey iron-fronted Tuttle Building on East Lake St. at the corner of State. It was built in 1856; the architect was John M. Van Osdel. Lloyd & Sons' Building, S. side of Lake St., east of State, and directly opposite the Tuttle Building, was of 1857. It was also by Van Osdel. There were other iron fronts on both sides of this block, and they all went down in the Great Fire of October 1871. The great Rookery Building by Burnham & Root has a fantastic cast-iron interior court with iron and glass skylight. The iron was fabricated by the Hecla Foundry in Brooklyn.
Cooperstown, N.Y. – 92 Main St. Three-storey iron front, 1862, by James Bogardus.
Halifax, N.S. – Four-storey iron front in a block of restored nineteenth-century commercial buildings near the waterfront. Ground floor grossly altered. Built before 1865. Architect probably C. P. Thomas.
Memphis, Tenn. – Clay Building, a large 4-storey iron front built before 1865. Architects Fletcher & Wintter. Demolished.
Portland, Ore. – There were tall, elaborate iron façades here that were destroyed for a riverside expressway. Now most of the cast iron is in the form of ground floor store fronts, many of which are elaborate and highly individual. Many buildings have fancy iron roof cornices and window caps. A well-known example, now gone, was the 3-storey Corbett Building, the iron for which was produced in the famous Baltimore, Md., foundry of Bartlett, Hayward & Co. (also known as Hayward, Bartlett & Co., or Bartlett, Robbins & Co.) The building was done before 1862.
Richmond, Va. – Stearn's block, Main St. Cast by Bartlett, Hayward. Still standing. Also the beautiful small iron façade of Branch & Co., stockbrokers (see p. 216), which is being protected and kept beautifully.
Rochester, N.Y. – Power Building, 16 W. Main St. Two large façades of cast iron. Architect Andrew Jackson Warner. Built 1870. Iron supplied by D. D. Badger's iron works in New York City.
Salem, Ore. – The elaborate 2-storey Ladd & Bush Bank of 1869, designed by John Nestor, was enlarged in 1967 by Skidmore, Owings & Merrill with identical cast-iron elements from a similar building (Ladd & Tilton Bank) which had been erected in Portland in 1868.
Salt Lake City, Utah – ZCMI department store (Zion's Cooperative Mercantile Institution), 15 S. Main St. Three storeys, entire iron front. Built 1876 with additions 1880 and 1902. Architects William Folsom and Obed Taylor. It has been disassembled, but is to be re-erected immediately (restoration architect Steven T. Baird).
Savannah, Ga. – Has many buildings with iron store fronts and masonry above. Store at S.W. corner Broughton and Bull Sts. Architect not known. Iron cast in the big Cornell Foundry in New York City prior to 1872. Store front at 121 W. Congress St. Iron cast by D. D. Badger, probably in the early 1860s.
Seattle, Wash. – No multi-storied iron fronts now, but several handsome ground floor store fronts, particularly in the vicinity of Occidental Square. In near-by Pioneer Square the charming iron and glass Pergola of 1909 – designed to shelter people waiting for horse cars, then trolleys, now buses – was recently restored, meticulously, with city funds with the backing of the mayor.
Wilmington, Del. – The Grand Opera House (built as the Masonic Temple and Grand Theater), 818 N. Market St. Elaborate 4-storey front in Second Empire style with mansard roof, 1872. Architect Charles L. Carson of Dixon & Carson of Baltimore, Md. Being carefully restored as Delaware's Center for the Performing Arts. Restoration architect is perfectionist Steven T. Baird of Salt Lake City.

Finally Margot Gayle also referred me to *The Origins of Cast-Iron Architecture in America*, ed. W. Sturgis Knight, New York 1970, a reprint of Badger's *Illustrations of Iron Architecture* (made by his firm) and Bogardus's *Cast iron buildings – their construction and advantages*.
26. *Space, Time and Architecture*, Cambridge, Mass. 1941, 134–38.
27. *Chicago Illustrated*, I, 1857.
28. The building has recently been demolished but fragments, at the time of writing, are waiting to be incorporated in the Worcester State College (according to Miss Nancy E. Gaudette, Librarian of the Worcester Collection).
29. *Newsletter of the Friends of Cast-Iron Architecture*, New York, September 1973. The Iron Block is on a corner at 205 E. Wisconsin Ave.; it has 5 storeys and two façades, all iron, by Badger of New York. The architect was George H. Johnson, the date 1860–61. (Information from Margot Gayle.)
30. H.-R. Hitchcock, *Rhode Island Architecture*, Providence 1939, reprint 1968, pl. 45.
31. So Professor W. B. O'Neal told me. He also mentioned to me a thesis on iron in Richmond building written by Ann Carter.
32. *AIA Guide to the Architecture of New Orleans*, 1959, fig. 58.
33. Reprinted in *Origins of Cast-Iron Architecture*, op. cit.
34. B. Foerster, *Architecture worth saving in Rensselaer County, New York*, Troy 1965, ills. 56 and 57. Information given me by Mr R. L. Lagasse, Director of the Troy Public Library.
35. The building is Nos. 221–225 Essex Street. Thanks to Margot Gayle and Colonel W. Hoxie for this information. See also *Salem News*, 8 July 1890 and *Salem Gazette*, 11 July 1890.
36. N. Pevsner, *Cheshire* (The Buildings of England), Harmondsworth 1971, 272 and ill. 89.
218 37. *A travers les arts*, Paris 1869, 76–77; and on Boileau see Garnier's pp. 31–32. On Boileau also C. Beutler, 'St Eugène und die Bibliothèque Nationale', in *Miscellanea pro Arte* (Schnitzler Festschrift), Düsseldorf 1965, 315–26.
38. J. C. Loudon, *An Encyclopedia of Cottage, Farm and Villa Architecture and Furniture*, London 1833. I quote from the 1842 ed., p. 675.
39. C. W. Condit, *The Rise of the Skyscraper*, Chicago 1952, 114 ff. and 169 ff.

The first real skeleton building in New York was the Tower Building by Bradford Lee Gilbert, 1888–90. But Condit calls the Produce Exchange of 1881–84 'nearly' skeleton (pp. 44–45). On Chicago see also Professor Condit's *The Chicago School of Architecture*, Chicago 1964.

40. Hautecoeur, op. cit., VII, 1957, 379.

41. My friend Professor Anna Zádor obtained the illustration and the information for me.

42. Paul Bourget in *Outremer*, Paris 1895, calls it cyclopean (p. 158).

220 43. Equitable, Tribune, Western Union, Park Row, Washington and many more are illustrated in Professor Weisman's paper, 'A New View of Skyscraper History', in *The Rise of an American Architecture*, ed. E. Kaufmann, Jr., New York 1970, 115–60. See also Professor Weisman's 'The Commercial Architecture of George B. Post', *JSAH*, XXXI, 1972, 176–203. For Buffington see my bibliography to this chapter.

221 44. The Monadnock Building has indeed no ornament, but it has instead subtle roundings in prominent places, first the incurved batter above the shops, then the bottom and the angles of the bay windows and finally the profile of the top cornice. This must be why Montgomery Schuyler called it 'the most successful of commercial structures'. See B. Hoffmann, *The Architecture of John Wellborn Root*, Baltimore 1973, chap. VII.

45. *Outremer*, op. cit.

46. The following data were all taken from two sources, both communicated to me by the Otis Elevator Company: *Otis Elevator Company; the first one hundred years*, 1953, and *The Story of Lifts*, 1963, a mimeographed symposium of which pt. I (to 1920) is by R. E. Allen, pt. VI (on escalators) by K. N. Pragnell.

47. The London Underground got its first escalator in 1911 – at Earls Court. About 1910 there was an escalator in a fashion store at Leipzig, the town where I grew up.

224 48. For illustrations of these and other German office blocks see, e.g., W. Müller-Wulckow, *Bauten der Arbeit* (Blaue Bücher), 1929 ed., and W. Pehnt, *Expressionist Architecture*, London 1974.

49. P. Collins, *Concrete*, London 1959.

50. *Concrete and Constructional Engineering*, I, 1906–07, 81. Also Collins, op. cit., 87 and pl. 21.

51. Collins, op. cit., 89 and pl. 26. Additional information was provided by my friend Margot Gayle.

14 Railway stations

BIBLIOGRAPHY

The bibliography of railway stations for the purpose of this book is very simple. My chapter is not much more than a digest of Carroll Meeks, *The Railroad Station*, New Haven, Conn. 1956, fortified on some technical matters and on recent buildings by M. Kubinszky, *Bahnhöfe Europas*, Stuttgart 1969. Meeks has twelve pages of bibliography, Dr Kubinszky two and a half. W. Schadendorf, *Das Jahrhundert der Eisenbahn*, Munich 1965, is a good book too. C. Barman, *An Introduction to*

Railway Architecture, London 1950, is brief and well illustrated. Henry-Russell Hitchcock in his *Early Victorian Architecture in Britain*, 2 vols., New Haven, Conn. 1954, has an excellent chapter on stations (I, 492 ff.). Of older literature the *Handbuch der Architektur* might still be consulted: Teil IV, Halbband 2, Heft 4 (*Empfängsgebäude der Bahnhöfe . . .*, by E. Schmitt), Leipzig 1911. – For the engineering aspects see (out of a large number of books) C. E. Lee, *The Evolution of Railways*, 2nd ed., London 1943; Hamilton Ellis, *British Railway History*, 2 vols., London 1954, 1959; Jack Simmons, *The Railways of England*, London 1961; and L. T. C. Rolt, *Victorian Engineering*, London 1970. – Finally on the Railway Age, two paperbacks: H. Perkin, *The Age of the Railway*, London 1970, and M. Robbins, *The Railway Age in Britain*, Penguin ed., Harmondsworth 1970 (hardback London 1962).

Seen by me too late for benefit to accrue: G. Biddle, *Victorian Stations*, Newton Abbot 1973 (the first detailed account of British stations from the start to *c.* 1900), and T. C. Barker and M. Robbins, *History of London Transport*, 2 vols., London 1974.

NOTES

p.225 1. I owe this reference to Dr Franz Kockel.

2. See C. E. Lee, *The Evolution of Railways*, 2nd ed., London 1943, and H. Jackman, *The Development of Transportation in Modern England*, 2nd ed., London 1962, 461 ff.

3. H. W. Dickinson and A. Titley, *Richard Trevithick*, Cambridge 1934.

4. L. T. C. Rolt, *George and Robert Stephenson*, London 1960.

5. One of the 'pre-railway' railways, Brecon-Eardisley, 1818–24, was 24 miles long.

6. H. Perkin, *The Age of the Railway*, London 1970, 113, 323.

7. M. Armstrong, *Fanny Kemble*, London 1938, 107–09. Quoted from Perkin, op. cit., 87.

226 8. W. Schadendorf, *Das Jahrhundert der Eisenbahn*, Munich 1965, p. v.

9. I am quoting from my own *The Englishness of English Art*, Harmondsworth 1964, 22–23 (hardback London 1956). My sources are given there.

10. For Manchester see my *South Lancashire* (The Buildings of England), Harmondsworth 1969, 293.

11. Recently very well restored and internally remodelled.

12. Nor does it promise well for the future.

13. This also was under reconstruction at the time of writing. The old station was outstanding for its date, the new one emphatically is not.

14. Ill. C. Meeks, *The Railroad Station*, New Haven, Conn. 1956, fig. 20. On London's stations two books have recently come out: A. A. Jackson, *London's Termini*, Newton Abbot 1969, and J. Betjeman, *London's Historic Railway Stations*, London 1972.

15. Schadendorf, op. cit.

16. See J. M. Richards, 'The Euston Murder', *Arch. Rev.*, CXXXI, 1962, 234–38.

Reprinted in A. and P. Smithson, *The Euston Arch and the Growth of the London, Midland and Scottish Railway*, London 1968.

227 17. A. B. Granville, *The Spas of England*, London 1841, I, 28.

18. Ill. M. Kubinszky, *Bahnhöfe Europas*, Stuttgart 1969, p. 223.

19. ibid., 118.

20. Ill. Meeks, op. cit., fig. 19.

21. ibid., fig. 63.

22. Ill. C. Barman, *An Introduction to Railway Architecture*, London 1950.

23. Ill. Kubinszky, op. cit., p. 113.

24. ibid., 112. I have not see the doctoral thesis on Eisenlohr by H. J. Cleeving, *Friedrich Eisenlohr und das Hochbauwesen der badischen Staatseisenbahnen*, Karlsruhe 1954.

228 25. Ill. Meeks, op. cit., fig. 68. Also H.-R. Hitchcock, *Rhode Island Architecture*, 1968 ed., 55.

26. Ill. Kubinszky, op. cit., 123.

27. ibid., 294.

28. III, 219–21.

29. Kubinszky, op. cit., 287.

30. Ill. Meeks, op. cit., fig. 22.

31. Ill. Kubinszky, op. cit., 109.

32. ibid., 100.

33. ibid., 84.

34. ibid., 262. See also J. Gantner and A. Reinle, *Kunstgeschichte der Schweiz*, IV, Frauenfeld 1962, 119–21. The book has several pages on Swiss stations.

35. Ill. Meeks, op. cit., fig. 39.

36. Ill. Kubinszky, op. cit., 67.

37. Ill. Meeks, op. cit., fig. 60, and Kubinszky, op. cit., 160.

38. Quoted from L. T. C. Rolt, *Victorian Engineering*, London 1970, 49.

39. Ill. Meeks, op. cit., fig. 112, and Kubinszky, op. cit., 89.

40. *Briefe an einen Architekten, 1870–1889*, 6th ed., Munich 1913, 84, 1 August 1879.

41. Ill. Kubinszky, op. cit., 88.

42. ibid., 136.

43. Further illustrations in Kubinszky, op. cit., 185–86 and Meeks, op. cit., fig. 14. On Brunel see L. T. C. Rolt, *Isambard Kingdom Brunel*, Harmondsworth 1970.

44. The main Brunswick station was a fine Classical building of 1846 with a triumphal arch in the middle and a semi-circular portico in the centre of the long side: ill. Kubinszky, op. cit., 117.

230 45. Ill. Kubinszky, op. cit., 239.

46. J. Simmons, *St Pancras Station*, London 1968.

47. For spans and other measurements see the tables in Meeks, op. cit., 169 ff., and Kubinszky, op. cit., 318 ff.

48. See the Scott chapter in my *Some Architectural Writers of the nineteenth Century*, Oxford 1972.

49. Ill. Meeks, op. cit., figs. 130, 133, 138, etc.

50. The shed spanned 200 feet.

51. Ill. Meeks, op. cit., fig. 107.

52. ibid., fig. 64.

53. Ill. Kubinszky, op. cit., 165.

54. ibid., 207.

232 55. *La stazione centrale di Milano*, Milan 1931, 93 ff.

56. See E. P. Alexander, *Down at the Depot*, New York 1970, chiefly 215–85.

57. Ill. Meeks, op. cit., figs. 169–70, 161–63 and 164–66 and 173.

58. ibid., figs. 188–89, and Kubinszky,

op. cit., 138. Professor Robert Judson Clark kindly drew my attention to the dependence of Karlsruhe on Olbrich's design of 1903 for Basel.

59. Ill. Meeks, op. cit., figs. 155–57, Kubinszky, op. cit., 111.

60. See Kubinszky, op. cit., 55–57.

61. Ill. Meeks, op. cit., figs. 186–87, Kubinszky, op. cit., 280–81.

234 62. Ill. Meeks, op. cit., fig. 190, Kubinszky, op. cit., 142; also W. Pehnt, *Expressionist Architecture*, London and New York 1973, ills. 93 and 132.

63. Ill. Meeks, op. cit., figs. 209–10, Kubinszky, op. cit., 211.

64. Ill. Meeks, op. cit., fig. 201. At the same time, it will be seen later (p. 252), Reims received a concrete market-hall.

65. Ill. Meeks, op. cit., fig. 204.

66. ibid., fig. 206, Kubinszky, op. cit., 149.

67. See my 'Patient Progress I, Frank Pick', in *Studies in Art, Architecture and Design*, London and New York 1968, II, 190–209.

68. Ill. Meeks, op. cit., figs. 212–13, Kubinszky, op. cit., 226–27.

69. Ill. Meeks, op. cit., figs. 216–17, Kubinszky, op. cit., 215.

70. Ill. Kubinszky, op. cit., 217 and 232. Nervi had made designs for Naples station: see *The Works of Pier Luigi Nervi*, London 1957, 96–97.

71. Ill. Kubinszky, op. cit., 228, 116, 157, 177.

72. ibid., 148–49.

73. ibid., 151.

15 Market halls, conservatories and exhibition buildings

BIBLIOGRAPHY

For market halls there is no adequate book. The nearest to adequacy is the *Handbuch der Architektur, Teil IV, Halbband 3 (Markthallen und Marktplätze*, by G. Osthoff and E. Schmitt), Darmstadt 1884, 326–95.

On conservatories A. Tschira, *Orangerien und Gewächshäuser, ihre Entwicklung in Deutschland*, Berlin 1939, is an excellent book with many examples and much documentation.

On exhibition buildings, E. Cornell, *De stora Utställningarnas Arkitekturhistoria*, Stockholm 1952, covers the ground admirably, but is unfortunately only available in Swedish. At the time of going to press, an English translation is in preparation. In English K. W. Luckhurst, *The Story of Exhibitions*, London 1951, is brief but helpful. Brief also and a help for the twentieth century is P. Carbonara, *Architettura pratica*, Turin 1954–62, vol. IV, tom. 2, 833 ff. (by Manfredi Nicoletti). Enormously long and totally unillustrated is A. Démy, *Essai historique sur les expositions universelles à Paris*, Paris 1907. Of yet older literature see A. Messel, *Austellungsbauten*, in *Handbuch der Architektur*, Teil IV, Halbband 6, Heft 4, Darmstadt 1893, 472–534. Far too little noticed is E. Schild, *Zwischen Glaspalast und Palais des Illusions* (Ullstein Bauwelt Fundamente), Berlin, Frankfurt and Vienna 1967, which also has chapters on early iron bridges, the great conservatories, the Bibliothèque Ste Geneviève and Baltard's Halles. In ad-

dition there is vol. I of the *Rapport général, Exposition universelle, 1889*, Paris 1890–92 (by A. Picard). I have not used this, but it is recommended in R. D. Mandell, *Paris 1900*, New York 1931. I was also unable to make use of Poirier, *Des Foires, des peuples, des expositions*, Paris 1958. J. Hix, *The Glass House*, London 1974, reminded me of some minor omissions (see e.g., n. 62 below). The excellent catalogue by Christian Beutler for the exhibition *Weltausstellungen im 19. Jahrhundert*, held at the Neue Sammlung, Staatliches Museum für Angewandte Kunst, Munich, in 1973, came too late for me to make full use of it.

NOTES

p.235 1. J. P. Desportes, 'Alavoine et la flèche de la cathédrale de Rouen', *Revue de l'art*, XIII, 1971, 48–62.

2. I have given more details and a brief bibliography of the structural use of iron in my *Pioneers of Modern Design*, Harmondsworth 1970 ed., 118 ff. and 231–33. Others of course have given far more details and a less brief bibliography.

3. L. Crema, *L'Architettura Romana (Enciclopedia Classica*, sezione III, vol. XII, tome I), Turin etc. 1959, 363; literature 364. Cf. also my p. 257.

236 4. On medieval market buildings see G. Nagel, *Das mittelalterliche Kaufhaus und seine Stellung in der Stadt*, Berlin 1971. Also F. Schröder – see n. 5 below.

5. There is no comprehensive up-to-date history of Bruges. Meanwhile the best for our purpose is F. Schröder, *Die gotischen Handelshallen in Belgien und Holland*, Munich and Leipzig 1914. But see also A. Duclos, *Bruges, histoire et souvenirs*, Bruges 1910, and still J. Gaillard's two books: *Ephémérides brugeoises*, Bruges 1847, and *Revue pittoresque des . . . ornements qui décoraient autrefois la ville de Bruges*, Bruges 1850. In addition M. Letts, *Bruges and its past*, Bruges 1924, can be recommended.

6. It is about 260 feet high now, even without the spire.

7. Schröder, op. cit.

8. The building was disastrously damaged in the First World War, but has since been rebuilt.

9. A. Vandenpeerebom, *Yprensia*, I, Bruges 1878.

10. J. Dhondt and P. de Keyser, *Gent*, Antwerp 1947.

11. C. Enlart, *Manuel d'architecture française*, pt. II, vol. I, 1929, 375 ff.

237 12. *Treatise on architecture, being the treatise by Antonio Averlino, known as Filarete*, ed. J. R. Spencer, 2 vols., New Haven, Conn. 1965. (Cf. above, p. 31.) Another edition is that of L. Grassi, Milan (Il Polifilo) 1972.

13. Francesco di Giorgio Martini, *Trattati di architettura, ingegneria e arte militare*, ed. C. Maltese, 2 vols., Milan (Il Polifilo) 1967, II, 363, 343–44. (Cf. above, p. 31.)

14. A. Dauphin-Meunier, *La Banque à travers les âges*, Paris 1917, 200, illustrates an engraving of 1616.

15. For the Steelyard see C. Knight, *London*, II, 1841, 285; for the Hansa in general see P. Böllinger, *The German Hansa*, London 1970 (French 1964), and still Schayes; for Antwerp H. C. Scribanius, S.J., *Origines Antverpiensium*, Antwerp 1610, and also J. B. van Mol, *Anvers*, Antwerp (1874), 146.

238 16. An exception and a curiosity are the Yorkshire piece halls, i.e. cloth halls, notably at Wakefield, Leeds and Halifax. At Leeds the first building of 1711 was replaced by a second in 1775. This had an open courtyard. Its façade is still there. (D. Linstrum, *Historic Architecture of Leeds*, Newcastle 1969, 21.) 1775 is also the date of the Halifax Cloth Market, a rectangle with 300 rooms in two colonnaded tiers: see my *Yorkshire, the West Riding* (The Buildings of England) 2nd ed., Harmondsworth 1967, 231 and pl. 63B). Similar and also an exception was the Leather and Skin Market at Bermondsey (i.e. London). This was completed in 1833 (Knight, op. cit., III, 1842, 17).

17. 6 vols., Paris 1869–76, V, 333.

18. II, Paris 1771, 424–30.

19. *Précis*, II, Paris 1809, 58 and pl. 13.

20. But he allows as exceptions Amiens, Brussels, Marseilles, Florence and Catania, the latter three illustrated in his *Recueil*, Paris 1801, pl. 14. The Halle au Blé is of course an exception too, though Durand calls it pretentious.

21. H. Rosenau, 'The Engravings of the Grands Prix of the French Academy of Architecture', *Arch. Hist.*, III, 1960, 34 and 132–33.

22. L. Hautecoeur, *Histoire de l'architecture classique en France*, V, 1953, 222; VI, 1955, 107–09. M. L. Biver, *Le Paris de Napoléon*, Paris 1963, 115–30. L. Bruyère, *Etudes relatives à l'art des constructions*, 2 vols., Paris 1823–28, Recueil IV.

23. Quatremère de Quincy in his *Dictionnaire historique de l'architecture*, Paris 1832 (II, 97–98) calls these two the most convenient and the largest, in this order.

24. Sigfried Giedion (*Space, Time and Architecture*, Cambridge, Mass. 1941) calls the roof of the Madeleine Market 1824, but that is wrong. C. L. G. Eck (*Traité de construction en poteries et fer*, Paris 1836, 65 and pl. 48) calls it recent, and Hautecoeur (op. cit., VI, 1955, 107–09) gives 1835 as the date. Eck names the designer: Veugny l'aîné. Eck also illustrates an iron roof for the Blancs-Manteaux Market but only as a project (*Traité de l'application du fer, de la fonte et de la tôle*, Paris 1841, 41 and pl. 31). However, L. M. Normand in 1843 (*Paris moderne*, II, pl. 143) illustrates the iron roof as existing.

25. Other American Grecian markets, e.g. that of 1841 at Charleston, S.C., are in T. Hamlin, *Greek Revival Architecture in America*, Oxford 1944. Specially interesting is the Meat Market in New Orleans by Jacques Tanesse, illustrated in 1813. It is of 25 bays with outer arcading and nave and aisles inside. For information on this I have to thank Professor Jessie Poesch and Mr Samuel Wilson, Jr.

26. C. L. V. Meeks, *Italian Architecture, 1750–1914*, New Haven, Conn. 1966, 158–59.

27. J. Taylor, 'Charles Fowler, Master of Markets', *Arch. Rev.*, CXXXV, 1964, 174–82.

28. J. Elmes, *Metropolitan Improvements*, published in 1828, already includes it. The iron roofs were added to Cubitt's in 1872, according to Mark Girouard in *Country Life*, 18 November 1965, 1308.

240 29. *Description of the Plan for a Revival of the Hungerford Market*. The market had

opened in 1682. Fowler says that he was first consulted in 1824.

30. The Hungerford Suspension Bridge had nothing to do with market or railway. It was a footbridge, built between 1836 and 1845, and when the railway demolished it the chains went for re-use to Brunel's Clifton Bridge at Bristol.

31. See A. Tschira, *Orangerien und Gewächshäuser, ihre Entwicklung in Deutschland*, Berlin 1939.

241 32. Rohault travelled to England in 1833, i.e. before starting on the *Serre*, and one recognizes that at once. See C. Rohault fils, *Serres chaudes . . .*, Paris (Musée d'histoire naturelle) 1837. I have to thank Madame Douault and M. Pierrot for information.

33. A. Hix, *The Glass House*, London 1974, 111–13.

34. *Arch. Hist.*, IV, 1961, 77–91. Also G. F. Chadwick, *The Works of Sir Joseph Paxton*, London 1961.

35. Quoted by Lady Longford in her outstanding *Victoria R.I.*, London 1964, 176, 587. Robin Mackworth Young sent me the text of the passages, and they are quoted here by gracious permission of Her Majesty the Queen.

36. J. Hix, 'Richard Turner', *Arch. Rev.*, CLII, 1972, 286–93.

37. There is no proper biography of Horeau. In its absence see G. Vapereau, *Dictionnaire universel des contemporains*, 3rd ed., Paris 1865, 902, and Thieme-Becker, *Künstlerlexikon*, XVII, Leipzig 1914, 506.

38. VI, 1848, 41.

39. J. K. Huysmans, *L'Art moderne*, Paris 1883. I quote from the 2nd ed., 1902, 237 and 239.

40. J. Doin, *Gaz. des b.-a.*, LVI (or per. IV, vol. XI), 11–29. My quotation is on p. 11.

41. Eck, *Traité de l'application*, op. cit., illustrates remarkably many Russian examples.

242 42. See K. W. Luckhurst, *The Story of Exhibitions*, London 1951, 63 ff., and much fuller E. Cornell, *De stora Utställningarnas Arkitekturhistoria*, Stockholm 1952.

43. On these industrial exhibitions see A. de Colmont, *Histoire des expositions des produits de l'industrie française*, Paris 1855, ills. 1 and 15. Similar trade shows were held in other countries as well. See now H. Kreisel, *Die Kunst des deutschen Möbels*, III (by G. Himmelheber), Munich 1973, 147–48, and especially note 376 which lists 169 such exhibitions between 1812 and 1850.

44. *L'Architecture et l'industrie comme moyens de perfection sociale*, Paris and Leipzig 1840. See also Cornell, op. cit., ills. 1 and 15.

45. Vapereau, op. cit., calls them 'études et dessins' and refers to what he calls 'Mémoires et Projets' published in 1846. But he also indicates a publication in 1837 and says that this included an exhibition building, a market hall and other public buildings, for instance a remodelling of the Imperial Library, now Bibliothèque Nationale.

46. The British Library has a loose sheet bound into a folio volume (1701.b.1) on which in a French text Horeau makes this statement. The *Rev. gén. de l'arch.*, VIII, 1849, 93, gives the date as 4 March 1848. The British Library also has a pamphlet by

Horeau called *Propositions for the Improvement of London*, London 1859 (906.k.6(9)), actually the catalogue of an exhibition of his own work held in London and the material for lectures in French and English (see my p. 246). In this are listed, side by side with later projects, the designs for an exhibition building with the date 1836.

47. *Rev. gén. de l'arch.*, VII, 1847, 410–11. The Château des Fleurs is described on pp. 254–55.

48. Reprinted in *Kleine Schriften*, Berlin and Stuttgart 1883, 484 ff.

243 49. Ill. Hautecoeur, op. cit., VII, 1957, 40.

50. V. Baltard and F. Collet, *Monographie des Halles Centrales de Paris*, Paris 1863. For the battle see *Gaz. des arch.*, VII, 1869–71, 337 ff.

51. *Paris herself again*, 5th ed. London 1880, 299.

52. *Entretiens*, Paris 1858–72, I, 333.

53. op. cit. (above, n. 39), 239.

54. E. Zola, *Le Ventre de Paris*, Paris 1873; *Oeuvres complètes* ed., 240. The phrase is taken over from Victor Hugo's passage in *Notre Dame de Paris* in which he states that while architecture dominated the past, printing is bound to dominate the future. Sala, op. cit. (above, n. 51), 295, called St Eustache 'the old Gothic-Renaissance church', which is very perceptive.

55. VIII, 92–93. Also Cornell, op. cit., pl. 29.

56. Of the literature on the Crystal Palace the following may be singled out. Best (and oldest) on the building is a lecture given by M. D. Wyatt, 'On the Construction of the Building for the Exhibition of the Works of Industry of all Nations', *Minutes of Proceedings of the Institution of Civil Engineers*, X, 1850–51, 127–65; pp. 166–91 give the discussion after the lecture (see my text, p. 244). Indispensable also is P. Berlyn and C. Fowler, Jun., *The Crystal Palace, its architecture, history and constructive marvels*, London 1851. Of more recent books see Y. ffrench, *The Great Exhibition, 1851*, London (1951), a serious work, then C. Hobhouse, *1851 and the Crystal Palace*, London 1937, N. Pevsner, *High Victorian Design*, London 1951 (reprinted in *Studies in Art, Architecture and Design*, London 1968, II), and more recently E. Schild, *Zwischen Glaspalast und Palais des Illusions*, Berlin, Frankfurt and Vienna 1967, and P. Beaver, *The Crystal Palace*, London 1970.

244 57. Henry Ashton (1801–72), when he was young, worked under Wyatville at Windsor Castle and Chatsworth. In 1838 he went to Holland and designed for the King a Tudor-Gothic country palace to be called Zorgvliet. Nothing came of it, and the Gothic range added to the Kneuterdijk Palace at The Hague in imitation of Christ Church Hall was designed by the King (H. W. M. van der Wijck, 'Koning Willem II als Bouwheer', in *Opus Musivum* (Ozinga Festschrift), Assen 1964, 415–38).

58. See my article in *Arch. Rev.*, CXLVIII, 1970, 257. On Turner see also Hix, op. cit. (above, n. 36).

59. op. cit. (above, n. 56), 166. For Gregory see p. 191.

245 60. Reprinted in full at the end of Christopher Hobhouse's book, op. cit.

61. *Wissen ist Macht – Macht ist Wissen*, address delivered in 1877. I am quoting

from F. J. Verpohl, 'Autonomie und Parteilichkeit', in *Autonomie der Kunst*, ed. M. Müller and others, Frankfurt 1972, 215.

62. Owen Jones in 1859 designed a People's Palace for Muswell Hill near London. It was to be 1,296 feet long with a central rotunda 200 feet in diameter and have eight towers. In 1861 Paxton designed for an exhibition to be held at St Cloud a glass palace 1,952 feet long with a central rotunda 328 feet in diameter and 360 feet high. The exhibition was not held. See Hix, op. cit. (above, n. 33), 146–49.

63. B. Silliman and C. R. Goodrich, *The World of Science, Art and Industry*, New York 1853.

In 1853 Dublin also held an international exhibition. The building (by John Benson) had a domed centre (Cornell, op. cit., ill. 72).

64. E. Roth, *Der Glaspalast in München*, Munich 1971.

65. W. Langewiesche, *Wolfs, Geschichten um ein Bürgerhaus*, Munich and Leipzig 1919, 402.

66. Pugin's Medieval Court from the 1851 Exhibition.

67. J. I. Hittorff, *Description de la rotonde des panoramas dans les Champs Elysées*, Paris 1842. See also K. Hammer, *Jakob Ignatz Hittorff*, Stuttgart 1968, 176–78. Later than both Hittorff and Bogardus is a design with suspended roof submitted by Alphonse Oudry for the 1867 exhibition. See F. Walch, *Das Gebäude der Pariser Weltausstellung 1867*, PhD thesis, Karlsruhe University 1967, 76 and fig. 246.

246 68. These measurements – of the built-over areas – are based on C. Beutler, *Weltausstellungen im 19. Jahrhundert*, catalogue of an exhibition at the Neue Sammlung, Staatliches Museum für Angewandte Kunst, Munich 1973. On pp. XXVIII, XXIX he provides sizes (in hectares) and numbers of visitors:

1851	London	8.4	6,039,195
1855	Paris	9.9	5,162,330
1862	London	9.5	6,211,103
1867	Paris	14.9	c. 11,000,000
1873	Vienna	16.2	7,254,687
1876	Philadelphia	30.3	10,165,000
1878	Paris	22.5	16,032,725
1889	Paris	21.2	32,250,297
1893	Chicago	81.0	27,329,000
1900	Paris	46.0	50,800,801

69. Hautecoeur, op. cit., VII, 1957, 316–17.

70. Ill. in Walch, op. cit., fig. 249; also Cornell, op. cit., ills. 88–89, and *The Builder*, XIX, 1861, 108. On the 1862 exhibition building as built see B. Bradford, 'The Brick Palace of 1862', *Arch. Rev.*, CXXXIII, 1962, 15–21.

71. Cornell, op. cit., ill. 90.

72. Walch, op. cit.

73. *Les Ouvriers européens*, Paris 1855 and *La Réforme sociale en France*, Paris 1864.

74. In his thesis (op. cit.) Dr Walch mentions among predecessors of the idea Napoleon III.

75. *Moniteur universel*, no. 260, 17 September 1867, 1214.

76. *Gaz. des arch.*, separately numbered supplementary volume to vol. V, 1867, 1.

77. *Rev. gén. de l'arch.*, XXVI, 1868, 201. Also Cornell, op. cit., ill. 92, and the curious

sheet in the British Library (above, n. 46).

78. See above, n. 46.

248 79. Baudot described the house in *Gaz. des arch.*, VI, 1868, 233–35. It had a plan with two splayed wings like E. S. Prior's The Barn at Exmouth of 1887 and Home Place at Holt of 1903–05 and like Lutyens' Papillon Hall of 1902–03, and very flush walls with broad flat frames, round brick panels and some small-scale Jacobean terracotta decoration on the top.

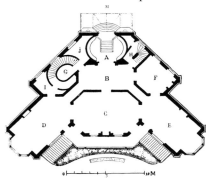

Horeau, house near Primrose Hill, London (*Gaz. des arch.*, VI, 1868)

80. The first of the three is illustrated in *Gaz. des arch.*, VI, 1868, 145–47, the other two are illustrated by Jeanne Doin, op. cit. (above, n. 40).

81. VI, 1868, 41 ff.

82. The little rhyme is: 'Hardwick Hall, more window than wall.' I was not able to use John Maass, *The Glorious Enterprise: the Centennial Exhibition of 1876 in Philadelphia*, Watkins Glen 1973.

83. *Portraits of Places*, London 1883, 79.

250 84. Quoted from *JSAH*, XXIX, 1970, 48.

85. *Revue des deux mondes*, XCIV, 1 July 1889. Quoted from R. D. Mandell, *Paris 1900*, New York 1931, 23.

86. Mandell, op. cit., 19 and 143 (n. 33). 143.

87. The most detailed account of the 1889 exhibition is A. Picard, *Rapport général, Exposition universelle, 1889*, Paris 1890–92.

88. See chap. X in D. Hoffmann, *The Architecture of John Wellborn Root*, Baltimore 1973.

89. ibid., 220.

251 90. On Chicago 1893 one should now look up M. Manieri-'Elia, 'Per una Città Imperiale', in *La città americana*, ed. G. Ciucci, Bari 1973. One of the illustrations is E. S. Jenison's proposal for one building covering 193 acres. The glass roof of the centre was to rise to 700 feet.

91. H. Phillips Fletcher, *The St Louis Exhibition 1904*, London 1905.

92. For the exhibition of 1900 see Mandell, op. cit., and A. Quantin, *L'Exposition du siècle*, Paris 1900. P. Jullian, *The Triumph of Art Nouveau, Paris Exhibition 1900*, London 1975, came too late for me. It is a piece of fantasy, flamboyance, and breathless preciosity, and it contains enviable quotations.

93. op. cit., VII, 1957, 464.

94. *Concrete*, London 1959, 71.

252 95. *Revue de l'art ancien et moderne*, VII, 1900, 253.

96. *Centralblatt der Bauverwaltung*, 1900, 157–58.

97. op. cit., VII, 1957, 457–59.

98. Ill. Hautecoeur, ibid., 455–70.

99. C. F. Marsh, *Reinforced Concrete*, London 1904, 421 (and for the Petit Palais 415–17). Also *Le Génie civile*, XXXIII, 1898, 53, XXXV, 1899, 289–94, and XXXVIII, 1900–01, 8.

100. Mandell, op. cit., 74.

101. ibid., 76.

102. ibid., 77.

103. Ill. *Concrete*, III, 1908–09. Also Collins, op. cit. (above, n. 94), 92.

253 104. J. Boehe, *Jugendstil im Theater (Die Darmstädter Künstlerkolonie und Peter Behrens)*, Vienna University (Institut für Theaterwissenschaft) 1969, I have not seen.

105. For bridges the Swiss engineer Robert Maillart had preceded Berg: Tavenasa 1905.

106. *Concrete*, II, 1907–08, 394, calls the largest concrete span that of a bridge in Fairmount Park, Philadelphia, which is 233 feet.

107. *Jahrbuch des Deutschen Werkbundes 1915*. Text by Peter Jessen.

254 108. *Arch. Rev.*, LXXXII, 1937, had a special number on the exhibition, written by J. M. Richards (Sir James Richards), and his admirable special numbers have gone on ever since: Glasgow 1938, vol. LXXXIV; Festival of Britain 1951, CX; Brussels 1958, CXXIV: Montreal 1967, CXLII; Osaka 1970, CXLVIII. For Paris 1937 P. Dupays in *L'Exposition internationale de 1937* and *Voyage autour du monde* describes all the buildings, but uncritically. No wonder – the catalogue of the British Library lists about 150 titles by Dupays.

256 109. R. Boyd, 'Germany', in the Expo number of *Arch. Rev.*, CXLII, 1967, 129 ff.

110. W. Marks, *The Dymaxion World of Buckminster Fuller*, New York 1960.

111. Hobhouse, op. cit. (above, n. 56), 179.

16 Shops, stores and department stores

BIBLIOGRAPHY

J. F. Geist, *Passagen*, Munich 1969, is about as near the perfect treatment of the history of a building type as can ever be hoped for. *Passagen* are shopping arcades.

For shopping as such D. Davis, *A History of Shopping*, London and Toronto 1966. This is the best we have, though confined to Britain. – For shops and department stores a good brief treatment is A. Adburgham, *Shops and Shopping, 1800–1914*, London 1964. A little on French shops is in L. Hautecoeur, *Histoire de l'architecture classique en France*, VI, Paris 1955, and VII, 1957. H. Lefuel, *Boutiques parisiennes du Premier empire*, Paris 1926, was mentioned to me too late for me to make use of it. A Geist, as it were, for shops and a Geist for department stores are lacking. D. Dean, *English Shop Fronts, 1792–1840*, London 1970, is an annotated collection of illustrations from pattern books. The change from Georgian to Victorian in terms of the shop window is treated in M. Eldridge, 'The Plate-Glass Shop Front', *Arch. Rev.*, CXXIII, 1958, 192–95. A. Artley, *The Golden Age of Shop Design: European Shop Interiors 1880–1939*, London 1975, a collection of photographs

of shops and department stores, will be published only after this book has gone to press.

On the department store there are many books, the majority of which I have alas not been able to use. I list the following:

(a) General: *Handbuch der Architektur*, Teil IV, Halbband 2, Heft 2 (*Geschäfts- und Kaufhäuser, Warenhäuser und Messpaläste, Passagen oder Galerien*, by K. Zaar and A. L. Zaar), Stuttgart 1902, is not very profitable. – H. Pasdermadjian, *The Department Store, its Origin, Evolution and Economics*, London 1954.

(b) In German: O. E. von Wussow, *Geschichte und Entwicklung der Warenhäuser*, Berlin 1906. – P. Göhre, *Das Warenhaus*, Frankfurt 1907. – A. Wiener, *Das Warenhaus*, Berlin 1912. – H. Schliepmann, *Geschäfts- und Warenhäuser*, 2 vols., Berlin and Leipzig 1913.

(c) In French: Hautecoeur (see above). – Vicomte G. d'Avenel, *Le Mécanisme de la vie moderne*, 5 ser., Paris 1896–1905, I, 1–90. – P. Jarry, *Les Magasins de nouveautés*, Paris 1948. – P. Giffard, *Les grands magasins*, Paris 1882. – F. Ambrière, *La Vie secrète des grands magasins*, rev. ed., Paris 1938. – L. Marcillon, *Trente ans de vie des grands magasins*, Nice 1924. – A. Saint-Martin, *Les grands magasins*, Paris 1900. – J. Michot, 'Evolution des grands magasins de nouveautés', *Science et industrie*, October 1925.

(d) For England and the United States: J. W. Ferry, *A History of the Department Store*, New York 1960.

NOTES

p.257 1. In a design by Inigo Jones the arrangement is still exactly the same: no. 355 of the Arts Council exhibition of 1973 (*The King's Arcadia: Inigo Jones and the Stuart Court Theatre*, catalogue by J. Harris, S. Orgel and R. Strong). The drawing is at Worcester College, Oxford.

2. C. Knight, *London*, V, London 1843, 392.

3. Author of *Anton Reiser*, a psychologically remarkable novel.

4. Quoted from D. Dean, *English Shop Fronts, 1792–1840*, London 1970.

5. Semicircular bows were not allowed under the London Building Act of 1774.

258 6. No. 62; quoted from Dean, op. cit. For illustrations of both Georgian and columnar see H. Dan and E. C. Morgan Wilmott, *English Shop Fronts old and new*, London 1907.

7. M. Eldridge, 'The Plate-Glass Shop Front', *Arch. Rev.*, CXXIII, 1958, 192–95.

8. Freiherr von Friesen, in a letter of 1 November 1840 written from London, mentions a whole shop window which was one sheet of glass. I owe the reference to this unpublished letter to Mrs C. C. Steinberg.

9. For Benson see *The Builder*, XXIV, 1866, 153 (cf. 179).

10. *Briefe an einen Architekten, 1870–1889*, 6th ed., Munich 1913, 89.

11. R. Hale Newton, *Town & Davis, Architects*, New York 1942, 62–63.

12. J. C. Krafft and N. Ransonnette, *Plans, coupes, élévations des plus belles maisons et des hôtels à Paris et dans les environs,*

Paris 1801–02. Also L. Hautecoeur, *Histoire de l'architecture classique en France*, V, Paris 1953, 107, 292.

13. Dean, op. cit., from L. and J. Taylor, *Designs for Shop Fronts*, 1792; also J. Young, *A Series of Designs for Shop Fronts*, 1828.

14. Dean, op. cit.

15. N. Whittock, *On the Construction and Decoration of the Shop Fronts of London*, London 1840, pls. 12, 15, 16.

16. To the best of my knowledge.

260 17. I saw this illustration in the Prints and Photographs Division of the Library of Congress. My thanks go to the staff there, who helped me in many other ways as well.

18. Dean, op. cit.

19. op. cit., pl. 17.

20. In the RIBA Drawings Collection.

21. op. cit., pl. 11.

22. *British Almanac*, London 1841, 247–48.

23. IX, 227.

24. See G. B. Tatum, *Penn's Great Town*, Philadelphia 1961. Professor Tatum kindly lent me the illustration.

25. II, Paris 1843, 83; IV, 1857 (395 rue St Honoré, by 'D', 1830; Café Frascati by Titeux Frénoy, 1840).

26. ibid., II, 134–38.

27. op. cit., VI, Paris 1955, 374, fig. 298.

28. op. cit. (above, n. 15), pl. 6 top and 13, also Eldridge, op. cit. (above, n. 7), 192.

29. *Marble Halls*, ed. Michael Darby and John Physick (catalogue of an exhibition at the Victoria and Albert Museum), London 1973, p. 102.

261 30. In England Chester has arcading with the curious speciality of two levels, one a few steps below street level, the other – which is the main shopping level – raised by some more steps. The arrangement is known as the Rows. See e.g. my *Cheshire* (The Buildings of England), Harmondsworth 1971, 132.

31. J. F. Geist, *Passagen*, Munich 1969, 238–40.

32. ibid., 79, where there is also a plan of the Pantheon in its 1834 form.

262 33. Knight, op. cit. (above, n. 2), 395–97.

34. *Paris Moderne*, II, Paris 1843, 139–40.

35. ibid., 4–8.

36. On Schinkel's *Kaufhaus* see P. O. Rave, *Karl Friedrich Schinkel, Lebenswerk: Bauten in Berlin*, III, Berlin 1962, 125–29.

263 37. Geist, op. cit., 257–60.

38. op. cit., 254–55.

39. The glass roof, according to Dr Geist (op. cit.) is later.

264 40. Geist, op. cit., 204.

41. The façades were rebuilt, south in 1911 and 1929–31 (by Beresford Pite), north in 1937.

265 42. *Civil Engineer and Architect's Journal*, XVIII, 1855, 247.

43. The City of Milan Improvement Company. On the board was incidentally Matthew Digby Wyatt, architect of the Cole circle. On the Galleria see, apart from the exhaustive treatment by Dr Geist (above, n. 31), F. Reggiori, *Milano 1800–1943*, Milan 1947, and G. Bandmann, 'Die Galleria Vittorio Emanuele', *Zs. f. Kunstgesch.*, XXIX, 1966, 89–110.

Halfway between the Galerie d'Orléans and Mengoni's Galleria are the Galeries St Hubert in Brussels, built in 1846–47. It is

said that in 1865 Mengoni visited their architect, J. P. Kuysenaar. The Brussels Galeries are 558 feet long, the Galleria 645. They also have a crossing with cross-arms though these are stunted. There is a glass tunnel-vault, and the style is a free Venetian Renaissance.

44. See apart from Geist, op. cit., Ada Louise Huxtable in *Progressive Architecture*, XXXVII, 1956, 139–40, and M. Peale Schofield in *JSAH*, XXV, 1966, 281–91.

45. P. Jarry, *Les Magasins de nouveautés*, Paris 1948, is the source of the following paragraphs. But one could also go to B. Gille, 'Recherches sur l'origine des grands magasins parisiens', *Mémoires de la Fédération des sociétés historiques et archéologiques de Paris et de l'Ile de France*, VII, 1955, 251 ff., of which Professor L. Gossmann told me.

266 46. Vicomte G. d'Avenel, *Le Mécanisme de la vie moderne*, I, Paris 1896, 10. I have been unable to find out anything about Kromm and his tradings. Nor have I been able to check whether Jarry is right (op. cit., 79) to give the date 1737 for the opening of Lamulle & Doublet's Au Mulet Chargé which sold 'clinquaillerie, armurerie, scellerie, accessoires d'écuries, limes et outils'.

47. op. cit., 70, 24.

48. op. cit., 46, 137, 100, 136.

49. *Oeuvres complètes* (*Comédie Humaine*, *Vie Parisienne* II), Paris 1913, 30–31. I don't know on what evidence Hautecoeur's reference to *prix fixes* (op. cit. – above, n. 12 – VI, 1955, 141) is based.

50. pls. 4 and 3.

51. Illustrated in Hautecoeur, op. cit., VI, 142.

52. op. cit., VII, 1957, 327–28.

53. A. Adburgham, *Shops and Shopping, 1800–1914*, London 1964, 137 ff.

267 54. *Rev. gén. de l'arch.*, XXX, 1873, 200 and pls. 50–53.

268 55. 2nd ser., V, 1876, 120 ff. and IX, 1880, 183 ff.

268 56. *Rev. gén. de l'arch.*, XXX, 11 and pls. 8–11.

57. Hautecoeur, op. cit., VII, 1957, 328–29.

269 58. *Enc. d'arch.*, 3rd ser., II, 1883, III, 1884, IV, 1885; pp. 1–35 of vol. IV are descriptive. The store was rebuilt after a fire in 1921 et seq., now in reinforced concrete, the central well being filled in.

59. F. Laudet, *La Samaritaine*, Paris 1933.

269 60. *Oeuvres complètes*, Paris 1927–29, XII. (The passages are given here in the translation of April FitzLyon, London 1957.) The *Oeuvres* volume also contains (pp. 459–988) notes by Zola for the book, e.g. several pages of minute description of the Bon Marché. Also contributions by Frantz Jourdain paying tribute to Zola, who had behaved to architects as if he were a real client. (Jourdain designed Zola's tomb in the Cimetière Montmartre.) As for Jourdain his view was that for stores 'en principe le fer seul' ought to be employed and that the impression aimed at ought to be 'gaie et lumineuse' (p. 461). For Zola and the Samaritaine see Jarry, op. cit. (above, n. 45), 75. Jarry also discusses Zola and La Paix, a *magasin de nouveautés* (p. 95).

61. J. W. Ferry, *A History of the Department Store*, New York 1960.

270 62. C. W. Condit, *The Chicago School of Architecture*, Chicago 1964.

63. A. S. Lambert, *The Universal Provider*, London 1938.

64. A. Briggs, *Friends of the People*, London 1956.

271 65. Ferry, op. cit., 277 ff.

66. Also Althoff at Dortmund by Kreis and Leonhard Tietz at Elberfeld, also by Kreis. Ill. *Jahrbuch des Deutschen Werkbundes 1913*, Jena 1913, pls. 67–71.

Leonhard was Hermann Tietz's nephew. His stores were higher priced. They are now called Kaufhof; Hermann Tietz has become Hertie.

67. P. Collins, *Concrete*, London 1959, 91 and pl. 28A. Also *Concrete*, I, 1906–07, 26–27.

68. p. 50.

69. And even preceded by Horta's Maison du Peuple, also in Brussels, of 1896–99, lately viciously destroyed. L'Innovation was destroyed by fire even more recently, in 1966.

70. D. Davis, *A History of Shopping*, London and Toronto 1966, 283.

71. Ferry, op. cit., 276.

72. *Woolworth's first seventy-five Years*, 1954. J. W. Winkler, *Five and Ten*, London 1940, is rather scrappy.

272 73. G. Baker and B. Funaro, *Shopping Centers*, New York 1951; W. Burns, *British Shopping Centres*, London 1959.

74. Ferry, op. cit. (above, n. 61), 78, 48.

75. vol. IV, tom. 2 (sect. 10), 1962, 767–68.

17 Factories

BIBLIOGRAPHY

There is no general history of factory buildings. There are plenty of books on factory buildings in the twentieth century (see below, n. 115) and they may or may not have a page or a number of pages on factories of the past.

The first attempt at coming to terms with factory buildings in one country is the article 'Fabrikbau' by Wolfgang Müller-Wiener in the *Reallexikon zur deutschen Kunstgeschichte* (begun by O. Schmidt, ed. L. H. Heydenreich and K. A. Wirth), instalments 67–68, Stuttgart 1971–72, cols. 847–80. – Early factories in Switzerland are summarized in J. Gantner and A. Reinle, *Kunstgeschichte der Schweiz*, IV, Frauenfeld 1962, 123–26. – In Belgium early factories are being recorded by M. Maurice Culot (see p. 284). – For France a great deal of material has been assembled, but nothing substantial has yet been published. The May 1973 issue of *Architecture Mouvement Continuité* (journal of the Société des Architectes diplomés par le gouvernement) was devoted to factories, in connection with the travelling exhibition 'L'Usine', organized by the Centre de Création Industrielle of Paris. The exhibition was at the Architectural Association, London, in 1975. It covered French factories from the beginning, but was very weak on dates for pre-twentieth-century buildings. – For one English county Jennifer Tann has provided a complete list of pre-twentieth-century factories: *Gloucestershire Woollen Mills*, Newton Abbot 1967. – Useful also for England is what E. P. Thompson himself calls the 'dense undergrowth' of footnotes in *The Making of the Working Class*, London 1963 (paperback 1968). – The best book on at least a period, the first half of the nineteenth century (in Lowell, Mass.), is John Coolidge, *Mill and Mansion*, New York 1942.

The crucial years of the introduction of iron into factory building are covered to perfection in three papers by Professor A. W. Skempton, the first and third written in collaboration with H. R. Johnson: 'William Strutt's Cotton Mills 1793–1812', *Transactions of the Newcomen Society*, XXX, 1955–57, 179–205; 'Evolution of the Steel Frame Building', *The Guild Engineer*, X, 1959, 37–51; and 'The First Iron Frames', *Arch. Rev.*, CXXXI, 1962, 175–86.

NOTES

p.273 1. E. Rücker, *Die Schedelische Weltchronik*, Munich 1973, 13.

2. M. Rooses, *Christopher Plantin*, 2nd ed., Antwerp 1897, 238–39.

3. vol. II, Paris 1771, 398.

4. 2nd ed., Bassano 1785, II, 281.

5. Quatremère de Quincy as late as 1832 still has not much more to say (*Dictionnaire historique d'architecture*, II, 92): 'Une manufacture est un bâtiment dont la condition première est l'utilité.' Hence simplicity and no luxury and no decoration.

6. A. W. Skempton and H. R. Johnson, 'The First Iron Frames', *Arch. Rev.*, CXXXI, 1962, 180 and 181. A curious reference is G. Walker, *The Costume of Yorkshire*, 1813–14: Cotton mills and similar large buildings for trade are 'now usually known under the general, though perhaps vulgar, denomination of factories'. Quoted from F. D. Klingender, *Art and the Industrial Revolution*, ed. Sir Arthur Elton, London ed. of 1972, 98. Just as curious is the German comment which is found in C. L. Stieglitz's *Enzyklopädie der Bürgerlichen Baukunst*, 5 vols., Leipzig 1792–98, II, 68–69: Manufacturing buildings are those where work is done by hand, without the use of fire; *Fabriken* are those where fire and the hammer are used. Stieglitz mentions iron, steel, porcelain, dyes, paper, tobacco, sugar, but not textiles.

7. H. Havard and M. Vachon, *Les Manufactures nationales*, Paris 1889.

8. E. Gerspach, *La Manufacture des Gobelins*, Paris 1892; A. Darcel, *Les Manufactures nationales des Gobelins*, Paris 1885.

274 9. At Vincennes before, where the start was 1740.

10. In 1876 Sèvres moved into a new building on a new site, at the south entry of the park of St Cloud. Architect: Laudin. For the history of Sèvres see G. Lechevallier-Chevignard, *La Manufacture de porcelaine de Sèvres*, Paris 1908. P. Verlet, *Sèvres, le XVIIIᵉ siècle*, Paris 1953, is architecturally no use.

11. Quoted from Havard and Vachon, op. cit.

12. G. Kubler, *Ars Hispaniae*, XIV, Madrid 1957, 240. More detailed but not seen by me: L. Pérez Bueno, *La Real Fábrica de Cristales de San Ildefonso de la Granja*, Madrid 1932. By the same author *Vidrios y vidrieras*, Barcelona 1942 and *Los Vidrios en España*, Madrid 1943. My thanks are due to Mr J. Almudevar of the Biblioteca

Nacional.

13. R. Taylor, 'Royal Tobacco Factory', *Arch. Rev.*, CXXVI, 1959, 267–68. Also *Ars Hispaniae*, op. cit., 275 ff.

14. M. Courtemisse, 'La Manufacture des draps fins Vanrobais au XVIIᵉ et XVIIIᵉ siècles', *Mémoires de la Société d'émulation d'Abbeville*, XXV (4th ser., IX), Abbeville 1922. I am grateful to Mlle Agache of the Abbeville Municipal Library for help about Vanrobais. In *Country Life*, CLIV, 1973, 82–88, Marcus Binney wrote about Bagatelle, Abraham van Robais' country house.

15. D. Smith, *Industrial Archaeology of the East Midlands*, Dawlish and London 1965. S. Glover, *The History of the County of Derbyshire*, 2 vols., Derby 1829, I, 247 and II, 423. Also J. M. Richards and E. de Maré, *The Functional Tradition in early Industrial Buildings*, London 1958, brief and beautifully illustrated.

275 16. N. Wibiral, 'Die Linzer Wollzeugfabrik', *Oberösterreichischer Kulturbericht*, XXII, 1968. W. Formann, 'Glanz und Ende der Linzer Wollzeugfabrik', *Linzer Aspekte*, 1970, 78–81. I wish to thank Dr G. Wachs, Director of the Linz Stadtmuseum.

17. E. Schweizer in *Basler Zeitschrift für Geschichte und Altertum*, XXVI, 1927, 32–42 and XXVII, 1928, 51–54. Also R. Traupel, *CIBA Rundschau*, Heft XCVII, January 1951, 3552–76. These references and some others were communicated to me by Archivar Dr Wackernagel at the Basel Staatsarchiv. On other Swiss *Industriebauten* see J. Gantner and A. Reinle, *Kunstgeschichte der Schweiz*, IV, Frauenfeld 1962, 123–26.

18. On the Rotes Haus see P. Schoenen, *Das rote Haus in Monschau*, Cologne 1968. Also a number of valuable papers by Professor R. Günter: 'Neue Aspekte zur Industrie-Architektur des 20. Jahrhunderts', *Impulse*, 1969–70, 9–26; 'Eine Wende in der Denkmalpflege', *Neues Rheinland*, 1970, no. 4; 'Zu einer Geschichte der technischen Architektur im Rheinland', Beiheft XVI of *Beiträge zur rheinischen Kunstgeschichte und Denkmalpflege*, Düsseldorf 1970, 343–72; 'Der Fabrikbau in zwei Jahrhunderten', *Archithese*, 34 plus 71, 34–51; Herr Professor Günter and Herr Michael Weisser in letters drew my attention to these articles. On the Augsburg Kattunfabrik see *Reclams Kunstführer*, I, Bavaria, 2nd ed., Stuttgart 1957, 17.

Other pre-machinery factories are a cloth mill at Luckenwalde of 1756 (p. 21 in W. Henn, *Bauten der Industrie*, I, Munich 1955), where the window band of the top floor marks the level of the looms – just as in English weavers' cottages – and a sugar refinery at Breslau (Wroclaw) of 1771. The latter is by Langhans, the architect of the Brandenburger Tor in Berlin. It is 17 bays long and has 5 floors and a centre with giant pilasters (W. T. Hinrichs, *Carl Gotthard Langhans*, Strassburg 1909, 24 and pl. 7).

19. *A History of Technology*, ed. C. Singer, F. J. Holmgard and A. R. Hall, 5 vols., Oxford 1954–58.

276 20. Quoted from Klingender-Elton, op. cit. (above, n. 6), 5.

21. Quoted from J. T. Ward, *The Factory System*, I, Newton Abbot 1970, 147 and 153.

22. R. S. Fitton and A. P. Wadsworth, *The Strutts and the Arkwrights, 1758–1830*, Manchester 1958.

23. C. L. Hacker, 'William Strutt of Derby', *Journal of the Derbyshire Archaeological and Natural History Society*, CXXX, 1960, 49–70. For Strutt's mills and some other early mills see the three outstanding papers by Professor Skempton in the Bibliography for this chapter. Professor Skempton also referred to the following papers and theses: W. H. Pierson, 'Notes on early industrial architecture in England', *JSAH*, VIII, 1949, 1–32; T. Bannister, 'The First Iron-Framed Buildings', *Arch. Rev.*, CVII, 1950, 231–46; W. D. Shepherd, *Early Industrial Buildings, 1700–1850*, thesis, RIBA, London 1950; Richards and de Maré, op. cit.

24. J. Harris, 'Cast Iron Columns', *Arch. Rev.*, CXXX, 1961, 60–61.

25. A. W. Skempton, 'Samuel Wyatt and the Albion Mill', *Arch. Hist.*, XIV, 1971, 53–73.

26. Arkwright's also was at the beginning of the mill of New Lanark, built in 1784 and later famous on account of Robert Owen (p. 278).

27. G. Unwin, A. Hulme and G. Taylor, *Samuel Oldknow and the Arkwrights*, Manchester 1924.

28. Skempton, op. cit., 1962 (above, n. 6), 176.

29. Quoted from my *Derbyshire* (The Buildings of England), Harmondsworth 1953, 32.

30. ibid., 104.

31. See my *Nottinghamshire* (The Buildings of England), Harmondsworth 1952, 96. Also M. D. George, *London Life in the Eighteenth Century*, Penguin ed., Harmondsworth 1966, 215 ff.

32. Quoted from Ward, op. cit. (above, n. 21), 144–47.

33. Penguin ed., Harmondsworth 1970, 114–17.

34. *The Poetical Works of William Wordsworth*, Oxford 1949, *The Excursion*, bk. VIII.

35. *The Complete Writings of William Blake*, Nonesuch ed., London 1957, 323. The lines are from *Vala*, 1797. The famous *A Memoir of Robert Blincoe*, 1832, may be the work of a man of sadistic leanings and thus not valid evidence (see Derbyshire Archaeological Society, *Derbyshire Miscellany*, suppl. X, 1966, ed. A. E. Musson), but it is still worth reading.

36. Ward, op. cit., 159.

37. ibid., 140–43.

277 38. It was not his first mill – see Skempton, op. cit., 1962 (above, n. 6), 178.

39. For Professor Skempton's papers see the bibliography to this chapter.

40. A. Freiherr von Wolzogen, *Aus Schinkels Nachlass*, 3 vols., Berlin 1862–63.

41. ibid., III, 34.

42. ibid., 43–44.

43. ibid., 57.

44. ibid., 78.

45. ibid., 73.

46. ibid., 96–97.

47. ibid., 112.

48. ibid., 113–14.

49. ibid., 141.

50. Quoted from L. Ettlinger, 'A German

Architect's Visit to England in 1826', *Arch. Rev.*, XCVII, 1945, 131–34. A volume of the Schinkel *Lebenswerk* (by M. Kühn) dealing with his journeys is in hand.

51. Wolzogen, op. cit., III, 122 and 119.

52. ibid., 123. Cf. J. Tann, *Gloucestershire Woollen Mills*, Newton Abbot 1967.

53. Wolzogen, op. cit., 123.

278 54. A. B. Granville, *The Spas of England*, London 1841, II, 19–21.

55. There is of course plenty of literature on Owen. I am going to quote only three recent and two older books: J. F. C. Harrison, *Robert Owen and the Owenites*, London 1970, *Robert Owen, Prophet of the Poor*, ed. S. Pollard and J. Salt, London 1971, and *Robert Owen, Prince of Cotton Spinners*, ed. J. Butt, Newton Abbot 1971. Still needed are Lloyd Jones, *The Life, Times and Labours of Robert Owen*, 2 vols., London 1889–90, and F. Podmore, *Robert Owen*, 2 vols., London 1906. Owen's *A New View of Society*, 1813–14, and his *Report to the County of Lanark*, 1820–21, exist as a Penguin Book, ed. V. A. C. Gattrell, Harmondsworth 1970.

56. Penguin ed., 95–96.

57. ibid., 49.

58. First presented in the *Report to the Committee for the Relief of the Manufacturing Poor* in 1817.

59. Owen's innovations, even if they were not fully successful, were surely more likely to achieve results than the innovation of the Butterly Coal Company, which was to provide all its employees with bibles (W. L. Burn, *The Age of Equipoise*, London 1964, 241).

60. Ward, op. cit. (above, n. 21), 131, from the *Penny Magazine*, 16 November 1833.

279 61. *Chartism*, Centenary ed., XXIX, 182. *Chartism* was published in 1839.

62. *Past and Present*, 1843, bk. III, chap. 2.

63. ibid. Southey in his *Colloquies* which were published in 1829 said more or less the same: 'the manufacturer uses his fellow creatures as bodily machines for producing wealth . . . a system which debases all who are engaged in it.' The white workers live 'in a state of servitude like the dark slaves'. (*Sir Thomas More, or Colloquies on the Progress and Prospect of Society*, 2nd ed., 1831, I, 169–70.)

64. *Sybil*, Penguin ed., Harmondsworth 1954, 178–81.

65. See my *Yorkshire, the West Riding* (The Buildings of England), 2nd ed., Harmondsworth 1967, 170.

66. ibid., 427–28. See A. Holroyd, *A Life of Sir T. Salt*, London 1871.

67. A. Ure, *The Cotton Manufacture of Great Britain*, 3 vols., London 1836, I, 296–314. Also H. Heginbothan, *Stockport, Ancient and Modern*, II, London 1892, 322–29, and O. Ashmore, *Industrial Archaeology of Lancashire*, Newton Abbot 1969, 48. My thanks are due to Mr. T. W. Skillern, the Reference Librarian of Stockport.

280 68. J. Coolidge, *Mill and Mansion*, New York 1942.

69. vol. XI, 1971.

70. Coolidge, op. cit., 29 and 10.

71. ibid., 31.

72. ibid., 157.

73. ibid., 177.

74. ibid., 182.

75. Concurrently, i.e. between 1826 and 1845, the population of Lowell grew from 2,500 to nearly 30,000 (Coolidge, op. cit., 45).

76. Fall River, Mass., Metacomet No. 6 Mill 1847; Lawrence, Everett Mill 1846–48.

77. For Rhode Island see also H.-R. Hitchcock, *Rhode Island Architecture*, 2nd ed., 1968, chap. IV (Slater Mill 1793, Old Belfry Mill 1813, also housing).

78. *Historic Cohoes*, 1971, with more literature. My thanks are due to Miss Melissa Ann Coury, Director of the Cohoes Public Library, and to Dr Michael J. Bednar (now at the University of Virginia), who carried out an architectural survey of Cohoes in 1971.

79. M. B. Dorgan, *History of Lawrence*, 1924. I am grateful for information to Mr T. J. A. Griffin, Librarian of Lawrence. Another large mill there was the Atlantic Cotton Mills, 600 feet long.

80. op. cit. (above, n. 69), 116–30.

81. Coolidge, op. cit., 46.

281 82. *American Notes*, Penguin ed., Harmondsworth 1972, 115–17. Dickens mentions that the working day is twelve hours and that children are employed, but neither the one nor the other seems to have given him food for thought.

83. *Western Life in the Stirrups*, Chicago 1965.

84. M. Chevalier, *Society, Manners and Politics in the United States*, Boston 1839, 169.

85. J. Turgan, *Les grandes usines*, Paris 1863–98, published in 373 issues and bound in 18 volumes plus one volume of a new series, sounds more useful than it is. The writing is popular, and the illustrations show more interest in processes and products than in buildings.

86. p. 102.

87. H. Chazelle, *Le Creusot, histoire générale*, Dole 1936. H. Chazelle and J. P. Jannot, *Une grande ville industrielle, Le Creusot*, 3 vols., Dole 1958. A. Fargeton, *Les grandes heures de Creusot et de la terre de Montcenis*, Le Creusot 1958. I have to thank M. Jean Pouillart for these references. I have used the book of 1936.

282 88. *Travels in France during the Years 1787, 1788, 1789*. I have used the edition of M. Bitham-Edwards, London 1889. Young spells Wilkinson *à la française*, Weelkainsong (226). In 1788 he visited another factory with Wilkinson's machinery, this one at Nantes (134). The job of both is given as casting and boring cannon. Young also visited a cloth mill at Châteauroux, and van Robais' mill at Abbeville (20, 8). On van Robais see my p. 274.

89. Where he employed 500 to 600.

90. *St Gobain presents its History* (1965).

91. A. Labouchère, *Oberkampf*, Paris 1866; H. Clouzot, *Histoire de la manufacture de Jouy, et de la toile imprimée en France*, 2 vols., Paris and Brussels 1928; and more literature.

92. The works are also shown in a painting attributed to J.-B. Huet in the town hall at Jouy (Clouzot, op. cit., pl. IV, there attributed to Boilly).

93. E. Kaufmann, 'Three Revolutionary Architects: Boullée, Ledoux and Lequeu', *Transactions of the American Philosophical Society*, Philadelphia 1952, 431–537, especially 510. Also M. Raval and J. C. Moreux, *Claude-Nicolas Ledoux*, Paris 1945, especially 160–80. In 1804 Ledoux published his *oeuvre* (*L'Architecture considérée sous le rapport de l'art, des moeurs et de la législation*) as built, or altered to stress the novelty of the buildings, or never built, or even hardly intended to be built. A second volume came out in 1847, i.e. long after Ledoux's death. It was edited by Daniel Ramée, son of the Franco-American J. J. Ramée who made the designs for Union College, Schenectady, N.Y.

94. Ledoux designed another factory in terms of a vast square. It is a cannon foundry, and the plan was to be a cross inscribed in the square. The four corners are pyramidal furnaces. (Ill. Raval and Moreux, op. cit., figs. 211–15.) Gilly incidentally also designed a group of symmetrically composed furnaces: A. Oncken, *Friedrich Gilly*, Berlin 1935, p. 133 (D 16) and pl. 32.

283 95. *Oeuvres complètes*, 6 vols., 2nd ed., 1841–45. H. Bourgin, *Fourier*, Paris 1905. V. Considérant, *Destinée sociale*, 3 vols., Paris 1835–44, I, 481 ff. is on the *phalanstères*. Also *La Grande Encyclopédie*, XXVI, 574–77.

96. *La Grande Encyclopédie*, XVI, 1133 ff.

97. R. Redlich, A. Dresen and J. Petry, *Geschichte der Stadt Ratingen von den Anfängen bis 1915*. Ratingen 1926, 236–40. Also J. Germes, *Ratingen im Wandel der Zeiten*, Ratingen 1965, 78, and M. L. Baum, *Johann Gottfried Brügelmann*, Rheinische Lebensbilder, no. 1, Düsseldorf 1961, 1–16. I want to thank Kulturamtsleiter H. H. Schmitz for having made these papers available to me and Herrn Michael Weisser for the photographs. My attention was first drawn to Ratingen by *Wolfs, Geschichten um ein Bürgerhaus*, the book by W. Langewiesche (Munich and Leipzig 1919) already mentioned, e.g. p. 161, n. 37 (and see below, n. 99).

98. From 6 to 10 years old, say Redlich *et al.*, from 10 to 12 says Germes.

284 99. *Wolfs*, op. cit., 63–82. *Wolfs* is a *roman à clef*. Wolf is the name given to the Lenssen family. Their trade was cotton spinning. The firm was originally Lenssen & Beckenbach. The Beckenbach progeny emigrated to Bradford. An illustration of the factory is in W. Strauss, *Geschichte der Stadt Rheydt*, 1897, 384. Their first steam engine was built by Harkort and installed in 1827. I have to thank Herrn R. Winkelmann, the Librarian of Rheydt.

100. The article 'Fabrikbau' in the *Reallexikon zur deutschen Kunstgeschichte*, although published in 1971–72 (instalments 67–68), was not seen by me until too late to make full use of it. It had not occurred to me to look for factory architecture in such an encyclopedia of art history. Yet the article written by Wolfgang Müller-Wiener and occupying over 30 columns (847–80) is the first attempt at coming to terms with the *Fabrikbau* in one country. The material is arranged according to industries. Textile buildings are most rewarding architecturally. Illustrations are few. Of the 1770s is Stanock, Kreis Oppeln (1775), which also had workers' housing and is composed on a circle, earlier than Ledoux, and the Weiss-

bach'sches Haus, Plauen (1777–78), 26 bays long and three and a half storeys high. Examples become much more frequent after 1810, but the structural use of iron seems to come in as late as the 1840s.

Wolfs (op. cit.) also refers to Oberlangenbielau in Silesia, the East German textile centre (227–28). Rioting at the Dierig factory (in 1841) is mentioned. (Gerhart Hauptmann's *Die Weber* has a note at the start that the events of the play took place in the 1840s at Kaschbach, Peterswaldau and Langenbielau; Hauptmann's grandfather was 'ein armer Weber' himself.) Too late for insertion into the text the Municipal Library of Wroclaw sent me I. G. Hennig, 'Die geschichtliche Entwicklung der Firma Christian Dierig', *Dierig-Blätter*, no. 2, 1936, 10–12 (with illustrations). The factories were for weaving and dyeing. The foundation stone was laid in 1804. Enlargement took place in 1820. In 1842 the main building was 7 bays and 5 storeys, with lower additions behind. The firm became an *Aktiengesellschaft* in 1928 and employed nearly 4,000 in 1936.

101. Article by M. Weisser in *Der Architekt*, XXIII, 1974, 203–06.

102. He generously told me much and sent me evidence.

103. C. Pierard, *La Cité et les ateliers du Grand Hornu.*

104. *Storia di Milano*, Milan (Fondazione Treccani), XII, 1959, 489 and 545.

286 105. W. G. Rimmer, *Marshalls of Leeds, 1788–1886*, Cambridge 1960, 203–06; D. Linstrum, *Historic Architecture of Leeds*, Newcastle 1969.

106. *Victorian London*, London 1972, 83. For the campanili see Sir R. Rawlinson, *Designs for Factories, Furnaces and other tall Chimneys*, London 1858.

107. C. Hadfield, *Atmospheric Railways*, Newton Abbot 1967.

108. I am very grateful to Dr K. K. Weber, whose monograph on Persius should soon come out. For all three engine houses Dr Weber sent me Xerox copies of *Architektonisches Album*, ed. F. Stüler, IV, 1842 (Glienicke), W. Grabner, 'Das maurische Dampfmaschinenhaus in Potsdam', *Natur und Heimat*, 1945, Heft III, and *Architektonisches Skizzenbuch*, 1852–86, XLI, 2, 3 and XXXIX, 6 (Babelsberg).

288 109. The building is presented e.g. in *Enc. d'arch.*, 2nd ser., V, 1876, and even earlier in Viollet-le-Duc's *Entretiens*, II, 1872, 334. Also in Turgan's *Grandes usines* (above, n. 85), XVIII, 1886.

110. P. Collins, *Concrete*, London 1959, 64–75. Collins (115–17) points out that St Jean de Montmartre, built in 1894 by Viollet-le-Duc's pupil Anatole de Baudot, made use not of true reinforced concrete, i.e. not of stone aggregate: the compression members are of brick, threaded with steel rods, and the tension members of reinforced cement. The brick walls and the brick vaulting cells could thus be kept very thin.

111. An American concrete factory pre Kahn is Kelly & Jones at Greenburg, Pa., of 1902. English examples are Rowntree's at York (illustrated in *Concrete and Constructional Engineering*, I, 1906–07, 303), Rawson's at Leicester (ibid., II, 1907–08, 309), and Siemens & Halske (ibid., III,

1908–09, 457).

112. G. Nelson, *The Industrial Architecture of Albert Kahn*, New York 1939. Also *The Legacy of Albert Kahn*, exhibition at the Detroit Institute of Arts, 1970, and, most recently, G. Hildebrand, *Designing for Industry; The Architecture of Albert Kahn*, Cambridge, Mass. 1974.

113. For this development see my *Pioneers of Modern Design*, latest ed., Harmondsworth 1973. But there is plenty of other literature. Closest to the events: *Die Kunst in Industrie und Handel, Jahrbuch des Deutschen Werkbundes 1913*, Jena 1913, and *Bauten der Arbeit* (Blaue Bücher), 2nd ed., 1929.

114. Ill. *Jahrbuch des Deutschen Werkbundes*, op. cit., 2–9 (Behrens), 11–17 (Poelzig), 30–31 (Marx). Also *Bauten der Arbeit*, op. cit., 20, 21, 27 (Poelzig), 25, 30, 31 (Alfeld), 7 (Marx).

115. On recent factory building there are plenty of books, mostly more of pictures than of text. I name (chronologically): *Architectural Forum*, September 1923 and September 1929. P. Schreber, *Industriebauten*, Stuttgart 1930. C. G. Holme, *Industrial Architecture*, London 1935. E. D. Mills, *The Modern Factory*, London 1951. A. Melis, *Gli edifici per le industrie*, Turin 1953. J. F. Munce, *Industrial Architecture*, New York 1960. K. H. Gerstner and T. Klaman, *Industriebauten der DDR*, Berlin 1962. G. Forti, *Architetture industriali*, Milan 1964. A. Hugon and R. Traverse, *Le Complex usinier*, Paris 1965. C. Cavallotti, *Architettura industriale*, Milan 1969. J. Winter, *Industrial Architecture*, London 1972.

List and sources of illustrations

anonymous designer, designs for a monument to Washington (*American Architect and Building News*, 1879. Victoria and Albert Museum, London)

1.28 Edinburgh, monument to the Napoleonic Wars on Calton Hill (Royal Commission on Ancient Monuments, Scotland. Crown copyright)

1.29 Edinburgh, Walter Scott Memorial (Tom Scott)

1.30 London, Albert Memorial (NMR)

1.31 New York, Statue of Liberty, skeleton

1.32 Leipzig, Völkerschlachtsdenkmal (Museum für Geschichte der Stadt Leipzig)

1.33 Voortrekker Monument, near Pretoria (by courtesy of the Publicity and Travel Department, South African Railways)

1.34 Moscow, Lenin Memorial (Novosti)

1.35 Ankara, Atatürk Memorial

1.36 Rome, monument to Victor Emanuel II (Mansell-Alinari)

2 Government buildings from the late twelfth to the late seventeenth century

2.1 Florence, Uffizi (Mansell-Alinari)

2.2 Como, Palazzo del Broletto (Mansell-Alinari)

2.3 Siena, Palazzo Pubblico (Mansell-Alinari)

2.4 Florence, Palazzo Vecchio (Mansell-Alinari)

2.5 Minden, Town Hall (Dr Franz Stoedtner, inh. Heinz Klemm)

2.6 Thorn (Torun), Town Hall: plan

2.7 Thorn (Torun), Town Hall (Dr Franz Stoedtner, inh. Heinz Klemm)

2.8 Middelburg, Town Hall (Rijksdienst v/d Monumentenzorg)

2.9 Rouen, Palais de Justice (CI)

2.10 Filarete, design for a town centre (Biblioteca Nazionale Centrale, Florence)

2.11 Francesco di Giorgio, designs for civic offices (Biblioteca Nazionale Centrale, Florence)

2.12 Antwerp, Town Hall (A.C.L., by courtesy of the Centre Belge d'Information et de Documentation, Brussels)

2.13 Rennes, Palais de Justice (Giraudon)

2.14 Rennes, Palais de Justice: plan (Archives, Rennes. Photo CI)

2.15 Amsterdam, Town Hall, now Royal Palace: plan (CI)

2.16 Amsterdam, Town Hall, now Royal Palace: Burgerzaal (Kunsthistorisch Instituut der Rijksuniversiteit, Utrecht)

2.17 Amsterdam, Town Hall, now Royal Palace (Rijksdienst v/d Monumentenzorg)

3 Government buildings from the eighteenth century: Houses of parliament

3.1 Dublin, Parliament House, now Bank of Ireland (Irish Tourist Board)

3.2 Dublin, Parliament House: section of the House of Commons (National Library of Ireland, Dublin)

3.3 Kent, design for Houses of Parliament for London: plan (Victoria

and Albert Museum, London)

3.4 Kent, design for Houses of Parliament for London: elevation (by courtesy of the Trustees of Sir John Soane's Museum, London)

3.5 Richmond, Va., State Capitol (Virginia State Library, Richmond)

3.6–9 Dobie and Thornton, designs for the U.S. Capitol, Washington, D.C.: elevations and plans (G. Brown, *History of the United States Capitol*, I, 1900. RIBA Library)

3.10 Paris, Ecole de Médecine: anatomy theatre (by courtesy of the Trustees of the British Museum, London)

3.11, 12 Latrobe, designs for the U.S. Capitol, Washington, D.C.: elevation and plan (G. Brown, *History of the United States Capitol*, I, 1900. RIBA Library)

3.13 St Petersburg (Leningrad), St Isaac's Cathedral: section of dome (A. R. de Montferrand, *L'Eglise Cathédrale de St Isaac*, 1845. RIBA Library)

3.14 Indianapolis, former Indiana State Capitol

3.15 Columbus, Ohio State Capitol (Martin Linsey)

3.16 Washington, D.C., U.S. Capitol (photo by courtesy of Professor H.-R. Hitchcock)

3.17 Chester, Shire Hall (John Mills, *Country Life*)

3.18 Paris, Palais Bourbon, Salle des Cinq Cents (J. de Joly, *Plans, coupes . . .*, 1840. RIBA Library)

3.19 Hereford, Shire Hall (A. F. Kersting)

3.20 Paris, Palais Bourbon (Archives Photographiques)

3.21 Paris, Palais Bourbon, Salle des Séances (J. de Joly, *Plans, coupes . . .*, 1840. RIBA Library)

3.22 London, Houses of Parliament, Scala Regia (by courtesy of the Trustees of Sir John Soane's Museum, London)

3.23 London, Houses of Parliament, throne (Crown copyright. Reproduced with the permission of the Controller of Her Majesty's Stationery Office)

3.24 London, Houses of Parliament (NMR)

3.25 London, Houses of Parliament, plan (copyright K. R. Mackenzie)

3.26 Ottawa, Houses of Parliament

3.27 Berne, Bundeshaus

3.28 Sir George Gilbert Scott, design for the Reichstag in Berlin (*Builder*, 1872)

3.29 Berlin, Reichstag (Dr Franz Stoedtner, inh. Heinz Klemm)

3.30 Budapest, Parliament (Archive of the Centre of Historical Monuments for Hungary, Budapest)

3.31 Vienna, Parliament (Dr Franz Stoedtner, inh. Heinz Klemm)

3.32 Bonn, Bundeshaus (Dr Franz Stoedtner, inh. Heinz Klemm)

3.33 Brasilia, Parliament buildings (by courtesy of the Brazilian Embassy in London)

4 Government buildings from the eighteenth century: Ministries and public offices

4.1 Kent, design for the Treasury, London (Guildhall Library, by

permission of the Corporation of the City of London)

4.2 London, Somerset House (Greater London Council Print Collection)

4.3 London, Board of Trade, known as the Treasury (A. F. Kersting)

4.4 St Petersburg (Leningrad), Admiralty (Novosti)

4.5 London, Foreign Office (RIBA Drawings Collection)

4.6 London, New Government Offices (B. T. Batsford Ltd)

4.7 Paris, Ministère des Affaires Etrangères, Quai d'Orsay

4.8 Paris, Louvre (Archives Photographiques)

4.9 Washington, D.C., Treasury (Public Buildings Service)

4.10 Washington, D.C., former State, War and Navy Office (now Old Executive Office Building) (Ronald Comedy, for HABS/NPS)

4.11 Washington, D.C., Old House Office Building (now Cannon House Office Building) (Jack E. Boucher, for HABS/NPS)

4.12 Washington, D.C., Rayburn House Office Building (Alan Fern 1973)

4.13 Washington, D.C., 600–800 Independence Avenue (Alan Fern 1973)

4.14 Bucarest, Ministry of Finance

4.15 Washington, D.C., James Forrestal Building (Alan Fern 1973)

4.16 Berlin, Air Ministry

4.17 Washington, D.C., Old Pension Building (Jack E. Boucher, for HABS/NPS)

5 Government buildings from the eighteenth century: Town halls and law courts

5.1 Lyons, Palais de Justice (photo C.R.D.P., Lyons)

5.2 London, Court of Chancery (by courtesy of the Trustees of Sir John Soane's Museum, London)

5.3 Boullée, design for a 'Palais Municipal' (Bibliothèque Nationale, Paris)

5.4 Boullée, design for law courts (Bibliothèque Nationale, Paris)

5.5 Bernard, design for law courts (A.-P. Prieur and P.-L. Van Cléemputte, *Collection des prix que la ci-devant Académie proposoit et couronnoit tous les ans*, Paris (Basan, Joubert & Van Cléemputte) 1796. By courtesy of Ben Weinreb Architectural Books Ltd, London)

5.6 Durand, design for law courts (J.-N.-L. Durand, *Précis*, II, 1809)

5.7 Birmingham, Town Hall (NMR)

5.8 Liverpool, St George's Hall (Eric de Maré, copyright The Gordon Fraser Gallery Ltd)

5.9 Leeds, Town Hall (by courtesy of Leeds City Council)

5.10 Paris, Palais de Justice, façade by Duc (Archives Photographiques)

5.11 Paris, Hôtel de Ville (Giraudon)

5.12 Manchester, Assize Courts

5.13 Manchester, Town Hall (NMR)

5.14 Scott, design for law courts for London (RIBA Drawings Collection)

5.15 London, Law Courts, *salle des pas perdus* (NMR)

5.16 Burges, design for law courts for

Index